RESEARCH HANDBOOK ON THE ECONOMICS OF PROPERTY LAW

RESEARCH HANDBOOKS IN LAW AND ECONOMICS

Series Editors: Richard A. Posner, *Judge, United States Court of Appeals for the Seventh Circuit and Senior Lecturer, University of Chicago Law School, USA* and Francesco Parisi, *Oppenheimer Wolff and Donnelly Professor of Law, University of Minnesota, USA and Professor of Economics, University of Bologna, Italy*

Edited by highly distinguished scholars, the landmark reference works in this series offer advanced treatments of specific topics that reflect the state-of-the-art of research in law and economics, while also expanding the law and economics debate. Each volume's accessible yet sophisticated contributions from top international researchers make it an indispensable resource for students and scholars alike.

Titles in this series include:

Research Handbook on Public Choice and Public Law
Edited by Daniel A. Farber and Anne Joseph O'Connell

Research Handbook on the Economics of Property Law

Edited by

Kenneth Ayotte

Northwestern University School of Law, USA

and

Henry E. Smith

Harvard Law School, USA

RESEARCH HANDBOOKS IN LAW AND ECONOMICS

Edward Elgar
Cheltenham, UK • Northampton, MA, USA

Published by
Edward Elgar Publishing Limited
The Lypiatts
15 Lansdown Road
Cheltenham
Glos GL50 2JA
UK

Edward Elgar Publishing, Inc.
William Pratt House
9 Dewey Court
Northampton
Massachusetts 01060
USA

A catalogue record for this book
is available from the British Library

Library of Congress Control Number: 2010927656

ISBN 978 1 84720 979 5 (cased)

Typeset by Servis Filmsetting Ltd, Stockport, Cheshire
Printed and bound by MPG Books Group, UK

Contents

Contributors

Barry E. Adler is the Bernard Petrie Professor of Law and Business and Associate Dean for Information Systems and Technology at the New York University School of Law, where he teaches in the areas of bankruptcy, contracts, corporate finance, and corporations. His numerous publications in these areas include *Foundations of Bankruptcy Law* (Foundation Press, 2005) and *Bankruptcy: Cases, Problems, and Materials* (co-authored with Douglas Baird and Thomas Jackson, 4th edn, Foundation Press, 2007).

Lee J. Alston is Professor of Economics and Director of the Environment and Society Program in the Institute of Behavioral Science at the University of Colorado at Boulder. Alston is also a Research Associate at the National Bureau of Economic Research. He has published numerous articles on historical and contemporary institutions with a focus on the United States and Brazil, as well as *Southern Paternalism and the American Welfare State: Economics, Politics, and Institutions in the South, 1865–1965* (co-authored with Joseph P. Ferrie, Cambridge University Press, 1999), *Titles, Conflict, and Land Use: The Development of Property Rights and Land Reform on the Brazilian Amazon Frontier* (co-authored with Gary D. Libecap and Bernardo Mueller, University of Michigan Press, 1999), and *Empirical Studies in Institutional Change* (co-edited with Thráinn Eggertsson and Douglass North, Cambridge University Press, 1996).

Benito Arruñada is Professor of Business Organization at Pompeu Fabra University and Barcelona GSE, where he teaches in the areas of organizations and markets, business economics and policy, and law and economics. He has published numerous articles and books on contracting, property rights, and organizations, including *The Economics of Audit Quality* (Springer, 1999), *Corporate Governance and Regulation* (Alianza, 1990), *Contractual Theory of the Firm* (Marcial Pons, 1998), and *The Economics of the Firm: A Contractual Approach* (Ariel, 1990).

Kenneth Ayotte is a Professor of Law at the Northwestern University School of Law. He was the recipient of the Dean's Award For Teaching Excellence in a Core Course (Corporate Finance) as an Assistant Professor of Finance and Economics at the Columbia Business School. He has taught and published in bankruptcy, corporate finance, and the economics of property law and legal entities.

Patrick Bolton is the Barbara and David Zalaznick Professor of Business, Finance, and Economics at Columbia Business School and a Research Fellow at the National Bureau of Economic Research. His teaching and research areas of interest are in contract theory and contracting issues in corporate finance and industrial organization. His publications in these areas include *Contract Theory* (co-authored with Mathias Dewatripont, MIT Press, 2005) and *Credit Markets for the Poor* (co-authored with Howard Rosenthal, Russell Sage Foundation, 2005).

Lee Anne Fennell is a Professor of Law at the University of Chicago Law School, where she teaches in the areas of property, land use, fair housing, local government, and torts. She has published widely in these areas and is the author of *The Unbounded Home: Property Values Beyond Property Lines* (Yale University Press, 2009).

William A. Fischel is a Professor of Economics and the Robert C. 1925 and Hilda Hardy Professor of Legal Studies at Dartmouth College, where he teaches a variety of courses in economics and law and economics. His numerous publications on regulatory takings and the economics of local government include *Making the Grade: The Economic Evolution of American School Districts* (University of Chicago Press, 2009); *The Homevoter Hypothesis: How Home Values Influence Local Government Taxation, School Finance, and Land-Use Policies* (Harvard University Press, 2001); *Regulatory Takings: Law, Economics, and Politics* (Harvard University Press, 1995); *The Economics of Zoning Laws: A Property Rights Approach to American Land Use Controls* (Johns Hopkins University Press, 1985).

Edwyna Harris is a Senior Lecturer in the Department of Economics at Monash University, where she teaches in the areas of environmental economics and economic history. Her research focuses on historical and contemporary institutions used to price and allocate water within Australia, particularly around the Murray River, and their efficiency implications.

Michael A. Heller is the Lawrence A. Wien Professor of Real Estate Law at Columbia Law School, where he teaches property, land use, and real estate law, and has served as the school's vice dean for intellectual life. He is the author of *The Gridlock Economy* (Basic Books, 2008) and co-editor with Merritt Fox of *Corporate Governance Lessons from Transition Economy Reforms* (Princeton University Press, 2006).

Keith N. Hylton is The Honorable Paul J. Liacos Professor of Law at the Boston University School of Law, where he teaches in the areas of law and economics; litigation theory; antitrust; labor and employment; and corporate law. He has published numerous articles in American law journals and peer-reviewed law and economics journals, as well as *Antitrust Law: Economic Theory and Common Law Evolution* (Cambridge University Press, 2003).

Daniel B. Kelly is an Associate Professor of Law and the Robert and Marion Short Scholar at the University of Notre Dame Law School. His research and teaching interests include property, land use, and natural resources law, as well as trusts and estates. His publications focus on the law and economics of takings and eminent domain.

Gary D. Libecap is Donald Bren Distinguished Professor of Corporate Environmental Management in the Donald Bren School of Environmental Science & Management and Professor of Economics at the University of California, Santa Barbara, a Research Associate at the National Bureau of Economic Research, and the Sherm and Marge Telleen Research Fellow at the Hoover Institution, Stanford University. He has taught courses and published numerous articles and books on property rights and the tragedy of the commons, including *Owens Valley Revisited: A Reassessment of the West's First Great Water Transfer* (Stanford University Press, 2007); *Titles, Conflict, and Land Use: The Development of Property Rights and Land Reform on the Brazilian Amazon Frontier* (co-authored with Lee J. Alston and Bernardo Mueller, University of Michigan Press, 1999); *The Federal Civil Service System and the Problem of Bureaucracy: The Economics and Politics of Institutional Change* (co-authored with R.N. Johnson, University of Chicago Press and NBER, 1994); and *Contracting for Property Rights* (Cambridge University Press, 1989).

Dean Lueck is Bartley P. Cardon Professor in the Department of Agricultural & Resource Economics, Professor of Economics (by courtesy), Professor of Law (by courtesy), and Co-Director of the Program on Economics, Law, and the Environment at the University of Arizona. He has taught courses and published widely on property rights, environmental economics, and the law and economics of natural resources, and is co-author with Douglas W. Allen of *The Nature of the Farm* (MIT Press, 2003).

Thomas W. Merrill is the Charles Evans Hughes Professor of Law at Columbia Law School. He has taught courses and published numerous articles in the areas of property, environmental law, administrative law, eminent domain, and the U.S. Supreme Court, as well as *Property (Oxford Introductions to U.S. Law)* (co-authored with Henry E. Smith, Oxford University Press, 2010), *Property: Principles and Policies* (co-authored with Henry E. Smith, Foundation Press, 2007), and *Property: Takings* (co-authored with David Dana, Foundation Press, 2002).

Bernardo Mueller is a lecturer in the Department of Economics at the University of Brasilia, where he has taught courses on Positive Political Theory of Regulation, Econometrics, Environmental Economics, and Brazilian Economic History. He writes on Positive Political Theory and Regulation, New Institutional Economics, and Environmental Economics, and is a co-author with Lee J. Alston and Gary D. Libecap of *Titles, Conflict, and Land Use: The Development of Property Rights and Land Reform on the Brazilian Amazon Frontier* (University of Michigan Press, 1999).

Carol M. Rose is the Ashby Lohse Professor of Water and Natural Resource Law at the University of Arizona College of Law and the Gordon Bradford Tweedy Professor Emeritus of Law and Organization and Professorial Lecturer in Law at Yale Law School. She teaches property, land use, environmental law, natural resources law, and intellectual property law. Her numerous publications include *Perspectives on Property Law* (co-edited with Robert C. Ellickson and Bruce A. Ackerman, 3rd edn, Aspen, 2000) and *Property and Persuasion: Essays on the History, Theory and Rhetoric of Ownership* (Westview, 1994).

Henry E. Smith is the Fessenden Professor of Law at Harvard Law School, where he also directs the Project on the Foundations of Private Law, and teaches in the areas of property, intellectual property, natural resources, remedies, taxation, law and cognitive science, and law and economics. He has written widely in these areas, including *Property (Oxford Introductions to U.S. Law)* (co-authored with Thomas W. Merrill, Oxford

University Press, 2010), *Property: Principles and Policies* (co-authored with Thomas W. Merrill, Foundation Press, 2007) and *Restrictiveness in Case Theory* (Cambridge Studies in Linguistics 78, Cambridge University Press, 1996).

Lior Jacob Strahilevitz is Deputy Dean, Professor of Law, and Walter Mander Teaching Scholar at the University of Chicago Law School, where he teaches courses on property, privacy, and intellectual property. His extensive writings in these areas include a book, *Information and Exclusion*, which is being published in 2010 by Yale University Press.

George Triantis is the Eli Goldston Professor at Harvard Law School, where he teaches and writes in the areas of bankruptcy, commercial transactions, contracts, and corporate finance. His recent publications include *Foundations of Commercial Law* (co-edited with Robert E. Scott, Foundation Press, 2009).

Martin Zelder is a Senior Lecturer in the Department of Economics at Northwestern University. He has published articles and book chapters in the areas of: the economics of the family (divorce, sex, love), law and economics (the Coase Theorem, penalizing academic fraud), and health economics (the implications of increased public health spending). He has held previous academic appointments at the University of Chicago, Australian National University, and the College of William and Mary.

Introduction
Henry E. Smith

Property rights and property systems vary along a large number of dimensions, and economics has proven very fruitful in analyzing these patterns and even the nature of the institution of property itself. In its early days, the efficiency of various features of property law dominated the economic analysis of property, like law and economics more generally. This first generation of economic analysis of property dovetailed with one of the prime legacies of the policy-oriented anti-formalist legal realism school that started in the 1920s: the bundle of rights or 'bundle of sticks' picture of property. On the 'bundle' view, property is simply a collection of rights, duties, privileges, liabilities, and so on, and attaching the label 'property' is more or less a matter of taste. Economically a 'property right' could be any of these individual sticks – any socially sanctioned expectation to be able to take valued actions with respect to a resource, availing against one or more others. So the expectation of sowing crops or building a house was property, as was the larger collection of property rights we might more conventionally call ownership. The task of economic analysis appeared to be to evaluate these sticks for their cost-effectiveness. As a grab bag of rules and other institutional features, property was no different from torts or contracts.

More recent economic analysis of property law has begun to address what is special about property. The chapters in this volume exemplify this new direction in the economic analysis of property law.

The first three chapters address the evolution of property rights out of open access, and the broad classes of systems that can result. In 'Property Rights, Land Settlement and Land Conflict on Frontiers: Evidence from Australia, Brazil and the US,' Lee Alston, Edwyna Harris, and Bernardo Mueller explore the emergence of de facto and de jure property rights on the frontier, where enforcement of property rights to land is marginally worthwhile. They present a demand-side model based on economic rents, political rents, and norms, to explain which combinations of first-, second-, and third-party specification and enforcement will tend to occur under which circumstances. Crucially, the lag between the specification and enforcement of de jure property rights can lead to violence. Moving beyond 'naïve' pure demand-side models for rights, they build in the supply-side response to the demand for property rights by incorporating the political economy of group formation, lobbying local and central authorities, and the preferences of members of other groups in the polity and the government(s). They apply this framework to the settlement of the frontier and emergence of property rights in Australia, the United States and Brazil, and show why Brazil exhibits the most conflict among settler-claimants.

At any given time, property systems are likely to mix elements of open access owned by no one, common property owned by groups, and private property owned by individuals and entities. Much confusion has surrounded the term 'Tragedy of the Commons,' popularized by Garrett Hardin.[1] Open access, in which anyone can use a resource, can lead to ruin if people benefit fully from appropriating units from the resource but bear only a fraction of the cost. Overall the structure is that of the Prisoner's Dilemma. Somewhat more constrained but with tragic tendencies that need to be kept in check is the limited commons, or group ownership, in which a closed group has use rights that may be further constrained by customs or other rules within the group. In 'Commons, Anticommons, Semicommons,' Lee Anne Fennell points out that many of the problems associated with the commons, in which many have use rights, and the anticommons,[2] in which many have veto (exclusion) rights, stem from the need to have different property regimes on different scales. For example, individual ownership of cattle and collective ownership of grazing areas benefit from the different scales but also open the door to strategic behavior. In this respect, the overlap of ownership regimes often present a semicommons in which some aspects of a resource are private and others are common.[3] In 'The Anticommons Lexicon,' Michael Heller explores the reasons why we have a less developed sense for the anticommons and its associated gridlock than we do for more familiar problems of the tragedy of the commons – and why this matters. Building on his earlier work on the anticommons – an ownership regime in which too many actors have a right to veto use (exclude) leading to underuse – he shows how the anticommons presents the mirror image to the tragedy of the commons in which too widely held rights of use lead to overexploitation (underexclusion).[4]

The next three chapters deal with a specific type of mixture of ownership regimes that could be called public and private. Thomas Merrill's chapter, 'Private Property and Public Rights,' provides a taxonomy of legal doctrines dealing with public property and public rights, and matches these up with economic justifications for publicness. Even if a system like American property law gives a prominent role to private property, various legal regimes and doctrines, ranging from the public domain, to the public trust to public use takings to public accommodations, among others, enhance the value of private property and serve public values. Economics provides some tools for thinking about the benefits of public property, including public goods, network effects, the dangers of monopoly, spillovers, and the difficulties in assembling fragmented rights. Normatively, Merrill identifies how two overarching principles operate to enhance the mixture of public and private aspects of property law – the *matching* of doctrines and economic rationales, and *subsidiarity* that directs the problem to the doctrine that involves the mildest interference with private rights.

A special publicness, in the sense of public goods and network effects, makes information so special that controversy surrounds what type of property to allow in information. Information as a resource benefits both from private investment and public-good-style use and so it is very often a semicommons. In 'Toward an Economic Theory of Property in Information,' Henry Smith explores how the thin notion of 'property rights' in the New Institutional Economics and Law and Economics needs to be extended to account for the information costs of delineation and enforcement in information as a resource itself. The nature of these information costs helps explain the structure of property rights as starting with exclusion (keep out, trespass) and moving in certain important contexts to governance regimes consisting of rules and standards of proper use. Because information as a property resource is associated with high delineation costs, it is more public than other forms of property, but the basic exclusion-governance architecture helps solve the problems of appropriating the returns to rival inputs in a complex system of interaction.

For example, employee inventions and joint ventures as well as the problems of licensing all benefit from the modularity supplied by the exclusion-governance framework. What combination of exclusion and governance is best for information as a resource, and for different regimes like patent and copyright, remains an empirical question. Suggestive evidence though can come from contracting in organizations.

The rise of private property out of open access or common property is a common Demsetzian theme, but Demsetzian evolution of property rights also includes the attenuation or disappearance of property rights with declining importance of spillovers or increasing delineation and enforcement costs – the familiar process in reverse.[5] So if resources become less valuable, it may at some point cease being worthwhile to assert property rights over that resource. On the individual level, such decisions involve a comparison of the costs and benefits of maintaining continued ownership. On the societal level, institutions may form to prevent externalities, in another example of the interplay between the private and the public. Lior Strahilevitz's chapter, 'Unilateral Relinquishment of Property,' explores the power of owners to abandon or destroy their property. Unlike sales, gifts, wills, inheritance, and even adverse possession, both abandonment and destruction involve a unilateral relinquishment of ownership. Many of the benefits (for example, low transaction costs) and costs (for example, externalities) stem from the unilateral nature of abandonment and destruction. After surveying these benefits and costs and the law's somewhat inconsistent response to them, the chapter proposes an economically informed rationalization of the law of abandonment and destruction. The law should liberally permit abandonment of positive value assets but encourage publicity and clarity (for example, by marking) and prohibiting certain forms of littering. As for destruction, Strahilevitz proposes to bring the law of living-owner and post mortem property destruction closer together, through a permissive regime of rights to destroy in wills subject to requirements that the owner made a public offer to sell a remainder interest in the property during the owner's lifetime. Such a requirement would allay concerns that the owner was not facing the full costs of the post mortem destruction. And subject to requirements such as paying off liens, the chapter argues that the law's differential treatment of the abandonment of real and personal property should likewise be abandoned. Overall the focus should be on reducing the information costs of unilateral transfers rather than outright prohibition.

Information costs have pervasive impacts on the institution of property, and to a far greater extent than contracts, property law standardizes the ways of owning. Because contracts are meant to serve the interests, sometimes idiosyncratic, of identified parties and these interests interact with resources subject to rights good against the world, the standardization of property and its interaction with contract feature prominently in many of the remaining chapters. The next two chapters deal explicitly with the theme of standardization in property law. In 'Standardization in Property Law,' Henry Smith offers an information cost theory of property communication. A central example of the standardization of property is the *numerus clausus* principle, which limits the number and types of property rights and channels changes in the basic menu to legislatures rather than courts.[6] Building on work with Thomas Merrill on the *numerus clausus*,[7] the chapter ties the standardization of property to the information-cost externalities involved in a system of in rem rights. The chapter extends this account to the role that the basic exclusion strategy serves in furnishing black-box-like modules within which owners and their activities are informationally irrelevant to outsiders – as in the simple rules of trespass. These modules are supplemented by an interface of use-based governance rules and standards (e.g. nuisance). The modularity of property law is related to formalism, which is a matter of degree. All communication is subject to a basic informational tradeoff: one can communicate in a more formal way with a wider audience or in a more information-rich fashion with a more limited audience (as in the prototypical contract) where everyone tends to be on the 'same wavelength.' In communicating with an in rem audience, parties have an incentive to externalize the costs of idiosyncratic communication to far-flung dutyholders and others. Property law addresses this externality through mandatory standardization by prescribing a *numerus clausus* of simple yet generative basic building blocks of property.

In their chapter, 'Covenant Lite Lending, Liquidity, and Standardization of Financial Contracts,' Kenneth Ayotte and Patrick Bolton model the role that mandatory standardization plays in reducing the costs of financial contracting and improving liquidity. In particular, they identity opportunities for financial contractors to appropriate value from unknowing third parties and show that rules that standardize contracts can serve as a commitment device against such demand-dampening pitfalls facing these other parties. Mandatory standardization thereby can improve the liquidity of secondary markets for loan contracts. The model also has implications for the current financial crisis. In good times such as an asset bubble, secondary purchasers of loan contracts will not be as scared off by the weakened covenants in loan contracts, because the costs of the moral hazard created by such 'covenant lite' contracting will only hurt purchasers in bad states. This equilibrium in good states can turn into one with pervasive 'lemons problems' when the bubble bursts and times are bad.

Standardization is often thought of as a constraint on the types of *division* of property rights, and the next three chapters deal with various types of division, between parties and/or states of the world. In general, the law provides for a menu of co-ownership arrangements that allow multiple parties to serve interests in situations in which a combination of multiple uses under a variety of circumstances maximizes resource value. In 'The Personification and Property of Legal Entities,' George Triantis analyzes entities, like corporations and other business organizations, as property, especially the central role played by the notion of legal personhood with its asset partitioning effect. The overlap and conflict between capital structure and governance structure is somewhat reminiscent of the interactions between different ownership structures (private, common, public) at the outset of the volume. In some situations different assets may call for different mixtures of debt and equity but capital structure is only allowed by the law to vary with legal personality. Yet separate entities can complicate the governance problem and reintroduce agency costs that unified organization structure is meant to address. In general, matching financial claims to asset types, governance tailoring, firm-internal capital market formation, and facilitation of the transfer of groups of firm assets may point in different directions. The chapter ends by asking whether the law should be changed to allow internal tailoring of financial and governance structures within firms and whether the law governing consolidation of multi-entity enterprises in bankruptcy should take more account of the reasons for asset partitioning.

Bankruptcy law itself divides property rights among claimants according to states of the world – solvency and insolvency. Barry Adler's chapter, 'Bankruptcy as Property

Law,' explores the role of bankruptcy law as property law and vice versa. The chapter points out that, despite the almost exclusive focus on bankruptcy law as process, bankruptcy law need not follow state law entitlements in all situations. Whether it does furnish its own substantive entitlements or follows those of state law, bankruptcy resolves competing claims to assets that cannot all be satisfied because of insolvency, and is thus property law. Among consensual and other adjusting creditors, the vindication of state law entitlements in bankruptcy may not matter much substantively and may prevent some forum shopping. But with respect to nonconsensual creditors, like accident victims, children who are owed support, and those injured by environmental contamination, bankruptcy law could furnish a better set of entitlements that would give nonconsensual creditors superpriority, thereby preventing the externalization of harms from consensual creditors to nonconsensual creditors. The chapter also points to how various aspects of property and contract law prevent externalization of harm by potentially insolvent actors, and thus function as bankruptcy law.

The winding up of conflicting claims is a function of another branch of law, marital property, which likewise allocates assets to spouses across different states of the world – falling under marriage and divorce. Martin Zelder's chapter, 'The Law and Economics of Marital Property,' models the incentives facing spouses both to contribute to marital and separate goods within the marriage and to get divorced in the shadow of outside options given divorce law's property division rules. The rules for property division and the grounds for divorce (fault versus no-fault) would not lead to different behavior in the absence of transaction costs: in a zero transaction cost world the spouses would in Coasean fashion bargain to the utility maximizing result (with varying distributions), but in our world the rules setting entitlements may matter to efficiency as well as distribution. Zelder provides a model that incorporates the joint product of marriage, the jointly created separate products, and separate spousal products, and shows how changes in the size of divorce settlements, the expanding scope of marital property (e.g. professional degrees), and no-fault divorce impact these three components through the behavior of the spouse with better outside options (traditionally and stylized as the husband) and the spouse with fewer outside options (traditionally and stylized as the wife). The model extends previous results about the conditions under which changes in the law affect spousal allocation of effort and incentives to pursue socially wasteful divorce, as well as the potential negative impact of no fault divorce on the more vulnerable spouse. The model draws support from empirical studies of the effects of no-fault divorce and sharpens the empirical questions for future research.

Closely related to the standardization of property are other notice-giving devices that ensure transactors and other third parties are aware of who owns what. The next two chapters deal with standardization, publicity, and notice issues surrounding property, and land in particular. In 'Property Titling and Conveyancing,' Benito Arruñada analyzes titling systems as a method of organizing the consent to transfer. A useful benchmark is privacy, in which the claims of original owners would prevail regardless of notice to later good faith claimants. In general, he shows that loosening property rights to make them enforceable by good faith purchasers may make rights more valuable than the loss of value from nonenforcement for original owners in such situations. As alternatives to the baseline of privacy, Arruñada then goes on to compare recordation, in which transaction-related documents are simply filed and indexed, and registration, in which an official determines the state of title in the course of accepting title documents. Each system makes different institutional demands, and in light of the theory he questions the oft-assumed cost advantage of recordation over registration. In a cross-country empirical study, the chapter shows that land records that are given more definitive effect tend to be accompanied by a stricter *numerus clausus*, apparently because an official who must give a determination of validity serves as a stand-in for the public and needs the information-cost-reducing effect of stricter standardization of property.

For land, property rights definition includes a description of the physical space covered by rights, through some sort of survey. In 'Land Demarcation Systems,' Gary Libecap and Dean Lueck compare land demarcation systems in various times and places. They focus on two primary systems and their variants. The metes and bounds system, which is decentralized and based on landmarks and angles, leads to a pattern of irregular land claims that tracks topography. The rectangular system is more centralized, and requires parcels to conform to a rectangular shape and in some systems, like the U.S. Public Land Survey System set up by the Land Ordinance of 1795, also requires all rectangular parcels to fit into a grid system based on markers defined in terms of latitude and longitude. They compare the two main systems in the United States in a comparative context. The regular interlocking shape and the standard location of the rectangular system provide substantial benefits, in light of Libecap and Lueck's empirical study of a natural experiment involving the Virginia Military District, a metes and bounds area in Ohio. The rest of Ohio, which was marked off in the public survey into townships and sections, etc., shows greater investment, more infrastructure, higher economic growth and less litigation than the Virginia Military District for long stretches of time. These findings suggest the superiority of the rectangular system in terms of incentives for land use, promotion of land markets and investment, and avoidance of border disputes.

Other conflicts between neighbors involve uses, and the next two chapters take up covenants and nuisance as devices for land use control. Covenants and easements – servitudes – in particular raise issues of recording and notice. In 'Servitudes,' Carol Rose explores the role of servitudes in coordination among neighbors and provides a framework for thinking about how the law addresses the special worries to which they give rise. She demonstrates how covenants partake both of in personam contract and in rem property and in what sense they are an alternative to zoning. Only through their running to successors in interest do servitudes enable the kind of commitment to patterns of land use that afford stability of expectations. Rose then shows how covenant law deals with the main worries to which covenants give rise: information or notice, renegotiability, and value over time. In particular, she highlights some of the problems servitudes pose to third parties. Informationally, any restrictions on servitudes are puzzling as long as they are reflected in land records. Nevertheless, in light of civil law comparisons, Rose argues that standardization and record systems may sometimes be supplements rather than alternatives to each other, and that some of the formalities that covenants are held to may reflect a more ex ante common law procedure involving juries. By contrast, the more flexible equitable servitude doctrine bears the traces of the judicial ex post decision making where jury control was not an issue. These worries and the characteristic solutions to them provide a descriptive explanation for and normative evaluation of the law's response to racially restrictive covenants, common interest communities, and conservation easements. In all these areas, many of the characteristic difficulties of covenants stem from their potential to reach out to the broader in rem set of actors in the world.

An alternative method of coordinating neighbors' land use is the tort of nuisance. In 'The Economics of Nuisance Law,' Keith Hylton takes up nuisance, which is a tort that protects property rights. After noting that transaction cost models of nuisance are designed to explain the contrast between trespass and nuisance, the chapter develops an externality model of nuisance. By taking into account both external costs and benefits, the chapter shows that imposing strict liability on a nuisance causes incentives facing private actors to roughly track social optimality when either of two conditions is satisfied: external costs of the activity substantially outweigh the external benefits, or there is a lack of reciprocity of the harms imposed by neighboring activities. Nuisance thus serves a regulatory function with respect to activity levels. This externality model helps explain the contours of nuisance, including the intentionality requirement, liability for abnormally dangerous activities, proximate cause, hypersensitive plaintiffs, and coming to the nuisance. Although the chapter focuses on the more finegrained rules governing identified parties and thus emphasizes the tort aspect of nuisance, the theory emphasizes situations in which external benefits *substantially* outweigh the external cost and those in which harms are *nonreciprocal*. These rough and ready tests bring out how nuisance reflects only a partial shift from crude exclusion rules to finegrained governance.

Eminent domain and takings implicate many of the themes of the economic analysis of property law, including the forms of property, externalities, hold outs, and the mixture of the public and the private. In 'Acquiring Land Through Eminent Domain: Justifications, Limitations, and Alternatives,' Daniel Kelly provides an economic analysis of the justifications for and limitations of eminent domain. Although eminent domain is often considered a solution to the holdout problem, holdouts come in different varieties with different implications for efficiency – strategic owners, numerous owners, and idiosyncratic owners. The chapter also explores other rationales for eminent domain, especially those sounding in positive externalities. On the 'limitations' side of the ledger, while valuation difficulties and the attendant risks of undesirable transfers receive much attention, secondary rent seeking and administrative costs can sometimes prove crucial. As alternatives to zoning secret purchasers, land assembly districts, and auction mechanisms are designed to solve some of the shortcomings of eminent domain. Kelly demonstrates that each of these alternatives carries with it a characteristic set of further problems. In particular, land assembly districts overcome many holdouts but do leave valuation problems and the possibility of socially undesirable transfers. Auction mechanisms benefit from strong theoretical support in the literature but they too are not immune from secondary rentseeking and might raise administrative costs. The chapter ends by noting that we are at the beginning of a true comparative analysis of the full range of institutions that deal with land assembly problems.

Finally, William Fischel's chapter, 'The Rest of Michelman 1967,' engages in an economic analysis of lesser known parts of Frank Michelman's landmark 1967 article on just compensation law. Most commentary has picked up on Michelman's Rawlsian and utilitarian criteria for takings law. But much of the rest of the article significantly qualifies these criteria and argues for skepticism about the state of takings law. In the most neglected aspect of the article, Michelman addresses institutional questions for implementing fairness, as a problem of choosing between a 'fairness machine' (politics) and 'fairness discipline' (judicial review). From a compromise between the need for judges to make subjective judgments in this area and the difficulty of doing so, Michelman derives a takings law remarkably like the one that unfolded in the decades since he wrote. Nevertheless, this 'test of fairness' in a variety of institutional vehicles remains a largely unfulfilled program.

The chapters in this volume suggest that the economic analysis of property is entering a new phase. A greater diversity of methods than ever – analytical, empirical, institutional – are being brought to bear on new questions regarding property's basic architecture.

NOTES

1. Garrett Hardin, The Tragedy of the Commons, 162 Science 1243 (1968).
2. Michael Heller, The Tragedy of the Anticommons: Property in the Transition from Marx to Markets, 111 Harv. L. Rev. 621 (1998).
3. Henry E. Smith, Semicommon Property Rights and Scattering in the Open Fields, 29 J. Legal Stud. 131 (2000).
4. James M. Buchanan & Yong J. Yoon, Symmetric Tragedies: Commons and Anticommons, 43 J.L. & Econ. 1 (2000).
5. Harold Demsetz, Toward a Theory of Property Rights, 57 Am. Econ. Rev. 347 (1967) (Papers & Proc.); see also Terry L. Anderson & P.J. Hill, The Evolution of Property Rights: A Study of the American West, 18 J.L. & Econ. 163, 170 (1975); David D. Haddock & Lynne Kiesling, The Black Death and Property Rights, 31 J. Legal Stud. S545 (2002).
6. Bernard Rudden, Economic Theory v. Property Law: The *Numerus Clausus* Problem, in Oxford Essays in Jurisprudence 239 (3d Series, John Eekelaar and John Bell, eds. 1987).
7. Thomas W. Merrill & Henry E. Smith, Optimal Standardization in the Law of Property: The *Numerus Clausus* Principle, 110 Yale L.J. 1 (2000).

1 Property rights, land settlement and land conflict on frontiers: evidence from Australia, Brazil and the US*

Lee J. Alston, Edwyna Harris, and Bernardo Mueller

INTRODUCTION

Australia, Brazil and the US are all physically large countries and each had different patterns of land settlement on their frontiers. In this chapter we will examine the way in which the extant property rights in each country affected settlement and in particular the potential and emergence of land conflict. Property rights, along with relative prices, provide the incentive for settlement and conflict on frontier lands. Property rights can be either formal or informal. By informal property rights we mean that the specification and enforcement of rights is either first person or second person enforcement, and not by a legal government or some other third party entity. First person specification and enforcement of property rights entails self-enforcement of property rights by the claimant. Second person specification of property rights may be done through social norms established through tradition or custom, or agreed upon rules of behavior determined by clubs or associations of various types, e.g. ranchers' associations and mining camps. When land is relatively abundant, informal property rights may suffice to entice settlement yet avoid conflict, but as land becomes scarcer and settlers more heterogeneous the potential for conflict increases. Government specification and enforcement of property rights generally emerges as resources become scarcer but not necessarily in time to avoid land conflict. Furthermore, though most governments ultimately specify property rights concerning settlement, many do not follow through with enforcement of property rights, and as a result land conflict may arise or increase. To the extent that the specification and enforcement of property rights by governments are clear and secure there will be little potential conflict, but historically the costs of such enforcement have been prohibitive.

In this chapter we first present a general model of the interaction between settlement and the emergence of property rights. The model will highlight the distinction between informal and formal property rights and the likelihood for land conflict. In subsequent sections we will discuss the settlement of three frontiers, along with the potential for and realization of land conflict. The frontiers include rural Australia, the arid Great Plains region of the US and the Brazilian Amazon. We are particularly interested in examining the emergence, sustainability, and collapse of commons arrangements.

I.   A MODEL OF LAND SETTLEMENT

Property rights affect the timing of settlement as well as the use of land. A full set of property rights includes the following: 1) the right to use the asset in any manner that the user wishes, generally with the *caveat* that such use does not interfere with someone else's property right; 2) the right to exclude others from the use of the same asset; 3) the right to derive income from the asset; 4) the right to sell the asset; and 5) the right to bequeath the asset to someone of your choice. If one possesses the full set of property rights, resources will be utilized optimally. But, a full set of property rights never exists because there are some margins of use that are too costly to specify and enforce, as Ronald Coase (1960) noted years ago: 'sometimes it costs too much to put the matter right.' As a result some attributes may be either *de jure* or *de facto* left as open access.[1] Individuals and groups have incentives to expropriate use rights over attributes that the state leaves as open access. For land settlement this could lead to different types of behavior which can dissipate the rental value of the land. If land is open to squatting on the basis of first possession then people will dissipate some resources in the race to claim land (Anderson and Hill, 1990). If land is left in open access, this will lead to overuse of the land in the familiar problem of the tragedy of the commons. Furthermore, unless occupants of land have a formal title to their land, which typically includes the coercive power of the state to evict trespassers, occupants will expend resources defending their claim. In the absence of formal titles to land, individuals will have an incentive to reach collective agreements to prevent trespass from outsiders as well as expend individual resources to demarcate and defend claims.

We illustrate in Figure 1.1 the 'demand' for more secure property rights as a function of its scarcity value. In Figure 1.1 the horizontal axis measures the relative scarcity of a given resource (from right to left) and the vertical axis measures the net present value that accrues to the owner of that resource.[2] Line *AE* shows that the net present value of the resource decreases as it becomes less scarce. In the case of land the measure of scarcity could be the distance of a plot of land to a market center, as transportation costs are often the main determinant of land value. An alternative measure of land scarcity could be soil quality. At point *E* land is so far from the market center or so abundant that the economic return is zero. The region *OGCDE* represents the net present value of land under an open access arrangement. *OH* represents the opportunity cost of the settlers with the lowest opportunity cost, given the costs of settling on the frontier. Settling on the frontier will vary considerably with climatic conditions. For example, the fixed costs of migrating and sustaining a subsistence standard of living are lower in tropical regions than in colder climates, where settlers may have to wait a year to plant and harvest crops. As such, distance *K* represents the economic frontier where it becomes worthwhile for labor to migrate to the frontier.[3]

At distances between points *J* and *K* open access conditions prevail, which means that property rights are not formally defined or enforced, but this does not affect the return to the resource given that it is still abundant relative to the competition for it. Though land is abundant, migrants find it worthwhile to establish norms pertaining to the amount of land claimed. This appears relatively easy to do because the settlers are relatively homogeneous with respect to their opportunity costs and typically other socio-economic characteristics. As the net present value increases, e.g. because of lower transportation costs or higher prices for the output of the land – represented here by an increase from *OHDK* towards *OGCJ* – new users arrive, yet they are able to get access to the resource without detracting much from the use of those who were already there. In region *OGCJ* resource users still tend to be relatively homogenous, but the return

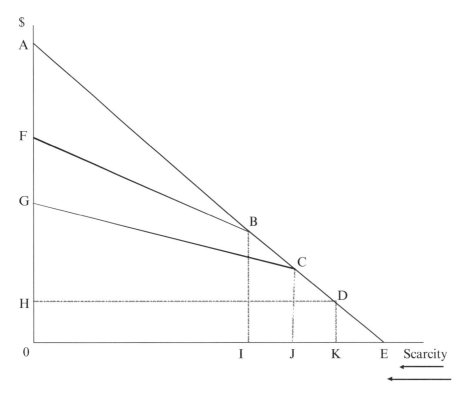

Figure 1.1   The demand for and evolution of property rights

from an open access resource is lower than moving to a limited commons. The increased relatively higher return from a commons arrangement creates the demand for informal property rights, which are sufficient to mitigate the otherwise existing dissipation of the rental stream. It is easier for homogeneous users to reach agreements concerning exclusivity for two reasons: 1) the claimants generally share similar cultural norms; and 2) in some instances there is a common collective good that will bring people together to reach agreements. With a common cultural background, potential disputes are easily defused as social pressure along with incentive to cooperate yields higher expected returns than confrontation. The most obvious collective good is common defense to prevent encroachments from potential claimants but a common yearly 'round-up' also served this function for ranchers on ranges operating as commons arrangements with exclusivity (Dennen, 1976).[4] Squatting prevails yet the absence of government-enforced private property rights does not pose significant costs.[5] Note that the emergence of informal property rights at this point is already a case of institutional change. We represent the higher return from switching from open access to collective or commons arrangements with the present value of *OFBCJ* compared to the lower value of *OGCJ* if the individuals do not reach a collective agreement. For land in the distances between *I* and *J* there is a gain to having informal property rights or norms of behavior, as opposed to open access, but not yet for having formally defined property rights. That is, the level of competition for land is sufficiently high that open access would lead to losses, but not sufficiently high for formal property rights to be an improvement over commons arrangements.

If scarcity values increase very quickly, e.g. a discovery of gold or rapidly rising relative prices, the demand schedules would shift out which would attract an influx of migrants. This new migration typically brings heterogeneous individuals with differing amounts of wealth or human capital, nationalities, cultures, or objectives. The informal institutions that developed can no longer cope with the increased competition for the resource. It becomes necessary to expend effort, time and money to assure continued possession of the resource and the income derived from it. This may involve incurring costs to exclude others or the cost from sub-optimal uses. It may also include the costs to lobbying for changes from informal to formal property rights. At some point it becomes beneficial in the aggregate to have officially defined and enforced property rights. We represent the increased value that would result from formally defined and enforced property rights as the pie-shaped area *ABF* which represents the increased value of land versus the next best commons arrangement for property rights. *ABF* is the potential rent that forms the basis for the demand for formal property rights. Nevertheless, the movement from a collective informal arrangement to a formal specification of property rights entails some redistribution which in turn generates the potential for conflict. The extent to which conflict emerges depends on several factors: 1) to the extent that the formal property rights sanction the existing *status quo* of 'first possession' there will be less conflict because the current occupants would view this as fair; and 2) the larger are the resources that the government devotes to enforcement the less actual conflict will emerge even if the occupants are not pleased with the redistribution from the new property rights arrangement. In our case studies we are most interested in the potential in conflict that results from the movement from collective informal arrangements to formal government specified property rights.

In our exposition we used distance as the proxy for scarcity but we could also use fertility of the soil or population density as alternative measures of scarcity.[6] The framework is flexible to allow for changes in technology, preferences or new market opportunities. For example, if the demand for the output of the land increases, the divergence between the rental streams from the various property rights regimes will emerge at distances further from the prior market frontier – currently at distance *OK* from the market center. The increase in net present value of the resource may not rise in a smooth and continuous manner as depicted in Figure 1.1, but rather in discrete jumps. Nevertheless the same logic holds. The shape of the present value curve will depend on the nature and characteristics of the change that affects the resource's relative scarcity. The main sources of change are technological innovations, changes in relative factor and product prices, and changes in the size of the market. For example, as we will see in our Australian example, the outflow of migrants from the exhausted gold fields induced an increased demand for land. An example of technological change affecting the returns to a resource is the invention of barbed wire that allowed 19th century cattlemen in the US west to confine their cattle, thereby increasing the return to selective breeding as well as better stocking practices (Anderson and Hill, 1975).[7]

Many of the early studies on the evolution of property rights simply assumed that as the area *ABF* became sufficiently large formal property rights would emerge. This notion has been termed the naïve theory of property rights, as it does not analyze the collective action problems or the politics that determine the supply of formal property rights (Eggertsson, 1990: 250). We will turn to the government supply of property rights in our case studies, but here we want to delve in more depth into the determinants of *OABI* versus *OFBI*, the differential value of the asset from formal secure property rights versus collective arrangements, and *OFBCJ* versus *OGCJ*, the differential value of the asset used in a commons arrangements versus an open access arrangement.

There are at least four incentives which lead to the dissipation of rents if formal property rights are not supplied at the optimal time: 1) incentives to usurp property rights from the existing holder; 2) incentives to defend your land against outsiders; 3) incentives to lobby for formal property rights; and 4) incentives for sub-optimal use of the resource. Efforts to usurp take place when individuals or groups perceive an expected gain from taking the asset away from the current holder. Efforts include time, money and violence. If the existing commons arrangement does not provide sufficient exclusivity to the present occupants the greater is the likelihood that the redistribution transpires.[8] The incentive to usurp and the incentive to defend are two sides of the same coin. From our reading of the literature, there is a strong 'home court' advantage in defending against outsiders. Smith (2002: S482) argues: 'In common-pool arrangements regimes, exclusion seems to be basic in the sense that efforts at exclusion are the first methods used to define property in a resource. The evidence from English land use is consistent with early exclusion.'[9] We also note that although the new holder may increase the value of the asset, the efforts to gain the asset are wasteful relative to a world where reallocation takes place via the market. Dissipation generally occurs when the specification of formal rights does not recognize the *status quo* commons arrangement but rather extends formal rights based on political access. The efforts to defend, together with the efforts by others to usurp, often lead to conflicts, which is one of the most wasteful forms of rent dissipation as the resource itself and human life may be destroyed in the process. As we will show in our case of the US, homesteaders expended resources lobbying the Government Land Office to enforce their formal rights over the informal rights of ranchers, but their efforts were for naught. Insecure property rights may also lead to dissipation through sub-optimal use of the land. In the US sub-optimal use resulted from migration to land in a race for property rights which in some instances meant migration past the economic frontier: point *K* in our Figure 1.1.

Supplying property rights is determined by the costs of definition, measurement, and enforcement. Groups supplying *de facto* rights also confront organizational costs because collective action is a public goods problem subject to free riding. Such organization is likely to create a net benefit that leads to informal property rights when groups are small, geographically proximate, have homogenous production technology, and share norms. Shared norms underpin cultural homogeneity which guides individual expectations about the behavior of other group members such as respect for property or equity. In turn, this creates focal points that provide coordination mechanisms which have mutual significance to participants (Zerbe and Anderson, 2001). Over time, increased competition for the resource brought about by rising values adds to the private costs of enforcement as the number of expropriators grows. This can lead to a breakdown of private collective action and encourage lobbying for the supply of *de jure* property rights by government. Government supply of formal rights (which may or may not support the *status quo*) involves the transfer of private monitoring and enforcement to the formal sector. These costs will affect the timing and extent of *de jure* property rights (Alston, Libecap, and Schneider, 1996). Titling costs rise as distance from the market center increases. For instance, at point *J* in Figure 1.1 supply of formal property rights is prohibitively costly given land values and distance from the market center. However, the return to supply of *de facto* rights by users themselves is positive. Moving past this point toward distance *I*, titling costs are lowered as distance from market center decreases. It is at this point that government faces positive returns, for instance via the ability to raise revenue from taxes, by allocating its scarce resources to *de jure* property rights. These positive returns correspond with the growing economic importance of productive output from the resource use making the government more willing to supply rights. For instance, as will be seen in our Australian case, as the value of wool production to export markets increased, the government sought to reaffirm squatters' *de facto* rights via the introduction of land licenses and, later, leases.

Nevertheless, as noted above, a shift from informal to formal rights may be associated with rent dissipation if formal rights do not recognize the *status quo*. In all three of our cases, some level of rent dissipation occurred because there was either a change in policy to reallocate existing rights to people outside the commons (Australia and the US) or due to a lack of clarity between the *de jure* rights of informal and formal claimants (Brazil). Lobbying by interest groups and their potential to pay political currency, for example, votes or campaign contributions, has the potential to increase the divergence between *status quo de facto* rights and government supply of *de jure* rights. The greater the divergence between supply of informal and formal rights, the greater the potential for more wasteful forms of rent dissipation, particularly violence.

II.   SETTLEMENT OF THE AUSTRALIAN FRONTIER

Settlement of the Australian frontier began in the late 1820s. Prior to the 1820s, population was concentrated around the original convict settlement at Botany Bay, New South Wales (NSW). NSW was the sole jurisdiction in eastern Australia until the mid 1800s.[10] As it was a penal colony, the British Colonial Office (BCO) in London determined economic and political policy, including land policies.[11] The representative of this office in NSW, the colonial governor, a military administrator, oversaw the implementation of directives received by the BCO. During the mid 1820s, the BCO attempted to concentrate settlement within an area known as the Nineteen Counties – the legal limits of settlement.[12] However, several factors caused the spread of population beyond these boundaries to the frontier: 1) population increases resulted in land scarcity within the settlement limits (Roberts, 1935);[13] 2) land prices within the Nineteen Counties were high, set at a minimum price of £1 per acre;[14] 3) growing demand and rising prices for Australian wool in Britain increased the net present value accruing from land settlement outside the boundaries (Imlah, 1950; Shergold, 1987, in Vamplew (ed.) 1987);[15] and 4) inadequate police numbers made the boundaries unenforceable.

Land occupation outside the Nineteen Counties was illegal and these settlers became known as squatters. Beyond the legal boundaries of the Nineteen Counties, land was not scarce and squatters occupied where they pleased – corresponding to the distances between points *J* and *K* in Figure 1.1. Australia's arid climate and economies of scale in wool production resulted in large land claims on the frontier, on average between 24,000 and 34,000 acres (Roberts, 1935).[16] Claims, referred to as 'runs', were not contiguous and a squatter employed at least one hut keeper on each parcel to enforce ownership against later arrivals. Property boundaries were vague, typically defined by natural features including rivers and marked trees. It would be expected that the combination of the lack of *de jure* rights and imprecise boundaries would increase the potential for conflict among squatters as scarcity increased. However, there is little evidence of actual conflict. In part, this may have been the result of enforcement by strategically placed huts and a physical presence of employees on runs; but there is also evidence that informal, *de facto* rights played a role. In some cases, informal agreements included a written contract between neighbors stating mutual respect for boundaries. If a dispute arose, arbitration by district squatters would determine the matter (Weaver, 1996). Moreover, Roberts (1924, 1935) and Weaver (1996) suggest that, at least during the early 1830s, prior to choosing a run, newcomers to an area would negotiate with any neighbors as to property boundaries. One of the earliest squatters in NSW noted:

> It is of great importance not to embroil the Establishment by disputes with neighbours, and (without, however, weakly giving away to unreasonable objections, and though distance is no doubt an objective), I think an extensive good Run, not subject to be encroached upon, may sometimes more than compensate for remoteness [Hogan Papers, 1830–4 quoted in Roberts, 1935: 278].

Norms also delineated *de facto* rights to prevent sheep stealing in the absence of branding (Fetherstonhaugh, 1917) and defined what constituted abandonment of a run (Weaver, 1996). Custom also determined the efficient number of sheep per flock at approximately 520 (Curr, 2001). Above 520 sheep, it was believed that pastures over which the flock travelled would be wasted and stronger sheep would consume the bulk of the grass. Given flock relocation often took place via the use of common stock routes, on which sheep still need to graze, norms dictating efficient flock size reduced the likelihood of overusing common pastures for relocation. These norms were collective goods that had private benefits, corresponding to differences between areas *OFBI* and *OGCJ* in Figure 1.1. This suggests that, like the first settlers on the US and Brazilian Amazonian frontiers, social norms developed among early squatters in Australia to reduce losses resulting from open access. By the late 1830s, increasing scarcity values led squatters to appeal to colonial administrators and the British government for recognition of their land rights and more secure *de jure* property rights.[17] However, unlike our Brazilian case study, this was not to access formal capital markets because mortgages and credit were acquired relatively easily from British banks in the colony and from private investors. Instead, it was to ensure that the rights of squatters were enforced against an increasing number of newcomers to the frontier brought about by the continuing pastoral boom.

As noted, the BCO determined colonial land policy which attempted to restrict population to the area within the Nineteen Counties. Nevertheless, expansion of settlement beyond the boundaries for wool production had resulted in NSW becoming a critical supplier of wool to British manufacturers, increasing incentives for the BCO to supply *de jure* property rights to squatters (Burroughs, 1967; Dingle, 1984). The BCO was reluctant to recognize titles for the land claims of squatters because this would require ceding Crown rights and potential revenue from later sale. Instead, the BCO introduced annual squatting licenses (An Act to Restrain the Unauthorized Occupation of Crown Land 7 Wm. IV., No. 4). The decision to use licenses to regulate squatting was based on recommendations from the colonial Governor, Richard Bourke, to the secretary of the BCO in which Bourke stated:

> I cannot avoid perceiving the peculiarities which, in this colony, render it impolitic and even impossible to restrain dispersion within limits that would be expedient elsewhere. The wool of NSW forms at present, and it likely long to continue, its chief wealth. It is only by free range over the wider expanse of native herbage which the colony affords that the production of this staple article can be upheld, at its present rate of increase in quantity, a standard of value in quality. The proprietors of thousands of acres already find it necessary, equally with the poorer settlers, to send large flocks beyond the boundary of location to preserve them in health throughout the year [Braim, 1846].

Under the license system, squatters paid £10 annually to occupy as much land as they pleased. Licenses gave squatters occupancy rights and were enforceable against all parties except the Crown. Therefore, the Crown could evict squatters at any time without compensation. Despite this, there continued to be an active market for squatters' runs.[18] The license system was enforced by Crown Lands Commissioners appointed in each of the seven districts outside the Nineteen Counties. Commissioners had authority to refuse license renewal and determine boundary disputes and claims of trespass. The BCO appointed border police to enforce the decisions of Commissioners should squatters fail to comply. Clause 10 of the legislation appointing Commissioners to each district, instructed them to act '*according to the established usages and customs of the Colony*' (emphasis ours).[19] Any departure from custom established by usage required government sanction (ANSW, 4/3660, Colonial Secretary Thomson to Lambie, 29 November, 1843). Therefore, licenses created a mix of both *de facto* and *de jure* property rights on the frontier. For much of the next decade, squatters continued to petition the colonial governor for greater ownership security. In other words, there was a growing demand for *de jure* property rights. A continuation of lobbying efforts indicates growing competition for land so that informal rights were no longer sufficient to protect the claims of squatters. It was at this point that increased potential value, the area measured by *ABF* in Figure 1.1, would accrue in a move away from a limited commons to formally defined and enforced property rights. Squatters secured greater *de jure* rights by the end of the 1840s with the introduction of leases accompanied by pre-emptive rights to a proportion of the land occupied. Leases could be granted for one, eight or 14 years depending on a run's location in the colony. Specifically, a run in 'settled' districts, that is, within the Nineteen Counties, could only acquire a one year lease; in 'intermediate' districts, that is, immediately surrounding the Nineteen Counties, a run acquired a five year lease; and in 'unsettled' districts, that is, on the frontier, 14 year leases were granted. Further, rentals were set at a minimum of £10 for 4,000 sheep with an increment of £2 10 shillings for every 1,000 sheep thereafter. Under these regulations, during the duration of the lease land could only be sold to the occupier. On a lease's expiration the extent of land subject to pre-emptive rights remained undefined, as did the cost of purchasing this area. As a result, the extent of *de jure* rights, specifically, the area subject to pre-emption, relied on government definition that was subject to change. This limited certainty over the extent of formal land rights under leases that persisted until land reform in the 1860s.

By the 1860s, NSW had been divided into four separate colonies: NSW, Port Phillip (Victoria), Moreton Bay (Queensland), and Van Diemen's Land (Tasmania).[20] On separation from NSW each colony was granted representative government, that is, the right to legislate over its own affairs, including land settlement. Nevertheless, each colony adopted similar land policies that followed broadly the same time line, beginning around 1860. Further, two guiding principles influenced reform in the majority of colonies: land selection before survey and phasing out the leases of squatters.[21] Reform was prompted by an influx of migrants during the gold rushes of the 1850s, shifting out demand schedules in the following decade.

Once gold supplies were exhausted, former miners' opportunity costs of moving to the frontier fell and many ex-miners wanted to turn to agriculture for a living. Pressured by the demands of ex-miners, the parliaments initiated policy changes in the 1860s that limited the extent of squatters' *de jure* rights, while increasing those of later claimants.[22] This increased the potential for conflict because the holdings of squatters not claimed under pre-emption were now subject to government sanctioned competition by 'selectors.' The potential for conflict between squatters and selectors was positively related to the extent of pastoral occupation in a colony. Moreover, the principle of selecting land before survey increased the potential for conflict due to the prevalence of information asymmetries.

District Land Agents employed by the Lands Departments recorded applications for land selection. Agents forwarded the applications to Departments for registration on a weekly basis. Once registered, a survey would be requested. However, prior to the survey taking place, the Lands Departments would update district maps as to the location and boundaries of the claim based on descriptions provided by applicants to Land Agents. District agents used the revised maps to record subsequent claims. Information asymmetries arose because neither Land Agents nor claimants were in a position to accurately define boundaries of selected land. These problems were only alleviated after a survey had taken place. Therefore, any delay between a land claim and survey increased the potential for conflict. For this reason, survey activity had a lagged effect on the potential for conflict. Consequently, a low number of surveys in any one year would increase the probability that some selections were invalidated in future years. Evidence from NSW suggests the lag between selection and survey was approximately nine to 12 months (Morris and Ranken, 1883).

Claims could be invalid for several reasons: 1) the parcel selected infringed on government reserves, that is, land set aside for public purposes such as access to water sources; 2) land selected was owned by squatters under pre-emptive rights. In part, the inability to accurately identify areas to which pre-emption applied was a result of imperfectly defined boundaries of squatters' properties that persisted over time. A typical description of squatters' boundaries:

It followed Mr. Whyte's ploughed line as far as a rock described by Mr. Grant as situated about 350 yards from a tea-tree sapling (should it not touch the rock to be drawn from the nearest point), then a straight plough-furrow to be drawn to the intersection of Mr. Henty's plough-furrow with a creek or marsh [Henty to Geelong Crown Lands Commissioner, quoted in Roberts, 1924: 179].

In turn, Crown Land Commissioners, responsible for recording the property boundaries of squatters within their districts, were often unable to exactly identify these areas. As a result, some areas opened for selection were legally retained by squatters under pre-emption. However, selectors and Land Agents had no way of knowing this until surveys had been completed and boundaries defined; and 3) claims could be invalid because land had been applied for earlier by another selector. As the number of surveys increased, a higher number of invalid claims would be identified and subsequently voided. However, in the years preceding survey, invalid claims were the source of potential conflict between squatters and selectors, as well as between selectors. Potential for conflict would also increase with the number of selections *per annum*.[23] As the number of selections increased so too would information asymmetries caused by inaccurate district maps resulting from survey delays. The greater the number of selections, the higher the probability that areas claimed formed part of squatting properties with unclear boundaries or incorporated land already claimed by another selector. Nevertheless, there is little evidence of actual violence occurring during the selection period (circa 1860 to 1880). Rather than a comparative violence potential mitigating violence, as we will see was the case in the US West, our explanation for the lack of conflict on the Australian frontier arises from the wealth advantage of squatters who had access to the Lands Office. Squatters used their wealth and influence to evade reallocation attempts, effectively insulating them against redistribution.

Loopholes in legislation also made it relatively simple for squatters to engage in evasion – a practice referred to as 'dummying.' Dummying involved squatters contracting with agents, often employees, to select part of their run, register the claim with the Department of Lands (often under false names), and then sell it back to the squatter for a small fee.[24] Dummying also included selecting land under family members' names, particularly children. The use of dummying implies two things: 1) squatters placed a higher value on the land than selectors; and 2) the size of pre-emption claims for squatters was too small (Harris, 2008).[25] In general, the evasion tactics succeeded, leading to the failure of selection policy to effectively redistribute colonial lands to smallholders. Roberts (1924) notes that in NSW over the period of selection eight sections out of every nine passed to original occupants and, by 1883, over eight million acres of colonial land was owned by 96 individuals. Two additional factors complemented the wealth advantage of squatters' ability to evade redistribution: 1) informational asymmetries on land quality concerning its suitability for agriculture; and 2) much of the area open to selection was arid, and unable to support small scale permanent agricultural production.[26] The inherent mobility advantages of sheep grazing made the activity drought tolerant, with sheep able to be moved long distances at low costs and, therefore, more suited to the more arid parts of the frontier. As a result, agriculture on the frontier produced a lower rental stream from land than did sheep grazing. This was compounded by the lack of transport infrastructure to urban markets and high costs of cyclical drought. The prematurity of promoting settled agriculture prior to it being profitable had the benefit of producing little actual conflict between squatters and selectors.[27]

III. SETTLEMENT OF THE US FRONTIER

There have been numerous studies on the overall pattern of settlement of land in the US. Indeed, the leading textbooks in economic history provide good overviews (Atack and Passell, 1994; Hughes and Cain, 2006; Walton and Rockoff, 2004). Here we want to focus on the settlement of the frontier in the Great Plains, which was initially occupied by cattlemen, following the expulsion of Native Americans.[28] We focus on the Great Plains because the land was relatively arid and as such its economic value at the time of settlement did not warrant paying the governmentally fixed price of $1.25/acre. Nevertheless, the region had economic value for ranching.[29] For the first arrivals the land was not scarce and ranchers were free to occupy where they pleased. In Figure 1.1 this corresponds to the region between distances *K* and *J*. This was the situation shortly after the Civil War and continuing through the decade of the 1870s. Because of the ruggedness of the Great Plains the land naturally consisted of a set of ranges. Dennen (1976: 424) defined a range 'as the watershed of a stream, with the provisions that cattle must drink water at least once a day, and the extent of a particular range is limited by the distance cattle can wander in 1 day. This is in the neighborhood of 5 to 10 miles.' The watershed was the basin between two valleys and cattle typically did not cross valleys but tended to meander within a valley. Over time it was difficult to establish exclusivity to an entire range because entrants would have an incentive to come to the range as long as the benefits to their cattle outweighed the costs that they imposed on the current occupants. In the early years of the post Civil War period, the costs were small. But, besides the externalities associated with grazing, once cattle with different owners occupied the same range the issue of ownership arose.

To establish ownership over their cattle, ranchers branded their cattle and ranchers need to have exclusivity to a single brand. On local ranges, it was simple enough for ranchers to recognize brands, but some cattle would stray across ranges, and over time ranchers acted collectively, first through local associations, later state-wide associations and subsequently with legislative approval. The first territorial legislative assemblies in Montana and Wyoming established registration systems (Anderson and Hill, 2004: 149). The registration system of brands established clear ownership and thereby facilitated sales of cattle and limited cattle rustling.

If branding was the only problem in establishing exclusivity then there would not have been any further need for collective action once a registration system was overseen by the government. But, ranchers faced two threats to the productivity of their ranges – this means that ranchers were now in the region between distances *I* and *J* in Figure 1.1. Current occupants of the range would have an incentive to overstock the range as long as the private benefit was positive. In addition outsiders would have the same incentive to enter a range as long as the private benefit was positive. Despite these gains, it is not obvious that cattlemen's associations would spontaneously emerge to solve these problems.[30] Three factors increased the likelihood that commons arrangements would emerge: 1) the number of ranchers on a single range was not large; 2) ranchers were quite homogeneous, facilitating cooperation; and 3) ranchers had to perform a roundup which not only had economies of scale but if performed multiple times inflicted costs on the cattle.

A 'roundup' was a bi-annual activity of collecting the cattle that roamed over the range. In the spring, the round-up allowed ranchers to assess damage from the winter and to brand calves. Assigning a brand to a calf was generally not difficult because calves did not stray far from their mothers. 'Maverick' calves, whose mothers presumably died over the winter, were sold at an auction to those participating in the roundup. During the spring and summer, cows grazed and gained weight making them ready for the market in the fall, which necessitated another roundup. In principle each rancher could perform his own roundup, but this had several problems. If a rancher performed his own roundup then he could steal the cattle of other ranchers, whereas if all ranchers on the range participated in the roundup the stealing was curbed. Moreover, a common roundup had two overarching advantages. A roundup was very labor intensive and there were economies of scale in having one roundup rather than several. The roundup was also stressful on the cattle that had to be herded together; and this disturbed their grazing. In short, given that a roundup made obvious sense, organizing into an association to prevent entry and overgrazing was less costly than it otherwise would have been.

The initial issue of an association was: who was in and who was out. To be a member of a cattlemen's association you had to have a range right. A rancher could gain a range right through several methods. The first rancher in the area acquired rights through 'first possession' which was a well respected norm.[31] Alternatively, ranchers could homestead some land under the provisions of the Homestead Act of 1862 which allowed the claimant title to 160 acres if he resided on the land and cultivated it for five years. A rancher could also file for a pre-emption claim, which meant that he had the right to purchase 160 acres at $1.25/acre when the government decided to put the land up for auction at some future date – land containing water was worth $1.25/acre – and many ranchers opted for this avenue.

After formation one of the first issues confronting a cattlemen's association was to exclude outsiders. This was accomplished by posting that the range was closed, generally through an announcement in a newspaper and not allowing a potential entrant to participate in the collective roundup.[32] Dennen (1976: 427) provides a succinct example of such a notice that was published in the Helena Montana *Daily Herald* of September 3, 1883:

> We the undersigned, stock growers of the above described range, hereby give notice that we consider the said range already overstocked: therefore we positively decline allowing any outside parties or any parties locating herds upon this range the use of our corrals, nor will they be permitted to join us in any roundup on said range from and after this date.

After preventing entry to limit overgrazing, the occupants of the range had to prevent two externalities: 1) because cows were sent to market and all calves went with them to the owner of the cows, ranchers had an incentive to put cows on the range but not bulls. Moreover, it mattered to all that the quality of the bulls was high; and 2) the total number of cows on the range had to be limited to prevent overgrazing with the result that cows did not put on sufficient weight to withstand the winter. The By-Laws of the Little Missouri River Stockmen's Association provided a clause stipulating the bull to cow ratio:

> It is the sense of this Association, and is hereby made binding on its members, that any man who shall hereafter turn out any female neat cattle upon the range shall place with them, at the time of the turning loose not less than seven (7) serviceable bulls for every one hundred (100) head of female cattle which are two years old and upward at that time; . . . Proved violation of

the above rule shall be deemed a proper subject for the complaint, the penalty to be decided by a majority of the Association present at the next meeting.[33]

Limiting overstocking on ranges was difficult because to a certain extent it was an ex-post problem in that, if the winter was expected to be mild, collectively you would want to stock more cattle than if ranchers expected a harsh winter.[34] In any event a procedure needed to be adopted to ensure overstocking relative to other members. On many ranges, the number of cattle that one could graze would be in proportion to water rights which were acquired through first possession, pre-emption claims, or homesteading. The ability of cattlemen's associations to prevent overstocking is mixed but the evidence is clear that in most cases the cattlemen's associations produced rents over the condition of open access. Evidence consistent with the production of rents was the monetary exchange of range rights:

> The agreements regarding such matters as the partition of the range and use of water became property rights and were frequently bought and sold as land is sold today. Once a man's range rights were determined, they were respected by all [Yost 1966: 129; quoted from Dennen 1976: 434].

Dennen (1976: 434) gives evidence of two transactions of range rights. Exclusive of the value of the cattle and land, Dennen estimates the value of range rights for two ranches and found that the value reached $200,000 for the sale of range rights on one ranch near the peak of prices in 1884. Dennen also found that some ranches carried range rights on their accounting books as a positive asset.

We also have considerable evidence that cattle survival rates were higher following the historically harsh winter of 1886–1887 for ranges that had an association versus ones that didn't. Mattison (1950: 190) describes the winter in North Dakota:

> Blizzards struck in the middle of November and continued. The snow, although melting and freezing, piled higher and higher. By January the ravines and coulees were almost level with snow. The snow lay for several feet on the plateaus and river bottoms – too deep for the cattle to get through to the grass. . . . During February, March and April, there was considerable speculation among the cattlemen as to what their losses would be.

The losses for the Little Missouri Stockmen's Association were so high that the members did not hold a general roundup in the spring of 1887 but waited until July (Mattison, 1950: 191, quoting from the *Dickinson Press,* April 23, 1887).[35] Across the West the winter of 1886–1887 was horrific. Loss rates varied inversely with the weight of cattle because cattle can live off their fat for a considerable period of time. In his archival research Dennen (1976) found that loss rates varied considerably across ranges in large part not due to variation in weather but rather due to the effectiveness of organizations to limit entry and prevent overgrazing. The loss rates in Montana ranged from 10% to 80–90% depending mostly on the degree of overstocking (Dennen, 1976: 432). Some overstocking was due to the inability to prevent open access, particularly along routes for cattle drives. On other ranges, the differences in stocking could be due to different expectations of weather or prices.[36]

Given the fact that very little of land grazed was under *de jure* secure property rights, one might have anticipated that there would be conflict. However, it appears that over the period following the Civil War to the early years of the twentieth century there was little open conflict amongst cattlemen. The reason seems straightforward. Once a cattlemen's association formed, it had a comparative advantage in violence over potential entrants and, moreover, the ability of excluding a potential entrant from participating in the collective roundup dramatically reduced the incentive to enter. There was some conflict between cattlemen and sheep herders on the public domain. This resulted from the inability to prevent entry for sheep herders through the exclusionary device of the roundup, which worked for cattlemen. To prevent intrusion onto what cattlemen's associations claimed as their range 'fences or force were the only successful protective measures' (Osgood, 1929: 189; quoted in Anderson and Hill, 2004: 167). Nevertheless, the sheep herders never posed a serious threat to the sustainability of cattlemen's associations, because the violence potential of ranchers collectively on a range trumped the violence potential of a sheepherder. Sheepherders did not naturally band together for a roundup because sheep herds grazed alone and were tended. To avoid conflict, sheepherders migrated to land not as well suited to cattle; more rugged and at higher elevations. The role for ultimately causing the demise of the commons arrangements fell to homesteaders.

Congress passed the Homestead Act in 1862. The Act allowed a claimant the right to a title to 160 acres of the public domain provided the claimant resided on the land for five years and paid a $10 registration fee. The largesse of the government should not be overstated because, by the time of the Homestead Act, most of the fertile land in the country had been purchased. Nevertheless, the post Civil War period brought a continued westward expansion of the railroads and massive immigration, both of which gave an increased incentive to settle and cultivate land in the Great Plains despite the aridity of the region. Because the government was still selling land at $1.25/acre, the land remaining for homesteading was generally used for ranching. Naturally, the less arid land was first settled, which meant that it took time for homesteaders to reach the ranching regions of west of the 100th meridian.[37] Homesteaders began moving into the Great Plains region in the 1880s.

By the time homesteaders began moving into the region many ranchers had fenced their ranges as a result of the invention of barbed wire. This enabled ranchers to better track their herds and prevent cattle from drifting onto other ranges. In addition it posed an obstacle for homesteaders who were reluctant to cut fences for fear of retaliation. In a direct conflict between a cattlemen's association and a single homesteader or even group of homesteaders, ranchers had a comparative advantage in violence. Instead of direct conflict we witnessed both ranchers and homesteaders seeking redress in the political arena.[38]

Since the settlement of the Great Plains, cattlemen petitioned Congress for more lenient land laws. Congress responded in 1879 with a commission to investigate the use of arid lands in the West. The Commission recommended that the homestead size be increased in the arid regions of the West from 160 acres to 2,560 acres. Despite the enthusiastic support of John Wesley Powell and other advocates familiar with conditions in the West, Congress opted to remain with the *status quo*. Undoubtedly this was the result of the large number of potential homesteaders and their political influence. Retaining the *status quo* meant retaining the *de jure* property right for homesteaders. Yet, the General Land Office (GLO) did little to enforce the rights of homesteaders against ranchers.

The reason for the inaction of the land office was twofold: the GLO was budget constrained and the ranching lobby had more influence through the executive branch which controlled the activities of the GLO. The GLO was under the control of the Interior Department. The Secretary of the Interior appointed the Commissioner of Land Office with no control over his appointment, except perhaps by the President. Until the early 1880s the GLO condoned the informal claims of ranchers and did nothing about the 'illegal fencing' of the public domain. During the term of Commissioner Noah McFarland (1881–1884) the GLO was flooded with letters from prospective home-steaders asking the GLO to intervene on their behalf. McFarland sent agents out west to determine the extent of illegal fencing and the GLO issued a report to Congress in 1884. Congress, which represented Homestead interests, passed anti-fencing legislation in 1885. Commissioner Sparks succeeded McFarland. Sparks appears to have been a dedicated civil servant and advocate of homesteaders. In 1886 he authorized the printing of the names of ranchers who had illegal enclosures on public lands. Furthermore, he persuaded the War Department to take down the illegal fences in Wyoming. Naturally, ranchers in Wyoming lobbied the Interior Department through their Congressmen to prevent action by the War Department. The process was at a stalemate until the Secretary of the Interior asked for the resignation of Commissioner Sparks and replaced Sparks with a new Commissioner who was sympathetic to the interests of ranchers. Subsequently, the GLO did not engage in any anti-fencing activity until the Presidency of Teddy Roosevelt in 1901. Nevertheless, Congress made it impossible for ranchers to formalize their large holdings by ending all cash sales of federal lands in 1891. As a result the informal commons arrangements of ranchers continued into the 20th century and were eventually replaced with government leases.

Ironically, Roosevelt, who was a rancher, sent out the cavalry to enforce the *de jure* rights of homesteaders. This resulted in a rapid increase in the number of homesteads filed in the Great Plains states.[39] The increased settlement by homesteaders prompted the move-ment of ranching activities onto more arid land in the West. Again there was little actual conflict because in a show of force between the cavalry and ranchers the cavalry would win hands down, so ranchers opted to move their livestock rather than fight. Throughout the period of the commons arrangements, circa 1870 to 1900, we found little evidence of con-flict resulting in violence because the outcome was always certain. The collective arrange-ments of ranchers into cattlemen's associations prevented entry onto ranges designated as closed because an entrant did not stand a chance against a group of ranchers. Similarly prospective homesteaders unless backed by the coercive power of state would lose in a violent conflict against ranchers. Eventually, when the government acted to enforce *de jure* property rights against the *de facto* property rights of ranchers, the ranchers backed down and allowed homesteaders in. The saga of the years under commons arrangements and the emergence of formal rights demonstrates the interplay of *de facto* versus *de jure* property rights and the important role of politics intermediating the two.

IV.   SETTLEMENT OF THE BRAZILIAN AMAZONIAN FRONTIER[40]

Until the mid-1960s the Amazon was virtually isolated from the rest of Brazil, with a total of only 6,000 kilometers of roads (only 300 km paved) for an area of over 5 million square kilometers. Fewer than 2.5 million people inhabited the region, mostly near the cities of Manaus and Belem, with most of the area subject to extremely low population densities. Economic activity was sparse and income *per capita* very low. This scenario fits the *OHDK* region of Figure 1.1 or possibly even the region to the right of distance *K*, as most economic activity would yield negative economic returns given the lack of infrastructure and markets. This situation started to change abruptly with the completion of the Belem–Brasilia highway in 1964 and with the great interest demonstrated by the new military dictatorship in occupying the Amazon and integrating it with the rest of the country. The overriding motivation behind this interest was geo-political, based on the military leaders' deeply held belief that foreign powers, especially the US, coveted the region for its riches and would eventually try to invade it. Secondary motivations were the desire to use the region as a demographic safety valve to alleviate social problems in other regions and the hope of encountering vast deposits of mineral wealth.

In the next two decades a continuous series of policies was devised and implementation initiated as a consequence of these motivations. The late 1960s and early 1970s was a period of very high economic growth that is known as the 'Brazilian Miracle', so that both the resources and the confidence existed in abundance to fuel the megalomaniacal schemes of taming the Amazon. What followed was a series of policies that had great physical, social, economic and environmental impacts on the region, though never quite what was originally anticipated, most often leading to unexpected and unintended consequences that would lead to the abandonment of the old plans and pursuit of a new line of action. Each of these sets of policies opened new areas and created situations where a varied mix of players competed for the rents that emerged. These players include landless peasants, settlers in official colonization projects, ranchers, large corporations pursuing fiscal incentives, mining companies, hordes of gold-diggers, Indians, priests, government officials from myriad different agencies, and hydroelectricity projects, among others. Government policies frequently pitted the players against one another in an explosive mix, because the government's policies were sufficiently coordinated to attract players to the focus areas but not enough to make the players act as the government intended. Corporations, for example, would create large ranches so as to receive fiscal incentives and tax breaks offered by the government, but would often not deign to actually stock them with cattle as the rates of return were often negative, leaving vast tracts of cleared land subject to invasion by landless peasants. Similarly the creation of colonization projects attracted not only the intended clients from southern Brazil, but also spontaneous multitudes of poor northeasterners that would often squat on land where it was rumored a road would eventually be built, in the hope of preempting a plot when rents would rise. With very little capacity to enforce its policies, the government lost agenda control and situations spiraled out of control. For example, the government was powerless against the conflicts that emerged and the inexorable devastation of the forest that inevitably followed. This process is described by Almeida (1992: 116) in a book about colonization in the Amazon:

> The decade of the 1970's was the peak of the colonization effort. . . . Huge populations followed, or even anticipated, the roads built by the state in an unprecedented northwesterly migratory flux. New social and physical infrastructure sharply increased land values on the frontier. Industrial and financial groups that previously had not been involved with land were attracted. A vast territory was added to the sphere of influence of the southern economy. Resources mobilized by the state were small compared to those demanded of Amazon occupation and were

insufficient to control the transformation process that was started. Not only were governmental resources insufficient for the Amazon frontier, but they suffered increasing competition from the Center-West's agro-industrial frontier, which gained importance throughout the decade.

In terms of our framework in Figure 1.1 this period experienced a sharp shift of the net present value lines upwards, bringing land that was beyond the frontier into the economic realm and transforming land that was in the *OGCJ* and *OHDK* region, where informal norms enforced property rights, into the region to the left of distance *I* where a lack of clear property rights resulted in rent dissipation and conflicts. It is important to stress the abrupt nature of the increase in land values, which rose not out of a conventional process of frontier evolution, but from an intense and unpredictable effort by the Brazilian government:

> These plans included an ambitious road-building program to link Amazonia with the Northeast and South, agricultural colonization schemes, and fiscal incentives to attract new industrial and agricultural enterprises. An administrative structure, which included a regional development agency and a regional development bank, was created to coordinate the implementation of these plans. . . . a key objective of Operation Amazonia was to attract private enterprise to the region. This was to be achieved through increased public expenditures on infrastructure – for example, roads, airports, telecommunications – and special fiscal incentives and credit lines for firms willing to establish operations in Amazonia [Mahar, 1989: 11 and 13].

In 1970 the focus of government policy shifted to the National Integration Plan (PIN – *Plano de Integração Nacional*) which concentrated on further road building and on directed colonization. The colonization projects were set up under the auspices of INCRA (National Institute for Colonization and Agrarian Reform), which was created in 1970. INCRA's mandate included the titling of federal land, colonization projects and subsequently land reform projects. Almeida (1992) is a detailed study of the costs of the government's directed colonization schemes of the 1970s. She concludes that the colonization of the Amazon frontier cost about $7.5 billion during that decade, with $4.1 billion going towards building roads, $0.182 billion spent on titling, $0.443 billion directly on settlement projects and $2.8 billion on other institutions such as schools, health care units and extension. Whereas the expenditures on roads, settlement projects and other institutions sharply increased the rents to holding land, the provision of formal property rights to mediate and discipline who would have access to those rights was clearly not sufficient to avoid the ensuing wasteful competition for rents. The early competition amongst a diverse group of settlers, some resorting to fraudulent titles, exacerbated the current difficulty of sorting out informal and formal property rights in the Amazon.

Figure 1.2 shows the growth of the network of roads that opened access to vast areas for the multiple types of social and economic actors. It also shows the availability of rural credit that spiked in the second half of the 1970s as the government became disillusioned with directed settlement as a means to occupy the region and switched instead to a strategy based on large operations – primarily cattle ranches. Subsidized credit and tax incentive schemes formed the basis of the government's revised strategy, available only to those with titled land. The fiscal incentives were highly attractive and increased dramatically the number of large landowners; many of the ranches purchased were quite large – over 25,000 hectares. Competition for land by all claimants increased because

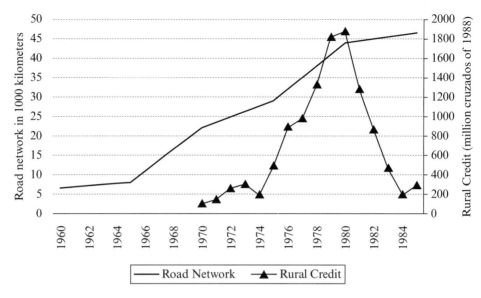

Source: Mahar, D. 1989. *Government Policies and Deforestation in Brazil's Amazon Region.* Washington: The World Bank.

Figure 1.2   A shock to the Amazon frontier: road network and rural credit

of the construction of roads. Claimants capitalized on the expected benefits from the fiscal incentives (for those with titled land) and the new roads and the fiscal incentives into higher land values. Gasques and Yokomizo (1986) analyzed a sample of subsidized projects and showed that the vast majority of settlers came in order to exploit the fiscal benefits and rarely achieved more than 10% of the ranching potential projected by the government. As we noted above, this situation of vast cleared yet unused plots of land, in the midst of masses of landless peasants that had been attracted by the possibility of settlement projects and the availability of roads, set the stage for numerous conflicts in the following decades. Indeed, Alston, Libecap and Mueller (1999) found a strong direct impact of the level of fiscal incentives in county-level regressions explaining the level of conflicts in the Amazonian state of Para.

Thus far we have described changes that led to an increase in land scarcity and rents in the Amazon since the 1960s. We now turn to a more detailed analysis of the property rights that emerged in this process. The spontaneous migrants had the right to squat on public land and were entitled to a use right after cultivating the land for a year and a day. After five years they had the right to a formal title. The squatters moved to the frontier as long as they more than covered their opportunity cost which we designated as *OHDK* in Figure 1.1. The migration was significant because with road building associated with the colonization projects, the government raised the return from being in the Amazon.[41] Squatters developed a set of norms associated with settlement. The norm was that you squatted on 100–150 hectares and others would respect your claim. Given the low scarcity of land there was no conflict amongst squatters. As scarcity values increased over time, squatters formed some informal commons arrangement for goods that had collective and private benefits, initially the region between distances *J* and *I* in our Figure 1.1. One collective good was the recognition and enforcement of the claims of others. As scarcity values increased further over time, squatters also organized to petition the government for legal titles which frequently were not forthcoming after five years. Squatters valued title not because of insecurity or for a lack of markets to exchange squatted claims but rather because it would help them access formal capital markets. The fact that they valued titles indicated that they had entered the region to the left of distance *I* in Figure 1.1. Despite increased scarcity values, social norms produced a commons arrangement that prevented violent conflict. This resulted from the homogeneous claims of the migrants as well as similar socio-economic backgrounds.

The settlement by colonists was similar to squatters though the government organized the settlement and provided more infrastructure. The size of plots was between 100 and 150 hectares, which was the norm chosen by squatters. The success of the colonization projects varied across the Amazon because the government did not always choose the land most suited to cultivation. The settlers as well did not possess as much local knowledge as the spontaneous migrants because many were recruited from the southern regions of Brazil. The colonists differed from the squatters in having more formal schooling, which may have made them better at accessing government services. The government did provide credit but they were slow in providing title, which hampered the ability to access credit. The colonists over time became essentially indistinguishable from the squatters except they were more likely to have a title. With or without a title social norms prevented conflict and ensured use rights for the claim.

The claimants who moved to the Amazon because of fiscal incentives differed significantly from the small landholders. In the case of large claimants, the rental stream from the land did not warrant their presence. In this sense it was induced premature settlement. Indeed many never moved but had managers who ran cattle operations. The rate of return from cattle in the 1970s and 1980s was presumably quite low, because stocking rates were very low or non-existent until the government began to enforce use as a condition for receiving tax credits. Over time the land did become more valuable and also provided a hedge against inflation, which until the 1990s was a major rationale for owning land. Without the fiscal incentives the large claimants would not have been in the Amazon because their opportunity costs were too high. But, their titled land rights set the pre-condition for subsequent land conflicts in the Amazon which continue to this day.

The titles to land carried the rights conveyed by the Civil Code which stipulated that you could use the land as you wished; you could sell the land; and you could enlist the coercive power of the state to evict trespassers. Until the 1980s most titled claimants felt secure with their holdings. But, over time squatters increasingly encroached on the large titled holdings because much of the titled land was of higher value than was available on the frontier of the public domain. Squatters also had a legal right to squat on private land because of a provision in the Brazilian Constitution. The historical Constitutions in Brazil (and reaffirmed in Article 191 of the 1988 Constitution still in force) gave squatters the right to occupy up to 50 hectares of privately owned land that was not put to use by the owner. If the squatter is not contested in his claim in five years he has the right to a title under adverse possession. Typically squatters would be contested, so little land was acquired in this manner.

Until squatters became better organized there was little actual violent conflict between the squatters and the titled owners of the land. The typical pattern followed by the actors was for squatters to occupy titled land, clear it and grow subsistence crops. Frequently, the owner was well aware of the occupancies and did not care. Indeed, clearing the land was viewed as improvement. At the time, when the owner wanted to use the land, he would ask the squatters to leave and generally pay them something for their improvements. A law was passed stating that owners pay squatters for improvements. This was not an enforceable law but a norm amongst owners developed such that it was common for them to pay for improvements. We do not have any hard data but the secondary literature argues that squatters were not fully compensated for improvements. Nevertheless, the squatters had no legal recourse because the large ranchers held sway over the local courts and squatters had difficulty in accessing the judicial system given their low levels of education.[42] At times some squatters who had banded together tried to resist an eviction, but the rancher had access to the local police as well as hired gunmen. In the face of overwhelming odds, most squatters opted to move on when asked to do so. The difference between this case and the case of ranchers in the US versus homesteaders is that in Brazil both had a legal right to be on the land. The similarity of the situations is that the ranchers had a greater violence potential and had better access to the political process, at least initially in Brazil and the US.

Beginning in the 1980s INCRA began to be less involved with colonization and more concerned with land reform based on compensated but forced expropriation for redistribution. The Constitution also gave squatters an opening. The Constitution stipulates that if land is not put into 'beneficial use' the state has the right to expropriate the land. This is a paid expropriation and can be contested in court, but it allowed INCRA to expropriate land and redistribute it to squatters. Squatters realized that if they invaded land, then INCRA would have a greater incentive to intervene to prevent bloodshed and, with luck, expropriate the land and give it to the squatters. However, because squatters had a comparative disadvantage in violence, the *status quo* prevailed. The situation began to change in the late 1980s and much more dramatically in the 1990s with the arrival of two groups which began to organize squatters and act as their advocates with the judicial system and media. As an outgrowth of the liberation theology movement in Brazil, some local priests became concerned with the well-being of the poor squatters. They helped organize meetings and encouraged some invasions of private land. They also stood up to powerful ranchers and several lost their lives in the process. Nevertheless, the liberation theology movement was the inspiration for the much more successful Landless Peasants Movement (MST – *Movimento Sem-Terra*).

The MST has gained momentum over time but the basic strategy has not changed. It organizes landless peasants into groups and unifies them in camps, providing them with sufficient food to survive. Their *forte* is their use of the media (Alston, Libecap and Mueller 2008). The MST decides on a target farm and makes a public announcement that it will invade a certain farm on a certain date. The reason for the public announcement is threefold: 1) it wants to sway public opinion in favor of the landless and thereby influence policy and budgetary allocations; 2) in making the invasion known publicly the MST hopes that the government will send in the military to prevent bloodshed; and 3) the MST hopes that INCRA will expropriate the invaded farm and redistribute the land to the group of invaders that it organized. The MST has been successful on all three fronts. The popularity of the President who controls the agenda in Brazil is negatively affected by occupations, prompting INCRA to expropriate more farms and settle more landless (Alston, Libecap and Mueller 2008). In addition the number of people killed in conflicts over land has declined, especially on land invasions organized by the MST.

What lessons can we learn from the settlement of the Brazilian frontier concerning property rights? The overriding lesson was that the prematurely induced settlement of the Amazon by titleholders over large tracts of land induced land conflict. Had the large landholders not been induced to settle land we anticipate that settlement would have occurred more in the fashion outlined in Figure 1.1 with property rights evolving over time from spontaneous migration and informal norms allocating and enforcing property rights to commons arrangements allocating and enforcing property rights as well as petitioning the government for the provision of titles. This argument takes on credence because this is the scenario that has transpired on much of the public domain in the Amazon. The biggest lesson is the imperative to avoid a legal conflict over *de jure* property rights. The Civil Code in Brazil is clear and transparent, giving the property rights to titleholders. The clause in the Constitution granting the government the power to expropriate land if the land is not in beneficial use is a catalyst for conflict. It allowed the MST to overtake the government in setting the agenda for land reform and has led to deaths and conflict. In a sense the beneficial use clause in the Constitution has given the MST a *de facto* property right to land in rural areas. This does not mean that Brazil should not engage in land reform but it does imply that Brazil should have a different land reform policy rather than ceding it to the MST.

V.   CONCLUDING REMARKS

In our theoretical framework there is a progression of settlement: from squatters, with norms; to commons arrangements with norms along with some second party enforcement; and ultimately to formally titled land. In all three case studies, the government intervened to encourage premature or inappropriate settlement which led to either actual conflict or the potential for conflict. The Australian case exhibited the least actual conflict between the heterogeneous settlers, the squatters who moved to the frontier to graze sheep and the selectors who moved to take up agriculture because of government policies. Little conflict emerged because by the time of the migration of the selectors the squatters were wealthy and politically connected and thereby better able to evade the law on limiting acreage. Moreover, the rental stream from the land was higher for grazing than settled agriculture so over time squatters could out-compete the agriculturalists for the land. The US case had a high potential for conflict but little conflict transpired because of the disproportionate violence advantage for ranchers over homesteaders. Ranchers moved to the frontier first and progressed from informal claimants with norms of settlement to more organized cattlemen's associations. Homesteaders subsequently attempted to settle on the land held informally by ranchers, but the ranchers through threats of violence dissuaded many potential homesteaders from filing claims. Instead the homesteaders took their grievances to the political arena though it took the government nearly 20 years to act on their behalf. Once the US cavalry came to the aid of homesteaders, ranchers backed down and moved further west. The Brazilian Amazon case exhibited the most actual violence which continues today. The original squatters, like the first settlers in Australia and the US, established norms protecting their claims from encroachment and, had the government not induced settlement of large ranching operations through tax incentives, we envision that the settlement process would have been peaceful and followed a natural progression dictated by the scarcity of land. The advent of ranchers in the Amazon with land closer to markets than the frontier available for squatters was a target for the squatters because of a clause in the Brazilian Constitution dictating that land should be put to beneficial use and allowing adverse possession. Nevertheless, at first, the ranchers had a dominant violence potential so squatters, when asked to vacate private ranches, typically left peacefully. Over time the squatters organized in larger groups of families such that their violence potential began to equal that of the ranchers. In addition, squatters strategically used the press to announce land invasions in order to bring the federal government into the conflict to limit bloodshed.

The establishment of norms by all original settlers shared certain characteristics: 1) the settlers limited the size of claims (or the number of sheep or cattle allowed to graze); 2) the claimants agreed to uphold the claims of others; 3) the claimants at some point banded together to exclude outsiders; and 4) the claimants petitioned the government for formal recognition of their claims as scarcity values increased. Except for ranchers, who had a collective roundup which naturally brought them together into an organization, the other claimants had to circumvent the free-rider problem. All managed to do so, though so far we are left with only a functionalist explanation. We hope to move beyond this explanation in future research.

NOTES

*   We thank Lee Cronk, Henry Smith and participants at a seminar on social norms at the Institute for Advanced Study in Princeton. Alston and Mueller acknowledge the support of NSF grant #528146. Alston thanks the STEP Program at Woodrow Wilson School at Princeton for their support as a Visiting Research Scholar during the Fall term of 2008.
1.   Barzel (1989) makes this point most explicitly and clearly.
2.   We expand on the framework developed in Alston, Libecap and Schneider (1996) and Alston, Libecap and Mueller (1999).
3.   Again in our figure, distance is the frontier but it could as easily be the quality of soil.
4.   A roundup in the spring was a yearly activity on the range which entailed capturing all the cattle on the range and sorting them according to their brands, and branding new calves, which never strayed far from their mothers. This activity was accomplished at lower cost if all ranchers engaged in the activity. It also enabled ranchers to monitor for overstocking the range.
5.   An example of informal arrangements includes cattlemen's associations in the 19th century US West (Dennen, 1976). See Anderson and Hill (2002); Eggertsson (1990); Ostrom (1990) and Umbeck (1981) for accounts of local groups allocating resources under 'common' arrangements. See Smith (2000) for an analysis of 'semi-commons' arrangements.
6.   The framework accommodates any force that increases (or decreases) the net present value of the land.
7.   We will expand on the role of cattlemen's associations in our US case study.
8.   Insecure property rights may also reduce the value of the resource to the usurper; however one would expect this effect to be smaller than the effect on the probability of successful appropriation.
9.   Smith (2002) gives numerous other examples consistent with current 'rights' holders using exclusion successfully to deter entrants. Acheson's (1987) discussion of the use of exclusion amongst lobster fishermen is a particularly good example consistent with 'home court' advantage. Smith (2002: S485) also makes the excellent observation that in deciding between governance and exclusion as mechanisms for controlling behavior on the commons 'a limit on behavior is pointless unless access is limited first.'
10.   Tasmania, Victoria, and Queensland became separate colonial jurisdictions during the 1850s.
11.   Captain James Cook declared the Australian east coast British territory in 1770. On settlement in 1788,

the British Crown declared the continent 'terra nullius': specifically, the land belonged to no one. This pronouncement implicitly denied the existence of ownership rights by first inhabitants, thereby dispossessing Australian Aboriginals under the British territorial claim. It followed that all land in Australia, unless expressly granted to individuals as freehold, was owned by the Crown.

12. Settlement concentration was in part a result of the need to restrain the convict element, but it was also attributable to the influential writing of colonial theorist, Edward Wakefield, an exponent of systematic colonization. Roberts (1924); Crowley (1980); and Kociumbas (1988) provide lengthy discussions of Wakefieldian theories.

13. Of significance is the increase in 'free' population (excluding military and convicts), that is, migrants entering NSW. During this period, free population increased from 12,846 in 1820 to approximately 50,000 by 1836 (Vamplew, 1987; Roberts, 1935).

14. Burroughs (1967) argues that £1 per acre was in excess of the productive value of colonial land due to enormous quality variation impacting its suitability for agriculture.

15. Imlah's (1950) wool price index for the United Kingdom uses Spanish, Leonesa, Saxon, and Australian price series to construct estimates from 1822 to 1880. Shergold's (1987) series (Table PC 106–107) in Vamplew (1987) is for Australian greasy wool 1850–1969.

16. Eighty % of Australia receives less than 600mm of rain *per annum*. On average, one sheep requires 3 acres of grazing land.

17. Burroughs (1967: 315–319) discusses in some detail the nature of squatters' lobbying activities in Britain during this period.

18. As you will see, early claimants in the US and the Brazilian Amazon were able to sell their informal claims indicating that the commons arrangements prevented dissipation.

19. An Act to continue and amend an Act intituled 'An Act to restrain the unauthorized occupation of Crown Lands' (2 Vic., No. 19, 1838).

20. Victoria was granted separation in 1850; Tasmania in 1856; and Queensland in 1859. Western Australia (WA) and South Australia (SA) were settled in 1827 and 1834 respectively, independently of NSW. WA, initially a free settlement, was founded by Captain James Stirling. However, in order to increase labor supply, in the 1830s it became a penal colony administered by the British Colonial Office. SA was established via Imperial legislation (South Australia Colonisation Act, 4&5 William IV).

21. WA and SA were the exceptions; WA remained a British colony until 1890, all land policy was determined by the British Colonial Office; and SA never introduced selection before survey.

22. By the 1860s universal male suffrage and removal of property ownership requirements limiting eligibility for election to colonial parliaments had occurred; these acted to reduce squatter representation and smooth the path of land reform. Limits to pre-emption in NSW allowed squatters to claim 320 acres and then one square mile in every 25 from their original holdings.

23. As you can see in the Appendix the number of selectors increased significantly over time, peaking in 1874.

24. In the US, ranchers also had hired men file for homestead claims for which the ranchers subsequently reimbursed their employees.

25. The restriction on size in arid areas parallels the US case.

26. The same situation arose in the US West where many homestead claims subsequently were abandoned because the land could not support agriculture (Libecap and Hanson, 2004).

27. The premature encouragement of settlement in the arid US West by homesteaders did not lead to much actual conflict but the premature encouragement through tax incentives in the Amazon for large ranching operations led to increased conflict.

28. There are many general accounts of the 'open range' period, including Briggs (1934); Nimmo (1884–1885); Osgood (1929); Pelzer (1936); and Sandoz (1958). Earlier authors used the term 'open range' when in fact they meant commons arrangements. We relied on these accounts for general overviews. On the specifics of cattlemen's arrangements and their economic rationale we relied heavily on Anderson and Hill (2004) and Dennen (1976).

29. Dennen (1976: 423) estimated the land was worth $1.00/acre for ranching.

30. Demsetz (1967) argued that property rights would spontaneously emerge to limit dissipation but this ignores the collective action problem.

31. In our Brazilian case study we will argue that squatters in Brazil also respected first possession. It appears as if first possession as a norm for allocating rights works well when scarcity is not high – distances J-K in Fig. 1.1. In subsequent work we will explore the use of first possession for claiming land in the Midwestern region of the US country prior to the land being open to settlers through auction. For an excellent analysis of the political economy of the use of first possession in the US Midwest see Kanazawa (1996). For the general use of first possession to allocate property rights see Lueck (2003) and Libecap (2007).

32. Teddy Roosevelt apparently infringed on the range rights of one of his neighbors and Roosevelt promptly removed his cattle (Mattison, 1950).

33. Quoted from Mattison 1950: 203.

34. Recent work in behavioral economics, borrowing from psychology or sociology, shows that humans, especially males, tend to be ex-post too optimistic.
35. Teddy Roosevelt was a member of the Little Missouri Stockmen's Association and was its president for several years.
36. To some extent human optimism may play a role. McCabe (2004) argues that for nomadic herds in present day Kenya and Tanzania the optimal strategy for herders is to stock as much as possible and periodically suffer large losses because of the inability to predict droughts.
37. The 100th meridian is typically designated as the longitude at which precipitation declines, making non-irrigated agriculture unprofitable in general unless prices are very high or rainfall better than average. The 100th meridian runs through North Dakota, South Dakota, Nebraska, Kansas, Oklahoma and Texas.
38. This section draws heavily on Alston, Libecap and Mueller (1998).
39. We note that not all of the increased settlement was the result of the activities of Roosevelt. Wheat prices recovered following the recession of the mid-1890s and remained high until 1920.
40. This section draws on Alston, Libecap and Mueller (1998 and 2000).
41. In terms of Figure 1.1, the line AE shifted out and to the right, prompting those with lowest opportunity costs to migrate first.
42. In our household surveys of small landholders in the Amazon we found that the mean years of formal education was two.

REFERENCES

Acheson, James M. 1987. 'The Lobster Fiefs Revisited: Economic and Ecological Effects of Territoriality in the Maine Lobster Industry' in Bonnie J. McCay and James M. Acheson (eds) *The Question of the Commons: The Culture and Ecology of Communal Resources*, Tucson: University of Arizona Press.

Almeida, Ana L.O. 1992. *The Colonization of the Amazon*, Tucson: University of Texas Press.

Alston, Lee J., Gary D. Libecap and Bernardo Mueller. 1998. 'Property Rights and Land Conflict: A Comparison of the U.S. Western and Brazilian Amazon Frontiers' in John H. Coatsworth and Alan M. Taylor (eds) *Latin America and the World Economy Since 1800*. Cambridge: Harvard University Press, 55–85.

Alston, Lee J., Gary D. Libecap and Bernardo Mueller. 1999. *Titles, Conflict, and Land Use: The Development of Property Rights and Land Reform on the Brazilian Amazon Frontier*. Ann Arbor, MI: The University of Michigan Press.

Alston, Lee J., Gary D. Libecap and Bernardo Mueller. 2000. 'Land Reform Policies: The Sources of Violent Conflict, and Implications for Deforestation in the Brazilian Amazon', *Journal of Environmental Economics and Management,* 39 (2), 162–188.

Alston, Lee J., Gary D. Libecap and Bernardo Mueller. 2008. 'Interest Groups, Information Manipulation and Public Policy: The Landless Peasants Movement in Brazil', Working Paper. University of Colorado.

Alston, Lee J., Gary D. Libecap and Robert Schneider. 1996. 'The Determinants and Impact of Property Rights: Land Titles on the Brazilian Frontier', *Journal of Law Economics and Organization*, 12, 25–61.

Anderson, Terry L. and Peter J. Hill. 1975. 'The Evolution of Property Rights: A Study of the American West', *Journal of Law and Economics*, 18 (1), 163–179.

Anderson, Terry L. and Peter J. Hill. 1990. 'The Race for Property Rights', *Journal of Law and Economics*, 33 (April), 177–197.

Anderson, Terry L. and Peter J. Hill. 2002. 'Cowboys and Contracts', *Journal of Legal Studies*, 31 (June), S489–S514.

Anderson Terry L. and Peter J. Hill. 2004. *The Not so Wild, Wild West: Property Rights on the Frontier*. Stanford, CA: Stanford University Press.

ANSW, 4/3660, Colonial Secretary. Main series of letters received 1826–1982.

Atack, Jeremy and Peter Passell. 1994. *A New Economic View of American History*. New York: W.W. Norton and Company.

Barzel, Yoram. 1989. *Economic Analysis of Property Rights*. New York: Cambridge University Press.

Braim, H.A. 1846. *A History of NSW: From its Settlement to the Close of the Year 1844*. New York: Bently Press.

Briggs, H.E. 1934. 'The Development and Decline of Open Range Ranching in the Northwest', *Mississippi Valley Review*, 20, 521–536.

Burroughs, Peter. 1967. *Britain and Australia 1831–1855: A Study in Imperial Relations and Crown Lands Administration*. Oxford: Clarendon Press.

Coase, Ronald. 1960. 'The Problem of Social Cost', *The Journal of Law and Economics*, 3, 1–44.

Crowley, F. 1980. *Colonial Australia 1788–1840*. Volume One. Melbourne: Nelson Press.

Curr, E.M. 2001. *Recollections of Squatting in Victoria, then called the Port Phillip District (from 1841 to 1851)*, 2nd edn. Melbourne: Melbourne University Press.

Demsetz, Harold. 1967. 'Towards a Theory of Property Rights', *American Economic Review*, 57 (2), 347–359.

Dennen, R.T. 1976. 'Cattlemen's Associations and Property Rights in the American West', *Explorations in Economic History*, 13, 423–436.

Dingle, Anthony. 1984. *The Victorians Settling*. Melbourne: Fairfax, Syme and Weldon.

Eggertsson, Thráinn. 1990. *Economic Behavior and Instituions*. New York: Cambridge University Press.

Fetherstonhaugh, Cuthbert. 1917. *After Many Days*. Melbourne: Cole Press.

Gasques, José G. and Clando Yokomizo. 1986. 'Resultados de 20 Anos de Incentivos Fiscais na Agropecuária da Amazônia', *XIV Encontro Nacional de Economia, ANPEC* 2, 47–84.

Harris, Edwyna. 2008. 'The Persistence of Correlative Water Rights in Colonial Australia: A Theoretical Contradiction', Discussion Papers. Department of Economics. No. 11/08.

Hughes, Jonathan and Louis P. Cain. 2006. *American Economic History*. Boston, MA: Addison Wesley.

Imlah, Albert, H. 1950. 'The Terms of Trade of the United Kingdom, 1798–1913', *Journal of Economic History*, 10 (2), 170–194.

Kanazawa, Mark T. 1996. 'Possession in Nine Points of the Law: The Political Economy of Early Land Disposal', *Explorations in Economic History*, 33, 227–249.

Kociumbas, J. 1988. *The Oxford History of Australia*. Volume One. Melbourne: Oxford University Press.

Libecap, Gary D. 2007. 'The Assignment of Property Rights on the Western Frontier: Lessons for Contemporary Environmental and Resource Policy', *Journal of Economic History*, 67 (2) (May), 257–291.

Libecap, Gary D. and Zeynep K. Hansen. 2004. 'Small Farms, Externalities, and the Dust Bowl of the 1930s', *Journal of Political Economy*, 112 (3) (June), 665–694.

Lueck, Dean. 2003. 'First Possession as the Basis of Property' in Terry L. Anderson and Fred S. McChesney (eds), *Property Rights: Cooperation, Conflict and Law*. Princeton, NJ: Princeton University Press.

Mahar, Denis. 1989. *Government Policies and Deforestation in Brazil's Amazon Region*. Washington, DC: The World Bank.

Mattison, Ray H. 1950. 'Roosevelt and the Stockmen's Association', *North Dakota History*, 17 (3) (July), 177–209.

McCabe, J. Terrence. 2004. *Cattle Bring Us to Our Enemies: Turkana Ecology, Politics, and Raiding in a Disequilibrium System*. Ann Arbor, MI: University of Michigan Press.

Morris, A. and G. Ranken. 1883. *Report of Inquiry into the State of Public Lands and the Operation of Land Laws*. New South Wales Legislative Assembly, Votes and Proceedings.

Mueller, Milton. 2002. *Ruling the Root: Internet Governance and the Timing of Cyberspace*. Cambridge: MIT Press.

Nimmo, J. 1884–1885. *Report on the Internal Commerce of the United States*. House Executive Document 7, Part 3, Serial 2295, 48th Congress, Second Session.

Osgood, Ernest Staples. 1929. *The Day of the Cattleman*. Chicago, IL: University of Chicago Press.

Ostrom, Elinor. 1990. *Governing the Commons: The Evolution of Institutions for Collective Action*. New York: Cambridge University Press.

Pelzer, L. 1936. *The Cattlemen's Frontier*. Glendale, CA: Arthur H. Clark Co.

Roberts, S.H. 1924. *History of Australian Land Settlement*. Melbourne: Macmillan Press.

Roberts, S.H. 1935. *The Squatting Age in Australia 1835–1847*. Melbourne: Melbourne University Press.

Sandoz, Mari. 1958. *The Cattlemen*. New York: Hastings House.

Shergold, P. 1987. 'Prices and Consumption' in W. Vamplew (ed.) *Australians Historical Statistics*. Melbourne: Fairfax, Syme and Weldon.

Smith, Henry E. 2000. 'Semicommon Property Rights and Scattering in the Open Fields', *Journal of Legal Studies*, XXIX (1), 131–170.

Smith, Henry E. 2002. 'Exclusion Versus Governance: Two Strategies for Delineating Property Rights', *Journal of Legal Studies*, XXXI (June), S453–S487.

Umbeck, John. 1981. 'Might Makes Right: A Theory of the Formation and Initial Distribution of Property Rights', *Economic Inquiry*, XIX, 38–59.

Vamplew, W. (ed.). 1987. *Australians Historical Statistics*. Melbourne: Fairfax, Syme and Weldon.

Walton, Gary W. and Hugh Rockoff. 2004. *History of the American Economy with Economic Applications*. Fort Worth: Dreyden Press.

Weaver, John C. 1996. 'Beyond the Fatal Shore: Pastoral Squatting and the Occupation of Australia 1826 to 1852', *American Historical Review*, 101 (4), 981–1007.

Yost, N.S. (1966). *The Call of the Range*. Denver: Sage Books.

Zerbe, R.O. and C.L. Anderson. 2001. 'Culture and Fairness in the Development of Institutions in the California Gold Fields', *Journal of Economic History*, 61, 114–143.

APPENDIX 1.1.   EXTENT OF SELECTION IN NSW AND VICTORIA 1862–1880

Year	*NSW* Number of selections[a]	*NSW* Number of selections (acres)[a]	*Victoria* Number of selections[b]	*Victoria* Number of selections (acres)[b]
1862	2,449	207,675		
1863	1,630	121,493		
1864	1,166	86,475		
1865	1,050	70,432		
1866	2,022	196,043		
1867	1,568	140,511		
1868	1,584	129,634		
1869	2,361	227,992		
1870	2,105	184,287	3,148	322,592
1871	2,117	195,043	5,248	487,256
1872	3,019	346,585	9,179	797,176
1873	4,761	619,386	8,144	1,063,066
1874	4,844	693,489	11,071	1,831,698
1875	4,632	738,523	7,091	183,520
1876	3,994	933,713	6,482	1,040,356
1877	3,578	715,440	7,017	1,126,492
1878	3,842	703,902	9,058	1,915,129
1879	2,625	468,121	6,688	1,032,214
1880	2,867	566,774	5,213	752,639

Notes:
[a]   Data compiled from Votes and Proceedings of the Legislative Assembly NSW, 1883.
[b]   Data compiled from Annual Reports of Department of Lands and Surveys, Victorian Parliamentary Papers, 1870–1880.

2 Commons, anticommons, semicommons*
Lee Anne Fennell

In recent years, theorists interested in the commons have increasingly broadened their gaze to take in two new entries in the property lexicon: the anticommons[1] and the semicommons.[2] Notwithstanding some excellent work comparing and contrasting these templates and their associated tragedies,[3] the literature lacks a cohesive account of how they relate to each other and to larger questions of incentive misalignment. Although scholars sometimes frame the commons, anticommons, and semicommons as conceptually distinct forms,[4] each is best understood as a lens for apprehending a single core, challenging fact about resource systems – their need to accommodate multiple uses that are most efficiently pursued at different scales, whether simultaneously or over time.[5] This chapter offers a brief introduction to the commons, anticommons, and semicommons models and shows how the three fit together in a unified theoretical framework.

I. THE COMMONS

Although the underlying idea is much older,[6] Garrett Hardin (1968) popularized the phrase 'tragedy of the commons' and illustrated it with an example involving an open-access pasture (ibid., 1244). Reasoning that each herdsman would bear only a fraction of the costs of grazing another steer but would internalize all of the benefits of doing so, Hardin predicted that the pasture would be overgrazed (ibid.). The same problem of incentive misalignment can lead people to underinvest in collective activities (communal farms or public television, for example), take too many resource units out of a given system (as by overfishing), or put too many 'bads' into a system (such as smog, litter, or email spam).[7]

Hardin's pasture fable conjures up a distinctively compelling brand of inefficiency: a self-contained system that is transparently suboptimal for its own participants. Because the exploiters and the exploitees are one and the same – Hardin's herders harmed only themselves – the label of 'tragedy' seems especially apt and uncontroversial. It is not a matter of one group benefiting at the expense of another, much less a question of whose interests should take priority. Rather, we see a group shooting itself in its collective foot through self-defeating behavior. Parties interacting in real-world resource systems rarely deliver and realize losses in such a cleanly symmetrical manner, but the stylized commons tragedy neatly excises thorny questions of distribution from the picture to focus attention on the unambiguous costs of self-interested actions.

A. The Commons Without the Tragedy

Despite its merits as a rhetorical device, the tragedy of the commons story often fails to square with reality. The fact that a resource is held in common need not spell disaster, as the successful management of many common-pool resources throughout history – including common grazing lands – attests (see, e.g., Dahlman 1980, 130–38; Ostrom 1990; Ostrom 2009). Refutations of Hardin's gloomy syllogism frequently begin by drawing a distinction between an open-access resource that anyone can exploit and a limited-access commons that is closed to all but its members (e.g., Ciriacy-Wantrup & Bishop 1975, 714–16; Eggertsson 2003, 75–76; Dagan & Heller 2001, 556–57) – what Carol Rose (1998b, 144) has aptly termed 'property on the outside.' The ability to exclude outsiders is an important prerequisite for a wide range of local, informal institutional solutions, even if it is not sufficient on its own to stave off tragedy (see, e.g., Ostrom 1990, 91–92; 2009, 32). Interestingly, the very features that lend power and elegance to the tragedy of the commons as a thought experiment – the closed system in which a small number of homogeneous individuals interact in reciprocal and symmetrical ways over time – may also allow real-world individuals to cooperate with each other in ways that avert tragedy (see, e.g., Ellickson 1991; Cole & Grossman 2010). Repeat play is especially important in this regard (see, e.g., Ellickson 1991, 164–65 (citing Axelrod 1984)).

There are also more fundamental reasons that tragedy may not follow from common ownership. First, misaligned incentives (that is, the existence of positive or negative externalities) can only generate inefficient results if they lead actors to choose differently than they would have under conditions of full internalization. This criterion will not always be met (see, e.g., Buchanan & Stubblebine 1962, 374–76; Dukeminier et al. 2010, 44–49; Haddock 2007). For example, people fishing from a remote pond may ignore the effects of their actions on others without triggering a tragic collapse of the fish population, if their decisions of whether and how much to fish would remain unchanged after taking into account the full social impact.[8] Similarly, people may add value by participating in a network such as a marketplace, festival, or road system without taking into account the positive spillovers their participation produces for others.[9]

Second, tragedy can only exist if it is technologically possible for the resource system to deliver different amounts of surplus as a result of individual choices.[10] Here it becomes important to clarify the sense in which struggles over finite resources can constitute commons tragedies. Consider a group of partygoers aggressively harvesting hors d'oeuvres from a buffet table's dwindling supply. Assuming no food is actually lost in the fray (and setting aside the important question of where the provisions came from in the first place), the outcome might seem to be a matter of pure distribution. Of course, the partygoers may derive varying amounts of marginal utility from the snacks, but we cannot be sure that the allocation produced by pushiness is inefficient – perhaps successfully aggressive food-harvesters are also higher valuers of food, on average.

To attribute tragedy to the spectacle, we must recognize not only the commons comprising the food itself, but also a second commons that is linked to the first, which we might call 'the party atmosphere' or, more broadly, 'the resource-gathering environment.' Actions that merely change the distribution of food harvested from the first commons may significantly degrade this second commons, whether in ways overt (injuries from tongs) or subtle (dampened conversation). Because each person may undertake individually rational but collectively costly efforts to get more of an underlying resource, a commons tragedy may cause even a fixed resource to yield up less total surplus to the group.[11]

Table 2.1   A Prisoner's Dilemma. Payoffs for (Rowena, Columbo)

	Columbo Refrains From Adding Cattle	Columbo Adds Cattle
Rowena Refrains From Adding Cattle	(0, 0)	(−7, 3)
Rowena Adds Cattle	(3, −7)	(−4, −4)

B.   The Prisoner's Dilemma

The commons tragedy and its connection to problems of scale can be better understood by boiling it down to its two-player structural equivalent, the Prisoner's Dilemma.[12] Like the tragedy of the commons, the Prisoner's Dilemma derives its analytic power from the transparent manner in which the parties make self-defeating choices. Consider a miniature version of Hardin's pasture that is shared by two ranchers, Rowena and Columbo.[13]

When we meet our protagonists, each has already added cattle to the pasture up to the socially optimal point. Each must now decide whether to add yet another animal. Doing so will generate ten in benefits and fourteen in costs; hence, it is a losing proposition from a societal standpoint. But consider things from, say, Rowena's point of view. Because she will internalize the full benefit (ten) from adding a steer, but will bear only half the cost (seven) inflicted on the pasture, she will enjoy a positive payoff of three by adding a steer. Her realization that Columbo will reason the same way does not change her decision. While Columbo's decision to add an animal drops Rowena's payoff to negative four in a world where she adds a steer as well, she would do even worse (negative seven) if she refrained from adding cattle in that state of the world. The dominant strategy for each player is to defect; hence, the lower righthand corner of Table 2.1 represents the Nash equilibrium (see Baird, Gertner, & Picker 1994, 21–22; 33–34).

C.   The Problem of Scale

The payoff structure of the Prisoner's Dilemma satisfies the preconditions for tragedy laid out above: the players make different decisions than they would if they were taking into account all the implications of their actions, and the resulting combination of blinkered choices produces less overall surplus for the pair. What accounts for this payoff structure? The usual focus of blame is each rancher's ability to externalize some of the grazing costs attributable to adding an animal to the commons, which is in turn a function of common ownership of the land. But the problem is just as much a result of the rancher's ability to fully *internalize* the grazing benefits associated with adding an animal. That ability to internalize benefits flows from a property system in which the rancher holds individual (or 'private')[14] property rights in the steer, and continues to hold those rights regardless of how much communal grass it ingests.[15] It is not, then, the commonly owned land alone that produces the rancher's dilemma; it is instead the mix of individual and common ownership.[16] The same is true of any other commons problem one might care to identify, from overfishing to shirking on a communal farm – although in some cases the private ownership in question is of one's person or one's labor rather than of a chattel or hunk of real estate (see Alchian & Demsetz 1973, 23–24).

Close analysis of the tragedy of the commons thus reveals an intriguing fact: The dilemma is driven by the presence of two (or more) activities that are being pursued at different scales and under different property arrangements.[17] The problem for Hardin's herders is only partly about the fact that grazing is pursued at a large scale and on commonly owned ground; it can be equally attributed to the fact that the raising of cattle is pursued through individual ownership of the animals. Furthermore, the mix of ownership types occurs under circumstances that permit private ownership to be used as a platform for offloading costs onto the commons, and that allow access to the commons to be used for the benefit of private property (the roving cattle). In other words, as will be developed further below, the prototypical commons tragedy grows out of an arrangement that looks a good deal like a semicommons – a system in which private and common property uses interact (Smith 2000).

If two resource uses conducted at different scales and under different ownership regimes generate payoffs like those shown in Table 2.1, we might examine the prospects for rescaling one use or the other to reduce the degree of mismatch. For example, the ranchers might conclude that grazing need not be undertaken on a large scale after all and respond with parcelization (see, e.g., Ellickson 1993, 1327–28). If individually owned cattle are grazed on individually owned plots of land, the costs of grazing fall on the same rancher who internalizes the benefits of it. But the redrawing of property lines need not move in the direction of more private ownership; commoners might instead place more elements under common ownership (Alchian & Demsetz 1973, 23). For example, the ranchers might decide that individual ownership of cattle is unnecessary and place the cattle themselves, as well as the grazing land, under common ownership.

A close analogue can be found in unitization, a prevalent approach for managing oil and gas reserves that underlie multiple parcels (see Libecap & Smith 2002, S595–96). If individual landholders are simply permitted to keep for themselves all the resource units they can extract from the common pool, an inefficiently high rate of depletion and attendant waste predictably results (see ibid., S591–93). Unitization agreements that maintain common ownership of the resource units after extraction and divide up the proceeds according to some predetermined rule alleviate this pressure toward overextraction (see ibid., S596). The goal is to create a collective body capable of making decisions in the same fully-internalized way as would a single owner, where the fugitive nature of the resource makes physical partition of the resource impracticable (see ibid, S595–96; see also Epstein 1993, 555–57).[18] Alternatively, one party could purchase oil or gas rights from all of the overlying landowners, along with any easements necessary to optimally exploit the resource (Libecap & Smith 2002, S593 & n.15 (citing Demsetz 1967, 357); see also Coase 1960, 16–17). Dean Lueck (1989) makes analogous points in the context of wildlife populations. As he explains, the fact that an animal herd (say, deer) has a territory that far exceeds the optimal land size for the land's most valuable use (say, farming) would not preclude ownership of the herd if the uses were compatible and if it were possible for all of the landowners to transact with each other or for an outsider to buy up 'deer population rights' from each of them (ibid., 301–03).

These moves involve delinking rights to the larger-scale resource from individual parcel ownership and consolidating them either in the hands of a single owner or in

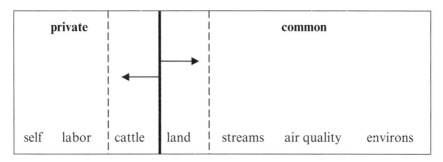

Figure 2.1 Mixed Ownership

the hands of a collectivity that will act as one. Both approaches eliminate the mismatch between ownership of the resource system and the resource units – the former by privatizing the resource system as well as the individual resource units, and the latter by collectivizing the units as well as the system. The transaction costs associated with accomplishing such shifts may be prohibitive, however. First, moving resource systems to private ownership or resource units to common ownership may be very difficult, especially if unanimous consent to the change is required.[19] This, as we will see, amounts to an anticommons problem. Second, to the extent that delinking uses from each other is costly or imperfect, a change in ownership for one use may require abandoning the most efficient scale of operation and ownership form for another use. In addition, the shift will inevitably create a new interface between privately and commonly owned elements that will carry costs of its own. Figure 2.1 illustrates this point.

The heavy vertical line in Figure 2.1 shows how a given resource system, such as a grazing pasture, might divide individually and commonly owned (or controlled) elements. A rescaling and associated ownership change can shift that line in one direction or the other, but it will not eliminate the line itself or the incentive problems that can occur when privately and commonly owned elements interact.

For example, parcelization would shift land to private ownership and thus move the line to the position of the rightmost dashed line. This removes the grazing misalignment flagged above, but the fact that resources like water and air are still experienced in common with one's neighbors may continue to distort incentives.[20] Similarly, moving to collective ownership of cattle remedies the dissonance between cattle ownership and land ownership, but creates a new abutment of private and common elements at the leftmost dashed line. As long as inputs to cattle care, including labor, remain individually owned, the temptation to shirk could replace the overgrazing tragedy with a tragedy of poor veterinary care or of other forms of neglect (see Alchian & Demsetz 1973, 23; Krier 2009, 150 n. 51). The question remains, of course, whether the new interface is less costly than the old one. Under some circumstances, shifting elements such as land into private ownership could reduce externalities and ease the bargaining burdens associated with accomplishing full internalization (Demsetz 1967, 356–57; Ellickson 1993, 1330–32), but that result depends crucially on the scale of the relevant activities and impacts (e.g., Sinden 2007, 587–94; see Ellickson 1993, 1334–35).

A shift in ownership represents just one of several ways of ameliorating a tragedy-prone payoff structure and the underlying problem of scale. Alternative approaches would allow uses to continue at different scales under existing ownership forms, but would adopt other measures designed to generate outcomes that look more like those that full internalization would produce.

D.   Addressing the Tragedy

The problem of incentive misalignment captured in Table 2.1 can be approached in two basic ways: coercively overriding each player's power to defect, or changing the relative payoffs of defection and cooperation.[21] The first possibility corresponds most closely to Hardin's (1968, 1247) idea of 'mutual coercion, mutually agreed upon,' and typically implies the state-wielded threat of force.[22] The second approach involves explicitly or implicitly repricing the alternatives so that the choice between them more closely reflects the full internalization of costs and benefits.

Repricing can take a variety of forms. First, the state (or other collective body) can tax defection or subsidize cooperation.[23] Setting penalties or rewards at levels that capture the previously externalized costs or benefits leaves each actor free to engage in cost-benefit comparisons incorporating the revised figures (see, e.g., Krier 1994, 452–53). Such an approach can accommodate heterogeneity among actors, such as unusually high costs of cooperation, in a way that directly coercive approaches cannot (see ibid.). But getting the prices right can be tricky (see, e.g., ibid.). Insufficient penalties (or rewards for restraint) may fail to avert tragedy, while excessive repricing may lead actors to engage in too little of a productive activity like ranching.

Price adjustments might also be nonpecuniary in nature. For example, a norm-based sanction and reward system may operate upon commoners in a manner closely akin to taxes and subsidies by inflicting the pain of social shaming or bestowing the pleasure of social inclusion and camaraderie (see, e.g., Sunstein 1996, 912–13; McAdams 1997, 355–75). Alternatively, norms might be inculcated in a manner that alters the players' internal calculus, so that cooperating brings a glow of satisfaction and defecting produces pangs of remorse and shame (McAdams 1997, 380–81; cf. Ullmann-Margalit 1977, 36–37). In this way, norms may become self-enforcing, diminishing or eliminating the need for monitoring and enforcement by the group (see McAdams 1997, 380–81).

Redrawing property lines represents an indirect way to accomplish repricing.[24] The potential to change the mix of private and common property, and thereby to alter the universe of costs and benefits that parties internalize and externalize, has already been noted. The redrawing of property boundaries can occur in other ways as well. Incentives to overdraw resources from the commons can be blunted by limits on the alienability of harvested resources (see, e.g., Rose-Ackerman 1985, 942–43; Epstein 1985, 978–88; Lueck 1989, 318–19; Hsu 2003, 870; Fennell 2009, 1429–33), by limits on use (e.g., Levmore 2002, S436), or even by limits on the owner's right to exclude others from the extracted resources (see Heller 1998, 675 & n. 246). All of these alternatives reduce the payoff associated with the noncooperative action and hence change ex ante incentives through a brand of repricing – although not without some attendant ex post costs.

Notwithstanding this array of solutions, the tragedy of the commons continues to present a foundational puzzle, one that James Krier (1992) termed 'The Tragedy of the Commons, Part Two': how could people locked in the tragedy's noncooperative equilibrium perform the impressive acts of coordination necessary to escape it? (ibid., 337). If private property rights were necessary to avert tragically misaligned incentives, for example, we need some account of how people overcame their incentive problems to create those property rights.[25] Rudimentary property rights might be explained by conventions in which one party's possession triggers deference by others (see, e.g., Krier 2009, 154–55 (discussing Sugden 2004)). But possession-based conventions would only sharpen the mismatch between private incentives and the social optimum when units are drawn out of a resource system that is too large to be reduced to individual control. Responding to these incentive misalignments requires coordination, whether it takes the form of assembling consent to a new system of property rights or employing a political apparatus to coerce cooperation (see, e.g., Krier 1992, 337–38). The anticommons model sheds light not only on the problems that may follow such changes, but also on difficulties in accomplishing these realignments in the first place.

II. ADDING THE ANTICOMMONS

Frank Michelman (1982) posited an imaginary regime that was the opposite of the commons, one in which no person could make use of a resource without obtaining permission from every other person (see ibid., 6, 9). This 'anticommons'[26] turned out to possess structural properties of more than mere theoretical interest. Although scholars had long realized that multiple vetoes over resource use could produce inefficiency (see, e.g., Arrow 1979, 25–26; Buchanan 1973, 73–74; Demsetz 1967, 354–55; Krier 1992, 335–36), Michael Heller (1998; 2008) made this structural dilemma salient and memorable through a series of vivid examples that developed, adapted, and applied Michelman's concept. For instance, Heller suggested that the puzzle of busy kiosks near empty storefronts in post-socialist Moscow could be explained by the fact that opening a store (but not a kiosk) required obtaining permits from multiple actors (Heller 1998, 633–40; 2008, xiv–xv, 143–56). James Buchanan and Yong Yoon (2000) followed up with a formal model of the dilemma, using the example of a parking lot that could only be accessed by patrons who obtained a parking pass from each of two independently operating ticket booths (ibid., 4–10).

The term 'anticommons' has since become shorthand for a broad class of problems requiring the assembly of permissions or entitlements, from land development to patent rights.[27] In each case, the worry is the same: that a value-enhancing assembly – one that could leave every party better off than the status quo – will fail to occur as a result of strategic holdout behavior and other transaction costs. Like the tragedy of the commons, the tragedy of the anticommons makes inefficiency transparent by creating a self-contained system in which participants make themselves worse off. But just as commonly owned property does not inevitably lead to a commons tragedy, the dispersal of veto rights does not automatically create an anticommons tragedy (Michelman 1985, 14–15; Heller 1998, 673–75; Heller 2008, 46).

A. When Is an Anticommons Tragic?

The problem of the anticommons is fundamentally a problem of assembly – whether of permissions, land, biotech patents, or something else.[28] Putting individually controlled fragments together to make a larger whole requires either obtaining the consent of the fragment-holders or overriding their refusal to consent, and dividing up the surplus (if any) that the resulting assembly will produce. If the individual pieces are protected by a property rule, these two operations are linked – consent of each entitlement-holder is required, and the price of the fragment may be set at whatever level the entitlement-holder chooses (Calabresi & Melamed 1972, 1092). Routine transaction costs and strategic behavior can make such reconfigurations prohibitively difficult, however, and the assembly may not occur (see, e.g., ibid., 1106–07). This is not necessarily tragic. Not all assemblies should occur, from an efficiency perspective. Fragments may be more valuable when kept in separate hands than when assembled into a whole (see, e.g., Heller 1998, 674–75); if so, there is no assembly surplus to be had.

Thus, diagnosing an anticommons tragedy requires more than pointing out fragments that could be put together and noting that they have not been so assembled. Those unassembled pieces could bespeak a tragically blocked aggregation, but they might instead represent an assembly that was just not worth doing, once everyone's interests were taken into account. A focus on the structural features conducive to tragedy can offer some, albeit incomplete, guidance. In the absence of monopoly power or 'thin markets' (see Merrill 1986, 75–77), a would-be holdout has no leverage and hence no incentive to strategically overstate her price. If she tries to do so, the assembler will simply obtain a substitute fragment from someone else who is willing to sell more cheaply, or create an assembly that leaves out the contested fragment (see, e.g., Cohen 1991, 358–59). Thus, anticommons tragedies are plausible only in settings where good substitutes are absent.

While it is not always easy to assess the availability of substitutes and hence the degree of monopoly power that a particular holdout might possess, examining the production function for assembly surplus may be helpful. Particularly conducive to holdout dynamics are lumpy or 'step' goods that do not deliver surplus in smoothly increasing increments as additional inputs are added, but rather provide a large shot of surplus all at once, when the assembly is complete (see, e.g., Taylor & Ward 1982, 353). If all of the components are necessary in order for any of the surplus to be enjoyed, the last holdout can command a high price – and, perceiving this, each fragment-holder will strive to be in that enviable position (see, e.g., Posner 2007, 62–63). In such a case it is possible (although by no means certain) that an assembly failure is attributable not to efficient fragmentation but to strategic behavior. In contrast, a fragment that will only add a relatively minor portion of the surplus that an assembly will produce or that is fungible with other readily available components can be much more readily jettisoned from the project. Such possibilities cabin strategic holdout behavior.

B. The Anticommons and the Commons

Both the commons and the anticommons tragedies feature self-interested choices that are collectively suboptimal. What, then, distinguishes the two dilemmas? Most writers on the anticommons tragedy, including Heller, strongly associate it with the underuse of resources (see, e.g., Heller 2008, 32–37; Buchanan & Yoon 2000, 1–2; Hsu 2003, 814). Although doing so offers an intuitive contrast with the example of resource overuse featured in Hardin's tragedy of the commons, the underuse/overuse dichotomy masks the structural nature of both tragedies. The anticommons tragedy is an assembly problem, nothing more and nothing less.[29] There is nothing in the nature of assembly – whether we are speaking of land, permission, intangibles, or anything else – that necessarily pushes us in the direction of intensified use.

To be sure, people often want to assemble fragments in order to engage in more intensive uses (for example, combine land parcels to develop a shopping center) but sometimes they want to do the opposite (such as buy up land parcels to construct a large, contiguous nature preserve). Similarly, the dispersed veto rights that characterize the anticommons can block actors not only from doing a particular thing (such as fishing from a pond) but also from creating a world in which actors are *not* doing that thing. Difficulty assembling consent to oil or gas unitization offers a case in point: the anticommons problem in that case, if unresolved, will result not in underuse of the resource, but continued overdrawing of it (see Heller 2008, 44). Heller's application of the anticommons model to efforts to coordinate conservation efforts further illustrates this point (ibid., 183–84). We can also find converse examples involving excessive draws against a common resource like space, which represent commons tragedies yielding too little use of a resource (see, e.g., Fennell 2004, 935; Heller 2011, n.44).

Another unstable distinction is that between too many 'use privileges' (associated with the tragedy of the commons) and too many 'exclusion rights' (associated with the tragedy of the anticommons) (see Heller 1998, 677). As the examples above suggest, sometimes parties keep valuable assemblies from occurring not by tacking 'keep out' signs on their property, but rather by engaging in uses (like polluting or drawing on a common pool) that keep people from being able to enjoy a desired resource (like an environment free of pollution or a common pool that remains viable over time). For similar reasons, identifying the anticommons with 'too much private property' (e.g., Heller 2001, 86) is incomplete. While individual holdings can certainly give rise to anticommons dynamics, assembly problems can also arise in contexts featuring too little private property.[30]

Returning to the patterns of strategic behavior that lie at the heart of the commons and anticommons dilemmas, respectively, offers a more promising distinction. Whereas the commons tragedy follows the strategic pattern of the Prisoner's Dilemma, the anticommons often resembles the strategic game of Chicken.[31]

C.   A Game of Chicken

Chicken gets its name from a potentially deadly (and, one would hope, largely fictional) game in which two drivers speed toward each other, each hoping the other will swerve first (see, e.g., Schelling 1966, 81–87; Baird, Gertner & Picker 1994, 43–45). There is one way to win the game (induce the other party to swerve first), and three ways to lose, in decreasing order of desirability: (1) swerve at the same time as the other party; (2) swerve first; and (3) crash into the other party. This same basic strategic interaction can be found in less dramatic contexts, such as negotiations between two parties (see, e.g, Baird, Gertner & Picker 1994, 43–45; Posner 2007, 62). A deal that will produce surplus is worth doing regardless of exactly how that surplus gets divided up, but each party would prefer to receive a larger share. Here, 'driving straight ahead' means getting more than one's share of the available surplus, 'swerving first' means taking less than one's share in order to facilitate the bargain, and 'crashing' means that the deal falls apart altogether.

In bargaining, as in roadway Chicken, one's best move depends on what the other

Table 2.2   Chicken Game. Payoffs for (Rowena, Columbo)

	Columbo Swerves	Columbo Drives Ahead
Rowena Swerves	(4, 4)	(1, 7)
Rowena Drives Ahead	(7, 1)	(0, 0)

party is going to do. Thus, unlike the Prisoner's Dilemma, Chicken does not feature dominant strategies that combine to produce a single Nash equilibrium; instead, there are multiple equilibria (see Baird, Gertner & Picker 1994, 44). A crash is by no means inevitable and indeed should be avoidable, but two players who misread each other or miscalculate about the total amount of surplus available may stick to positions that, in combination, preclude the successful completion of an efficient deal. We need not worry about the crash outcome in competitive markets; a party who insisted on a supernormal share of surplus would only hurt herself, metaphorically crashing into a wall, while the other party would go on to trade with a less problematic partner. But holdout problems similar to those discussed above can appear in situations of bilateral monopoly, where neither party has access to alternative trading partners (see, e.g., Posner 2007, 62).

Returning to the earlier interaction between Rowena and Columbo illustrates not only how the game of Chicken works, but also how the tragedy of the anticommons connects to the tragedy of the commons. When we last saw them, our protagonists were locked in a Prisoner's Dilemma, each tempted to add more cattle than would be efficient. If they could agree among themselves to refrain from adding the extra ungulates, the tragedy of the commons could be averted, and a surplus of eight – the difference between the payoffs in Table 2.1's upper left ('both refrain') and lower right ('both add') cells – could be enjoyed between them. Each would be better off with even a little of this surplus but each would prefer to get more of it rather than less. Their attempts to assemble the acts of forbearance that will produce the surplus, and their struggle over how that surplus will be divided, makes up the Chicken game depicted in Table 2.2.[32]

Each player must choose whether to 'swerve' by ceding surplus to the other, or 'drive ahead' by insisting on the bulk of the surplus. The outcome in the lower-right corner is the 'no deal' or 'crash' outcome in which all of the available surplus is lost, dispreferred by both parties. However, each party will try to play the strategy of 'drive ahead' if she thinks the other party can be bullied into swerving. The concern here is not that one party or the other will get an 'unfair' share of the surplus; that may be a problem for independent normative reasons, but it is a question of distribution rather than efficiency (see, e.g., Cohen 1991, 352–53). Rather, the worry is that each will push too far, miscalculate, and contribute to a crash. The crash in question involves nothing other than failure in contracting – long recognized as the true root of inefficiency in resource use (see Coase 1960, 15–17; Cheung 1970). What the anticommons analysis illustrates, however, is that externalities in common-pool contexts can flow not only from the absence of a right to contract or flaws in the contract stipulations themselves (see Cheung 1970, 50–52), but also from parties strategically standing on their rights and refusing to engage in beneficial bargains.

Although these two-player games are helpful for examining strategic interactions, the prototypical anticommons problem, like the prototypical commons tragedy, is a multi-player game. This is not a coincidence. While two-party bargains can sometimes lead to impasse, the risk of the 'crash' outcome is greatly magnified when many different parties hold independent vetoes on an assembly of entitlements. Misreadings and miscalculations become more likely in the many-player case, and mundane transaction costs associated with identifying and communicating with the other parties rise as well (see, e.g., Ellickson 1993, 1330–31; Demsetz 1967, 354–57; Posner 2007, 62–63). Seen in this light, a potential anticommons problem lies between every garden-variety commons problem and its solution. Put differently, the anticommons problem and its underlying Chicken Game structure shed light on an important aspect of the contracting problems that can perpetuate commons tragedies.

D.   Linked Tragedies and Solutions

The example above shows one connection between the anticommons and the commons, but the relationship between these models requires further exploration. Recall again the slate of solutions to the tragedy of the commons: mandating cooperation, or repricing the choice between cooperation and defection. One mechanism for repricing involves redrawing property lines so that actors better internalize the costs and benefits of their choices. Implementing this alternative may involve granting various actors ownership or control of individual fragments or parcels – a rightward shift of the vertical line in Figure 2.1. The anticommons literature has stressed the potential difficulty in later reassembling those resulting fragments into a unified whole.[33] This line of reasoning emphasizes the link between commons and anticommons tragedies that has received the greatest amount of scholarly attention: a 'propertized' solution to the tragedy of the commons may create a tragedy of the anticommons (see, e.g., Heller 2008, 18).

   This is an important point, but the analysis underlying it is incomplete in at least two respects. First, the inefficiency produced, if any, is not unique to the propertized solution, but could stem from any response to a tragedy of the commons that is premised on errors or faulty assumptions about the most efficient use of the resource over time. A commons from which all commoners have been coercively banished by the government is just as 'tragic' (assuming some use of the commons would be optimal) as one that no commoner can assemble sufficient permission to enter. What propertization adds to the story, at least potentially, is a heightened level of stickiness. Unlike fines or bans that can be politically undone on less than unanimous consent, property fragments are often thought to be particularly difficult to reassemble. But other institutional responses to commons dilemmas can also prove problematically resistant to change (see Daniels 2007), and political overrides can also apply to property interests, as through eminent domain.[34] Moreover, easy access to political overrides is not an unmixed blessing; good as well as bad interventions into commons tragedies can be undone. In some cases, the stickiness in arrangements that stems from propertization can actually enhance efficiency over time (see Bell & Parchomovsky 2003).

   A second, more fundamental inadequacy in the usual connection drawn between the commons and the anticommons can be seen by returning to Figure 2.1's vertical line dividing the realms of individually and commonly owned property. The anticommons tragedy is usually thought to stymie only leftward moves of that dividing line – that is, moves that would increase the domain of the commons relative to the domain of individual ownership. But rightward moves that take elements out of the commons and place them under individual ownership can also be blocked by interested stakeholders (see, e.g., Dahlman 1980, 187; Rose 1998a, 97). Solving the tragedy of the commons in any manner, whether through redrawing property lines or otherwise, requires actors to give up something – their current untrammeled access to the resource in question (Krier 1992, 335–36). To the extent that such access represents something like a property interest, an effort to aggregate consent to a plan of forbearance may itself present an anticommons dynamic (see, e.g., Heller 2008, 183–84).

We might, therefore, expect holdout problems analogous to those anticipated in moving from private to common property to beset attempted moves in the other direction.[35] In other words, it is not only propertized *interventions* into a commons tragedy that can produce an anticommons tragedy; an anticommons dynamic can also interpose itself between a commons tragedy and its solution. This is precisely the point that was illustrated above when the original Prisoner's Dilemma (commons dilemma) between Rowena and Columbo in Table 2.1 morphed into Table 2.2's game of Chicken (anticommons dilemma) once they began to negotiate a solution.

The anticommons theorist might respond that it is politically and legally easier to forcibly aggregate the forbearance necessary to solve a commons dilemma than it is to aggregate other kinds of entitlement fragments (see Heller 1999, 1195–96). Framed more broadly, perhaps the political capacity to move from common to private property is greater than the capacity to move from private property to the commons. Yet we have seen moves in both directions, and a variety of accounts exist for how and why such moves occur (see, e.g., Demsetz 1967; Field 1989; Levmore 2002; Wyman 2005; Bell & Parchomovsky 2009). Without more information about the underlying efficiency stories, it is difficult to know whether too few shifts of one type or another have occurred, much less whether anticommons dynamics are to blame.

One more take on the problem also deserves attention: conferring property rights may be essential to aggregating (or gathering the political will to impose) forbearance. Consider here the prevalence of 'grandfathering' provisions within legislation designed to curtail draws against common pool resources (see, e.g., Rose 1998a, 97; see also Nash & Revesz 2007, 1730; Levmore 1999, 1665–66). If it is impossible to move from one inefficiently fragmented entitlement pattern without introducing a newly fragmented ownership pattern, we should not lament the fact that the new arrangement 'propertizes' – in fact, it may be replacing a less efficient form of de facto propertization. On this account, property – and the veto power it confers – does not only feature in anticommons tragedies, but may also be essential to overcoming them.

III.   SCALE AND THE SEMICOMMONS

Resource systems, as we experience them on the ground, are never solely composed of individually owned or commonly owned elements. Instead, we constantly encounter interacting mixtures of private and common property.[36] In developing the notion of the 'semicommons,' Henry Smith (2000) focused attention on a subset of these interacting elements – those in which 'both common and private uses are important and impact significantly on each other' (ibid., 132). In the remaining space, I will examine how this subset, as well as the larger category of mixed property regimes, relates to the commons, the anticommons, and the unifying problem of scale.

A.   Seeing the Semicommons

As Smith (2000, 132) explains, medieval farming and grazing arrangements constituted a semicommons: pieces of farmland were individually owned but the land as a whole was shared for grazing purposes. In the open field arrangement, grazing alternated with farming in a seasonal cycle (ibid.), but this sequential feature is not essential to the notion of a semicommons. What is important is that the ownership arrangements reflected the different scales at which two activities – farming and grazing – were best undertaken (see ibid.; Dahlman 1980, 132). Rather than hold farmland in contiguous blocks or parcels, the commoners who shared the grazing land each held a number of physically dispersed strips (see Ellickson 1993, 1388–90 & fig. 3). While a variety of reasons for this arrangement have appeared in the literature, including the diversification of risk (e.g., McCloskey 1989), Smith (2000, 146–54) has emphasized its role in controlling strategic behavior. Interspersing farmland holdings dampens the incentives that commoners might otherwise have to use their private holdings or their access to the common grazing land strategically to burden or benefit particular parcels; the physical layout binds together the fates of many different owners (ibid.).

The farming and grazing semicommons contained a built-in solution to the problems presented by mixtures of private and common property. However, the notion of the semicommons extends to interacting mixtures of common and private property whether or not they are managed in this manner.[37] Nonetheless, it has been viewed as a relatively narrow category of mixed property. In what Smith (2000, 161) has termed 'true semicommons property,' the commonly and privately owned elements 'cover the same physical resource,' such as land. The incentive structure also differs from that of the prototypical commons in which each rancher must bear 1/n of the costs of an added animal (ibid., 139; Bertacchini, De Mot & Depoorter 2009, 165–66). In a semicommons, privately owned elements (such as sheep) may be used to impose costs not indiscriminately on the commons as a whole but selectively on other people's privately owned elements (such as farming lands); similarly, commoners might use their access to the commons to benefit their own private property at the expense of other parties' property (for example, by attempting to direct trampling sheep elsewhere) (see Smith 2000, 132; Bertacchini, De Mot & Depoorter 2009, 165–71).

Thus cabined, a semicommons is indeed distinguishable from the stylized commons in which defecting means proportionally harming every member of the group, oneself included. But the prototypical commons with its homogeneous players and perfectly symmetrical payoffs operates more as a simplified model than as an approximation of reality. Because producers of externalities rarely bear a perfectly proportionate share of the costs they impose, real-world situations classified as commons dilemmas often hew much closer to the semicommons model. More broadly, the challenges brought to light by the semicommons – operations at multiple scales and the resulting interaction of different ownership regimes – encompass the tragedies of both the commons and the anticommons, whether considered in prototypical or contextualized form.

On this account, the semicommons is less a distinctive property type than a manner of seeing – a lens or frame through which to view existing or proposed arrangements that involve activities at different scales, whether simultaneously or over time. I have already suggested that tragedies of the commons are driven by the incentive misalignments produced by differently scaled activities under different ownership regimes. These mixed regimes are usefully illuminated by the semicommons analysis. We can now examine how the anticommons fits in.

B.   The Commons, the Anticommons and the Semicommons

Recall that what pulls incentives out of alignment in a tragedy of the commons is not common ownership alone, but rather the interface between private and common ownership. As discussed above, that interface can be altered either by parcelizing more of what is commonly owned or bringing under common ownership more of what is privately owned. Neither move eliminates the potential for strategic interaction between privately and commonly owned elements. As long as spillovers exist, parcelization is incomplete. Similarly, any system of common ownership incorporates private elements to the extent that it leaves individuals with some control over their own bodies and labor (see Alchian & Demsetz 1973, 23–24). Nonetheless, changing the mix of common and private property may produce a new mixed regime that aligns better with the scale of events affecting the actors' returns (see Ellickson 1993, 1325–35).

Accomplishing the reconfiguration of property rights, however, requires either obtaining or overriding the consent of the parties affected, and somehow distributing the resulting surplus. This is where the anticommons comes in. If the parties are given a veto over the reconfiguration, an anticommons dynamic may keep it from happening. As discussed above, this may not be a bad thing; it depends on whether the present configuration is more or less efficient than the proposed revision, which in turn depends (at least in part) on questions of efficient scale. Similarly, once a reconfiguration of ownership occurs, an anticommons dynamic may lock it in place. Again, this could be benign (if the reconfiguration is, and remains, efficient) or tragic (if the reconfiguration was undertaken in error or becomes inefficient over time). To maintain greater flexibility, we might attempt to draw (or redraw) property lines in a way that simultaneously accommodates multiple scales, builds in future reversibility, or both.

A focus on reversibility suggests an interesting direction in which the logic of the semicommons might be extended. Thus far, the semicommons literature has focused on the simultaneous or 'temporally interleaved' use of resources (Smith 2002, S481). Such a mixed ownership regime might accommodate multiple activities that can be most efficiently pursued concurrently at different scales. But there is an analogous problem of accommodating differently scaled uses of resources *over time* – what we might characterize as a temporal semicommons.[38] For example, individual pieces of land might be most efficiently held as individual homesteads at Time 1, but might be more valuable when combined to form some larger development or preserve at Time 2. Just as the judicious drawing of property boundaries can allow activities to be pursued simultaneously at different scales under different ownership rubrics – that is, without private ownership wrecking things for the commons, or vice versa – so too might property be crafted in a manner that allows a resource to be used in different configurations at different times.[39]

Thus, the semicommons idea, writ large, speaks to the fact that it is efficient to have property configured in different ways under different circumstances, whether those circumstances occur at the same time or at different times. Allowing those different property arrangements to coexist (whether in space or over time) requires defeating or precluding strategic behavior. The mechanisms employed in the traditional semicommons bear a striking resemblance to some of the strategies that have been developed to deal with reconfiguration challenges over time, as the next section explains.[40]

C.   Toward Strategy-Proof Solutions

The existence of historic semicommons demonstrates that it may be efficient, at least for a time, to maintain operations on multiple scales and take other measures to align incentives. As Smith (2000, 132) explains, '[a] semicommons need not be tragic where the benefits from operating on multiple scales outweigh the costs of strategic behavior and its prevention.' Thus, awareness of the semicommons prompts us to consider various forms of strategy-proofing as alternatives to altering the mix of privately owned and commonly owned elements within a resource system, where different efficient scales of operation exist for different uses.

The scattered pattern of farmland ownership within common grazing fields shows how mechanism design can harness self-interest and defeat strategic behavior. As Smith observes, the system works in part by making boundaries more obscure and rendering it more difficult to tell whether a particular act will be to one's benefit or detriment (Smith 2002, S480–81). This idea of veiling decisionmakers from crucial information about the personal implications of their decisions also underlies a broad range of strategies for eliciting unbiased information and advancing distributive goals, from the 'veil of ignorance' thought experiment in Rawlsian analysis, to the 'one divides, the other chooses' strategy for dividing up cakes (and other things) (see Smith 2000, 165; see also Rawls 1971, 85, 136–42; Brams & Taylor 1996, 8–12). While the physical interspersal that blurs boundaries in medieval grazing fields is not feasible in many settings, the idea of generating useful uncertainty can be transplanted to solve otherwise intractable problems.

For example, liability rules can sidestep holdout problems that preclude efficient entitlement rearrangements over time, but their efficacy depends upon reliable valuations of the entitlements in question (Calabresi & Melamed 1972, 1107–08). Getting entitlement holders to accurately report their own valuations is obviously difficult when a party knows in advance whether a higher or a lower number will be to her benefit (see, e.g., Ayres & Talley 1995, 1030). Consciously constructing situations in which that information is veiled or blurred – as where a stated valuation is made not only a basis for receiving compensation but also a basis for paying a tax – can help to alleviate the problem of strategic misstatements (see, e.g., ibid.; Tideman 1969, 51–69; Levmore 1982; Fennell 2005).[41] While such a tactic may seem to take us far afield from the semicommons, the genius of the semicommons solution similarly resides in its capacity to render the implications of stratagems unclear, and hence deter them.

CONCLUSION

Our tour of the commons, anticommons, and semicommons has revealed a number of connections among these models, but the overarching theme of scale deserves special emphasis. Property forms attempt to match the scale of the relevant activity, but resources are often used in multiple ways, spillovers are ubiquitous, and privately and commonly owned elements are always interacting. The commons literature highlights one facet of this interaction: the mismatch between private and collective returns to a given act.

The anticommons shows us how difficult it can be to solve a commons problem through a rearrangement of property rights, as well as how difficult it can be to undo any solution that we manage to cobble together. While these are interesting points in their own right, we must ask why all this assembly – whether of consent to a consolidation of property interests, or of forbearance with respect to a common pool resource – is necessary in the first place. The answer involves changes over time in the efficient scale of activities. Regardless of whether a contemplated move will involve more individually owned property or more commonly owned property, getting those who hold a stake in the resource to agree to the shift can implicate the anticommons holdout dynamic.

Our understanding of both the commons and anticommons can be enriched by the semicommons analysis, which highlights both the problems associated with using resources on multiple scales and the potential efficiency of this arrangement when undertaken in conjunction with strategy-proofing measures. Incentive-compatible mechanisms not unlike those used in the spatial semicommons can help to build reversibility into property arrangements so that activities can be pursued at different scales not only concurrently but also consecutively.

NOTES

*   Portions of this chapter are adapted from Fennell 2004. I am grateful to Kenneth Ayotte, Daniel Cole, Elinor Ostrom, James Krier, Sarah Larson, Somabha Mohanty, Henry Smith, Lior Strahilevitz, and participants in the Indiana University Workshop in Political Theory and Policy Analysis for comments on earlier drafts. Prisca Kim, Catherine Kiwala, and Eric Singer provided excellent research assistance.
1.   The anticommons was first conceptualized by Frank Michelman (1982, 6, 9; 1985, 6–7) and later adapted and applied by Michael Heller (1998; 2008).
2.   The term 'semicommons,' as used in this chapter, was coined by Henry Smith (2000) to refer to interacting private and common property uses. A different usage appears in Levmore 2002, S422 (referring to a system of 'open access and restricted use').
3.   A recent paper modeling the relationships among these three templates is Bertacchini, De Mot & Depoorter 2009. Scholarship addressing the relationship between the commons and the anticommons includes, for example, Michelman 1985; Buchanan & Yoon 2000; Hsu 2003; Fennell 2004; Munzer 2005; Vanneste et al. 2006; and Heller 2011.
4.   For example, Heller (2001) characterizes the anticommons as a fourth 'ideal type,' that can take its place alongside private property, common property, and state property, while recognizing that real-world property systems often combine elements of these types. See also Heller 2011, figs 3.2 & 3.9 (presenting the commons and anticommons as different ends of a spectrum that has private property at its center).
5.   The issue of multiple scales has been closely associated with the semicommons (see, e.g., Smith 2000; Bertacchini, De Mot & Depoorter 2009), and scale also receives extensive attention in Ellickson 1993. Other discussions of scale as it relates to the ownership and use of property include, for example, Lueck 1989, 300–303; Heller 1999, 1221–22; and Sinden 2007, 556–61, 585–93.
6.   Antecedents to Hardin's analysis, including the work of Aristotle, are noted in Ostrom 1990, 2–3.

Important economic treatments of common pool resources include Warming 1911 [1983]; Gordon 1954; Demsetz 1967; and Cheung 1970.

7. The literature on resource dilemmas is vast. For some examples see Ostrom, Gardner & Walker 1994, 8–15 (discussing 'appropriation' and 'provision' problems); Libecap & Smith 2002 (overextraction of oil); Thompson 2000, 250 ('overdrafting' of water); Ellickson 1993, 1326 (overharvesting and shirking in communal farming); Eggertsson 2003, 76–78 (discussing 'supply side' and 'demand side' effects of open access regimes). The distinction between 'resource units,' such as fish, and 'resource systems,' such as fisheries, is emphasized in Hess & Ostrom 2003, 121; see also Lueck 2003, 202 (distinguishing between resource 'stocks' and 'flows').

8. See, e.g., De Alessi 2003, 91 (observing that '[o]pen access does not present a problem as long as the supply of a resource is so great relative to the demand that there is no (net) gain from conserving or improving it'); Rose 1986, 717–18 (discussing 'plenteous' goods); see also Epstein 1994, 28 (observing that when water is abundant, diversion may 'produce private gains that exceed the losses to the commons').

9. Carol Rose (1986, 767–70) refers to the potential for such interaction and associated spillovers as 'the comedy of the commons.' She notes, however, that a risk of underinvestment exists that might be countered by legal doctrines that help to encourage rather than discourage such participation. See ibid. at 768–71.

10. See, e.g., Ostrom, Gardner, and Walker 1994, 15–16 (characterizing 'suboptimal outcomes' and the capacity to improve matters through 'institutionally feasible alternatives' as preconditions of a common-pool resource dilemma); Michelman 1985, 5–6 (observing that 'degradability' is required for a 'supposedly tragic common').

11. Tragedies of the resource-gathering commons are not limited to 'fixed pot' resources, although they may receive special attention in that context. See, e.g., Posner 2007, 36 (discussing wasteful competition to recover treasure from a shipwreck); see also Anderson & McChesney 2003, 5 (discussing wasteful competition for open-access resources).

12. The Prisoner's Dilemma captures the choice faced by each of two prisoners who are questioned separately about their joint crime and must decide whether to stay silent (cooperate) or testify (defect). Under the payoff structure presented, each player does better by defecting, regardless of what the other prisoner does, even though the pair would do better jointly if both cooperated. See, e.g., Baird, Gertner, & Picker 1994, 33–34; Goetz 1984, 8–17. The structural equivalence between the Prisoner's Dilemma and the tragedy of the commons has been frequently noted. See, e.g., Ostrom 1990, 3–5; Baird, Gertner, & Picker 1994, 34; Michelman 1985, 9. Even though institutional arrangements can change the game and forestall tragedy (see Cole and Grossman 2010), it remains useful to frame the baseline incentive structure that prompts such arrangements as a Prisoner's Dilemma.

13. For similar applications of the Prisoner's Dilemma to the overgrazing problem, see Baird, Gertner, & Picker 1994, 34; Ostrom 1990, 3–5.

14. Consistently with much of the commons literature, I use 'private' here to designate individual ownership, even though commonly owned resources can also be 'privately' held by the commoners. See Krier 2009, 144–45.

15. See Lueck 2003, 202 (discussing appropriation of resource units from commonly owned stock).

16. See Alchian & Demsetz 1973, 22–23 (describing the problematic 'incongruity' between ownership forms that exists whenever a resource can be converted to private ownership by removing it from a communal resource system). The significance of the juxtaposition of private and common ownership to resource dilemmas has also been noted in, for example, Krier 2008, 11 & n. 29; Lueck 2003, 202; Heller 1998, 675 n. 246 (with attribution to William Miller); and Gordon 1954, 135.

17. See supra note 5 (collecting citations relating to scale).

18. In order to get all owners to agree to unitization, however, a form of partitioning – dividing the resource into different physical areas or temporal phases – may be used, despite its potential to pull incentives out of alignment. Libecap & Smith 2002, S590–91; S597–S606.

19. In the oil and gas context, many jurisdictions have addressed these difficulties through compulsory unitization laws that permit a specified majority to impose unitization on dissenters – a solution that carries its own risks. See Libecap & Smith 2002, S596, S606–07; see also Mohan & Goorha 2008 (analyzing the potential for ex post bargaining and hold-up problems in incomplete unitization contracts).

20. See Demsetz 1967, 356 (making this point in the context of a dam that affects a neighbor's water levels), cited and discussed in Krier 2009, 141; Rose 1998a, 95 (noting land's adjacency 'to other resources, notably air, water, and wildlife stocks,' that 'are considerably more difficult to divide into individual properties'); Sinden 2007, 556–61, 586–93 (emphasizing the problems that larger-scale phenomena, such as ecosystems, present for private property solutions).

21. These strategies can be carried out through a variety of institutional arrangements. See, e.g., Ostrom 1990, 8–21 (critiquing the dichotomy between governmental and private property solutions and suggesting that

local institutional arrangements offer an alternative); Heller 2008, 24 ('There are three distinct approaches [to commons tragedies]: privatization and markets, cooperative engagement, and political advocacy and regulation.').

22. See Ostrom 1990, 8–9 (discussing potential role of 'Leviathan' in resolving commons tragedies).

23. This basic approach equates to Pigouvian taxation, which endeavors to bring the net private and social impacts of a given action into alignment through state-imposed taxes or subsidies. Pigou 1932, 172–203. Because taxes are coercively imposed, they too might be classed within Hardin's 'mutual coercion' prescription. See, e.g., Krier 1992, 334–35.

24. See Smith 2000, 162–63 (discussing how boundaries may operate not only as prices but also as 'sanctions' that produce a large discontinuity in payoffs).

25. As Krier (1992) notes, this puzzle has long been recognized in the literature. See ibid., 338–39 n. 44 (collecting citations). For more recent discussions see, e.g., Krier 2009; Rose 1998a.

26. See Michelman 1985, 6–7 (defining and discussing the 'anti-common'); Ellickson 1993, 1322 n. 22 (referencing the 'anticommons' and attributing the idea to Michelman 1982).

27. See, e.g., Heller 1998; Heller & Eisenberg 1998; Heller 2008. Some scholars have questioned the fit between the theoretical anticommons problem and various real-world phenomena, especially with respect to patents. See, e.g., Epstein & Kuhlik 2004; Mann 2005, 999–1009; Walsh et al. 2005; but see Heller 2008, 66–69 (discussing and critiquing conclusions drawn from Walsh et al. 2005).

28. Heller (2008) suggests that anticommons or 'gridlock' problems have become more prevalent because '[t]oday, the leading edge of wealth creation requires assembly.' Ibid., xiv.

29. For a contrary view and a narrower reading of the term 'anticommons' see Katz 2010: 104–11. The point in the text is a functional one based on the typical structure of the problems that have been associated with the anticommons tragedy. See Fennell 2004, 933–64 (advocating and developing a functional taxonomy that eschews some of the distinctions that have been drawn between commons and anticommons tragedies).

30. It is an empirical question whether anticommons dynamics are more likely to block moves from private property to common property than moves in the opposite direction. For discussion, see infra note 35 and accompanying text.

31. Goetz (1984, 35–36) explicitly associated Chicken with land assembly problems, which have in turn been identified as an important category of anticommons tragedies (see, e.g., Heller 2008, 107–21).

32. This insight (without the Chicken label) was captured in Demsetz 1967, 354–55 (explaining that an effort to solve a commons problem by mutual agreement may be blocked by a 'hold-out' who, in the meantime, retains 'the right to work the land as fast as he pleases'). See also Krier 1992, 335–36 (discussing Demsetz's work and presenting an example involving excessive tree-chopping, in which '[e]ach chopper is effectively a monopolist whose agreement is essential to saving any trees'). But see Wyman (2005, 132) (suggesting that solutions to resource dilemmas are less vulnerable to holdouts than Demsetzian accounts assume because '[i]n practice . . . the collective-choice rules for altering property rights rarely require unanimity among the affected parties').

33. This argument rests on the 'Humpty Dumpty' claim that assembling fragments is more difficult than breaking apart unified entitlements. See, e.g., Heller 1999, 1169; Parisi 2002.

34. Entitlements can also be made more easily reversible by design, as through the use of liability rules that effectively extend a call option to nonowners. See, e.g., Morris 1993, 852; Calabresi & Melamed 1972, 1092, 1107.

35. Whether there is an asymmetry in the ease with which these two kinds of moves can be accomplished is an interesting question. Experimental work by Vanneste et al. (2006) found that people playing board games in three-person groups behaved less cooperatively in wielding the right to hold out than in accessing a common pool resource. These results might suggest that the form of ownership or problem frame is psychologically significant. Ibid. 117; cf. Andreoni 1995; Nash 2009. That fact might bear in turn on people's relative willingness to agree to moves from common to private property and vice versa. However, the very attempt to assemble agreement might itself cause interests in a commons to be recast psychologically as private property rights.

36. See, e.g., Michelman 1985, 13 ('[A]ny practicable, real-world so-called private property regime must contain large doses of both common and anti-common.').

37. In later work, Smith (2005; 2008) has suggested that other, differently managed resources – telecommunications and water – share the semicommons structure. Other authors have employed the semicommons in other contexts. See, e.g., Heverly 2003, 1164–83 (information); Loren 2007, 274–79 (creative works); Fennell 2008, 1102–03 (neighborhoods and metropolitan areas).

38. The text refers to multiple efficient scales that abut each other in time rather than space. A different facet of the relationship between time and the semicommons involves the use of rotation systems and similar mechanisms to avoid strategic behavior, providing a temporal analogue to the scattered farming strips. See Smith 2000, 165–66.

39. For a discussion of the adaptation of systems over time to changing conditions, such as the transportation advances that made the medieval open-field arrangement unnecessary, see Janssen, Anderies, & Ostrom 2007.
40. Doctrines that limit the degree of fragmentation that can occur in the first place can also serve to address reconfiguration challenges over time (see Heller 1999, 1176–82; see also Ellickson 1993, 1374; Michelman 1982, 15–16).
41. This family of approaches has inspired a large literature and presents numerous complications. For example, obtaining truthful valuations will only be possible if certain design parameters are satisfied (Plassmann & Tideman 2009).

REFERENCES

Alchian, Armen A. and Harold Demsetz. 1973. 'The Property Right Paradigm'. *Journal of Economic History*, 33, 16–27.
Anderson, Terry L. and Fred S. McChesney. 2003. 'Introduction: The Economic Approach to Property Rights'. In Terry L. Anderson and Fred S. McChesney (eds) *Property Rights: Cooperation, Conflict, and Law*. Princeton, NJ: Princeton University Press, 1–11.
Andreoni, James. 1995. 'Warm-Glow Versus Cold-Prickle: The Effects of Positive and Negative Framing on Cooperation in Experiments'. *Quarterly Journal of Economics*, 110, 1–21.
Arrow, Kenneth J. 1979. 'The Property Rights Doctrine and Demand Revelation Under Incomplete Information'. In Michael J. Boskin (ed.) *Economics and Human Welfare: Essays in Honor of Tibor Scitovsky*. New York: Academic Press, 23–39.
Axelrod, Robert. 1984. *The Evolution of Cooperation*. New York: Basic Books.
Ayres, Ian and Eric Talley. 1995. 'Solomonic Bargaining: Dividing a Legal Entitlement To Facilitate Coasean Trade'. *Yale Law Journal*, 104, 1027–1117.
Baird, Douglas G., Robert H. Gertner and Randal C. Picker. 1994. *Game Theory and the Law*. Cambridge, MA: Harvard University Press.
Bell, Abraham and Gideon Parchomovsky. 2003. 'Of Property and Antiproperty'. *Michigan Law Review*, 102, 1–70.
Bell, Abraham and Gideon Parchomovsky. 2009. 'The Evolution of Private and Open Access Property'. *Theoretical Inquiries in Law*, 10, 77–102, www.bepress.com/til/default/vol10/iss1/art4.
Bertacchini, Enrico, Jef De Mot and Ben Depoorter. 2009. 'Never Two Without Three: Commons, Anticommons and Semicommons'. *Review of Law & Economics*, 5 (1), 163–76, www.bepress.com/rle/vol5/iss1/art8.
Brams, Steven J. and Alan D. Taylor. 1996. *Fair Division: From Cake-Cutting to Dispute Resolution*. Cambridge: Cambridge University Press.
Buchanan, James M. 1973. 'The Institutional Structure of Externality'. *Public Choice*, 14, 69–82.
Buchanan, James M., and W. Craig Stubblebine. 1962. 'Externality'. *Economica*, n.s., 29, 371–84.
Buchanan, James M., and Yong J. Yoon. 2000. 'Symmetric Tragedies: Commons and Anticommons'. *Journal of Law and Economics*, 43, 1–13.
Calabresi, Guido and A. Douglas Melamed. 1972. 'Property Rules, Liability Rules, and Inalienability: One View of the Cathedral'. *Harvard Law Review*, 85, 1089–1128.
Cheung, Steven N.S. 1970. 'The Structure of a Contract and the Theory of a Nonexclusive Resource'. *Journal of Law and Economics*, 13, 49–70.
Ciriacy-Wantrup, S.V. and Richard C. Bishop. 1975. '"Common Property" as a Concept in Natural Resources Policy'. *Natural Resources Journal*, 15, 713–27.
Coase, R.H. 1960. 'The Problem of Social Cost'. *Journal of Law and Economics*, 3, 1–44.
Cohen, Lloyd. 1991. 'Holdouts and Free Riders'. *Journal of Legal Studies*, 20, 351–62.
Cole, Daniel H. and Peter Z. Grossman. 2010. 'Institutions Matter! Why the Herder Problem Is Not a Prisoner's Dilemma'. *Theory and Decision*, 69, 219–31.
Dagan, Hanoch and Michael A. Heller. 2001. 'The Liberal Commons'. *Yale Law Journal*, 110, 549–623.
Dahlman, Carl J. 1980. *The Open Field System and Beyond: A Property Rights Analysis of an Economic Institution*. Cambridge: Cambridge University Press.
Daniels, Brigham. 2007. 'Emerging Commons and Tragic Institutions'. *Environmental Law*, 37, 515–71.
De Alessi, Louis. 2003. 'Gains from Private Property'. In Terry L. Anderson and Fred S. McChesney (eds), *Property Rights: Cooperation, Conflict, and Law*. Princeton, NJ: Princeton University Press, 90–111.
Demsetz, Harold. 1967. 'Toward a Theory of Property Rights'. *American Economic Review* (Papers and Proceedings), 57, 347–59.

Dukeminier, Jesse, James E. Krier, Gregory S. Alexander and Michael H. Schill. 2010. *Property*. 7th edn. New York: Aspen Publishers.

Eggertsson, Thráinn. 2003. 'Open Access Versus Common Property'. In Terry L. Anderson and Fred S. McChesney (eds), *Property Rights: Cooperation, Conflict, and Law*. Princeton, NJ: Princeton University Press, 73–89.

Ellickson, Robert C. 1991. *Order Without Law: How Neighbors Settle Disputes*. Cambridge, MA: Harvard University Press.

Ellickson, Robert C. 1993. 'Property in Land'. *Yale Law Journal*, 102, 1315–1400.

Epstein, Richard A. 1985. 'Why Restrain Alienation?' *Columbia Law Review*, 85, 970–90.

Epstein, Richard A. 1993. 'Holdouts, Externalities, and the Single Owner: One More Salute to Ronald Coase'. *Journal of Law and Economics*, 36, 553–86.

Epstein, Richard A. 1994. 'On the Optimal Mix of Private and Common Property'. In Ellen Frankel Paul, Fred D. Miller, Jr. and Jeffrey Paul (eds) *Property Rights*. Cambridge: Cambridge University Press, 17–41.

Epstein, Richard A. and Bruce N. Kuhlik. 2004. 'Is There a Biomedical Anticommons?' *Regulation*, 27 (Summer), 54–58.

Fennell, Lee Anne. 2004. 'Common Interest Tragedies'. *Northwestern University Law Review*, 98, 907–90.

Fennell, Lee Anne. 2005. 'Revealing Options'. *Harvard Law Review*, 118, 1399–1488.

Fennell, Lee Anne. 2008. 'Homeownership 2.0'. *Northwestern University Law Review*, 102, 1047–1118.

Fennell, Lee Anne. 2009. 'Adjusting Alienability'. *Harvard Law Review*, 122, 1403–65.

Field, Barry C. 1989. 'The Evolution of Property Rights'. *Kyklos*, 42, 319–45.

Goetz, Charles J. 1984. *Cases and Materials on Law and Economics*. St Paul, MN: West Publishing.

Gordon, H. Scott. 1954. 'The Economic Theory of a Common-Property Resource: The Fishery'. *Journal of Political Economy*, 124–42.

Haddock, David D. 2007. 'Irrelevant Externality Angst'. *Journal of Interdisciplinary Economics*, 19, 3–18.

Hardin, Garrett. 1968. 'The Tragedy of the Commons'. *Science*, n.s., 162, 1243–48.

Heller, Michael A. 1998. 'The Tragedy of the Anticommons: Property in the Transition from Marx to Markets'. *Harvard Law Review*, 111, 621–88.

Heller, Michael A. 1999. 'The Boundaries of Private Property'. *Yale Law Journal*, 108, 1163–1223.

Heller, Michael A. 2001. 'The Dynamic Analytics of Property Law'. *Theoretical Inquiries in Law*, 2, 79–95.

Heller, Michael A. 2008. *The Gridlock Economy: How Too Much Ownership Wrecks Markets, Stops Innovation, and Costs Lives*. New York: Basic Books.

Heller, Michael A. 2011. 'The Anticommons Lexicon'. This volume.

Heller, Michael A. and Rebecca S. Eisenberg. 1998. 'Can Patents Deter Innovation? The Anticommons in Biomedical Research'. *Science*, n.s., 280, 698–701.

Hess, Charlotte and Elinor Ostrom. 2003. 'Ideas, Artifacts, and Facilities: Information as a Common-Pool Resource'. *Law & Contemporary Problems*, 66, 111–45.

Heverly, Robert A. 2003. 'The Information Semicommons'. *Berkeley Technology Law Journal*, 18, 1127–89.

Hsu, Shi-Ling. 2003. 'A Two-Dimensional Framework for Analyzing Property Rights Regimes'. *U. C. Davis Law Review*, 36, 813–93.

Janssen, Marco A., John M. Anderies and Elinor Ostrom. 2007. 'Robustness of Social-Ecological Systems to Spatial and Temporal Variability'. *Society and Natural Resources*, 20, 307–22.

Katz, Larissa. 2010. 'Red Tape and Gridlock'. *Canadian Journal of Law and Jurisprudence*, 23, 99–123.

Krier, James E. 1992. 'The Tragedy of the Commons, Part Two'. *Harvard Journal of Law and Public Policy*, 15, 325–47.

Krier, James E. 1994. 'Marketable Pollution Allowances'. *University of Toledo Law Review*, 25, 449–55.

Krier, James E. 2008. 'The Evolution of Property Rights: A Synthetic Overview'. University of Michigan Law School, Public Law and Legal Theory Working Paper No. 131, John M. Olin Center for Law & Economics Working Paper No. 08-021 (November 24, 2008). Available at http://ssrn.com/abstract=1284424.

Krier, James E. 2009. 'Evolutionary Theory and the Origin of Property Rights'. *Cornell Law Review*, 95, 139–59.

Levmore, Saul. 1982. 'Self-Assessed Valuation Systems for Tort and Other Law'. *Virginia Law Review*, 68, 771–861.

Levmore, Saul. 1999. 'Changes, Anticipations, and Reparations'. *Columbia Law Review*, 99, 1657–1700.

Levmore, Saul. 2002. 'Two Stories About the Evolution of Property Rights'. *Journal of Legal Studies*, 31, S421–51.

Libecap, Gary D. and James L. Smith. 2002. 'The Economic Evolution of Petroleum Property Rights in the United States'. *Journal of Legal Studies*, 31, S589–608.

Loren, Lydia Pallas. 2007. 'Building a Reliable Semicommons of Creative Works: Enforcement of Creative Commons Licenses and Limited Abandonment of Copyright'. *George Mason Law Review*, 14, 271–328.

Lueck, Dean. 1989. 'The Economic Nature of Wildlife Law'. *Journal of Legal Studies*, 18, 291–324.

Lueck, Dean. 2003. 'First Possession as the Basis of Property'. In Terry L. Anderson and Fred S. McChesney (eds) *Property Rights: Cooperation, Conflict, and Law*. Princeton, NJ: Princeton University Press, 200–26.

Mann, Ronald J. 2005. 'Do Patents Facilitate Financing in the Software Industry?' *Texas Law Review*, 83, 961–1030.

McAdams, Richard H. 1997. 'The Origin, Development, and Regulation of Norms'. *Michigan Law Review*, 96, 338–433.

McCloskey, Donald N. 1989. 'The Open Fields of England: Rent, Risk, and the Rate of Interest, 1300–1815'. In David W. Galenson (ed.) *Markets in History: Economic Studies of the Past*, Cambridge: Cambridge University Press, 5–51.

Merrill, Thomas W. 1986. 'The Economics of Public Use'. *Cornell Law Review*, 72, 61–116.

Michelman, Frank I. 1982. 'Ethics, Economics and the Law of Property'. In J. Roland Pennock and John W. Chapman (eds) *Nomos XXIV: Ethics, Economics and the Law*, New York: New York University Press, 3–40.

Michelman, Frank I. 1985. 'Is the Tragedy of the Common Inevitable?'. Remarks at Property Panel, AALS, January 1985. Unpublished manuscript, on file with author.

Mohan, Vijay and Prateek Goorha. 2008. 'Competition and Unitization in Oil Extraction: A Tale of Two Tragedies'. *Review of Law & Economics*, 4 (1), 519–61, www.bepress.com/rle/vol4/iss1/art24/.

Morris, Madeline. 1993. 'The Structure of Entitlements'. *Cornell Law Review*, 78, 822–98.

Munzer, Stephen R. 2005. 'The Commons and the Anticommons in the Law and Theory of Property'. In Martin P. Golding and William A. Edmundson (eds) *The Blackwell Guide to the Philosophy of Law and Legal Theory*. Malden, MA: Blackwell Publishing, 148–62.

Nash, Jonathan Remy. 2009. 'Packaging Property: The Effect of Paradigmatic Framing of Property Rights'. *Tulane Law Review*, 83, 691–734.

Nash, Jonathan Remy and Richard L. Revesz. 2007. 'Grandfathering and Environmental Regulation: The Law and Economics of New Source Review'. *Northwestern University Law Review*, 101, 1677–1733.

Ostrom, Elinor. 1990. *Governing the Commons: The Evolution of Institutions for Collective Action*. Cambridge: Cambridge University Press.

Ostrom, Elinor. 2009. 'Design Principles of Robust Property Rights Institutions: What Have We Learned?'. In Gregory K. Ingram and Yu-Hung Hong (eds) *Property Rights and Land Policies*. Cambridge, MA: Lincoln Institute of Land Policy, 25–51.

Ostrom, Elinor, Roy Gardner and James Walker. 1994. *Rules, Games, and Common-Pool Resources*. Ann Arbor, MI: University of Michigan Press.

Parisi, Francesco. 2002. 'Entropy in Property'. *American Journal of Comparative Law*, 50, 595–632.

Pigou, A.C. 1932. *The Economics of Welfare*. 4th edn, Repr., London: Macmillan and Co., 1962.

Plassmann, Florenz and T. Nicolaus Tideman. 2009. 'Applying Marginal Cost Pricing: Efficiency and Fairness in Takings and Land Assembly, and Accuracy in Assessment, All in One Fell Swoop'. Working Paper. Available at: http://works.bepress.com/florenz_plassmann/1.

Posner, Richard A. 2007. *Economic Analysis of Law*. 7th edn. Austin, TX: Aspen Publishers.

Rawls, John. 1971. *A Theory of Justice*. Cambridge, MA: Belknap/Harvard UP.

Rose, Carol M. 1986. 'The Comedy of the Commons: Custom, Commerce, and Inherently Public Property'. 53 *University of Chicago Law Review*, 53, 711–81.

Rose, Carol M. 1998a. 'Evolution of Property Rights'. In Peter Newman (ed.) 2 *The New Palgrave Dictionary of Economics and the Law*. London: Macmillan, 93–98.

Rose, Carol M. 1998b. 'The Several Futures of Property: Of Cyberspace and Folk Tales, Emission Trades and Ecosystems'. *Minnesota Law Review*, 83, 129–82.

Rose-Ackerman, Susan. 1985. 'Inalienability and the Theory of Property Rights'. *Columbia Law Review*, 85, 931–69.

Schelling, T.C. 1966. 'Uncertainty, Brinksmanship, and the Game of "Chicken"'. In Kathleen Archibald (ed.) *Strategic Interaction and Conflict: Original Papers and Discussion*. Berkeley, CA: Institute of International Studies, University of California, 74–87.

Sinden, Amy. 2007. 'The Tragedy of the Commons and the Myth of a Private Property Solution'. *University of Colorado Law Review*, 78, 533–612.

Smith, Henry E. 2000. 'Semicommon Property Rights and Scattering in the Open Fields'. *Journal of Legal Studies*, 29, 131–69.

Smith, Henry E. 2002. 'Exclusion Versus Governance: Two Strategies for Delineating Property Rights'. *Journal of Legal Studies*, 31, S453–87.

Smith, Henry E. 2005. 'Governing the Tele-Semicommons'. *Yale Journal on Regulation*, 22, 289–314.

Smith, Henry E. 2008. 'Governing Water: The Semicommons of Fluid Property Rights'. *Arizona Law Review*, 50, 445–78.

Sugden, Robert. 2004. *The Economics of Rights, Co-operation, and Welfare*. 2nd edn; Basingstoke: Palgrave Macmillan.

Sunstein, Cass R. 1996. 'Social Norms and Social Roles'. *Columbia Law Review*, 96, 903–68.

Taylor, Michael and Hugh Ward. 1982. 'Chickens, Whales, and Lumpy Goods: Alternative Models of Public-Goods Provision'. *Political Studies*, 30, 350–70.

Thompson, Barton H., Jr. 2000. 'Tragically Difficult: The Obstacles to Governing the Commons'. *Environmental Law*, 30, 241–78.

Tideman, T. Nicolaus. 1969. 'Three Approaches to Improving Urban Land Use'. Ph.D. dissertation, University of Chicago.

Ullmann-Margalit, Edna. 1977. *The Emergence of Norms*. Oxford: Clarendon Press.

Vanneste, Sven, Alain Van Hiel, Francesco Parisi and Ben Depoorter. 2006. 'From "Tragedy" to "Disaster": Welfare Effects of Commons and Anticommons Dilemmas'. *International Review of Law and Economics*, 26, 104–22.

Walsh, John P., Charlene Cho and Wesley M. Cohen. 2005. 'View from the Bench: Patents and Material Transfers'. *Science*, 309, 2002–03.

Warming, Jens. 1911. 'On Rent of Fishing Grounds'. In Peder Andersen, '"On the Rent of Fishing Grounds": A Translation of Jens Warming's 1911 Article, with an Introduction', translated by Peder Andersen and Kirsten Stentoft. *History of Political Economy*, 15 (1983), 391–96.

Wyman, Katrina Miriam. 2005. 'From Fur to Fish: Reconsidering the Evolution of Private Property'. *New York University Law Review*, 80, 117–240.

3 The anticommons lexicon

*Michael A. Heller**

When I was drafting this chapter, my computer spell-checker kept underlining *underuse* with red squiggles. *Underuse,* it seems, is not a word in Word. These squiggles are a signal: the nonexistence of a word can be as telling as its presence.

When we lack a term to describe some social condition, it is because the condition does not exist in most people's minds. When the opposite of overuse is not considered a word, it is unsurprising that we have overlooked the hidden costs of anticommons ownership. We cannot easily fix the problem until we have created a shared language to spot tragedies of the anticommons. That's the task of this chapter.[1]

COMMONS AND ANTICOMMONS

To understand the underuse dilemma, it is helpful to start with overuse in a commons.[2] Aristotle was among the first to note how shared ownership can lead to overuse: 'That which is common to the greatest number has the least care bestowed upon it . . . each thinks chiefly of his own, hardly at all of the common interest; and only when he is himself concerned as an individual.'[3]

Why do people overuse and destroy things that they value? Perhaps they are short-sighted or dim-witted, in which case reasoned discussion or gentle persuasion may help. But even the clear-headed can overuse a commons, for good reasons. The most intractable overuse tragedy arises when individuals choose rationally to consume a common pool of scarce resources even though each knows that the sum of these decisions destroys the resource for all. In such settings, reason cuts the wrong way and gentle persuasion is ineffective. In other words, I do what's best for me, you do what's best for you, and no one pays heed to the sustainability of the shared resource.

Ecologist Garrett Hardin captured this dynamic well when he coined the phrase *tragedy of the commons*.[4] In 1968 he wrote, 'Ruin is the destination toward which all men rush, each pursuing his own best interest in a society that believes in the freedom of the commons. Freedom in a commons brings ruin to all.'[5] Since Hardin wrote these lines, thousands have identified additional areas susceptible to overuse and commons tragedy.[6]

In addition, Hardin's metaphor inspired a search for solutions. Most solutions revolve around two main approaches: regulation or privatization. Suppose a common lake is being overfished. Regulators can step in and decide who can fish, when, how much, and with what methods. Such direct 'command-and-control' regulation has dropped from favor, however, partly because it fails so often and partly because of disenchantment with socialist-type regulatory control.

These days, regulators are more likely to look for some way to privatize access to the lake. They know that divvying up ownership can create powerful personal incentives to conserve. Harvest too many fish in your own lake today, starve tomorrow; invest wisely in the lake, profit forever. Extrapolating from such experience, legislators and voters reason – wrongly – that if some private property is a good thing, more must be better. In this view, privatization can never go too far.

Until now, ownership, competition, and markets – the guts of modern capitalism – have been understood through the opposition suggested by Figure 3.1. Private property solves the tragedy of the commons. Privatization beats regulation. Market competition outperforms state control. Capitalism trounces socialism. But these simple oppositions mistake the visible forms of ownership for the whole spectrum. The assumption is fatally incomplete.

Figure 3.1   The standard solution to commons tragedy

Privatizing a commons may cure the tragedy of wasteful overuse, but it may inadvertently spark the opposite. English lacks a term to denote wasteful underuse. To describe this type of fragmentation, I coined the phrase *tragedy of the anticommons.*[7] The term covers any setting in which too many people can block each other from creating or using a scarce resource. Rightly understood, the opposite of overuse in a commons is underuse in an anticommons.

This concept makes visible the hidden half of our ownership spectrum, a world of social relations as complex and extensive as any we have previously known (see Figure 3.2). Beyond normal private property lies anticommons ownership. As Lee Anne Fennell writes, 'To simplify a little, the tragedy of the commons tells us why things are likely to fall apart, and the tragedy of the anticommons helps explain why it is often so hard to get them back together.'[8]

Figure 3.2   Revealing the hidden half of the ownership spectrum

Often, we think that governments need only to create clear property rights and then get out of the way. So long as rights are clear, owners can trade in markets, move resources to higher valued uses, and generate wealth. But clear rights and ordinary markets are not enough. The anticommons perspective shows that the *content* of property rights matters as much as the *clarity*. Wasteful underuse can arise when ownership rights and regulatory controls are too fragmented.

Making the tragedy of the anticommons visible upends our intuitions about private property. Private property can no longer be seen as the end point of ownership. Privatization can go too far, to the point where it destroys rather than creates wealth. Too many owners paralyze markets because everyone blocks everyone else. Well-functioning private property is a fragile balance poised between the extremes of overuse and underuse.

THE MAGICAL PARKING LOT

So far, I've introduced the nutshell version of the commons and anticommons. To understand the concepts more fully, imagine you've discovered an empty paved lot near Times Square in New York City. At first, the parking paradise is free and open to all. No one tickets or tows. You park and go to the theater. No problem. Later, you tell friends, who park there too. No problem. But then others notice, and soon the lot is jammed. Cars are blocked in. Doors are dinged. Fights break out. The lot becomes a scary place. You pay to park elsewhere.

This overused lot is an example of a tragedy of the commons. It's a tragedy because every parker is acting reasonably, but their individual actions quickly sum to collective disaster. Similarly, if a single shepherd has access to a field, the result is well-trimmed grass and fat sheep. But open the field to all shepherds, each of whom may add sheep without regard to the others, and soon there may be nothing left but bare dirt and hungry animals.

Overuse tragedies are everywhere: species extinction, ozone depletion, and highway congestion. After Garrett Hardin popularized the 'tragedy of the commons' metaphor in 1968, people gained a new language for a phenomenon that was widely experienced, but had been difficult to name. The concept helped people give voice to then-emerging concerns about environmental degradation.

Metaphors can be powerful. The tragedy of the commons concept revealed hidden links among innumerable resource dilemmas, large and small. Spotting this shared structure helped people identify shared solutions. For example, the International Association for the Study of the Commons brings together a global network of scholars, policymakers, and practitioners, while the Digital Library of the Commons hosts an online database that cites about fifty thousand articles related to the commons.[9]

How do we solve such tragedies? There are three distinct approaches: privatization and markets, cooperative engagement, and political advocacy and regulation. Bear in mind that each solution has an analogue on the anticommons side of the property spectrum.

Private property and market transactions can solve overuse tragedy. Recall that in the parking example, you were the first to discover the empty lot. You might claim ownership for yourself based on your original discovery and first possession. Being first is a standard (but not necessarily fair or efficient) way to hand out rights in resources. Another path to private ownership passes through state control. The state might reject your claim of original discovery and instead appropriate the lot and auction it to the highest bidder or transfer it quietly to a crony. However the lot arrives in private hands, it will likely be managed better than if it had remained open to all. Owners can profit if they spruce up the lot, repave it perhaps, paint lines, and keep it clean, safe, and well used. As a parker in a private property regime, you lose the freedom of the commons but gain order and access.

The moral justifications for private ownership are controversial for philosophers, but as a practical matter, moving to private property often does prevent overuse in a commons. Harold Demsetz, author of the leading economic theory of ownership, argues that this 'conservation effect' is the main reason private property emerges in, and provides a benefit to, society.[10]

Because of our private-property focus, we tend to overlook cooperative solutions to overuse dilemmas. Cooperative solutions are often small-scale, context-specific, local, and not reliant on legal structures – thus invisible. In the case of our magical parking lot, notes under windshields, gossip on the street, and other neighborly devices can coordinate the parkers. Parkers may figure out how to keep the parking lot running smoothly without state coercion or private ownership. In *Governing the Commons,* Ostrom demonstrated that close-knit communities around the world have succeeded in managing group property without tragic outcomes.[11] There are thousands of stories of successful cooperation that preserve contested resources and promote overall social welfare.

Finally, state coercion can solve overuse. Cooperative mechanisms may break down if there are too many newcomers coming and going, if people don't really know each other, or if it is otherwise hard to discipline deviants. Then, parkers may move from polite notes under windshields to breaking antennae, purposely scratching cars, slashing tires, and fistfights. The state might assert ownership over the lot, put up a gate, and hand out or sell parking permits. But bureaucracy is costly and often capricious. Political pressure may lead to bizarre uses of the lot. States are rarely nimble or efficient parking-lot operators. Public ownership and management can eliminate the tragedy of the parking-lot commons, but they may create new costs and inconveniences for the parkers.

The Magical Parking Lot and the Anticommons

Privatizing a commons may cure the tragedy of wasteful overuse and lead to orderly parking; but it also may inadvertently spark the opposite, a lot that no one can use. The phrase *tragedy of the anticommons* describes this problem of wasteful underuse. Though the anticommons concept refers at its core to fragmented ownership, the idea extends to fragmented decision-making more generally. Resource use often depends on the outcome of some regulatory process. If the regulatory drama involves too many uncoordinated actors – neighbors and advocacy groups; local, state and federal legislators; agencies and courts – the sheer multiplicity of players may block use of the underlying resource.

How could the parking lot become an anticommons? Recall that underuse in an anticommons is the mirror image of overuse in a commons. Much can go wrong when politicians privatize state-owned resources, when resources are owned for the first time, or when owners divvy up property later on. For example, in privatizing the lot, politicians might not want to annoy parkers who are also voters. So they might give free parking spots based on every parker's previous use of the lot. (This is approximately how U.S. regulators have allocated ocean fishing quotas and tradable pollution permits.) If there are thousands of parkers, but say one hundred spots, dozens might have to share each spot. Assembling the fractional shares back into a usable parking lot would require too many deals. Even if each parker behaved reasonably, bargaining is costly. And many of us are not reasonable, especially at seven o'clock in Times Square when shows are about to start. So the 'privatized' lot may sit empty and unused – an anticommons.

Now substitute sheep in a meadow for the parkers in the lot. If a common field were privatized down to the square inch, no shepherd would be able to graze a single sheep. The same might happen if innumerable heirs separately owned scattered strips of an ancestor's farm. In an anticommons, the grass may be lush and tall and unused; in a commons, it may be picked bare. In both cases, the pasturage can be wasted and the sheep starve.

The parking lot and shepherd's field show that creating private property can solve the problem of overuse in a commons. But privatization can go too far. When it does, we can tip into an anticommons, and again everyone loses. Adding the concepts of underuse and anticommons makes visible a new frontier for private bargaining, political debate, and wealth creation. Our goal should be to find the sweet spot for property rights, between commons and anticommons.

WHY *UNDERUSE* SHOULDN'T BE SQUIGGLY

My tales of the magical parking lot are a bit of a sleight of hand. They give a succinct overview of overuse and underuse, commons and anticommons. But *underuse* and *anticommons* are still squiggly. My spell-checker suggests *undersea* and *anticommunist* as replacements. The balance of this chapter explains why these words should enter our everyday lexicon. We need an easy way to bridge the language gap.

Besides highlighting the language problem, the squiggles prompted me to look around the Internet at overuse and underuse. Googling *overuse* yielded 4.5 million hits in late 2008, while *underuse* generated only 140,000. (*Commons* had 240 million hits and *anticommons* had 40,000.) To me, the data immediately suggest two possibilities: either overuse is about thirty times more important a social problem than underuse, or we are only about 3 percent as aware of underuse as we should be. You will not be surprised to learn I believe the latter to be correct.

To understand the Google results, start with overuse. According to the *Oxford English Dictionary*, *overuse* entered the language as a verb in the early 1600s. One of the earliest usages is as apt today as it was centuries ago: 'When ever we overuse any lower good we abuse it.' By 1862, the noun form was well recognized: 'The oyster beds are becoming impoverished, partly by over-use.'[12]

Overuse continues to mean 'to use too much' and 'to injure by excessive force,' definitions that have been stable for hundreds of years. Many of Google's top links for *overuse* come from medicine. Doctors diagnose 'overuse syndrome' and dozens of 'overuse injuries' – injuries from too much tennis, running, violin playing, book reading, whatever. So what is the opposite of overuse?

Ordinary use. The opposite of injuring yourself through too much use and excessive force is staying injury free by using an ordinary amount of force. Instead of abandoning an activity, do it in a reasonable, sustainable way. In medicine as in everyday language, the opposite of overuse is ordinary use (Figure 3.3). Since the 1600s, overuse and ordinary use have been an either–or proposition. Either you will feel pain in your elbow, or you will be able to play happily, if not well. When you overuse a resource, bad things happen. It is much better to engage in ordinary use.

Figure 3.3   Ordinary use as the end point

How do we achieve ordinary use? Recall the problem of the magical parking lot. The usual solutions to tragedies of the commons are, as I've mentioned, privatization, cooperation, and regulation. These three solutions map onto the traditional view that ownership can be organized into three basic types of property: private, commons, and state (Figure 3.4).[13]

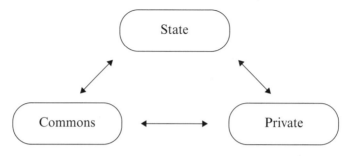

Figure 3.4   The trilogy of ownership

We all have strong intuitions about private property, but the term is surprisingly hard to pin down. A good starting point comes from William Blackstone, the foundational eighteenth-century English legal theorist. His oft-quoted definition of private property is 'that sole and despotic dominion which one man claims and exercises over the external things of the world, in total exclusion of the right of any other individual in the universe.'[14] In this view, private property is about an individual decision maker who directs resource use.

Commons property refers to shared resources, resources for which there is no single decision maker. In turn, the commons can be divided into two distinct categories. The first is *open access,* a regime in which no one at all can be excluded, like anarchy in the parking lot or on the high seas. Mistakenly, the legal and economics literatures have long conflated the commons with open access, hence reinforcing the link between commons and tragedy. The second type of commons has many names, but for now let's call it *group access,* a regime in which a limited number of commoners can exclude outsiders but not each other. If the ocean is open access, then a small pond surrounded by a handful of landowners may be group access. Group access is often overlooked even though it is the predominant form of commons ownership and often not tragic at all.[15]

State property resembles private property in that there is a single decision maker, but differs in that resource use is directed through some process that is, in principle, responsive to the needs of the public as a whole. In recent years, state property has become less central as a theoretical category: the cold war is over, most socialist states have disappeared, intense state regulation of resources has dropped from favor, and privatization has accelerated. Today, for many observers, the property trilogy can be reduced to an opposition of private and commons property, what one scholar calls simply 'all and none' (Figure 3.5).[16]

Figure 3.5   The familiar split in ownership

I believe a substantial cause of our cultural blindness to the costs of fragmented ownership arises from this too simple image of property. Note how the commons–private opposition tracks the overuse–ordinary use opposition. The former implies that there is nothing beyond private property; the latter suggests that we cannot overshoot ordinary use. Together, these oppositions reinforce the political and economic logic of the global push toward privatization. We assume, without reflection, that the solution to overuse in a commons is ordinary use in private ownership. This logic makes it difficult to imagine underuse dilemmas and impossible to see the uncharted world beyond private property.

The New World of Use

According to the *OED*, *underuse* is a recent coinage. In its first recorded appearance, in 1960, the word was hedged about with an anxious hyphen and scare quotes: 'There might, in some places, be a considerable 'under-use' of [parking] meters.' By 1970, copy editors felt sufficiently comfortable to cast aside the quotes: 'A country can never recover by persistently under-using its resources, as Britain has done for too long.' The hyphen began to disappear around 1975.[17]

In the *OED*, this new word means 'to use something below the optimum' and 'insufficient use.' The reference to an 'optimum' suggests to me how *underuse* entered English. It was, I think, an unintended consequence of the increasing role of cost-benefit analysis in public policy debates. What happens when we slot underuse into the opposition in Figure 3.3? Although the result seems simple, it leads to conceptual turmoil (Figure 3.6).

Figure 3.6   The new spectrum of use

In the old world of overuse versus ordinary use, our choices were binary and clear-cut: injury or health, waste or efficiency, bad or good. In the new world, we are looking for something more subtle – an 'optimum' along a continuum. Looking for an optimum level of use has a surprising twist: it requires a concept of underuse and surreptitiously changes the long-standing meaning of overuse. Like Goldilocks, we are looking for

Figure 3.7   Goldilocks' quest for the optimum

something not too hot, not too cold, not too much or too little – just right. Figure 3.7 suggests how underuse changes our quest.

How can we know whether we are underusing, overusing, or optimally using resources? It's not easy, and not just a matter for economic analysis. Searching for an optimum between overuse and underuse sets us on the contested path of modern regulation of risk, an inquiry that starts with economic analysis but quickly implicates our core beliefs. We have to put dollar values on human lives and on the costs of overuse and underuse behaviors – a process filled with moral and political dilemmas. I note this difficult topic to show that finding the optimum requires the idea of *underuse* and that this new word in turn transforms the meaning of *overuse*. Overuse no longer just means using a resource more than an ordinary amount. The possibility of underuse reorients policy making from relatively simple either–or choices to the more contentious trade-offs that make up modern regulation of risk.

The Tragedy of the Anticommons

Adding the idea of 'underuse' sets the stage for the anticommons. Looking back at Figures 3.3–3.7, you can see there is a gap in our labeling scheme. We have seen the complete spectrum of *use,* but not the analogous spectrum of *ownership*. What form of ownership typically coincides with squiggly underuse? The force of symmetry helped reveal a hidden property form. Figure 3.8 shows my path to the anticommons.

Figure 3.8   An ownership puzzle

I coined the term *tragedy of the anticommons* to help make visible the dilemma of too fragmented ownership beyond private property. Just as the idea of 'underuse' transforms the continuum of resource use, 'anticommons' transforms the continuum of ownership. It shows that the move from commons to private can overshoot the mark (Figure 3.9). When privatization goes too far, resources can end up wasted in an unfamiliar way.

Figure 3.9   The full spectrum of ownership

Seeing the full spectrum of ownership has another benefit. Our understanding of commons ownership may help inform solutions to anticommons tragedy. To start, consider the distinction between open access (anarchy open to all) and group access (property that is commons to insiders and private to outsiders). This distinction can do some work on the anticommons side of the spectrum as well. The conventional wisdom has often overlooked group access, but we don't have to.

HOW GROUP PROPERTY WORKS

Under the right conditions, groups of people succeed at conserving a commons resource without regulation or privatization.[18] Cooperation can get us to optimal use. Under what conditions does cooperation work, and what does that teach about fixing underuse dilemmas?

At the extreme of open access, group norms don't stick. For example, anyone can fish for tuna on the high seas. Tuna fleets work in relative isolation, and their catches can be sold anonymously to diverse buyers. Conservation norms, such as voluntary limits on fishing seasons, may gain little traction. Gossip and other low-cost forms of policing don't work for wide-ranging international fleets. Unless states intervene, overuse is hard to avoid. Whales were saved from extinction more through naval powers enforcing international treaties than through gossip at the harbor bar.

The state can sponsor hybrid solutions. What if the state asserted ownership over lobsters and fish, and then created private rights (such as licenses and tradable quotas) that complement cooperative solutions? Often, such hybrid regimes lead to fairer and higher-yielding results than informal group access can achieve. For example, in Australia, the government issues licenses for a sustainable number of lobster traps and enforces strict harvesting limits. Lobstermen can wait to harvest until the lobsters mature, or they can sell their government-created rights, secure in their markets and property. With far less fishing effort, this system yields more and bigger lobsters than U.S. lobstermen catch either in coastal harbor gangs or on the open ocean.[19]

Hybrid systems are the cutting edge of natural resource management: examples include not only tradable fishing quotas, but also carbon-emission markets and transferable air-pollution permits.[20] These solutions can work far beyond lobsters and tuna, even beyond natural resources generally. They may reach the edge of high-tech innovation.

Lessons From the Commons

Solutions to commons property dilemmas give clues to solving anticommons tragedy. For *open access*, like the high seas, states must command resource use directly or create hybrid rights, such as fishing quotas. The anticommons parallel to open access is *full exclusion* in which an unlimited number of people may block each other. With full exclusion, states must expropriate fragmented rights or create hybrid property regimes so people can bundle their ownership. Otherwise, the resource will be wasted through underuse. There is, however, one important respect in which full exclusion differs from open access: an anticommons is often invisible. You have to spot the underused resource before you can respond to the dilemma.

Group access in a commons also has an anticommons parallel: *group exclusion* in which a limited number of owners can block each other. Recall the multiple owners of our magical parking lot. For both group access and group exclusion, the full array of market-based, cooperative, and regulatory solutions is available. Although self-regulation may be more complex for anticommons resources,[22] close-knit fragment owners can sometimes organize to overcome anticommons tragedy. For group exclusion resources, the regulatory focus should be support for markets to assemble ownership and removal of roadblocks to cooperation.

Group property on the commons or anticommons side of private ownership is exponentially more important than the rare extremes of open access or full exclusion. Much of the modern economy – corporations, partnerships, trusts, condominiums, even marriages – can be understood as legally structured group property forms for resolving access and exclusion dilemmas.[23] We live or die depending on how we manage group ownership. Now, we can see the full spectrum of property, as shown in Figure 3.10.

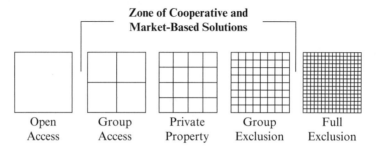

Figure 3.10   The full spectrum of property, revealed[21]

SYMMETRY IN COMMONS AND ANTICOMMONS

After I proposed the possibility of anticommons tragedy, economist and Nobel laureate James Buchanan and his colleague Yong Yoon undertook to create a formal economic model. They wrote that the anticommons concept helps explain 'how and why potential economic value may disappear into the "black hole" of resource underutilization.'[24] According to their model, society gets the highest total value from a resource – say, the magical parking lot – when a single decision maker controls its use. As more people can *use* the lot independently, the value goes down – a tragedy of the commons. And as more people can *block* each other from the lot, the value also goes down symmetrically – a tragedy of the anticommons.[25]

After developing their proof and showing how the anticommons construct may apply to a wide range of problems, Buchanan and Yoon concluded that 'the anticommons construction offers an analytical means of isolating a central feature of sometimes disparate institutional structures. . . . [People] have perhaps concentrated too much attention on the commons side of the ledger to the relative neglect of the anticommons side.'[26]

The Economics of the Anticommons

In recent years, economic modeling of the anticommons, including game theory approaches, has become quite sophisticated.[27] At the simplest level, anticommons theory can be understood as a legal twist on the economics of 'complements' first described by Antoine-Augustin Cournot in his 1838 *Researches into the Mathematical Principles of the Theory of Wealth*[28] (and discovered independently by Charles Ellet in 1839 in his work on railway tariffs[29]). Anticommons theory is a partial corrective for modern economic models that focus on 'substitutes' and often neglect the role of 'complements.'[30] What's the difference?

In Figure 3.11, Railways A, B, and C are substitute ways to get from here to there. Say the fare is 9. If railway A finds a way to provide service for 8, it will win riders. B and C must become more efficient to keep up. In markets with robust substitutes, competitors have incentives to innovate, lower prices, and thereby indirectly benefit society as a whole. By contrast, Railways D, E, and F are complements. When inputs are complementary, generally you want all or none of them.

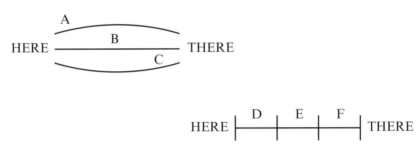

Figure 3.11   Substitutes versus complements

Again, assume the fare from here to there is 9. D, E, and F each charge 3. Railway D knows that if you want to ride, you must buy its ticket. So why innovate? Instead, D may *raise* its fare to 5, hoping that E and F lower theirs to 2 each. But why would E and F go along? More likely, they too would raise fares, so the total exceeds 9, and ridership falls below the optimal level. With complementary competition, incentives to innovate are blunted: if D did lower fares, then E and F just might raise theirs.

It's the same problem if D, E, and F are complementary patents instead of railways. Then innovators face what economist Carl Shapiro calls a 'patent thicket,' a lot of phantom tollbooths on the route to commercializing new technology.[31] Cournot proved that in markets dominated by complements – whether railways or patents – we can get higher overall social welfare if D, E, and F merge. Here, monopoly trumps competition. Anticommons theory, in turn, moves from railways and patents to ownership and regulation generally. All these concepts describe facets of the same dilemma: too many uncoordinated owners or regulators blocking optimal use of a single resource.

To date, the most debated application of anticommons theory has been in the area of drug patents and innovation. The field was sparked in part by my article with Rebecca Eisenberg on the anticommons in biomedical research.[32] Since then, there has been a flurry of follow-on papers, studies, and reports, many of which conclude that patents should be harder to obtain, in part to avoid potential anticommons tragedy effects.[33] In their 2009 book, *The Patent Crisis*, Dan Burk and Mark Lemley review the most recent literature on patents and biotech innovation and conclude that, 'the structure of the biotechnology industry seems likely to run high anticommons risks,' particularly when companies are attempting to bring products to market.[34] However, the empirical basis for finding that anticommons effects are stifling innovation remains inconclusive.[35] In addition, the anticommons framework has been used to analyze ownership across the high tech frontier, ranging from Thomas Hazlett's work on broadcast spectrum ownership to Rosemarie Ham Ziedonis' study of technology patents.[36]

It's not just high tech that's susceptible to anticommons tragedy. Cutting edge art and music are about mashing up and remixing many separately owned bits of culture.[37] Even with land, the most socially important projects require assembling multiple parcels.[38] Innovation has moved on, but we're stuck with old-style ownership that's easy to fragment and hard to put together.

The Empirical Cutting Edge

Anticommons theory is now well established, but empirical studies have yet to catch up. How hard is it to negotiate around ownership fragmentation? How much does ownership fragmentation slow down technological innovation? Does the effect vary by industry? It is difficult to measure discoveries that should have been made but weren't, industries that could exist but don't. We are just starting to examine these conundrums.

In 2006, a team of law, economics, and psychology researchers reported experimental findings that reject the presumed symmetry of commons and anticommons. They find that anticommons dilemmas 'seem to elicit more individualistic behavior than commons dilemmas' and are 'more prone to underuse than commons dilemmas are to overuse.' The researchers conclude that 'if commons leads to "tragedy," anticommons may well lead to "disaster."'[39]

These preliminary findings of bargaining failure around anticommons ownership may help provide some insight into otherwise puzzling economic phenomena. For example, some of the world's biggest energy companies have for years failed to agree on joint management of oil and gas fields they own together. If one company pumps the oil too fast, it can wreck the pressure in the gas field; if the other extracts gas too fast, it traps the oil. American law has offered them an effective legal tool, called 'unitization,' to overcome anticommons tragedy and smooth joint management of divided oil and gas interests. Yet firms block each other year after year.[40]

How can this be? Oil units aren't a case of two spiteful neighbors arguing over a broken backyard fence. They involve arm's-length business negotiations between savvy corporations. Everyone has good information about the underlying geologic and technical issues. The gains from cooperation are in the billions of dollars. Why doesn't one firm sell its interest to the other? Why don't the firms merge? What's going on? The experimental studies are beginning to give us explanations rooted in the psychology of the anticommons. Even the most sophisticated businesspeople can fail to reach agreement when a negotiation is framed in anticommons terms.

ROUNDING OUT THE LEXICON – A CAVEAT ON MONOPOLY

In rounding out the anticommons lexicon, there are some caveats: first, my lexicon focuses on one form of underuse, the tragedy that arises when ownership is too fragmented. Here, *multiple* owners block each other from using a scarce resource. Underuse can also arise in the monopoly context, when a *single* owner blocks access to a resource. This situation may be tragic, but it is not an anticommons in my sense of the term.

In the old economy, many companies held monopolies – Ma Bell, railways, local water utilities. Society gained the economic benefits of scale and scope from allowing these sectors to be monopolized. The state policed against abuse of monopoly power through complex rate regulation and oversight. Phone lines were cheaper and more available than in many other countries. The costs of these monopolies were often invisible, like deferred and dampened innovation.

In an information economy, any piece of intangible property, such as a patent, is also a monopoly. We award patents because monopoly profits create incentives to invent and because patents give inventors incentives to disclose their discoveries (without patents people might prefer to invent things they could keep secret). On the other hand, drugs would be cheaper and lives could be saved if competitors could make generic copies at will. To balance the values of innovation, disclosure, and competition, Congress keeps shifting the bundle of rights that a patent confers.

The dilemmas of any individual monopoly in the old or new economy are a great topic – for the antitrust volume in this series. For better or worse, these quandaries are familiar. We do not, however, have much experience dealing with the interaction of ownership fragments or an array of blocking patents. The anticommons lexicon addresses not monopoly per se, but ownership multiplicity.

A Caution on Absolutes

When talking about an anticommons, stay away from absolutes. First, you shouldn't assume that anticommons ownership is inevitably tragic.[41] If we lived in a world where people had perfect information and could bargain with each other at no cost, they could avoid anticommons tragedy every time (just as, in a perfect world, there would be no commons tragedy, or for that matter, tragedy of any sort).[42] In practice, however, bargaining is never free, people shirk duties and hold out for payoffs, and there are cognitive limits that shape owners' decisions. In the real world, anticommons ownership is not necessarily tragic, but it does tend that way.

Second, it's theoretically possible that an anticommons may face overuse instead of underuse.[43] For example, consider real estate development along the California coast. It's a mess. Multiple community groups, environmentalists, neighbors, and government agencies may each prefer different versions of a project. Even in that regulatory morass, though, *overbuilding* may occur if it is sufficiently costly to exercise each right to veto development. Every opponent of development may prefer to go surfing and hope the others sit through the boring public hearings. If enough people opt for a free ride, a project might face *too little* opposition, not too much. It's an empirical question whether the California coast tips toward over- or under-building. That said, in most cases I've seen, anticommons regulation tends to be associated with too little economic development, not too much.[44]

The Comedy of the Anticommons – or Underuse by Design

The final caveat comes from legal theorist Carol Rose, who noticed the economic and social benefits of what she calls 'the comedy of the commons.'[45] Certain resources, such as roads and waterways, are sometimes owned most efficiently in common. As Rose points out, creating and enforcing private-property rights is itself costly; sometimes these costs exceed the gains, not just economically but also socially. Village greens and town halls may strengthen communities in ways that are socially valuable but hard to quantify in monetary terms.

Rose's insight is equally true on the anticommons side – there are both economic and social reasons that we may prefer group exclusion to sole ownership. For example, it's possible that creating multiple vetoes may help preserve a treasured resource against transient political pressures for development – for instance, Central Park in New York City or Indian burial grounds in Arizona.[46] Similarly, 'conservation easements' intentionally use anticommons ownership to foster environmental goals.[47] (With a conservation easement, the owner sells or gives away the right to develop land, gets a tax break, and retains the right to continue a current use such as farming.) The underuse created by split ownership may be justifiable if the environmental gains exceed fragmentation costs. On balance, though, I'm skeptical. What happens a generation from now when communities want to reduce sprawl but face a patchwork of easements that make 'in-fill' development prohibitively difficult? Many conservation easements look to me like potential anticommons tragedies.[48]

The 'comedy of the anticommons' insight suggests that sometimes, for some resources, we should promote little or no use. Most of the time, for most resources, however, some positive level of use will be socially most valuable. Underuse is rarely the optimum.

TOWARD A NON-SQUIGGLY LANGUAGE

We have millennia of practice in spotting tragedies of the commons. When too many people fish, fisheries are depleted. When too many people pollute, we choke on dirty air. Then, we spring into action with market-based, cooperative, and legislative solutions. Similarly, we have a lot of experience spotting underuse caused by a particular monopoly owner. We have created regulatory bodies that know (more or less) what to do with such dilemmas.

But underuse caused by multiple owners is unfamiliar. The affected resource is hard to spot. Our language is new. A tragedy of the anticommons may be as costly to society as the more familiar forms of resource misuse, but we have never noticed, named, debated, or learned how to fix underuse. How do we stumble into the problem of too many owners? How do we get out? As a first step, underuse in a tragedy of the anticommons should be squiggly no more.

NOTES

*   This chapter is adapted from Chapter 2 of Michael Heller, The Gridlock Economy: How Too Much Ownership Wrecks Markets, Stops Innovation, and Costs Lives (2008). Thanks to Seth Davis for invaluable research assistance.

1.   The fullest account of anticommons theory and solutions appears in The Gridlock Economy. For excerpts, reviews, and further resources on the anticommons, see www.gridlockeconomy.com. *See also* Commons and Anticommons (Elgar Publishing, Economic Approaches to the Law Series) (ed. Michael Heller, 2010) (collecting and reprinting, in two volumes, the key scholarly articles on the theory and economics of commons and anticommons property).

2.   Modern-day analysis of the problems of common pool resources can be traced back 100 years to the work of Jens Warming. *See* Henry E. Smith, *Semicommon Property Rights and Scattering in the Open Fields*, 29 J. Leg. Stud. 131, 138n.18 (2000) (tracing this intellectual history, from the 1911 work by Jens Warming, to its independent discovery in 1954 by H. Scott Gordon and later extension by Steven N.S. Cheung in 1970); Jens Warming, *Om 'Grundrente' af Fiskegrunde*, 49 Nationaløkonomisk Tidsskrift 495 (1911), *translated in* Peder Andersen, *'On Rent of Fishing Grounds': A Translation of Jens Warming's 1911 Article, with an Introduction*, 15 Hist. Pol. Econ. 391 (1983); Jens Warming, *Aalegaardsretten*, 69 Nationaløkonomisk Tidsskrift 151 (1931); H.S. Gordon, *The Economic Theory of a Common Property Resource: The Fishery*, 62 J. Pol. Econ. 124 (1954); Steven N.S. Cheung, *The Structure of a Contract and the Theory of a Non-Exclusive Resource*, 13 J. Law & Econ. 49 (1970).

3.   Aristotle, The Politics and The Constitution of Athens (ed. Steven Everson, trans. Benjamin Jowett, 1996), 33. Before Aristotle, Thucydides noted that people 'devote a very small fraction of time to the consideration of any public object, most of it to the prosecution of their own objects. Meanwhile each fancies that no harm will come to his neglect, that it is the business of somebody else to look after this or that for him; and so, by the same notion being entertained by all separately, the common cause imperceptibly decays' History of the Peloponnesian War (trans. Richard Crawley, 1910), bk. 1, sec. 141.

4.   Garrett Hardin, *The Tragedy of the Commons*, 162 Sci. 1243, 1244 (1968). Hardin's metaphor builds on, and popularizes, the economic analysis of common pool resource dilemmas by Warming, Gordon, and Cheung. *See supra* note 2 (citing sources). The power of Hardin's rhetoric sometimes exceeded the reach of his data. For example, he used the grazing commons as a core example of tragedy. *Id.* at 1244. However, as Henry Smith argues, Hardin's characterization does not well capture the dynamics of grazing commons such as the medieval open-field system. First, at the theoretical level, a grazing commons can be better understood as a 'semicommons' in which commons and private rights both are significant and can interact. Smith, *supra* note 2, at 132, 134–38. Second, as an empirical matter, peasants often devised methods such as scattering and boundary placement that successfully and for long periods addressed strategic behavior problems. *Id.* at 144–54, 161–167. In addition, Hardin's work overlooks the important distinction between 'open access' and 'limited access commons.' On the implications of this distinction for common pool resource dilemmas, see *infra* note 15 and accompanying text.

5.   Hardin, *supra* note 4, at 1244.

6.   *See, e.g.,* 'The Digital Library of the Commons,' http://dlc.dlib.indiana.edu.

7.   Michael A. Heller, *The Tragedy of the Anticommons: Property in the Transition from Marx to Markets*, 111 Harv. L. Rev. 621, 624 (1998). In turn, my term builds on earlier conceptual work by Frank Michelman. *See id.* at 667–69 (discussing evolution of the concept); *see also* Frank J. Michelman, *Ethics, Economics and the Law of Property*, in 24 Nomos 3 (1982) (discussing the 'regulatory regime').

8.   Lee Anne Fennell, *Common Interest Tragedies*, 98 Nw. L. Rev. 907, 936–37 (2004). See also the chapter in this volume by Lee Anne Fennell, 'Commons, Anticommons, and Semicommons.'

9.   On the IASC, see www.iascp.org. On the Digital Library of the Commons, see http://dlc.dlib.indiana.edu/dlc/.

10.   *See* Harold Demsetz, *Toward a Theory of Property Rights*, 57 Am. Econ. Rev. 347, 354–59 (Pap. & Proc. 1967).

11.   *See generally* Elinor Ostrom, Governing the Commons: The Evolution of Institutions for Collective Action, 1–28 (setting out the theoretical framework); Elinor Ostrom, *Coping with Tragedies of the Commons*, 2 Ann. Rev. Pol. Sci. 493 (1999) (discussing solutions).

12.   *Oxford English Dictionary,* 'overuse,' http://ed2.oed.com/cgi/entry/00168291.

13.   On the property trilogy, see Michael A. Heller, *The Dynamic Analytics of Property Law*, 2 Theo. Inq. L. 79, 82–92 (2001). Most property regimes are best described as mixtures of these basic categories. *See, e.g.,* Smith, *supra* note 2 (defining semicommons property); *see also* Richard A. Epstein, *On the Optimal Mix of Private and Common Property*, 11 Soc. Phil & Pol. 1 (1994); Dean Lueck & Thomas J. Miceli, *Property Rights and Property Law*, in Handbook of Law and Economics, vol. 1, at 183, 190–99 (eds. M. Polinsky & S. Shavell, 2005).

14. William Blackstone, *Commentaries on the Laws of England: In Four Books,* bk. 2, *2.
15. On open access versus group access property, see Thráinn Eggertsson, *Open Access versus Common Property*, in PROPERTY RIGHTS: COOPERATION, CONFLICT, AND LAW (eds. Terry Anderson & Fred McChesney), 74–85. *See also* Leuck & Miceli, *supra* note 13, at 190–95 (defining and discussing property forms); Carol M. Rose, *Left Brain, Right Brain, and History in the New Law and Economics of Property*, 79 OR. L. REV. 479, 479–88 (2000). I advocate that we use the term *liberal commons* to describe many forms of legally sanctioned group ownership. *See generally* Hanoch Dagan & Michael A. Heller, *The Liberal Commons*, 110 YALE L.J. 549 (2001).
16. YORAM BARZEL, ECONOMIC ANALYSIS OF PROPERTY RIGHTS 71 (1989).
17. OED, 'under-use, *n.*,' http://dictionary.oed.com/cgi/entry/50265168.
18. *See, e.g.* ROBERT C. ELLICKSON, ORDER WITHOUT LAW: HOW NEIGHBORS SETTLE DISPUTES 167–83 (1991); S. Kopelman, M. Weber & D. Messick, *Factors Influencing Cooperation in Commons Dilemmas: A Review of Experimental Psychological Research*, in THE DRAMA OF THE COMMONS (E. Ostrom ed., 2002), 113–56.
19. *See generally* John Tierney, *A Tale of Two Fisheries*, New York Times, Aug. 27, 2000, Magazine section, at 40; JAMES ACHESON, LOBSTER GANGS OF MAINE (1988).
20. *See* Carol M. Rose, *Expanding the Choices for the Global Commons: Comparing Newfangled Tradable Allowance Schemes to Old-Fashioned Common Property Regimes*, 10 DUKE ENV. L. & POL'Y FORUM 45 (1999); Carol M. Rose, *The Several Futures of Property: Of Cyberspace and Folk Tales, Emission Trades and Ecosystems*, 83 MINN L. REV. 129–82 (1998).
21. I develop an early version of this spectrum in Michael A. Heller, *The Boundaries of Private Property*, 108 YALE L.J. 1163, 1194–98 (1999).
22. *See* Ben Depoorter & Sven Vanneste, *Putting Humpty Dumpty Back Together: Pricing in Anticommons Property Arrangements*, 3 J.L. ECON. & POL'Y 1 (2007).
23. *See* Dagan & Heller, *supra* note 15, at 552–54; *see also* Hanoch Dagan & Carolyn J. Frantz, *Properties of Marriage,* 104 COLUM. L. REV.75 (2004).
24. James Buchanan & Yong J. Yoon, *Symmetric Tragedies: Commons and Anticommons*, 43 J. L. & ECON. 1, 2 (2000).
25. *Id.* at 8.
26. *Id.* at 12.
27. *See* Francesco Parisi, *Entropy in Property*, 50 AM. J. COMP. L. 595 (2002); Francesco Parisi, Norman Schulz & Ben Depoorter, *Fragmentation in Property: Towards a General Model*, 159 J. INST. & THEO. ECON. 594 (2003); see also Fennell, *Common Interest Tragedies, supra* note 8 (arguing that tragedies of the commons are best modeled as prisoner's dilemma games and anticommons as chicken games).
28. ANTOINE-AUGUSTIN COURNOT, RESEARCHES INTO THE MATHEMATICAL PRINCIPLES OF THE THEORY OF WEALTH (1838) (Nathaniel T. Bacon trans., 1897), 99–104 (secs. 55–57, introducing theory of complements). On the current usefulness of Cournot's insights, see Hal R. Varian, *In Europe, G.E. and Honeywell Ran Afoul of 19th-Century Thinking*, New York Times, June 28, 2001, Bus. sec., at 2. Today, 'Cournot complementarity' usually describes the multi-product problem; when one input producer and a downstream manufacturer both have market power, economists may call it 'double marginalization.' In either case, merger or vertical integration is a standard solution.
29. CHARLES ELLET, JR., AN ESSAY ON THE LAWS OF TRADE IN REFERENCE TO THE WORKS OF INTERNAL IMPROVEMENT IN THE UNITED STATES (1839). For a description of Ellet's contribution, see C.D. Calsoyas, *The Mathematical Theory of Monopoly in 1839: Charles Ellet, Jr.,* 58 J. POL. ECON. 162 (1950).
30. On the problem of complements in an information economy, see HAL R. VARIAN, CARL SHAPIRO, AND JOSEPH V. FARRELL, THE ECONOMICS OF INFORMATION TECHNOLOGY: AN INTRODUCTION 43–45 (2004). On the interaction of substitutes and complements in the anticommons context, see Giuseppe Dari-Mattiacci & Francesco Parisi, *Substituting Complements*, 2 J. COMP. L. & ECON. 333 (2006).
31. Carl Shapiro, *Navigating the Patent Thicket: Cross Licenses, Patent Pools, and Standard Setting, in* INNOVATION POLICY AND THE ECONOMY (Adam B. Jaffe et al. eds., 2001), at 119; *cf.* DAN L. BURK & MARK A. LEMLEY, THE PATENT CRISIS AND HOW THE COURTS CAN SOLVE IT 75–78, 86–92 (2009) (distinguishing anticommons and patent thickets in the patent context).
32. Michael A. Heller & Rebecca S. Eisenberg, *Can Patents Deter Innovation? The Anticommons in Biomedical Research*, 280 SCI. 698 (1998); *see generally* HELLER, GRIDLOCK ECONOMY, *supra* note 1, at 49–78 (Chapter 3, 'Where are the Cures?,' reviewing ten years of scholarship and debate on anticommons effects in drug development).
33. *See id.* at 65 (discussing three influential policy-oriented reports that argue for patent reform based on anticommons concerns). These reports include Federal Trade Commission (FTC), TO PROMOTE INNOVATION: THE PROPER BALANCE OF COMPETITION AND PATENT LAW AND POLICY (2003), www.ftc.gov/os/2003/10/innovationrpt.pdf; National Academy of Sciences, Committee on Intellectual Property Rights in the Knowledge-Based Economy, PATENT SYSTEM FOR THE 21ST CENTURY, www.nap.edu/catalog.php?record_id=10976; National Research Council of the NAS, Committee on Intellectual Property

Rights in Genomic and Protein Research and Innovation, REAPING THE BENEFITS OF GENOMIC AND PROTEOMIC RESEARCH: INTELLECTUAL PROPERTY RIGHTS, INNOVATION, AND PUBLIC HEALTH (2006), www. nap.edu/catalog.php?record_id=11487.

34. BURK & LEMLEY, *supra* note 31, at 89.

35. Several survey-based studies have questioned whether anticommons tragedy is blocking academic biomedical research. *See, e.g.,* John P. Walsh, Ashish Arora, & Wesley M. Cohen, *Effects of Research Tool Patents and Licensing on Biomedical Innovation, in* PATENTS IN THE KNOWLEDGE-BASED ECONOMY (eds. Wesley M. Cohen & Stephen A. Merrill, 2003), 285–340, at 324, www.nap.edu/catalog.php?record_id=10770 (concluding that there is 'little evidence of routine breakdowns in negotiations over rights, although research tool patents are observed to impose a range of social costs and there is some restriction of access'); REAPING THE BENEFITS, *supra* note 33 (extending results through second Walsh survey); John P. Walsh, Charlene Cho, & Wesley M. Cohen, *View from the Bench: Patents and Material Transfers*, 309 SCI. 2002–03 at 2003 (2005); *see also* Richard A. Epstein & Bruce N. Kuhlik, *Is There a Biomedical Anticommons?* 27 REGULATION 54 (2004) (presenting theoretical arguments against the prevalence of a biomedical anticommons); BURK & LEMLEY, *supra* note 31, at 89 (arguing that anticommons tragedy effects appear more likely at product stage than in research phase). In my view, a legal system that leads academic scientists to break the law routinely cannot be good or sustainable social policy. *Cf.* Kara Moorcroft, *Scofflaw Science: Avoiding the Anticommons through Ignorance*, 7 TULANE J. TECH. & INTEL. PROP. 71, 80–85 (2005). In addition, increased patenting appears to be associated with delayed publication and dissemination of scientific knowledge. *See* Fiona Murray & Scott Stern, *Do Formal Intellectual Property Rights Hinder the Free Flow of Scientific Knowledge? An Empirical Test of the Anti-Commons Hypothesis*, 63 J. ECON. BEHAV. & ORG. 648 (2007). Finally, the empirical studies to date do not address gridlock in the commercial context. Commercial scientists cannot easily be patent pirates. Infringement is too discoverable, forbearance by competitors too unlikely, and potential liability too high. When commercial drug developers abandon research because of anticommons problems, the loss would not show up in surveys such as those by Walsh. *See* BURK & LEMLEY, *supra* note 31, at 87–89. It's hard to know how to quantify gridlock, in part because it involves testing a counterfactual: what cures would we have if people could work together more easily?

36. On the anticommons in the telecom context, see HELLER, GRIDLOCK ECONOMY, *supra* note 1, at 79–106 (Chapter 4, 'You Can't Hear Me Now'). *See also* Thomas W. Hazlett, *Spectrum Tragedies*, 22 YALE J. REG. 242 (2005); Rosemarie Ham Ziedonis, *Don't Fence Me In: Fragmented Markets for Technology and the Patent Acquisition Strategies of Firms*, 50 MGMT. SCI. 804 (2004).

37. On the anticommons in the copyright context, see HELLER, GRIDLOCK ECONOMY, *supra* note 1, at 9–16 (Chapter 1, 'The Tragedy of the Anticommons,' discussing tragedy in filmmaking, art, history, and music), 27–30 (Chapter 2, 'Welcome to the Lexicon,' discussing the anticommons in online search, such as Google Books). *See also* Francesco Parisi & Ben Depoorter, *Fair Use and Copyright Protection: A Price Theory Explanation*, 21 INTL REV. L. & ECON. 453 (2003).

38. On the anticommons in land, see HELLER, GRIDLOCK ECONOMY, *supra* note 1, at 107–42 (Chapter 5, 'Block Parties, Share Choppers, and BANANA Republics,' detailing anticommons tragedies and solutions in land resources). *See, e.g.,* Mark D. West & Emily M. Morris, *The Tragedy of the Condominiums: Legal Responses to Collective Action After the Kobe Earthquake*, 51 AM. J. COMP. L. 903 (2003); Russell S. Sobel & Peter T. Leeson, *Government's Response to Hurricane Katrina: A Public Choice Analysis*, 127 PUBLIC CHOICE 55 (2006); Thomas J. Miceli & C.F. Sirmans, *Partition of Real Estate; or, Breaking Up Is (Not) Hard to Do*, 29 J. LEG. STUD. 783 (2000).

39. Sven Vanneste, et al., *From 'Tragedy' to 'Disaster': Welfare Effects of Commons and Anticommons Dilemmas*, 26 INTL REV. L. & ECON. 104 (2006). Follow-up studies looked at why negotiations fail when presented in anticommons form. They found more failure as the number and complementarity of fragment owners increase. Also, as uncertainty increases, losses become even more pronounced. Depoorter & Vanneste, *supra* note 21, at 21–23.

40. On the costs of 'excessive anarchy' in the oil industry, see Gary D. Libecap & James L. Smith, *The Economic Evolution of Petroleum Property Rights in the United States*, 31 J. LEG. STUD. S589 (2002). The same tragedy affects excessive pumping of groundwater. *See* Barton H. Thompson Jr., *Tragically Difficult: The Obstacles to Governing the Commons*, 30 ENVIRO. L. 241, 250 (2000).

41. These points are developed in Heller, *supra* note 7, at 676.

42. *See generally* Ronald H. Coase, *The Problem of Social Cost*, 1 J.L. & ECON. 1 (1960).

43. Fennell develops this insight in her theory of common interest tragedies, see *supra* note 8, at 934–37.

44. Just as an anticommons theoretically may lead to overuse, it is possible for a commons to be associated with underuse. *See id.* For a real-world example, see William W. Buzbee, *The Regulatory Fragmentation Continuum, Westway, and the Challenges of Regional Growth*, 21 J. L & POL. 323 (2005).

45. Carol M. Rose, *The Comedy of the Commons: Custom, Commerce, and Inherently Public Property*, 53 U. CHI. L. REV. 711 (1986); *see also* Rose, *supra* note 15; Robert C. Ellickson, *Property in Land*, YALE L.J. 1315, 1336–38 (1993).

46.   On the potential use of an anticommons to preserve Central Park, see Abraham Bell and Gideon Parchomovsky, *Of Property and Antiproperty*, 102 MICH. L. REV. 1, 3–4, 31–36, 60–61 (2003).

47.   *See* Julia D. Mahoney, *Perpetual Restrictions on Land and the Problem of the Future*, 88 VA. L. REV 739, 785 (2002).

48   *See id.* at 785–86 (discussing the potential for anticommons tragedy that conservation easements may create).

4 Private property and public rights
Thomas W. Merrill

> An essential element of individual property is the legal right to exclude others from enjoying it. If the property is private, the right of exclusion may be absolute; if the property is affected with a public interest, the right of exclusion is qualified. – Louis D. Brandeis[1]

The public/private distinction has long played a central role in debates about the institution of property. Lawyers schooled in the common law and economists who write about property tend to accept the validity of the distinction between private property and public rights. They assume that most scarce resources are owned by someone as property, and the owner has broad discretionary authority over the use and disposition of the resource. This discretionary 'gatekeeper' power is qualified in exceptional circumstances by considerations of public rights. But individuated control by owners remains the norm. This conventional perspective is captured in the statement of Justice Brandeis quoted above.

The Legal Realist movement that began in the 1920s sought to debunk the public/private distinction, along with other fundamental categories in legal thought.[2] The Realists argued that all legal rights depend on collective recognition and enforcement, so all rights – including property rights – are effectively public. To single out some legal entitlements as 'private,' the Realists argued, is to engage in empty rhetoric or beg the question about the appropriate balance of authority between the individual and the state. The Realists and their successors also thought the state should play an active role in producing a more egalitarian distribution of resources. This function, they argued, should proceed free of any preconceptions that privilege 'private property' from claims on the general pool of resources in the society.

The Realist insight that property rights depend on collective recognition and enforcement is generally accepted today. Relatively few lawyers or economists regard property as a 'natural right,' in the sense of a divine or inalienable right. It does not follow, however, as some of the more extreme Realists and their followers claim, that the distinction between property and public rights is meaningless. As Morris Cohen, himself a Realist property scholar, recognized, property can be viewed as a delegation of authority from society to particular individuals to exercise 'sovereign' authority over particular resources.[3] Such a strategy for organizing the management of resources plausibly generates greater collective benefits than other strategies, such as control by state bureaucracies. Moreover, the perception that social welfare is affected by the distribution of resources does not mean that specific assets should be periodically reassigned by the state to promote greater equality. It may be better to preserve private ownership of specific assets, and meet distributional concerns through general tax and social welfare programs.[4] In any event, this chapter proceeds on the assumption that the public/private distinction is a meaningful and important one in describing certain features of a system of property rights.

75

I begin by surveying the leading legal doctrines that qualify private property in the name of public rights. This is followed by a review of various concepts that economists have developed to analyze the same problems. I will then sketch some ways in which economic understandings may be of assistance in determining which doctrine of public rights (if any) is most appropriate to deploy in response to particular problems.

I.   PROPERTY AND PUBLIC RIGHTS: A SURVEY OF LEGAL DOCTRINES

Private property plays an extremely important role in modern societies, and confers a broad range of discretionary managerial powers and prerogatives on owners. But private property rights are qualified in a great many ways by what the Romans called the *jus publicum* or the public right. Limitations on private property rights grounded in some conception of the *jus publicum* are far more numerous and important than might at first appear.[5] With a little manipulation – but not too much – we can say that all start with the letter 'P' and most have the word 'public' in them, thereby revealing a common heritage of sorts.

Before undertaking the survey of legal doctrines, a number of qualifications are necessary at the outset. First, public rights do not equate with public ownership. By public rights, I refer to various limitations on the domain of property and on the rights of property that have been recognized in order to protect interests thought to inhere collectively in the general public. These limitations typically apply to privately owned and publicly owned property alike.[6]

Second, I consider only those legal doctrines that embody some conception of rights that belong to the public as a collectivity, as opposed to rights which members of the public hold as individuals. This does not exhaust the many duties imposed on private property holders.[7] Private property rights are also qualified by doctrines designed to protect *other* private rights; the actions of trespass and nuisance would be obvious examples. Similarly, private property rights are qualified in many ways designed to promote the overall utility of a system of property rights; rules against restraints on alienation and the Rule against Perpetuities would be examples.

Third, I also ignore certain field-specific or resource-specific doctrines that could also be characterized as recognizing public rights. Examples might include the fair use doctrine in copyright, a privilege of experimental use in patent law, a general privilege to hunt on unenclosed rural land, and doctrines of correlative rights in water law.

Fourth, private property owners are frequently required to pay taxes in order to fund a variety of public functions. These tax obligations also impinge upon the autonomy of private owners, but again I do not consider this phenomenon as reflecting any distinct legal doctrine embodying some conception of public rights in property.

Fifth, I make no comprehensive attempt to describe the source or legal status of different public rights doctrines. Thus, I will not inquire in every case whether a doctrine is grounded in federal or state law, or whether it is based on constitutional law, statutory law, or common law. This omission would have to be rectified in a more complete account.

The Public Domain

One of the broadest public rights concepts is that of the public domain, which refers generally to a storehouse of resources open to all and subject to claiming of private rights. In American law, the primary referent historically is to the federal public domain – a vast tract of land originally comprising some 1.4 billion acres stretching from the Appalachian Mountains to the Pacific Ocean. In the nineteenth century, the federal government was regarded as temporarily holding this land as a trustee until it could be claimed in various ways by settlers.[8] Not all the land was claimed, however, with the result that a huge amount remains today – about thirty percent of the entire land mass of the United States. Over time attitudes toward this federal public domain have changed dramatically, such that today the notion that it is a storehouse of resources open to claiming is much attenuated. Federal lands are increasingly regarded as simply one type of public property, subject to gatekeeper control by the land management agencies of the federal government, and a strong preservationist sentiment has arisen that is hostile to further private claiming. Still, a tradition of open access remains as a legacy of the public domain status of these lands. National forests, wilderness areas, wildlife refuges, national parks, and federal rangelands are all generally open to the public, even if they are not subject to further claiming of private rights, and even if permissible uses in these areas are tightly regulated.

Another meaning of public domain, grounded in a metaphorical extension of the original concept, concerns intellectual goods like ideas, images, stories and songs. Sometimes intellectual goods are protected by private exclusion rights we call intellectual property. This includes patents, copyrights, and trademarks, along with lesser rights such as the right of publicity. But this protection is exceptional. The great mass of intellectual goods remains in an open access state, which has come also to be called the public domain.[9] If we indulge in a bit of Platonism, we can imagine that this version of the public domain consists of all ideas, images, tunes, and stories that will ever exist. Only a fraction of these have been 'discovered' and claimed as intellectual property. The others which have yet to be discovered, together with those for which intellectual property rights have expired, are open to all who might venture forth to find and enjoy them.

The concept of the public domain in its original sense was not seen as a limitation on private property rights. It was, instead, a state of affairs antecedent to the creation of private property – the raw material out of which private rights could be claimed. Yet the concept of the public domain has the potential to become a limitation on private property rights, insofar as we adopt 'anti-enclosure' measures designed to slow down withdrawals from the public domain or hasten the return of resources subject to private exclusion rights to the public domain as quickly as possible.[10] The larger the public domain, and the more impediments to claiming of private rights from the public domain, the smaller the quantum of private property rights.

Moreover, to the extent we adopt policies designed to protect the public domain from private claiming, we may also choke off private rights established at an earlier point in time when private claiming was encouraged or at least tolerated. We have already seen significant evidence of this in the context of the federal public domain lands. The rise of preservationist policies has resulted in restrictions on access to private 'inholdings,' and de facto moratoria on the development of many mineral leases and other private rights.[11] In the domain of intellectual goods, a growing movement to protect the 'creative commons' against enclosure has arisen.[12] This movement has captured the allegiance of a large portion of the academic community, and there are signs of its influence in recent judicial opinions evincing skepticism toward intellectual property rights.[13] In general, the higher the barriers to establishing private exclusion rights in the public domain, the more the concept of the public domain acts as a limitation on the creation and exercise of private rights.

Public Trust

Certain types of resources, nearly always owned or controlled by the state, are said to be impressed with a public trust that prevents them from being subject to private exclusion rights. In the terminology introduced by Calabresi and Melamed, public trust resources are protected by an inalienability rule.[14] Any attempt to transfer these resources into private hands or to block the public from gaining access to them is said to violate this public trust. Resources protected by the public trust doctrine therefore share the open access feature of the public domain, but lack the potential for private claiming. Public trust resources are in effect frozen in a 'public' state for all time.

The public trust doctrine is potentially a powerful limitation on the scope of private property. Resources subject to the public trust ordinarily cannot be turned into private property, and any attempt at privatization can be reversed without compensation, since the power of alienation was not included in the original title. Some environmentalists have been attracted by these features, seeing the public trust as a device for undoing private property rights and replacing them with public rights without having to pay for the rights so acquired.[15] This of course presupposes that public control would yield more environmentally-friendly management practices than private control, which is unproven in general and contrary to experience in many circumstances.[16]

In practice, the public trust doctrine has been of relatively modest significance, as courts have largely confined it to resources closely associated with navigable waterways.[17] States vary in their definition of 'navigable,' with some limiting it to tidal waters, some extending it to all waters navigable by commercial vessels, and some going further to include all floatable waters. States also vary in how far beyond navigable waters the trust extends, with nearly all states including the bed of navigable waterways, most states the banks and shores to the high water mark, some states to the dry sand area between the high water mark and the vegetation line, and at least one (California) extending the trust to the tributaries of navigable waterways.[18] Finally, there is variation in what interests are protected, with a few states limiting the trust to commercial navigation and fishing, but most extending it to include also recreational interests like pleasure boating and swimming. Still, notwithstanding vigorous advocacy to the contrary, it is striking that the doctrine has largely failed to jump the banks of navigable waterways and march inland.

When the public trust applies to a resource, it is presumptively inalienable. But how strongly this inalienability rule is entrenched is also subject to considerable variation. Some states treat the trust as a limitation on the title to lands acquired from the federal government upon statehood, which makes modification virtually impossible.[19] Others locate the trust in the state constitution, which makes modification difficult but not impossible.[20] In still others, the trust obligation can be modified by ordinary legislation. Also, states vary in terms of whether interests lesser than the fee can be alienated. If long term leases to commercial entities are permitted (as they are in Illinois for example[21]), then there is not much difference between public trust resources and private property.

Public Streets, Highways, and Navigable Airspace

Highways and streets, like navigable waterways, tend to be held in an open access state, and there is a strong tradition of public ownership and control. By and large, this is a matter of custom and statute rather than any general doctrine of public rights.[22] For historical reasons, the public trust doctrine is not usually invoked in this context, although the interest in maintaining free access to streets and highways is closely analogous to the interest in maintaining access to navigable waterways. Similarly, navigable airspace has been declared a resource open to the public, subject to extensive regulatory oversight. Thus, a private landowner cannot sue to enjoin airplane overflights, because navigable airspace above the land is regarded as public.[23] But this understanding is grounded in statutory interpretation, not any common law doctrine of public rights.

Public ownership of streets and highways is not universal. Private turnpikes were common in the nineteenth century, and private tolls roads are re-appearing in many places in the twenty-first. Similarly, railroads in the US always have been and remain largely private enterprises. Congestion pricing, which would condition access to public streets upon payment of a fee or tax, is a possibility in the future, although a recent proposal to adopt such a system in downtown Manhattan was defeated due to opposition from commuters. Even if privately owned, transportation infrastructures would almost certainly be subject to public accommodation or public utility-type duties preventing discrimination and unreasonable charges, as discussed below.

Although there is no general public rights doctrine associated with streets, highways, and airspace, there are a number of more discrete doctrines that allow the public to create open access rights of way without any formal transfer of title by the landowner, and these doctrines can act as a qualification of private property rights.[24] Public prescription allows a public way to be created by continuous adverse use by the public, that is, use without the consent of the landowner. Customary rights can be invoked to declare a public way through longstanding use from 'time immemorial.' Perhaps most interestingly, public dedication allows a public way to be created when a map or plat has been presented to the public showing a street or road, and members of the public have relied on this representation.[25] Except in the context of beaches (considered further in Part III), these doctrines are largely of historical interest today. New construction of roads, highways, rail lines or airports today is nearly always accomplished by the use of eminent domain.

Public Use Takings

The government has the power of eminent domain, which means it can take private property by compulsory means in return for payment of just compensation. The Fifth Amendment and state constitutions have been interpreted as limiting this power to takings for some 'public use.' Here, it is possible to say the concept of public rights functions as a limitation on a limitation. The power of eminent domain is a limitation on private property, and the public use requirement is a limitation on the power of eminent domain. But we can also put the matter more directly: The government has the power to compel transfers of private property for public uses, but not otherwise. So understood, the power of eminent domain is yet another doctrine of public rights.

Takings for public use occur most frequently in connection with transportation networks, and thus exhibit a strong continuity with the public rights doctrines previously considered. The most common use of eminent domain is to acquire land for the construction of public thoroughfares such as highways and streets. During the railroad boom of the nineteenth century, railroads were also heavy users of eminent domain. Other networks which transport inanimate things, such as electric transmission lines, telephone lines, natural gas pipelines, water lines, and sewers, are also beneficiaries of eminent domain. More controversially, eminent domain has also come to have broader uses, including urban renewal and economic redevelopment projects.

There are some important institutional differences in the way the 'public' inquiry plays out in the context of eminent domain relative to the other public rights doctrines we are surveying. Perhaps the most important is that eminent domain requires the payment of just compensation. When private property must give way to public rights in the eminent domain context, the property owner has the solace of an award of money compensation, generally equal to the fair market value of what is taken. This arguably justifies a broader conception of public rights in this context than might apply in other areas, where subtractions from private rights are not compensated. In addition, eminent domain is a governmental power, which must be initiated through some type of legislative or administrative process. These processes are necessarily somewhat costly, both in terms of time and expense but also in terms of the opportunity for triggering political opposition to the use of the power. These additional costs make the exercise of eminent domain somewhat self limiting.[26]

What is a public use that will justify a compulsory transfer of property? This has long been controversial, and the courts have not been able to reach a consensus on a definition that has any real content. From time to time, the public use limitation has been construed to mean public access: the acquired property must be literally open to 'use by the public,' which would tend to limit the power to transportation networks and public buildings and parks. But the dominant interpretation, certainly the US Supreme Court's interpretation of the federal public use requirement grounded in the Fifth Amendment, requires only that the taking must serve some legitimate 'public interest.'[27] This is an exceedingly broad standard that would seemingly justify any forced exchange that has a plausible public rationale. Yet, state courts applying state constitutions have sometimes invalidated proposed takings for failing to satisfy the public use requirement, even as broadly defined to mean the public interest. For example, although the US Supreme Court has approved takings to promote local economic development projects managed by private developers,[28] some state courts have held that property can be taken for economic development only if it is blighted.[29]

Public Nuisance

One who uses his property in such a way as to create an unreasonable interference with rights common to the public can be charged with committing a public nuisance. The paradigmatic example historically was blocking a public highway or navigable waterway (such interferences were also known as purprestures). Again, we see the centrality of the public thoroughfare to the understanding of public rights. Nevertheless, the understanding of what constitutes a public nuisance long ago spread beyond the narrow context of blocking public highways. The generalization of the concept occurred in an incremental fashion, through a process in which courts and legislatures both participated. Courts were willing to extend the action to include other types of activity thought to injure rights common to the public, such as widespread pollution or the operation of houses of prostitution. Legislatures intervened to declare that certain specified activities were public nuisances, such as selling tainted foods or running gambling operations.

It is not clear that the resulting hodge-podge of disfavored activities can be reduced to any overarching principle. The *Restatement (Second) of Torts* sought to assimilate public nuisance to the tort of private nuisance, and in so doing suggested that public nuisance, like private nuisance, is defined by judicial weighing of the benefits and costs of the challenged conduct.[30] But the historical record, which reveals a process of slow accretion of specific instances of disfavored conduct through legislative and judicial analogizing from earlier examples, belies this characterization. Typically, courts and legislatures make no effort to calibrate benefits and costs in determining whether something is a public nuisance, so we do not know the relationship between costs and benefits in any given case.

Public nuisance always was and remains a judicial action.[31] Originally the action was prosecuted by Crown Attorneys in the name of the King. Today the state attorney general or the public prosecutor is ordinarily the moving party. Starting in the sixteenth century, English courts began permitting private parties who had sustained special injury from a public nuisance to maintain an action,[32] and this option continues to be recognized in most American jurisdictions. The traditional remedy for conduct found to be a public nuisance was an order in the nature of an injunction requiring the defendant to abate the nuisance. Private plaintiffs who claim and prove special injury can obtain an award of damages.

Police Power

Probably the broadest and most indefinite public limitation on property rights is the concept of the police power. The term originated in federalism cases decided by the US Supreme Court in the early nineteenth century, where it referred to the general mass of powers reserved to the states after the delegation of enumerated powers to the federal government and specific federal constitutional limitations on state power were subtracted.[33] Toward the end of the nineteenth century, the concept of the police power came to refer more narrowly to the power of the states to protect the health, safety, and morals of the public. The Supreme Court, in the famous *Lochner* decision,[34] opined that the police power did not justify purely redistributive legislation, such as re-doing the terms of an employment contract voluntarily entered into by competent adults. Thus, the police power could not be used to limit hours worked or to raise wages. Similarly, the police power could not be used to override an agreement waiving the protection of property against subsidence caused by mining, even if such an agreement might seem improvident in hindsight.[35]

The *Lochner* era's exclusion of redistributive legislation from the scope of the police power has long since been repudiated. Today, the police power undoubtedly includes redistributive measures, such as providing a social safety net for the poor. Thus, for example, rent controls and mandatory warranties of habitability are today regarded as legitimate forms of police regulation, as are zoning laws, environmental laws, workplace safety regulations, and anti-discrimination laws. From time to time, efforts have been made to limit the scope of the police power to the range of conduct that would be actionable as a public nuisance.[36] Yet since the conception of a public nuisance is defined by accumulated precedent (judicial and legislative), it is not clear that such a limitation has any coherent content. In any event, restrictive definitions of the police power have generally been rejected.[37]

Notwithstanding the failure to identify any conceptual core for the idea of the police power, the Supreme Court has identified some constitutional limitations on how far legislatures can go in limiting private property rights in the name of the police power. Under the due process clauses, police regulations must have a rational basis, and if they are made retroactive, the decision to make them retroactive must be independently justified.[38] Ordinarily these limits are readily satisfied. The principal constitutional limitation today is supplied by the regulatory takings doctrine. This says, in effect, that if a police regulation has an impact that is functionally equivalent to an exercise of eminent domain, the government must pay just compensation to the owner, just as if eminent domain had in fact been used.[39] The Court has said government measures that authorize a permanent occupation of property and measures that deprive owners of all economic value, unless the activity being regulated would be a common law nuisance, will nearly always be regarded as regulatory takings.[40] Other limits on the use of property, like zoning regulations, are subject to a balancing test that usually results in a finding of no taking.[41]

A key difference between public nuisance and the police power is that the former refers to a judicial action and the latter to a legislative or regulatory action. This has important implications for the type of controls that each doctrine authorizes. Conduct that a court declares to be public nuisance will ordinarily be remedied by a prohibitory injunction directing that the conduct cease or abate. Conduct that the legislature or a regulatory agency seeks to control pursuant to the police power is subject to a much wider array of regulatory tools.[42] The conduct can be prohibited, with violators subject to criminal sanctions; the conduct can be taxed in an effort to limit the frequency with which it occurs ('sin taxes'); the conduct can be channeled, as through the adoption of zoning ordinances that permit it to take place in certain areas but not others, and so forth. Police regulations are also generally prospective, and thus allow property owners more opportunity to avoid them or adjust to them before they take effect. Public nuisance judgments are typically made after the fact, and hence can have a more disruptive impact on owner expectations.

Public Enforcement

One reason the line of demarcation between public and private is important is the state action doctrine. Governmental or 'state action' as it is generally called is subject to a wide array of legal restrictions that do not apply to nongovernmental or private action.

The individual rights provisions of the Constitution, such as the First Amendment's protection of freedom of speech, the Fourth Amendment's protection against unreasonable searches and seizures, and the equal protection and due process clauses, apply only to state action. Similarly, there are many statutory constraints that apply only to governmental action. A partial list would include the Administrative Procedure Act and the Freedom of Information Act and their state analogues, obligations to prepare environmental impact statements before undertaking new development of resources, restrictions on the use of no-bid contracts, and Davis–Bacon prevailing wage rules. As a rule, the management and control of public property is state action and hence is burdened with these and other legal restrictions that do not apply to the management and control of private property.[43] For example, an auditorium owned by the government will not be allowed to engage in viewpoint discrimination, such as renting only to Democrats but not Republicans, whereas an auditorium that is privately owned is free to engage in viewpoint discrimination.[44]

One might think the many obligations that attach to public property because of the state action doctrine would not pose any qualification on private property. This is not true, however, because in several contexts the Supreme Court has held that *public enforcement* of private rights constitutes a form of state action. Consequently, when private property owners call upon the authority of the state to enforce or implement their prerogatives of ownership, this may trigger the obligations that would attach to a similar effort by the government to enforce the prerogatives of public property.

Many of the decisions that equate public enforcement with state action involve race discrimination, and were rendered in the period before statutes were adopted in the 1960s and afterwards limiting, as a matter of police power regulation, the ability of private property owners to discriminate on the grounds of race. In the most famous of these decisions, *Shelley v. Kraemer*,[45] the Supreme Court held that judicial enforcement of privately-negotiated racial covenants running with the land is state action and hence is prohibited by the Equal Protection Clause of the Fourteenth Amendment. The effect was to deny public enforcement to covenants that previously had been recognized as an incident of property rights in land. In the aftermath of *Shelley*, the Court came close to ruling that bringing a trespass action to exclude African Americans from segregated lunch counters is also state action.[46] But it drew back after Congress enacted the Civil Rights Act of 1964 outlawing discrimination in public accommodations connected with interstate commerce, including restaurants.[47]

Not all the decisions equating public enforcement of private rights with state action involve discrimination. The Court has also held that certain types of judicial procedures for recovering possession of property, including common law replevin actions, involve state action.[48] Consequently, an individual seeking to use these procedures to recover property must comply with due process notice and hearing requirements, just as a public entity would. The use of self help is less likely to be characterized as state action.[49] Paradoxically, therefore, the use of public enforcement to protect property rights is more encumbered with procedural protections than is the use of self help, although from a functional perspective the need for additional protection is arguably greater in the latter context.

One can see why judges and lawyers would be drawn to extending state action to encompass public enforcement of private rights. Most lawyers support the values enshrined in the Bill of Rights and other restrictions on government action. If society benefits from having the government respect freedom of speech, equal protection, and due process hearing rights, then why shouldn't private property owners respect freedom of speech, equal protection, and due process hearing rights if they seek public enforcement? A possible answer is that blurring the distinction between private property and public rights in this fashion greatly limits owner autonomy. Managerial discretion is compromised, and efficiency and innovation burdened. There is a tradeoff between public and private rights, and caution is in order before pushing one too far at the expense of the other.

Few courts or commentators appear to be eager to extend the state action theory to *all* public enforcement of private rights. No one suggests, for example, that courts cannot enforce a construction contract between a private property owner and a private building contractor unless the contractor complies with Davis–Bacon prevailing wage requirements that apply to government construction projects.[50] But the theory that would allow *Shelley* to stand while drawing the line short of characterizing all public enforcement as state action has proven to be elusive.[51]

Public Accommodations

Certain enterprises that open their doors to the public are classified as public accommodations, a status which subjects them to duties to avoid economic discrimination and price gouging in dealing with the public. The origins of the concept of public accommodation are murky. Blackstone spoke in a single passage of the special legal duties of common carriers, inn-keepers, and common callings, such as farriers and tailors.[52] Later, it seems, the concept narrowed to businesses linked to travel, namely common carriers like coaches, steamboats, and trains, plus inns and roadhouses.[53] These enterprises, as public accommodations, could not arbitrarily exclude travelers when they had available space, and could not change exorbitant rates. Modern anti-discrimination laws including Title II of the Civil Rights Act have further expanded the concept of public accommodations to include restaurants and places of entertainment. These laws, of course, outlaw discrimination in the form of segregation based on race and other protected classes like gender and religious affiliation, something that was not clearly included within the concept of discrimination under the common law.

Behaving in a fair and nondiscriminatory manner is a virtue, and not surprisingly some courts have been eager to expand the concept of public accommodations to promote what they regard as virtuous behavior by property owners. The New Jersey Supreme Court, in particular, has ruled that Princeton University, Atlantic City gambling casinos, and the Boy Scouts are either public accommodations or are subject to duties of public accommodations, in order to advance a more inclusive policy by these institutions toward political demonstrators, card counters, and openly gay scoutmasters, respectively.[54] But of course, there is a tradeoff between expansions of public accommodation duties and the loss of institutional autonomy, analogous to the tradeoff discussed in connection with expanding the state action doctrine to include public enforcement of private rights.

Expansion of the state action doctrine and extensions of the concept of public accommodations both represent encroachments of public rights into areas previously reserved for owner discretion. The triggering mechanisms are different: close involvement with the government in the case of the state action doctrine; opening one's property to the public in the case of public accommodations. But the relevant tradeoffs are analogous.

Public Utilities

Related to the concept of public accommodation is the idea of the public utility. This was defined in a famous nineteenth century case as any enterprise providing a service 'affected with the public interest,'[55] an extremely vague formulation that offers little guidance as to its scope. In practice, public utilities tend to be large firms in network industries that provide basic services like electricity, natural gas, water, sewage disposal, and land-line telephony, although historically other enterprises like grain elevators have also been included in the concept. Public utilities are often subject to pervasive regulation that requires firms to adhere to published tariffs describing their rates and services, subjects rates and services to oversight by public regulatory authorities, and restricts the ability of providers to decline service to high cost customers. Public utility duties therefore apply to a smaller subset of property owners than do public accommodation duties. But where they apply, public utility duties constrain the freedom of owners much more extensively than do public accommodation requirements.

Interestingly, the public utility idea has been weakening in recent years as a basis for subordinating private property to concerns about public rights.[56] Many industries previously subject to public utility duties, including the railroad, trucking, and airline industries, have been extensively deregulated. In these industries, competition and private contracting are now thought to be a more effective way of assuring adequate service and reasonable rates. Other industries, including wholesale electric and natural gas distribution and local telephony, have been partially deregulated, with mixed results. Still other industries, including cable television and internet service providers, have successfully resisted the imposition of traditional public utility duties. Here we see an interesting countermovement to the trend with respect to other legal doctrines, where public duties are generally expanding at the expense of private rights.

Summary and Generalizations

A few generalizations can be drawn about these nine doctrines or clusters of doctrines of public rights. Notice that some doctrines are restrictions on title whereas others are restrictions on use. The doctrines at the top of the list, including the public domain, the public trust, the public right-of-way doctrines, and public use takings, involve inalienability rules or compulsory transfers of title.[57] These doctrines prohibit private ownership or compel the loss of private ownership previously enjoyed. They tend to be narrow in scope (public trust), of little contemporary relevance (the public right of way doctrines), limited to unclaimed resources (public domain), or are moderated by a compensation requirement (public use takings). The other doctrines entail more delineated restrictions on particular uses of private property.[58] Public nuisance, the police power, and public enforcement (the state action doctrine) focus on the regulation of uses that cause general social harms; public accommodations and public utilities impose affirmative duties that restrict owners of affected properties from engaging in certain types of conduct thought to be abusive. The police power is the most ill-defined and open-ended of these doctrines. But because of the regulatory takings doctrine, exercises of the police power that are tantamount to a transfer of title are in effect converted into exercises of the power of eminent domain, thus effectively limiting the police power to regulations of particular harmful uses.

A second thing to note is how many of the doctrines are concerned with transportation networks or access to private property more broadly. The public trust doctrine in practice is limited to navigable waterways and associated resources; public use takings are primarily used to acquire rights of way for streets or highways or utility lines; public nuisance in its original signification referred to blockages of navigable waterways or public roads; public accommodations duties historically applied primarily to travel-related industries; and public utilities are understood to be firms dedicated to transporting people (common carriers) or things (electricity, gas, etc.) from one place to another. Even the public domain can be regarded as a doctrine designed to ensure public access to as-yet unclaimed resources. Clearly a number of the doctrines, including public use takings, public nuisance, and the police power, have been expanded beyond this central concern. Nevertheless, the core of the public rights doctrines is concern with ensuring that holders of private rights remain interconnected and can engage in free exchange and communication with each other.

A third observation is that the nine doctrines vary widely in their contemporary significance. Today, takings for public use and especially the police power dominate all else. In considerable measure, this is because earlier limitations on these doctrines – notably *Lochner*'s refusal to extend the police power to redistributive regulations and the limitation of the power of eminent domain by many states in the nineteenth century to projects accessible by the public – required recourse to other, more specific public rights concepts. Doctrines like public accommodations, public utilities, and public enforcement can be seen as stand-ins designed to legitimate certain kinds of restrictions on the use of property (like anti-discrimination laws and rate regulation) which were arguably outside the scope of the police power in its *Lochnerian* conception. Once nearly all limitations were removed from the police power, these doctrines retreated to a position of largely vestigial significance. Similar observations can be made about the public domain, the public trust, and the public right of way doctrines. These doctrines can be seen as understandings designed to maintain public access rights in a world in which government had few resources and limited capacity to own and control transportation facilities. Once governments acquired significant powers of taxation and large bureaucracies, eminent domain became the logical means for acquiring property for use in transportation networks.

II   PUBLIC RIGHTS: ECONOMIC CONCEPTS

Let us now shift focus and consider public rights from an economic perspective. Here, mercifully, there are fewer relevant concepts. I will mention five distinct economic rationales for qualifying or limiting property rights in order to promote social welfare. As we shall see, some of these concepts map fairly directly onto certain legal doctrines. Others are either narrower or broader than the legal doctrines, or in some cases cut across multiple doctrines. The lack of perfect fit suggests that familiarity with economic concepts may sharpen our understanding of the function of the legal doctrines, or may convince legal actors to broaden, narrow, or conceivably abandon some of these doctrines.

One way to bring some unity to these concepts is through the idea of transaction costs. If we adopt Coase's thought experiment about an imaginary world of no trans-actions costs,[59] we quickly find that problems associated with private exclusion rights largely disappear. Costless bargaining, in some cases on a massive scale, would yield re-arrangements of rights that would eliminate most of these problems, insofar as they restrict the aggregate wealth of society. Reversing the logic, we can say that transaction costs are the explanation for most of the shortcomings of a regime of private property.

This integration of economic concepts is useful in identifying precisely which features of particular situations make contractual or other voluntary solutions unlikely. To be sure, 'transaction costs' covers a wide range of impediments to exchange, and virtually any argument for modifying property rights in order to achieve some public good can be described in terms of transaction costs. Nevertheless, the integration may be of assistance in choosing among the nine public rights doctrines as potential solutions.

Closely related to transaction costs – indeed, one might say inseparable from transaction costs – is the idea of externalities.[60] An externality occurs when one person engages in some activity that affects the welfare of one or more other persons, and this effect is not reflected in property values or contractual opportunities of the person engaging in the activity.[61] As Coase intuited, externalities are a function of transaction costs. The higher the transactions costs, the more likely that private rights will generate externalities, either because of incomplete specification of property rights or incomplete contracts. This suggests that the circumstances in which economic analysis would support a qualification of private exclusions rights can also be characterized as ones in which externalities loom large.

Public Goods

Public goods are defined as goods from which it is not possible to exclude potential users and/or goods as to which consumption does not increase the costs of providing the good to other users. Public goods, in cumbersome terminology favored by economists, are either 'nonexcludable' or 'nonrivalrous' or both.[62] Classic examples of public goods, such as national defense and a clean environment, usually partake of both defining conditions. Conceptually, however, these defining conditions are distinct, and may in some cases diverge. They also have different implications for identifying appropriate limits on private property rights.[63]

Excludability is a function of technology. Land is thought to be an excludable good, because it is relatively easy to erect fences or other barriers to access, that is, the technology of exclusion is relatively cheap. The ocean has traditionally been regarded as nonex-cludable, because it has been difficult to imagine how one would enforce exclusive rights to ocean parcels at a reasonable cost. But perhaps with the development of satellite sur-veillance technology and GPS monitoring this will change. City streets provide an even more striking illustration of the relationship between technology and exclusion. Streets have traditionally been regarded as an open access, non-excludable good. But congestion pricing schemes recently adopted in London and Oslo using transponders, automated cameras, and computers show that streets can be made excludable – at a cost. Notice that in all these examples (land, oceans, streets) the good is rivalrous in some ranges of usage, that is, consumption of the good by one person precludes (to some degree, however small) consumption by others.

The difference between rivalrous and nonrivalrous goods can be described in terms of the way the marginal costs of production change as levels of consumption rise. If a good is rivalrous, then there is a positive marginal cost of producing additional units of the good. This is because the good is finite in quantity and the consumption of one unit will require drawing upon increasingly scarce inputs in order to produce additional units of the good. If the good is nonrivalrous, then the marginal cost of consuming an additional unit of the good is zero. The good (once created) is in effect infinite in supply, in the sense that consumption of one unit has no effect on the marginal cost of producing additional units of the good. This feature, when present, provides a strong reason for encouraging or subsidizing the production of the good, since the correct price for any good having a marginal cost of zero, from an allocational efficiency perspective, is zero.

Many goods are nonrivalrous at some ranges of usage but become rivalrous as usage increases. An interstate highway is a good example. If there are relatively few vehicles using the highway, then the addition of another car will impose little or no cost on other users. As usage rises, however, congestion sets in. In a rush hour traffic jam, each additional car slows the movement of traffic by a small but measurable amount. This imposes costs in the form of additional delay on all other vehicles using the highway. In the aggregate, the costs of each additional vehicle can become quite substantial.

There is at least a strong correlation between whether a good is rivalrous or nonrivalrous and whether it is tangible or intangible. Tangible goods – land, buildings, vehicles, clothing, food – tend to be rivalrous, in that consumption of the good by one person precludes consumption by another and hence increases the marginal costs of producing additional units. Intangible goods such as intellectual goods – ideas, stories, images – tend to be nonrivalrous. Once I have whistled 'Dixie' in your presence you can start whistling Dixie without in any way impairing my ability to continue whistling Dixie, and it does matter to either of us how many other people are busy whistling Dixie. Notice that intangibles can be made excludable by law (i.e., by creating intellectual property rights) even if they are nonrivalrous.

Some goods are partial public goods. My beautiful flower bed is a private good insofar as I can exclude others from entering the bed to sniff the flowers, but it is a public good insofar as I cannot stop passersby from gazing at it. (Excludability in this case is the key; if I erect a tall fence I can make the view excludable.) Other goods are localized public goods, in the sense that they are public goods only within a delineated area. A local park would be an example.

Public goods are usually regarded as positive things, in that they improve the aggregate welfare of society. Conceptually one could also speak of public bads, like air pollution, which are also nonexcludable and/or nonrivalrous. But the elimination of a public bad can be regarded as a public good. Action taken to eliminate a bad which is nonexcludable and/or nonrivalrous will itself ordinarily have a nonexcludable and/or nonrivalrous quality, so we can probably ignore public bads as a distinct phenomenon, and consider only public goods, understood also to include elimination of public bads.

Public goods analysis suggests that private property is a potential impediment to the production of public goods because of the excludability feature. If excludability is not possible with respect to some good, because the technology of exclusion is too expensive relative to the benefits of exclusion, then a system of private property rights will under-produce such a good. This is because private property owners cannot capture (through exclusion) the benefits to the public of providing the good. Nonrivalrousness is also rele-vant to the normative assessment of private property, insofar as someone given exclusion rights to a nonrivalrous good is likely to charge a positive price for access to the good. If the marginal cost of consumption is zero, however, then the correct price for access to the good from the perspective of allocative efficiency should be zero. This implies that the good should be held in an open access state, without any private exclusion rights.

If transaction costs were zero, as in Coase's thought experiment, then individuals would contract with each other until the most efficient providers of public goods pro-duced the socially optimal quantity of public goods. There would be no need for collec-tive intervention, beyond the enforcement of contracts. In the case of pure public goods like national defense, this is obviously too fantastic to take seriously. The transaction costs of achieving collective agreement would be so enormous the enterprise would never get off the ground. This helps explain why the provision of public goods is commonly assumed to require some type of collective decision making process and coercion of individual property owners (for example through taxation).

Insofar as public goods are nonexcludable, private individuals who supply public goods (intentionally or unintentionally) cannot expect to capture the full social benefit of their endeavors. For this reason too, public goods would often be undersupplied in a system that relies solely on private property rights and voluntary exchange of rights through contracts. Some public goods would still exist under such a system where owners of private property have sufficient incentives to create such goods given the private gains they expect to realize. For example, owners of radio stations provide radio program-ming, which has the attributes of a public good, because they expect to reap a profit from selling advertising along with the programs.[64] Nevertheless, other public goods like national defense require collective action, and this necessitates some qualification of private property rights. In the most common case, individuals will be taxed in order to generate funds which are then devoted to the provision of public goods. Yet a desire to promote the collective provision of public goods may also explain some public rights doctrines, such as the public domain, public trust doctrine, or takings for public use.

Any collective provision of public goods raises difficult problems because individual valuations of the public good will diverge. These differential preferences mean that some preference-aggregating decisional rule must be adopted for determining how much will be spent on providing public goods. Take clean air for example. Just because clean air is a public good, it does not follow that the cleaner the better. Removing all pollutants from the air would be extraordinarily expensive, and might entail a policy of eliminat-ing all industry. So determining the optimal cleanliness of the air requires a balancing of benefits and costs through some collective decision making procedure.

In this light, it is problematic to give individuals the right to demand some level of pro-vision of public goods, since the individuals who step forward as private enforcers may be outliers who place a higher valuation on the public good than does the median citizen. This has been offered as an explanation for why we have standing rules that restrict the ability of individuals to enforce public goods.[65] It also provides a clue as to why public nuisance law has traditionally been enforced by public officials rather than private citizens, and why the police power is implemented by legislatures and public agencies exercising delegated legislative authority rather than by courts. In each case these limitations assure that the level of public goods is determined by officials accountable to the public, which means the level of public good provision is more likely to approximate the preferences of the median citizen than would be the case if any self-appointed watchdog could determine the desired level of public goods.

Network Effects

Distinct from public goods is the idea that certain resources become more valuable as more people use them. This is encapsulated in the saying, 'the more the merrier,'[66] and has come to be known as network effects. Common examples include languages, computer operating systems, telephone systems, and internet sites like Facebook. In each case, the system becomes more valuable as more persons join, because increasing the number of participants increases the value to all others who participate in the system.[67]

Goods that have network effects need not be and indeed typically are not public goods. The telephone system, for example, is not a public good, insofar as each person who signs up for service can be charged for the service (the good is excludable) and typically only one person can use a line at any time (the good is rivalrous). Nevertheless, telephone service becomes more valuable to each user as each additional user is added to the system, because there are more people to communicate with by telephone.[68]

The transaction cost framework can again be applied to network effects. Network effects are a particular kind of positive externality generated by increasing participation rates. If transaction costs were zero, then the providers of goods with network effects could re-negotiate contracts with purchasers on a continuing basis to capture these positive externalities through their pricing, i.e., by recomputing the price every time the size of the network expands or shrinks. In practice, this type of continual re-contracting would be prohibitively expensive, and not surprisingly we do not see it, although some crude approximations no doubt exist. Certainly, it is not clear that public regulation is more likely to produce better pricing than private contracting.[69]

Another issue raised by network effects is that it may make sense, from an aggregate welfare perspective, to pursue cross-subsidization strategies – over-charging low cost customers and under-charging high cost customers – in order to increase overall participation rates. An example would be a universal service mandate requiring telephone companies to provide service in high cost rural areas, which are paid for in part by charges paid by low cost customers in urban areas.[70] Again, whether collective intervention is needed to secure this outcome may depend on context. If the phone company has a monopoly in the service area, it will have an incentive to cross-subsidize in order to make the system more valuable to all users. If competitive entry is allowed, cross subsidies may be eliminated as rival providers 'cream skim' low cost customers by offering them lower prices. Thus, the introduction of competition into telephone markets may necessitate public regulation in the form of mandatory cross-subsidization through universal service obligations.

Yet another device for encouraging network effects is to enforce a very low access price or even a price of zero for goods characterized by network effects. Some of the literature on open source software suggests that pricing access to basic computer operating programs at zero is desirable insofar as it will encourage the development of the maximum number of application programs.[71] Once again, it is not clear that it is appropriate to mandate such pricing policies by government fiat, as opposed to tolerating them when adopted voluntarily. Nevertheless, some enthusiasts for open source software and other aspects of the 'creative commons' have embraced the idea of preserving the public domain as a way of enhancing network effects related to digital networks and intellectual goods more generally.[72]

Monopoly

A familiar economic argument for regulating private property rights is the prevention of monopoly. All property rights confer a monopoly, insofar as the right to exclude also gives the owner of a resource unilateral authority to determine output and set prices for access to the resource in question. In the ordinary case, the monopoly conferred by property is unobjectionable. If there are dozens of farms in a given valley, each farmer has a monopoly over his own farm. But competition among the farmers will constrain the behavior of each farmer-monopolist, such that output and prices will be determined by market forces. Monopolies are troubling only when they confer market power, that is, when they give the monopolist the power to influence market prices through adjustments in output. With market power, the right to exclude confers the right to demand supra-competitive prices and exact other measures that diminish social welfare.

Again, if transaction costs were zero monopoly would not interfere with the efficient allocation of resources. Those holding monopoly resources and those seeking access to these resources would eventually agree on an exchange that maximizes the sum of their valuations of the resource. The presence of monopoly would likely affect the distribution of wealth, with the monopolists gaining a larger share of social output at the expense of those without monopoly power. But the allocation of resources would be unaffected. There are a number of variations on the monopolist with market power. Whether contractual exchange is a plausible means of overcoming the problem depends on context.

At one extreme we have the phenomenon of natural monopoly. A natural monopoly arises in a market in which the average cost of producing an additional unit of output is always higher than the marginal cost at all relevant levels of production.[73] The usual reason for this is that one or more inputs into the production process are characterized by very large economies of scale. For example, an electric power company requires a very large expenditure on fixed plant, in the form of generating facilities, distribution lines, transformers, and so forth. The marginal cost of delivering an additional kilowatt of power may be tiny – a small amount of fuel consumed by a generating plant perhaps. But the enormous cost of the fixed plant investment, when spread over all the units of output, yields a higher average cost for the kilowatt of power. The problem this creates is that if prices in a competitive market are driven toward marginal cost, then the power company will never recover all its costs (average costs times total output) and will go bankrupt. Here, contractual solutions are unrealistic, given the large number of affected parties. Rather, it is probably necessary to confer a monopoly franchise on a single power company, and then subject its pricing and output decisions to some form of public regulation in order to allow it to recover its average costs, but not to charge the full monopoly price. Accordingly, natural monopolies are often associated with the idea of public utility regulation.

Another variation is the idea of a situational or locational monopoly. This refers to private property that has market power only because of certain circumstances that may be transient or dependent on the location of customers. An example would be a hardware store that has the only supply of snow shovels in a community when a freak snowstorm hits. The hardware store has market power over snow shovels, given the transient imbalance between supply and demand in the local market. Another example would be a solitary taxicab at an airport taxi stand at 4:00 a.m. when a long delayed flight arrives. The cab is in a position to charge a very large fare to deliver a passenger to her desired destination. Situational or locational monopolies are usually regulated by social norms, but sometimes are controlled by regulations, such as requiring that all charges for taxicabs be metered. There is some association historically between locational monopolies, particularly those associated with travel, and the idea of public accommodations.[74]

A third variation, which plays a particularly large role in property law, is the idea of bilateral monopoly. This is a situation combining a local monopoly and a local monopsony, in other words where there is only one buyer and one seller of a particular resource. Suppose A builds a garage on what he thinks is his own land, but it turns out that the land is owned by his neighbor, B. In order to preserve the garage, A needs to buy additional land from B. B has a monopoly vis-à-vis A in the sale of garage-preserving land. Yet at the same time, A has a monopsony vis-à-vis B, in that A is the only one seeking to buy additional land under a garage from B. Bilateral monopolies commonly arise from boundary mistakes, improperly formalized easements, disputes over fixtures, lease extensions, and similar situations. They can give rise to prolonged and acrimonious bargaining, and occasionally result in the use of eminent domain or the application of implied easement theories.

Spillovers

Perhaps the most frequently-encountered economic rationale for qualifying private exclusion rights is based on activities engaged in by one land owner that affect the use and enjoyment of other land owners. I will call these interactive land use effects 'spillovers.'[75] Pollution is a familiar example. Land use spillovers are the most commonly-cited form of externalities, although as previously suggested nearly all economic concepts that justify modification of exclusion rights can be reframed in terms of externalities.

Spillovers, like externalities more generally, can be either positive or negative. Suppose O dumps waste oil in her backyard, which seeps into an aquifer that serves as the source of well water for neighboring property owners. If O is not required to compensate her neighbors for their loss, then O has created a negative spillover. Alternatively, suppose O discovers a leaking oil tank on her property, left by a previous owner, and removes it, with the result that the well water of the neighbors improves. If the neighbors are not required to pay restitution to O for her expenses in cleaning up the aquifer, then O's action has created a positive spillover through her actions. As this example suggests, whether something is regarded as a negative or positive spillover depends critically on our identification of the baseline against which the spillover is analyzed.

It is important to emphasize that spillovers justify public intervention only if they are true externalities, in the sense of effects that are not reflected in the value of the actor's property rights or in opportunities to contract among the persons affected. If A's view of the ocean is blocked by B, but A has accepted a payment of compensation in advance from B in return for the obstruction, this is not an externality and hence not an economically-relevant spillover. Similarly, if C keeps well-stocked bird feeders on his land, which allow D to enjoy the sight and sounds of songbirds, this is not a spillover if D has offered to pay for the bird feed.

Sometimes action by one set of parties in a contractual relationship will have a spillover effect on third parties due to changes in prices, usually described as 'pecuniary' externalities. Suppose E constructs and maintains an extremely popular resort hotel, which has the effect of increasing the profits earned by F, who operates a nearby gasoline filling station. Here E's action changes the demand for gasoline by hotel patrons, which creates a positive spillover for a third party, F. Economists generally argue that these pecuniary effects should be ignored, since their primary effect is only to redistribute income rather than change the allocation of resources in society.[76]

The transaction cost perspective is often invoked in discussing spillovers. This was Coase's principal example in introducing the concept of transaction costs. And indeed, it is often more realistic to imagine that contractual exchange might provide a solution to various spillover problems than it is to think that contracting might solve problems of public goods, network effects, or monopoly.[77] Much depends, however, on context. If large numbers of persons are affected by a spillover, holdouts and freeriders are likely to interfere with any effort to reach a consensual agreement on limiting negative spillovers (or encouraging positive ones). Even if only two parties are involved, this can be described as a form of bilateral local monopoly, especially if one or both do not have easy exit options. As we have seen, bilateral local monopolies often prove impervious to contractual solutions.

Spillovers, especially negative ones, are usually associated with regulations of the use of land. The judicial interdiction of public nuisances is typically aimed at activity that produces widespread negative spillovers. Police regulations, including zoning laws and environmental regulations, typically have similar objectives.

Assembly of Rights

The final economic concept is probably the least familiar, although it is highly germane to the study of public rights. This is the idea that private exclusion rights can frustrate large-scale undertakings because of the difficulty of assembling the required rights.[78] This is sometimes referred to in the literature as the 'anticommons' problem, although strictly speaking a true anticommons – where everyone has the right to exclude everyone else from a resource – is so rare it is practically unheard of. More often, the term anticommons is used to refer to situations where large numbers of rights need to be assembled under common ownership or control in order to undertake some socially worthwhile project.[79]

Examples of assembly problems are legion. Consider a project that requires a long corridor of access rights, such as the right of way for a railroad, pipeline, or highway. If the only way to develop such a corridor were through voluntary purchases of rights, particular owners who own parcels located along the corridor might refuse to sell or would hold out for a disproportionate share of the gains from the project. In some circumstances it is possible to use preexisting corridors, which explains why highways often follow old Indian trails, rail lines snake along river banks, and utility lines are buried under city streets. In other circumstances, alternate routes and detours might be possible responses to holdouts. But at some point these zig-zags become prohibitively expensive or inconvenient in assembling corridors.

Another example is assembling the site for a superstore, like a Home Depot or Costco (often referred to in the USA as a 'big box store'). These stores require a large footprint, both because of the size of the store and associated warehouse space, but also because of the imperative of providing a large parking lot for customers. Finding such a site along the fringes of urban areas is not difficult, where agricultural land or other 'Greenfields' can be purchased and configured in extra-large parcels suitable for big box development. But firms that wish to locate big box outlets in previously developed urban areas will face greater challenges in locating a site with a large enough footprint. In some cases abandoned factories or rail yards can be acquired for these purposes. But if multiple small parcels must be purchased and assembled for the site, a potential holdout problem may again be confronted. Various stratagems may be used to try to circumvent these problems, including the use of undisclosed buying agents, but these too entail costs not associated with Greenfield development.

A third example is assembling intellectual property licenses for purposes of engaging in research or the publication of works that draw on multiple prior publications. Certain types of medical research may require purchasing licenses from multiple patent holders covering different segments of the human genome.[80] Or the production of a documentary film or an anthology of writings from different authors may require obtaining permissions from large numbers of content providers. The ultimate example of an assembly problem may be the GoogleBooks project, which seeks to create a digital database that includes every book ever published, including many still under copyright protection.

The assembly problem, more so than even the spillover problem, is a story about transaction costs. Where assembly is at issue, typically there is no ambiguity about the scope or definition of the relevant property rights. The problem is purely one of the negotiating costs, including overcoming holdout and freerider problems. As one would predict, therefore, significant amounts of assembly occur without any invocation of public rights. Big box store development in dense urban areas does occur, often without any direct public intervention to facilitate land assembly. Documentary films get made and anthologies are published, without recourse to any doctrine of public rights. These projects entail significant transaction costs, but the enterprisers who undertake them often conclude that the transaction costs are worth incurring in light of the benefits that will accrue from the assembly of rights. Yet we also see significant amounts of assembly that is facilitated by the invocation of public rights doctrines, most prominently public use takings (and their intellectual property analogue, compulsory licensing), but also public access rights doctrines and the public trust doctrine.

Summary and Generalizations

Economists deploy five different concepts in describing the limitations of a world divided into distinct private property rights. Each of these concepts can be redescribed in terms of transaction costs. The first three concepts – public goods, network effects, and monopoly – are rarely analyzed in terms of transaction costs, because providing public goods, promoting network effects, and regulating monopolies by negotiating voluntary agreements among all affected persons would ordinarily be impossible, making this perspective unhelpful. (Situational and bilateral monopolies are partial exceptions to this generalization. In these contexts we do see consensual exchange, although it can be difficult.) The last two concepts – spillovers and assembly of rights – are much more commonly considered in terms of transaction costs, because here we do often see solutions in the form of consensual exchanges of rights. Not always of course. Many spillover and assembly problems defy contractual solutions, and are dealt with by applying some doctrine of public rights. But when considering these problems (as well as situational and bilateral monopolies), the possibility that a contractual solution may be forthcoming without the invocation of public rights doctrines should always be kept in mind.

The one exception to the transaction cost perspective is found in the alternative definition of public goods as being 'nonrivalrous.' This refers to the fact that some goods can be consumed (at least through some range of usage) without imposing any additional costs on other consumers. If a good is nonrivalrous, either because of its intangible nature or because the good is so plenteous at current levels of consumption that additional consumption effectively imposes no cost (think of adding another person to the world who breathes oxygen), then this provides a justification for limiting private exclusion rights that is independent of transaction costs. Here we see a possible economic justification for limiting the domain of private property rights – at least in some kinds of resources – that diverges from the more standard arguments grounded in the costs of collective action to maximize private values. Imposing time limits on intellectual property rights in order to assure that intellectual goods return to the public domain and are priced at zero would be a prime example.

III   TWO NORMATIVE GUIDELINES: MATCHING AND SUBSIDIARITY

To what extent can economic concepts help guide our application of legal doctrines of public rights? The foregoing surveys, legal and economic, yield two general observations.

First, public rights are not merely subtractions from private rights. Public rights do qualify property rights, but on balance private property is much more valuable because of public rights. This is true both in terms of the overall utility of the system of private property and the value of particular private holdings. As we have seen, public rights facilitate exchange and interconnection among owners of private property, by promoting transportation and other infrastructural networks. Public rights also serve to limit abuses of monopoly power, and facilitate regulation of widespread nuisances and other harms that damage property. Private property is worth much more when it is enmeshed in a web of public rights than it would be in a world consisting solely of private rights.[81]

Second, there is also obviously a danger of overburdening private property with too many obligations to the public or obligations that cut too deeply into the prerogatives of private owners. Private property works well as a system for organizing the management of resources because it concentrates responsibility for particular resources on particular owners, in a one resource/one owner fashion.[82] This concentration of authority maximizes incentives to extract value from resources, since the residual gains from good management will be captured by the singular owner. Such concentration of authority also permits ready assignment of responsibility when the management of resources breaks down. It is easier to impose affirmative duties on particular persons who can be identified as being uniquely accountable for each resource. Assigning resources to singular owners also facilities the exchange of rights. It is much easier for one owner to decide whether to sell or modify rights to a resource than it is for a community or group to agree on such a disposition.

In short, private property needs public rights, but the advantages of having a system of private property can be compromised by having too many public rights or ones that are ill-suited to the needs of the situation. The trick is to strike the right balance. I suggest two normative guidelines that might assist in this process.

The first can be called the 'matching' principle. A system of private exclusion rights creates a variety of problems, to which public rights doctrines are a response. (Not the only response, of course. Contracts and social norms also provide solutions to problems created by exclusion rights.) Insofar as legislatures and courts decide to qualify private property with some conception of public rights, ideally they should select the public rights doctrine that offers the best match or fit with the problem.

The second normative guideline can be called the 'subsidiarity' principle.[83] The idea here is that private property should be qualified only to the extent necessary to correct some problem associated with private exclusion rights. Every qualification of private property by some doctrine of public rights dilutes the concentration of responsibility that makes private property such a valuable social institution. If a system of private property is generally desirable because of its features of cost internalization, attribution of responsibility, and facilitation of transfers, then we should not want to impair the system of private rights more than is necessary to overcome particular problems associated with a system of exclusion rights. Consequently, a principle of subsidiarity should be applied by legislatures and courts in deciding which if any public rights doctrine to deploy.

The Matching Principle

The matching principle says that one should choose the public rights doctrine that most closely approximates the economic problem created by a system of private exclusion rights. The idea, as Stephen Breyer put it in a somewhat related context, is 'to correctly match the tool to the problem at hand.'[84] As we have seen, some public rights doctrines serve as qualification on title; others limit particular uses. Some are broad; others more narrow. It makes sense to pick the doctrine that best matches the particular problem created by exclusion rights, in order to avoid the frustration associated with enforcing a doctrine that does not work, not to mention the waste of resources this entails. The foregoing discussion suggests many examples of matches, and correspondingly of potential mismatches. I will highlight only a few for purposes of illustration.

Consider the public utility concept. Public utility regulation, as it has evolved over time, is tailored to deal with industries having natural monopoly features, principally network industries with high fixed costs. This suggests that the bundle of constraints on private ownership associated with the public utility doctrine should be reserved for

industries that are natural monopolies. Industries that do not share this attribute probably should not be subject to full blown utility treatment. For example, the market for
residential tenancies may suffer from a variety of imperfections, such as asymmetric
information between landlords and tenants. But it cannot plausibly be described as a
natural monopoly. A system of rent controls with periodic adjustments based on rate-
of-return type administrative proceedings, characteristic of utility regulation, is therefore
an overly intrusive public response to whatever imperfections inhere in residential rental
markets. Treating residential rental property as a public utility is a mismatch.[85]

Or, consider public nuisance law. Public nuisance liability is well matched to controlling spillovers, such as pollution, or engaging in an enterprise likely to promote criminal
activity. But public nuisance law is not well matched to regulating other problems, such
as expanding network effects or overcoming barriers to assembly of rights. Public subsidies or cross subsidization are more appropriate tools for promoting network effects.
And public access doctrines or public use takings are more appropriate for overcoming
assembly problems.

Admittedly, identifying the proper match can be difficult where there is disagreement
about the correct characterization of the economic problem. Consider in this light the
controversy over whether it is proper to use eminent domain to facilitate private commercial development, such as the construction of big box retail stores. The legal doctrine
says that such a use of eminent domain is proper only if this is a 'public use,' yet the
relevant authorities provide no clear guidance as to whether condemnation for economic
development purposes is a legitimate public use. Economic concepts can shed light on
the underlying controversy, but probably cannot resolve it.

One way to view the issue is that public use means the provision of public goods.[86] On
this analysis, the power of eminent domain can only be used to create goods that have
(at least in significant part) the attributes of nonexcludability and/or nonrivalrousness.
For example, eminent domain could be used for projects related to national defense, law
enforcement, environmental protection, and public transportation, since these projects
are thought to have attributes of public goods. But it would be implausible to say that the
construction of a big box retail store is a public good.[87] The store may produce a number
of benefits – for consumers, employees, suppliers, and shareholders – but these benefits
can largely be captured through private contracts, that is, they are excludable and rivalrous. To be sure, like most economic activity, the big box store will generate some positive (pecuniary) externalities, like increased customer traffic for nearby merchants. But
the ratio of excludable to nonexcludable benefits is very large, making it inappropriate to
justify the use of eminent domain for the site of a big box store on the ground that this
will promote the provision of a public good.

Another way to view the issue, however, is that 'public use' includes other economic
objectives like facilitating the assembly of rights. The developer of a big box store is
likely to ask for the power of eminent domain only if the site requires the assembly of
multiple parcels of land or the developer has encountered other serious transaction cost
problems. If significant assembly is required, then the big box store is likely to encounter
holdouts and strategic behavior, just as the city would in building a new highway or a
railroad would in developing new rail line. So if we cash out public use in terms of assembly of rights, the use of eminent domain to provide sites for big box stores may well be
permissible.

Notice that when we reframe the public use controversy in terms of economic concepts, the appropriate scope of eminent domain boils down to how high the transaction cost barriers must be before the power can be invoked. If we insist that the power be used only for goods that are nonexcludable, then we are demanding a very high transaction cost barrier before the power can be deployed. To say a good is nonexcludable is to assert that, under existing technology, exclusion is prohibitively expensive, and hence the good ordinarily cannot be assembled through voluntary exchange of rights.[88] If we allow the power to be used to facilitate assembly of rights, then we are willing to let the power be used in settings where transaction costs are low enough that voluntary exchange of rights often occurs without public intervention (even if it is costly). Here, well-formed property rights and excludability are taken for granted; the only impediments to exchange are holdouts and strategic bargaining. The economic perspective thus helps us see why the debate over the meaning of public use is so intractable. There is no bright line between high and low transaction costs; rather there is a continuum from impossibly high to relatively low. Consequently, there is no natural or logical point at which to draw the line and say public use lies on one side but not the other.

The Subsidiarity Principle

A second normative guideline for choosing among public rights doctrines is subsidiarity, meaning that one should select the doctrine that corrects the problem with the least interference with private rights. Here the concern is not with picking a doctrine that fails to work (or fails to work at an acceptable cost), but rather with picking a doctrine that works but is more intrusive on private rights than necessary. As noted above, private property rights perform many valuable functions, including creating incentives for good management, assigning responsibility for poor management, and facilitating exchange. Every time some doctrine of public rights is invoked to qualify private rights, these advantages are diluted. It makes sense, therefore, to select public rights doctrines that correct problems associated with exclusion with the least intrusion upon private ownership.

An illustration of how the subsidiarity principle might operate is provided by the controversy over public access to beaches, especially the 'dry sand' area between the mean high water line and the vegetation line, which is typically owned as private property. There is growing public demand for unobstructed access to dry sand beaches bordering the oceans or large inland lakes like the Great Lakes. This demand relates almost exclusively to recreational use; there is no suggestion that the public wants access to dry sand beaches to engage in mineral extraction, commercial fishing, or to claim sites for temporary housing. The agitation for recreational breach access has resulted in litigation in which claimants have asserted a variety of public rights theories, including the public trust doctrine and various public right of way doctrines, such as customary rights, public prescription, and public dedication.[89] Occasionally eminent domain has been used to acquire beach rights for public use. California has sought to use the police power to obtain public access to private beach properties.[90]

In economic terms, what is the nature of the problem posed by private exclusion rights in dry sand beaches? This is not a public goods problem; such beaches are excludable and rivalrous assets (at least when they are crowded). It is somewhat more plausible to think that network effects may be at issue. At least if one imagines that beaches perform a function similar to singles bars, the more people packed onto a beach, the higher its value for beach users.[91] But match-making is not the only recreational use of beaches; many prefer long solitary walks or contemplating sunsets. Monopoly is not the problem, at least not in the sense of natural monopoly. Many different owners control a portion of the dry sand beach. Nor do spillovers appear to characterize the issue. Private land owners complain about the public littering their properties, not the other way around.

The best economic characterization would seem to be that beach access is an assembly of rights problem. What is desired is a corridor of beach. Many members of the public would like access to dry sand beaches, some to take long unobstructed walks and others to reach more desirable stretches of beach. Ownership of private rights along the beach corridor is highly fragmented, making holdouts and strategic bargaining an impediment to voluntary assembly efforts. Private negotiation of access rights is made even more difficult given that the demand for beach access is episodic and unpredictable, creating an assembly problem on the demand side as well as the supply side.

If this characterization is correct, it can help us to focus in on the proper public rights doctrine under the subsidiarity principle. A transfer of full title to dry sand beach properties, as under the public trust doctrine, is probably overkill. The public is not interested in using beaches to gain access to navigation or in excavating minerals from beaches. A compulsory transfer of access rights under the police power also seems inappropriate. The owners have not imposed a spillover on others but are simply exercising their right to exclude. Using the police power to compel owners to permit entry on their land is inappropriate absent some nexus between harm-generating conduct and the transfer of rights to the public, as the Supreme Court has held.[92] This narrows the field to the public right of way doctrines and public use takings. Eminent domain is clearly the less intrusive option here. Under the public right of way doctrines, a public easement would be declared as a matter of law; if eminent domain is used, owners would be compensated for the taking of a public easement. The subsidiary principle therefore generates a relatively clear answer to the question of which public rights doctrine is best suited to providing public access to heretofore private beach properties: public use takings.

CONCLUSION

Private property is qualified by a bewildering array of public rights doctrines. If applied unthinkingly and aggressively, these doctrines could undermine the system of private rights. Economic analysis can help us understand the rationale for these doctrines, and can assist us in determining when particular public rights doctrines should be applied. If correctly applied with the aid of the matching principle and the subsidiarity principle, public rights doctrines can make private property more, rather than less, valuable and secure.

NOTES

1. International News Service v. Associated Press, 248 U.S. 215, 250 (1918) (dissenting opinion).
2. *See, e.g.*, BARBARA H. FRIED, THE PROGRESSIVE ASSAULT ON LAISSEZ FAIRE: ROBERT HALE AND THE FIRST LAW AND ECONOMICS MOVEMENT ch. 3 (1998) (discussing 'The Empty Idea of Property Rights').

3. Morris Cohen, *Property and Sovereignty*, 13 CORNELL L. Q. 8 (1927).
4. *See, e.g.,* Louis Kaplow & Steven Shavell, *Why the Legal System is Less Efficient Than the Income Tax in Redistributing Income*, 23 J. LEGAL STUD. 667 (1994).
5. The best general discussion of public rights doctrines, which is nevertheless incomplete in several respects, is Carol Rose, *The Comedy of the Commons: Custom, Commerce, and Inherently Public Property*, 53 U. CHI. L. REV. 711 (1986).
6. One exception to this generalization, considered in Part I below under the heading of public enforcement, is the state action doctrine, which imposes certain restrictions on public ownership that do not apply to private ownership. It is also possible that doctrines of sovereign immunity and preemption might eliminate some restrictions on public ownership that would ordinarily apply to privately owned property.
7. *See* Michael A. Carrier, *Cabining Intellectual Property through a Property Paradigm*, 54 DUKE L. J. 1, 52–81 (2004) (cataloguing 50 legal doctrines that limit conventional private property rights).
8. *See* Pollard v. Hagan, 44 U.S. (3 How.) 212, 224–25 (1845).
9. *See, e.g.,* JAMES BOYLE, THE PUBLIC DOMAIN (2008).
10. *See, e.g.,* James Boyle, *The Second Enclosure Movement and the Construction of the Public Domain*, 66 LAW & CONTEMP. PROBS. 33 (2003).
11. *See, e.g.,* Clouser v. Espy, 42 F.3d 1522 (9th Cir. 1994) (upholding a denial of motorized access to a mining claim surrounded by public wilderness land).
12. *See, e.g.,* LAWRENCE LESSIG, FREE CULTURE: HOW BIG MEDIA USES TECHNOLOGY AND THE LAW TO LOCK DOWN CULTURE AND CONTROL CREATIVITY (2004).
13. *See, e.g.,* eBay Inc. v. MercExchange, L.L. C. 547 U.S.388, 396–97 (2006) (Kennedy J. concurring) (voicing concerns about abuses of patent rights by patent trolls).
14. Guido Calabresi & A. Douglas Melamed, *Property Rules, Liability Rules, and Inalienability: One View of the Cathedral*, 85 HARV. L. REV. 1089, 1111–15 (1972).
15. The environmentalist infatuation with the public trust doctrine began with Joseph Sax, *The Public Trust Doctrine in Natural Resource Law: Effective Judicial Intervention*, 68 MICH. L. REV. 471 (1970), who in fact viewed the public trust as more of an administrative law than a property doctrine.
16. *See* Thomas W. Merrill, *Private Property and the Politics of Environmental Protection*, 28 HARV. J. L & PUB. POL'Y 69 (2004).
17. *See* Robin Kundis Craig, *A Comparative Guide to the Eastern Public Trust Doctrines: Classifications of States, Property Rights, and State Summaries*, 16 PENN ST. ENV. L REV. 1 (2007) (providing a useful compendium of state public trust doctrines in 31 states).
18. National Audubon Society v. Superior Court, 658 P.2d 709 (Cal. 1983).
19. Illinois Central R. Co. v. Illinois, 146 U.S. 387 (1892).
20. *E.g.,* Hawaii Const., art. XI, § 1.
21. *See* Friends of the Parks v. Chicago Park District, 786 N.E. 2d 161 (Ill. 2003) (upholding 40 year lease of a stadium built on public trust lands to Chicago Bears football team).
22. The Romans recognized a category of things – including roads, harbors, and bridges – called *res publicae*, which were understood to belong to the public and to be open to the public by operation of law. *See* Carol M. Rose, *Romans, Roads, and Romantic Creators: Traditions of Public Property in the Information Age*, 66 LAW & CONTEMP. PROBS. 89, 96–100 (2003).
23. United States v. Causby, 328 U.S. 256, 260–67 (1946) ('The air is a public highway, as Congress has declared.').
24. For an overview, see Rose, *supra* note 5 at 723–27.
25. *See, e.g.,* City of Chicago v. Ward, 169 Ill. 392, 48 N.E. 927 (1897) (relying on plat notation to recognize public right to maintain a city park free of buildings).
26. See Thomas W. Merrill, *The Economics of Public Use*, 72 CORNELL L REV. 61, 74–81 (1986).
27. *See, e.g.,* Hawaii Housing Auth. v. Midkiff, 467 U.S. 229, 241–43 (1984).
28. Kelo v. City of New London, 545 U.S. 469 (2005).
29. *See, e.g.,* Norwood v. Horney, 853 N.E. 2d 1115 (Ohio 2006); County of Wayne v. Hathcock, 684 N.W. 2d 765 (Mich. 2004).
30. American Law Institute, Restatement (Second) of Torts § 821B and comment e (1977).
31. For a history of public nuisance enforcement, see Denise E. Antolini, *Modernizing Public Nuisance: Solving the Paradox of the Special Injury Rule*, 28 ECOL. L. Q. 755 (2001).
32. Anon., Y.B. Mich. 27 Hen. 8, f. 26, pl. 10 (1535).
33. *See* D. Benjamin Barros, *The Police Power and the Takings Clause*, 58 U. MIAMI L. REV. 471 (2004).
34. Lochner v. New York, 198 U.S. 45 (1905).
35. *See* Pennsylvania Coal Co. v. Mahon, 260 U.S. 393 (1922).
36. *See* Lucas v. South Carolina Coastal Council, 505 U.S. 1003, 1020–32 (1992); RICHARD A. EPSTEIN, TAKINGS: PRIVATE PROPERTY AND THE POWER OF EMINENT DOMAIN 112–25 (1985).

37. Indeed, the modern conception of the police power is so vast and nebulous that it is questionable whether it can still be called a doctrine of public rights, in the sense of a doctrine defining rights shared by the public as a whole, as opposed to a shorthand reference for government power. At its core, however, the doctrine covers what would have to be regarded as public rights, such as the rights to a clean and safe environment.

38. *E.g.*, Usery v. Turner Elkhorn Mining Co., 428 U.S. 1, 16–18 (1976).

39. *See* Lingle v. Chevron U.S.A. Inc., 544 U.S. 528, 539 (2005); DAVID A. DANA & THOMAS W. MERRILL, PROPERTY: TAKINGS 4–5; 86–93 (2002).

40. Loretto v. Teleprompter Manhattan CATV Corp., 458 U.S. 419 (1982) (permanent physical occupations); Lucas v. South Carolina Coastal Council, 505 U.S. 1003 (1992) (complete loss of economic value).

41. *See* Penn Central Transp. Co. v. City of New York, 438 U.S. 104 (1978).

42. *See* Henry Monaghan, *The Supreme Court, 1974 Term – Foreword: Constitutional Common Law*, 89 HARV. L. REV. 1, 28–29 (1975) (discussing the greater remedial flexibility of legislatures relative to courts).

43. This is an exception to the generalization in the introduction that privately owned and publicly owned property are subject to similar rights and duties vis-à-vis the public.

44. Conversely, private rights are often accorded greater protection under law than public rights. For example, private rights holders are more likely to be able to demand a judicial trial before those rights are abrogated or qualified than one who has a public right. *See generally* Gordon G. Young, *Public Rights and the Federal Judicial Power: From Murray's Lessee Through Crowell to Schor*, 25 BUFF. L. REV. 765 (1986).

45. 334 U.S. 1 (1948).

46. *See* Bell v. Maryland, 378 U.S. 226 (1964).

47. *See* 42 U.S.C. § 2000a (2000).

48. Fuentes v. Shevin, 407 U.S. 67 (1972).

49. *See, e.g.*, Flagg Brothers, Inc. v. Brooks, 436 U.S. 149 (1978) (sale of goods in custody of warehouse to pay debt did not entail state action).

50. *See* 40 U.S.C. §§ 3141–44 (2006).

51. *See* Mark D. Rosen, *Was Shelley v. Kraemer Incorrectly Decided? Some New Answers*, 95 Cal. L. Rev. 451 (2007) (surveying a variety of theories endorsed by different judges and commentators).

52. 3 WILLIAM BLACKSTONE, COMMENTARIES *164.

53. *See* A.K. Sandoval-Strausz, *Travelers, Strangers, and Jim Crow: Law, Public Accommodations, and Civil Rights in America*, 23 LAW & HIST. REV. 53 (2005).

54. *See* Dale v. Boy Scouts of America, 734 A.2d 1196 (NJ 1999), *rev'd on other grounds*, 530 U.S. 640 (2000) (holding that the Boy Scouts are a 'place of public accommodation' under New Jersey law); Uston v. Resorts International Hotel, Inc., 445 A.2d 370 (NJ 1982) (holding that casino could not exclude card counter without permission of state Casino Control Commission); State v. Schmid, 423 A.2d 615 (NJ 1980) (holding that Princeton University did not have right to exclude protestors from its property).

55. Munn v. Illinois, 94 U.S. 113, 126–27 (1877).

56. *See* Joseph D. Kearney & Thomas W. Merrill, *The Great Transformation of Regulated Industries Law* 98 COLUM. L. REV. 1323 (1998).

57. Sometimes the transfer is only of an easement. But this too is regarded as a type of property right, and generally has an indefinite duration.

58. *Cf.* Henry E. Smith, *Exclusion versus Governance: Two Strategies for Delineating Property Rights*, 31 J. LEGAL STUD. S453 (2002) (contrasting property rights grounded in exclusion with rights based on regulation of particular uses).

59. R.H. Coase, *The Problem of Social Cost*, 3 J. L. & ECON. 1 (1960).

60. *See* Steven N.S. Cheung, *The Structure of a Contract and the Theory of a Non-Exclusive Resource*, 3 J. L & ECON. 49 (1970).

61. For an overview of the literature on externalities, with particular reference to property, see STEVEN SHAVELL, FOUNDATIONS OF ECONOMIC ANALYSIS OF LAW 77–109 (2004).

62. *See* RICHARD MUSGRAVE & PEGGY MUSGRAVE, PUBLIC FINANCE IN THEORY AND PRACTICE 8–9 (5th ed. 1989).

63. For a discussion that disaggregates excludability and rivalrousness, see Brett M. Frischmann, *An Economic Theory of Infrastructure and Commons Management*, 89 MINN. L. REV. 917, 942–56 (2005).

64. When private incentives are sufficient to supply public goods without public intervention the situation is said to involve 'irrelevant externalities.' *See* David D. Haddock, *When Are Environmental Amenities Policy-Relevant?*, 44 NAT. RES. J. 383 (2004) James M. Buchanan & William Craig Stubblebine, *Externality*, 29 ECONOMICA 371 (1962).

65. *See* Eugene Kontorovich, *What Standing is Good For*, 93 VA. L. REV. 1663 (2007). Kontorovich advances his argument in the context of constitutional rights, such as the right to free speech, which can be seen as a type of public good at least in some instances. The argument is fully applicable to other public goods

like clean air. Indeed, we would regard it is unthinkable to all allow individuals to demand a given level of national defense.

66.   *See* Rose, *supra* note 5, at 768.
67.   *See* Michael L. Katz & Carl Shapiro, *Network Externalities, Competition, and Compatibility*, 75 AM. ECON. REV. 424, 426–27 (1985). For an overview of possible applications of the concept, see Mark A. Lemley & David McGowan, *Legal Implications of Network Economic Effects*, 86 CAL. L. REV. 479 (1998).
68.   *See* James B. Speta, *Handicapping the Race for the Last Mile?: A Critique of Open Access Rules for Broadband Platforms*, 17 YALE J. REG. 39, 78–81 (2000).
69.   This is arguably a broad lesson of deregulation of transportation industries, including airlines, railroads, and trucking. These industries exhibit network effects, insofar as the more customers who use these networks, the more service options become available for other customers. Yet regulated pricing, designed to prevent 'discrimination' between low-cost and high-cost customers, very likely thwarts the full development of these industries. A regime of contract-based pricing has generated more service options.
70.   *See* 47 U.S.C. § 254 (2000) (delegating authority to the FCC to establish universal service obligations for telecommunications service providers).
71.   *See, e.g.*, YOCHAI BENKLER, THE WEALTH OF NETWORKS: HOW SOCIAL PRODUCTION TRANSFORMS MARKETS AND FREEDOM (2006).
72.   *See, e.g.,* Boyle, *supra* note 9; Lessig, *supra* note 12.
73.   *See, e.g.,* DENNIS CARLTON & JEFFREY M. PERLOFF, MODERN INDUSTRIAL ORGANIZATIONS 101–03 (3rd ed. 2000).
74.   *See* Bruce Wyman, *The Law of Public Callings as a Solution to the Trust Problem*, 17 HARV. L. REV. 156, 159 (1903).
75.   Economists often use the term 'spillovers' to refer to any type of externality. Here I am using the term to refer to a subset of externalities – those associated with incompatible land uses by different owners or mutually beneficial land uses by different land owners.
76.   *See* Brett M. Frischmann & Mark A. Lemley, *Spillovers*, 107 COLUM. L. REV. 257, 271–75 (2007) (describing the traditional view but arguing that pecuniary externalities are more relevant in analyzing intellectual goods).
77.   Although the elimination of many spillovers can create a public good, as in the case of air pollution control, other spillovers involve only small numbers of parties and have no public goods aspects. *See, e.g.*, Hendricks v. Stahlnaker, 380 S.E. 2d 198 (W.V. 1989) (construction of water well interferes with neighbor's construction of septic (sewage) field, and vice versa).
78.   *See, e.g.*, Michael Heller & Rick Hills, *Land Assembly Districts*, 121 HARV. L. REV. 1465, 1472–74 (2008) (discussing the problem in the context of land assembly).
79.   *See generally* MICHAEL HELLER, THE GRIDLOCK ECONOMY (2008).
80.   *See* Michael A. Heller and Rebecca S. Eisenberg, *Can Patents Deter Innovation? The Anticommons in Biomedical Research*, 280 SCIENCE 698 (1998); *cf.* John P. Walsh et al., *When Excludability Matters: Material Versus Intellectual Property in Academic Biomedical Research*, 36 RES. POL'Y 1184 (2007).
81.   For an analogous argument, in which the public rights doctrines that connect private rights are characterized as 'infrastructure,' see Frischmann, *supra* note 63.
82.   Concurrent ownership, as through tenancies in common and joint tenancies, may be thought to be an exception to the principle of singular control. But in practice, these forms of ownership are limited to close knit family relations, where informal norms dictate a de facto singular manager or a division of managerial responsibilities. When the number of owners gets too large or disagreements arise and become acute, the action for partition allows a quick and automatic exit from shared ownership, and the property is either split up or sold, establishing singularity of control.
83.   Subsidiarity in European law refers to the principle that 'action should be taken at the lowest level of government at which particular objectives can adequately be achieved.' George A. Bermann, *Taking Subsidiarity Seriously: Federalism in the European Community and the United States*, 94 COLUM. L. REV. 331, 338 (1994). I am extending the idea to mean that private rights should be qualified by the least intrusive doctrine of public rights consistent with achieving particular objectives.
84.   STEPHEN BREYER, REGULATION AND ITS REFORM 191 (1982).
85.   *See* Lawrence Berger, *The New Residential Tenancy Law – Are Landlords Public Utilities?*, 60 NEB. L. REV. 708 (1981) (spelling out the details).
86.   Richard Epstein has endorsed this perspective. *See* TAKINGS, *supra* note 36, at 166–69.
87.   *Cf.* Daniel D. Polsby, *What If This is as Good as It Gets?*, 2 GREEN BAG 2D 115, 122 (1998) (offering a variety of imaginary arguments politicians might make in support of characterizing government programs as providing public goods, including providing public subsidies for mohair production).
88.   Except in the case of irrelevant externalities, as in the radio broadcasting example. *See* note 64 *supra*.
89.   *See, e.g.*, David J. Bederman, *The Curious Resurrection of Custom: Beach Access and Judicial Takings*, 96 COLUM. L. REV. 1375 (1996).

90. *See* Nollan v. California Coastal Comm'n, 483 U.S. 825, 828–29 (1987) (describing program by California Coastal Commission to condition issuance of building permits on agreement to permit public use of private beaches).

91. *See* Rose, *supra* note 5 (suggesting that the demand for beach access reflects a human need for 'sociability').

92. *See* Nollan, *supra* note 90; Dolan v. City of Tigard 512 U.S. 374 (1994).

5 Toward an economic theory of property in information
Henry E. Smith

I. INTRODUCTION

In what sense is intellectual property property? In what sense should it be? These questions would be a lot simpler to answer if we had a good definition of property, before we try tackling the nature and purpose of property rights in information. In this Chapter, I argue that part of the controversy over intellectual property stems from inadequacies in the economic theory of property rights.

Most economists do not put much stock in labels, and 'property' is no exception. New Institutional Economics (NIE) is all about 'property rights,' but the definitions of property in NIE are surprisingly incongruent with traditional notions of property in the law. In this, both law-and-economics and the NIE tend to strip away what is distinctive about property. For many purposes this is just fine. For most economists, property rights are stable expectations of an ability to take certain actions with respect to a resource and to enjoy the return from these resource-centric actions.[1] Thus, someone who has rights to pick berries on Blackacre has property rights (as it happens, a right that would be called a 'profit' at common law). Someone who has fee simple title has property rights to Blackacre of a more sweeping sort. This larger package could, as some would have it, be regarded as a collection of specific rights: the right to collect berries, the right to plant crops, the right to build a house etc., etc. If so, then fee simple ownership of Blackacre differs from the berry-picking profit quantitatively: a fee simple owner has a larger set of expectations of acting and benefitting with respect to Blackacre. In this Chapter, I argue that this merely quantitative bundle-of-rights picture is not only an inadequate theory of property in general but falls especially short when it comes to property rights in information.

Instead I will argue that for reasons of information cost, a different view of property must be incorporated into the NIE and that this picture of property allows us to ask the right questions about intellectual property. To return to our Blackacre example, what the fee simple owner of Blackacre holds can alternatively be summarized by saying that A has a right to keep others generally (including B) off the land or to give permission, as A sees fit, coupled with a liberty to make use of Blackacre in a variety of largely unspecified ways. This definition of property differs from the quantitative bundle-of-rights view in two ways.[2] First, the set of activities or uses is generally not specified. Instead, a boundary is defined over which A is gatekeeper, and this set-up indirectly protects a collection of interests in use that usually need not be separately specified. Although extensionally this is equivalent to having a bundle of profits (for berries, corn) and other use rights, from the point of view of delineation it is not equally costly to set up. The former, boundary-based method is more cost-effective.

Second, the set of people who must respect this boundary or get permission from A is an open-ended one – the right is in rem. So again the set of dutyholders is equivalent to an enumeration of all the people in society (B, C, D, . . .), but capturing it as 'everyone else' is far cheaper.[3]

In both respects – interests in use and dutyholders – the indefinite approach is much cheaper in terms of information cost. The right to Blackacre is a black-box-like *module*, in the sense that what happens inside is of limited relevance to dutyholders who are told to simply keep off. Tortfeasors need not know who the owner is or what she is doing in order to know to keep off and so not to interfere. Likewise, one can navigate the world of personal property like cars in a parking lot by not taking any car one does not own, with no need to know who the owner is or how the car is being used.[4] Furthermore, the broad-brush approach in each case allows A to alter the configuration of rights to uses and the status of dutyholders. The owner also has the right within limits to alter the interface between this package of rights and the outside world as with covenants, easements and leases.[5] As long as the law's prescribed standard set of building blocks is preserved, the owner can subdivide and modify the duties by contract.[6]

It is the indirectness and indefiniteness of property that are crucial to the rationale for property rights in information.[7] Because information is usually nonrival there is no purpose to be served by exclusive rights to consume it. A wide variety of theories of intellectual property have been put forth, with varying degrees of relevance to specific areas of intellectual property, but these theories mostly do not depend on the allocation of rights that is emphasized on the bundle-of-rights view. Information per se does not call for exclusive rights. And to the extent some of these theories do call for limited rights, the quantitative expansion of them does not receive any justification. Instead, it is the need for appropriation of *rival* inputs surrounding the use of information, such as labor and lab space in discovering it and commercializing it, that call for property rights that feature the informational shortcuts – the indirectness in the set of interests protected and the indefiniteness in the set of dutyholders.

I will start by surveying briefly a variety of theories of intellectual property. Many of these theories do not particularly point to property rights in the traditional sense, as opposed to direct government rewards, auctions, and the like. I then turn to three approaches to the appropriation problem – contracting, unjust enrichment with tracing, and intellectual property rights. Each is used over some overlapping and shifting domains. An information cost theory of property based on modular rights and their interfaces allows us to capture some of the contours of rights regimes and partially explain their development over time.

II.   THEORIES OF INTELLECTUAL PROPERTY

Information can be valuable, but unlike many other valuable resources it usually exhibits both features of public goods: nonrivalness and nonexcludability. As for nonrivalness, one consumer can enjoy the plot of a play or practice a useful invention without preventing another from doing so. With rivalness, if more than one person tries to eat the same apple or till the same soil, the two uses conflict. Because, by contrast, with many nonrival information goods additional consumption can occur at zero or near-zero marginal cost, a competitive market will drive the price for a unit – a song file, for example – towards zero. One well-known problem is that the fixed costs in making this flow of marginal units possible need to be covered; these costs include the costs of creation and commercialization. Alternatively, people using rival resources (labor, lab space, and the like) as inputs will sometimes need some mechanism to appropriate the value from combining these resources with nonrival information.

As for non-excludability, it is possible to keep secrets, and to prevent people from acting in certain ways that relate to information – for example, patent liability for practicing an invention. But these forms of protection are difficult, and some uses of information are almost impossible to prevent.[8] For example, it would be prohibitively costly to prevent people from thinking about any idea without the 'idea owner's' permission. This difficulty with exclusion lies at the heart of Arrow's paradox of information: a seller cannot convince a potential buyer of the value of information without revealing it, but then the potential buyer has the information already and won't pay for it.[9] Methods of overcoming this paradox include not only intellectual property rights, but also reputation, ownership of physical assets (or one's own human capital) complementary to the information, warranties, and so forth. For example, a person with a reputation for having good ideas can offer an idea to another on the understanding that he will get paid if the other uses it. Without such a reputation this deal is not possible because the idea might be something the other already knew or could have found out easily. A simple contract by itself will not do. A partial substitute is the elaborate doctrine on idea submissions. Here usually some form of novelty is required, at least to the offeree, if not novelty in a more absolute sense.[10] Sometimes quasi-contract can apply based on the behavior of the parties, especially if the recipient solicited the idea. Thus for example, if someone proposes an idea for a tourist center near a pipeline, and the company proceeds with the project, a court will look for novelty in order to apply property-like remedies but may apply quasi-contract if the idea was solicited.[11]

Economic theories are not the only possible explanations or justifications for intellectual property rights – competitors include labor-desert theories and personhood – but the US intellectual property system, especially in its core aspects of patent and copyright, is conventionally thought to sound in either Lockean or utilitarian concerns.[12] Probably the most traditional theory and the one that potentially applies most widely across areas of intellectual property is the *reward theory* – that IP rights are rewards for creation of information goods. Intellectual property rights allow creators of information, especially authors and inventors, to reap a return, which in turn provides an incentive to create in the first place. Addressing the problem of nonrivalness, the idea is that the reward will cover the costs of creation (including the opportunity cost of the creator's effort) because a competitive market will not allow cost recovery from the sale of units at the competitive price, which would equal the zero or close-to-zero marginal cost of the additional use.[13]

The main problem with reward theory is that it tells us very little about what form rewards should take. An all-knowing and benevolent social planner could dole out rewards directly. Or the government could buy out patents or auction patents off but keep most of them.[14] On reward theories, the main issue is the *size* of the reward. In this they are reminiscent of the quantitative theory of property rights, only the quantity now is totally one-dimensional: the size of the monetary reward.

Like the reward theory, many other economic theories of intellectual property focus on some activity of the creator.[15] Some of these theories are mainly of relevance to patents. Thus, patents give an incentive to disclose an invention rather than keep it secret.[16] Patents allow inventions to be exploited commercially without keeping them secret. For useful information that *can* be kept secret, we need some other reason to give it patent protection (if nothing else, the difficulty of specifying which inventions could be kept secret and which couldn't). Others see patents as preventing a wasteful race to invent. Economists starting in at least the 1960s noticed that multiple potential claimants for the patent monopoly/reward could engage in wasteful competition (rentseeking).[17] The rent-seeking theories analogize patent protection to problems of first possession in regular property. The solution there is often to give rights where one claimant is in a much better position to claim (heterogeneity of claimants), and one view is that patent law prevents wasteful races by picking a clear winner early.[18] Conversely, some see patents as giving others an incentive to design around; the promotion of designing around counsels for narrow patents that encourage follow-on inventors.[19]

One activity that forms the basis for a theory with application to patent law and perhaps beyond is *commercialization*. A cluster of related theories stresses the similarity of patents and ordinary property in promoting commercialization. Judge Giles Rich theorized that rewards for inventors are not the centerpiece of patent law but rather that patents encourage those engaging in a wide range of activities to bring an invention – already created in the sense of invented – to market in useful products.[20] On Edmund Kitch's related prospect theory, a patent gives a right to develop an idea, but unlike Rich's commercialization theory, prospect theory emphasizes further inventive activity and the coordinating role of the inventor.[21]

Judge Rich cited the example of Herbert Spencer's 'invalid chair,' which Spencer deliberately did not patent but which no one would market without the exclusive rights of a patent.[22] The chair was invented, but according to Rich the commercialization would have taken place if someone had had a patent. In commercialization theory, private property plays its familiar role in delegating decisions to an owner who then can coordinate development of the invention. Property thus serves as a basis for further contracting.[23] The commercialization theory emphasizes the owner of the patent, who need not be the inventor. The inventor may well not be the one who can best develop or commercialize the invention, but the inventor can sell the patent or license it to others who can. These theories also have a strong entrepreneurial element. The 'entrepreneur' here may – but need not – be the inventor himself.

Inputs to commercialization are not all nonrival – that is, some *are* rival – and exclusive rights over inventions have to be compared with other methods of establishing property rights over inputs. In keeping with the emphasis on the similarities to regular property, commercialization theorists often assert that the patent monopoly often does not (or does not necessarily) give market power.[24] Commercialization theorists emphasize how many patents go into a 'product' as defined by consumer demand. If so, coordination and valuation become very difficult. Whether this leads to contracting or to a patent thicket (a form of anticommons) are empirical questions.[25]

Although commercialization theory is most often proposed for patent law, it is occasionally cited as a justification for copyright and trademark. In these latter areas the commercialization theory is much more controversial, but to the extent one accepts it, it does point to more property-like treatment. Consider trademark. The traditional theory was the avoidance of consumer confusion, and more recently and controversially trademark dilution can lead to liability.[26] For example, the holder of the Kodak mark might object to its being used in connection with bicycles even though no one would be confused into thinking that the bicycles were made by the manufacturer of photographic equipment.[27] Anti-dilution calls for a more propertized view of trademark, and the idea is in part that the more blanket protection encourages not the development of new or inventive marks but their commercialization. The question here is whether commercialization is important enough and would be furthered enough through stronger trademarks to justify the increased cost of expanding liability.[28]

All of the above theories take as their starting points some benefit that intellectual property rights encourage – invention, commercialization, the promotion of good types of racing behavior, or the suppression of bad racing – but all intellectual property rights, like all property rights in general, come at a cost. Any prevention of access carries with it costs of foregone use, but this is particularly important in the case of a nonrival resource. And the more that use of information is interactive in the sense of benefiting from network effects and cumulative creation, the greater are these costs.

Considering these costs, one looks for some clear benefits on the other side that can only be supplied by intellectual property rights. But here is where the economists' thin definition of property becomes a stumbling block. If all property rights do is determine the size of a reward or allow owners to manage the variance in the returns from information, then buy-outs or auctions are theoretically better than intellectual property rights. They do less to impede access to nonrival information, and they provide the same quantitative rewards. Perhaps there is some administrative cost advantage in intellectual property rights over grants or auctions, but this is not obvious. And putting these administrative costs aside, auctions or liability rules look very attractive indeed, compared to NIE-style 'quantitative' property rights. If intellectual property rights are to receive a positive and normative explanation, quantitative rewards for creation cannot be the whole story.

III.   PROPERTY IN NIE AND LAW

The thin notion of property rights or entitlement does not follow necessarily from the assumptions of the New Institutional Economics. On the contrary, a more complete view of the costs and benefits of various entitlement structures carries the NIE further. An NIE that incorporates the information costs of entitlement delineation and enforcement can provide an explanation for the contours of rights and their changes over time. Interestingly, this more complete NIE-inspired account of property accords in a rough fashion with the legal detail of intellectual property regimes.

In the next Part, I will turn to some specific IP regimes, but to see how property rights in information work, it will be useful to compare three theoretically possible approaches, which are in fact used in various domains of activity involving valuable information. For transaction cost reasons, these three institutional frameworks – contracting, unjust enrichment with tracing, and property in the legal sense – have overlapping and shifting domains. It is the relative domains of these three methods for managing the complexity of interactive activities over information – which include not just creation but also development, marketing, and follow-on invention – that need an explanation, which an NIE enriched with notions of bounded rationality and modularity can provide.

Traditional property law and its alternatives differ in their degree and type of modularity. All systems of interacting agents who face issues of appropriation and access form a complex system. A complex system is one in which internal interactions are many and multiplex such that is it difficult to infer the properties of the whole from the properties of its parts.[29] Any change to an element of the system can in principle affect any other element or combination of elements directly or indirectly. The number of possibilities rises at least exponentially (in the literal sense). So in a fully interconnected system change is so unpredictable through such ripple effects that change may not be an option, leading to rigidity. The choice, in other words, is between near-chaos and rigidity. One way out of this bind is to break up the system into semi-autonomous components (modules).

Modularization depends on the system being what Herbert Simon termed 'nearly decomposable.'[30] A nearly decomposable system consists of a pattern of interactions such that module boundaries can be drawn so that interactions are intense within the module but sparse and constrained between modules. This allows for information hiding: decisions in one module can be made largely without regard to what is happening in other modules, with the only constraint being the satisfaction of the interface conditions. Modularity has been a key concept in many areas ranging from evolutionary biology to cognitive science, software, and organization theory. To take one example, teams writing software tend to be modular, often reflecting the structure of programs. By contrast in a nonmodular structure, any part could potentially impact every other, requiring superhuman efforts at acquiring and tracking information.

Property modules allow for bundling that is not captured by regarding a bundle as the mere sum of its constituents. In property, the exclusion strategy results in property being not just a bundle of sticks but something more – something that high transaction costs preclude us from accomplishing by contract. One of the functions of property is that it is a shortcut over all the bilateral contracts (or regulations) that would have to be devised for every pair of members of society in all their various interactions (A's right to grow corn on Blackacre as against B's trampling, same against C, etc.; A's right to park a car on Blackacre as against B, etc., etc). And intellectual property law provides a modular platform for the interactions of parties, especially when it comes to commercialization. Although exclusive rights have their costs – and because of the nonrivalness of information itself these costs are more apparent in intellectual property than in property – the modular bundling in intellectual property can serve to manage the complexity of coordinating rival inputs to commercialization.

A thought experiment captures the role that modularity plays in the basic architecture of property and intellectual property. Legal relations are superimposed on a set of actors and activities. Let M be the set of m actors and L the set of interactions between them. This can be modeled by a graph with nodes M and links L. A world in which the legal system tracked every potential interaction would be modeled by the full graph, in Figure 5.1 for $m = 10$. Pick one node, say m_{10}. Compare the value of the least valuable link with the cost of the complexity it adds. The benefits of the link are likely to be linear, especially because other links can serve as substitutes. But from a complexity point of view, the

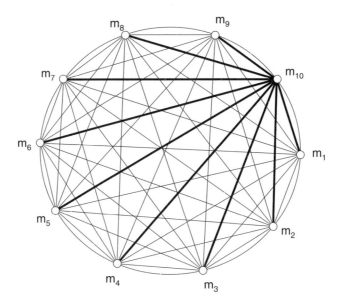

Figure 5.1   Complete graph, m = 10

last link, say (m_{10}, m_5), causes each of the nodes to link indirectly with every other node. Thus, as is familiar in modularity theory, the complexity costs are at least exponential.[31] In the complete graph (for the fully nonmodular system), each added node m_n adds $n - 1$ links to the system, as illustrated in Figure 5.1 by means of the heavy lines for the links radiating from node m_{10}. This suggests that anything close to the nonmodular system will be far from optimal.

In many systems including the property-tort-contract-restitution system, i.e. basic private law, most links will not be very relevant, or will be weak. (Each link can be associated with a strength, but for simplicity's sake we assume for now that all links are of equal strength.) Although the level of modularity that is most suited to a system depends on empirical evidence that we only partially possess, as mentioned earlier there is a large literature on optimal modularization. Thus, in our example, if the system is nearly decomposable, we can group the system into modules. An easy case is illustrated in Figure 5.2. In this example all the nodes within each module are interconnected. As for relations between modules, they are much more sparse. Here the pattern of interactions indicates three modules with the interface between the left $(m_6\text{-}m_7\text{-}m_8)$ and bottom $(m_2\text{-}m_3\text{-}m_4\text{-}m_5)$ modules consisting of the link (m_4, m_7), the interface between the right $(m_1\text{-}m_9\text{-}m_{10})$ and bottom modules consisting of the links (m_4, m_9) and (m_1, m_2), and the interface between the left and right modules consisting of the link (m_1, m_6). If we wanted further modularization one or more of these four interface links would have to be suppressed, at some positive cost.

It is worthwhile to consider now how the complexity of actors' interactions in appropriation and access to information might be guided by three types of institutions: contracting, restitution with tracing, and property.

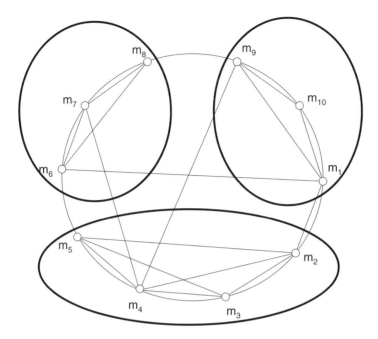

Figure 5.2   Modular system, m = 10

A.   Contracting

In accordance with Coase's thought experiment of the zero transaction cost world, it is customary to think of contracting as an alternative institutional arrangement.[32] It is true that in a zero transaction cost world any institutional arrangement that operates without costs would theoretically maximize wealth. But because the contract is a basic unit of analysis and the gains from trade are familiar, the full contracting environment is the conventional benchmark.

The idea of gains from trade is a familiar one, and bilateral contracts can be easily envisioned as exploiting gains from trade. Of course there are obstacles to achieving these gains because the costs of contracting are positive. In a positive transaction cost world, some of these contracts might not occur, making the initial setting of the 'entitlement' potentially relevant from a wealth-maximizing point of view.

In a world of no transaction costs all the necessary appropriation could occur with no sacrifice of access, all by means of consensual contacts. In such a world it would not matter what the initial entitlements were; everyone would bargain their way to the wealth-maximizing result given the initial entitlements. In the case of a nonrival resource like information, any value to be gained through additional access would occur through contracts. Perfect price discrimination, which would eliminate the deadweight loss, would be just one of the many possible costless contracts in the zero transaction cost world.

Moreover, other problems associated with the appropriation–access tradeoff would also be costlessly solved through contracts in the absence of transaction costs. Employees and their employers would contract for the optimal level of inventive efforts and development, idea submitters would overcome Arrow's paradox of information and would costlessly bargain with those who can use their ideas, and in general any licensing that has any positive value would happen. Either full control of ideas by the originators or a universal public domain could be the starting point.

In a world of positive transaction costs, such contracts may or may not occur, and when they do they consume resources. This makes the institutional-choice question central. One issue with universal contracting in principle is its contribution to complexity. Consider the employee invention again. Without intellectual property rights, the set of all the inputs contributed by anyone in the firm might impact the value of any other. The problem of keeping separate what the employee contributed in her personal capacity versus as an employee would multiply. Contracts would have to sort out the claims to value made by any of the firm's stakeholders (and possibly persons further afield who claim to be idea submitters) on the value of the final output.

Returning to Figure 5.1, the links in the full graph could be interpreted as potential contracting channels. If so, one might ask whether the possibility of contracting keeps all the links alive and therefore makes the modularity-based theory inapplicable. To this it can be pointed out that the law of property does *not* allow unlimited contracting. One interpretation of mandatory standardization in property, through the *numerus clausus* and related devices,[33] is that property prevents contracting from undermining the basic modular architecture of the system.

B.   Tracing and Restitution

Another alternative to intellectual property would be a generalization of the law of tracing.[34] Tracing allows a plaintiff's claim to relate to a succession of assets and to follow the assets into remote hands. Thus if B steals A's car, sells it for $10,000 and puts the money in B's own bank account, A can claim the $10,000 in the account. Because B is a wrongdoer, presumptions work in A's favor. So if the bank account had $5,000 before 'A's' $10,000 was added, B adds the $10,000 and then withdraws $5,000 to bet at the racetrack, A can claim B's winnings. It is presumed that B used A's $10,000 to win at the track. If, however, B loses the $5,000 at the track, then we trace A's claim to the amount still in the account. Sometimes tracing claims can follow an asset in a transfer from B to C, for example if B stole A's car and gave it to C. American law with only a few exceptions enables A to claim the car back even if C paid for it, leaving C with a claim against B.[35] The law, however, does not allow unlimited tracing, and makes tracing available mainly where the primary actor involved is a wrongdoer.

We could imagine generalized tracing, where property claims were made in the narrowest fashion and the claims would float around, impacting those who interact with the assets in question. Thus, A might improve an object and have a lien that travels with the object into remote hands. We could imagine various liens interacting with each other, extinguishing each other, and so on. The more levels of tracing we allow and the more general the contexts in which we allow it, the closer we come to a property system that would look like the complete graph in Figure 5.1. In intellectual property, someone would on this hypothetical system be able to claim an inventive contribution – the light bulb is the famous example – and then 'trace' its effects to remote hands and make a claim against all remote beneficiaries.

Our property system is not like this, and it is worthwhile to consider why it is not. The full tracing system would be like coupling a tort law with no limits like foreseeability or duty constraints with an unlimited law of unjust enrichment.[36] Actual tort law places severe limits on which contextual variables are relevant,[37] and unjust enrichment is even more limited in its scope with respect to nonconsenting parties.[38] Property law limits interdependencies even more severely, as we have seen. Most of the possible interactions between any arbitrary pair of actors are weak or nonexistent. So ruling them out in principle is low cost. At the same time ruling such interactions out – simplifying the interface between modules – is likely to decrease complexity costs for the reasons discussed earlier.

C.   Property in Information and Rights to Things

What this thought experiment shows is that some (severe) limits on interdependencies are likely to be worthwhile and that the basic property element in property and intellectual property can be seen as serving this limiting function. What we still need is a theory of which modules and interfaces are (and should be) chosen, and how decentralized the modularization of the system should be. Work on community structure and optimal modularization can be a source of testable hypotheses. In particular, the application of network theory, community structure, and the notion of the strength of ties in social networks is well-established.[39] These theories, along with the organizational modularity literature, draw in turn on general modularity theory. These implications I leave for further work, but modularity theory provides some hypotheses about the tradeoffs in IP and some pointers to empirical evidence.

Intellectual property employs the same strategies as regular property, ranging from exclusion to governance, but because information is a special type of resource, the combinations of these strategies will differ from one IP regime to the next and from IP to regular property. Nevertheless, the same basic architecture of defining a modular thing and using on/off exclusion rights as a starting point, supplemented with rules of proper use, can be discerned even in IP. I will turn in the next section to how this approach to delineation allows for coordination of various parties who might commercialize information.

The economics of intellectual property tends to emphasize either one of two facets of the problem – the need for incentives or the nonrivalness of information – neither of which does much to explain the details of the delineation issues in a static or dynamic sense. As mentioned earlier, the need for creators to appropriate does not explain why 'quantitative' thin property rights (in the sense usually assumed in the NIE or 'entitlements' in law and economics) wouldn't suffice, thereby obviating broad exclusion rights for owners of IP. On the other side, an exclusive focus on the nonrivalness of information, although likewise important, misses the benefits that modular exclusion based structures can provide in terms of managing the complexity of coordination. For example, the law of employee inventions and the establishment of joint ventures are facilitated through the asset-partitioning effect of IP rights.[40] Moreover, a regime such as patent in which uses are hard to delineate separately relies more heavily on exclusion than does the more tort-like copyright law, in which governance regimes like fair use loom much larger.[41] As we will see in the next Part, a simple model of the supply and demand for different delineation strategies can capture these differences as well as their trajectory over time. A singular emphasis on either incentives or public goods faces great difficulties in this regard.

Like other resources that are hard to delineate and have public goods aspects, such as water and radio spectrum, intellectual property tends towards a mixture of public and private rights.[42] The modularity of exclusion can help deal with the problems of an information semicommons. In a semicommons, private and common property regimes overlap and interact. This interaction raises the potential for strategic behavior through the enhanced access from the overlap.[43] A tangible (and elaborate) semicommons was the medieval open field system in which the access afforded by throwing open the entire set of privately owned strips to common grazing during fallow periods and right after harvest allowed strategic behavior, such as favoring one's own parcel with manure or trashing others' with excessive trampling of sheep.[44] The benefits and costs of this type of access-through-overlap are more likely in the case of intellectual property: access to information is more difficult to prevent and impeding access to nonrival information is presumptively undesirable.[45] Doctrines like fair use in copyright can be regarded as an overlap between private rights and the public domain, and as a very complicated interface between the two.

But by relying on exclusion as well as governance, the interface conditions provided by intellectual property law make the complexity entailed by this multiple use easier to manage. As in regular property intellectual property helps contracting parties get together and to coordinate their inputs. For example, someone who commercializes an invention by using labor and lab space to make the invention more attractive to consumers or to producers of downstream products need only focus on her contribution and the claims of others (supplemented by whatever contractual license terms are considered worthwhile). Likewise, the owners of those claims need attend only to a subset of the information that the other input owners claim, supplemented by license terms. As in regular property, exclusion in intellectual property rights is not absolute. IP rights are meant to furnish notice to draw contracting parties together.[46] Nonetheless, any property system, including patent, copyright, and the other branches of intellectual property law, must face the question of what combination of exclusion modules and governance interfaces will most cost-effectively bring parties together and allow them to engage not only in a division of labor but also in a specialization of information.

Which degrees of exclusion and governance are called for and how best to manage a semicommons are empirical questions. Recitation of the benefits of open access in terms of nonrivalness or the benefits of entitlements in terms of incentives tells us very little about the shape those entitlements should take or the forms of protection they should receive. If we are to have property rights, why are they not very thin sticks to engage in very specific uses? If someone invents a new compound, why would a patent cover all uses instead of pre-identified ones (fuel-additive, lubricant, etc.)? If the public domain is important why don't we specify the public rights stick by stick? Lumpiness in delineating rights has its advantages, and the on/off quality of the exclusion strategy allows complexity to be managed through modularity. Where necessary, governance can be used to tailor these solutions – to enrich the interface conditions between modules, as is the case with copyright fair use.

Modularity theory has the potential to be helpful in developing new empirical strategies for studying property. First of all, modularity theory provides an explanation for why certain aspects of property have been more amenable to conventional economic analysis than others. Governance rules – such as covenants, easements, nuisance, and zoning – are more like the rules of contracts and torts and impinge on identified persons. For this reason, we can try to connect variation in those rules with a micro theory of individual behavior. And the behavioral response to changes in the rules is likely described by some linear function. If so, some parts of property law are more susceptible to this approach than others. Thus, the refinements and extensions of the governance strategy can more easily be isolated, and regimes with and without them might present sufficient variation against a nearly constant (or at least unbiased) backdrop of the rest of the property regime.

But what of the exclusion strategy? The bundle-of-rights view would regard this as one more feature that can be turned on or off, or dialed up or down. And in a narrow sense that is true. But if the exclusion strategy is a primary vehicle through which property attains a modular structure, we have to be on the look out for more systemic effects. These are not likely to be easy to isolate, for several reasons. There is a danger in isolating chunks of the property system that do not constitute a module. If we allow such pseudo-components to vary, we are either likely to mistake what true variation is or we are likely not to find anything interesting. On the flip side, modularity theory generates hypotheses about what constitutes a 'component' worth studying. In other words, the modularity-based theory gives us some handle on the granularity of the economic phenomenon.

Likewise, the information-cost theory directs us to potential case studies. One method for doing so is to look at smaller structures like business organizations and joint ventures to get a suggestive idea about larger property issues. This of course is fraught with perils relating to the scalability of the structures in question. But as one avenue of investigation, this is likely to be worthwhile. As a starting point, I turn to some comparative statics below.

More generally, we first need a theory that gives us candidates for what constitutes a component of the system in order to ask the right questions. All empirical work requires a theory, and I am suggesting that the theory needed in NIE to study property rights needs more of an architecture than suggested by the conventional view of property as an arbitrary collection of bare entitlements without much internal structure.

Appropriation versus access is the central tradeoff in intellectual property. On the access side, exclusion rights are costly because they deny access to a nonrival resource. Consumption is being denied that would cover marginal cost. Intellectual property, like property and organizations, can be seen as the solution of a complex coordination problem of attributing outputs to inputs. In the intellectual property area, different actors combine inputs with something that can be said to belong to the public. As long as the innovator's or commercializer's rival input is valuable enough and the overall coordination problem of investment, appropriation, and consumption is complex enough, the theory of systems and our experience with human artifacts should lead us to expect a major role for modular solutions.

In this Part I have emphasized the benefits of modularity in terms of managing complexity. These benefits do not come without cost. Modularization may preclude interdependencies of some value or may overlook interdependencies that exist and cause unanticipated trouble.[47] Relatedly, conditions can change and call for a different modularization. Although under a wide variety of circumstances, modular systems evolve more easily than nonmodular systems, modular systems can get stuck at local optima depending on how much modules can vary and whether variation is random or rationally selected.[48] Particularly promising are studies of modularity that allow for decentralized search and sporadic intervention by a control module (like official decisionmakers or other coordinating institutions) or special intermodular communication (like contracting) in order to improve the evolutionary path of the modular system under changing conditions.[49]

IV.   APPLICATIONS

As we have seen, the information cost theory shows how intellectual property rights could be part of the solution to the appropriation–access tradeoff. Whether and to what extent they are justified in these terms requires empirical analysis. The information cost theory of property leads to a number of testable propositions and helps explain the contours of the intellectual property system.[50] I first turn to some simple comparative statics which allow some rough predictions of the direction of change in IP systems. Next I turn in particular to the benefits of modular IP in terms of asset partitioning and coordinating inputs to developing information as a resource. Finally, I show how the information cost theory of modular IP also helps explain the law's response to the problem of IP compatibility.

A.   Comparative Statics

The information-cost theory generates predictions about the likely direction of changes in property rights, in a Demsetzian sense.[51] We do not need to know the exact size of various quantities in order to be able to predict a move from exclusion towards governance or vice versa. Consider a simple model of exclusion and governance, and a few of the propositions that one can derive from it. A graphical version of this model with the cost structures of exclusion and governance can be illustrated as in Figure 5.3, with Wealth (W) depicted on the y-axis and precision (p) depicted on the x-axis.[52]

The marginal cost of exclusion (MCE) starts out low at low levels of precision, but increases rapidly. First cuts at defining a resource and preventing the most basic forms of theft by all sorts of pilferers and trespassers will use informational variables (proxies) with this cost structure. But fences and such measurement devices are not good at regulating uses in a finegrained way. By contrast, informational variables of the governance type start out with high marginal costs (MCG).

Dynamically, as marginal benefit shifts outward (inward) we expect, in Demsetzian fashion an increase (decrease) in property rights activity.[53] But because the supply curve is made up of components reflecting the various strategies, we can predict a shift from exclusion to governance (or in a more elaborate version of the model, a finegrained effort at exclusion).[54] An example would be the increasingly stringent rules governing the use of grazing commons in medieval and early modern England before enclosure.[55]

Moreover, as the various components of the supply curve of property rights – the individual strategies – differ or change in cost, we can predict shifts in the relative reliance on exclusion and governance. For example, we can compare patent law and copyright law

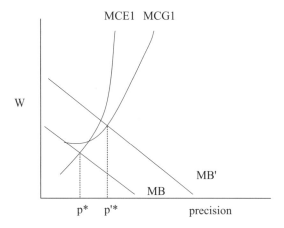

Figure 5.3   Exclusion and governance for a resource

in terms of the relative difficulty of setting up modular exclusion-style boundaries versus individualized governance-style rules of use, to explain why patent law is more property-like than copyright (as well as some changes in these areas over time).[56] Likewise, exclusion in the case of water is difficult and the high cost of modularization helps explain why water law has – both in its riparian and, more surprisingly, in its prior-appropriation versions – been more reliant on governance regimes than other areas of property.[57]

B.   Modular Intellectual Property and Asset Partitioning

Indirect intellectual property rights allow transacting parties to cooperate without delineating the rights to their inputs. This is important in joint ventures. Each of the participants in the joint venture can use its rival inputs to develop and commercialize a combination of joint and individual projects at low delineation cost. It is not that exclusive rights to information are useful per se. That is, the asset-partitioning function of intellectual property is important because it partitions the related *rival* assets and inputs at the same time.[58] In this way the partitioning effect and the attribution of returns in a team-production-type problem are closely related.[59] As modularity promotes specialization in organizations and production teams generally,[60] there is evidence that intellectual property rights promote specialization in firms.[61]

The modular structure of exclusion-based intellectual property rights also makes other types of contracting more tractable. Robert Merges has argued that intellectual property rights facilitate contracting by making precontractual liability possible and enforcement more flexible.[62] Sometimes this happens precisely because intellectual property rights serve as a convenient reference point even in advance of or apart from any need to delineate more accurate provisions relating to particular possibly unforeseeable (rival) inputs. For example, intellectual property rights can make the law of employee inventions simpler.[63] If independent invention were a defense to patent law, it would be very difficult to allocate rights as between employers and employees without the constant threat of defection.

All of this is not to say that intellectual property rights are always necessary or desirable or that stronger is always better. It does suggest that in considering the empirical question of what kinds of rights make sense, the modular structure of intellectual property rights potentially carries benefits. Otherwise, the indirectness between the mechanism and its purpose – an indirectness even greater than the sometimes controversial indirectness in regular property[64] – appears as an unmitigated problem. And pointing to incentives does not provide a complete explanation. Going back to the NIE definitions of property rights, if we knew the mean return from assets and all options were known and could be valued, there would be far less reason to have a property rights system for information at all, rather than some system of direct rewards or restitution with tracing.

One main issue here is notice, and in particular the most cost-effective method of furnishing it. Although systematic and centralized property records do often provide effective notice (most notably in the case of land),[65] it is an empirical question how they stack up against other methods in any given type of situation.[66] Other methods include standardization, equitable doctrines of notice (which apply in personam and not in rem), and doctrines absolving those encountering rights from liability. Where a legal device falls between in personam contract and in rem property, we should expect intermediate strategies to deal with the potentially large but still limited set of dutyholders.[67]

When notice is the issue it is important to keep in mind that it is not information that is scarce but rather *attention*, as Herbert Simon pointed out a long time ago.[68] Thus, even where land records or notices printed on a product may give notice in some sense, there might still be reasons to force a standardized format (as in the case of nutrition information or the terms of consumer loans). Even the land records are not a 'data dump' but limit the types and form of documents that are permitted to be recorded. Format can matter. For example, a rule that rent is incompatible with fee ownership means that once one knows that an interest is a fee simple, one can stop looking for information along this dimension. Similar problems arise in contract, and are solved with a different mix of private and public solutions, such as making contracts shorter or enforcing reasonable consumer expectations.[69]

One reason that servitudes present a problem of informational detail is that they implement a governance strategy. Basic exclusion (e.g., 'keep off,' boundaries) is a platform upon which we can build governance regimes, i.e. rules of proper use. Governance rules refine and supplement the basic exclusionary regime when particular use conflicts are important enough. Governance rules in the law can be contractual, from common law, or from some combination of statute and regulation.[70] Servitudes are a largely private governance regime. One possibility here is that courts have little problem with servitudes as long as they can be said to refine and supplement the basic exclusionary regime. Servitudes that are not refinements but rather unrelated (e.g., the sale or lease of a shop partially in return for free haircuts) or more than a mere refinement (e.g., going outside the copyright baseline by controlling rights to criticize) present information problems that normal governance regimes do not.

C.   Intellectual Property Compatibility

Licensing has implications for the modular structure of intellectual property. Licensing occurs at the interfaces between IP modules and, through licensing, transactors can modify those interfaces.

Intellectual property servitudes arise in the context of licensing. An intellectual property license is like an easement in real property in that the default is nonrevocability of the license. But intellectual property servitudes are highly contractual. The question becomes what limits, if any, the law should impose on intellectual property servitudes and why. The law has always been more suspicious of personal property servitudes than in real property, but this area of the law has been undertheorized.[71] Recently Molly Van Houweling has explored the 'new servitudes' in intellectual property, examining how they implicate some of the traditional concerns with servitudes both more and less than real and personal property servitudes do.[72] In particular, she shows how licenses can conflict downstream, as in the cases of the GPL Version 2, under which the original Linux kernel was created and licensed, and the Wikipedia GNU Free Documentation License.[73] These licenses mandate that further works incorporating the licensed material be made available on the same terms; the problem comes when these terms of openness are detailed and potentially conflict with later visions of openness. A later work may incorporate material licensed in two conflicting ways. This is a general problem with licenses that are meant to apply to somewhat remote and indefinite parties. The conflict is somewhat reminiscent of water law, in which property rights definition is difficult because it is desirable or unavoidable that water rights interlock tightly (the return flow issue in first appropriation is a dramatic example).[74]

In both IP servitudes and water law, the difficulty of delineating with respect to the resource leads to complex interfaces between modules. For a variety of purposes, we need refinements (governance), which complicate this interface when uses interact (e.g., nuisance and servitudes). One difference among land, chattels, and intangibles is that the exclusion strategy is easier to carry out for tangible property. The baseline is clearer: in the case of land, there is a physical bubble that corresponds to the module that the exclusion strategy provides. In intellectual property by contrast, attempts at exclusion are necessarily artificial. Thus, it is easier for servitudes in intellectual property to lack reference to an exclusion baseline. Admittedly, some have reference to a relatively clear ex ante baseline, as with the Creative Commons licenses favoring use within the scope of the copyright.[75] But some licenses do not use this baseline and instead go beyond it (as where rights to criticize are contracted away).[76] The conflicting license issue would not arise if intellectual property were more naturally modularized: the problem is that these servitudes can in principle be about anything and interact in any way with each other. The modularity of land rights through spatially defined exclusion limits the extent to which servitudes will come into conflict. Owners will be aware of what a servitude will 'cover' (almost literally) in the case of land.[77] Unlike land, software as a resource does not ensure this.

Complex interfaces can reduce transferability, as in the case of water. In some kinds of property, those setting up property desire liquidity, and this is more than enough incentive for standardization (financial instruments are sometimes an example).[78] In other cases, idiosyncratic rights (fancies) may 'pollute' the general informational atmosphere, increasing information costs for others.[79] The resulting general need for others to be on the lookout for additional types of information in no predetermined format can present an externality that exceeds the benefits of the idiosyncrasy to the transacting parties.[80] The private incentives for liquidity and the size of the externality, therefore, partly determine the need for standardization. Moreover, as long as the state is involved in enforcing property rights, there can be economies of scope in the state taking on the standardization function.[81]

Many of the issues raised in this Chapter manifested themselves in *Quanta Computer v. LG Electronics, Inc.*,[82] a case recently decided by the U.S. Supreme Court. In that case, the Federal Circuit had taken a wholly contractarian approach, concluding that the patent exhaustion doctrine did not apply to a method patent, allowing the patent holder to license a firm without at the same time licensing that firm's customers.[83] The Supreme Court, however, reversed, holding that patent exhaustion was mandatory and that servitudes on intellectual property, including patent related restrictions on use downstream from a licensee, would not run to remote purchasers.[84] But these problems of servitudes perched between property and contract suggest intermediate possibilities. Van Houweling, for example, suggests that the distinction made in earlier Supreme Court cases between commercial producing entities and individual consumers (the latter of whom may have more of an everyday expectation of permission to use a physical article) is potentially a good rule of thumb.[85] For one thing, those manufacturing under a license are a more expert audience with more at stake than consumers.[86] Accordingly, there is less reason for the law to worry about the processing costs of closer, more expert duty holders, particularly those with actual notice.

V.   CONCLUSION

The New Institutional Economics employs a thin notion of property under which most expectations of deriving value from a resource count as 'property rights.' Under these definitions the prospect of a government reward or rights arising under a contract to transfer information would be property rights. Without more, the NIE definition of property is very similar to the bundle of rights picture of property that legal theorists have inherited from the Legal Realists. In other words, any right that the NIE would label a property right would count as a bundle and could be labeled an 'entitlement' or 'property.' By contrast, the traditional motion of property as a right to a thing good against the world focuses attention on certain aspects of property as being architecturally important. The basic architecture of modular exclusion and interfaces of governance rules manifests itself in dynamic changes in intellectual property, in the asset-partitioning function of intellectual property, and in the issue of the compatibility of intellectual property rights. It is these architectural features that result from the information costs involved in the appropriation/access tradeoff that bring property and intellectual property closer together – rather than simply providing quantitative rewards.

NOTES

1. See, e.g., Armen A. Alchian, Some Economics of Property Rights, 30 Il Politico 816 (1965), reprinted in Armen A. Alchian, Economic Forces at Work 127, 130 (1977) ('By a system of property rights I mean a method of assigning to particular individuals the "authority" to select, for specific goods, any use from a nonprohibited class of uses.').
2. For present purposes, I am not distinguishing between rights and privileges. The exclusion strategy based on the right to exclude protects many interests in use without further delineation, making them look like

privileges or liberties. But when a given use comes into view in an important resource conflict, it may be singled out as a right.

3. Wesley Hohfeld tried to analyze in rem rights as a collection of in personam rights. Wesley Newcomb Hohfeld, Fundamental Legal Conceptions as Applied in Judicial Reasoning, 26 Yale L.J. 710 (1917), reprinted in Wesley Newcomb Hohfeld, Fundamental Legal Conceptions as Applied in Judicial Reasoning and Other Legal Essays 65–114 (Walter Wheeler Cook, ed. 1923). Others have emphasized that 'in rem' means availing against not only a large but also an indefinite set of dutyholders. See, e.g., Albert Kocourek, Rights in Rem, 68 U. Pa. L. Rev. 322, 322 (1920); Thomas W. Merrill & Henry E. Smith, The Property/Contract Interface, 101 Colum. L. Rev. 773, 783–86 (2001) (breaking notion of in rem legal relation into elements of numerosity and indefiniteness of dutyholders).

4. See, e.g., J.E. Penner, The Idea of Property in Law 29–30, 71 (1997).

5. Henry E. Smith, Intellectual Property as Property: Delineating Entitlements in Information, 116 Yale L.J. 1742 (2007).

6. Thomas W. Merrill & Henry E. Smith, Optimal Standardization in the Law of Property: The *Numerus Clausus* Principle, 110 Yale L.J. 1 (2000); Smith, this volume.

7. Henry E. Smith, Institutions and Indirectness in Intellectual Property, 157 U. Pa. L. Rev. 2083 (2009).

8. R. Polk Wagner, Information Wants To Be Free: Intellectual Property and the Mythologies of Control, 103 Colum. L. Rev. 995 (2003).

9. Kenneth J. Arrow, Economic Welfare and the Allocation of Resources for Invention, in The Rate and Direction of Inventive Activity: Economic and Social Factors 609, 615 (Nat'l Bureau of Econ. Research ed., 1962) ('[T]here is a fundamental paradox in the determination of demand for information; its value for the purchaser is not known until he has the information, but then he has in effect acquired it without cost.').

10. See Mary LaFrance, Something Borrowed, Something New: The Changing Role of Novelty in Idea Protection Law, 34 Seton Hall L. Rev. 485 (2004). New York now takes an intermediate approach under which novelty in general (to all) is required for misappropriation but only novelty to the defendant is required in quasi-contract. Apfel v. Prudential–Bache Securities Inc., 81 N.Y.2d 470 (1993); see also Nadel v. Play-By-Play Toys & Novelties, Inc., 208 F.3d 368 (2d Cir. 2000).

11. See Reeves v. Alyeska Pipeline Service Company, 926 P.2d 1130 (Alaska 1996).

12. See, e.g., Robert P. Merges & Jane C. Ginsburg, Foundations of Intellectual Property 21 (2004) (noting that the '"utilitarian" view of intellectual property is widely held to be the intellectual foundation for U.S. intellectual property law'); Justin Hughes, The Philosophy of Intellectual Property, 77 Geo. L.J. 287 (1988) (analyzing Lockean justifications close to Founders' vision and more European-style Hegelian theories).

13. On the problems of marginal cost pricing as a benchmark for subsidies, see John F. Duffy, The Marginal Cost Controversy in Intellectual Property, 71 U. Chi. L. Rev. 37 (2004).

14. See, e.g., Michael Abramowicz, Perfecting Patent Prizes, 56 Vand. L. Rev. 115, 123–24 (2003); Steven Shavell & Tanguy van Ypersele, Rewards Versus Intellectual Property Rights, 44 J.L. & Econ. 525, 534–45 (2001).

15. For a summary of a wide range of theories of patent law, see A. Samuel Oddi, Un-Unified Economic Theories of Patents – The Not-Quite-Holy-Grail, 71 Notre Dame L. Rev. 267 (1996).

16. See, e.g., Rebecca S. Eisenberg, Patents and the Progress of Science: Exclusive Rights and Experimental Use, 56 U. Chi. L. Rev. 1017, 1028–30 (1989).

17. Yoram Barzel, Optimal Timing of Innovations, 50 Rev. Econ. & Stat. 348 (1968); Jack Hirshleifer, The Private and Social Value of Information and the Reward to Inventive Activity, 61 Am. Econ. Rev. 561 (1971); see also Mark F. Grady & Jay I. Alexander, Patent Law and Rent Dissipation, 78 Va. L. Rev. 305 (1992).

18. Dean Lueck, The Rule of First Possession and the Design of the Law, 38 J.L. & Econ. 393, 399–403 (1995).

19. State Indus. v. A.O. Smith Corp., 751 F.2d 1226, 1236 (Fed. Cir. 1985) ('One of the benefits of a patent system is its so-called 'negative incentive' to 'design around' a competitor's products, even when they are patented, thus bringing a steady flow of innovations to the marketplace.'); F. Scott Kieff et al., Principles of Patent Law 70–71 (4th ed. 2008).

20. See Giles S. Rich, The Relation Between Patent Practices and the Anti-Monopoly Laws, 24 J. Pat. Off. Soc'y 159, 177–81 (1942) (arguing that promoting the commercialization of inventions is the most important function of patent law); see also F. Scott Kieff, Property Rights and Property Rules for Commercializing Inventions, 85 Minn. L. Rev. 697 (2001) (arguing for commercialization theory).

21. Edmund W. Kitch, The Nature and Function of the Patent System, 20 J.L. & Econ. 265, 276–77, 284 (1977) (discussing, inter alia, the role of patent prospect in giving 'the patent owner . . . an incentive to make investments to maximize the value of the patent,' including investments in manufacture, distribution, and market development).

22. Giles S. Rich, The Relation Between Patent Practices and the Anti-Monopoly Laws, 24 J. Pat. Off. Soc'y 85, 179 (1942).
23. See, e.g., F. Scott Kieff, Coordination, Property, and Intellectual Property: An Unconventional Approach to Anticompetitive Effects and Downstream Access, 56 Emory L.J. 327 (2006); Robert P. Merges, A Transactional View of Property Rights, 20 Berkeley Tech. L.J. 1477 (2005); Paul J. Heald, A Transaction Costs Theory of Patent Law, 66 Ohio St. L.J. 473 (2005).
24. See, e.g., Edmund W. Kitch, Elementary and Persistent Errors in the Economic Analysis of Intellectual Property, 53 Vand. L. Rev. 1727, 1729–31 (2000); see also Herbert Hovenkamp, Federal Antitrust Policy: The Law of Competition and Its Practice §10.3c (2d. ed. 1999) ('[M]ost patents confer absolutely no market power on their owners.'); but cf. Mark A. Lemley, The Economics of Improvement in Intellectual Property Law, 75 Tex. L. Rev. 989, 1048–67 (1997) (arguing for importance of market power with respect to improvers).
25. See, e.g., Eric G. Campbell et al., Data Withholding in Academic Genetics: Evidence from a National Survey, 287 J. Am. Med. Ass'n 473, 477 (2002) (reporting that 47% of academic geneticists said that another academic had refused at least one of their requests for data or materials associated with a published article at least once in the preceding three years); Stephen Hilgartner & Sherry I. Brandt-Rauf, Data Access, Ownership, and Control: Toward Empirical Studies of Access Practices, 15 Knowledge 355, 359, 363–66 (1994) (discussing strategic issues involved in decisions to grant access to data); Fiona Murray & Scott Stern, Do Formal Intellectual Property Rights Hinder the Free Flow of Scientific Knowledge? An Empirical Test of the Anti-Commons Hypothesis, 63 J. Econ. Behav. & Org. 648 (2007) (finding modest effect of property rights on flow of information); Carl Shapiro, Navigating the Patent Thicket: Cross Licenses, Patent Pools, and Standard Setting, in 1 Innovation Policy and the Economy 119 (Adam B. Jaffe et al. eds., 2001); John P. Walsh et al., Effects of Research Tool Patents and Licensing on Biomedical Innovation, in Patents in the Knowledge-Based Economy 285 (Wesley M. Cohen & Stephen A. Merrill eds., 2003) (noting that a survey of industry participants found that patents on research tools generally have not caused much breakdown or even restricted access as anticommons theory would suggest, and documenting various solutions to the fragmentation problem, including licensing, inventing around, infringing, public disclosure, and litigation); John P. Walsh et al., Patents, Material Transfers and Access to Research Inputs in Biomedical Research 2 (Sept. 20, 2005), http://tigger.uic.edu/~jwalsh/WalshChoCohenFinal050922.pdf. Problems seem to be greater in the case of materials transfer than sharing of data. John P. Walsh et al., View from the Bench: Patents and Materials Transfers, 309 Science 2002, 2002 (2005); see also Rebecca S. Eisenberg & Arti K. Rai, Harnessing and Sharing the Benefits of State-Sponsored Research: Intellectual Property Rights and Data Sharing in California's Stem Cell Initiative, 21 Berkeley Tech. L.J. 1187, 1200 n. 47 (2006) (discussing studies surveying geneticists on sharing of data and materials).
26. See, e.g., Rochelle Cooper Dreyfuss, Expressive Genericity: Trademarks as Language in the Pepsi Generation, 65 Notre Dame L. Rev. 397 (1990); Stephen L. Carter, The Trouble with Trademark, 99 Yale L.J. 759 (1990).
27. See Eastman Kodak Co. v. Kodak Cycle Co., 15 Rep. Pat. Cas. 105 (1898).
28. The dilution theory has been criticized for overpropertizing trademark. See, e.g., Jessica Litman, Breakfast with Batman: The Public Interest in the Advertising Age, 108 Yale L.J. 1717 (1999).
29. Herbert A. Simon, The Sciences of the Artificial 195 (2d ed. 1981) (1969).
30. Id. at 195–98 (describing a nearly decomposable system as one 'in which the interactions among the subsystems are weak but not negligible'). See also 1 Carliss Y. Baldwin & Kim B. Clark, Design Rules: The Power of Modularity (2000); Managing in the Modular Age: Architectures, Networks and Organizations (Raghu Garud et al. eds., 2003).
31. Here they are factorial. See generally Modularity in Development and Evolution (Gerhard Schlosser & Günter P. Wagner eds., 2004); Lauren W. Ancel & Walter Fontana, Plasticity, Evolvability, and Modularity in RNA, 288 J. Experimental Zoology 242 (2000); Günter P. Wagner & Lee Altenberg, Complex Adaptations and the Evolution of Evolvability, 50 Evolution 967 (1996); John J. Welch & David Waxman, Modularity and the Cost of Complexity, 57 Evolution 1723 (2003).
32. See R.H. Coase, The Problem of Social Cost, 3 J.L. & Econ. 1 (1960).
33. See Merrill & Smith, supra note 6; Smith, this volume.
34. See, e.g., Peter Birks, Mixing and Tracing: Property and Restitution, in 45 Current Legal Problems 69, 84 (1992) (exploring tracing in restitutionary claims); Dan B. Dobbs, Law of Remedies: Damages-Equity-Restitution §6.1 (2d ed. 1993) (discussing the necessity of tracing); Peter B. Oh, Tracing, 80 Tul. L. Rev. 849, 876 (2006) (examining remedial tracing in equity and at common law).
35. See, e.g., Joseph William Singer, Introduction to Property § 16.2.5 (2d ed. 2005). Other legal systems favor good faith purchasers in more circumstances. See, e.g., Saul Levmore, Variety and Uniformity in the Treatment of the Good-Faith Purchaser, 16 J. Legal Stud. 43 (1987). Purchasers with notice are generally not protected. See generally Benito Arruñada, Property Enforcement as Organized Consent, 19 J.L. Econ. & Org. 401 (2003).

36. Here we are considering the law of unjust enrichment as a mechanism for appropriation. On restitution as an interest in intellectual property, see Wendy J. Gordon, On Owning Information: Intellectual Property and the Restitutionary Impulse, 78 Va. L. Rev. 149 (1992).

37. See James M. Anderson, The Missing Theory of Variable Selection in the Economic Analysis of Tort Law, 2007 Utah L. Rev. 255.

38. Andrew Kull, Rationalizing Restitution, 83 Cal. L. Rev. 1191, 1196 (1995); Emily Sherwin, Restitution and Equity: An Analysis of The Principle of Unjust Enrichment, 79 Tex. L. Rev. 2083 (2001); but cf. Hanoch Dagan, The Law and Ethics of Restitution (2004) (arguing for an expansive role for restitution).

39. See, e.g., Aaron Clauset, M.E.J. Newman & Christopher Moore, Finding Community Structure in Very Large Networks, 70 Phys. Rev. E 70, 066111 (2004); M.E.J. Newman, Modularity and Community Structure in Networks, 103 Proc. Natl. Acad. Sci. USA 8577 (2006). For a discussion and an application to community custom, see Henry E. Smith, Community and Custom in Property, 10 Theoretical Inquiries L. 6 (2009).

40. See infra notes 58–63 and accompanying text.

41. Smith, supra note 5.

42. Henry E. Smith, Governing Water: The Semicommons of Fluid Property Rights, 50 Ariz. L. Rev. 445, 475–77 (2008).

43. See Henry E. Smith, Semicommon Property Rights and Scattering in the Open Fields, 29 J. Legal Stud. 131, 131–32, 138–44 (2000).

44. See id. at 134–38, 144–54.

45. See, e.g., Robert A. Heverly, The Information Semicommons, 18 Berkeley Tech. L.J. 1127 (2003); Lydia Pallas Loren, Building a Reliable Semicommons of Creative Works: Enforcement of Creative Commons Licenses and Limited Abandonment of Copyright, 14 Geo. Mason L. Rev. 271 (2007); Smith, supra note 5, at 1765–66; Henry E. Smith, Governing the Tele-Semicommons, 22 Yale J. on Reg. 289, 291–96 (2005); Smith, supra note 43, at 131–32, 138–44, 166–67; Peter K. Yu, Intellectual Property and the Information Ecosystem, 2005 Mich. St. L. Rev. 1, 11–12.

46. See F. Scott Kieff, On Coordinating Transactions in Information: A Response to Smith's Delineating Entitlements in Information, 117 Yale L.J. Pocket Part 101 (2007). Much recent criticism has focused on failures in the notice-giving function of patent law. James Bessen & Michael J. Meurer, Patent Failure: How Judges, Bureaucrats, and Lawyers Put Innovators at Risk 29–72 (2008). Giving discretion to examiners and judges to deny more patents eliminates the notice problem along with the patents that are denied, but for those that remain the property rights may wind up more unclear than ever. Part of the problem may be solved by using damages as an alternative to injunctions as a limited equitable safety valve. See Smith, supra note 7, at 2125–32.

47. See Oliver Baumann, Coordinating Search in Modular Systems: The Value of (Temporary) Integration (Munich School of Management Draft Mar. 21, 2008), available at SSRN: http://ssrn.com/abstract=1113174.

48. See Stefano Brusoni et al., The Value and Costs of Modularity: A Problem-Solving Perspective, 4 Eur. Mgt. Rev. 121 (2007) (exploring tradeoff between speed of search through modularity and lock in to sub-optimal solutions); Luigi Marengo et al., Decomposability and Modularity of Economic Interactions, in Modularity: Understanding the Development and Evolution of Complex Natural Systems 835 (Werner Callebaut and Diego Rasskin-Gutman eds., 2005). Baldwin & Clark, supra note 30, assume a rationally designed search.

49. Baumann, supra note 47.

50. This Part draws on material from Smith, supra note 7.

51. Henry E. Smith, Exclusion Versus Governance: Two Strategies for Delineating Property Rights, 31 J. Legal Stud. S453, S477–78 (2002).

52. For a discussion of how to operationalize precision, see id., at S467–79.

53. See, e.g., Terry L. Anderson & P.J. Hill, The Evolution of Property Rights: A Study of the American West, 18 J.L. & Econ. 163 (1975); Harold Demsetz, Toward a Theory of Property Rights, 57 Am. Econ. Rev. 347 (1967) (Papers & Proc.); Smith, supra note 51.

54. Smith, supra note 51, at S464–78. Here for simplicity I assume the strategies act independently of each other, in part to evaluate the 'bundle' approach on its own terms.

55. Id. at S478–83.

56. Smith, supra note 5, at 1799–1819.

57. Smith, supra note 42.

58. See Paul J. Heald, A Transaction Costs Theory of Patent Law, 66 Ohio St. L.J. 473, 480–84 (2005) (arguing that intellectual property has an asset partitioning function like organizational law).

59. Id. at 487–99 (discussing team production issues in involving intellectual property).

60. See Baldwin & Clark, supra note 30.

61. See Ashish Arora & Robert P. Merges, Specialized Supply Firms, Property Rights, and Firm Boundaries,

13 Indus, & Corp. Change 451, 452 (2004) (arguing from model and suggestive empirical literature that strong intellectual property rights lead to specialization in firms); see also Daniel W. Elfenbein, Publications, Patents, and the Market for University Inventions, 63 J. Econ. Behav. & Org. 688, 690 (2007) (discussing intellectual property marketplaces and selectivity issues).

62. See Robert P. Merges, A Transactional View of Property Rights, 20 Berkeley Tech. L.J. 1477, 1479 (2005) (stating that specific aspects of property law 'encourage the making of real-world deals').

63. Robert P. Merges, The Law and Economics of Employee Inventions, 13 Harv. J.L. & Tech. 1, 21 & n. 69 (1999) (recognizing a greater emphasis on teamwork and cooperative tasks in patent law).

64. See Henry E. Smith, Mind the Gap: The Indirect Relation between Ends and Means in American Property Law, 94 Cornell L. Rev. 959 (2009).

65. See Alfred F. Conard, Easement Novelties, 30 Cal. L. Rev. 125, 131–33 (1942) (arguing that enforcement of easements should not be objectionable on grounds of novelty as long as there is notice); Richard A. Epstein, Notice and Freedom of Contract in the Law of Servitudes, 55 S. Cal. L. Rev. 1353, 1354 (1982) (arguing for freedom of contract in the area of covenants and easements as long as land records provide notice).

66. See Merrill & Smith, supra note 6, at 43–45 (describing other methods of meeting third-party informational needs).

67. Thomas W. Merrill & Henry E. Smith, The Property/Contract Interface, 101 Colum. L. Rev. 773, 776–77 (2001) (discussing the differences in the legal doctrines associated with areas mixing contract rights and property rights due to the costs and benefits associated with different types of rights).

68. Herbert A. Simon, Designing Organizations for an Information-Rich World, in Computers, Communication, and the Public Interest 37, 40–41 (Martin Greenberger ed., 1971) (noting that an abundance of information results in a scarcity of attention).

69. See Henry E. Smith, Modularity in Contracts: Boilerplate and Information Flow, 104 Mich. L. Rev. 1175, 1176 (2006) (discussing boilerplate language in contracts).

70. For the role of governance regimes in intellectual property, see Smith, supra note 5, at 1784–98.

71. See, e.g., Zechariah Chafee, Jr., Equitable Servitudes on Chattels, 41 Harv. L. Rev. 945, 977–87 (1928) (surveying the case law and explaining objections to equitable servitudes on chattels); Zechariah Chafee, Jr., The Music Goes Round and Round: Equitable Servitudes and Chattels, 69 Harv. L. Rev. 1250, 1254–56 (1956) (acknowledging the scarcity of authorities addressing equitable servitudes on chattels). For a recent contractarian argument, see Glen O. Robinson, Personal Property Servitudes, 71 U. Chi. L. Rev. 1449, 1449–55 (2004).

72. Molly Shaffer Van Houweling, The New Servitudes, 96 Geo. L.J. 885, 924–50 (2008). Incompatibility of intellectual property can sometimes be remedied by modularity. See, Smith, supra note 7; Joachim Henkel & Carliss Baldwin, Modularity for Value Appropriation: Drawing the Boundaries of Intellectual Property (Harvard Business School Finance Working Paper No. 09-097), available at SSRN: http://ssrn.com/abstract=1340445.

73. Van Houweling, supra note 72, at 941–43.

74. See supra note 57 and accompanying text.

75. Van Houweling, supra note 72, at 938–39.

76. See id. at 938 (providing Microsoft's Vista EULA as an 'example of a license that in fact imposes limitations that exceed the baseline restrictions of copyright').

77. If, however, we followed the Legal Realists and asserted that there is no core to the bundle of sticks of rights in land, the situation would be much more similar to the one Van Houweling identifies for information goods.

78. See Merrill & Smith, supra note 6, at 47–48. But moral hazard in financial contracting is possible under certain circumstances, and this can provide a rationale for mandatory standardization. See Ayotte & Bolton, this volume.

79. Merrill & Smith, supra note 6, at 26–34 (differentiating the information costs for originating parties, potential successors in interest, and other market participants).

80. Id. at 31–33.

81. Id. at 51.

82. 128 S. Ct. 2109 (2008).

83. Id. at 2113.

84. Id.

85. Van Houweling, supra note 72, at 932–39 (evaluating the different notice and information costs of licensing practices).

86. Henry E. Smith, The Language of Property: Form, Context, and Audience, 55 Stan. L. Rev. 1105, 1173–77 (2003) (examining specialized audiences in various areas of intellectual property).

6 Unilateral relinquishment of property
*Lior Jacob Strahilevitz**

Suppose you have property that you would like to get rid of. There are five basic avenues for doing so. Sale is probably the first option that springs to mind, and this can be effectuated through a voluntary transfer (at a flea market, say), or involuntary transfer (as when the government exercises eminent domain). Donation is another obvious means of parting with a resource. Less obviously, but no less critically, you can get rid of property through sheer passivity: if a trespasser settles on your land and uses it as a normal person would for years, the trespasser eventually becomes its owner through adverse possession. These three mechanisms for losing title to property have been covered at great length in the legal literature.

Rather little has been said about the two other mechanisms for relinquishing property: abandonment and destruction. They will be the subject of this chapter. The important commonality between abandonment and destruction is their unilateral nature. Sales, gifts, and adverse possession all require bilateral interactions, but abandonment and destruction permit the owner of a resource to relinquish it without requiring any action by a third party. These two avenues for losing property turn out to be common, important, widely practiced, and largely undertheorized. Perhaps as a result of that last attribute, the law of abandonment and destruction is poorly thought through and in need of reform.

I. ABANDONMENT

On an ordinary Wednesday in August of 2008, there were 77 separate listings in the 'Free Stuff' section of Chicago's Craigslist directory.[1] The items made freely available ranged from items highly desirable (an entertainment center in great condition, a working Gilbranson organ, televisions and microwave ovens) to those that might be useful to a niche population (a Hewlett Packard inkjet cartridge, VHS tapes of the motion pictures Free Willy *and* Free Willy 2, wooden doors from a colonial house built in 1938) to the nearly worthless (a broken refrigerator, one cubic yard of dirt from a landscaping project, 'tons of river rocks'). All were offered by their owners on a first come, first served basis. In most cases, the items were kept inside the owner's home, and a claimant would need to make arrangements with the owner to haul off the property. But the owners would not be picky; the first claimant would take the advertised property home. In a few cases, such as the broken refrigerator, the item had been left by the owner in an alley or another publicly accessible spot, and the Craigslist advertisement described its location.[2] Craigslist is not alone in matching up would-be abandoners with potential claimants – another national organizational called freecycle.org offers a similar service, with high levels of participation. And it is not only personal property that is widely slated for abandonment. In rural, depopulated areas of Kansas, Nebraska, and North Dakota, local governments have made free land available to anyone who is willing to build a house on it and move in.[3] And in urban centers, the problem of abandoned dwellings is significant, accounting for 23,000 dwelling units in New York City in 1996, and fully 1.3% of all urban residential housing units in the Northeastern United States two decades earlier.[4]

A. Why Do People Abandon Property?

Why would someone abandon property? This question lies at the core of any serious inquiry into this body of law. As discussed below, there may be a number of reasons why an owner might regard abandonment as an attractive strategy for transferring property. The most significant advantages of abandonment are that it allows an owner to avoid the transaction costs associated with a consensual transfer and the decision costs associated with determining the identity of the most appropriate transferee. Other reasons why abandonment might prove attractive include altruistic or reciprocal motivations, a desire to sell ancillary goods, and efforts to enhance one's reputation or derive entertainment value.

It is commonly assumed that property is only abandoned when it becomes worthless or when the costs of removing the property exceed its market value. Yet the case law reflects numerous instances where property with positive market value is abandoned, and contemporary experience suggests that this behavior remains common. By exploring the different types of non-negative value properties that are nevertheless abandoned, we can make headway toward determining precisely what the law of abandonment ought to say.

Positive market value assets present the most interesting abandonment puzzles. For example, consider baseballs hit into the stands at major league ballgames. Thanks to *Popov v. Hayashi*, the Barry Bonds home run ball dispute, we now have clear case law holding that a baseball is the property of major league baseball at the time the pitcher throws it, but that it becomes abandoned property the moment it flies off a hitter's bat and out of play.[5] Some of these baseballs have significant monetary value. For example, Mark McGwire's 70th home run ball sold for $3 million, and the ball at issue in *Popov* sold for $450,000. One might appropriately wonder why Major League Baseball does not retain title to balls hit into the stands, as the National Basketball Association and National Football League evidently do. The answer is straightforward – major league baseball seems to have concluded that the opportunity to capture abandoned baseballs at ballparks induces fans to attend games. Thus, by abandoning valuable property, but limiting the potential claimants of that property almost entirely to paying fans, major league baseball plausibly maximizes its own profits. Major league baseball is not the only entity to recognize that abandonment might lend itself to profit-maximization by opening up ancillary revenue streams. One clever Craigslist poster offered a free HDTV that was in need of expensive repairs, and noted, 'As an added bonus, you can buy the [TV] stand for 50 bucks!'[6]

Now for some less straightforward cases. Devon, England, has been celebrating the Hot Pennies Ceremony for more than 750 years. During the ceremony, town residents in the buildings throw buckets of coins into the streets, where they are scooped up by the crowds below. Although the ceremony has now become a successful tourist attraction – consistent with the major league baseball explanation of abandoned baseballs

– its origins were rather different. By town lore, the items tossed into the streets were initially coins that had been heated to high temperatures 'so that rich people could amuse themselves by witnessing poor people burning themselves.' [7] In an updated echo of this ancient ceremony, athletes, musicians, models, and other public figures have gained notoriety by tossing large denomination bills into the air. In hip-hop culture the practice has been referred to as 'making it rain,' and media accounts have popped up around the globe describing the practice, with one sports columnist referring to it as a 'tradition' among athletes. [8] Boxing champion Floyd Mayweather, Jr. has become famous for the practice of tossing stacks containing $10,000 in hundred dollar bills into the air so that he can see fans scramble for them. [9] So too football player Pacman Jones, who was arrested after allegedly tossing tens of thousands of dollars into the air at a Las Vegas strip club, sparking a violent melee. [10] The practice of abandoning caches of cash is evidently a strategy for accomplishing any number of rational objectives: garnering attention, signaling wealth, or being entertained (for people with unusual entertainment preferences).

B. Costs of Abandonment

There are two leading problems associated with abandonment. First, abandonment may create confusion as to the state of ownership of property. Second, abandonment may result in the deterioration of an asset's value during the time period that it remains abandoned. Moreover, in some cases involving worthless property, abandonment may externalize disposal costs onto society. In other cases involving valuable property, abandonment may spark violent squabbling among would-be claimants.

Consider the confusion problem first. The legal treatment of abandoned property differs from that of lost or mislaid property. Abandoned property belongs to the first person to find it and take possession. [11] The finder of lost property typically prevails over anyone other than the true owner or a prior possessor. [12] Finally, mislaid property typically goes to the landowner on whose property the item in question was found subject to the rights of the true owner. [13] When an individual stumbles upon chattel property, it can be quite difficult to discern whether it is abandoned, lost, or mislaid, and thus difficult for the finder to determine his rights and responsibilities.

The deterioration problem is also nearly universal in cases of abandonment. To the extent that property forms a portion of a jurisdiction's tax base, abandonment may result in an ownership lag whereas gifts and sales do not. The lag also means that a productive societal asset generates no wealth for a period of time. This lag is particularly troublesome in the case of an asset whose quality or value will decline the longer it remains unpossessed by an owner. The classic example would be abandoned homes, which may suffer from burst pipes, vandalism, use by criminals, or vermin infestations if they remain unoccupied for a significant period of time. [14] Once again, with most abandoned assets, the goal of law should be to reduce the time during which property remains abandoned.

Two mutually exclusive costs of abandonment are disposal costs (in the case of negative market value property) and race costs (in the case of positive market value property). The former are best exemplified in the context of environmentally contaminated real property, where CERCLA tries to impose cleanup costs on owners who try to abandon their land. The latter are best exemplified by the *Popov v. Hayashi* dispute referenced earlier. If a particularly valuable property like a million dollar baseball is to be abandoned, one can expect that many claimants will invest in capturing it, and those who seek to do so may try to obtain some advantage over their competitors by engaging in violent acts.[15] The criminal violence at the nightclub where Pacman Jones 'made it rain' provides further illustration.[16] Finally, permitting abandonment may encourage non-sustainable uses of a resource.[17]

C. The Law of Abandonment

In some contexts, American law permits property abandonment quite broadly. In others, the law takes a far more restrictive tack.[18] A permissive regime is one in which the abandonment of property by its owner is typically lawful, and the first person who takes possession of the property becomes its new owner, with rights good against the entire world. Setting aside pets and hazardous waste, this is the rule that governs the majority of abandoned chattel property. While there may be time, place, and manner restrictions on such abandonment (via anti-littering laws or attractive nuisance tort causes of action, say), the law's attitude is appropriately characterized as permissive. Hence, a newspaper publisher may leave two thousand copies of its newspaper in a publicly accessible place, to be read (or not) by whomever wants to pick up some free reading,[19] and the law recognizes the placement of trash in a dumpster as lawful abandonment, enabling third parties to dumpster dive legally.[20]

Prohibition regimes sometimes arise in the context of chattel property. For example, most American states explicitly categorize the abandonment of pets or livestock as animal cruelty, punishable as a misdemeanor.[21] One rationale for the prohibitory rule is that an unowned animal may create negative externalities by spreading disease, breeding strays, or colliding with vehicles, for example. The dominant explanation for the prohibitory rule, however, likely stems from the animals' status as living things that are capable of suffering. The abandonment of an animal will in most cases substantially diminish the animal's welfare. The criminal prohibition against abandonment thus encourages owners to relinquish ownership in a manner that will be less harmful to the animal in question by donating the animal to an animal shelter.[22]

The Prohibition regimes are most visible in the context of real estate. The leading case here is *Pocono Springs Civic Association v. MacKenzie*,[23] which held that perfect title to real property cannot be abandoned. Note, however, that lesser interests in land are treated differently. The conventional account holds that at common law, corporeal hereditaments like fee simple interests could not be abandoned, but incorporeal interests (e.g., easements, mineral interests, and licenses) could.[24] This account is incorrect as a matter of logic. Because the abandonment of real property necessarily entails indifference as to the identity of the subsequent owner,[25] it is wrong to refer to the abandonment of an incorporeal hereditament. When such an interest is 'abandoned,' the interest in question reverts to the owner of the previously burdened estate. For example, if an oil and gas interest is abandoned, any deposits on the land come to be owned by the fee simple owner. It is thus accurate to say that real property cannot be abandoned under the common law. Forfeited yes, abandoned no.

In any event, the traditional explanation for the distinction in the legal treatment of corporeal and incorporeal is historical. Essentially, in the English feudal system, the crown could not tolerate the non-ownership of land between the time of abandonment and reclamation because no feudal incidents would be paid in the interim.[26] Superficially, there would appear to be a contemporary analog to these feudal incidents that would justify the law's antagonism toward the abandonment of real property. Real property taxes are the modern-day equivalent of feudal incidents. Hence state and local governments might conclude that the trouble with abandonment is that for some period of time, there will be no one to pay a tax bill, even though the abandoned parcel presumably requires some expenditure of state resources (e.g., for preventing crime on the property or maintaining nearby roads). Under scrutiny this static argument for the common law rule breaks down. Real property that is abandoned, like chattel property that is abandoned, often has negative market value, in which case the state should not be levying taxes against it. To the extent that the state does levy taxes, it does so on the basis of outdated information about the resource's value. If the property in question has positive market value, then it should be taxed by the state, but it should also be claimed by a new owner in short order. If nobody claims such property, it suggests the presence of severe informational asymmetries. Namely, would-be owners of the land might not know of its availability, might worry about whether it has actually been abandoned, or might infer from the fact of abandonment that the property in question is actually a negative value asset.

A better argument for the common law rule prohibiting abandonment of the fee simple interest in land tackles the problem not from the static perspective outlined above, but from a dynamic one. Namely, a regime that prevents individuals from abandoning real property might encourage them to use the property in a more sustainable way. We can look to the Brazilian rain forests for an example of how the common law might improve social welfare. In Brazil, it is common for ranchers to chop down portions of the Amazon rain forest, use the land quite intensively for ranching cattle, and then, typically within eight years, abandon the land, which has become worthless scrubland thanks to overgrazing.[27] The rancher then moves on to greener pastures (or forests) and begins the process anew. As a civil law country, Brazil does not prohibit the abandonment of real property.[28] Were it to prohibit abandonment, the law might encourage land owners to evaluate their own practices with a longer time horizon in mind, shifting strategies from slash-and-burn to techniques more in line with maximizing the long term value of the property. On this account, the common law rule regarding abandonment might function as a defense against hyperbolic discounting or economic conditions that encourage short-sighted uses of land.[29]

II. THE RIGHT TO DESTROY

When asked to resolve cases where one party seeks to destroy her property, courts have reacted with great hostility toward the owner's destructive plans. Despite the existence of a norm that tolerates the burial of wedding rings, courts might well refuse a decedent's humble request to wear such jewelry for eternity.[30] If a testator orders her executor to destroy her home upon her death, the law probably will render the executor unable to carry out her wishes.[31] And if a landlord requests the city's permission to demolish a venerable but badly burned building that has become an eyesore, a teetering hazard, and a financial burden, the government can thwart her wishes.[32] Confronted with arguably hard cases and high stakes, many American courts have rejected the notion that an owner has the right to destroy that which is hers.

A.   An Ex Ante Perspective on Destruction

The trend of curtailing destruction whenever presented with an opportunity is somewhat puzzling, because it runs counter to so many well-established cultural norms. For example, the destruction of diaries and other papers is commonplace, even when those written works have enormous economic value. As *Nixon v. United States* makes clear, American Presidents repeatedly have destroyed diaries, correspondence, and other personal effects, either during their lifetimes or via will.[33] Throughout the nation's history, a powerful custom existed giving the President ownership of his presidential papers.[34] Private ownership of these papers evidently entailed a right to destroy them. According to the D.C. Circuit's opinion, there are 'numerous examples of Presidents willfully and intentionally destroying their presidential papers.'[35] They include Van Buren, Garfield, Arthur, Grant, Pierce, and Coolidge.[36] The heirs of Presidents Harding and Fillmore also destroyed large numbers of presidential papers following the deaths of those Presidents.[37] Some of Abraham Lincoln's papers were destroyed by his heirs as well.[38] The destruction of these papers occurred even though the Library of Congress repeatedly approached Presidents and their heirs, offering 'fancy sums' to purchase collections of presidential papers.[39] Presidents and presidential descendants well understood the economic and historical value of their official papers and nevertheless set them ablaze. Numerous Supreme Court Justices behaved likewise.[40] These Presidents and other public officials were not behaving irrationally. Rather, they were destroying the papers to protect their privacy and the privacy of their associates.[41]

Largely in response to the fallout from Watergate and the Nixon papers dispute, Congress enacted the Presidential Records Act of 1978,[42] prospectively abolishing private ownership of presidential papers.[43] The Act makes it difficult for the President to destroy any of the presidential papers that are produced during his tenure. The President may not dispose of any records that have 'administrative, historical, informational, or evidentiary value,'[44] a category that presumably includes virtually all presidential records.[45] If the President wishes to destroy presidential records that lack administrative, historical, informational, and evidentiary value, he may petition the Archivist of the United States for permission to do so. If the Archivist further concludes that said records are of no 'special interest to the Congress' and that 'consultation with the Congress regarding the disposal of these particular records' is not 'in the public interest,' then he may provide the President with written authorization to destroy the records in question.[46]

One strongly suspects that given a President's inability to destroy important papers, and given the hassle associated with destroying even the most insignificant scrap of presidential parchment, a rational President whose rights are restricted by the Presidential Records Act of 1978 will create a less interesting paper trail than his relatively unconstrained predecessors. When in doubt, the President simply will decline to memorialize an important idea or communication.[47]

Historic preservation of buildings presents an interesting illustration of this ex ante perspective in the real property context. Historic preservation statutes typically limit the rights of landowners to demolish buildings that have been designated as landmarks.[48]

When someone tries to destroy his own property, and courts have a chance to prevent the destruction, loss aversion may convince courts to prohibit destruction.[49] This is particularly true in cases involving homes and other buildings. Judges may grow fond of vintage buildings or defer to people who love buildings that have long been part of a neighborhood landscape. Judges, legislators, and ordinary citizens have a much more difficult time imagining the structures that will replace these venerable buildings, even though virtually every landmark building in a major city stands on a site that was previously occupied by some other structure.

For much of the nation's history, the judiciary's absolutist notions of ownership trumped these tendencies to preserve the old regardless of the cost to the new. So when it considered *People ex rel. Marbro Corp. v. Ramsey* in 1960, an Illinois court found it quite natural to hold that a building owner was entitled to a demolition permit where the costs of repairing and maintaining a historically significant building were high and where the owner would still lose money operating the building if it were fully renovated at the public's expense.[50] Implicit in this holding is the sensible view that destroying a building in order to maximize the value of the land on which it sits is not property destruction at all – rather it is an improvement to the parcel as a whole.

Three decades later, the notion of absolute ownership had receded to the point where courts ratified ill-considered policies that forced landowners to expend large sums maintaining teetering buildings. In one such case, *J.C. & Associates v. District of Columbia Board of Appeals & Review*, the District of Columbia Court of Appeals denied a property owner's request to destroy a fire-damaged building that, in the opinion of several experts and a city building inspector, was on the brink of collapse.[51] The building had been designated a historic landmark before the fire, but the fire had rendered it an eyesore and the costs of rehabilitating it appeared prohibitive to several experts who testified or filed reports.

Some commentators have argued that the possibility of future landmark designation and the associated limitations on future uses will discourage property owners from commissioning great buildings.[52] I agree with William Fischel that this precise possibility is a 'bit far-fetched.'[53] Under existing laws, the time lag between a building's groundbreaking and its designation as a historic landmark is usually long enough that any concerns about future landmarking will be discounted by most developers.[54] That said, there will be instances in which the decisions a building owner makes *after* the completion of construction affect the building's chances of being designated a historic landmark. For example, the owner of a building that has some historic or architectural merit – but that will not become eligible for landmark designation for ten more years – might maintain the exterior of the building poorly or remove the most architecturally interesting ornamentation in the years preceding landmark eligibility.[55]

Those who wish to limit the right to destroy further, however, propose to eliminate the time lag that currently causes developers to discount the possibility of future landmark designation when designing a new building. Joseph Sax argues that '[w]e already have well-established systems for classifying and protecting historic structures, and it would be a rather small step to create a new category that designates distinguished, newer architectural masterworks, and offers them some protection.'[56] Sax then suggests that governments could adopt a range of regulatory options to protect new architectural triumphs.

Sax's proposal is no 'small step.' Restricting the alteration or destruction of new buildings could have enormously deleterious consequences with respect to developers' incentives to commission great architectural works. Such a developer would be locking in a particular parcel to its current use perpetually, without regard to changes in market conditions or social tastes. The developer also would need to invest substantial resources in ensuring that the architect selected the appropriate designs and building materials, because the local government could deter or even preclude functional or aesthetic changes at a later date.[57] Contemporaneous limitations on the destruction or modification of buildings also deny landmark commissions the hindsight and perspective that can be so useful in evaluating a building's merits. Simply put, the destruction or modification of a new building is usually supported by compelling circumstances. The prospect of immediate limitations on the right to destroy almost certainly would do more harm than good and substantially dampen builders' incentives to commission great works.

Whatever the economic consequences of immediate landmarking, Sax sees a moral basis for imposing such requirements on the owners of new buildings:

> [W]hile the patrons (or owners) of an important work of architecture were not obliged to engage with a masterwork, having done so they have by their own voluntary act potentially made the community *worse* off than it would have been if they had never acted. It is insufficient to say that the work would not have existed without their patronage. For they have diverted the time and effort of an artist from other work he might have done, and that – in other hands – might have been better protected . . . .[58]

According to Sax, the patron who decides to destroy a great building has wasted the architect's time and prevented him from working on other masterpieces that would have been preserved for generations.

Sax's argument ultimately is unconvincing. Great architects have strong economic and artistic motivations for seeing that their better works are preserved for future generations. Architects are thus good agents for the public. But there are things besides preservation that great architects are trying to maximize when negotiating projects with clients. Architects typically want clients who can offer substantial resources, high-profile building sites, favorable zoning environments, hands-off supervision, and many other perks. Renowned architects will select their projects based on a combination of all these factors, and there will be difficult tradeoffs among them. It therefore seems strange to impose preservation requirements on clients, without simultaneously mandating that clients fully fund architects' visions (and happily pay for unanticipated overruns), provide large building sites that maximize architects' flexibility, generously pay off neighbors and zoning board officials to ensure that their objections do not limit the architects' freedom of action, and so on.

Requiring the preservation of great buildings may ensure that some beautiful and potentially influential designs never get built. The 1893 Chicago World's Columbian Exposition provides perhaps the most famous example of an architect trading off permanence for other project attributes. The visionary architect Daniel Burnham oversaw the construction of glorious white buildings made of plaster of Paris and hemp fibers. The buildings were temporary structures, but they proved profoundly influential, helping to usher in a neoclassical revolution in architecture and providing a blueprint for the great Chicago civic structures that would be built in the decades that followed.[59] Had Burnham's 'Great White City' been built of anything sturdier, it never would have been as large, nor would it have been built as quickly, as cheaply, or as magnificently. Permanence is neither a necessary nor a sufficient condition for great architecture. There is a place in our landscape for gorgeous sandcastles.

In short, there can be a clear connection between property destruction and creation. When individuals and businesses destroy valuable property, they often do so for rational reasons. Denying owners the right to destroy property that becomes embarrassing, unfashionable, unproductive, or obsolete threatens the impulses that spur future creation.

B.   Destruction Via Will

The most prominent set of cases prompting concerns about waste involve efforts by landowners to destroy property via will.[60] The leading case, which articulates the approach courts most frequently follow,[61] is *Eyerman v. Mercantile Trust Co.*[62] The *Eyerman* court was called upon to decide whether a provision in the will of Louise Woodruff Johnston ought to be enforced. The will directed her executor to have Johnston's attractive house on St. Louis's Kingsbury Place razed, the land underneath it sold, and the proceeds from the land sale transferred to the residue of the estate.[63] Johnston's beneficiaries evidently did not object to the razing of the home, but the neighbors did, and one month after Johnston's death they convinced the city government to have Kingsbury Place declared a historic landmark.[64] The neighbors then sought injunctive relief to prevent Johnston's executor from razing the home, arguing, inter alia, that the destruction would depress property values in the neighborhood.[65]

The court held that the provision directing the executor to destroy the home was unenforceable on public policy grounds. In the court's words, 'Destruction of the house harms the neighbors, detrimentally affects the community, causes monetary loss in excess of $39,000.00 to the estate and is without benefit to the dead woman.'[66] Such destruction, the court held, was simply intolerable in a 'well-ordered society.'[67] While this waste of resources and damage to third parties cautioned against permitting Johnston's wishes to be carried out, the court saw no countervailing justification for respecting those wishes: 'No reason, good or bad, is suggested by the will or record for the eccentric condition.'[68] Seeing nothing but caprice in Johnston's instructions, the court refused to respect them.

American property law ordinarily deems the individual property owner to be in the best position to evaluate how her property should be used. Exceptions arise in two primary circumstances: (1) where certain uses will engender negative externalities, and (2) where the owner lacks the capacity to make a rational judgment about how the property should be used. Although the *Eyerman* court primarily focuses on the negative-externalities point in the destruction context, its characterization of Johnston's will as 'eccentric' and its emphasis on Johnston's failure to explain her motivations suggests that the second consideration was important there, too.

There is one justification for restricting the rights of people to destroy their property via will that emerges repeatedly in the literature and case law. As the *Eyerman* court put it:

> While living, a person may manage, use or dispose of his money or property with fewer restraints than a decedent by will. One is generally restrained from wasteful expenditure or

destructive inclinations by the natural desire to enjoy his property or to accumulate it during his lifetime. Such considerations however have not tempered the extravagance or eccentricity of the testamentary disposition here on which there is no check except the courts.

On this account, and the account of other judges,[69] we only defer to the person who is willing to put her money where her mouth is by destroying property while she might still live to enjoy it.

The court's analysis of posthumous destruction misses the mark. The *Eyerman* court is correct that upon her death Johnston had no incentive to preserve the house. But she did not draft her will on her deathbed. On some earlier date, when she did create her will, Johnston knew she wanted to spend the remainder of her life living in her home. She faced a choice about what to do with the remainder interest in her home. If she wanted, she could have retained a life estate in her home and sold the remainder interest to a third party for a substantial sum of money. She then could have used that money immediately to improve the quality of her life. If she wished to destroy the home, by contrast, she would have to forgo this present income from the sale of the remainder. So by forgoing a substantial amount of current income and retaining fee simple ownership over her home, Johnston did put her money where her mouth was. The closer Johnston got to death, the higher the value of the remainder interest she was forgoing, and the greater her current monetary sacrifice.

To be sure, the testator can always change her mind and alter the destructive provisions of her will. Because wills are revocable until death, one might argue that writing such a provision into a will entails no immediate sacrifice. But this tempting argument should be resisted. The testator does not know when she will die. Nor does she know that her efforts to amend the will at a subsequent date will be effective. They might not be, because of lack of capacity, bad legal advice, or judicial error. Executing a valid will, then, necessarily creates a risk that the testator will not be able to prevent the destruction, even if she might change her mind in the future. It is akin to lighting a fuse that is connected to a bomb, where the fuse has an indeterminate length. The person who lit the fuse can always try to extinguish the flame if he changes his mind, but there is a real chance he will be unable to do so before the bomb explodes.

A destructive will provision represents an immediate sacrifice in other respects as well. First, a savvy testator is well advised to use an attorney to amend a will, thereby generating legal costs for altering the status quo. Second, the persistence of a destructive will provision would deter transactional partners who are aware of its existence by creating legal complexity or uncertainty. For both these reasons, inserting a destructive provision into a will is immediately costly.

That cost will not always suffice to deter destructive intentions, and for some testators the cost will be trivial. For example, there will be circumstances where a property owner has little use for additional wealth. A dying property owner might liquidate future interests in order to pay for expensive medical intervention, a private hospital room, travel costs for old friends and relatives who wish to visit her one last time, and the like. But some wealthy individuals have more than enough money to cover even the most lavish end-of-life expenditures. In such cases, where the additional income to be gained from a sale of future interests in one's property is essentially superfluous, there would be a stronger case for limiting the owner's power to destroy that which is hers. If, however, the decision to destroy property is made by an owner who faces ordinary resource constraints or who does not anticipate her imminent demise, the case for deferring to those wishes is strong.

More serious problems arise if an individual destroys property either because he does not recognize the potential to obtain immediate income in exchange for the sale of a future interest or because he underestimates the value of a remainder interest in the property. Destruction in either case might well make society worse off. In the former case, the owner fails to realize that sparing the property might benefit both himself and society in general. In the latter case, the owner might falsely believe destruction to be the property's highest-value use.

III.   RATIONALIZING THE LAW OF ABANDONMENT AND DESTRUCTION

Having reviewed the motivations for abandonment and destruction, the different types of property that might be abandoned or destroyed, and the existing legal regimes governing abandonment and destruction in the United States, it is appropriate to ask how, if at all, the law might be improved.

A.   Abandonment and Destruction Compared

The common law requires that the party seeking to demonstrate abandonment of property establish two elements. First, the owner must have intended to relinquish all interests in the property, with no intention that it be acquired by any particular person. Second, there must be a voluntary act by the owner effectuating that intent.[70] If property is abandoned, then it belongs to the first person who subsequently takes control over it.[71] Although it is the second element that often looms large in abandonment litigation, the first is worth emphasizing for analytical purposes. True abandonment entails an individual relinquishing property to *no one in particular*. Abandonment thus provides a property owner with a low-cost way to 'roll the dice' as to the identity of the subsequent owner, and in this way it differs from virtually all other forms of uncompensated relinquishment, where the subsequent taker or class of takers will be identified with particularity. This 'roll of the dice' element is important, because it means that a great deal of what is commonly called 'abandonment' in the law actually is more akin to forfeiture.[72]

Insofar as it necessarily entails a roll of the dice, abandonment has something in common with most sales. A generally underappreciated attribute of an auction or other sale is that the seller typically rolls the dice as to the identity of the subsequent owner. Sellers are usually indifferent to the identities of subsequent owners because that indifference is likely to maximize the sale price. With abandonment, randomization of course must have some different function. An owner might prefer to randomize with respect to the identity of property's subsequent owner because of a desire to reduce decision costs. Seen in these terms, abandonment has significant social value as the way to gratuitously transfer property while minimizing these costs. Destruction will be less attractive, by contrast, from a decision costs perspective. Because destruction is irreversible, fear of feeling regret may cause the owner of a resource to spend a lot of time thinking about whether it should be destroyed.

The transaction costs savings associated with abandonment also can be significant. Suppose an owner has a positive market-value asset that he no longer wants. Consider the alternatives to abandonment. A sale will bring the owner revenue, but may also require the expenditure of time, money, and effort. If the market for a product is well-developed, then the owner will be drawn toward a sale. For that reason the rise of eBay probably resulted in a large decline in the prevalence of abandoned property.[73] But even in a nation of ubiquitous eBay access and scores of eBay drop centers, many owners still opt for abandonment via Craigslist or simply putting chattel property on the sidewalk. From this we can infer that the transaction costs of even eBay sales are not negligible. Sellers must compose an advertisement for the product, specify the auction's duration, communicate with the winning bidder about payment and shipping, arrange for shipping, and run the risk that the buyer will defraud them. A repeat player seller may well find it worth his while to lawyer up as well, so as to reduce the risk that he will be sued if buyers emerge from their transactions unhappy or if the property sold injures its purchaser. Destruction is similar to abandonment from the transaction costs perspective – if disposal is straightforward then an owner need not transact with anyone.

The transaction costs of gifts are not negligible either. In deciding upon a recipient for a gift, the donor must evaluate that donee's preferences and existing assets. No donor wants to be the resented gift giver who donates something that the recipient does not want but feels guilty discarding. Then, having decided upon a recipient, the donor must arrange for delivery, which again will entail the costs and inconvenience of a trip to the post office or across town to the recipient's home.

In short, both sales and gifts are bilateral transactions, and such transactions necessarily entail transaction costs. In some cases, the property to be transferred is sufficiently valuable that these transaction costs are easily overcome. But where the property in question does not have a particularly high value, and where the nature of the property raises the transaction costs of a sale or gift (e.g., a bulky item, like a refrigerator, or an item that cannot be sent via the mail readily, like a firearm), the likelihood that the owner will opt for a unilateral means of relinquishment increase.

The universe of unilateral means of relinquishment is limited to abandonment and destruction. Once we realize that, we develop a better understanding of the dangers of restricting abandonment too much. With respect to a positive market-value asset, society is generally better off if the owner opts for abandonment over destruction. Permitting destruction and forbidding abandonment of these assets would be folly. With respect to a negative market-value asset, the reverse is often true. Even this simple axiom, however, must be subject to a minor caveat concerning race costs and a major caveat concerning asset bundling.

Let us take up the minor caveat first. If abandonment of a positive value asset causes a large number of people to engage in violent jostling or other tortious behavior to be the first to retrieve the asset, then society suffers. Having said that, it is difficult to imagine a violent race being sparked by the abandonment of an asset that has insufficient market value to warrant a sale. It is conceivable, however, that with respect to valuable property where the expected disposal costs are low, the transaction costs of a bilateral transfer are high, and the expected risk of a violent race is high, destruction, rather than abandonment, is social welfare maximizing. Though these cases can be expected to be rare, this analysis suggests that society's openness toward abandonment ought to be a function of the baseline level of law-abiding behavior in society.

Now consider the major caveat. There are two kinds of negative value assets. The first is a resource with no intrinsic value, such as a rotting animal corpse, a spent battery, or a sound recording by William Hung. For these assets, society certainly prefers that the owner destroy the asset rather than abandoning it, which externalizes the disposal costs to society. The second is a resource that comes bundled with a liability that exceeds its positive intrinsic value. The paradigmatic example is a home worth $50,000 with tax liens against it totaling $75,000. Here, destruction of the underlying asset is the worst case scenario, because it eliminates a productive resource and imposes a $75,000 loss on the lienholder. Permissive abandonment – a rule that would allow the owner to walk away from the resource and the liability – is not as bad, because it preserves the intrinsically valuable asset while imposing the same loss on the lienholder, though it may well spark a violent race. The superior rule, however, is one that prohibits abandonment and requires the lien holder to foreclose on the property and force its sale. The lienholder can now auction off an unencumbered asset, presumably fetching a $50,000 return, resulting in a loss of only $25,000. Foreclosure thus dominates permissive abandonment because it forestalls the violent race and provides the lienholder with some security in the event of a default, which will have beneficial ex ante effects on a lienholder's propensity to extend credit.

There are other important considerations that bear on the question of whether the law should attempt to shift owners between abandonment and its alternatives. Abandonment is the method of intentionally relinquishing property that most frequently gives rise to confusion costs. This is a legitimate reason for curtailing the practice. Sales and gifts are rarely confusing, though it might not seem that way to law students and legal academics because cases involving ambiguity are a staple of law school casebooks.[74] There can be no confusion about the ownership of property that has been destroyed. But historically, when property has been abandoned, the result is ambiguity that imposes costs on the third parties who are charged with respecting in rem rights.[75] To push the point further, as the fraction of seemingly unpossessed property that is abandoned rises, the odds that lost or mislaid property will be returned to its rightful owner fall.[76] Finally, abandonment is more likely than sales and gifts to result in erroneous transfers of an asset from its highest value user. Whereas the negotiations involved in a sale and the communication typically associated with a gift provide a property owner with valuable information about how third parties assess the value of an asset, the unilateral nature of abandonment deprives the resource owner of this information, raising the likelihood of a mistake. Notably, however, abandonment dominates destruction on this score, because the latter is irrevocable and the former is not. If nobody claims property that an owner has abandoned, the prior owner is as entitled as anyone else to retake possession.

B.   An Informational Intervention in the Law of Abandonment

Positive market value properties present the most compelling case for a permissive rule regarding abandonment. In the case of such property, transfer represents a welfare improvement over maintaining the status quo. The thorny question is whether the law should restrict abandonment so as to privilege other forms of property transfer, such as sales or gifts. In order for policymakers to make an optimal decision about whether and when to permit the abandonment of a piece of positive market-value property they would need to know, at the very least, (a) the propensity of race participants to resort to illegal acts in order to capture that abandoned property, (b) the effects that the marginally increased prevalence of abandoned property would have on the propensity for finders to help reunify lost and mislaid property with its owners, (c) the likely time lag before someone will claim it, (d) the decay rate of the property in question, and (e) the magnitude of the transaction costs, decision costs, and warm glow associated with hypothetical bilateral transfers of the same property. To describe these as difficult empirical questions would be a vast understatement. They are essentially unsolvable. And whereas the property owner might be well-positioned to respond to private information about the factors (d) and (e), factors (a), (b), and (c) represent externalities that will have no bearing on the abandoning owner's decisionmaking. What is a common law court or an administrative agency in a licensing regime to do?

The sensible legal response is one that seeks to control most of the negative externalities associated with the abandonment of positive market value properties by supplementing the information that is available to members of the public. This can be done by encouraging an abandoning owner to (1) mark abandoned property as 'abandoned' and (2) advertise the availability of property on one of the many free Internet forums that have sprung up to alert consumers to the availability of 'free stuff.' These measures will reduce confusion and lag time costs. Optimally, this would be done through tax policy, giving abandoned property of this sort some of the same tax advantages that property donated to charity presently receives. Alternatively, the law might regard property abandonment that does not comport with steps 1 and 2 a misdemeanor, akin to littering, or it might enforce laws prohibiting the destruction of property. Owners wishing to rid themselves of property would still find that abandonment represents the lowest transaction cost option for doing so, especially if destruction is taken off the table.

Permitting abandonment, provided that adequate publicity is given to the abandoned property, will mitigate all the negative externalities associated with abandonment save one: race costs. If there is reason to believe that violent races are likely to occur, and will have large costs when they do occur, then requiring that abandonment be publicized will entail more races, with more participants, resulting in more violence. So what is the evidence on that score? It does not appear that violent races to capture abandoned property occur with much frequency, *Popov v. Hayashi* and Vegas strip clubs aside. Even if Americans have a high propensity to engage in violent races, it does not seem terribly plausible that the social costs from marginally more races would trump the reduction in lag time, decay costs, confusion costs, and the greater warm glow associated with higher rates of utilization of abandoned property.

Even if violent races would be frequent and costly in a legal regime that permitted publicized abandonment, those costs could be mitigated through property doctrine. The law might both require publicity via Craigslist or one of the other information clearinghouses that have emerged, and provide the first person who puts in an online claim to receive a time-limited window during which only she could lawfully take possession of the abandoned asset. Put another way, after I announced that I was abandoning a dining room set, the first person to note in a linked follow-up posting on Craigslist that she was putting in a claim would get an exclusive two hour window to take possession.

If she failed to take possession within that timeframe, the dining room set would be up for grabs once again. Although such a regime would slightly increase lag time costs, it would substantially curtail violent races, so such a doctrinal tweak would make sense in high violence environments.

C. Informational Interventions in the Law of Destruction

Whatever one thinks about the right of a living person to destroy her property, it is harder, instinctively, to develop sympathy for the owner who wishes to destroy her property via will. The interests of the dead generally do not count in a utilitarian calculus, except insofar as individuals worry about what happens to them after they die and take actions during life to safeguard their graves, legacies, or descendants' welfare.

In explaining the law's uneasiness with will provisions directing the destruction of property, scholars have noted the potential for people affected by destruction to persuade the living owner to reconsider. Adam Hirsch makes the argument succinctly:

> Living persons face the . . . social repercussions of their actions; dead persons do not. One consequence is that a testator can, if she is so inclined, wash her hands of her dependents, without suffering the opprobrium that a living person would bear for such behavior. Death spares the testator from interpersonal costs.[77]

Hirsch thus argues that a testamentary destroyer avoids having to witness the consequences of her actions to her heirs and immunizes herself against the social retaliation that might follow.

Judge Posner offers a related explanation for courts' resistance to testamentary destruction. If the destroyer is alive at the time of the destructive act, affected neighbors or kin might be able to persuade her to alter her course. The person who destroys her property via will, on the other hand, is no longer susceptible to such persuasion.[78] Someone who has written a destructive provision into her will can keep her intentions secret, precluding third parties from trying to persuade her to preserve her property. Courts construing destructive wills have been troubled by the prospect that a testator might have changed her mind if only she had known certain facts not available at the time.[79]

Hirsch's and Posner's arguments are not without force. But it is hard to establish definitively which way they cut. Assuming that testators care about their reputations after death, we might be particularly worried when a court refuses to honor a person's wishes at a time when she no longer can respond. A court deciding whether to enforce a destructive will provision would have to do so without the benefit of the owner's testimony regarding her motivations. This happened in *Eyerman*. Such hearings are one-sided affairs where no party advocates the decedent's expressed interests or explains her motivations. By contrast, the possibilities for judicial error will be lower during the homeowner's lifetime, when the destroyer and those opposed to the destruction both have an opportunity to explain their positions and critique each other's arguments in open court.

Even setting aside this point, Posner and Hirsch both suppose that (1) a living donor's destruction of property will be noticed by those who would prefer that the property be preserved, and (2) a living donor who destroys property will be susceptible to persuasion or social sanction. It is not clear that both presumptions would hold true in most of the property-destruction cases where valuable resources are at stake.

First, chattel property usually can be destroyed surreptitiously by a living owner. There is little reason to think that owners generally will consult third parties before electing to destroy the chattels in question. Indeed, to the extent that living people care about their reputations after death, directing the destruction of a chattel via will probably attracts more attention than destroying it during life. Because posthumous chattel destruction must be spelled out in a will, one anticipates that some testators who believe their heirs will object to this destruction will be deterred from putting destructive instructions in their wills. To them, surreptitious destruction during life will be the preferred route – heirs might never learn about what they had lost.

Second, in many instances the living owner of destroyed property will not stick around long enough to be ostracized. Take the paradigmatic home-destruction case of *Eyerman*. By attempting to destroy the home via her will, Johnston indeed escaped the social ostracism of her neighbors. But had she destroyed the home during her lifetime, said destruction would have required Johnston to move elsewhere, where she may have escaped her neighbors' disapproval. Since it appears that Johnston's relatives, the would-be beneficiaries, did not object to the home's razing,[80] it is not clear that she would have suffered serious social repercussions in the wake of the destruction. Presumably, the primary opportunity for norm enforcement would have arisen during the window of time necessary to obtain a demolition permit.

Still, persistent concerns that the dead have 'nothing to lose' by destroying property make courts reluctant to permit testamentary destruction. To be sure, a sophisticated living testator demonstrates her seriousness of purpose by forgoing the present income that could result from the sale of a future interest in the property. At the same time, some people may destroy their property because they do not realize that they have the opportunity to retain a life interest in it and sell the remainder for present cash, or because they underestimate the amount of money that a remainder interest will fetch. Finally, some percentage of those who attempt to destroy property are incapable of making rational judgments.

In short, there are some instances where respecting destructive will provisions is welfare enhancing and other instances where it is not. Is the appropriate legal response a strict anti-destruction rule? Hardly. An owner's exercise of any property right – the right to exclude, the right to mortgage, or the right to sell – can diminish social welfare in certain circumstances. But the law does not respond to this possibility by eliminating the property right in question. Rather, the law recognizes the persistence of the right but imposes limitations on how it can be exercised.[81] This raises the following question: Is there a legal rule that can help courts distinguish between the types of posthumous destruction that ought to be permitted and those that ought to be prohibited? Namely, we want a rule that addresses our concerns about: testators underestimating the value of the future interest in property slated for destruction; testators using the will process to dodge efforts to persuade them to preserve valuable property; would-be owners never learning about the existence of property until after it has been destroyed; and testators lacking testamentary capacity.

Property law can respond to all these concerns through a rather simple requirement: destructive instructions contained in wills shall be honored only if the owner, during his lifetime, notified the public of the opportunity to purchase a future interest in the property. For example, a testator interested in destroying his home would earn the right to do so by auctioning off a remainder interest following his life estate, or by negotiating with a reverse mortgage company over the purchase of such an interest. In the case of an auction, the testator would establish a minimum reserve price, which could be kept secret by the testator, and if no bid exceeded the reserve price, the testator would not be obliged to sell. If the owner's reserve price was exceeded by a bidder or the government decided to condemn the future interest, then the property would be spared from destruction. But if no bid exceeded the would-be destroyer's minimum asking price, then the owner would have demonstrated that he valued destruction of the property more than anyone else valued its preservation. Turning down the highest bid for a future interest would give owners safe harbor to destroy their property via will.

Note that this policy lever addresses all the concerns that have prompted the divergent legal treatment of testamentary and inter vivos destruction. From a welfarist perspective, where the owner of property has forgone a market price for the property's future interest, he has earned the right to consume that future interest by destroying the property. Moreover, the policy would substantially lower the transaction costs associated with monitoring living people's decisions to destroy property. Marketing future interests in the property would alert community members and heirs apparent to the owner's intentions while they were still in a position to influence him to change his mind.[82]

A major advantage of this approach is that it would facilitate the condemnation of property that might benefit the community more generally. By acquiring a future interest, the government would be paying less than the full market value for the property in fee simple, while simultaneously ensuring that the property would be spared from destruction. Posthumous condemnation in right-to-destroy cases necessarily thwarts the wishes of the testator without conferring any meaningful benefit on him. Condemnation during the testator's lifetime thwarts his wishes too, but it at least provides him with money that he can enjoy during the rest of his life.

Finally, the process of marketing a future interest in anticipation of one's death will require that the testator have some sophistication and a capacity to plan for the future. One imagines, therefore, that those lacking testamentary capacity rarely will be able to jump through the appropriate hoops. And while legal counsel can be expected to facilitate this process, the decision to consult counsel regarding such intentions seems, independently, to offer some evidence of the testator's capacity. By conditioning testamentary destruction on some efforts during life to alienate a future interest, the law can ensure that the would-be destroyer was not ignorant of the opportunity to convert a future interest into present value.

For all these reasons, the law should harmonize its treatment of inter vivos and posthumous destruction in cases where the posthumous destroyer has marketed the future interest in the property and elected to forgo the full market value of this future interest. Such a rule will make all testamentary destroyers behave like sophisticated market actors and enable them to weigh the costs and benefits of property destruction.

Although at first glance destruction and abandonment would appear to have only a little bit in common, that turns out not to be the case upon close reflection. Not only does the unilateral nature of abandonment and destruction entail important similarities, but the law dealing with both property rights has the same lacuna. Welfare-reducing destruction typically arises when an owner underestimates the market value of a resource. Welfare-reducing abandonment generally occurs when an owner overestimates the demand for a resource and thinks he is engaging in a charitable act or when potential claimants are not made aware of the availability of a desirable resource quickly enough. In both instances, optimal legal doctrines would ensure that these information asymmetries are corrected. But instead of pursuing that objective, insufficiently imaginative courts develop prohibitions on abandonment and destruction that may prevent some welfare-reducing acts of destruction and abandonment but surely prevent a good many welfare-enhancing uses of property as well.

D.   Treating Land Differently

Land's indestructibility entails an absence of case law regarding the right to destroy it. Not so for abandonment. The abandonment of chattel property is generally permitted, but the abandonment of corporeal interests in real property is flatly prohibited. The doctrine looks to the nature of the property rather than its value. It is worth asking whether there is anything about land that justifies its disparate treatment.

Land differs from chattel property in three relevant respects: (a) it is immobile, (b) it cannot be destroyed; and (c) a sophisticated recording system is already in place for land throughout the United States.[83] Real property's immobility eliminates the possibility that it will be lost or mislaid, which reduces the significance of confusion costs in the policy-making calculus. Real property's indestructibility reduces the damage associated with the decay of a resource.[84] The presence of a recording system means that there already exists, and long has existed, a low-tech version of Craigslist, which might function as an effective clearinghouse for information about abandoned property, thereby reducing confusion and lag-time costs. In short, the unique attributes of land suggest that the problems created by abandonment are *more significant* in the context of chattels than they are in the context of real property. On this reasoning, the rule regarding the abandonment of real property should be at least as permissive as the rule regarding chattel property.

Alas, there are two complicating factors. First, if abandoned real property has a higher propensity than abandoned chattel property to have negative value, then the common law rule might make sense. Put another way, the real versus chattel property distinction on its own would not make sense, but the law would be justified because real property is a good proxy for negative value in the abandonment context. Unfortunately, reliable data about the proportions of abandoned real and chattel property that have negative value is in short supply.

Second, we must consider the relationship between adverse possession law and the law of abandonment. Adverse possession may function as a substitute for abandonment, though it is an awkward one. Permissive entry will not ripen into adverse possession.[85] What the thwarted abandoner therefore must do is either incur the transaction and decision costs associated with a sale or gift to a willing recipient, or engage in an elaborate kabuki performance with a trespasser, whereby the abandoner pretends that he objects to the trespasser's entry. This latter approach will not be attractive to a real property owner, precisely because adverse possession takes so long – typically six to ten years – for title to transfer.[86] This lag creates a great deal of uncertainty for the would-be-transferor, who may see a trespasser work the land for five years, only to move elsewhere, likely requiring the would-be-transferor to start from scratch.

Given that abandonment would be far more attractive than adverse possession for a land owner who wishes to lose his interest in land, what could possibly explain why the law might prohibit the abandonment of land but permit its transfer via adverse possession? To put the point even more persuasively, we might ask why the law would favor consensual transfers of land masquerading as nonconsensual transfers of land over genuinely consensual transfers of land? There is no persuasive answer to this question. The conventional response would be that adverse possession ensures that someone who values the property is using it at all times. But this response fails once we recognize that a trespasser will hesitate to improve another's land with gusto in the period before the statute of limitations runs and that abandonment law can have a role in reducing the consequences of lag time by requiring that the owner advertise his act of abandonment. Indeed, it is striking to compare the very sensible law of chattel property, which makes transfer via adverse possession rather difficult[87] and transfer via abandonment easy, to the bizarre law of real property, where the reverse is true.

Assuming real property that is abandoned is not overwhelmingly characterized by negative value, the common law rule embraced in *Pocono Springs* and numerous similar common law cases should be overruled. With respect to positive market value property, the law should permit abandonment of corporeal interests, requiring only that the owner record a notice of abandonment, so that all parties interested in the land will learn of its availability, and the claimant records his interest in the land, so third parties and government taxing authorities are informed of the title transfer. With respect to negative market value property, the same considerations relevant in the chattel context have enough force to warrant similar treatment for real and chattel property. An owner seeking to abandon land should be able to do so upon paying off liens or improving the property sufficiently to give it positive market value.[88] An owner should not be forced to find a seller to take the property off his hands in order to be rid of it, in light of the substantial transaction costs associated with land sales.

CONCLUSION

There has not been much sustained attention given to the issue of property's abandonment, and until recently the same has been true of property's destruction. This review of the law, economics, and sociology of abandonment and destruction suggests that this lack of attention has resulted in the generally lackluster content of property law with respect to these subjects. In particular, two essential distinctions that are well embedded in the common law ought to be eliminated: the divergent legal treatment of abandoned chattels and real property, and the divergent treatment of inter vivos and testamentary destruction. A careful analysis reveals that while there may be some reasons to treat the abandonment of real property differently, land's abandonment should not be prohibited categorically, and the same is true of testamentary destruction. Rather, the law of abandonment should focus on the economic value of the asset that is slated for abandonment and the steps the owner takes to make third parties aware of the opportunity to claim it. Similarly, the law of destruction should highlight the question of whether the owner of property took steps, during life, to demonstrate that he valued its destruction more than third parties valued its preservation. In short, many of the negative externalities associated with abandonment or destruction stem from information costs, and the law should intervene in the spirit of reducing information asymmetries, not reducing the owner's freedom to use his property as he sees fit.

NOTES

*   The author thanks Ben Foster for energetic research assistance, and the Morton C. Seeley Fund and John M. Olin Foundation for research support. This chapter draws heavily on Lior Jacob Strahilevitz, *The Right to Destroy*, 114 Yale L.J. 781 (2005), and Lior Jacob Strahilevitz, *The Right to Abandon*, 158 U. Pa. L. Rev. 355 (2010).
1.   *See* http://Chicago.craigslist.org/zip/ (visited Aug. 14, 2008).
2.   *See* http://Chicago.craigslist.org/chc/zip/795812089.html (visited Aug. 14, 2008).
3.   *See, e.g.*, Laura Bauer, *Property Giveaway, Trying to Halt the Population Slide: Towns Tout Free Land to Lure New Residents*, Kansas City Star, Jan. 29, 2007, at A1; www.kansasfreeland.com/ (visited Aug. 15, 2008).
4.   Benjamin P. Scafidi et al., *An Economic Analysis of Housing Abandonment*, 7 J. Housing Econ. 287, 288 (1998).
5.   Popov v. Hayashi, No. 400545, 2002 WL 31833731, at *3 (Cal. Super. Ct. Dec. 18, 2002).
6.   *See* http://Chicago.craigslist.org/nwc/zip/795820052.html (visited Aug. 14, 2008).
7.   Bradley Gerrard, *Town Cashes in as Hot Pennies Rain Down on a Money-Mad Crowd*, Express & Echo (Exeter, UK), July 23, 2008, at 3.
8.   Tom Knott, *Blath Following Pro Athlete Tradition*, Wash. Times, June 6, 2008, at C1.
9.   Norm Clark, *Waxworks Visitors Casts Vote Early*, Las Vegas Rev. J., Nov. 12, 2006, at 4A, available in 2006 WL 19743500; Paul Hayward, *A Fight for Survival?*, Daily Mail, June 23, 2007, at 115, available in 2007 WLNR 11869796.
10.   Greg Moore, *The Mash-Up: Live in a Fantasy This Week in Video Games, This Week in Sports, Pop Culture Mash-ups*, K.C. Star, Feb. 25, 2007, at C15. There is some dispute as to whether Jones was throwing the money at exotic dancers, abandoning it generally, or just tossing it in the air with the hopes of reclaiming it. He was arrested after allegedly striking a dancer who was grabbing some of the bills.
11.   Popov, 2002 WL 31833731, at *3.
12.   *See, e.g.*, Armory v. Delamirie, 93 Eng. Rep. 664 (K.B.1722); Ganter v. Kapiloff, 69 Md.App. 97, 103 (1986).
13.   McAvoy v. Medina, 11 Allen 548, 549 (Mass. 1866).
14.   *See* Scafidi et al., *supra* note 4, at 288; Note, *A Nuisance Law Approach to the Problem of Housing Abandonment*, 85 Yale L.J. 1130, 1132–33 (1967).
15.   *See* Popov, 2002 WL 31833731, at *6. In the *Popov* case, where the baseball in question was valuable enough to be claimed by someone in short order, and it was likely going to be found located in a finite space, there was no need to have 20,000 fans in position to track down the ball.
16.   *See supra* text accompanying note 10.
17.   *See infra* text accompanying notes 27–29.
18.   There are other types of legal regimes governing abandonment, including escheat regimes (whereby the state takes title to abandoned property), licensing regimes (whereby a state agency gets to decide when to permit abandonment), and encouragement regimes (whereby the law promotes property abandonment). For a lengthier discussion of these regimes, see Lior Jacob Strahilevitz, *The Right to Abandon* (working paper 2009).
19.   *See* Right Reason Publications v. Silva, 691 N.E.2d 1347, 1351 (Ind. App. 1998).
20.   *See* Long v. Dilling Mech. Contractors, 705 N.E.2d 1022 (Ind. App. 1999); *but see* Sharpe v. Turley, 191 S.W.3d 362, 367 (Tex. App. 2006).
21.   *See, e.g.*, Al. St. Ann. §S 13A-11-14 & 13A-11-240 (requires unnecessary or unjustifiable pain to result); Ariz. Stat. Ann. § 13-2910; Ark. Stat. Ann. § 5-62-101 (requires knowing abandonment); Cal. Penal Code § 597.1(a) (animal abandonment is a misdemeanor); Col. Rev. Stat. Ann. § 18-9-202 (intentional abandonment of cat or dog or knowing abandonment of another animal is a misdemeanor).
22.   There is some similarity here to laws that provide parents with the opportunity to abandon babies at fire stations and other designated places without fear of criminal liability. *See, e.g.*, Eric Eckholm, *Law's Effect: An Iowa Girl is Abandoned in Nebraska*, N.Y. Times, Oct. 9, 2008, at A15.
23.   667 A.2d 233 (Pa. 1995).
24.   Fender v. Heirs at Law of Smashum, 581 S.E.2d 853, 856 (S.C. App. 2003); James C. Roberton, *Recent Development – Abandonment of Mineral Rights*, 21 Stan. L. Rev. 1227, 1228 (1969).
25.   *See infra* note section III.A.

26. Roberton, *supra* note 24, at 1228 n. 13.
27. Uma Lele et al., Brazil Forests in the Balance: Challenges of Conservation with Development 19 (2000).
28. Roberton, *supra* note 24, at 1228 n. 13; Angus Lindsay Wright & Wendy Wolford: To Inherit the Earth: The Landless Movement and the Struggle for a New Brazil 271 (2003).
29. The example suggested in the text may be more simplistic than the real world environment. In Brazil, it is evidently the case that some deforestation results from squatters clearing land so as to obtain informal property rights to it. *See* Lele et al., *supra* note 27, at 34; Andrea Cattaneo & Nu Nu San, *The Forest for the Trees: The Effects of Macroeconomic Factors on Deforestation in Brazil and Indonesia*, in Cheryl A. Palm et al. (eds), Slash-and-Burn Agriculture: The Search for Alternatives 170, 183–85, 192 (2005).
30. *See* Meksras Estate, 63 Pa. D. & C.2d 371, 373 (C.P. Phila. County 1974).
31. *See* Eyerman v. Mercantile Trust Co., 524 S.W.2d 210, 217 (Mo. Ct. App. 1975).
32. *See* J.C. & Assocs. v. D.C. Bd. of Appeals & Review, 778 A.2d 296, 308–09 (D.C. 2001).
33. 978 F.2d 1269, 1279–80 (D.C. Cir. 1992). Years after the D.C. Circuit's remand, I worked on this case for the Nixon estate, researching issues relating to just compensation for his presidential papers.
34. *Id.* at 1282–84.
35. *Id.* at 1279.
36. *Id.* at 1279–80.
37. President Fillmore willed his presidential papers to his son, and the son's will directed that all the presidential papers be destroyed. *Id.* at 1291. President Harding's widow destroyed many of his papers following Harding's death. *Id.* at 1294.
38. Jonathan Turley, *Presidential Papers and Popular Government: The Convergence of Constitutional and Property Theory in Claims of Ownership and Control of Presidential Records*, 88 Cornell L. Rev. 651, 660 (2003).
39. *Nixon*, 978 F.2d at 1282–83 (internal quotation marks omitted).
40. Joseph L. Sax, Playing Darts with a Rembrandt: Public and Private Rights in Cultural Treasures 94–95 (1999).
41. Turley, *supra* note 38, at 718, 731.
42. 44 U.S.C. §§ 2201–07 (2000).
43. *Id.* § 2202.
44. *Id.* § 2203(c).
45. 'Personal records,' which are documents that do not concern the President's official duties, are excluded from the Act, and can be destroyed by the President. *Id.* § 2201(2)(B)(ii), (3).
46. 44 U.S.C. § 2203(c), (e). Executive Order 13,233, 3 C.F.R. 815 (2002), issued by President George W. Bush, strengthens the hand of the President vis-à-vis the Archivist if the President wishes to restrict access to certain papers. Turley, *supra* note 38, at 671–76. Notably, the Executive Order does not restore the President's traditional power to destroy presidential papers. *Id.* at 687.
47. Nixon v. United States, 978 F.2d 1269, 1280 (D.C. Cir. 1992) (quoting William Howard Taft, Our Chief Magistrate and His Powers 34 (1916)).
48. *See, e.g.*, Kalorama Heights Ltd. P'ship v. D.C. Dep't of Consumer & Regulatory Affairs, 655 A.2d 865, 869 (D.C. 1995); *see also* Susan Rose-Ackerman, *Inalienability and the Theory of Property Rights*, 85 Colum. L. Rev. 931, 954 (1985) (noting that the New York City landmarks law 'only rarely allows demolition' of historic buildings).
49. *See* Georgette C. Poindexter, *Light, Air, or Manhattanization?: Communal Aesthetics in Zoning Central City Real Estate Development*, 78 B.U. L. Rev. 445, 500 (1998).
50. 171 N.E.2d 246, 247–48 (Ill. App. Ct. 1960).
51. 778 A.2d 296, 298, 299–300 (D.C. 2001). The District presented evidence to suggest that the building was salvageable. *Id.* at 300.
52. *See, e.g.*, Mendes Hershman, *Critical Legal Issues in Historic Preservation*, 12 Urb. Law. 19, 28 (1980).
53. William A. Fischel, *Lead Us Not into Penn Station: Takings, Historic Preservation, and Rent Control*, 6 Fordham Envtl. L.J. 749, 754 (1995).
54. *See* Gregory A. Ashe, *Reflecting the Best of Our Aspirations: Protecting Modern and Post-Modern Architecture*, 15 Cardozo Arts & Ent. L.J. 69, 71 (1997) (discussing the thirty-year time lag required under New York City's historic preservation law); Angela C. Carmella, *Landmark Preservation of Church Property*, 34 Cath. Law. 41, 43 (1991) (noting that the minimum age required for a building to be landmarked can range from twenty-five to seventy-five years).
55. Richard A. Posner, Economic Analysis of Law 67 (5th ed. 1998).
56. Sax, *supra* note 40, at 199.
57. During the 1980s, several new skyscrapers clad in Carrara marble had to be resurfaced because the marble unexpectedly failed in cold-weather conditions and had the potential to fall off the buildings. Michael Arndt, *Amoco Tower's Fate May Be Carved in Stone*, Chi. Trib., May 22, 1988, §7 at 4. Most famously,

Chicago's 1,136-foot Amoco Building (now Aon Center) had its marble replaced with granite seventeen years after its construction, at a cost of $60 to $80 million. Lindsey Tanner, *Amoco Caught Between Rock, Hard Place*, WASH. POST, Mar. 31, 1990, at E16.

58. SAX, *supra* note 40, at 58.
59. DONALD L. MILLER, CITY OF THE CENTURY: THE EPIC OF CHICAGO AND THE MAKING OF AMERICA 380–85 (1996).
60. See, e.g., In re Estate of Jones, 389 A.2d 436 (N.H. 1978) (construing a will, unpersuasively, so as to defeat testator's directions that buildings be razed as a condition of property's devise to forest conservation group); In re Estate of Beck, 676 N.Y.S.2d 838 (Sur. Ct. 1998) (honoring a destructive will provision, where testator and city had contracted, during life, for the building's demolition); In re Will of Pace, 400 N.Y.S.2d 488 (Sur. Ct. 1977) (refusing to honor a destructive will provision); National City Bank v. Case Western Res. Univ., 369 N.E.2d 814 (Ohio Ct. Com. Pl. 1976) (honoring a destructive will provision where testator had indicated that she wanted her home destroyed to prevent its reuse as a boarding house or commercial establishment); In re Wishart, 129 N.B.R.2d 397 (1992) (prohibiting the destruction of the testator's horses via will).
61. Richard A. Posner, Economic Analysis of Law 559 (5th ed. 1998).
62. 524 S.W.2d 210 (Mo. Ct. App. 1975).
63. *Eyerman*, 524 S.W.2d at 211–12.
64. *Id.* at 219. The applicable landmark law evidently did not bar owners from destroying their landmarked property.
65. *Id.* at 211, 213 (majority opinion).
66. *Id.* at 214.
67. *Id.* at 217.
68. *Id.* at 214.
69. *See* In re Will of Pace, 400 N.Y.S.2d 488, 492 (Sur. Ct. 1977).
70. *See, e.g.*, Campbell v. Cochran, 416 A.2d 211, 221 (Del. Sup. Ct. 1980); Griffis v. Davidson County Metro. Govt., 164 S.W.3d 267 (Tenn. 2005).
71. Haslem v. Lockwood, 37 Conn. 500 (1871).
72. Bright v. Gineste, 284 P. 2d 839, 842–43 (Cal. App. 1955).
73. *See generally* David Lucking-Reiley, *Pennies from eBay: The Determinants of Price in Online Auctions*, 55 J. Indus. Econ. 223 (2007) (discussing the mechanics of auctions on eBay).
74. *See, e.g.*, Gruen v. Gruen, 496 N.E.2d 869 (N.Y., 1986) (ambiguity in a famous gifts case); Newman v. Bost, 29 S.E. 848 (N.C. 1898) (ambiguity in another famous gifts case); *cf.* Raffles v. Wichelhaus, 2 Hurlstone & Coltman 906 (1864) (ambiguity in a famous contracts case).
75. *Cf.* Thomas W. Merrill & Henry E. Smith, *Optimal Standardization In The Law Of Property: The Numerus Clausus Principle*, 110 Yale L.J. 1 (2000).
76. Finders of lost and mislaid property do not become its owners. Rather, they have duties to return the property to its true owner, a prior possessor, or, in some cases, the owner of the land on which the property was found. Finders of abandoned property have no such duty.
77. Adam J. Hirsch, *Bequests for Purposes: A Unified Theory*, 56 Wash. & Lee. L. Rev. 33, 72–73 (1999).
78. POSNER, *supra* note 55, at 558–59.
79. *See* Nat'l City Bank v. Case W. Reserve Univ., 369 N.E.2d 814, 818–19 (Ohio Ct. Com. Pl. 1976); *In re* Capers Estate, 34 Pa. D. & C.2d 121, 129 (C.P. Allegheny County 1964).
80. *See* Eyerman v. Mercantile Trust Co., 524 S.W.2d 210, 218 (Mo. Ct. App. 1975) (Clemens, J., dissenting) ('By its decision, the court officiously confers a 'benefit' upon testamentary beneficiaries who have never litigated or protested against the razing.').
81. *See, e.g.*, State v. Shack, 277 A.2d 369 (N.J. 1971) (limiting exercises of a landowner's right to exclude legal aid and health care workers from his land, based on the competing rights of the migrant workers who worked and lived on the property); Folgueras v. Hassle, 331 F.Supp. 615, 624 (W.D. Mich. 1971) (adopting, on similar facts, *Shack*'s reasoning as the correct interpretation of Michigan trespass law); State v. Decoster, 653 A.2d 891, 894 n. 3, 896 (Me. 1995) (citing *Shack* and *Folgueras* with approval in a state civil rights act case involving a landowner's attempt to exclude third parties who wish to visit employees residing on the landowners' property); 67 Md. Op. Atty. Gen. 4 (1982), at *2('Based on our review of the law, we find the New Jersey Supreme Court's approach in *State v. Shack* to be particularly sound, an approach that, we believe, Maryland courts are likely to follow in achieving a fair accommodation of these competing rights and interests.') (citation omitted).
82. A company in the reverse mortgage industry similarly would have an incentive to alert neighbors and interested government officials to the possibility of destruction so as to gauge the fair market value of the remainder interest.
83. Douglas Baird & Thomas Jackson, *Information, Uncertainty, and the Transfer of Property*, 13 J. Legal Stud. 299, 309–10 (1984) (noting the first and third of these attributes).

84. Note that this is true for land but not for buildings or other improvements.
85. RICHARD R. POWELL, POWELL ON REAL PROPERTY, 95.01[5][a] (Michael Allan Wolf ed., rev. vol. 2008) (noting that use consistent with the true owner's use cannot be sufficiently hostile to be adverse possession).
86. JESSE DUKEMINIER ET AL., PROPERTY 115 (6th ed. 2006).
87. *See* O'Keefe v. Snyder, 416 A.2d 862 (N.J. 1980) (holding that adverse possession of chattels should be displaced by the discovery rule, which dictates that the statute of limitations start running only when the true owner reasonably knows or should know the whereabouts of the property and the identity of its possessor); Guggenheim Found. v. Lubell, 569 N.E.2d 426 (N.Y. 1991) (holding that the statute of limitations does not run until the true owner demands return of chattel property and a good faith purchaser refuses to hand it over).
88. If the landowner in question is the party that polluted it, abandoning the property would not relieve the polluter of the legal liabilities resulting from that pollution. *See* Ronald G. Aronovsky, *Federalism and CERCLA: Rethinking the Role of Federal Law in Private Cleanup Cost Disputes*, 33 Ecology L.Q. 1, 12–13 (2006) (describing CERCLA as a congressional response to the proof, causation, and statute of limitations problems that often thwarted common law nuisance claims for contamination).

7   Standardization in property law
*Henry E. Smith**

I.   INTRODUCTION

One of the most striking features of property law is that it is far more standardized than contract law. The main purpose of contract is to serve the parties' joint objectives, and the law allows contracting parties a great deal of leeway to customize their agreements. By contrast, property law starts with the need to establish a basic set of entitlements. Aside from the very hypothetical world of some political philosophers, the members of society never got together and consented to the various claims people made to particular resources. Instead, the law provides a framework for establishing, transferring, and enforcing basic claims to resources. In doing so the law allows only a finite set of defined basic types of property right. In civil law systems this mandatory standardization is termed the '*numerus clausus*', which means 'closed number' of property forms. In common law countries, especially the United States, standardization is more of an implicit feature of the property system, and is correspondingly weaker. Nonetheless, all post-feudal property systems standardize, more or less, the basic building blocks of the property system. The question is Why? If particular parties find that some other form of property would serve their purposes better why shouldn't they be allowed to craft what they want? Why is property law so different from contract law in this respect?

   This puzzle has called forth a number of explanations that are less than satisfying.[1] One is that the *numerus clausus* is an example of outmoded formalism of one sort or another. Some would see it as a vestige of feudalism even though in its modern form the *numerus clausus* was an instrument of *eliminating* feudalism:[2] in the name of standardization, reformers abolished the feudal incidents and local customs of the feudal past.[3] Others see the *numerus clausus* as a vestige of the nineteenth century, but its persistence and pervasiveness belie this dismissal.[4] Yet others might see it as a vestige of pre-legal-realist (pre-1930s) formalism, but the same charge has been leveled against earlier versions of the law of contract and torts. Nonetheless, property has been much more resistant to realist-inspired contextualized decisionmaking, despite a large amount of scholarship suggesting the loosening of the standardized aspect of property.[5] Indeed many from across the spectrum of economic approaches see the *numerus clausus* as largely irrelevant as long as one can achieve one's objectives by contract, and these objectives can be communicated to others via registries (at least in the case of land).[6] Finally, some see the *numerus clausus* as a device to prevent excessive fragmentation of property.[7] While it is true that fragmentation can be a problem, the *numerus clausus* does little to prevent it. What the *numerus clausus* does is limit the *types* of fragmentation – not its amount. Thus one can divide a fee simple into a life estate and a remainder and into various other sets of pieces, and this limitation is the essence of the *numerus clausus*. But the *numerus clausus* does *not* limit the number of co-owners or the number of times that one subdivides across time – think of a life estate followed by a remainder in life estate followed by a remainder in life estate . . . followed by a remainder (in fee simple). No limit on fragmentation there.

These attempts to explain – or to dismiss – the *numerus clausus* overlook how the *numerus clausus* reflects a basic problem of information costs faced by any property system.[8] The traditional definition of property is a right to a thing good against the world – it is an in rem right. The special in rem character of property will form the basis of an information-cost explanation of the *numerus clausus* and standardization in property.[9] In rem rights are directed at a wide and indefinite audience of dutyholders and other affected parties, who would incur high information costs in dealing with idiosyncratic property rights and would have to process more types of information than in the absence of the *numerus clausus*. Crucially, parties who might create such idiosyncratic property rights are not guaranteed to take such third party processing costs into account. There is thus an information cost externality, and the *numerus clausus* is one tool for addressing this externality. Other devices include title records and technological changes in communication.

By contrast the 'modern' view espoused by legal scholars and economists alike is that property is a bundle of rights (or, more metaphorically a 'bundle of sticks') and that each stick governs a relationship between persons.[10] This can be a useful analytical device, but it is no accident that property governs a wide range of impersonal relationships and resource uses, without making direct reference to the identity of persons or uses. I know to keep off Blackacre or not to steal a car from a parking lot without needing to know what the land or the car is being used for, how virtuous the owner is – or who (or what) the owner is. Nor need courts delve into these matters. The things defined by the basic exclusion strategy mediate the relation between often anonymous parties.

Part II will set out briefly how the *numerus clausus* works and in what ways property is standardized. In particular, the external simplicity of the basic building blocks of property allows them to combine in flexible ways. Because of this modular structure, the standardization of property gives rise to smaller frustration costs than might appear at first. Part III picks up on these observations to present an explanation of the *numerus clausus* based on the informational externalities to remote third parties. This externality is more serious with in rem rights, directed as they are at remote parties, than with in personam contracts. A simple model is presented to show that the existence and relative size of the externality follows from some minimal assumptions about the goals of contract and property respectively. Some further implications of this information-cost theory are taken up in Part IV, where I show that the information-cost theory helps explain the relation of standardization to title registries, the problem of running of servitudes, the role of custom, and complexity externalities in financial engineering. Part V concludes.

II.   STANDARD FEATURES IN PROPERTY

The law prescribes a much greater degree of standardization for property than for contract. Those aspects of property that implicate third parties most – the in rem aspects of property rights – are subject to limitations on the basic types and to various notice-giving devices like registries. Because the basic set of types can combine in generative ways, a very limited menu of property forms can accomplish most purposes for which in rem rights are employed.

A.   Standardization through the *Numerus Clausus* Principle

Although the law standardizes property in many ways, standardization in property starts with the defined and closed number of basic ways of owning resources, a principle known as the *numerus clausus*. This term is borrowed from civil law, which is much more explicit about the standardization of property than is the common law, and American law in particular.[11]

In the common law, the *numerus clausus* is closely identified with the 'catalog of estates.' The catalog is largest for interests in land. (There is a similar, though possibly simpler and smaller, catalog of interests in personal property.) The largest interest is a fee simple absolute (or full ownership, in personal property). The basic fee simple (and other interests) can be carved up in a limited number of ways.[12] One can break the fee simple into an interest that lasts for the life of a natural person – called a life estate – followed by a reversion or a remainder (of various subvarieties). Or one can break the fee simple absolute into a fee simple that can end upon a specified event (for example 'to A as long as the premises are used for hospital purposes, then to B'). These so-called defeasible fees – fee simple determinable, fee simple subject to condition subsequent, and fee simple absolute subject to executory limitation – are followed, respectively, by the possibility of reverter, the right of entry, and the executory interest. In addition to these freehold estates, there are the leasehold interests – the term of years, the tenancy at will, and the periodic tenancy.[13]

The catalog of present estates and future interests is the most dramatic example of the *numerus clausus* and standardization in property. Some other legal dimensions are standardized in a similar fashion. There is a list of only two or three forms of direct co-ownership: the tenancy in common, the joint tenancy (with right of survivorship), and (in some places) the tenancy by the entirety (for married couples only).[14] So the present and future interests discussed earlier can be held in these co-ownership forms. For example, A and B might hold an executory interest in Blackacre as co-tenants or joint tenants. Co-ownership forms are limited, but the number of co-owners is not limited. Theoretically, 100 persons could co-own an asset.

One reason that forms of direct co-ownership can be few and simple is that parties have a great deal of freedom to customize their relations among themselves and creditors by using *organizational forms* like the partnership, the corporation, and the trust (to which I return in the next section). These forms might be termed 'entity property,'[15] and while not completely customizable, they offer an increasing amount of flexibility (especially with the addition of new forms like the limited liability partnership). Interestingly, the most standardized aspect of entity property arises where organizations govern in rem relations, which is consistent with the information-cost theory of the *numerus clausus*.[16]

Nonpossessory interests are also standardized in that American property law recognizes four basic forms: easements, covenants, equitable servitudes, and profits. As we will see, English law imposed even greater standardization on servitudes, because land records furnished less of a substitute method of reducing information costs.

Other legal dimensions are standardized as well. For example, leasehold interests can be transferred in assignments or subleases.[17] An assignment is roughly speaking an outright transfer taking the first tenant mostly out of the picture, whereas a sublease transfers something less than this and leaves the primary tenant primarily liable to the landlord. The distinction between an assignment and a sublease matters in terms of who owes duties to whom (especially the duty to pay rent), and one can imagine that people might want some customized collection of such rights and duties. Although the landlord, the prime tenant, and the assignee or subtenant can contract for new relations, transfers of existing leasehold interests by a tenant will be taken to fit into one of the two boxes provided by the law – assignment and sublease. As is often the case where the *numerus clausus* operates, courts may speak of searching for the parties' intent, but here the relevant intent is which of the prescribed boxes most closely approximates what the parties were trying to achieve.[18] This is a far cry from the customizability of contract.

More generally, the *numerus clausus* and standardization in property law are relevant at the edges of contract law itself. Contract rights can sometimes be transferred. This possibility might be thought to contradict any distinction between contract and property. But appearances are deceiving. When contract rights are transferred they are packaged as property such that their internal detail matters less to the transfer.[19] Indeed the law of *choses in action* (literally making a 'thing' out of a contract) imposes standardization on the property packaging that a contract wears when it implicates remote parties. In other words, contract rights are mostly owned in one basic property form: full ownership. Contract rights can be retained or (sometimes) transferred, but we don't have future interests in contracts. For more complex transfers and carving up of contract rights, one needs to use a trust, which, as we will see, allows complexity to be managed though a specialized modular structure.

More generally, the law has the effect of reducing information costs to third parties who encounter contract rights. First, in the tort of interference with contract, the third party to be liable must know of the contract and does not have a duty to inquire whether a potential contracting partner would have to breach another contract.[20] Second, tortfeasors need not inquire into contractual relations because only property rights are protected under the pure economic loss doctrine. For example, if A damages a boat owned by B and rented to C, A is liable to B for the market value of the damage but not for C's particular lost profits. Liability as between B and C is not relevant to A. The property right in B is a module within which the interdependencies between B and C are information that is hidden. A and B interact through the property interface only.[21] Finally, contract interpretation itself seems to be more formalistic – in the sense of relying relatively less on context, especially idiosyncrasies supplied by the parties – when questions of third party beneficiaries arise.[22]

More seriously constraining is the application of the *numerus clausus* to restraints on alienation. The leading English case on what we would call the *numerus clausus* is *Keppell v. Bailey.*[23] In that case parties were not permitted to enforce contractual restrictions on the use of property – there a requirement to purchase all limestone for the works from a particular quarry and to ship the limestone on a particular railroad – as property rights in the hands of successors. (Equity courts stepped in and cabined this flat-out rule against enforcing covenants against successors, as long as they had notice.[24] I return to the role of equity and its consistency and complementarity with the *numerus clausus* below.)

What is particularly interesting is that the Chancellor in *Keppell* voices an objection to idiosyncratic forms of property that foreshadows the explanation given by Merrill and me in previous work, and elaborated upon below. The Chancellor expressed the concern about what have come to be known as 'fancies':

> There can be no harm to allowing the fullest latitude to men in binding themselves and their representatives, that is, their assets real and personal, to answer in damages for breach of their obligations. This tends to no mischief, and is a reasonable liberty to bestow; but great detriment would arise and much confusion of rights if parties were allowed to invent new modes of holding and enjoying real property, and to impress upon their lands and tenements a peculiar character, which should follow them into all hands, however remote. Every close, every messuage, might thus be held in several fashion; and it would hardly be possible to know what rights the acquisition of any parcel conferred, or what obligations it imposed.[25]

The problem with 'fancies' (the term is a take off on this passage) is that other people will be confused. The concern with fancies forms the germ of the information-cost explanation of the *numerus clausus*.

B. The Flexibility of Standardized Modular Building Blocks

One might think that a list of some ten basic interests would be too constraining, but if anything the list is too long. We could probably make do with one defeasible fee (and allow tailoring within the basic type), or possibly even one generic present and one generic future interest.[26] Why is such a short list enough to serve the multifarious objectives of parties?

Two answers suggest themselves, and dovetail with the information-cost theory discussed below. First, the property forms in the *numerus clausus* are not the end of the story: they are building blocks from which complexes of rights can be created. Crucially they have the property of *recursiveness*: the interests can nest within themselves, as where a life estate is followed by a remainder in life estate followed by a remainder in life estate . . . followed by a remainder (in fee simple). Generally a small set of rules (as small as one rule) can generate an infinite set of outputs if one of the rules is recursive (i.e. it can apply to its own output, or, in other words, the rule feeds itself).[27] This is true of natural language, where a finite grammar can capture the infinite set of sentences of a language like English, because some rules, such as the rule that forms subordinate clauses, can be repeatedly used on itself: Pat said that Chris believed that the cat is sick.[28] The set of property forms has a Lego-like interface with each other that allows the generation of complex structure out of a small set of simple parts. In this, property forms are like a basic grammar or 'pattern language' of property.[29]

Modularity is the key to managing complexity in this as in many other situations. A system is complex when it has many interdependencies. In a nonmodular system any change to any element can in principle impact another element directly, or through any path however long. This pattern of dense interdependencies makes such systems either unpredictable, if changed, or excessively rigid, in order to avoid unpredictable change from these ripple effects. A partially decomposable system allows chunks or components of the system to be partially walled off and the interconnections between these chunks and the rest of the system are deliberately limited (sometimes even at the expense of interdependencies that might have some value).[30] Interactions and interdependencies can be intense within such modules but are defined and relatively sparse across the interface with other modules. The key is that the interface allows only certain information though; the rest is 'hidden' in the module.

Consider some examples of modularity from organizations.[31] A simple pre-modern example would be a team of smiths making an iron pothook for a team of cooks. Within each team, the members interact intensively on the production process. But the smith-cook system is nearly decomposable into a smith-module and a cook-module. At the interface, the design specifications of the pothook (strength, resistance to heat, size, shape) travel from cooks to smiths (along with payment) and the pothook travels in the reverse direction. All the other details of the production process are relevant only within the smith module, and the details of how the hook is used in cooking food are relevant only with the cook-module. Activities in each module can take place independently, as long as the interface conditions – notably the design parameters of the pothook – are respected. An innovation within one team-module can take place without worrying about ripple effects on the other team. To take a more recent and more complex example, the production of a laptop with a disk drive involves multiple teams that interact much more intensively than the smiths and cooks. Nevertheless, modularity can play some role in creating options for flexible actions within teams in this more complex setting. Because the interaction across interfaces is more intense, interfaces may require more elaborate transactions and even formal contracts to govern potential opportunistic behavior. Modularity is a key design principle in many areas and is important in evolutionary theory, cognitive science, computer hardware and software, as well as all sorts of engineering and architecture.

Modularity plays a key role in making the standardization of property possible. Property rights can be standardized because they combine recursively, and because of modularity these interconnections can be very few, thus allowing much of what goes on inside a package of property rights not to be relevant to the outside world. As we will see, property rights 'mesh' with neighboring property rights and show network effects with more far flung property rights. The outside interfaces make this possible at reasonable cost.

The second reason why a short list of allowed property forms is not seriously constraining in terms of party objectives is that much can be accomplished in trust – and in fact is.[32] The settlor, who sets up the trust by designating a set of assets as the trust corpus (or res), can engage in many types of complicated carving up of interests as long as they are beneficial interests. The trust presents a relatively simple face to the world (in rem) and is, with a few exceptions for parties with notice, governed by the legal ownership of the trustee. The beneficial interest can be more complicated but the complications are mostly relevant within the trust (in personam) to the beneficiary, the trustee, and the settlor. Trusts are like simple property on the outside, and a potentially idiosyncratic third-party beneficiary contract on the inside.[33] From the outside, people who do not want to deal with the complexity of the trust can avoid assets designated as being held in trust. Thus, the trust itself serves as a modular structure that hides idiosyncratic information and presents a relatively simple interface to the outside world. And for those third parties who would have the hardest time dealing with trust-internal complexity – say tortfeasors – the trust is largely irrelevant.

C.   Intermediate Situations

Property is further characterized by a number of other mandatorily simple rules. The pattern of standardization is no accident. The most basic aspects of property are the ones most likely to be parsed by distant and impersonal audiences. (Don't trespass; don't steal.) This pattern of standardization is highly consistent with the basic architecture of property as well.[34] Property delineation strategies range from exclusion to governance. An exclusion strategy defines a thing and uses rough proxies to announce a rule of keep off. Trespass to land is the paradigmatic example. By contrast, a governance strategy focuses in on given uses and prescribes proper behavior with respect to the resource. Governance rules are more tailored and context-specific. Often they are directed to a smaller more defined group of dutyholders. Thus in nuisance, the governance regime holds between neighbors. In covenants, the right holder and dutyholder are defined by the contract. (And covenants only run, i.e. bind successors in interest, if certain more standardizing requirements like touch and concern are met.) Zoning too is more fine-grained than a basic exclusion regime. Thus those aspects of property that are aimed at the widest and most impersonal audience tend to be the most standardized and we allow greater information intensiveness as we move out from this core to the refinements that are relevant to more defined subgroups.

More generally, situations between the fully in rem and the in personam present themselves, and a preliminary inquiry reveals that the degree of mandatoriness and formalism applying in these intermediate situations falls between the degree of standardization characteristic of the *numerus clausus* on the one hand and the customizability of core contract law on the other. As Merrill and I have shown elsewhere, in rem rights avail against many parties and those dutyholders tend to be anonymous or indefinite.[35] But rights can avail against dutyholders that have only one of these properties: the class dutyholders may be large but definite, as in mass contracts, or the dutyholders may be indefinite but not numerous, as with successors in interest. And each of the features – numerosity and indefiniteness – falls along a spectrum. Information costs rise as we increase numerosity and indefiniteness. In situations falling between in personam and in rem we tend to find intermediate levels of mandatoriness and standardization. These intermediate approaches usually take the form of protective strategies, which make certain forms difficult or prohibitive where we fear the dutyholders will not understand the content of the legal relation at reasonable cost. The implied warranty of habitability in landlord and tenant law, in which minimum standards (usually drawn from a local housing code) are read as a warranty into leases, protects the tenants as purchasers of housing services.[36] This interpretation of the implied warranty of habitability (IWH) makes it a close cousin of consumer protection law. Other protective strategies exempt the potential dutyholder from an obligation to inquire. Thus, tortfeasors must respect property rights but have no duty to inquire into the contractual arrangements surrounding property that the tortfeasor might damage (an example would be a rented car). The other class of intermediate strategies also is reminiscent of consumer protection law: rules mandating the giving of notice. So for example, equitable estates in trusts, which as we have seen are mostly in personam (against the trustee), often cannot be enforced against third parties unless notice of the beneficial interest is given.

D.   Judicial and Other Institutional Approaches to Standardization

The *numerus clausus* has implications for institutional choice. In the first instance the *numerus clausus* is a norm of judicial forbearance from innovating – or allowing parties to innovate – in the basic set of property forms. Change in the menu of forms is left largely to legislatures.[37] But because the *numerus clausus* is largely an unspoken design principle in American law, courts have given it impressive but less than complete adherence.

When parties veer from the closed list of forms, courts in keeping with the *numerus clausus* will force the parties' choice into one of the set of pigeonholes provided by the law. Because, as we have seen, the list of prescribed forms in the *numerus clausus* is a flexible set of basic building blocks, parties usually do not need to deviate from the approved list in order to meet their objectives. So cases raising the *numerus clausus* directly tend to involve oddities or poor drafting. A recurring problem is leases 'for the duration of the war.' The law provides for tenancies at will, periodic tenancies, terms of years (and perhaps tenancies at sufferance). Courts faced with a lease for the duration of war or a lease for life will usually enforce it as a periodic tenancy, which automatically renews after a given period, or a tenancy at will, which can be unilaterally terminated by either party at any time.[38] A few courts have modified the terms of years to count an event like the ending of the war as determinate enough for the term of years.[39] This is consistent with the *numerus clausus* (although a stretch) because it redefines the pigeonhole 'term of years' rather than simply enforcing the lease as written without regard to its place on the *numerus clausus* list. Or a court might recast the lease (in effect redraft it) in order to achieve the same objective but within the confines of the *numerus clausus*. So for example a lease for the duration of the war could be reformulated as a lease to end in 50 (or 99, or 999) years or the 'end of the war' whichever comes sooner. This would count as a term of years under the usual definition and the parties could have chosen it themselves. The only difference between this and a lease for the duration of the war on its own terms comes from wars lasting longer than 50 years (or 99 or 999, as the case may be).[40]

Interestingly, the semi-recognition of the *numerus clausus* (not by that name) in American law has led to some confusion at the margins. Most of the time the *numerus clausus* operates as an unstated constraint on creating new forms, with the occasional nod to the 'fixed' catalog of estates. The leading case, if there is one, is *Johnson v. Whiton*,[41] in which Justice Holmes interpreted a will as an attempt to create a new kind of inheritance, in essence a new fee tail-like estate, which he disallowed. Because the testator's goals and the will were both of unclear import, the case is not as crisp an example as one might wish for.[42] Because of the unstated aspect of the *numerus clausus* in traditional common law, courts sometimes fail to recognize when it should apply. Thus, in an atypical but casebook-friendly case, *Garner v. Gerrish*,[43] Judge Wachtler comes perilously close to recognizing a lease for life. Most courts enforce this as a tenancy at will or a periodic tenancy.[44] The New York Court of Appeals in *Garner* basically enforces the lease as a life estate (which is certainly on the *numerus clausus* list of forms) but implies in dictum that it is a lease too.[45] Fortunately for the court, questions like whether landlord/tenant protections (e.g. the implied warranty of habitability) would apply were not presented and one can only guess how those questions would be resolved. The problem is that when a principle has no name it is easier to ignore or to dismiss as a relic of feudalism (again with more than a little irony).[46] This makes having a theory of what the *numerus clausus* does all the more important, not least because a more explicit awareness of the *numerus clausus* and its purposes in lowering information costs might itself serve to reduce information costs.

Even if courts do respect the *numerus clausus* and refrain from innovating in the area of basic property forms, the closed list of property forms in the *numerus clausus* is not fixed for all time. Instead the *numerus clausus* directs courts to avoid innovation in the basic forms of property and to leave such changes to legislatures.[47] When removing or adding or changing property forms, the legislature has advantages over courts in terms of announcing the change and making the adjustments necessary, such as creating new replacement forms. To take one example, legislation abolishing dower and curtesy in the nineteenth century also introduced the spouse's elective forced share in compensation.[48]

Although property is a common-law subject, innovation by courts in the inventory of property rights has been rare. Probably the area with the most judicial innovation – and thus the loosest version of the *numerus clausus* – is what might be termed 'non-core' intellectual property. The main forms of intellectual property – copyright, patent, trademarks, and trade secret – are a closed set. Moreover, creating new copyright-like or patent-like rights at the state level would be preempted by the federal copyright and patent statutes, either statutorily or directly under the U.S. Constitution. The Supreme Court has gone quite far in striking down specific laws as preempted by copyright or patent.[49]

But state courts have innovated more in areas like the right of publicity.[50] Under pressure from private litigants, especially in celebrity-heavy jurisdictions like California and Tennessee, some courts pushed the right of publicity, which allows people to control their public images for commercial purposes, from its origins in the privacy torts towards a more thing-based entitlement. The tendency has been for the right of publicity to survive the person's death and to pass by will or intestacy. Statutes have played an important role in the development of the right of publicity, but in this area of non-core intellectual property courts have innovated more than they usually do when it comes to basic property forms. Otherwise legislatures have overwhelmingly taken the lead in modifying the list of property forms under the *numerus clausus*, especially considering that property is a common-law subject.

Another non-core intellectual property area that has formed a battle ground in the *numerus clausus* (if not under that heading) is the tort of misappropriation. Misappropriation had at one time the potential to provide a legal right to reap where one sows, and the closest it came to this broad application was in the famous case of *International News Service v. The Associated Press*.[51] In that case, the Supreme Court held that the tort of misappropriation could protect a news organization against a competitor that used its news stories while they still had value as hot news. The Court was concerned with freeriding and the disincentive to collect news. In dissent Justice Brandeis pointed out the expansive nature of this approach,[52] and later cases, especially in opinions by Second Circuit judge Learned Hand, cabined reap-where-you-sow misappropriation to hot news.[53] So one might say that courts added a property right in hot news to the *numerus clausus*, but skepticism, based in part on concerns sounding in information costs, has limited its scope and prevented *INS* from becoming a generator of new property rights. But a close look at the majority opinion in *INS* also reveals an implicit concern with information costs in property: even the majority was quite careful to call the right against misappropriation a quasi-property right, availing only against competitors and not an in rem right good against people generally. (Discussing a news story around the water cooler would not violate the quasi-property right.) Even though the majority in *INS* was sympathetic to arguments sounding in the reap-where-one-sows principle, even the majority was uncomfortable with vindicating it through the mechanism of a fully in rem property right.

Moreover, *INS* was itself an equity case, which the Court was at great pains to point out, repeatedly.[54] Equity was in theory cabined off jurisdictionally and substantively from presenting the full-blown information costs of in rem rights. The tort of misappropriation has its origins partly in equity, which was at one time administered in a parallel court system. Equity focused more on individualized justice and fixing the defects of the common law. Nevertheless both jurisdictionally and substantively equity courts were encouraged to exercise this authority in ways that can be viewed as minimizing information costs. In theory equity would act only in personam, not in rem, thus limiting the direct impact of equitable decisions to parties.[55] In general, third parties would not need to know about the equities of a situation unless at the very least the third party had notice. And one substantive rule of thumb directed equity courts not to alter property rights, i.e. in rem rights that present the largest third-party information costs.[56]

III. STANDARDIZATION AND THIRD-PARTY INFORMATION COSTS

This Part will introduce an information-cost theory of the *numerus clausus* and show how the information costs presented by property follow from very general principles of communication.[57] At the outset, it is important to recognize what we mean by information costs. Information can be costly, in terms of efforts at gathering it, and this is an important category of information costs. But information costs also extend to the costs of processing information. If a piece of information is not readily usable (data dump) or is in an unfamiliar format, users need to incur more costs in dealing with the information. Most generally, as Herbert Simon pointed out long ago, information is not scarce but human attention is.[58] The more we build bounded rationality into our models, the more importance the scarcity of mental resources will take on.

Property and contract are used by different kinds of parties. At its core, property is an in rem right, which means that it avails against all others. This in rem aspect causes given property rights to be informationally relevant for a wider audience than are typical contract rights. Standardization is one response to third-party information costs, in addition to publicity devices such as registries. Information costs would not be a problem if they were fully borne by those causing them. But to some classes of actors, the information costs of idiosyncratic rights are partially externalized. In particular, parties creating property rights may find idiosyncrasy beneficial to themselves but they will bear only a fraction of the information costs. Furthermore those creating rights will often be in a better position to avoid information costs than the nonconsensual dutyholders who are expected to respect rights or who wish to acquire other rights. Because property rights are in rem they are broadcast to more than the parties – they bind everyone, including successors and potential violators. By introducing a new type of right – and the

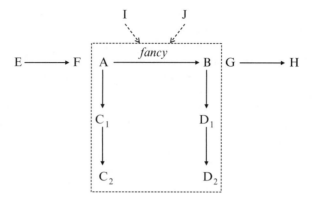

Figure 7.1   The classes of affected parties

possibility of new types along as yet un-thought-of dimensions – they increase what other unrelated parties must be on the look out for.

A.   Third-Party Information Costs

The problem of third-party information costs in property is an example of a communicative tradeoff in law and language more generally. At the same cost one can communicate in an information intense way with a small defined audience or in a more stripped down way with a larger more indefinite audience.[59] Information intensiveness can be thought of as the density of information: the amount of information conveyed per unit of communication cost. In natural language one can communicate in a more compressed way when the audience shares a lot of background knowledge. Stating 'It's cold in here' is a way of asking someone near a window to close it. But if the person lacks the background knowledge (the social conventions and knowledge of windows), the speaker would need to give far more explicit – and lengthier – instructions. In general, language is more formal the less its interpretation varies by context, and usually achieving this effect of formalism requires more effort (and usually more length). Thus formalism – and standardization – are called for when the audience of dutyholders and enforcers cannot be expected to share a lot of background knowledge about context.

The communicative tradeoff in the case of in rem property rights involves several kinds of audiences. This can be illustrated with Figure 7.1 on the extended privity relationship: What is the externality when someone creates an idiosyncratic property right? Consider a hypothetical in which 100 people own watches and can buy and sell them.[60] What if A sells B a time share in a watch, say a 'Monday only' watch and retains the rest of the days of the week? This affects the parties to the transaction, A and B. It also affects those they might turn around and sell to – their successors in interest – and those people's successors in interest and so on – the Cs and Ds. But if the market mechanism of capitalization is working then the bad effects of the idiosyncrasy on the Cs and Ds should affect the price in the hands of their predecessors all the way back to A and B. If so (and that is an if), then there is no externality from A and B's point of view. Things change, though, when we consider the other parties in the diagram. Other people transacting in other watches now have more to be on the lookout for.[61] They will have to figure out whether they are getting all the days of the week for the watches they are buying, and other sellers will have more convincing to do. But the externality does not stop there. In the absence of a *numerus clausus* principle, the other watch owners will have to be on the lookout for *as yet unimagined* dimensions of idiosyncrasy – there is in principle nothing to stop people from coming up with other strange property rights in watches – like a right to use a watch only on even days, or a watch that is associated with an unusual remedy (like half damages on even days and double damages on odd days).

Finally, there will be those who interact with watches in a nonconsensual way, those who might damage a watch, or enter a parcel in the case of land (Is and Js). Property law keeps things simple: when interacting with cars in the parking lot, I need not know very much. Interestingly, it is the simplest and most standardized parts of property that are relevant to potential violators. The law of trespass is most relevant to potential entrants, and it sends a simple message of keep off.[62] Somewhat more detailed is the law of nuisance, but this governance strategy is directed at neighboring landowners. Even more clearly directed at in personam dutyholders are covenants and easements, until they apply to successors, in which case they implicate somewhat more remote parties.

Moreover, complexity raises another externality problem. Idiosyncratic rights may not mesh well with each other. Consider water rights.[63] Because of the nature of the resource, exclusion is difficult, and much of water law is a governance regime. Riparianism, based as it is on reasonable use of a common resource, is a classic governance regime. But even prior appropriation, which at first blush allows the assertion of property rights in water, is more of a governance regime than is conventionally thought; the rights are delimited (and often measured) in terms of use, and prior appropriation allows downstream appropriators to make claims to return flow. This may make sense from a static point of view, but because of the context-specificity of the water right it is harder to transfer. If the nature of the interlock were allowed to be nonstandard the water right would be even harder to transfer because it would be even more tethered to a specific context.

The meshing of property rights is related to their alienability. Many property rights do not need to 'mesh' beyond the information costs of those trying to discover their legal attributes. If I own a table my use of it does not interact with others' use of tables. Property used in consumption with network effects is different: televisions and telephones need to have standardized interfaces with the rest of the system.[64] In property, the rights and duties of neighboring parcels do interlock and that is why the 'interface' between the packages of rights of neighboring landowners is more complex than in personal property. Water law is an extreme example of interdependency. Governance regimes fill out these more complex interfaces. But the cost of a complex interface is reduced alienability. And it is under the heading of alienability that property law manages some of the non-meshing externalities we are now considering. Idiosyncratic covenants would make personal property hard to divorce from its context and port as a module to a new context. Even in real property where the land does not move, moving a parcel to a new use will be more difficult the richer the interface is between the parcel and its surroundings. A rich interface is inevitable, but one must trade off the complexity of the interface to handle conventional externalities (noise, odor, etc.) on the one hand and the simplicity to avoid the problems of potential conflict especially in the face of changing conditions and desired uses on the other.

An analogy to money is helpful. It is surprisingly difficult to explain the use of money because other goods with other features might provide a unit of account and store of value. And invocations of 'liquidity services' are inherently vague. But interestingly, an information-cost theory of money helps explain what we might mean by liquidity services.[65] By coinciding on one standard good (especially one that is itself easy to measure) with standardization, it becomes worthwhile to break a single transaction (say wheat for oil) into two transactions (wheat for money and money or oil).[66] The whole point of money is its negotiability: one need not inquire into its history.[67] Thus a good faith holder can get good title to cash, even from a thief. But in this respect money is an extreme example of what the *numerus clausus* does to property: it modularizes by hiding information and presenting an extremely simple and easy-to-measure face to the world, thereby providing liquidity.

B.   A Simple Model

The externality in the *numerus clausus* stems from information costs associated with idiosyncratic property rights that are not fully borne by the creators of those rights. The size of this externality depends on the type of the recipient of information. This problem is an example of audience design,[68] and in this Part I will present a model in which the *numerus clausus* is a solution to an inherent tradeoff in all communication.

As mentioned earlier, communication to socially closer audiences can rely more on background knowledge. In particular, messages can be compressed because it is not as costly for such audiences to 'fill in the blanks.' Consider again the example of someone asking someone else to close a window by saying 'It's cold in here.' Sociolinguists have demonstrated that communication tends to be more formal in the sense of relatively invariant to context when the audience is socially closer.[69] This can be measured by the occurrence of pronouns over nouns, because the former require more context for their interpretation (most notably in figuring out the antecedent). One aspect of formalism is that information must be spread out over a more explicit message. Information is quantifiable, as is the cost or length of a message.[70] Thus in more impersonal settings, the information rate (information per unit of communication cost) or intensiveness is lower than in more close-knit social contexts. Thus, audiences that are more socially distant, more numerous, more indefinite can be lumped together and called more 'extensive', and it is for such audiences that we expect communication to be less intensive: the message is spelled out such that information is spread out with respect to communication cost. Thus, at the same cost one can communicate intensively with a less extensive audience or less intensively with a more extensive audience.

Before turning to the model, note that in personam and in rem legal relations are a special case of extensiveness of the audience. In personam parties are few and definite, whereas in rem parties are more numerous and more indefinite. According to the communicative tradeoff, we should prefer communication to be more intensive in in personam contexts and less so in in rem contexts. And most of the time this is likely to be true, without any special effort. As in human language communication, of which this is merely a special case, most of the time people will adjust for the nature of their audience. But in the case of in rem rights communicators will trade off wholly internalized benefits from idiosyncrasy and compressed communication against only part of the costs to audiences. The problem is that people will not adjust enough to the extensive audience. Most of the time this is not a problem, although in certain high stakes situations, like air traffic

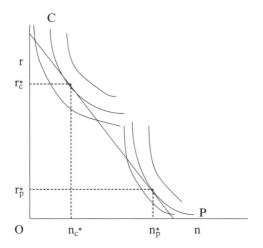

Notes:
n = audience size
r = information rate
C = isobenefit for contract
P = isobenefit for property

Figure 7.2   The communicative trade-off

control and oil tankers, we do mandate standardized ways of communicating because we worry that extensive audiences may be misled.[71] Likewise in consumer protection a mandatory format is sometimes mandated.

We can analyze the tradeoffs in the in personam versus in rem situations using a simple isocost model. If one holds the costs of producing and receiving a message about legal relations constant, a communicator, for example one deciding how to divide property rights, then trades off the intensiveness of the communication with the extensiveness of the set of contexts into which the communication can fit. What about the benefit side? In Figure 7.2, we place the information rate (r) on the y axis and the extensiveness of the audience (n) on the x axis. (Remote audiences are one of the many types of contexts that the information must reach, and in a more general model we might build an index of remoteness of all the contexts.[72]) The isocosts reflect a budget to be allocated between average information rate (intensiveness) and the compatibility with context (here extensiveness of the audience). Points along the line connecting the two axes in Figure 7.2 all represent different combinations of information rate and extensiveness of the audience that are equally costly. We focus on one isocost but additional isocost lines to the northeast in the Figure, not drawn here, would involve a greater level of cost. On any isocost line, the actor communicating can spell things out more (be more formal), which will cause the rate of information per unit of communication cost to decrease. Ideally, as one increases the extensiveness of the audience one would be more formal (lower r) or increase the amount of cost incurred (move to an isocost to the northeast). In the model we assume that the optimal amount of communication cost to incur has already been determined given the parties' objectives. The question is the allocation of the cost: for the same cost, one can communicate at a high information rate to an in personam audience (high r, low n), or at a low information rate (formally) with an in rem audience (low r, high n), and combinations in between.[73]

In personam and in rem differ on the benefit side as well. On the benefit side, different combinations of intensiveness and extensiveness will present different levels of benefits depending on the goals one is seeking to achieve. Contract and property in particular are different in terms of their goals. In a contract, it is essential that the parties understand and act on their rights and duties, but the arrangement is of limited relevance to third parties, other than enforcers (and occasionally third-party beneficiaries, assignees, tortious interferers, and the like).[74] (As we have seen, the law engages in a mild form of modularization for the non-party actors in the contract situation.) By contrast, in property we have a wide rage of affected parties, including successors, other transactors, and potential violators. Thus in property, communicating information, at a given cost, will produce different value with respect to the level of extensiveness of the audience. In property, many in the set of dutyholders can contribute most to the owner's plan by simply keeping off. For those parties, more than minimal information ('keep off') does not have much incremental value.

This more complicated picture on the benefit side is reflected in the different isobenefit curves for largely in personam contract versus largely in rem property (or at least their prototypical versions, with intermediate cases not being shown here). Isobenefit curve C (mnemonic for contract) and those parallel to it reflect high benefits from communicating a lot to a few and rapidly diminishing returns to additions to the audience.[75] By contrast, the isobenefit curve P (mnemonic for property) and those parallel to it, reflect great benefits from communicating a little (low r) to a wide audience but diminishing returns to more information per unit of delineation effort.[76] So again we are comparing the benefits available for investment of given levels of communication cost, and because of different goals, a given level of benefit is distributed differently in the contract and the property situation. So for example, the lowest of the drawn curves represents a given level of benefits, but the C-version and the P-version reflect the faster tradeoff of benefits of intensiveness with greater extensiveness in the case of contract than in the case of property, and vice versa. Again, the fence or the no trespassing sign will work much of the time. As property requires more elaborate interfaces, as between neighboring landowners, the isobenefit curve would stretch from looking like P to looking more like C. Likewise, as contracts become more mass produced and in particular where they rely on modular and very standardized components like boilerplate, the isobenefit will likewise shift from being like C in the direction of P.[77] Because the concern here is with the *numerus clausus* and the in personam versus in rem distinction, I will concentrate on the extreme cases.

In either situation, the optimal mix of intensiveness and extensiveness is found where the budget line is tangent to the highest of the isobenefit curves it intersects with. In the core contract-like case, this tangency point is at point $(n_c{}^*, r_c{}^*)$, where curve C is tangent to the isocost. So the in personam right will involve intensive information directed at few people. In the case of the core property-like case with the isobenefit curve P, the tangency point is at $(n_p{}^*, r_p{}^*)$, and the in rem right will be characterized by less intensive but more extensive information (directed at a wider, more indefinite audience).

This model does allow us to derive a prediction about the relative sizes of the externality in the two situations, in personam contract versus in rem property. Externalities emerge on the extensive margin, precisely because the more distant and impersonal the

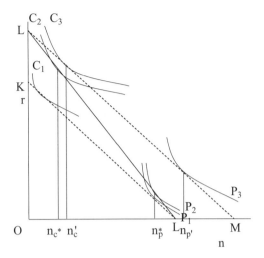

Notes:
n = audience size
r = information rate
C_1, C_2, C_3 = isobenefit curves for contract
P_1, P_2, P_3 = isobenefit curves for property

Figure 7.3   The divergent communicative trade-off

audience, the less their activities matter directly to the one creating the right.[78] People will take into account the benefits and costs of communication to those they deal with, but potential audiences that are more distant – especially those not in privity with the communicator – will incur processing costs that, in the absence of legal intervention, would not be brought home to the communicator. Transactors might for example find idiosyncrasies in the remedy for violation of a property right as between themselves to be worthwhile, but the employment of such idiosyncratic remedies against trespassers or those committing nuisances could come as a surprise. Likewise, idiosyncrasies in the division and transfer of a particular instance of property may open up new dimensions of investigation in unrelated transactions (e.g. the Wednesday-only watch), especially if transactors are unconstrained as to the format for the information. As we will see, land records are not a data dump, and systems in which records are more definitive tend to exhibit a more stringent standardization of property forms.[79] Simple forms like 'fee simple' do not reduce information costs if someone can use these words to mean something else or can defeat expectations associated with familiar forms in a cryptic fashion. In this respect, property forms are a lot like weights and money, which are subject to similar efforts at standardization.[80]

Because property is directed at the widest audience, it is most subject to informational externalities and is the most appropriate area for a mandatory rule like the *numerus clausus* that keeps the information rate down to manageable levels for remote audiences.[81] Extensiveness is a stand-in for several sorts of social distance between communicator and audience.

Figure 7.3 derives the relative sizes of the externalities from the nature of the budget constraint and the different goals of contract and property as reflected in the isobenefit curves. The externality in each case stems from the fact that to a communicator the costs of reaching extensive audiences and distant contexts will appear to be less than they are. The 'apparent' isocost, line LM, i.e. the isocost as it appears to the communicator, is less steep than the actual line LL, which is the 'full' isocost line that reflects all the costs of the communication.

Those creating rights are overly inclined toward reaching extensive audiences and contexts, and this externality is greater in property than in contract. The externality will increase with the excess of the extensiveness chosen over the optimal level (generically, $n' - n^*$). Consider the contractual situation. In the contract situation the full-cost line LL is tangent with the isobenefit curve C_2 which is the highest level of (net social) benefit attainable with this budget. At that optimal point the extensiveness of the audience is at n_c^* where the full-cost line LL is tangent with the isobenefit curve C_2. Similarly for n_p^*, in the property situation. In each case (of contract, property), the communicator will believe himself to be facing the less steep budget line LM that makes the tradeoff appear to favor extensiveness more than it actually does. This divergence results in the communicator believing that he can attain a higher level of benefit than is socially optimal.[82] As the optimal degree of extensiveness increases (as it does in the property as opposed to the contract situation), the gap between the full and apparent budget line becomes larger; a larger and more indefinite audience and more contexts give rise to additional costs that are not brought home to the communicator. If, as one would expect, the externality correlates with the divergence of the extensiveness of the audience from its optimal level it is easy to see that the externality is larger in the case of property than in the case of contract. In the case of contractual provisions, this externality is smaller than the case of property because $n_c' - n_c^* < n_p' - n_p^*$. The size of the communication costs relates to audience size, and the model here captures how the informational externality in property is larger. The *numerus clausus* keeps property simple by mandating transactors to hew more closely to the actual rather than the apparent budget line (LL rather than LM).

At first blush this intervention through the *numerus clausus* may seem counterintuitive, because generally with more at stake we would expect more complexity to be worth incurring. But higher stakes can lead to efforts at greater standardization and modularization. In particular, where modularization has greater benefits, we might expect private parties and public authorities to expend efforts on keeping things simple and standardized. Particularly if the kind of processing costs here are basic to human cognition, the fact that judges or other interpreters will themselves need to process legal communication will have a tendency to lead parties to keep things simple and for the third-party decisionmakers themselves to favor or even mandate simplicity.[83]

One reason that standardization through the *numerus clausus* still seems to have a role to play even where property is covered by a system of title records is that standardization is simply not that costly. Because property rights combine in various ways, one can accomplish with a small set of standardized forms most of the objectives one might want to achieve with property. This is because property rights are recursive, as noted earlier. A recursive rule is one that feeds itself. In natural language the rule that forms clauses with 'that' (*that*-clauses) is recursive: one can form a *that*-clause out of a *that*-clause plus a verb followed by *that*, with no bound on embedding. ('John said that Mary believed that Pat said that . . . .') Likewise, the rule breaking a remainder into a life estate and a remainder can be applied in nested fashion: life estate followed by a remainder in life estate followed by a remainder in life estate . . . followed by a reminder in fee simple. Basic property forms are like Lego blocks because of their all-purpose generativity. Because the basic property forms are recursive and therefore the system is highly generative, standardization does not present high frustration costs.[84] It may require more effort and cost to figure out the right combination of permitted basic forms to achieve a given objective than under a system of freely customizable property, and in that sense the *numerus clausus* is like a tax on complexity (and as we will see a tax on externalized complexity costs).[85] But the *numerus clausus* does little to prevent objectives from being reached, even if indirectly.[86]

Finally, the critique of the *numerus clausus* that it is a form of formalism does have some point. But the critics mistake the nature and function of the formalism involved in the *numerus clausus*. Formalism in communication systems can be defined as invariance to context, and this is inherently a matter of degree.[87] The *numerus clausus* allows property rights to be understandable without the degree of reliance on context that would be required if parties could create fancies – lend an in rem character to their idiosyncratic rights. The information-cost theory provides an answer to the oft-quoted Holmesian aphorism that 'it is revolting to have no better reason for a rule of law than that so it was laid down in the time of Henry IV.'[88] Far from being mindless, some degree of formalism in the in rem context is almost inevitable: remote third parties at some point will stop inquiring into the context of property rights and either incur liability or engage in drastic avoidance strategies.

IV.   FUTHER IMPLICATIONS

The information-cost theory of property can explain aspects of standardization beyond the *numerus clausus* itself. First, the *numerus clausus* is not the only method of managing information costs. In the case of land and a few other resources, registries provide information for interested parties. The *numerus clausus* and registries can be supplements, but also complements under various circumstances. Second, an aspect of property that presents a borderline case for standardization is servitudes. The information-cost theory sheds some light on the stakes involved in the tests for whether servitudes should run to successors. Third, the conflict over the role of custom raises the *numerus clausus* question, and proponents of widespread incorporation of custom often seek to undermine the *numerus clausus*. Finally, some property interests, especially those resulting from financial contracting, raise the problem of complexity externalities and suggest some role for the *numerus clausus* and mandatory standardization to contain them.

A.   The *Numerus Clausus* and Registries

It need not be the case that standardization is the *only* response to third-party information costs. Title records can reduce third-party information costs as well. How does the availability of registries affect the *numerus clausus*?

In some circumstances, the *numerus clausus* and title records are substitutes.[89] This is particularly true where there are no title records. In England systematic title records did not come until legislation in 1925 that both increased reliance on land registration and *at the same time* radically reduced the number of estates.[90] And it was in England, lacking systematic land registration in the nineteenth century, that the *numerus clausus* applied more strictly than in the United States. If there are no title records, the informational burden of idiosyncrasies on third parties is very great and simplification can be expected to be very important. Many theorists believe that title records make standardization through the *numerus clausus* unnecessary – that in other words the *numerus clausus* and title records are always substitutes and that title records generally dominate as a solution to the problem of giving third parties notice of property rights.[91]

The position that notice cures all overlooks some of the functions of the *numerus clausus* as well as empirical evidence that suggests that standardization and title records are not always substitutes.[92] As argued above, title records may gain in effectiveness if they are standardized in their format. The many problems with bad title records and inadequate indexes attest to this problem. Among the ways that title records can be easier to use is to require property itself to come in standardized forms. Once one has discovered that an interest is a fee simple or a lease, one need not search for information that will contradict the basic features of these forms. It is true that as title records become cheaper and easier to use, most recently by being digitized, we can expect some loosening of the *numerus clausus*.[93] Something similar arguably happened when title records got started and more forms were allowed.

But there is a limit to the ability of title records to replace standardization. Title records come in two main types, with variations.[94] In registration, found in Germany and Australia among other countries, an official (the registrar or the like) will inspect documents before placing them in the land records, and will guarantee their validity. Fees sometimes cover insurance in case of mistakes. By contrast, in recordation, characteristic of France and the United States, transactional documents are filed and users of the records must search in order to evaluate title. The search is often carried out by title companies with their own set of parallel records and they often also issue or arrange for title insurance. It appears that systems with more definitive land records (in the direction of registration as opposed to recordation) tend to have a stricter *numerus clausus* – that is they allow fewer forms.[95] Apparently, the registrar, in passing on the validity of the interests to be filed, cannot be expected to process large amounts of idiosyncrasy. The registrar is a stand-in for the in rem public, and the up-front information costs of the registrar are correlated with a more stringent *numerus clausus*.

Title records and the *numerus clausus* can go hand in hand in another way, by working together. Systems of recordation sometimes impose standardization *through* the land records. Recordation systems tend to allow more idiosyncrasy than do registration systems. In some recordation systems, as in France, an interest will not be given in rem effect through the land records unless it is standardized.[96] Even the American system of recordation only allows documents of certain types to be recorded,[97] although most standardization occurs in the attempt ex post to fit an interest into one of the boxes defined by the *numerus clausus*.

It is an empirical question how much title records reduce the need for standardization. Again, even title records can benefit from a standardized format. And if property involves a basic set of building blocks, the records will be easier to search. Recall that in registration systems – in which land records are taken very seriously – the *numerus clausus* tends to be more, not less strict. Moreover, not all dutyholders will be expected to consult the title records.[98] For those who interact with property in a nonconsensual way there is a need to keep things simple. And for types of property – like much of personal property – that is not subject to title records, standardization can be expected to be – and is – even more stringent than in the case of land. Although there is little law on the subject, if anything personal property is subject to a smaller set of legal estates and future interests than is real estate.[99] And personal property servitudes are more restricted in their ability to bind successors.

B.   Servitudes

Servitudes present an interesting borderline case for standardization. The rules for servitudes in real, tangible personal, and intellectual property differ greatly. Because of the many unresolved empirical issues, the information-cost theory can only structure the inquiry and provide tentative prescriptions.

In real property, transactors can tailor servitudes, but traditionally the law places limits on the ability of servitudes to run to successors.[100] As we have seen, successors in interest are remote parties but not as remote as true third parties. If capitalization is working, problems faced by successors will impact today's price for the parcel in question. But problems remain. Not only may capitalization fail to work, we might worry about whether complex servitudes will cause property not to mesh well with other property in the sense discussed above. As Carol Rose points out, servitudes can reduce the 'renegotiability' of property.[101] How much of a problem this presents in particular cases is a difficult question. Furthermore, sometimes this meshing will impact true third parties, as where neighbors try to devise a local property regime through covenants. Such localized regimes serve as a crystalized version of custom but may burden outsiders with excessive information costs. More substantively, such covenants can violate wider policies, as in the case of racially restrictive covenants.[102]

Currently, the level of mandatoriness in the law of servitudes is controversial. Traditional doctrines like 'touch and concern' which limited the ability of a servitude to bind successors in interest to only those servitudes that 'touch and concern' the land, have demonstrated staying power in the face of reform efforts aimed at greater customizability and freedom of contract.[103] Although the possible function of tests like touch and concern has been very elusive,[104] it is worthwhile to consider whether touch and concern may serve to standardize the package of servitudes to those that refine the basic default package of rights in land. Promises to furnish haircuts to landlords or neighbors would be an unusual and unexpected 'refinement' of the basic package of rights and duties of landowners. By contrast a restriction on building height would be easily seen as a refinement. The possible function of touch and concern and its relation to standardization in property law remains a topic for further work.

Personal property servitudes have long been regarded with disfavor.[105] Although some have called for greater freedom in this area,[106] the problems of information costs should not be dismissed too lightly. For one thing, most personal property is not subject to registries, which are a main source of information about servitudes in real property. The problems of meshing and being on the look out for whole new dimensions of idiosyncrasy are problems, and reducing the scope for servitudes to run to successors in personal property is one solution. On the flip side, the benefits of servitudes on much personal property are not that great, because much personal property does not last very long.

Servitudes on intellectual property present special problems.[107] Sometimes they do intersect with issues of personal property servitudes, as in the case of restrictions on a patented article sold to another party. Do the restrictions travel into the hands of remote purchasers? Here the information costs faced by competitors and consumers are quite different. Thus, while the Supreme Court's recent decision in *Quanta Computer v. LG Electronics, Inc.*[108] may seem to enforce a stringent and mandatory version of the patent exhaustion doctrine under which a license will automatically apply to the licensee's downstream customers, a more finegrained approach makes more sense.[109] For example, the running of servitudes in intellectual property could be more restricted in the case of consumers than commercial parties,[110] or the patent exhaustion doctrine could operate as a strong default rather than a mandatory rule.

One way to frame the problem of information costs and servitudes is to ask whether it makes sense to allow transactors to modify the interface between property rights through the servitudes in question. The touch and concern requirement would ask if a servitude can be regarded as a refinement of a modular right or not. Servitudes that make little reference to the property baseline would be suspect, for example promises to give haircuts. Likewise, intellectual property servitudes that go beyond the copyright baseline would also be good candidates for striking down as property rights.[111]

C.   Custom

Custom and the role it should play in law raise some tensions with the *numerus clausus*. The information-cost theory of standardization in property has implications for the role custom should play.[112]

The *numerus clausus* is in tension with a robust role for custom in the law. If the law incorporates custom in all the details from its context in a community of origin and applies it more widely, the legalized custom can place large informational demands on people in this wide audience. In terms of the model above, unmodified custom is intensive communication that presents large information costs with more extensive audiences. Indeed the history of the *numerus clausus* in civil law is marked by the effort to abolish the customs of feudalism and to make property more marketable (for a more extensive audience).

As I have argued elsewhere, one aspect of the incorporation of custom into the law is a process of stripping it down, simplifying it, and making it more formal.[113] On the information-cost theory this is to be expected and is desirable as an effort to keep information costs manageable. The formalization of custom as part of its incorporation into the law is closely related to the *numerus clausus*. For example, one approach to problems like hot news in *International News Service v. The Associated Press*[114] would, as Richard Epstein argues, be to adopt the customs of the news business, which evidently do provide for some protection of hot news.[115] But before we can conclude that this is a good idea we have to consider information costs imposed on more extensive audiences, as implicitly recognized by the majority opinion in its emphasis on misappropriation rights as quasi-property binding only on competitors.

The tension between the *numerus clausus* and custom is illustrated by current controversies in some East Asian countries over the role of custom in law.[116] Those who would like to see a loosening of the *numerus clausus* espouse a role for custom, which would allow more finegrained detail and local and industry variation into the basic building blocks of property. However these controversies get resolved, the information-cost theory suggests that the burden on extensive audiences should be an important consideration.

D. Complexity Externalities

Another source of idiosyncratic information that impacts third parties is the complexity of the products of recent financial engineering. One problem for the *numerus clausus* is the need to figure out when parties have enough (or too much) incentive to standardize even in the absence of mandatory rules like the *numerus clausus*. Generally speaking, where actors care more about resale they will standardize more (think of purchasers of condominiums in a common interest community). People will not create idiosyncratic rights when resale is important enough to the return they anticipate. Thus in financial markets we generally expect standardization to emerge, at least in mature markets.[117] Recent problems with collateralized debt obligations and other advanced instruments whose markets froze in the financial meltdown of 2008 suggest (among other things) some role for mandatory standardization of some financial devices. In rising markets and bubbles in particular, we might worry that those who should object to complexity will have insufficient incentive to investigate or refuse to trade.[118] Whether the solution to this problem comes from better monetary policy to prevent bubbles, better financial regulation to prevent the build-up of systemic risk, or more standardization of financial products is left open for further work.

V. CONCLUSION

Information costs help explain the *numerus clausus* and ground it in a fundamental difference between property and contract – the in rem versus in personam distinction. Because transactors creating idiosyncrasies enjoy all the benefits but a fraction of the costs faced by in rem audiences, there is a rationale for the law to step in to standardize property. Property law furnishes a modular structure with constrained interfaces, and the *numerus clausus* provides the basic building blocks of the system. Because the building blocks can combine recursively and in a generative way, the system does not present as high frustration costs as a system that required a tailor-made property form for each purpose. The information-cost theory of the *numerus clausus* also helps explain the relation of standardization in property to registries, the role of standardization in servitudes, the limited role of custom in the law, and the possibility of complexity externalities.

NOTES

*   Email: hemsith@law.harvard.edu.
1.   Bernard Rudden, Economic Theory v. Property Law: The *Numerus Clausus* Problem, in Oxford Essays in Jurisprudence 239 (3rd Series, John Eekelaar and John Bell, eds. 1987) (setting out *numerus clausus* problem and discussing possible explanations); Thomas W. Merrill & Henry E. Smith, Optimal Standardization in the Law of Property: The *Numerus Clausus* Principle, 110 Yale L.J. 1, 42–58 (2000)

(critiquing previous explanations of the *numerus clausus* based on anti-fragmentation, notice-cures-all, and irrelevance).

2. See, e.g., Curtis J. Berger & Joan C. Williams, Property: Land Ownership and Use 211–12 (4th edn 1997).

3. See John Henry Merryman, Ownership and Estate, 48 Tul. L. Rev. 916, 938–43 (1974).

4. When Hansmann and Kraakman claim that the *numerus clausus* has no basis in the common law, they are simply wrong descriptively. Henry Hansmann & Reinier Kraakman, Property, Contract, and Verification: The *Numerus Clausus* Problem and the Divisibility of Rights, 31 J. Legal Stud. S373, S416–17 (2002). Part of the problem is that their narrow focus on verification costs – the costs of convincing a purchaser that a seller has the rights to sell – leads them to overlook the more pervasive role played by information costs that arise from nonstandard formats of information and that face more impersonal audiences such as potential violators of property rights. Because they focus on a subset of the information costs treated in Merrill and Smith, supra note 1 – verification costs are a proper subset of information or 'measurement' costs – their account predictably comes up short as an explanation for mandatory standardization.

5. See, e.g., Susan Bright, Of Estates and Interests: A Tale of Ownership and Property Rights 546, in Land Law: Themes and Perspectives (Susan Bright & John Dewar eds. 1998) (stating that English judges have 'bolt[ed] the door' on existing categories of property and '[I]t is about time that the door was opened and new rights admitted on a more principled basis').

6. Richard A. Epstein, Notice and Freedom of Contract in the Law of Servitudes, 55 S. Cal. L. Rev. 1353 (1982); see also Alfred F. Conard, Easement Novelties, 30 Cal. L. Rev. 125, 131–33 (1942).

7. Michael A. Heller, The Boundaries of Private Property, 108 Yale L.J. 1163, 1176–78 (1999); Francesco Parisi, Entropy in Property, 50 Am. J. Comp. L. 595 (2002).

8. Merrill & Smith, supra note 1, at 4, 33.

9. Id.

10. Thomas W. Merrill & Henry E. Smith, What Happened to Property in Law and Economics?, 111 Yale L.J. 357 (2001).

11. See Rudden, supra note 1, at 240; John Henry Merryman, Policy, Autonomy, and the *Numerus Clausus* in Italian and American Property Law, 12 Am. J. Comp. L. 224 (1963).

12. See, e.g., Thomas F. Bergin & Paul G. Haskell, Preface to Estates in Land and Future Interests 19–80 (2nd edn 1984).

13. See, e.g., William B. Stoebuck & Dale A. Whitman, The Law of Property §§ 6.14–20 (3d edn 2000).

14. See id., ch. 5.

15. Thomas W. Merrill & Henry E. Smith, Property: Principles and Policies ch. 6 (2007).

16. John Armour & Michael J. Whincop, The Proprietary Foundations of Corporate Law, 27 Oxford J. Legal Stud. 429 (2007).

17. Thomas W. Merrill & Henry E. Smith, The Property/Contract Interface, 101 Column. L. Rev. 773, 820–33 (2001).

18. See, e.g., Jaber v. Miller, 239 S.W.2d 760 (Ark. 1951).

19. Merrill & Smith, supra note 1, at 54–55; J.E. Penner, The 'Bundle of Rights' Picture of Property, 43 UCLA L. Rev. 711, 802–03, 810–13 (1996).

20. Richard A. Epstein, Inducement of Breach of Contract as a Problem of Ostensible Ownership, 17 J. Legal Stud. 1 (1987); see also Fred S. McChesney, Tortious Interference with Contract Versus 'Efficient' Breach: Theory and Empirical Evidence, 28 J. Legal Stud. 131 (1999).

21. Henry E. Smith, Law and Economics: Realism or Democracy?, 32 Harv. J.L. & Pub. Pol'y 127, 140–42 (2009).

22. Henry E. Smith, The Language of Property: Form, Context, and Audience, 55 Stan. L. Rev. 1105, 1186–88 (2003).

23. 2 My. & K. 517, 39 Eng. Rep. 1042 (Ch. 1834).

24. Tulk v. Moxhay, 2 Ph. 774, 41 Eng. Rep. 1143 (Ch. 1848).

25. 2 My. & K. at 535–36.

26. For some proposals to simplify the system of estates and future interests, see, e.g., Restatement of the Law (Third), Property: Wills and Other Donative Transfers (Draft); Thomas P. Gallanis, The Future of Future Interests, 60 Wash. & Lee L. Rev. 513 (2003); Lawrence W. Waggoner, Reformulating the Structure of Estates: A Proposal for Legislative Action, 85 Harv. L. Rev. 729 (1972).

27. For an engaging introduction, see Douglas Hofstadter, Gödel, Escher, Bach: An Eternal Golden Braid 127–57 (1979); see also, e.g., Joseph R. Shoenfield, Recursion Theory (2000).

28. See, e.g., Ivan A. Sag & Thomas Wasow, Syntactic Theory: A Formal Introduction 36, 259 (1999).

29. The notion of a 'pattern language' has been influential in architecture. See Christopher Alexander et al., A Pattern Language: Towns, Buildings, and Construction (1977). More generally, what I am suggesting is that property has an architecture, so the analogy is quite apt. Furthermore modularity serves a very similar role in all fields where an 'architecture' is used to manage complexity, including most clearly

computer hardware and software. See Christopher Alexander, Notes on the Synthesis of Form (1964) (exploration of design principles with an emphasis on architecture but which were influential in computer software); Herbert A. Simon, The Sciences of the Artificial 195–98 (2d ed. 1981) (1969); see also 1 Carliss Y. Baldwin & Kim B. Clark, Design Rules: The Power of Modularity (2000).

30. See Simon, supra note 29; Baldwin & Clark, supra note 29.
31. These examples are drawn from Carliss Y. Baldwin, Where Do Transactions Come From? Modularity, Transactions, and the Boundaries of Firms, 17 Indus. & Corp. Change 15, 166–74 (2008).
32. John H. Langbein, The Secret Life of the Trust: The Trust as an Instrument of Commerce, 107 Yale L.J. 165, 165, 177–78 (1997); Henry Hansmann & Ugo Mattei, The Functions of Trust Law: A Comparative Legal and Economic Analysis, 73 N.Y.U. L. Rev. 434 (1998).
33. Merrill & Smith, supra note 17, at 843–49. Thus in the longstanding debate as to whether trusts are property or contract – with Scott versus Maitland a century ago and more recently Hansmann & Mattei versus Langbein, we can reconcile the positions by explaining the trust as a hybrid whose property-like and contract-like features are not random: trusts are largely property-like and standardized with respect to in rem parties and more contract-like and customizable to the in personam internal parties (settlor, trustee, beneficiary). Id. The main complication stems from the protection of beneficial interests against third party transferees with some kind of notice of the trust. This special form of protection falls short of in rem in the sense that personal notice is required. But information costs are lessened by the lack of a duty to inquire on the part of transferees.
34. Henry E. Smith, Exclusion Versus Governance: Two Strategies for Delineating Property Rights, 31 J. Legal Stud. S453 (2002).
35. Merrill & Smith, supra note 17, at 783–89.
36. Id. at 825–27.
37. Merrill & Smith, supra note 1, at 58–68.
38. National Bellas Hess, Inc. v. Kalis, 191 F.2d 739 (8th Cir. 1951); Stanmeyer v. Davis, 321 Ill. App. 227, 53 N.E. 2d 22 (1944); Lace v. Chantler, 2 All E.R. 369 (K.B. 1944).
39. See Smith's Transfer & Storage Co. v. Hawkins, 50 A.2d 267, 268 (D.C. 1946).
40. 2 Powell on Real Property § 16.03[4][b] at 16–68.
41. 159 Mass. 424, 34 N.E. 542 (1893) (Holmes, J.).
42. See Merrill & Smith, supra note 1, at 20–23.
43. 63 N.Y.2d 575, 473 N.E.2d 223 (N.Y. 1984).
44. Compare Thompson v. Baxter, 119 N.W. 797 (Minn. 1909) (life estate) with Nitschke v. Doggett, 489 S.W. 2d 335 (Tex. Civ. App. 1972), vacated on other grounds, 498 S.W. 2d 339 (Tex. 1973) (tenancy at will); Kajo Church Square, Inc. v. Walker, 2003 WL 1848555 (Tex. App. Apr. 9, 2003) (same).
45. 473 N.E.2d at 225.
46. Id. at 224–25.
47. Merrill & Smith, supra note 1, at 58–68.
48. Id. at 15, 60, 65.
49. See, e.g., Kewanee Oil Co. v. Bicron Corp., 415 U.S. 470 (1974) (holding that trade secret law is not preempted by federal patent law); Bonito Boats, Inc. v. Thunder Craft Boats, Inc., 489 U.S. 141 (1989) (holding that Florida anti-plug mold statute was preempted by patent law).
50. See Merrill & Smith, supra note 1, at 20.
51. 248 U.S. 215 (1918).
52. Id. at 262–67 (Brandeis, J. dissenting).
53. See Cheney Brothers v. Doris Silk Corp., 35 F.2d 279 (2d Cir. 1930) (L. Hand, J.) (denying protection to dress designs under the tort of misappropriation).
54. 248 U.S. at 236–37, 239–40.
55. See, e.g., Howard W. Brill, The Maxims of Equity, 1993 Ark. L. Notes 29 (1993); Roger Young & Stephen Spitz, SUEM – Spitz's Ultimate Equitable Maxim: In Equity, Good Guys Should Win and Bad Guys Should Lose, 55 S.C. L. Rev. 175, 177 (2003) (listing nine equitable principles used by the South Carolina courts, including '[e]quity follows the law' and '[e]quity act in personam, not in rem').
56. Charles M. Gray, The Boundaries of the Equitable Function, 20 Am. J. Legal Hist. 192, 202–06 (1976) (illustrating how courts of equity were prohibited from addressing real estate disputes).
57. See Merrill & Smith, supra note 1; Smith, supra note 22; Henry E. Smith, Modularity in Contracts: Boilerplate and Information Flow, 104 Mich. L. Rev. 1175 (2006).
58. Herbert A. Simon, Designing Organizations for an Information-Rich World, in Computers, Communication, and the Public Interest 37, 40–41 (Martin Greenberger ed., 1971) (noting that an abundance of information results in a scarcity of attention).
59. Smith, supra note 22.
60. Merrill & Smith, supra note 1, at 26–34; see also Hansmann & Kraakman, supra note 4, at S416.
61. Those dividing property rights have an incentive to divide them in such a way as to divert value to

themselves, and the *numerus clausus* can serve as a commitment device to lower the information costs of buyers fearing such moral hazard. Kenneth Ayotte & Patrick Bolton, Optimal Property Rights in Financial Contracting (Draft July 2007), available at SSRN: http://ssrn.com/abstract=989225; see also Eric Bennett Rasmusen, Explaining Incomplete Contracts as the Result of Contract-Reading Costs, Advances Econ. Analysis & Pol'y, 2001, available at www.bepress.com/bejeap/advances/vol1/iss1/art2/index.html (follow 'View the Article' hyperlink) (explaining short contracts as a commitment device by contract drafter against placement of hidden traps).

62. See, e.g., Carol M. Rose, Rethinking Environmental Controls: Management Strategies for Common Resources, 1991 Duke L.J. 1, 9–36; Smith, supra note 34.

63. Henry E. Smith, Governing Water: The Semicommons of Fluid Property Rights, 50 Ariz. L. Rev. 445, 475–77 (2008).

64. Legal instruments can exhibit network effects. See, e.g., Marcel Kahan & Michael Klausner, Standardization and Innovation in Corporate Contracting (Or, 'The Economics of Boilerplate'), 83 Va. L. Rev. 713 (1997); Marcel Kahan & Michael Klausner, Path Dependence in Corporate Contracting: Increasing Returns, Herd Behavior, and Cognitive Biases, 74 Wash. U. L.Q. 347 (1996); Marcel Kahan & Michael Klausner, Corporations, Corporate Law, and Networks of Contracts, 81 Va. L. Rev. 757 (1995).

65. See Armen A. Alchian, Why Money?, 9 J. Money, Credit and Banking 133 (1977); Karl Brunner & Allan H. Meltzer, 61 Am. Econ. Rev. 784 (1971).

66. Alchian, supra note 65.

67. See Merrill & Smith, supra note 1, at 42 (discussing measurement costs and negotiability).

68. Smith, supra note 22.

69. See, e.g., Jean-Marc Dewaele, How to Measure Formality in Speech: A Model of Synchronic Variation, in Approaches to Second Language Acquisition (Kari Sajavaara & Courtney Fairweather eds., 1996).

70. See C.E. Shannon, A Mathematical Theory of Communication (pts. 1 & 2), 27 Bell Sys. Tech. J. 379–82 (1948), 27 Bell Sys. Technical J. 623 (1948) (developing a theory of information based on quantity), reprinted as Claude E. Shannon & Warren Weaver, The Mathematical Theory of Communication (1949); see also R.V.L. Hartley, Transmission of Information, 7 Bell Sys. Technical J. 535 (1928) (developing notion of 'amount of information'); see also Fred I. Dretske, Knowledge & the Flow of Information 3–26 (1981) (adapting information theory to individual messages).

71. Merrill & Smith, supra note 1, at 49.

72. Smith, supra note 57, at 1207–14.

73. To avoid asymptotic isocost lines, the origin depicts the minimal unit of information being communicated to one person.

74. In contract theory, this comes under the heading of verification costs, which despite typical assumptions of contract theory fall on a sliding scale. See George G. Triantis, The Efficiency of Vague Contract Terms: A Response to the Schwartz-Scott Theory of U.C.C. Article 2, 62 La. L. Rev. 1065 (2002).

75. Contracts between a few sophisticated and numerous unsophisticated parties might be somewhat closer to the curves for property than are contracts between a few identified and fully informed parties. For factors that make some contractual situations somewhat 'intermediate' between prototypical contract and property, see Merrill & Smith, supra note 17, at 799–809; Smith, supra note 22, at 1151–53.

76. All the curves are concave because information rate and information extensiveness are not perfect substitutes: one has to give up more and more of one input to achieve the same amount of benefit with substitution of the other input.

77. Smith, supra note 57, at 1207–08.

78. Smith, supra note 22, at 1139–48, 1153–57.

79. See infra notes 89–97 and accompanying text.

80. See supra notes 65–67 and accompanying text.

81. See Merrill & Smith, supra note 1, at 24–42; Smith, supra note 22, at 1157–62.

82. There is another way to derive the externality, as discussed in Smith, supra note 22, at 1154 n.174. By selecting along line LM when from a social point of view one cannot do better than LL, the private actor is in effect selecting along a budget line KL. This is the actual tradeoff being made along LM taking social cost into account: KL shares a point with LL on the x-axis but is parallel to line LM. When the private actor believes he is at point M, he is really at point L on the x-axis. The actor nonideally trades off r and n at the rate reflected in line LM (and parallel line KL), i.e. at a rate of $-OL / OM$. Notice that KL is tangent to the lowest drawn isoquants for contract, and property (C_1, P_1), again reflecting lower social benefits than in the case of C_2 and P_2.

83. Smith, supra note 22, at 1155–60.

84. Merrill & Smith, supra note 1, at 35–38.

85. Id. at 35.

86. Some theorists have hypothesized that the *numerus clausus* is a constraint on private legislation and focuses on regulating the public aspect of property. See Nestor M. Davidson, Standardization and

Pluralism in Property Law, 61 Vand. L. Rev. 1597 (2008). This substantive approach dovetails to some extent with the information cost theory of in rem rights, but the public regulation theory has more difficulty explaining why heavily regulated areas of property like landlord-tenant are subject to 'intermediate' strategies that fall short of stringent standardization; why the *numerus clausus* limits judicial, not just private, innovation in property forms; and why the law of torts is characterized by more judicial innovation than is the law of property.

87. Francis Heylighen, Advantages and Limitations of Formal Expression, 4 Foundations of Science 25, 49–53 (1999); Smith, supra note 22, at 1167–90.
88. Oliver Wendell Holmes, The Path of the Law, 10 Harv. L. Rev. 457, 469 (1897); Merrill & Smith, supra note 1, at 6 & n.14 (quoting examples).
89. Smith, supra note 22, at 1170–71.
90. See Law of Property Act 1925, 15 & 16 Geo. 5, c. 20 (reducing number of legal estates to two, limiting legal concurrent tenants, and defining trust for sale); Land Registration Act 1925, 15 & 16 Geo. 5, c. 21 (setting up title registration system).
91. Richard A. Epstein, Notice and Freedom of Contract in the Law of Servitudes, 55 S. Cal. L. Rev. 1353 (1982).
92. Merrill & Smith, supra note 1, at 43–45.
93. Id. at 42.
94. See, e.g., Benito Arruñada & Nuno Garoupa, The Choice of Titling System in Land, 48 J.L. & Econ. 709 (2005); Joseph T. Janczyk, An Economic Analysis of the Land Title Systems for Transferring Real Property, 6 J. Legal Stud. 213 (1977).
95. Benito Arruñada, Property Enforcement as Organized Consent, 19 J.L. Econ. & Org. 401, 416–20 (2003).
96. 3 Marcel Planiol & Georges Ripert, Traité Pratique de Droit Civil Français: Maurice Picard, Les Biens § 3 ¶ 48 (2d edn 1952).
97. See, e.g., John C. Murray, Defective Real Estate Documents: What Are the Consequences?, 42 Real Prop. Prob. & Tr. J. 367 (2007).
98. Merrill & Smith, supra note 17, at 849 & n. 264.
99. Merrill & Smith, supra note 1, at 17–18.
100. Stoebuck & Whitman, supra note 13, ch. 8.
101. See Rose, this volume.
102. See id.
103. Restatement (Third) of Property: Servitudes § 2 (2000); Susan F. French, Symposium on Servitudes, Part II, Can Covenants Not To Sue, Covenants Against Competition and Spite Covenants Run With Land? Comparing Results Under the Touch or Concern Doctrine and the Restatement Third, Property (Servitudes), 38 Real Prop. Prob. & Tr. J. 267 (2003).
104. See, e.g., A. Dan Tarlock, Touch and Concern is Dead, Long Live the Doctrine, 77 Neb. L. Rev. 804 (1998); Jeffrey E. Stake, Toward an Economic Understanding of Touch and Concern, 1988 Duke L.J. 925.
105. See, e.g., Zechariah Chafee, Jr., Equitable Servitudes on Chattels, 41 Harv. L. Rev. 945, 977–87 (1928) (surveying the case law and explaining objections to equitable servitudes on chattels); Zechariah Chafee, Jr., The Music Goes Round and Round: Equitable Servitudes and Chattels, 69 Harv. L. Rev. 1250, 1254–56 (1956) (acknowledging the scarcity of authorities addressing equitable servitudes on chattels).
106. Glen O. Robinson, Personal Property Servitudes, 71 U. Chi. L. Rev. 1449, 1449–55 (2004).
107. Molly Shaffer Van Houweling, The New Servitudes, 96 Geo. L.J. 885, 924–50 (2008).
108. 128 S. Ct. 2109 (2008).
109. Henry E. Smith, Institutions and Indirectness in Intellectual Property, 157 U. Pa. L. Rev. 2083 (2009).
110. Id. at 2124–25; Van Houweling, supra note 107, at 932–39 (discussing consumers and notice of servitudes).
111. How they should be treated as attempted bilateral non-assignable contracts is another question.
112. This section is based on Henry E. Smith, Community and Custom in Property, 10 Theoretical Inquiries L. 6 (2009).
113. Id.
114. 248 U.S. 215 (1918).
115. Richard A. Epstein, *International News Service v. Associated Press*: Custom and Law as Sources of Property Rights in News, 78 Va. L. Rev. 85 (1992).
116. See Yin Tian, Reflection on the Criticism of *Numerus Clausus*, 1 Front. L. China 92, 94–95 (2006) (discussing and citing literature).
117. Merrill & Smith, supra note 1, at 47.
118. Cf. Ayotte & Bolton, this volume.

8 Covenant lite lending, liquidity, and standardization of financial contracts
*Kenneth Ayotte and Patrick Bolton**

1 INTRODUCTION

The last decade has witnessed many rapid changes in corporate financial practice. Perhaps most important among these is the expansion of securitization to corporate loans. Through securitization, corporate loans are originated and sold into investment vehicles that issue securities called Collateralized Loan Obligations (CLOs). A common justification for securitization is that it allows for otherwise illiquid corporate loans to be transformed into more liquid securities that can be easily traded in secondary markets.[1]

Though the channel through which this 'liquidity creation' occurs is not fully understood, a common explanation is that the process of pooling a large volume of loans allows third-party rating agencies, and the asset managers that assemble these pools, to create standardized securities that are easier to value than the individual, idiosyncratic loans that back the securities.[2] This standardization occurs through several channels. First, credit rating agencies publish and use a standardized process to determine ratings for CLOs and the underlying assets in the loan pools.[3] For example, assumptions regarding loan recovery in default, an input into the rating process, use standard formulae based on the priority ranking of the loan in the capital structure. Asset managers also provide standardization of the product offered to investors through the collateral restrictions in their organizational documents. These restrictions provide a list of characteristics to which the manager must adhere in assembling the loans in the pool.

A noteworthy feature of this type of standardization is that it is *open-ended*: while the composition of CLO loan pools, and the process used to generate ratings, is often based on a closed set of loan characteristics, these characteristics do not provide a complete description of the rights and obligations in each loan contract being originated and sold. Loans may include various clauses and covenants that are not included in these fixed sets; moreover, the specific contractual language may modify the lenders rights in important ways that a standardized rating model may not capture.

The goal of this chapter is to investigate the impact of standardization on the liquidity and composition of financial contracts. Following the property law literature approach (Merrill and Smith 2000, 2001), we model standardization as a technology that reduces the contract reading costs of potential buyers (in our case, buyers of debt contracts, such as CDO investors). Using the same tension as in our earlier work (Ayotte and Bolton 2008), the originator of a loan contract and the borrower may have the incentive to include contractual terms that redistribute value from unknowing third parties (here, loan buyers) when reading costs are present. Third parties are rational, and anticipate the possibility of these redistributive terms. As a result, the liquidity of loan contracts in secondary markets is affected, as well as the borrowing and investing decisions of firms.

Our model generates findings that relate to recent developments in credit markets. In particular, one trend accompanying the recent boom in loan securitization was the rapid weakening of contractual covenants in loan agreements. This trend, which has become known as *covenant-lite lending*, became commonplace during the boom in loan securitization, and has become substantially less common as the securitization market has slowed. Our model explains this empirical correlation. When an open-ended standardization technology is introduced to a market, it becomes cheaper to disclose information about certain features of a contract at low cost. If these features reveal enough about the loan, the loan may be sold without any further investigation by the buyer. If she has rational expectations, however, the loan buyer will anticipate that the loan originator and borrower will write the contract so that all of the unobserved terms of the contract are unfavorable to her. The buyer's willingness to pay will be based on the expectation of a covenant-lite contract.

We find that under *open-ended standardization*, two equilibria are possible. In one equilibrium, covenant-lite contracts are written and sold in secondary markets. These contracts are more liquid because they reduce reading costs for buyers, but because of their covenant-lite features, they fail to limit over-borrowing and excess continuation by the borrowing firm in bad states of the world. This equilibrium is more likely in good times (when good states are expected in the future with high probability), because the costs of moral hazard created by covenant-lite loans arise only when bad states of the world occur.

If the benefits of liquidity are low or agency costs are high, a second equilibrium is possible, with covenant-strong contracting and illiquid loans that are held by the originator. In this equilibrium, the secondary market for loan sales is subject to the familiar 'lemons problem'. Beliefs are such that any loan that is sold is believed to be covenant-lite, and thus subject to a large price discount. Knowing this, the originator instead chooses to write a more valuable, covenant-strong contract that prevents over-borrowing in the bad state of the world, holding this loan to maturity. Thus, our model rationalizes the perspective of Standard and Poor's, who wrote, presciently, about the covenant-lite lending trend in 2007:

> Liquidity has helped the loan market evolve from strictly buy-and-hold to a trading market, making covenants less compelling. When a lender held a loan for the duration, the ability to control the situation was much more important than it is now, when the secondary market is fairly liquid. . .Right now, with default rates at record lows and borrowers generally able to buy covenant relief on the cheap, there is little cost in giving up [typical covenants absent in covenant lite loans]. In the future, however, when the cycle turns, lenders will grow more demanding.[4]

Our model is intended to serve only as a starting point to investigate these issues, but we expect that further investigation may generate additional insight in future work. For example, the standard logic in finance is that senior securities should be the most liquid, because their value is less sensitive to private information about the firm's future cash flows (Gorton and Pennacchi 1990). In our model, the source of asymmetric information is the terms in the debt contract. When contractual terms become the source of asymmetric information, one might expect that a senior loan would be *less* liquid than a junior loan (or equity), because an effective guarantee of seniority requires a host of specific covenants to create it, while an absence of seniority does not. Thus, senior loans may require greater investigation by lenders than junior loans with respect to the details of the contract.

2   RELATED LITERATURE

The liquidity benefits of standardized contracts due to lower reading costs has been posited in the financial economics literature, and associated with securitization (Amihud and Mendelson 1988). But to our knowledge, the trade-offs from the issuer's perspective have not been formalized. The formal theoretical economics literature on standardization to date, in our view, can be viewed alternatively as theories of contractual innovation. The primary trade-offs in these works relates to the choice between an existing set of contracts with well-known properties and the innovation of a new contract with potentially valuable but also potentially unknown features.

Sussman (1999) studies the decision of a potential innovator to create a new contract, at a privately incurred cost. New contracts can be valuable in this model by allowing more efficient risk-sharing across states than the existing, standard contracts provide. The innovator, whose monopoly over the new contract is only temporary, cannot recoup the entire value added of the new contract. Thus, under-innovation occurs, and the extent of new innovation depends on the characteristics of the existing standard contracts.

Gale (1992) is closer to our model, in that potential buyers must incur costly investigation to understand the full implications of contracts. In Gale's model, the potential buyer investigates his own utility function, rather than the contract itself, to find out whether the new contract's features are well-adapted to his preferences. Multiple equilbria can arise due to network efficiencies in sharing the idiosyncratic risk of a new security. If a potential buyer expects others to investigate, then he may investigate as well, because he can share the idiosyncratic risk of the new security with other buyers. If he expects others will not investigate, then he might not investigate either and choose to hold standard securities whose properties are well-known.

Empirical evidence in Rajan, Seru and Vig (2008) is closely related to some of the trade-offs we model here. Rajan, Seru and Vig (2008) find that the increasing prevalence of loan securitization resulted in two related forces. First, loan interest rates became more closely tied to easily describable, standardized 'hard information' such as borrowers' credit scores and the loan-to-value ratio. At the same time, models that predict default based on these variables, using data from a regime with low securitization, under-predicted default rates when securitization became more prevalent. These authors hypothesize that lenders spent less time and effort gathering information that is more costly to observe by the ultimate loan buyers ('soft information' such as subjective evaluation by a loan officer), since the originating lenders planned on selling these loans. Our model considers the possibility that hidden information is in non-standardized contractual terms, instead of borrower characteristics. Also, loan buyers in our model are rational and do not misprice loans in equilibrium. Nevertheless, our model does predict that the prices of sold loans will depend more on standardized information, and non-standardized, hidden information will be unfavorable to the ultimate loan buyer.

2.1 A Brief Summary of Ayotte and Bolton (2008)

This chapter follows closely from our earlier work on optimal property rights in financial contracting (Ayotte and Bolton 2008). In that paper, the central problem concerns a lender (P2), who must expend a cost to observe pre-existing rights in a borrower's (A's) property that were transferred by contract to an earlier lender (P1). Since A ultimately internalizes these reading costs, he would like to reduce them by committing to P2 that assets will be available to repay his loan.

This commitment is not possible without the law, however. P2 is unwilling to lend without expending reading costs because he is aware that P1 and A have an incentive to collude against him if he does not. They might write a contract, for example, that transfers all of A's rights in his assets to P1, making them unavailable to satisfy P2's claim when it comes due. With this in mind, P2 insists that A pay for a sufficient level of due diligence expenditures to assure P2 that there will be sufficient assets available to pay him at the final date. The due diligence serves as a valuable signal: if A is willing to help P2 investigate into his prior contracts, he must believe that P2 will lend after the investigation.

The law provides a credible commitment that reduces these costs of investigation and thereby the cost of borrowing. If P2 is confident that the law will refuse to enforce a transfer of rights that is particularly damaging to him, he might be willing to lend after a less costly investigation. In equilibrium, this makes A better off.

Our model generates several comparative statics that drive optimal legal restrictions on property rights. In particular, we find that an optimal law refuses to enforce transfers of rights to P1 by A when these rights are a) more costly to observe, b) less likely to reduce A's agency costs, and c) more redistributive from P2.

This chapter builds from our earlier work. In this chapter, the key tension is not between an early lender and a later lender, but instead between the early lender and a loan buyer. Standardized contracts serve a role similar to legal restrictions in our earlier work, in that they provide a minimum guarantee to a loan buyer and thus make the loan buyer more willing to participate. To our knowledge, standardization has not been modeled as a means of providing this commitment.

3 MODEL

3.1 Technological Assumptions

We extend our model of a firm in Ayotte and Bolton (2008) comprising a single project that requires two rounds of financing from two different lenders. At date 1, a wealthless agent (A) is endowed with a valuable idea, and must raise an amount of i_1 from a principal ($P1$) to start the project. To continue the project at date 2, the agent requires an additional cash input of i_2 from a second principal ($P2$). To focus on the interface between principal $P1$'s and $P2$'s claims, we shall make the restrictive assumption that $P2$ can contribute no more than the required investment outlay i_2 and that $P1$ cannot contribute the entire amount $i_1 + i_2$. Between dates 1 and 2 (call this date 1.5), $P1$ may suffer a liquidity shock, described in detail below. Also, both principals operate in competitive lending markets, all parties are assumed to be risk-neutral, and there is no discounting.

If the project receives two rounds of financing (i.e. it is continued at date 2 rather than liquidated) it produces a random cash flow at date 3. If the project does not receive the required funding at date 2, it is liquidated for a known value $L > 0$. The final cash flow outcome depends on the realization of the state of nature at date 2, which becomes observable to $P2$ and A at date 2 before the continuation decision is made. We allow for two states of nature, $\hat{s} \in \{s_g, s_b\}$. The good state of nature, s_g, occurs with probability π and the bad state, s_b, with probability $1 - \pi$. As is standard in this literature, we assume that $\hat{s}$ is non-contractible.

In the bad state of nature, the project yields a cash flow of X at date 3 with probability p and with probability $(1 - p)$ the project yields no cash flow but a liquidation value γL, where $\gamma < 1$. In the good state of nature, the cash-flow outcome of the project depends on the agent's effort choice $e \in \{0,1\}$ at date 2. If the agent chooses $e = 1$ then the project yields a final cash flow X with certainty. If the agent chooses $e = 0$, the project succeeds with probability p, as in the bad state of nature. The agent's private cost of choosing high effort ($e = 1$) is $c > 0$, and the cost of $e = 0$ is normalized to zero.

3.2   Parameter Assumptions

The parameter assumptions are identical to those in Ayotte and Bolton (2008); we repeat them here for convenience. We shall restrict ourselves to a subset of parameter values for which the optimal contract for $P1$ and A, and for $P2$ and A, is such that continuation with high effort is optimal in the good state and liquidation at date 2 is optimal in the bad state.

For ease of exposition, we will use the notation R_g to denote the maximum pledgeable income to $P1$ in the good state, conditional on continuation with effort:

$$R_g \equiv X - \frac{c}{1 - p} - i_2 \qquad (8.1)$$

To see that this is the maximum pledgeable income to $P1$, note that in order to encourage A to choose high effort, A requires a sufficient stake w_g in the output when the project succeeds. An optimal contract will pay the agent w_g when the cash flow is X and 0 if output is 0. Thus, in order to elicit effort from A, the following incentive compatibility constraint must be satisfied:

$$w_g - c \geq pw_g$$

which reduces to

$$w_g \geq \frac{c}{1 - p}.$$

Therefore, the maximum pledgeable income to all lenders is $X - \frac{c}{1-p}$. Since $P2$ will not participate unless he receives an expected payment equal to his monetary contribution, $P2$ must be repaid i_2. Thus the maximum pledgeable income to $P1$ is as in (8.1).

With this notation, the parameter restrictions we maintain throughout this chapter are:

Assumptions:
A1)

$$X - c - i_2 > L$$

The first assumption tells us that in the good state, continuation with high effort is economically efficient relative to liquidation.

A2)

$$pX + (1 - p)\gamma L - i_2 < L$$

Assumption A2 says that continuation with low effort is inefficient relative to liquidation; hence liquidating the project will be optimal in the bad state at date 2. Assumptions A1 and A2 together imply also that high effort is efficient relative to low effort in the good state.

A3)

$$\pi R_g + (1 - \pi)L \geq i_1$$

Assumption A3 implies that the first-best action plan, which involves continuation in the good state with effort and liquidation in the bad state, can generate enough cash flow to repay $P1$ for his loan. Since we assume that $L < i_1$, A3 also implies that $R_g > L$; i.e. continuation with effort produces more pledgeable income to $P1$ than liquidation in the good state.

Finally, we shall also assume that:

A4)

$$X - R_g \geq \frac{i_2}{p}.$$

As we will show in the next section, assumption **A4** implies that $P1$ may be at risk of *dilution* of his claim in the bad state even if he writes a debt contract that makes him senior to $P2$, if $P1$ does not also limit $P2$'s borrowing. This assumption implies that $P1$ will require a negative covenant in his loan contract in addition to seniority in order to elicit the first-best action plan by A.

3.3   Contracting Assumptions

The agent A and principal $P1$ can write a bilateral long-term debt contract $C_1 = \{i_1, F_1, \xi_1, \Phi_1\}$ at date 1. Similarly, the agent and principal $P2$ can write a bilateral debt contract $C_2 = \{i_2, F_2, \xi_2\}$ at date 2. Each bilateral contract specifies the amount the principal agrees to lend i_j and a repayment F_j at date 3. The contracts can also specify whether $P1$ takes a *security interest* in the final cash flow or not ($\xi_j \in \{0, 1\}$, where 1 = secured, 0 = unsecured). Consistent with US debtor–creditor law, a security interest gives the lender seniority over any unsecured lender, and seniority over any other secured lender that arrives later in time.[5]

Most important to this chapter, the contract between $P1$ and A can also include a *negative covenant*, which states a maximum amount Φ_j that A is allowed to repay any subsequent lender at date 3.[6] We assume that this negative covenant gives $P1$ a property right that is good against $P2$: if the negative pledge is violated by $P2's$ loan, then $P2's$ loan would be voided, giving him no rights to collect from A. In this chapter, unlike in Ayotte and Bolton (2008), $P2$ is assumed to be fully aware of $P1$'s loan with no reading costs. In contexts where $P2$ has actual knowledge, negative covenants have been enforced against subsequent lenders as property rights.

We also rule out the possibility for now that $P1$ is available to monitor the firm, or to renegotiate his contract with A at date 2 after the realization of the state of nature s_j. Thus, $P1$ is a passive lender who can only lend at date 1 and collect at the final date. This assumption is admittedly strong, but is made to demonstrate in the simplest possible fashion the potential conflicts between $P1$ and $P2$ when they lend at different points in time.

The key economic issues in this chapter are as follows. First, the agent's repayment obligations F_j must be low enough that the agent has an incentive to put in high effort ($e = 1$) in state s_g. Second, F_1 must be sufficiently low to make room for continuation financing by $P2$ at date 2, whenever continuation is efficient. Third, $P1$ faces a threat of dilution of the value of his claim F_1 in the bad state at date 2, when the agent issues a new claim F_2 to $P2$. As we have already mentioned and show below, making $P1$ senior to $P2$ is not a sufficient protection against dilution in our setup, so a negative covenant in $P1's$ contract will be necessary to prevent inefficient dilution.

3.4   Liquidity Preferences and Loan Sales

Liquidity demand of $P1$ is modeled as follows: at date 1.5, after signing contract C_1 but before the state of nature $\hat{s} \in \{s_g, s_b\}$ is realized, $P1$ requires cash (perhaps to originate new loans) and thus values the ability to sell the loan. Formally, we assume that any payment $P1$ receives after date 1.5 is discounted by a factor $\delta < 1$: a contract worth V to an outside buyer with no liquidity needs is worth δV to $P1$. The liquidity demand of $P1$ (δ) is known to all parties at date 1.

We assume a competitive market of potential loan buyers (call a buyer $B1$) with no liquidity needs, willing to buy loans at their perceived fair value at date 1.5. These investors can be thought of as investors such as pension fund managers or other investors that purchase CDO securities. Key to our problem, though, these buyers are imperfectly informed about the details of the loan contracts offered for sale. If $P1$ and A expect that $B1$ is willing to pay a high enough price, they might water down the terms of the loan agreement through weak covenant protection, knowing they can sell it to $B1$ at an inflated value. We assume that $P1$ and A can act as a coalition that maximizes their joint surplus. That is, any benefit to A from cheating $B1$ can be shared with $P1$ through side payments.[7]

To keep the problem simple, we make two strong assumptions about the relationship between the loan buyer $B1$ and seller $P1$. First, we assume that although $B1$ is aware of the production technology of the firm (i.e. the parameters X, p, π, etc.), he is completely uninformed about the specifics of the loan contract $C1$ in the absence of any standardization. The lack of information about loan contracts is realistic in the securitization context, in which many investors hold small stakes in many individual loans. CDO issuances are often backed by hundreds of loans, many of which are purchased by asset managers after the CDO securities are issued to investors. It is rare for a CDO investor to examine the individual loan contracts that comprise the loan pool; instead, these investors are likely to rely on standardized information, such as credit ratings and the prospectus that describes the key characteristics of the individual assets.

Second, in restricting B1 to buy the entire loan or nothing, we abstract from any contracting between P1 and B1, which is undoubtedly important in practice. In many securitizations, for example, the loan originators hold equity in the SPV as a means of eliminating the asymmetric information problems that are relevant here. Though optimal contracts between loan buyers and sellers can mitigate these problems, recent developments suggest that they do not eliminate them.

4 OPTIMAL CONTRACTING WITH NO INFORMATION COSTS

4.1 First-best Contract

Suppose a benevolent, social welfare-maximizing planner could observe the state of the world and make all investment and effort decisions. Under the assumptions above (**A1–A4**), the social planner would choose to fund the project, to continue the project in the good state at date 2 while at the same time choosing high effort ($e = 1$), and to liquidate the project at date 2 in the bad state. This first-best action plan would maximize social welfare, which is given by

$$\pi(X - c - i_2) + (1 - \pi)L - i_1$$

Even though the state of the world is not contractible, in Ayotte and Bolton (2008), we show that the following contract will result in a first-best outcome:

Proposition 1 *Under assumptions A1 to A4, an optimal contract between P1 and A is the following: A receives i_1 at date 1, and promises P1 a repayment*

$$F_1 = \frac{i_1 - (1 - \pi)L}{\pi},$$

at date 3. P1 takes a first-priority security interest in the final cash flow, and P1 has a right to void any loan to A made before date 3 whose repayment exceeds $\Phi_1 = i_2$.

The best response for P2 and A at date 2 is to sign a new loan contract only in the good state specifying a loan of i_2 in return for a (riskless) junior claim of i_2 at date 3.

Proof see Ayotte and Bolton (2008).
In order to implement the first-best, P1 requires not only priority over P2 (through the security interest), but also that A make a credible commitment not to borrow more than i_2. If this negative pledge were not included, then in any contract that allows for

continuation with effort in the good state, $P2$ and A would have the incentive to continue the firm inefficiently at $P1's$ expense in the bad state.

To see this, recall that under assumption **A4**, $X > R_g + \frac{i_2}{p}$. To achieve continuation with effort in the good state F_1 must be no larger than R_g, leaving $X - R_g > \frac{i_2}{p}$ available to offer to $P2$. In the bad state, $P2$ would be willing to lend i_2 and take an unsecured (junior) debt claim with face value $F_2 = \frac{i_2}{p}$. Then A would receive an expected payoff from continuation of

$$p(X - F_1 - F_2) > p\left(X - R_g - \frac{i_2}{p}\right) > 0,$$

which is strictly higher than what A gets in liquidation.

A negative pledge clause that limits $P2's$ repayment to i_2 prevents this excess continuation problem. Since $P2$ understands that A can offer no more than i_2, $P2$ is willing to lend in the good state (since repayment occurs with certainty) but not in the bad state (since the possibility of failure requires a face value above i_2). Thus, the negative pledge clause makes the first-best outcome achievable even though the state is non-contractible.[8] We will refer to the first-best contract between $P1$ and A in Proposition 1 as a *covenant-strong contract* since it includes the negative pledge, and denote this contract C_1^{fb}.

5   OPTIMAL CONTRACTING

5.1   The Contracting and Trading Game with No Standardization

Recall that the timing of the contracting game proceeds as follows:

1. At date 1, $P1$ and A agree on a contract $C1$ and $P1$ extends a loan of i_1 to A.
2. At date 1.5, $P1$ decides whether to sell his loan to $B1$. In the event of a sale, the loan sale game works as follows:
    a. $B1$ forms a belief about the loan contract. Let v_1 denote this belief.
    b. $P1$ decides whether or not to make a take it or leave it offer to sell his loan to $B1$. An offer is a price y_1 at which the loan will be sold if $B1$ agrees.
    c. If an offer is made, $B1$ examines the contract and updates his belief to $v(\Omega_1)$ based on Ω_1, the observable component of the contract C_1. $B1$ then decides whether or not to buy the loan at the given price.
3. At date 2, all parties observe the state of the world. A approaches $P2$ to negotiate contract $C2$. If $P2$ lends i_2, then the project continues to date 3. Otherwise, the project liquidates.
4. At date 3, if the project has been continued, cash flows are realized and the parties holding loans collect from A according to the rights specified in their contracts.

We assume that the loan buyer has pessimistic beliefs. Specifically, the buyer's belief function $v(C_1)$ assumes that the contract being sold is as unfavorable to the buyer as possible, given the loan characteristics that the buyer observes. While these beliefs are convenient, they are not crucial to our qualitative results.

With this structure in hand, it is easy to see that loans will be illiquid when buyers are uninformed. We formalize this in the following proposition:[9]

Proposition 2 *Under no standardization, loans are illiquid and covenant-strong: there does not exist any pure strategy Perfect Bayesian Equilibrium with loan sales. P1 and A write the first-best contract C_1^{fb}.*

The intuition for the first part of the proposition is simple. If the buyer observes nothing about the loan he buys, and his beliefs are pessimistic, he will assume that any loan offered for sale is worthless. Given these beliefs, $B1$ is not willing to pay any positive price. This, in turn, makes $P1$ willing to forgo any attempt to sell the loan.

The implications of illiquid secondary markets has an important effect on the details of the loan contract actually written between $P1$ and A. Since $P1$ expects the loan to be illiquid, the contract between $P1$ and A is written without regard to the buyer – this implies that the parties will write the first-best contract.[10]

We now turn to an analysis of open-ended standardization and its effects on optimal contracting.

5.2   Optimal Contracting with Open-Ended Standardization

We model open-ended standardization as follows. Suppose a technology exists that allows the loan buyer to observe some, but not all, characteristics of the loan he buys at a low cost. As before, this assumption is intended to capture the type of standardization process involved in the securitization of bank loans. When a collateral manager assembles a loan portfolio, he creates a prospectus for investors that describes certain characteristics of the loans that will be assembled in the pool. This provides some important information to investors, who need not read the details of every loan contract purchased by the pool.

In our model, suppose that this technology allows the loan buyer, at zero cost, to observe i_1, F_1, and ξ_1, but not Φ_1. In other words, the loan buyer knows the interest rate and whether the loan is secured (and thus senior), but is not aware of the specific contractual covenants in the loan that are intended to prevent excess continuation in the bad state.

Unlike the previous case, under open-ended standardization the loan buyer can be guaranteed that the minimum value of the loan is above zero. Specifically, the minimum value of a loan at date 1.5 that is secured, and has face value $F_1 \leq R_1$ is

$$V_{lite}(F_1) = \pi F_1 + (1 - \pi)(pF_1 + (1 - p)\gamma L)$$

V_{lite} is the minimum value that $B1$ can ascribe to the loan when $P1$ offers to sell it at date 1.5. Given what $B1$ can observe, the worst case scenario is a contract that completely omits the negative pledge term Φ_1, thus allowing A to continue inefficiently in the bad state and diluting $B1$. Call this contract C_1^{lite}. Alternatively, the first-best loan contract C_1^{fb} has the following value to the buyer:

$$V_{fb}(F_1) = \pi F_1 + (1 - \pi)L$$

Compared to the no-standardization case, open-ended standardization provides more of a guarantee about the loan's characteristics and limits the asymmetric information between loan buyer and seller.

Now, consider how $P1$ and A will set F_1. To keep the problem simple, we suppose that F_1 is set at the level that allows $P1$ to break even under a covenant-lite contract, whenever $P1$ plans to offer a loan for sale. If $P1$ writes a covenant-lite contract, then continuation will not be prevented in the bad state, so the face value of the debt F_1^l satisfies

$$i_1 = \pi F_1^l + (1 - \pi)(pF_1^l + (1 - p)\gamma L)$$

Rearranging, we get

$$F_1^l = \frac{i_1 - (1 - \pi)(1 - p)\gamma L}{\pi + (1 - \pi)p}$$

When $P1$ plans to hold the loan, F_1^s is set so that $P1$ breaks even given that the contract is covenant-strong:

$$F_1^s = \frac{i_1 - (1 - \pi)L}{\pi}$$

As a result, the loan market can now become more liquid as the next proposition illustrates.

Proposition 3 *Under open-ended standardization, two pure strategy equilibria are possible: an equilibrium with liquid, covenant-lite loans, and an equilibrium with illiquid, covenant-strong loans.*

Consider the observable components of the contract C_1: i_1, F_1, ξ_1}. Effectively, this allows $B1$ to know the interest rate and whether the loan is secured, but not whether the loan includes the negative pledge covenant. Given this contract and $B1$'s beliefs, the buyer is willing to pay $V_{lite}(F_1)$ if the loan is offered for sale, which assumes that the covenant is missing (or completely ineffective).

Now, consider the incentives of $P1$ and A when they write C_1. Two cases are relevant. First, suppose that the cost of liquidity to $P1$ is small relative to the difference in values between a covenant-lite and covenant-strong loan. Call this Case 1:

$$\delta V_{fb}(F_1^s) > V_{lite}(F_1^s) \tag{8.2}$$

Then, if $P1$ has a covenant-strong contract, he prefers to hold it and suffer the liquidity cost rather than sell it, given $B1$'s beliefs that the contract is covenant-lite. In this case, the trade-off in writing a covenant-strong contract is the liquidity cost to $P1$. The benefit is the expected gains from preventing inefficient dilution in the bad state. Thus, the incentive compatibility condition under which $P1$ and A write a covenant-lite contract is given by[11]

$$(1 - \delta)V_{fb}(F_1^s) > (1 - \pi)(L - pX - (1 - p)\gamma L + i_2)$$

or

$$(1 - \delta)(\pi F_1^s + (1 - \pi)L) > (1 - \pi)(L - pX - (1 - p)\gamma L + i_2) \qquad (8.3)$$

The left-hand side is the expected liquidity cost to the $P1$ and A coalition from holding a loan when a liquidity shock occurs. The right-hand side is the expected efficiency loss from continuation in the bad state, which $P1$ and A bear in equilibrium. If the inequality holds, then $P1$ and A would prefer to write a covenant-lite contract, which is sold whenever $P1$ suffers a liquidity shock, at a fair price. If this inequality does not hold, then the equilibrium will feature covenant-strong, illiquid contracts.

The second case (Case 2) occurs when $P1$'s liquidity demand is large enough that $P1$ would prefer to sell a covenant-strong loan even if it is subject to the discount due to $B1$'s pessimistic beliefs. This will be true when $\delta V_{fb}(F_1^s) < V_{lite}(F_1^s)$. Then the above inequality becomes

$$V_{fb}(F_1^s) - V_{lite}(F_1^s) > (1 - \pi)(L - pX - (1 - p)\gamma L + i_2)$$

If this inequality holds, then $P1$ and A prefer to write a covenant-lite contract which is sold when $P1$ suffers a liquidity shock, at a fair price. This expression can be reduced to

$$X - F_1^s > \frac{i_2}{p}$$

which is always true, given assumption A4. Thus, the parties always prefer a covenant-lite contract if liquidity demand is high enough.

Corollary 4 *The liquid, covenant-lite equilibrium is more likely when:*
a) *the probability of the bad state is lower (higher π);*
b) *originators' liquidity needs are higher (lower δ)*

When economic times are good, and defaults are unlikely to occur, loan buyers are less concerned about the absence of contractual terms that would impose discipline on borrowers in bad states. As a result, there are two effects: they are willing to pay a high price for loans, despite their information disadvantage. This makes Case 2 more likely to occur, which is a covenant-lite equilibrium. Second, within the Case 1 region, a covenant-lite equilibrium occurs if and only if

$$(1 - \delta)(\pi F_1^s + (1 - \pi)L) > (1 - \pi)(L - pX - (1 - p)\gamma L + i_2)$$

Given the definition of F_1^s, the left-hand side of the inequality is always equal to $(1 - \delta)i_1$, which is independent of π. The right-hand side is the expected efficiency loss from excess continuation in the bad state, and is decreasing in π. This implies that the covenant-lite equilibrium is more likely to occur when π is high. Intuitively, within Case 1, $P1$ and A trade off the cost of holding an illiquid, covenant-strong loan contract with the expected losses from inefficient continuation. As π rises, the costs of inefficient continuation fall.

Part (b) of the Corollary is also important. The liquidity discount can be interpreted as a cost to $P1$ of funds required for new lending. In boom periods (when $P1$ has valuable loan opportunities), selling loans is more valuable because it frees up capital to make new loans (Drucker and Puri 2006). Thus, we would expect δ to be low during a credit boom, when lenders perceive that the opportunity cost of funds is high. However, in a downturn δ is higher and π is lower, so that $P1$ is both less eager to sell the loan and more concerned about limiting excess continuation in the bad state. As credit markets deteriorated in 2007, loan opportunities dried up and bad states became more likely. Our model explains that both of these conditions lead to more covenant-strong lending with less liquidity.

The formal model is intended as a starting point to investigating these issues. In the next subsections, we explore in turn how our analysis might be extended to the liquidity of junior loans, to capture closed-ended standardization, and to the role of the law in achieving standardization.

5.2.1 Sales of junior loans

In the formal model, we considered sales of $P1's$ senior loan to an outside buyer. Suppose instead that $P2$ has liquidity needs ($\delta < 1$) with respect to its junior loan. $P2$ seeks to sell her loan in a competitive secondary market to some buyer $B2$ at an interim date 2.5 (between the date of $P2's$ loan and the final cash flow).

Similar to our analysis above, suppose there are no information asymmetries with respect to $P1's$ loan – all parties are fully informed about C_1, but $P2$ has private information about $C2$. Consider the incentives of the various parties under open-ended standardization. Specifically, suppose a loan buyer $B2$ can observe the standard terms $\{i_2, F_2\}$ but not whether the loan is secured (ξ_2) or any negative pledge covenants (Φ_2).

Under these assumptions, we expect that the first-best contracts will be written by $P1$ and $P2$. $P2$ lends only in the good state, since the negative pledge in the first-best contract C_1^{fb} makes it unprofitable for $P2$ to extend a loan in the bad state. When $P2$ lends in the good state, his loan will be fully liquid: $P2$ will always be able to sell the loan to $B2$ at its fundamental value (i_2). The intuition for this is simple. Unlike the senior loan C_1, which requires several contractual terms to guarantee its value, the optimal contract C_2 is unsecured debt, and does not contain a negative pledge covenant. Thus, there is less scope for opportunism in the contractual terms of a junior loan than there is in a senior loan. The buyer expects a worst-case scenario given the terms he observes, but with a junior loan, the worst-case scenario is in fact the optimal contract.

The idea that junior loans are always liquid, while senior loans can be illiquid, runs against standard theories in corporate finance that find the opposite (Gorton and Pennacchi 1990). When asymmetric information concerns the firm's future cash flows, senior securities are more liquid because their value is less sensitive to private information. In this model, the asymmetric information is about the terms of the contract, not the firm's cash flows. A senior loan requires more contractual terms to be effective. Relative to junior loans, this increases the asymmetry of information between loan buyers and sellers, which can make senior loans particularly illiquid.

This logic is a starting point, but should not be overstated, because we have not fully explored the interactions between loan buyers when there is asymmetric information about both C_1 and C_2. Here, the issues become substantially more complicated. A loan buyer $B2$ would be interested in knowing not only about the details of the contract C_2

that he is buying, but also about the contract C_1, which can affect the value of C_2 in a meaningful way. Moreover, $P1$ and A will structure their contract in response not only to $B1$, but also to whether $P2$ expects to sell his loan to $B2$. Whether senior or junior loans are more liquid in a more complicated model is left for future work.

5.2.2 Closed-ended standardization

The open-ended standardization we consider in the formal model assumes that $P1$ and A can always include in their loan agreement extra terms that $B1$ cannot observe. In the loan securitization context, this is realistic, but it is not true in all cases that involve buying and selling of credit risk. For instance, consider credit default swap contracts. These contracts allow one party to purchase credit insurance from another party to protect against a default of some reference entity. These contracts are standardized by the International Swaps and Derivatives Association (ISDA), a trade organization comprised of large players in this market. The ISDA has standard-form contracts that allow the parties to a swap contract to tailor various terms (the price, the reference security, the default event, etc.). But importantly, the ISDA form is closed-ended: the options given to the parties to tailor the contract are fixed in advance in the standard contract.

In a richer model, one might expect a trade-off between open- and closed-ended standardization. For example, because of its closed-endedness, terms outside this closed set might be valuable for some borrowers to limit agency costs. But if the standard form becomes open-ended enough to include these terms, and they are sufficiently costly to discover, this increases the scope for contracting parties to include opportunistic terms that redistribute value away from the potential loan buyer.

5.2.3 Law and standardization

This chapter focuses on private means of achieving standardization, but has not explored the role of the law in enhancing liquidity of contracts. It is possible for the law to standardize contracts so as to limit asymmetric information about contractual terms, thus making them more liquid.

One example of this is the law's treatment of negotiable instruments under Article 3 of the Uniform Commercial Code (UCC). The intent of this area of law is to enhance the liquidity of loans in the secondary market by limiting the required investigation by a buyer into the loan transaction. Specifically, a loan buyer who qualifies as a 'holder in due course' takes free of any 'personal defenses' that may be asserted by the borrower (A) against his original lender (P1). For example, suppose that A gives $P1$ a note in exchange for goods that $P1$ promises to deliver, and $P1$ fails to deliver. $P1$ sells the note to $B1$, who does not know about $P1's$ failure to deliver the goods. If $B1$ is considered a holder in due course, he has the right to collect the full amount of the note from A. This frees up $B1$ from knowing the entire details of the relationship between $P1$ and A and makes the note more liquid as a result.

The law also adds value in some cases by standardizing the forms of notice that are available to third parties. The law of security interests in personal property, governed by Article 9 of the UCC, is one prominent example. In order to have a right that binds third parties (like buyers and other lenders), a lender must provide notice to the world by recording their interest in a registry that other lenders can check. This notice is standardized and includes only basic information, such as the creditor's name and a categorical description of the collateral subject to the security interest. This standardization has an important benefit in reducing information acquisition costs of third parties. Suppose, for example, that a lender is interested in being secured by a borrower's inventory. If this lender checks the registry and finds that the only prior security interest is in the borrower's accounts receivable, then the inventory lender knows that she can obtain a first priority position with respect to the inventory; she need not inquire any further into the details of the contract between the receivables lender and the borrower. While there are many other characteristics that would affect the ultimate value of the loan (the borrower's likelihood of default, the lender's expected recovery when her claim exceeds the value of the inventory, etc.), the inventory lender can be guaranteed a baseline minimum level of protection at a very low investigation cost. Smith (2006, 2010) refers to this concept as *modularity*, and argues that it is a common observed feature in the standardization of property rights.

While there are examples of standardization within the law that enhance liquidity and limit opportunism, there are important open theoretical questions in this area. As the ISDA and securitization examples illustrate, market participants may have the incentive and ability to create open-ended and closed-ended standardized forms. This raises the question, why is the law necessary to create standardization? Under what circumstances are private attempts to standardize subject to market failures that require legal intervention?

6.   CONCLUSION

In this chapter, we have conducted a preliminary investigation into standardization of financial contracts as a means of reducing reading costs by third-party loan buyers. We show, however, that standardization is not a panacea. When loan buyers can acquire more information about the underlying loan at low cost, this enhances the liquidity of loan contracts. But this liquidity, in turn, creates incentives for the loan originator and borrower to water down the features of the contract that the loan buyers do not observe. Even if loan buyers are rational and incorporate the expectation of this 'covenant-lite' lending behavior into the price of the loan, these terms will not be used in equilibrium, only when bad economic times are perceived as unlikely. When bad times do arise, however, lenders respond by writing covenant-strong illiquid debt contracts.

We have left many important and interesting questions as open areas for future research. In particular, the role of legal intervention as a mandatory standardization device, and the different ways that standardization can operate, is a promising topic for future theoretical research in the law and economics of property.

NOTES

*   We would like to thank Ed Morrison, David Skeie, and Henry Smith for helpful discussions and suggestions on this draft.
1.   For example, the definition of securitization in Investopedia: 'Securitization is the process of taking an illiquid asset, or group of assets, and through financial engineering, transforming them into a

security. . .This market is extremely large, providing a significant amount of liquidity to the group of mortgages, which otherwise would have been quite illiquid on their own.'

2. The Encylopedia of Finance (Lee and Lee, 2006) defines securitization as: 'Pooling loans for various purposes into standardized securities backed by those loans, which can then be traded like any other security'.

3. See, for example, 'Global Cash Flow and Synthetic CDO Criteria', Standard and Poors Structured Finance, March 21, 2002. In addition, rating agencies license computer programs to CLO asset managers that allow these managers to generate predicted ratings for their CLO securities by inputting a predetermined set of characteristics of their loan pools (Benmelech and Dlugosz, 2009).

4. 'CDO Spotlight: The Covenant-Lite Juggernaut Is Raising CLO Risks – And Standard & Poor's Is Responding' Standard and Poor's Ratings Direct, June 12, 2007.

5. This implies that if A gives security interests to both lenders, $P1$ has priority over $P2$ by virtue of being first in time.

6. Since $P2$ is the last lender in our simple model, this term is obviously relevant only for $P1$.

7. One way to motivate this scenario is through an 'origination fee' that A pays $P1$. Another is a second loan that $P1$ holds rather than sells.

8. If $P2$ can take a claim on A's personal assets (his dividend from the firm at the end of date three) then he would be equally happy to lend into an inefficient continuation in the bad state. Thus $P1$'s right to restrict alienability must extend beyond the corporate form and also to A's assets more generally in order to effectively shut down $P2$'s loan.

9. We omit formal proofs in this chapter, but the informal intuition follows the proposition in the text.

10. The result may seem paradoxical, in that the loan buyer's pessimistic beliefs about a worthless loan are not confirmed by the loan that $P1$ and A actually write. Moreover, $P1$ loses liquidity by virtue of $B1's$ beliefs: on the equilibrium path, there are potential gains from trade that are not exploited when $P1$ suffers a liquidity shock. But the perfect bayesian equilibrium (PBE) requires only that strategies are consistent with beliefs on the equilibrium path. $P2$ believes that any loan offered for sale is worthless; given these beliefs, $P1$ refuses to offer the loan for sale, knowing any positive price will be rejected.

11. If the expression holds at F_1^y, it holds a fortiori for F_1^j, which will be the equilibrium F_1 in a covenant-lite equilibrium.

REFERENCES

Amihud, Y. and H. Mendelsohn. (1988). 'Liquidity and Asset Prices: Financial Management Implications', *Financial Management*, 17, 5–15.

Ayotte, K. and P. Bolton. (2008). 'Optimal Property Rights in Financial Contracting', Working Paper.

Benmelech, E. and J. Dlugosz. (2009). 'The Alchemy of CDO Credit Ratings', NBER Working Paper 14878.

Drucker, S. and M. Puri. (2009). 'On Loan Sales, Loan Contracting, and Lending Relationships', *Review of Financial Studies*, 22 (7), 2635–2672.

Gale, D. (1992). 'Standard Securities', *Review of Economic Studies*, 59, 731–755.

Gorton, G. and G. Pennacchi. (1990). 'Financial Intermediaries and Liquidity Creation'. *Journal of Finance*, 45, 49–71.

Lee, C.F. and A.C. Lee. (2006). *Encyclopedia of Finance.* Springer Science and Business Media, Inc.

Merrill, T. and H.E. Smith. (2000). 'Optimal Standardization in the Law of Property: The Numerus Clausus Principle', *Yale Law Journal*, 110 (1), 1–70.

Merrill, T. and H.E. Smith. (2001). 'What Happened to Property in Law and Economics?', *Yale Law Journal*, 111, 357–398.

Rajan, U., A. Seru and V. Vig. (2008). 'The Failure of Models that Predict Failure: Distance, Incentives and Defaults', Working Paper.

Smith, H.E. (2006). 'Modularity in Contracts: Boilerplate and Information Flow', *Michigan Law Review*, 104, 1175–1221.

Smith, H.E. (2010). 'Standardization in Property Law', Working paper.

Sussman, O. (1999). 'Economic Growth With Standardized Contracts', *European Economic Review*, 43 (9), 1797–1818.

9 The personification and property of legal entities
George Triantis*

Property rights in productive assets are commonly held by legal entities rather than individuals. Only persons can own property, and the law defines persons to include organizations such as corporations, partnerships, and trusts (referred to collectively hereafter as 'entities' or 'firms'). This chapter addresses the related issues of the justification for firm ownership of property and the efficient division of assets among distinct legal entities.[1] In brief, firm ownership coordinates the productive activity of self-interested individuals. Earlier scholarship by economists suggested that the allocation of *control* over assets reduces the inefficiencies of incomplete contracts caused by imperfect information. Thus, economic integration brings assets into common ownership to avoid or simplify contracting. These theories, however, do not distinguish between assets owned directly by an individual and assets controlled indirectly through an entity. They also do not distinguish between assets held within a single entity and assets partitioned among multiple entities within common control. More recent literature fills this gap by explaining the legal significance of the boundaries of distinct entities, whether or not they fall under the control of a single owner.

The starting point for understanding firm boundaries is the observation that the person who is best situated to control the use of an asset may not be in the best position to finance its use. Berle and Means (1932) famously noted that the corporation is a vehicle for achieving such separation and that the separation raises significant and costly conflicts between owners and managers. This chapter explains how the deliberate drawing of firm boundaries can reduce these agency costs and thereby lower the cost of financing productive activity. In particular, the discussion focuses on the advantages of tailoring financing (or capital structure) to asset type. The law presents significant challenges to the goals of tailoring. Although optimal financing terms are often asset-contingent, the law favors entity-based rather than asset-based financing. In particular, the law requires considerable uniformity in the manner in which assets are financed and governed within a single entity, and the law raises obstacles to collaborative efforts across legal entities (the trade of goods, services, or capital across firm boundaries) even if they are held under common control.

Part I reviews the economic theories explaining the allocation of *control* over asset groups and, specifically, the justifications for the integration of assets under common control. Given the wealth constraints and risk aversion of individuals, external financing is often needed to enable the desired accumulation of assets; that is, ownership of the economic returns must be separated from control. Yet, this separation itself causes information problems (moral hazard and adverse selection) that afflict financial contracts. Part II demonstrates that the division of assets into distinct legal entities allows for the tailoring of financial contracts to asset types which, in turn, mitigates the information problems and reduces the cost of financing. The division of assets between entities, however, raises new costs: notably, (a) the partitioning of internal capital markets that facilitate the movement of capital from one use to another (Part III) and (b) the legal hurdles to collaboration between related firms, despite the presence of common control (Part IV). This framework might explain the conditions under which asset partitioning occurs, as well as the choice among alternative corporate restructurings involving divestitures (e.g., spin-offs, equity carveouts or securitizations) and combinations (e.g. mergers or acquisitions).

Part V briefly describes how enterprises may wish to keep in a discrete entity assets that they intend to sell as a group, in order to reduce the transaction costs of such future alienation. The chapter then concludes with suggestions for future research.

I.   ECONOMIC BOUNDARIES OF CONTROL

In 1937, Ronald Coase inquired why a significant portion of productive activity is carried out within firms rather than by contract between individuals. This question has since spawned a large body of scholarly literature on the theory of the firm. Coase argued that a firm can rely on the hierarchical authority ('fiat') of its management to avoid the transaction costs of contracting with employees in the face of uncertainty. Since then, other scholars have focused particularly on the danger of opportunistic hold-up, which arises where one party to an exchange can increase the surplus from trade by making relationship-specific investments, but where information problems impede complete contracting (e.g., Klein et al., 1978; Williamson, 1975). Contracts are incomplete when they fail to specify efficient obligations for all possible future contingencies. This may be the case because the parties cannot anticipate all contingencies or they find it infeasible to provide for all of them. In addition, the parties may be asymmetrically informed in ways that prevent them from specifying the optimal performance obligations in each future contingency. And, even if they could provide for each future contingency, contract enforcement is costly and error-prone because the court might not be able to verify all relevant facts.

Parties may complete their contracts in order to achieve efficient trade ex post, either by renegotiating their deal or asking a court to fill the gaps. Both litigation and renegotiation give rise to opportunistic behavior, particularly hold-up strategies, that distorts ex ante incentives to make specific investments. If one party has made an investment specific to the anticipated exchange, the other party may exploit a gap or ambiguity in the contract to appropriate the value of this investment. She may threaten to withhold performance in order to force a favorable renegotiation of the terms of trade. In anticipation of this renegotiation, parties are reluctant to make specific investments that cannot be protected by contract (e.g. R&D expenditures: Aghion and Tirole (2004)), and this reduces the expected value of exchanges. Efficient incentives might be restored if both sides make reciprocal investments. Otherwise, according to the early literature on hold-ups, this problem can be avoided by integrating the two parties in a single hierarchical firm, where bosses make specific investment and employees must follow their commands.

A hierarchical structure might also improve the prospects for ex post efficiency – for example, the decision whether or not to execute the exchange as agreed upon or how much effort to invest in it. In fact, ex post efficiency is viewed by some authors as a more significant concern in business ventures than the vulnerability of specific investment (e.g., Baker, Gibbons and Murphy, 2006). Whereas the hold-up literature assumes that information becomes symmetrical ex post in order to allow for efficient renegotiation, information problems in fact often persist to disrupt renegotiation. Given that renegotiation cannot ensure ex post efficiency and that a court might not be able to verify all pertinent facts, a feasible contract may simply give one party discretion over some term of the contract. For example, if it is not clear which color widget would yield the greatest surplus, the contract may allow the buyer to choose the color sometime after contracting. This may be preferable over contracting initially for a red widget and relying on renegotiation: if the seller were unaware of the value of the blue widget to the buyer, she might demand too high a price in renegotiation, leaving the buyer with no choice but to pay for the less valuable red widget. The advantage is particularly clear if the parties' interests are unlikely to conflict too much (e.g. the blue widget is much more difficult to manufacture than the red) (Simon, 1951).[2] Yet, this contract solution is effective in avoiding opportunism only to the extent that contract enforcement is cheap and accurate. In this light of the reality of imperfect contract enforcement, the hierarchical structure within a firm provides an alternative mechanism for delegating discretion: the employer can direct its employee to manufacture the blue widget.

In reality, however, a boss can no more compel an employee to follow an order (instead of quitting) than she could specifically enforce a simple contract (Alchian and Demsetz, 1972). Therefore, the mere establishment of a hierarchy within a firm cannot resolve the ex ante and ex post inefficiencies of incomplete contracting. Within or outside a firm, agency problems abound: an employee or contractor may invest too little in firm-specific human capital, each may exert too little effort in the performance of his duties and each may appropriate firm assets in the form of excessive perquisites or otherwise (Jensen and Meckling, 1976).

Given that contracts are inherently incomplete and that the law does not permit coercive authority to be exercised directly over the actions of individuals, economists have looked for other means by which parties may delegate discretion and power. One tool is the control that accompanies ownership of physical assets that are critical to the production of the contracting surplus. Grossman, Hart and Moore, for example, suggest that allocating control over unique assets to parties who could make the most significant relationship-specific investments gives them greater bargaining power to retain the fruits of their specific investment (Grossman and Hart, 1986; Hart and Moore, 1990; Hart, 1995). Within a firm, shareholders have the authority to remove assets from their managers' control, and a creditor has the right to take control in the event of default. These ownership rights are the source of power and important discipline against agency conflicts with managers. In some cases, power does not rely on formal property rights. Rajan and Zingales (2000) note that physical resources are less significant in today's economy than assets over which property rights cannot be asserted: such as relationships, reputation and human capital. In these cases, an employer can use its access to a key resource, such as client relations or the complementarities among the human capital of different personnel, as leverage against a reluctant employee.

These theories explain that the control over key assets, whether vindicated by property rights or otherwise, can mitigate residual agency problems left unresolved by incomplete contracting, but they do not address the advantage of organizing collaborative activity in firms qua legal entities. They have little to say about the legal boundaries of discrete business entities. In particular, these theories do not distinguish among an individual owner, a single firm and a family of affiliate companies controlled by the same majority stockholder. The importance of entity financing is revealed when the assumptions of risk neutrality and boundless wealth are relaxed, and third party financing becomes necessary. External financing gives rise to a distinct set of contractual conflicts, between investors and managers (Berle and Means, 1932). To some degree, therefore, integration substitutes the problems of *financial* contracting for those of incomplete *commercial* contracting.

Entity ownership of property is important in addressing the problems of third party financing. If individual A acquires the assets of individual B – or, if firm A vertically integrates with firm B – the acquirer needs to finance the acquisition and the deployment of the assets. Productive assets, like A and B, are usually held in one or more firms in order to improve *financing* efficiency, rather than to address the challenges of incomplete contracts for goods or services. To a large degree, financing efficiency depends on the ability to match capital and governance structures with the types of assets being financed. The law makes it difficult, however, to achieve such tailoring to subsets of assets within a single firm. Thus, under current law, an enterprise must split asset groups among distinct entities in order to tailor. Yet, while financing may be more efficient when the assets are separated, separation between firms resurrects the need to enter into incomplete contracts to exploit efficiencies from the joint use of assets. This tension is explored in Part III. In sum, the decision to integrate two pools of assets in a single firm or to separate them into distinct firms, has significant and conflicting efficiency implications.

II.   THE LEGAL BOUNDARIES OF A FIRM

A.   Capital Structure Tailoring[3]

Only a legal person has the capacity to enter into a contract. To contract, a party must have standing to sue and be sued, and must be entitled to hold property against which the contract may be enforced. The law endows some entities with the rights of a person, including the capacity to enter into legally enforceable contracts. Given that individuals have rights to contract, what is the advantage of contracting through legal entities? The benefit comes from pledging different subsets of assets to different obligations (Mahoney, 2000; Hansmann and Kraakman, 2000). In particular, the discussion below explains that (a) there are benefits from tailoring financial contracts to asset types and (b) under current law, such tailoring can be accomplished only by separating different asset types into distinct legal entities.

Three features of the boundaries around firm property are significant for our purposes. First, one entity cannot encumber the assets of another without the latter's consent.[4] Thus, the assets of one entity are shielded from the claims and enforcement rights of creditors of another person. The legal recognition of debts as personal protects the firm's assets from the claims against the firm's owner, as well as against other firms controlled by the same owner (Hansmann and Kraakman, 2000).

Second, *all* firm assets are generally available to satisfy the firm's debts. It is difficult for a firm to insulate some of its assets from its creditors or to divide the residual claim in different groups of assets between two classes of shareholders, unless they are removed to a separate legal entity. If a corporate division purchases inventory on credit, for example, judicial enforcement of that obligation can reach any asset of the corporation and is not limited to the inventory or the division to which it is delivered. Security interests and tracking stocks only partially segregate and shield assets; both contracts provide payoffs out of all firm assets when the firm is dissolved or liquidated (Triantis, 2004; Iacobucci and Triantis, 2007). Secured creditors have a higher priority against collateral assets, but they can also assert a personal claim against all firm assets (subject to marshalling restrictions). Under some circumstances, even non-recourse secured claims have general recourse against firm assets: for instance, they become recourse claims in Chapter 11 bankruptcy reorganizations. On the equity side, the tracking stockholder is entitled to share in the residual payoff following the dissolution of the firm. Thus, a firm's capital structure must be firm-wide; to tailor capital structure to asset-types, asset pools must be split into distinct entities (Iacobucci and Triantis, 2007).

The third important feature consists of the set of significant formalities and restrictions on the dealings that the law imposes on transactions between related firms, whether commercial or financial, in order to protect the interests of minority shareholders or creditors of the distinct entities. Thus, a parent company cannot shift capital between subsidiaries as easily as an integrated firm may move funds among divisions (Triantis, 2004). Moreover, the affiliated subsidiaries are compelled by corporate and debtor–creditor laws to deal with each other at arm's length (Iacobucci and Triantis, 2007).

The benefits of tailoring capital structure to asset types are multifaceted and highly significant. While the scholarship on financial contracting is voluminous, several broad themes demonstrate that optimal capital structure varies with the type of asset or venture being financed. Much of financial contracting is motivated by the problems of imperfect information: asymmetric information between the outsider investor and the insider entrepreneur or manager, and agency problems due to costly and error-prone enforcement of contractual controls on behavior. The dual concerns with the insider's private information and the unchecked risk of misbehavior explain much of the financial contracting of an enterprise (e.g., Jensen and Meckling, 1976; Myers, 1977; Myers and Majluf, 1984). The following asset-type contrasts, among others, bear accordingly on capital structure choices: (1) growth opportunities versus assets in place, (2) liquid versus illiquid assets, (3) risky versus non-risky assets, and (4) the degree to which asset values are vulnerable to exogenous and systemic volatility. First, the valuation of growth opportunities depends on information that is available only to insiders (for example, R&D projects and other trade secrets), while mature industries tend to be more transparent. Second, agency problems are more significant when managers can convert firm assets into private benefits, and some assets are more prone to such appropriation. In particular, managers can more easily convert liquid than illiquid assets to their private use. Third, investors are concerned about the volatility of assets because of the risk of insolvency and often wish to diversify this risk. Fourth, the contribution of management to asset values is often difficult to observe when the values are susceptible to significant exogenous risks.

The benefits from tailoring hinge on the sensitivity of optimal design of financial contracts to the characteristics of firm assets. To the degree that the capital structure demand of asset types within a firm diverge, the cost of capital may be lowered by segregating asset types into distinct entities. For example, suppose that both asset group A and group B are most efficiently controlled by the same individual, but that the optimal shareholding of this individual is 60% in A and 40% in B. This combination is easily achieved by dividing the assets into firms A and B, both of which are controlled by a holding company. If the asset groups are held instead as divisions in a single entity, the entity would have a 'blended' capital structure that reflects both asset groups and the interaction between them: for example, the controlling shareholder might hold a 50% equity stake.

The principal function of entity ownership of property is to reduce the cost of financing productive ventures by permitting the tailoring of capital structure to asset-type. As noted earlier, legal obligations are personal and, with few exceptions, a creditor can reach any of the assets of a debtor. Thus, the decisions to incur debts are firm-wide. Two ventures may call for different debt–equity ratios, so that separating the ventures between two entities allows each venture to have its optimal amount of debt and equity financing (Leland, 2007; Iacobucci and Triantis, 2007) Indeed, the evidence indicates that spin-offs create firms with significantly different leverage than their originators have, both before and after the divestiture, which reflects the differences in asset types (e.g. Mehotra et al., 2003; Dittmar, 2004). Mehotra et al. (2003) report that 'it is not uncommon for company documents to state that a spin-off would allow heterogeneous business units to establish capital structures that are better suited to the nature of their assets or growth prospects' (at 1362).

The tailoring of leverage to asset types encompasses many other features of debt contracting, and this cannot be done within a single firm. This is demonstrated in the scenario presented in Hansmann and Kraakman (2001). If a hotel and an oil refining venture are held in separate corporations, then the respective assets can be pledged to back the obligations to different lenders (see also Hansmann and Mattei (1998) on the use of the trust entity to partition assets). This tailoring of debt claims to asset types yields a number of potential benefits. Hansmann and Kraakman (2001) suggest that the borrower can thereby exploit the specialized screening and monitoring of one or both lenders. The lender to the hotel business can concern itself only with monitoring the hotel assets, and the oil refining lender can similarly focus its monitoring in oil refining. This may reduce the cost of borrowing if one or both lenders have comparative advantage in screening and monitoring the respective set of assets.[5] The partitioning may yield other efficiencies as well. The portfolio of one lender may be better suited to diversify or otherwise accommodate the risk in venture A. Or, it may be that venture B requires relatively little monitoring and can be financed by relatively passive bondholders, rather than by incurring the higher cost of a delegated monitor such as a bank.

The exploitation of screening and monitoring efficiencies was the explanation offered by a number of authors for secured credit (e.g. Jackson and Kronman, 1979; Schwartz, 1981; Levmore, 1982). For example, a secured creditor could focus its monitoring efforts on the collateral, while unsecured creditors could monitor the remaining assets or the value of the synergies created by the joint use of the assets. Yet, such partitioning within a firm is less effective than between firms because of the right of secured creditors to enforce their claim against all assets of the debtor. Moreover, the bankruptcy process is well known to 'bleed' secured creditors somewhat, leaving them exposed to share as unsecured claimants some of the losses from insolvency (see, e.g. Scott, 1986). The desire to partition assets and insulate one group (often, receivables) from the bankruptcy of the other, has led to the use of special purpose entities in structured finance and securitizations. These entities often sell debt securities of tiered priority, whose market value depends on the expectation that the entity will be 'bankruptcy remote'.[6]

The choice between public and private debt is determined partly by monitoring considerations, but also by the feature that private debt is more easily renegotiated than public debt (Triantis and Daniels, 1995). Financial institutions are better suited to financing groups of assets with significant synergies (or going concern surpluses), particularly where exogenous shocks may cause insolvency and necessitate financial restructuring. If an enterprise includes ventures that are different in these respects, partitioning the ventures into distinct entities may reduce capital costs. In particular, assets with higher liquidation values and lower susceptibility to exogenous shocks may be financed by public debt and those with lower liquidation values and greater insolvency risk may be financed by bank debt.

In a related manner, partitioning between firms also shields one venture from the bankruptcy cost arising from another failed venture. If insolvency leads to the liquidation of the latter venture, the healthy one can continue intact without the cost of bankruptcy lawyers and accountants, the threat of inefficient liquidation, or distraction to management (Hansmann et al., 2006). On the other hand, combining the two ventures in one firm diversifies the risk of the assets and lowers the probability of insolvency and bankruptcy costs.

The same asset-based characteristics that govern efficient partitioning among lenders are also the source of potential benefits from tailoring stockholding to asset type. Investors with specialized screening and monitoring skills may pay more for stock in one or the other venture alone. Moreover, the risk of one venture alone may offer the market a 'pure play' in that venture, that may meet diversification (or other) needs of a group of investors. As noted below, ventures that would benefit from closer monitoring may have more concentrated ownership than transparent assets. Issuing stock separately in a venture may also invite information intermediaries, such as analysts, to follow those assets separately, allowing the market to 'unpack' their value. As noted earlier, the separate equity financing of such assets can only be done by removing them to a distinct legal entity.

The optimal concentration (or dispersion) of ownership offers a good example of tailoring opportunities. Finance theory suggests that the optimal concentration is a function of asset type under the following tradeoff. The larger the proportion of shares held by a single person, the more she internalizes the fortunes of the firm. If she is a manager, her decision-making incentives improve and, if she is not, her incentives to monitor improve. On the other hand, the owner of a large block of stock sacrifices some of her ability to diversify the nonsystematic risk of firm assets as well as the ability to trade shares in a liquid market. In addition, as a controlling shareholder acquires a large proportion of the votes, she is increasingly insulated from the market for corporate control and proxy contests from other shareholders. Such protection can lead to increase in consumption of private benefits at the expense of overall firm value. As a general matter, then, concentrated ownership is more valuable when the optimal monitoring investment is high; but concentration is less valuable when asset values are risky, managerial entrenchment causes inefficient private-benefit extraction, and there is otherwise a vibrant market for corporate control. Thus, for example, an unregulated venture highly dependent on R&D

and vulnerable to the exogenous shocks of international trade may benefit more from the monitoring of a concentrated owner than a regulated or conventional manufacturing enterprise, yielding opportunities for private benefit consumption by managers or controlling shareholders.

To the extent there is a market for an entity's stock, trading in the stock reveals information about the value of the venture that would be less clear if the venture were part of an integrated issuer. This is a significant consideration in the design of performance-based compensation. The inability to issue stock that closely tracks the value of a division of an integrated firm constrains the ability of firms to provide performance-based compensation to the divisional managers, because they would benefit (or lose) from the performance of other divisions. A firm can compensate a divisional manager on the basis of the division's performance, as reflected in the firm's financial statements. If it seeks to exploit market rather than accounting information, however, it is limited to the market price of its firm-wide shares. Thus, partitioning assets offers valuable opportunities to tailor managerial compensation. It can also enhance recruiting and retention efforts because the manager is not subject to the risk of performance failures of other divisions.

Finance experts focus on the stock-side tailoring benefits in justifying the creation of a new entity and the divestiture of assets in spin-offs and equity carve-outs (e.g., Schipper and Smith, 1986; Allen, 1998; Daly et al., 1997). For reasons outlined above, tracking stocks cannot yield these benefits and are therefore much less frequent than either spin-offs or carve-outs. In particular, business enterprises and commentators suggest that, by creating a legal interest in the partitioned assets, the divestitures offer investors a new security (the 'pure play') and more specialized coverage by securities analysts. In addition, the new stock can be issued to executives to align their compensation more closely to the value of the venture, as well as to recruit or retain talented management. In 2008, Motorola announced that it would split its company into two publicly traded companies, and it invoked explicitly the benefits of tailoring. The CEO and President announced that 'Creating two industry-leading companies will provide improved flexibility, more tailored capital structures, and increased management focus – as well as more targeted investment opportunities for our shareholders.'[7]

The foregoing discussion focused on the tailoring of the distribution of financial interests and claims among investors. The governance or control rights in a firm may also be tailored. Given that governance choices typically entail personal obligations, in the sense described earlier, the segmenting of assets in different firms may be necessary for tailoring. For example, although covenants in debt contracts may apply to the use of specific assets (e.g., a covenant to insure or not to sell a key asset), all assets of the firm are pledged and are affected by a default. A violation of the covenant leads to acceleration of the maturity of the loan and entitles the lender to enforce against any or all the assets of the firm. Thus, a covenant that may be appropriate with respect to one group of assets may be undesirable when that asset group is combined with others because of the wider impact of the default sanction. If the contract cannot be renegotiated or refinanced, for example, there is a risk of inefficient liquidation. The integration of asset groups may be inefficient if it leaves the firm with a choice between two crude alternatives: to include the asset-specific covenant and bear the firm-wide consequences of violation or exclude the covenant and bear the cost of diluted incentives.

Corporate governance is firm-wide in other respects, as well. Each corporation chooses a single state of incorporation, which determines both the corporate statute and the courts that enforce state governance laws. For example, by selecting an incorporation state and its charter provisions, a firm chooses among various duties of care to bind its directors, as well as among alternative standing rules allowing shareholders to bring derivative suits to enforce such duties. Directors owe fiduciary obligations to the firm as a whole, to maximize the value of the entire firm without regard to the value of any subdivision. As noted earlier, tracking stocks reflect imperfectly the value of the tracked division because they entitle the investor to participate in the residue of the entire firm. If tracking stock carries voting rights, those rights are to vote for directors on the firm's board. A single board typically sits at the top of each firm's governance hierarchy. Moreover, in cases involving fiduciary claims asserted by tracking stockholders, courts have declined to apply a fairness scrutiny to transactions that have disparate impact on tracked divisions (Triantis, 2004).[8]

Given that firms issue firm-wide equity interests and have unitary boards that owe duties to entire firms, it follows that only entire firms and not asset subgroups (or divisions) may be subject to hostile takeover bids. This is a significant constraint because some ventures would benefit more than others from the discipline imposed on inefficient managers by the market for corporate control. If a raider seeks control over a division alone, it must first assume control over the entire firm and then dispose of the other assets. Therefore, a firm's defenses against hostile acquisitions are firm-wide: poison pills, staggered boards and dual class recapitalization affect all assets in a firm. A firm cannot offer shareholders the discipline of exposing only some of its ventures to the discipline of the market for corporate control. Instead, the ventures must be split between distinct legal entities that can proceed to adopt different strategies toward future acquisitions. In fact, the anti-takeover provisions in the corporate charters of spinoffs often differ from those of their parents (Daines and Klausner, 2004).

III. TENSION BETWEEN LEGAL SEPARATION AND ECONOMIC INTEGRATION

The discussion thus far raises a tension between the motivation of economic integration and financial tailoring. A supplier and a customer might vertically integrate under common ownership in order to avoid the transaction costs of contracting. The owner, however, may be inclined to seek financial capital from outside investors either because of wealth constraints or risk aversion. This gives rise to the informational problems that drive much of the analysis of optimal capital structure and that might be mitigated by tailoring through legal partitioning (while maintaining common control). In order to enjoy both benefits of economic integration and financial tailoring, the two ventures may be brought within common control but in distinct affiliate firms. While spinoffs and carveouts both exploit the benefits of separate legal entities, they differ in their effect on control. In a spinoff, the shares of the new entity are distributed as a dividend to the shareholders of the original firm, who may then sell them. In a carveout, the original firm maintains a controlling interest as a parent of the new entity, while the minority interest is sold in a public offering. Each of the spun-off and carved-out firms has a distinct capital structure: including a state of incorporation, a separate board, and different creditors. The carved out firm, however, remains under the same control. Information is more easily transferred between the parent and the carved-out subsidiary, and the costs of collaboration between the firms are correspondingly lower.

Legal partitioning, however, can undermine the gains from economic integration, even if the distinct legal entities remain under common control. Corporate and debtor–creditor law compel the two affiliates to transact at arm's length, a requirement that can be enforced by minority shareholders. Where assets A and B are held in different legal firms under common control, they may be understood to have a common 'owner', but their joint use must be the subject of contract and cannot be determined by fiat. Otherwise, they risk having their boundaries disregarded by a court on the grounds that one firm is the alter ego or agent of the other (or, alternatively, doctrines of veil piercing or enterprise liability) and this would undermine the benefits of tailoring financial claims. Moreover, each party to the contract is a distinct legal entity with its own governance; each has different shareholders and/or creditors and a different board of directors. This resurrects transaction costs of various kinds, although the transaction costs are likely to be lower because there is less information asymmetry. Any contract between the two affiliates will be a related-party transaction and required to be authorized by a vote of disinterested shareholders or directors, and perhaps also pronounced by a court to be fair. Arguably, minority shareholders in each firm might require their respective boards to exploit gaps and uncertainties in the contracts in order to benefit their respective firms. These conflicts of interest, which threaten to lower the combined value of the parent and subsidiary, are absent when assets are legally and economically integrated in a single entity.[9]

It is not surprising therefore that elaborate contracts are drafted when firms spinoff or carve out some of their operations in a new firm. Iacobucci and Triantis (2007) describe the complex contract that was drafted when AT&T spun off its wireless division, in order to preserve the synergistic gains between the wireless and wireline businesses. Similarly, an elaborate contract was necessary when Air Canada partitioned its frequent flyer program, Aeroplan, as a wholly owned limited liability partnership in 2002. Aeroplan evolved into a loyalty marketing company serving other large consumer product companies. It was restructured in 2007 as an income trust, and a 12.5% interest was sold in an initial public offering. Air Canada's 2007 annual information form describes five major and complex agreements between the related companies.[10]

IV.   INTERNAL CAPITAL MARKETS TRADEOFF[11]

Firms usually prefer to fund new investments or operations with internal capital – cash from operations, asset sales or secured borrowing. An enterprise faces informational obstacles that raise the cost of external capital. The outside investor knows that insiders of the firm have private information about the prospects of future profitability. The firm's decision to sell stock may indicate that insiders believe the stock is overvalued. To a lesser degree, this may occur also with the sale of debt. The investor is therefore likely to ask for a premium rate of return. The narrower the asymmetry, the smaller the premium: thus, firms may borrow at lower rates from their bank than from public debt markets (Myers and Majluf, 1984).

Information asymmetries are narrower or absent between two firms owned by the same parent. However, the legal obstacles noted in Part III that disrupt contracting between affiliates also impede capital movements across affiliates (Triantis, 2004). Consider an enterprise with lines of business A and B and suppose they are divisions within a single entity. The managers may move capital between the two divisions with relative ease: they can divert A's cash flow to B, or borrow against A's assets to finance a venture in B. If A and B are in separate entities, however, the law imposes significant obstacles to the movement of capital. A's cash flow cannot simply be diverted. A might loan the funds to B, or it might guarantee repayment of a loan from a third party. Alternatively, A might pay a dividend to the parent who can use it to invest new equity in firm B. Legal obstacles impede such movement of capital between related entities, particularly if they have minority stockholders or different creditors. Under corporate law, minority shareholders can challenge and delay contracts between affiliates as related-party transactions, compelling ratification votes and perhaps judicial scrutiny of their fairness. In addition, a court may find that a fraudulent transfer has occurred if A transfers funds to B or guarantees the repayment of B's debts, for less than reasonably equivalent value and while B is insolvent or undercapitalized. The payment of a dividend by an undercapitalized subsidiary may also be contrary to corporate law, as well as being a fraudulent transfer. In addition, there may be tax regulations that similarly require that capital transfers occur on arm's length terms. In contrast, there are no such restrictions on the movement of capital between divisions of a single entity.

Internal markets have advantages and disadvantages, and the breaking up of internal markets by segregating assets into distinct entities sometimes yields a net benefit. Both informational obstacles and legal frictions are avoided when a firm uses internal capital. A multi-divisional firm can reallocate capital from one division with no profitable opportunities to finance the investments of another division in a growth industry. The advantage is the speed and ease with which the integrated firm can react to changing conditions, by redeploying capital from one venture to a more profitable opportunity. This is particularly helpful when the cost of external capital, from public markets or private institutions, is increased by the presence of information asymmetries as to the value and prospects of the firm. On the other hand, managers with the discretion to make these decisions may pursue private benefits rather than maximizing the value of the firm. Indeed, if one envisages the firm as a hierarchy in which headquarters allocate internal capital among divisions, then resources may be expended by divisional owners to lobby for an allocation skewed in their favor (e.g. Harris and Raviv, 1996). Moreover, the ultimate allocation may not be the most efficient (Scharfstein and Stein, 2000).

If the advantages of internal markets are outweighed by the agency and influence cost problems, legal partitioning may be desirable. In this way, any movements of capital between ventures must be done at market rates, with the formalities of arm's length contracting and with the approval of disinterested shareholders. So, while mergers can create internal markets within single entities, divestitures may be motivated by the elimination of cross-subsidization and the discipline of requiring managers to prove their value in capital markets (e.g. Allen, 1998; Triantis, 2004).

V.   ASSET IDENTIFICATION AND ALIENABILITY

William Widen (2007) writes that legal entities are convenient vessels by which to transfer groups of assets. Therefore, if a parent company acquires a subsidiary, it may preserve the firm as a subsidiary rather than legally transferring the assets into the parent, in order to minimize the additional cost of asset transfers at the time of the acquisition, as well as to facilitate a potential future sale of those assets as a group. Transfers of stock can be completed at lower cost than the discrete transfers of individual firm assets. Widen observes in practice, however, that corporate groups seek also to maximize the gains from the economic integration of assets, by ignoring the corporate boundaries between affiliates and treating them effectively as divisions or departments. The group effectively forms an internal market for capital, labor and even physical assets. Thus, the identity of the subsidiary entity 'hibernates' until it is needed to facilitate a future sale of all, or substantially all, its assets.

The disregard of corporate boundaries has legal consequences: a court is more likely to allow creditors to disregard the boundaries as well, thereby undermining attempts to tailor financial claims. However, if the purpose of the separate entity is not tailoring but rather what Widen calls 'asset identification', then the pooling of assets to pay creditors is consistent with the intended capital structure. Widen notes that creditors frequently deal with corporate groups on the understanding that, in the event of insolvency, all assets in the group will be available to satisfy all third party liabilities. His observations that creditors seem to tolerate the disregard of corporate boundaries for the purposes of decision-making within a group and that they regularly consent to deemed consolidation[12] of the group in bankruptcy reorganizations, are consistent with this view of the entity as a vessel for future asset sales, rather than for tailoring financial claims.

Widen is careful not to suggest that all lending to corporate groups is done on this basis; he notes in particular the importance of partitioning in the case of structured finance or securitized assets. He correctly argues that, where financing is intended to be tailored to asset groups, the legal partitioning among subsidiaries is often supplemented by covenants that protect the boundaries of the discrete entities: in particular, covenants prohibiting mergers or other combinations between entities, engagement in new lines of business, significant asset transfers, and the disregard of corporate formalities. Investors might also wish to proscribe sales of stock in the debtor and changes in control, but these are less common than the aforementioned covenants that preserve the integrity of the asset pool and its going concern. A related argument has been advanced recently by Ayotte and Hansmann (2009) in connection with the contracts of a firm. The authors argue that the separate legal entity creates transferable bundles of contracts. They assert that some contracting partners wish to prevent the assignment of their individual contracts (via anti-assignment provisions in the contract), without impeding the ability of the entrepreneur to cash out, or to finance the operations by selling interests or claims against the value of the bundle.

CONCLUSION

This Chapter explains that property is held by entities rather than individuals in order to lower the cost of financing productive assets, particularly where financing is desirable to integrate assets under common control. The discussion reviews four categories of efficiency benefits from dividing assets among discrete entities: matching financial claims and interests to asset types; tailoring governance; splitting internal capital markets; and facilitating asset group transfers. There is a substantial body of empirical work indicating that divestitures such as spinoffs, carveouts and structured finance yield gains from many of these features.

The law plays an important role in yielding these benefits: by endowing the legal capacity of persons to firms, shielding assets of one entity from the claims against another requiring firm-wide capital structure decisions in many respects, and impeding the free flow of capital across firm boundaries. The analysis described here provides a positive explanation for these sets of legal rules, but it leaves a number of interesting normative legal issues – in corporate, securities and bankruptcy law – to future research. Two interesting lines of inquiry have been suggested in the foregoing discussion. First, should American law relax its requirement of uniform capital structure within a firm, to allow for greater financial and governance tailoring within firms? Elgueta (2009) reports that civil law jurisdictions permit the partioning of property into pools of assets within a single entity. Each pool can be bonded to a different purpose and pledged only to creditors whose claim is connected to that purpose. Second, the resolution of a number of normative issues concerning the treatment of multiple-entity enterprises in bankruptcy – for example, substantive consolidation or the enforcement of intercorporate guaranties – seem to hinge on the motivation for the partioning of assets. In particular, the decision to consolidate such enterprises or to subordinate inter-affiliate claims might depend on whether the separate entities were used for tailoring or for simply asset identification or regulatory compliance?

NOTES

* I thank the John M. Olin Center for Law, Economics and Business at Harvard Law School for financial support. I am indebted to Edward Iacobucci, with whom I developed the theory of tailored capital structure in Iacobucci and Triantis (2007), and Henry Hansmann, for a number of valuable conversations about asset partitioning. I thank the editors, Ken Ayotte and Henry Smith, for their helpful comments on an earlier draft.
1. In the law and finance scholarship of the 1970s and 1980s, the predominant paradigm of the corporation was the nexus of contracts. E.g., Jensen and Meckling, 1976; Easterbrook and Fischel, 1991. The scholarship described in this chapter raised the salience of the ownership rights vested in the corporation, its legal personification, and particularly the significance of its boundaries. A related scholarly vein examines the property-like features of mandatory corporate law rules that bind third parties dealing with the firm, even without their consent. These property features are valuable in economizing on information costs. E.g., Armour and Whincop, 2007; Merrill and Smith, 2007.
2. This tradeoff anticipates also the evaluation of internal capital markets, discussed in Part IV, infra.
3. This section and Part III draw extensively from the analysis in Iacobucci and Triantis (2007), so specific references to that article are omitted throughout.
4. Courts occasionally invoke common law doctrines (such as alter ego, agency, veil piercing, enterprise liability, and of course fraud) to extend liability from one firm to another when the entities themselves have disregarded their separate personality. Widen (2007) finds, however, that substantive consolidation of affiliates in the bankruptcy proceedings of large firms is fairly common. See Part V infra.

5. The partitioning of assets into distinct legal entities has the effect of limiting the effective liability for torts or regulatory fines arising out of the hazardous activities of either the individual or the corporation. It also may work to the disadvantage of less sophisticated creditors who may be unaware of the partitioning. E.g., LoPucki, 1996. There is some disagreement among commentators as to whether such judgment proofing motivates a significant formation of separate legal entities (e.g. White, 1998).

6. The matching of asset types with lender types is sometimes reinforced by contractual provisions ('single-purpose entity' covenants) in loan agreements that constrain the borrower from engaging in any other business or acquiring any new assets. They also require the borrower to keep its affairs separate and apart from those of any other entity.

7. *Motorola Commences Process to Create Two Independent Industry-Leading Companies*, March 26, 2008, PRNewswire-First Call. The company proposed to create two companies, Mobile Devices and Broadband & Mobility Solutions. It put the spinoff plans on hold in October 2008 while it cut its workforce and addressed other internal restructuring issues.

8. Another asset-contingent governance choice is the proportion of inside, outside and independent directors on a firm's board. The optimal proportion is a function of asset type. In particular, outsiders are better suited to more traditional industries where assets are fairly transparent and there are temptations for management. In contrast, growth industries have relatively little slack and are more difficult for outsiders to monitor, even while sitting on the board.

9. Ayotte and Gaon (2009) similarly observe in the context of bankruptcy that, if there are synergies between the assets in special purpose entities and those of the originating entity, their separation into distinct entities may make the preservation of going concern value more difficult.

10. Air Canada, Initial Annual Information Form 42–44 (March 27, 2007). Air Canada's parent, ACE Aviation Holding disposed of its remaining interest in Aeroplan in 2008, so that the companies are no longer affiliates.

11. This section summarizes Triantis (2004).

12. The consolidation is 'deemed' because the separate legal entities are preserved, while the assets are pooled for the purpose of determining the distributions to which all third-party creditors are entitled.

REFERENCES

Acemoglu, Daron, Simon Johnson and Todd Mitton. (2009). *Determinants of Vertical Integration: Financial Development and Contracting Costs*, 64 J. Fin. 1251.

Aghion, Philippe and Patrick Bolton. (1992). *An Incomplete Contracts' Approach to Financial Contracting*, 59 Rev. Econ. Stud. 473.

Aghion, Philippe and Jean Tirole. (2004). *The Management of Innovation*, 109 Qu. J. Econ. 1185.

Alchian, Armen and Harold Demsetz. (1972). *Production, Information Costs, and Economic Organization*, Am. Econ. Rev. 777.

Allen, Jeffrey W. (1998). *Capital markets and corporate structure: the equity carve-outs of Thermo Electron*, 48 J. Fin. Econ. 99.

Armour, John and Michael J. Whincop. (2007). *The Proprietary Foundations of Corporate Law*, 27 Oxford J. Legal Stud. 429.

Arora, Ashish and Robert P. Merges. (2004). *Specialized Supply Firms, Property Rights and Firm Boundaries*, 13 Ind. & Corp. Change 451.

Ayotte, Kenneth and Stav Gaon. (2009). *Asset Backed Securities: Costs and Benefits of Bankruptcy Remoteness* (working paper).

Ayotte, Kenneth and Henry Hansmann. (2009). *Legal Entities as Transferable Bundles of Contracts* (draft May).

Baker, George, Robert Gibbons and Kevin J. Murphy. (2006). *Contracting for Control* (draft March 21).

Berle, Adolf and Gardiner Means. (1932). *The Modern Corporation and Private Property* (rev. edn 1968)

Blair, Margaret M. (2003). *Locking in Capital: What Corporate Law Achieved for Business Organizers in the Nineteenth Century*, 51 UCLA L. Rev. 387.

Bolton, Patrick and David S. Scharfstein. (1998). *Corporate Finance, the Theory of the Firm, and Organizations*, 12 J. Econ. Persp. 95.

Coase, R.H. (1937). *The Nature of the Firm*, 4 Economica 386.

Daines, Robert M. and Michael Klausner. (2004). *Agents Protecting Agents: An Empirical Study of Takeover Defenses in Spinoffs* (Stanford U. Law Sch. Working Paper, December 16).

Daley, L., Vikas Mehrotra and R. Sivakumar. (1997). *Corporate Focus and Value Creation: Evidence from Spinoffs*, 45 J. Fin. Econ. 257.

Dittmar, Amy. (2004). *Capital Structure in Corporate Spin-Offs*, 77 J. Bus. 9.
Easterbrook, Frank H. and Daniel R. Fischel. (1985). *Limited Liability and the Corporation*, 52 U. Chi. L. Rev. 89.
Easterbrook, Frank H. and Daniel R. Fischel. (1991). *The Economic Structure of Corporate Law*. Cambridge, MA: Harvard University Press.
Elgueta, Giacomo Rojas. (2009). *Divergences and Convergences of Common Law and Civil Law Traditions on Asset Partitioning: A Functional Analysis*, U. Penn. (working paper), available at: http://ssrn.com/abstract=1395342.
Gertner, Robert, David Scharfstein and Jeremy Stein. (1994). *Internal versus External Capital Markets*, 109 Qu. J. Econ. 1211.
Grossman, Sanford J. and Oliver D. Hart. (1986). *The Costs and Benefits of Ownership: A Theory of Vertical and Lateral Integration*, 94 J. Pol. Econ. 691.
Halpern, Paul, Michael Trebilcock and Stuart Turnbull. (1980). *An Economic Analysis of Limited Liability in Corporation Law*, 30 U. Toronto L.J. 117.
Hansmann, Henry and Reinier Kraakman. (2000). *The Essential Role of Organizational Law*, 110 Yale L.J. 387.
Hansmann, Henry and Ugo Mattei. (1998). *The Functions of Trust Law: A Comparative Legal and Economic Analysis*, 73 NYUL. Rev. 434.
Hansmann, Henry, Reinier Kraakman and Richard Squire. (2006). *Law and the Rise of the Firm*, 119 Harv. L. Rev. 1333.
Harris, Milton and Arthur Raviv. (1996). *The Capital Budgeting Process: Incentives and Information*, 51 J. Fin. 1139.
Hart, Oliver. (1995). *Firms, Contracts, and Financial Structure*. New York: Oxford University Press.
Hart, Oliver and John Moore. (1990). *Property Rights and the Nature of the Firm*, 98 J. Pol. Econ. 1119.
Iacobucci, Edward and George Triantis. (2007). *Economic and Legal Boundaries of Firms*, 93 Va. L. Rev. 515.
Jackson, Thomas H. and Anthony Kronman. (1979). *Secured Financing and Priorities Among Creditors*, 88 Yale L.J. 1143.
Jensen, Michael and William Meckling. (1976). *Theory of the Firm: Managerial Behavior, Agency Costs and Ownership Structure*, 3 J. Fin. Econ. 305.
Klein, Benjamin, Robert Crawford and Armen Alchian. (1978). *Vertical Integration, Appropriable Rents, and the Competitive Contracting Process*, 21 J. L. & Econ. 297.
Leland, Hayne E. (2007). *Financial Synergies and the Optimal Scope of the Firm: Implications for Mergers, Spinoffs, and Structured Finance*, 62 J. Fin. 765.
Levmore, Saul. (1982). *Monitors and Freeriders in Commercial Corporate Settings*, 92 Yale L.J.49.
LoPucki, Lynn M. (1996). *The Death of Liability*, 106 Yale L.J. 1.
Mahoney, Paul G. (2000). *Contract or Concession? An Essay on the History of Corporate Law*, 34 Ga. L. Rev. 873.
Mehotra, Vikas, Wayne Mikkelson and Megan Partch. (2003). *The Design of Financial Policies in Corporate Spin-Offs*, 16 Rev. Fin. Stud. 1359.
Merrill, Thomas W. and Henry E. Smith. (2007). *Property: Principles and Policies*, ch. VI. New York: Foundation Press.
Myers, Stewart. (1977). *The Determinants of Corporate Borrowing*, 5 J. Fin. Econ. 147.
Myers, Stewart C. and Nicholas S. Majluf. (1984). *Corporate Financing and Investment Decisions when Firms Have Information that Investors do not Have*, 13 J. Fin. Econ. 187.
Rajan, Raghuram G. and Luigi Zingales. (2000). *The Governance of the New Enterprise*, in X. Vives, ed., *Corporate Governance*.
Scharfstein, David S., Robert Gertner and Eric Powers. (2002). *Learning about Internal Capital Markets from Corporate Spinoffs*, 57 J. Finance 2479.
Scharfstein, David S. and Jeremy Stein. (2000). *The Dark Side of Internal Capital Markets: Divisional Rent-Seeking and Inefficient Investment*, 55 J. Finance 2537.
Schipper, K. and A. Smith. (1986). *A Comparison of Equity Carve-outs and Seasoned Equity Offerings*, 15 J. Fin. Econ. 153.
Schwartz, Alan. (1981). *Security Interests and Bankruptcy Priorities: A Review of Current Theories*, 10 J. Legal Studies 1.
Scott, Robert E. (1986). *Through Bankruptcy with the Creditors' Bargain Heuristic*, 53 U. Chi. L. Rev. 690.
Simon, Herbert. (1951). *A Formal Theory of the Employment Relationship*, Econometrica 293.
Stein, Jeremy C. (1997). Internal Capital Markets and the Competition for Corporate Resources, 52 J. Fin. 111.
Stout, Lynn A. (2005). *On the Nature of Corporations*, U. Ill. L. Rev. 253.
Triantis, George G. (2004). *Organizations as Internal Capital Markets: The Legal Boundaries of Firms, Collateral, and Trusts in Commercial and Charitable Enterprises*, 117 Harv. L. Rev. 1102.

Triantis, George G. (2000). *Financial Slack Policy and the Laws of Secured Transactions*, 29 J. Legal Stud. 35.

Triantis, George G. and Ronald J. Daniels. (1995). *The Role of Debt in Interactive Corporate Governance*, 83 Calif. L. Rev. 1073.

White, James J. (1998). *Judgment Proofing: A Response to Lynn LoPucki's the Death of Liability*, 107 Yale L.J. 1363.

Widen, William. (2007). *Corporate Form and Substantive Consolidation*, 75 Geo. Wash. L. Rev. 237.

Williamson, Oliver E. (1975). *Markets and Hierarchies: Analysis and Antitrust Implications*. New York: Free Press.

Williamson, Oliver E. (1979). *Transaction-Cost Economics: The Governance of Contractual Relations*, 22 J. L. & Econ. 233.

10 Bankruptcy as property law
Barry E. Adler

What *must* bankruptcy law be? As it turns out this question has a simple answer. There is exactly one function bankruptcy law must serve. It must govern mutually insupportable obligations. Or, one might say, any law that governs mutually insupportable obligations is bankruptcy law. That is, bankruptcy law is property law.

To understand this claim, consider first what almost anyone would see as a typical bankruptcy setting. A borrower arrives on hard times, unable to repay her debts in full and with liabilities that exceed her assets. Her creditors seek to collect, but cannot get blood from a stone, so not all of them will succeed; i.e., the debtor is insolvent. There are many things that bankruptcy law *could* do in response to this debtor's financial crisis. The law could, for example, stay the creditors' individual collection efforts in favor of a collective process and discharge the debtor from her obligations, in whole or in part. Indeed American bankruptcy law does each of these things for individual and corporate debtors. But the law needn't do either. There is only one thing bankruptcy law must do, if there is to be law at all in this situation: it must decide which of the creditors, if any, gets the debtor's assets. Put another way, because creditors of an insolvent debtor have conflicting claims against assets, bankruptcy law must establish which of the creditors has a superior interest in those assets. This is a function of property law too.

This point has been overlooked because bankruptcy law has become associated so closely with *process* – the substitution of collectivization for unilateral creditor collection – and because, except through its provision of process, Congress has largely deferred to state law on questions of property rights. But whether the federal government or the states provide the rules, there must be some way to determine who prevails when claims conflict; such determination is the essence of bankruptcy law and it is also property law. The first part of this chapter explores this theme further and describes how process myopia has led Congress to overlook an important opportunity for reform of bankruptcy entitlement: priority for tort claims.

The second part of this chapter shifts perspective. Just as it has not been universally understood that the question of insolvency, a standard bankruptcy law topic, is truly a property law topic, it has also been less than fully understood that other basic law doctrines reflect insolvency concerns. This idea is briefly expounded below.

1. PROCESS VERSUS PROPERTY

The notion that bankruptcy is and should be about process begins with a narrow, lawyer's view of bankruptcy law not as a mechanism for resolving an insolvent debtor's conflicting obligations, but rather as a particular set of federal statutes that governs the case of such a debtor. In the United States, the current incarnation of such statutes, the Bankruptcy Code,[1] was enacted in 1978, more or less in its current form, and covers both individual and corporate debtors. Since its enactment, the Code's process-centric approach has become identified with a single case, *Butner v. United States*.[2] *Butner* was decided under law that predates the current Code, but its principle survives to this day.

In *Butner*, a debtor corporation filed a petition for arrangement under the Bankruptcy Act. At the time of the petition, the debtor owned mortgaged real estate. As part of the bankruptcy process, an agent was appointed to collect rents on the mortgaged property and to apply the rents to the mortgage claims. For a time, the mortgagees received those rents. Eventually, however, the arrangement was discarded and the debtor, while in default on the mortgages, was adjudicated bankrupt.[3] Upon such adjudication, a bankruptcy trustee replaced the agent, who was dismissed. Butner, the holder of a second mortgage on the real estate, requested that the property be abandoned to him, subject to the first mortgage. The court opted for a sale of the property instead, though, and Butner did not explicitly seek sequestration of rents pending the sale. Consequently, for the nine months between the adjudication and the sale, the trustee collected rents on the property but, unlike the former agent, did not have instructions to apply those rents to mortgage payments. The trustee claimed the collected rents on behalf of the debtor's general creditors while Butner claimed them as subject to its security interest in the real estate.

Under applicable state law, that of North Carolina, the debtor remained owner of land subject to mortgage and remained entitled to rents from that land until the mortgagee took actual or constructive possession of the land. Thus, even though the debtor was in default, a mortgagee could not establish a security interest in rents until it took possession. A receiver, such as the agent, could establish constructive possession in favor of a mortgagee, but such possession terminated upon the receiver's dismissal. Under applicable state law, a mortgagee ordinarily could acquire actual possession through a foreclosure proceeding, but bankruptcy removed the property from the foreclosure remedy. State law, therefore, instructed Butner to foreclose while federal law prohibited that very action.

At the time of the *Butner* opinion, some lower courts had taken pity on the mortgagee in states such as North Carolina and held that on 'equitable principles' the debtor's bankruptcy adjudication in and of itself established the mortgagee's security interest in the rents.[4] In *Butner*, the Supreme Court put an end to this, holding instead that if a mortgagee wanted to establish an interest in the rents but was prohibited from doing so, the mortgagee need only request that the bankruptcy court sequester funds or permit a foreclosure, the result of which would be to provide the mortgagee with constructive or actual possession, respectively. That is, the Supreme Court did not object to the mortgagee's acquisition of a security interest that did not exist under state law at the time of the bankruptcy adjudication, but rather the Court objected to the automatic creation of such an interest upon the adjudication.

An analogy to a child's game comes to mind. When the mortgagee in *Butner* said 'may I have the rents, please,' the Supreme Court denied the request because the mortgagee did not say 'Simon Says, may I have the rents please.' To be sure, one might defend the Court's decision on the ground that a mortgagee entirely asleep at the time of a bankruptcy adjudication should not benefit in bankruptcy court from inattention that would have led it to neglect foreclosure, and an interest in rents, had there been no bankruptcy. But if a mortgagee is awake, as was Butner, the requirement that it request sequestration or foreclosure is likely to be little more than a technical trap for the unwary, as it was for

Butner.[5] In any event, once the rule is established, little may turn on the outcome as all but the indolent will toe the line.

Although *Butner* is widely regarded as a case that establishes the general primacy of state law entitlements in bankruptcy, the case did not present a dispute between a state-law property interest and a conflicting bankruptcy property interest (which would have been decided, without doubt, in favor of the latter).[6] The Court identified no bankruptcy provision or policy that would limit the secured creditor's right to rents. In *Butner*, the bankruptcy process simply threatened to interfere with a state law entitlement that Congress apparently did not intend to displace. *Butner* may seem, then, little more than a prescription for courts to fill in procedural details where needed to harmonize bankruptcy and state law. To see that more is at stake, one needs to look beyond the facts of the case.

Butner is not just a case, but a *principle*. The principle, as stated by the Court itself, is simple: 'Property interests are created and defined by state law.'[7] The Court explains why, in its view, this should be so: 'Uniform treatment of property interests by both state and federal courts within a State serves to reduce uncertainty, to discourage forum shopping, and to prevent a party from receiving "a windfall merely by reason of the happenstance of bankruptcy."'[8] Note that missing from this list is any suggestion that state law is inherently the appropriate source of authority, based either on federalism or institutional competency.[9] Given the facts of *Butner*, which presented a question of how a mortgagee was to establish its interest in rents, this is not surprising. Little but consistency turned on the outcome and little but consistency justified the holding (if anything did). Put another way, it would be hard to identify a right versus wrong answer on the substance.

As opposed to the *Butner* case, the *Butner* principle has been applied to situations in which the result clearly matters. For example, in *BFP v. Resolution Trust Corp.*,[10] a debtor invoked the Bankruptcy Code's fraudulent conveyance provision to challenge the legitimacy of a quickly conducted pre-bankruptcy foreclosure sale that complied with state law but that the debtor claimed yielded an insufficient sale price. The Court held that any price at a foreclosure sale is adequate if the sale is non-collusive and consistent with state law. That is, state law not federal law determines the extent of a mortgagee's property interest in collateral, an interest that bankruptcy law will not cut back for the benefit of the debtor or the debtor's general creditors. For another example, in *Nobelman v. American Savings Bank*,[11] a debtor invoked a loan modification provision of the Bankruptcy Code in an attempt to alter a mortgage obligation that could not be changed under state law. The Court denied the modification and permitted the mortgagee to enforce the terms of its security interest under state law. In each of these cases, a party identified a provision of bankruptcy law that arguably supplanted a creditor's state law entitlement: to dispose of collateral in one case and to the payment terms of a loan in the other. In each case, however, the Supreme Court, relying on *Butner*, narrowly interpreted the Code provision so as to honor state law. Whether the Court was right or wrong in these cases, the decisions significantly affected the parties' respective rights.

The *Butner* principle not only guides judicial interpretation of Bankruptcy Code provisions – such as in *BFP* and *Nobelman* – but also reflects the structure of the Code itself. While there are exceptions – such as special priority granted to some tax claims[12] – the Bankruptcy Code often expressly or indisputably defers to state law entitlements. For example, if a corporate debtor is to reorganize in bankruptcy, the reorganization plan must honor what is known in bankruptcy jargon as 'absolute priority.' This means that a debtor cannot retain collateral for a secured loan unless the plan provides a secured creditor with what a court deems to be full compensation for that collateral,[13] and a junior creditor or a shareholder cannot receive any property under a plan unless senior claims are fully satisfied,[14] again according to the court's estimation. Under the absolute priority rule, investors are paramount; no provisions are made for payments to other constituents of the debtor, such as employees without claims or communities that might be injured if the debtor ceased operation. These priorities, so honored, are defined by state law.[15]

With this in mind, consider the important question of whether a corporate debtor in bankruptcy should reorganize or liquidate. Debtors' equity-appointed management, with the acquiescence of bankruptcy courts, sometimes engineer the reorganization and continuation of firms that, some argue, would be worth more if allowed to die in piecemeal liquidation; despite the absolute priority provisions just mentioned, the result may be a shift of value away from senior claims to junior claims or interests or to those without claims but who rely on the firms' survival.[16] The holders of senior claims sometimes object, but may be overridden, or may simply go along to avoid costly delay or litigation expense.[17] (Neither proponents of questionable reorganization plans nor the judges who approve them deny the applicability of the absolute priority rule, but rather champion or accept disputed valuations of the firms that would, if correct, satisfy the rule.) The continuation of failed firms was a more common pattern in the recent past, before secured creditors began aggressively to insinuate themselves into the Chapter 11 reorganization process,[18] but the threat of continuation bias exists despite creditor control of a bankruptcy case,[19] and the current credit crisis may cause secured creditors to recede and return us soon to the days of debtor control.

Those who defend continuation bias as a social good favor protection of corporate employees and communities that would suffer from liquidation even while the creditors prospered.[20] (The government's sponsorship of the recent Chrysler and General Motors bankruptcy cases well illustrates this sentiment.) Those who oppose continuation bias may remain agnostic on the question of whether law should protect a business' non-investor constituents, but feel that any such protection should be independent of a company's capital structure or financial situation. That is, these agnostics do not believe that a debtor in bankruptcy should be obliged to consider the interests of employees or communities while outside of bankruptcy firms owe no such consideration and can instead favor the entitlements of investors.[21] Put simply, those who oppose special bankruptcy law treatment of non-investor constituents invoke the *Butner* principle.

Proponents of strict adherence to state-law entitlement have been described, aptly, as 'proceduralists,'[22] as they believe that bankruptcy law – or, more precisely, corporate bankruptcy law – should do little more than serve as a collectivized debt recovery mechanism. For a proceduralist, the right to collect, as opposed to how, should be determined by state law. This notion of collectivization as bankruptcy law's fundamental purpose, most closely associated with Thomas Jackson and his frequent co-author Douglas Baird,[23] stems from the observation that creditors, left to their own devices, might race with one another to grab an insolvent debtor's assets, wasting effort and perhaps destroying synergy as they separate assets one from the other. On this view, bankruptcy law's key contribution is to stay individual creditor collection and impose an orderly process for the disposition of a firm's assets. Accordingly, bankruptcy law can take non-bankruptcy entitlements as given, as nothing in bankruptcy's collectivization function depends on any alteration of those entitlements.

Bankruptcy law *can* serve its collectivization function without alteration of non-bankruptcy entitlement, but this does not imply that it *should*. I have argued elsewhere that bankruptcy law should *not* provide a collectivization process, which, in my view, debtors can better adopt contractually where desired.[24] But even if one were to assume that process is a proper function for bankruptcy law, the law can, in theory, *both* solve the problem of the creditors' grab race and adopt substantive entitlements that differ from nonbankruptcy entitlements. As to why this would be a bad idea, at least according to the proceduralists, one must return to the Supreme Court's rationale in *Butner*. And that rationale now deserves careful attention. Where there is no substantively right or wrong answer, little may be required to justify a devotion to consistency, but when there are important distinctions in substantive alternatives, as there frequently are, such justification must be able to carry more weight.

Turning, then, to the *Butner* rationale, there are three purported benefits of consistency between bankruptcy and nonbankruptcy entitlements: the reduction of uncertainty; the avoidance of windfall; and the avoidance of forum shopping. The idea that adherence to state-law entitlement will reduce uncertainty is simple enough, but can easily be overstated. After all, judicial interpretation, state or federal, is by its nature uncertain until solid precedent is established, at which point certainty may be achieved. One might imagine that bankruptcy courts could create special bankruptcy entitlements about as certain as those of state law. Consider, next, avoidance of windfall. The *Butner* Court does not say why, if there is one outcome in bankruptcy and another outside, that the outcome *in* bankruptcy is the windfall as opposed to the other way round. Windfall, then, is in the eye of the beholder and does not seem an independent basis to favor state law entitlement. Moreover, the possibility that a creditor will gain from the bankruptcy forum would be anticipated by the debtor and other creditors and in a competitive capital market would be factored into the creditor's interest rate, which would be relatively lower; the gain once realized, then, would in no sense be a windfall. This leaves forum shopping. It is on forum shopping that proceduralist scholars tend to rely.

Here is a simple illustration of what is traditionally meant by forum shopping: Abel has a grievance with Baker. Forum A and Forum B are otherwise identical except that Forum A will award Abel damages for her grievance while Forum B will not. Abel and Baker live near Forum B and can have their dispute adjudicated in that forum at low cost. Abel, however, has an option to bring her dispute in Forum A; adjudication there will impose high costs on all parties. Despite the greater transactions cost, Abel chooses Forum A. The higher transactions cost is a forum-shopping cost, one that would disappear if Forum A and Forum B provided the same substantive entitlements.

The proceduralist defense of the *Butner* principle is, in essence, that different entitlements in, as opposed to outside of, bankruptcy would be the equivalent of the above illustration, with the bankruptcy process the analog to costly Forum A. The concern is, or has been, that if there existed special bankruptcy entitlements, parties who would benefit from those entitlements would have a perverse incentive to invoke the potentially cumbersome and costly bankruptcy machinery – described colorfully in one account as a 'Feast for Lawyers'[25] – even if the debtor is not otherwise a good candidate for the process. However, like the significance of certainty or windfall, the forum-shopping concern is easy to overstate.

Note that, in general, a bankruptcy entitlement – such as whether a security interest should be honored fully – establishes priority among creditors, not between creditors and their debtor. Thus, with few exceptions, it would be a creditor with an incentive to exploit a special bankruptcy entitlement, if any.[26] Under current law, however, a creditor cannot force a debtor into bankruptcy against her or its will unless the debtor has failed to pay debts as they come due.[27] If one imagines that almost every such debtor would be a good candidate for bankruptcy regardless of how assets would be distributed to creditors within bankruptcy, then the transactions cost of bankruptcy would *not* be wasted.[28] In this case, any costs truly attributed to forum shopping could easily be outweighed by a competing interest in favor of a special bankruptcy entitlement.

This said, there may yet be circumstances under which adherence to nonbankruptcy entitlement is sensible, even if that entitlement is suboptimal. Consider the debate, noted above, over whether Chapter 11 should favor continuation even if liquidation maximizes the return to investors. Assume, for the sake of argument, that as a matter of good social policy no business should be able freely to terminate its operation at the expense of workers and community even if investors would profit from such termination. Assume further that outside of bankruptcy businesses are not so constrained and may terminate at will. Assume, finally, that debt is generally valuable, as a device to discipline managers, for example.[29] Under these circumstances, it is theoretically possible that a constraint on bankruptcy liquidation would be inferior to a bankruptcy rule that followed the suboptimal nonbankrutpcy entitlement. This could be the case if, for example, a firm reduced its debt load in an attempt to avoid not the transactions cost of bankruptcy but the termination constraint. A firm that issued little debt and thus stayed out of bankruptcy would not face a restriction on termination, and so society could lose the benefits of debt and not gain the assumed benefits of liquidation restriction.

Perversion of capital structure, with no or little offsetting gain, is worth avoiding, and whether such cost in the above illustration is properly attributed to forum shopping, or to something closely related, is merely semantic. But such outcome is no more than a theoretical possibility. A little bit of a good thing may be worse than nothing, as the above illustrates, but it may be better too. The question is an empirical one. In any case, the above assumes, for the sake of argument, that restriction on business termination is socially optimal. There are arguments to the contrary, that restriction on termination raises a firm's ex ante cost of capital and may sacrifice more jobs and communities at the formation stage than it saves at the failure stage.[30] So while it may be correct that continuation bias in bankruptcy is ill advised, the reason may not be forum shopping or anything related. It may be simply that such bias is itself bad substantive policy, in or out of bankruptcy. More generally, despite the risk of capital structure perversion, it may be difficult to conceive of a good substantive bankruptcy rule – or, put differently, a good allocation of property rights – the benefits of which are better forgone just because the rule is inconsistent with applicable nonbankruptcy law.

The only case made so far, if any has been made, is that the rationale behind the *Butner* principle may not be as powerful as it first appears. Still, a claim that a principle may be relatively unimportant is not a claim that it is wrong. To make out the latter claim requires at least a single plausible story that bankruptcy law adherence to state law entitlement is mistaken. The treatment of nonconsensual claims is such a story.

There is little reason to change current bankruptcy law's deference to state law in the priority among consensual claims – i.e., among investors. State law honors contractual priority arrangements, among senior and subordinated bondholders, for example, and between creditors and shareholders, because each such investor explicitly or implicitly agrees to its place in the priority hierarchy and presumably pays for its claim or interest accordingly. It is unremarkable that bankruptcy law follows state law in this regard.

State law also reasonably addresses priority where subordination among investors is not by mutual agreement. For example, a debtor might pledge the same collateral to two different creditors on account of different loans. If the debtor cannot fully repay both loans, state real estate mortgage law or Article 9 of the Uniform Commercial Code will establish priority between the claims.[31] States may differ somewhat in how they establish priority in real estate mortgages, under their own versions of Article 9, or by reference to a race for a judgment lien on unencumbered assets. But the differences among jurisdictions are small and the applicable rules almost always sensible. Notice is the key element in such a contest. A perfected interest – one good against later claims – requires some form of public notice, usefully warning other potential lenders whether that notice is provided by filing in an appropriate records office or by having a sheriff seize property on behalf of a lender who seeks to become a lien creditor. It is hard to see how a special rule in bankruptcy would serve any additional purpose, though it would offend notions of federalism and could inhibit experimentation among jurisdictions. Similarly, the Bankruptcy Code's deference to state law exempt-property rules for individual debtors – provisions that remove property from creditor reach – is largely unobjectionable, at least so long as a debtor does not change the rules on his creditors by moving to a new state before filing a bankruptcy petition.[32]

To a large extent, then, current bankruptcy law's adherence to state law seems reasonable. Not all creditors are lenders, however. In a small number of bankruptcy cases, tort creditors (or other nonconsensual claimants) are owed significant sums. State law generally treats such claims as general obligations that, outside of bankruptcy, are subject first to any perfected security interest then to a creditors' race. The first to establish a judgment lien on any of a debtor's unencumbered assets has priority. And if there are no or few unencumbered assets from which a nonconsensual creditor can collect, the result is that the nonconsensual creditor simply loses. In bankruptcy, this system of state law priority translates into a ratable return for nonconsensual creditors who share priority with other general creditors, all junior to any perfected security interest, which survives a bankruptcy petition.

There is little to support so low a priority for nonconsensual claims. Standard economic analysis suggests that nonconsensual claims should have the highest priority, even above that of secured claims.[33] Otherwise investors – shareholders and lenders together – can externalize the risk of a debtor's operation and internalize the benefits. A classic example is where a cab company pledges all of its cars to secured creditors (or, the economic equivalent, leases rather than owns them) then simply folds if a negligently driven taxi runs down a pedestrian who successfully sues the company.[34] Beyond anecdote, although the evidence is mixed, there is reason to believe that companies use capital structure to externalize risk.[35] This result not only strikes most as unfair based on any theory of justice, but reflects excessive activity and insufficient precaution by risky actors.

Proceduralist arguments notwithstanding, then, useful bankruptcy reform might include highest priority – i.e., a special property interest – for nonconsensual claims. Holders of such claims would include accident victims, sufferers of environmental contamination, children owed support, and others who have no relationship with a debtor or an insufficient opportunity to bargain with the debtor prior to the injury that gave rise to their claims. Recently, Congress has come round partially to this view. In 2005, the Bankruptcy Code was amended to provide high priority – just below that of secured claims – for individuals owed 'domestic support obligations' such as alimony or child support.[36] Perhaps Congress will eventually go further, offering even higher priority and to *all* nonconsensual claims. Such reform would not certainly be beneficial. Other considerations might predominate, federalism, for example. But the case against priority for nonconsensual claims is yet to be made. And despite the proceduralist arguments, the substantive question of priority for nonconsensual claims is one Congress should address rather than duck, because the establishment of property rights among holders of mutually insupportable obligations is a core function of bankruptcy law, one that is made just as certainly by affirmative action as by deference to alternative authority.[37]

2.   INSOLVENCY AS PART OF BROADER DOCTRINE

To make the case that bankruptcy law is in fact property law, I attempted to strip away the widely held belief that bankruptcy law is essentially about process. With process gone, what remains is the observation that bankruptcy law must settle conflicting claims to assets. That is, I've argued that bankruptcy law serves a role traditionally understood as property law. Here, I'd like to shift perspective and show that some legal issues from other areas of the law address what are in essence insolvency questions and thus can be resolved by reference to principles traditionally understood as part of bankruptcy law.

To begin, I contend that although property law may have functions beyond the settlement of conflicting claims, this function – also a bankruptcy function – is more deeply embedded in property law, qua property law, than may be ordinarily understood. Consider that Black's Law Dictionary defines property in 'the strict legal sense [as] an aggregate of rights which are guaranteed and protected by the government.'[38]

This broad property definition, seemingly independent of insolvency matters, brings to mind a case familiar to every first-year law student, one in which a landowner conveys the same parcel to two different buyers.[39] The question presented is who owns the land. That is, which of the transferees would the government protect and which one would it evict. Unsaid, or at least underappreciated, is that this paradigmatic property law case is, in essence, a paradigmatic *insolvency* case. The outcome is interesting if, perhaps only if, the original landowner is unable fully to satisfy the conflicting obligations she has created. Otherwise one buyer would receive the land while the other would receive alternative compensation. There would be no harm.

The background rule in a case such as this is *nemo dat quod non habet* (one cannot give what one does not have). But this does not mean that the first transferee will prevail, because recording statutes provide an exception. Here, if the second transferee is a bona fide purchaser – i.e., one who buys without notice of the earlier transaction – she will prevail if she records her interest first;[40] the initial transferee could have protected himself from this outcome by promptly recording his interest, which would have put the second transferee on actual or constructive notice of the earlier interest. A rule such as this that bases priority on a public filing – like the Uniform Commercial Code's similar rule for conflicting security interests in personalty – is useful because it allows a purchaser who has provided public notice to rely on her ownership interest even if she cannot rely on the seller, that is, if the seller becomes insolvent or, to say the same thing, subject to mutually insupportable obligations. So here, even a most basic property law case is conceptually also a bankruptcy law case, at least if bankruptcy law is defined by reference to the function of insolvency resolution rather than its process.

Aspects of the restitution doctrine can similarly be integrated into this paradigm. Take the concept of the constructive trust, under which a victim fraudulently deprived of funds can claim a property interest in any of the funds he can trace into the hands of the perpetrator.[41] Here, the constructive trust is an application of the *nemo dat quod non habet* property doctrine as it rests on the notion that one who wrongfully obtains assets has no title, which remains with the victim. But the wrongdoer is also a debtor of his victims and so, just as in the case of the twice-sold house, the constructive trust may matter only where the wrongdoer is insolvent. From this perspective, as suggested by Emily Sherwin,[42] one may wonder why a victim who can trace his funds should have priority over other creditors, including victims whose funds the fraudfeasor has already spent. A better approach would ask whether the conflicting claims of victims are sufficiently similar that they should share priority. This question – a property law question – is traditionally associated with bankruptcy law.

The connection between property law and the resolution of conflict among creditors is, moreover, an important one, in particular, for our current economy. As Karl Llewellyn said in a related context, sane law must go beyond mere notions of passing title to property and account for the fact that a modern transaction rarely 'resembles that of three hundred years ago: where the whole transaction can be accomplished at one stroke, shifting possession along with title, no strings being left behind – as in a cash purchase of an overcoat worn home.'[43] Although he did not say so expressly, the sane law that Llewellyn called for to address the strings left behind is, at its heart, also sane *bankruptcy* law because those strings matter most to law when they represent conflicting claims that cannot all be satisfied.

In more recent scholarship, there has been an interesting discussion about the meaning of property law. Tom Merrill and Henry Smith, for example, champion the 'in rem' nature of property as salient and observe that property law is essential in its ability to provide standard forms of rights, which serve as 'social glue' for interactions within society.[44] Although their emphasis is on how in rem rights can, under certain circumstances, reduce information costs, Merill and Smith recognize, as I do here, the significance of reliance on these rights where in personam obligations would be insufficient.[45] Ken Ayotte and Patrick Bolton make a similar point in a discussion of property rights and financial contracting.[46] Henry Hansmann and Reinier Kraakman focus particularly on the role of notice in property law,[47] and in a context related to the one I identify here, argue that corporate law – long considered a set of contract default rules – serves primarily the property law function of asset segregation in the face of inconsistent claims.[48]

These are generally helpful developments. These developments are also specifically helpful to my theme here, as the conception of property law advanced is a conception of property law as bankruptcy law.

The nexus between bankruptcy law and property law not only allows for a cross-pollination of ideas within those fields, it also has implications for other areas of basic private law. As an example, consider the contract law doctrine of substantial performance and material breach. Where this doctrine is applicable, a party to a contract who substantially performs can demand performance, or an expectation remedy, from her counterparty. An insubstantial breach entitles the counterparty to damages, but not to walk away from the contract. By comparison, if a party has committed an uncured material breach (does not substantially perform), the counterparty is free to disregard the contract and may withhold his own performance with impunity.

The line between substantial and insubstantial performance – or between immaterial and material breach – is not a bright one, and courts struggle over the distinction. Section 241 of the Restatement (Second) of Contracts describes a number of factors that courts consider when determining whether a breach is material. The first factor listed is not surprising: 'the extent to which the injured party will be deprived of the benefit which he reasonably expected.'[49] This factor may not be particularly helpful, as anyone who speaks English would implicitly know that a greatly injurious breach is likely to be a 'material' one, but helpful or not the relevance of the factor is straightforward. The second factor listed may require more thought: 'the extent to which the injured party can be adequately compensated for the part of that benefit of which he will be deprived.'[50] Why, one might ask, does the availability of compensation matter in a determination of whether a breach is or is not 'material'? One might imagine that the question of materiality would be prior to that of compensation.

This conundrum evaporates once one recognizes that the doctrine of substantial performance and material breach can be characterized in part as a bankruptcy doctrine, that is, one about property rights applied to address insolvency. To see this, consider the consequences of a contract rule that *never* released a party from his obligation (absent his counterparty's permission) regardless of how egregious the counterparty's breach.

Were damages awards from breach always fully compensatory, a rule that required performance in all events might seem sensible, as such a rule would protect the parties' respective interests.[51] That is, a breaching party would be obligated to pay for the injury caused by her breach but could count on the value of the return performance for which she contracted; even if an initial breach portended future breaches, therefore, the victim of breach ultimately would be made whole and the victim as well as the party in breach would receive the benefit of her bargain. Moreover, a party who could count on her counterparty's performance despite her own breach would be free from concern that a mere minor defect in her performance would relieve her counterparty of any obligation under the contract, a concern that might lead a party to invest too much in precaution to prevent breach or invest too little in reliance on her counterparty's performance.[52]

One might ask, then, why a failure of substantial performance should ever relieve a victim from her contractual obligations. An answer arises from an analysis of the parties' incentives when a breaching party will not be fully responsible for his contractual obligations. A breaching party might escape such obligation if the victim's injury is difficult to prove,[53] but even if nominal damages awards are, or could be made, fully compensatory on average, the possibility of the breaching party's insolvency remains. A rule that permitted an insolvent party to demand performance despite its incapacity or unwillingness to perform in turn could, as Dick Craswell has noted,[54] allow the insolvent party to profit from continuation, or threatened continuation, of a contractual project even if such continuation is or would be inefficient (including where a solvent party would repudiate the contract and pay damages rather than allow its own obligation to increase with its counterparty's performance).[55] Put simply, even a project with a negative net present value – i.e., a poor gamble – may be attractive to a party whose insolvency means that it will not have to pay its obligations fully at least unless the other party's performance is sufficient to restore the party's solvency.[56] And while an insolvent party's counterparty could himself terminate the contract, if he did so without right, he would become the breaching party and would lose the ability to sue for the lost benefit of his contractual bargain, a suit that might have some value even against an insolvent party; faced with a choice between financing an inefficient project at his own expense and sacrificing a valid claim, or compromising such claim in an ex post negotiation, the counterparty would be deprived of the benefit of his bargain, a deprivation that could, moreover, skew his ex ante investment incentive.

A determination that an uncured breach is material and performance thus insubstantial – like the related requirement of adequate assurance as a precondition to performance[57] – can eliminate or mitigate an insolvent party's advantage from inefficient continuation,[58] an advantage the finance literature calls an overinvestment problem.[59] Such elimination or mitigation is accomplished through what is in essence a grant to the breach victim of a property interest in her own performance, which she can withhold unless the insolvent party's due performance is proffered as payment of the insolvent party's obligation.[60] This priority scheme limits the insolvent party's ability to gamble with other people's money in much the same way that priority for ordinary early lenders limits a debtor's ability to so gamble. The latter limitation is one that Alan Schwartz, alone and with Yeon-Koo Che, has explained in the context of contests among creditors for bankruptcy priority.[61] The analysis here, then, is an illustration of contract law as bankruptcy law, and as property law as well.

CONCLUSION

When claims over assets conflict, bankruptcy law determines which claimant will prevail and own the assets. This is also a role of property law. Thus, in an important sense, property law is bankruptcy law. This fact is frequently overlooked because bankruptcy law has become associated with the Bankruptcy Code, a federal statute that provides the procedure for the resolution of conflicting claims, but generally leaves substantive entitlement to state law. Obscured in this delegation of substance is the possibly beneficial role the federal government could play if it moved from a process-oriented bankruptcy law approach to a substantive one and established sensible property entitlements. Specifically, the Bankruptcy Code could provide priority for nonconsensual claims even though state law offers no such priority. Such a change could induce forum shopping, as holders of nonconsensual claims might force debtors into bankruptcy to obtain an entitlement available only there. But such forum-shopping concerns are easily exaggerated because any debtor unable to satisfy all of its claims – consensual as well as nonconsensual – is perhaps a good candidate for bankruptcy regardless of the entitlements provided by the process.

Once bankruptcy law is seen as a source of property law, other links between insolvency and legal doctrine come into view. For instance, fundamental principles of property law, or contract doctrine, can be seen at least in part as responses to insolvency problems. These observations help promote a unified approach to legal questions, whether traditionally understood as belonging to one set of doctrines or another.

NOTES

1. *See* 11 U.S.C. 101 et seq. (2006).
2. 440 U.S. 48, 55 (1979).
3. The concept of 'adjudication as a bankrupt' is from the 1898 Bankruptcy Act; there is no such adjudication under current law.
4. *See, e.g.,* In re Pittsburgh-Duquesne Development Co., 482 F.2d 243 (3rd Cir., 1973).
5. Under the Bankruptcy Code today, if the mortgagee has a security interest in real property and that interest extends to rents, the security interest continues in rents collected after the commencement of the bankruptcy case. See Bankruptcy Code 11 U.S.C. §552(b) (2005). Under these circumstances, the mortgagee need make no request for sequestration or foreclosure. Note, however, that in *Butner* the underlying mortgage did not cover rents.
6. No one doubts Congress' authority to intervene as it wishes. *See* id. *See also* 11 U.S.C. §546(b)(2), which today permits a secured creditor to perfect a security interest through notice rather than seizure of collateral where, under state law, perfection through seizure would trump even earlier perfected interests.
7. 440 U.S. 48, 55 (1979). The Court repeatedly affirms the principle. *See, e.g.*, Releigh v. Illinois Dep't of Revenue, 530 U.S. 15, 20 (2000); BFP v. Resolution Trust Corp., 511 U.S. 531, 545 (1994); Nobelman v. American Savings Bank, 508 U.S. 324, 329 (1993); Barnhill v. Johnson, 503 U.S. 393, 398–99 (1992).
8. Id. quoting Lewis v. Manufacturers National Bank, 364 U.S. 603, 609 (1961).
9. As described in the text, in *Butner*, the law in question was state law. The Court uses the phrase 'state law' more broadly than is accurate, however. A more exact version of the Court's statement about entitlements established by state law would have been a statement that entitlements are established by substantive nonbankruptcy law, which occasionally includes federal law, such as on patent rights, e.g. This said, as a general matter, entitlements are established by the states and so the Court's failure of precision is understandable. For the same reason, I refer here and hereafter to 'state law' rather than substantive nonbankruptcy law.
10. 511 U.S. 531 cited in note 7.
11. 508 U.S. 324, cited in note 7.
12. *See, e.g.*, 11 U.S.C. §507(a)(8).
13. *See* 11 U.S.C. §1129(b)(2)(A).
14. *See* 11 U.S.C. §1129(b)(2)(B), (C).
15. *See, e.g.*, 11 U.S.C. §502(b), which determines claim allowance by reference to 'applicable law.'
16. Although empirical study is difficult, in part because firms are not randomly selected for continuation or liquidation, there is theory to support a continuation bias, at least when equity controls the reorganization process of large firms. *See, e.g.*, Arturo Bris, Alan Schwartz, and Ivo Welch, *Who Should Pay for Bankruptcy Costs?*, 34 J. LEGAL STUD. 295, 329 (2005); George G. Triantis, *Financial Slack Policy and the Laws of Secured Transactions*, 29 J. LEGAL STUD. 66-68 (2000). Not all agree that such bias exists, however. *See, e.g.*, Elizabeth Warren and Jay L. Westbrook, *The Success of Chapter 11: A Challenge to the Critics*, 107 MICH. L. REV. 603 (2009). And there is evidence that courts do not succumb to any such bias for small-firm debtors. *See* Edward R. Morrison, *Bankruptcy Decision Making: An Empirical Study of Continuation Bias in Small-Business Bankruptcies*, 50 J. L. & Econ. 381 (2007).
17. One might imagine that holders of senior claims would favor bankruptcy distributions inconsistent with absolute priority – though not if a result of inefficient continuation – if these distributions included payments to or benefits for an insolvent debtor's managers or shareholders. Anticipation of such payments or benefits might convince the managers or shareholders to bring the firm into bankruptcy early rather than remain outside of the process and wastefully gamble the debtor's assets in the hope of an unlikely reversal of fortune. There is evidence that insolvent debtors' managers and shareholders deprived of

bankruptcy distributions delay bankruptcy filings. *See* Barry E. Adler, Vedran Capkun, and Larry Weiss, Value Destruction in the New Era of Chapter 11 (unpublished manuscript, 2009). But anticipation of absolute priority violations may exacerbate a debtor's risk prior to its insolvency, so it is not clear that such deviation would be productive on balance or, thus, in the interest of senior creditors. See Barry E. Adler, *Bankruptcy and Risk Allocation*, 77 CORNELL L. REV. 439 (1992).

18. *See* Douglas G. Baird and Robert K. Rasmussen, *The End of Bankruptcy*, 55 STAN. L. REV. 751 (2002).
19. *See* Barry E. Adler, *Bankruptcy Primitives*, 12 AM. BANKR. INST. L. REV. 219 (2004).
20. *Cf.* Elizabeth Warren, *Bankruptcy Policy*, 54 U. CHI. L. REV. 775 (1987) (favoring distributional interests of employees, suppliers, and customers who are not creditors).
21. *See* Douglas G. Baird, *Loss Distribution, Forum Shopping, and Bankruptcy: A Reply to Warren*, 54 U. CHI. L. REV. 815 (1987).
22. *See* Douglas G. Baird, *Bankruptcy's Uncontested Axioms*, 108 YALE L. J. 573 (1998).
23. *See* Thomas H. Jackson, *Translating Assets and Liabilities to the Bankruptcy Forum*, 14 J. LEG. STUD. 73 (1985); Baird cited id.; and Baird cited in note 21.
24. *See* Barry E. Adler, *A Theory of Corporate Insolvency*, 72 NYU L. REV. 343 (1997); Barry E. Adler, *Financial and Political Theories of American Corporate Bankruptcy*, 45 STAN. L. REV. 311 (1993).
25. *See* Sol Stein, BANKRUPTCY: A FEAST FOR LAWYERS (1999).
26. There are some exceptions. In In re Telecom Express, Inc., 384 F.3d 108 (3rd Cir., 2004), e.g., managers of a solvent debtor that had already terminated its business had the firm file for bankruptcy in an attempt to apply a special bankruptcy limitation on a landlord's claims and to thus increase the return to the debtor's shareholders. This bankruptcy case served no legitimate purpose and was dismissed.
27. *See* 11 U.S.C. § 303.
28. In fact, there is evidence that a debtor's managers and shareholders, who do not fare well in bankruptcy, resist bringing firms into bankruptcy even when the firms could benefit from the process. *See, e.g.*, Adler, Capkun, and Weiss, cited in note 17. In this case, any pressure a creditor might apply to force a debtor into bankruptcy could enhance social welfare rather than reduce it.
29. For the functional benefits of debt, *see, e.g.*, Michael C. Jensen, *Agency Costs of Free Cash Flow, Corporate Finance, and Takeovers*, 76 AM. ECON. REV. 323, 324 (1986) (propounding 'control hypothesis' of debt creation); Sanford J. Grossman and Oliver D. Hart, *Corporate Financial Structure and Managerial Incentives*, in John L. McCall (ed.), THE ECONOMICS OF INFORMATION AND UNCERTAINTY 107 (1982) (arguing that debt forces managers to be profit maximizing or risk losing benefits of their positions upon bankruptcy); Stephen A. Ross, *The Determination of Financial Structure: The Incentive Signaling Approach*, 8 BELL J. ECON. 23 (1977) (describing debt as signal of firm quality). Debt may also offer the issuer tax benefits in the deduction of interest payments from corporate income, though a firm that favored debt for this reason would not serve efficiency.
30. Compare Warren with Baird, cited in notes 20 and 21, respectively. *See also* Alan Schwartz, *A Normative Theory of Business Bankruptcy*, 91 VA. L. REV. 1999, 1261–64 (2005); Robert K. Rasmussen, *An Essay on Optimal Bankruptcy Rules and Social Justice*, 1994 U. ILL. L. REV. 1, 27–41 (1994).
31. *See* UCC §9-101 et seq.
32. *See* 11 U.S.C. §522. On exempt property and jurisdiction jumping, *see generally* Marcus Cole, *The Federalist Cost of Bankruptcy Exemption Reforms*, 74 AM. BANKR. L.J. 227, 230–36 (2000) (relying on empirical evidence to find jurisdiction jumping relatively limited, but nevertheless 'demonstrably real and symbolically potent.').
33. *See, e.g.*, Henry Hansmann and Reinier Kraakman, *Toward Unlimited Shareholder Liability for Corporate Torts*, 100 YALE L.J. 1879 (1991) (collecting sources and arguing even against shareholder limited liability where plaintiff is tort victim).
34. *See* Walkovsky v. Carlton, 223 N.E. 2d 6 (NY, 1966). More generally, whenever a company subject to potential tort liability operates for a time on funds obtained through secured finance, the priority of the secured claims is an example of risk externalization. *See, e.g.*, In re Chrsyler, 576 F.3d 108 (2nd Cir., 2009), vacated as moot (December 14, 2009) (describing payment of sale proceeds of debtor's assets going entirely or almost entirely to secured creditors even though tort victims will be unable to pursue the assets in the hands of the purchaser).
35. A recent study suggests that at least some firms do not exploit potential tort claimants to the fullest extent possible. *See* Yair J. Listokin, *Is Secured Debt Used to Redistribute Value from Tort Claimants in Bankruptcy? An Empirical Analysis*, 57 DUKE L.J. 1037 (2008). This finding does not imply, however, that the effects described are nonexistent, only that they may not always be large. These results are, in any case, called into question by Barry E. Adler and Vedran Capkun, The Externalization of Risk (unpublished manuscript, 2009).
36. *See* 11 U.S.C. §507(a)(1).
37. This is not to say that states are incapable of enacting such changes. But they have not and their inaction is not necessarily a reason for Congress to refrain as well.

38. BLACK'S LAW DICTIONARY (1979).
39. *See, e.g.*, Lessee of Ewing v. Burnet, 36 U.S. 41 (1837), a principal case found, e.g., in Thomas W. Merrill and Henry E. Smith, PROPERTY: PRINCIPLES AND POLICIES (2007); Charles M. Haar and Lance Liebman, PROPERTY AND LAW (2d ed. 1985).
40. In a pure notice jurisdiction, as opposed to a race-notice jurisdiction, the second transferee as a bona fide purchaser would prevail even without winning the race to record.
41. *See* RESTATEMENT (THIRD) OF RESTITUTION AND UNJUST ENRICHMENT §54(1) (2006).
42. *See* Emily Sherwin, *Unjust Enrichment and Creditors,* 27 REV. LITIGATION 141 (2007). *Cf.* Cunningham v. Brown, 265 U.S. 1 (1924) (victims of the original Ponzi scheme ordered to share ratably in available assets despite claim of constructive trust by the later contributors among them).
43. Karl N. Llewellyn, *Through Title to Contract and a Bit Beyond,* 15 N.Y.U. L. REV. 159, 167 (1938).
44. *See* Thomas W. Merrill and Henry E. Smith, *The Property/Contract Interface,* 101 COLUM. L. REV. 773, 795 (2001); *see also* Thomas W. Merrill and Henry E. Smith, *What Happened to Property in Law and Economics?,* 111 YALE L.J. 357 (2001).
45. Merrill and Smith, *Property/Contract Interface,* id. at 791 and note 66 (collecting sources).
46. *See* Kenneth Ayotte and Patrick Bolton, Optimal Property Rights in Financial Contracting (unpublished manuscript, 2007), available at http://ssrn.com/abstract=989225.
47. *See* Henry Hansmann and Reinier Kraakman, *Property, Contract, and Verifiability: The Numerus Clauses Problem and the Divisibility of Rights,* 31 J. LEGAL STUD. 373 (2002).
48. *See* Henry Hansmann and Reinier Kraakman, *The Essential Role of Organizational Law,* 110 YALE L.J. 387, 390–93 (2000).
49. RESTATEMENT (SECOND) OF CONTRACTS § 241 (1981).
50. Id. at § 241 (b). Five factors are listed in all, but the others are not relevant to the discussion here.
51. The result would grant each party the benefit of his bargain but would not necessarily be ideal. The expectation remedy does not properly align incentives in all cases, and can lead to overinvestment by a promisee. *See, e.g.*, Robert Cooter, *Unity in Tort, Contract, and Property: The Model of Precaution,* 73 CAL. L. REV. 1 (1985). A more complete explanation is beyond the scope of this chapter.
52. For a discussion of the importance of precaution and reliance, *see, e.g.*, Richard Craswell, *Contract Remedies, Renegotiation, and the Theory of Efficient Breach,* 61 S. CAL. L. REV. 629, 646–50 (1988).
53. *See* RESTATEMENT (SECOND) OF CONTRACTS § 241(b), comment c (1981). *See also, e.g.*, First Interstate Bank of Idaho v. Small Business Admin., 868 F.2d 340 (9th Cir. 1989).
54. *See* Richard Craswell, *Insecurity, Repudiation, and Cure,* 19 J. LEG. STUD. 399 (1990); *see also* Charles J. Goetz and Robert E. Scott, *The Mitigation Principle: Toward a General Theory of Contractual Obligation,* 69 VA. L. REV. 967 (1983).
55. There are countervailing factors, beyond the scope of this chapter, that qualify this result. *See* Alexander J. Triantis and George G. Triantis, *Timing Problems in Contract Breach Decisions,* 41 J. L. & ECON.163 (1998), which suggests that judicial valuation error in damages calculations – particularly in the value of a breach victim's termination option – can induce premature repudiation.
56. An insolvent party may well have a perverse continuation incentive even if she cannot immediately consume her counterparty's performance. Such incentive could stem from her hope that the product of her counterparty's performance would restore her to solvency. In that event, unlikely though it may be, the party could then pay the counterparty in full for such performance and retain any excess value. If the gamble failed, the party would only then renege.
57. A party who has reason to be insecure about her counterparty's performance can, under some circumstances, withhold her own performance until she receives adequate assurance of her counterparty's performance. *See* RESTATEMENT (SECOND) OF CONTRACTS § 251 (1981); UCC §2-60. Consider as well the hoary equitable doctrine that prevents an insolvent party who has not himself performed from demanding specific performance. *See, e.g.*, H.C. Horack, *Insolvency and Specific Performance,* 31 HARV. L. REV. 702, 713 (1918). *See also* UCC §2-702, which permits a seller of goods on credit to withhold delivery if the buyer is insolvent.
58. *See, e.g.*, Lary v. U.S. Postal Service, 472 F.3d 1363 (9th Cir. 2006) (material breach found in part because promisor was unable to pay a money judgment). Reported cases in which a breach is deemed material because of a promisor's inability to pay are rare, but the relevance of ability-to-pay is not disputed.
59. This use of 'overinvestment' is traditional in finance literature, which directly addresses insolvency issues and which I am here attempting to integrate into contract analysis. This use of the term is not standard for the contracts literature, which reserves 'overinvestment,' or its counterpart 'underinvestment,' for investment prior to the realization of a state that will determine whether performance of a contract is efficient. What I call overinvestment in this example, the standard contract literature would call inefficient ex post performance. There is no substantive distinction, however.
60. *Cf.* Geotz & Scott, cited in note 54 at 990, describing a party's suspension of performance as security against a counterparty's nonperformance.

61.   *See* Alan Schwartz, *A Theory of Loan Priorities*, 18 J. LEGAL STUD. 209, 214–18 (1989); *see also* Yeon-Koo Che and Alan Schwartz, *Section 365, Mandatory Bankruptcy Rules and Inefficient Continuance*, 15 J.L. ECON. & ORG. 441, 441–46 (1999) (describing inefficient investment incentives under anti–ipso facto provisions of the Bankruptcy Code).

11 The law and economics of marital property
Martin Zelder

1. INTRODUCTION

For the purposes of economic analysis, marital property can be construed in two different but complementary (and sometimes overlapping) ways: (1) the formal legal sense, and (2) the functional practical sense. Marital property, as defined formally/legally, refers to property acquired during marriage and thereby (typically) subject to division upon divorce. Marital property can also be defined in a functional/practical sense as assets which provide consumption flows that can be used to make transactions within both marriage and divorce. It is worth brief consideration and comparison of these two senses of marital property, and how they have been affected by developments in law and in economics.

In regard to formal/legal marital property, the law is clearly instrumental in determining its scope and the extent to which it is transferred between spouses. To be specific, at the time of divorce, property is classified either as marital (and necessarily subject to division) or separate (and not necessarily subject to division). Furthermore, the legal system then sets standards or guidelines as to the appropriate magnitude of post-divorce transfers.

As for functional/practical marital property, it can be construed as assets which yield consumption flows which can be used for transacting within marriage and divorce. In recent years, economic analysis of spousal transacting has identified a fundamental issue, transferability, which critically influences the effect of legal rules governing marriage and divorce (and changes in them). The implications of limitations on transferability, and of changes in legal rules, will be explored in the subsequent sections.

2. MODELING MARRIAGE, DIVORCE, AND MARITAL PROPERTY

Prior to considering the advances made by economic analysis of marital property, and some remaining unconfronted issues, it is worthwhile to formulate a simplified model of marriage and divorce as a framework for evaluating what we know and wish to know. To begin with, define M as the quantity of household output produced within marriage. M is a function of time inputs t_{HM} and t_{WM} provided, respectively, by husband H and wife W:[1,2]

$$M = M(t_{HM}, t_{WM}) \tag{11.1}$$

For analytical purposes, M can usefully be divided into proportions of *marital* property (the fraction m) and *separate* property (the corresponding fraction 1-m). In this context, m represents the fraction of marital output M which the couple understands to be treated (upon divorce) as 'marital property' under the law.

For each spouse, total time T is divided between the production of M and the production of individual explicitly separate outputs, denoted M_{HS} and M_{WS} for H and W, respectively. Hence, the production functions for these explicitly separate outputs are:

$$M_{HS} = M_{HS}(t_{HS}) \qquad\qquad (11.2A)$$

$$M_{WS} = M_{WS}(t_{WS}), \qquad\qquad (11.2B)$$

where t_{HS} and t_{WS} represent time by H and W, respectively, in producing their own separate outputs (and, hence, time *not* spent producing M).[3] Total time T for each spouse is then given by:

$$T = t_{HM} + t_{HS} = t_{WM} + t_{WS} \qquad\qquad (11.3)$$

Within marriage, marital property mM is divided between H and W, with H receiving the fraction b and W receiving the remaining $1 - b$.[4] In addition, the rest of M, i.e., the output $(1 - m)M$, is an additional source of 'separate' property (beyond M_{HS} and M_{WS}). Specifically, $(1 - m)M$ represents the amount of separate property arising from the *joint* efforts of H and W, as opposed to M_{HS} and M_{WS}, which constitute separate property arising from *individual* efforts of H and W. The jointly-created separate property $(1 - m)$ M is divided within marriage, with H receiving the share h and W receiving the share $1 - h$. Thus, H's jointly-created separate property within marriage is $h(1 - m)M$, while W's jointly-created separate property within marriage is $(1 - h)(1 - m)M$.[5]

Given these definitions, the income or consumption of each spouse[6] within marriage can be specified:

$$M_H = bmM + M_{HS} + h(1 - m)M \qquad\qquad (11.4A)$$

$$M_W = (1 - b)mM + M_{WS} + (1 - h)(1 - m)M \qquad\qquad (11.4B)$$

where M_H is H's total consumption within marriage and M_W is W's total consumption within marriage. Each consumption expression contains three terms, in order: each spouse's share of marital property mM, each spouse's individually-created separate property, and each spouse's share of jointly-created separate property $(1 - m)M$.

The motivation to stay married, or get divorced, comes from random shocks to M_H and M_W. Specifically, there are three shocks: Φ is a *marriage*-specific shock, Φ_H is a shock specific to H, and Φ_W is a shock specific to W. Each shock is assumed to be normally distributed with mean 0. It is necessary to assume some source of uncertainty in order to depict the possibility of divorce in a model of rational marital status choice such as this one. More precisely, after H and W marry, these shocks are revealed as unexpected gains or losses associated with remaining married to one another (or alternatively, unexpected losses or gains associated with getting divorced). In practice, these shocks arise because H and W have incomplete information about their degree of compatibility and also about their own individual future opportunities with other potential mates. The shocks are modeled as additive, with income in divorce described as follows:

$$D = mM + \Phi \tag{11.5A}$$

$$D_H = a(mM + \Phi) + M_{HS} + h(1 - m)M + \Phi_H \tag{11.5B}$$

$$D_W = (1 - a)(mM + \Phi) + M_{WS} + (1 - h)(1 - m)M + \Phi_W, \tag{11.5C}$$

where D is marital property available upon divorce, a is the share of D obtained by H upon divorce, $1 - a$ is the share of D obtained by W upon divorce, D_H is H's total consumption upon divorce, and D_W is W's total consumption upon divorce. Given this setup, conditions for (Kaldor-Hicks) efficient divorce (11.6) and inefficient divorce (11.7) can be specified:

$$M_H + M_W < D_H + D_W$$
$$\Phi + \Phi_H + \Phi_W > 0 \tag{11.6}$$

$$M_H + M_W > D_H + D_W$$
$$\Phi + \Phi_H + \Phi_W < 0 \tag{11.7}$$

Based on the definitions of each spouse's marriage income (M_H, M_W) in equations (11.4A) and (11.4B) and each spouse's divorce income (D_H, D_W) in equations (11.5B) and (11.5C), expressions denoting each spouse's gains/losses from divorce can be constructed. The most interesting cases to consider are those in which one spouse gains from divorce, while the other gains from continued marriage, as these cases are the ones most vulnerable to an altered outcome as a result of legal change. Suppose for concreteness (but without loss of generality) that H gains from divorce while W gains from continued marriage. The gain from divorce experienced by H is therefore:

$$\Delta D_H = D_H - M_H$$
$$= [a(mM + \Phi) + M_{HS} + h(1 - m)M + \Phi_H] - [bmM + M_{HS} + h(1 - m)M]$$
$$= (a - b)mM + a\Phi + \Phi_H > 0 \tag{11.8}$$

The corresponding gain from marriage experienced by W is thus:

$$\Delta M_W = M_W - D_W$$
$$= [(1 - b)mM + M_{WS} + (1 - h)(1 - m)M]$$
$$\quad - [(1 - a)(mM + \Phi) + M_{WS} + (1 - h)(1 - m)M + \Phi_W]$$
$$= (a - b)mM - (1 - a)\Phi - \Phi_W > 0 \tag{11.9}$$

Equations (11.8) and (11.9) present a stylized depiction of these gains/losses. A central term in both expressions is $(a - b)mM$. Because a and b are H's share of marital property mM within divorce and marriage, respectively, $(a - b)mM$ describes H's gain, in terms of increased mM, within divorce. Conversely, $(a - b)mM$ also signifies W's gain, in terms of increased mM, within marriage.[7] As specified here, H's gain to divorce derives from three elements: his increased/decreased share of marital property within divorce, his share of the marriage-specific shock Φ, and his person-specific shock Φ_H. Similarly, W's gain to continued marriage derives from three elements: her increased/decreased share of marital property within marriage, her avoidance of her share of the divorce-specific shock Φ, and her avoidance of the person-specific shock Φ_W. The expressions for both H and W reflect the fact that each spouse's consumption from separate property drops out of (11.8) and (11.9), as a result of the assumption that the value of separate property is unaffected by divorce. In subsequent analysis, however, legal rules will be seen potentially to affect the allocation of time to the production of separate-property-based consumption. As well, subsequent analysis will address how legal rules (and changes in them) have affected the size and transferability of ΔD_H and ΔM_W.

In addition to describing ΔD_H and ΔM_W, it is important at this juncture to outline the conditions under which H and W choose their time allocations to maximize utility, and how this compares with the socially optimal time allocations. Consider first the social optimality problem. Both H and W allocate time given the possibility that divorce occurs with probability π. Expected incomes I_H and I_W can be defined for each as follows:

$$I_H = (1 - \pi)M_H + \pi E(D_H)$$
$$= (1 - \pi)[bmM + M_{HS} + h(1 - m)M] + \pi[amM + M_{HS} + h(1 - m)M]$$
$$= bmM + \pi(a - b)mM + h(1 - m)M + M_{HS} \tag{11.10}$$

$$I_W = (1 - \pi)M_W + \pi E(D_W)$$
$$= (1 - \pi)[(1 - b)mM + M_{WS} + (1 - h)(1 - m)M]$$
$$+ \pi[(1 - a)mM + M_{WS} + (1 - h)(1 - m)M]$$
$$= (1 - b)mM + \pi(b - a)mM + (1 - h)(1 - m)M + M_{WS} \tag{11.11}$$

These expected income equations indicate that H and W each receive their (bargained) shares of mM (b for H, $1 - b$ for W) plus/minus the difference between a and b if divorce occurs (with probability π). Also, the value of separate property is retained whether or not marriage continues, with H receiving $h(1 - m)M + M_{HS}$, and W receiving $(1 - h)(1 - m)M + M_{WS}$.

Social optimality entails maximizing the sum of their expected incomes I_T, where:

$$I_T = I_H + I_W$$
$$= [bmM + \pi(a - b)mM + h(1 - m)M + M_{HS}]$$
$$+ [(1 - b)mM + \pi(b - a)mM + (1 - h)(1 - m)M + M_{WS}]$$
$$= M + M_{HS} + M_{WS} \tag{11.12}$$

Maximizing this with respect to t_{HM} and t_{WM} yields two first-order conditions:

$$\frac{\partial M}{\partial t_{HM}} = \frac{\partial M_{HS}}{\partial t_{HM}} \qquad (11.13A)$$

and

$$\frac{\partial M}{\partial t_{WM}} = \frac{\partial M_{WS}}{\partial t_{WM}} \qquad (11.13B)$$

Intuitively, (11.13A) states that H spends the efficient amount of time, t_{HM}^{S*}, in household production of M when its social marginal benefit is equated with its social marginal cost. Equation (11.13B) is the analogous condition that determines the socially optimal time allocation for W, t_{WM}^{S*}.

These conditions can be compared with privately optimal choices when H and W incompletely internalize external benefits of their time-allocation choices. While complete internalization is certainly possible, it is realistic to suppose that difficulties in monitoring and enforcing bargains might lead to incomplete internalization.[8] For concreteness, imagine that each allocates time to satisfy Nash equilibrium: each treats the other's time allocation as given in maximizing his or her own utility. Hence, H chooses t_{HM} to maximize:

$$I_H = (1 - \pi) M_H + \pi D_H$$
$$= bmM + \pi(a - b)mM + h(1 - m)M + M_{HS} \qquad (11.10)$$

This yields the first-order condition:

$$[(1 - \pi)bm + \pi am + h(1 - m)]\frac{\partial M}{\partial t_{HM}} = \frac{\partial M_{HS}}{\partial t_{HM}}, \qquad (11.14)$$

which indicates that H equalizes the private marginal benefit and private marginal cost of t_{HM}, defining the private optimum t_{HM}^{P*}.[9] Evaluation of (11.14) reveals that the private marginal benefit, $[(1 - \pi)bm + \pi am + h(1 - m)]\partial M/\partial t_{HM}$, is less than the social marginal benefit derived in (11.13A), $\partial M/\partial t_{HM}$, because $0 < [(1 - \pi)bm + \pi am + h(1 - m)] < 1$. Consequently, less time is devoted by H to the production of M than is socially optimal: $t_M^{P*} < t_{HM}^{S*}$.

The other spouse, W, chooses t_{WM} to maximize:

$$I_W = (1 - \pi) M_W + \pi D_W$$
$$= (1 - b)mM + \pi(b - a)mM + (1 - h)(1 - m)M + M_{WS} \qquad (11.11)$$

This implies the corresponding first-order condition for W:

$$[(1 - \pi)(1 - b)m + \pi(1 - a)m + (1 - h)(1 - m)]\frac{\partial M}{\partial t_{WM}} = \frac{\partial M_{WS}}{\partial t_{WM}}, \qquad (11.15)$$

reflecting her equating of private marginal benefit and private marginal cost, and defines the private optimum t_{WM}^{P*}. Analogously to H, her private marginal benefit of effort, $[(1 - \pi)(1 - b)m + \pi(1 - a)m + (1 - h)(1 - m)]\partial M/\partial t_{WM}$, is also less than her social marginal benefit, $\partial M/\partial t_{WM}$, because $0 < [(1 - \pi)(1 - b)m + \pi(1 - a)m + (1 - h)(1 - m)] < 1$. Consequently, less time is devoted by W to the production of M than is socially optimal: $t_{WM}^{P*} < t_{WM}^{S*}$.

3.   THE ROLE OF THE LAW

The important role of family law in determining outcomes pertaining to marriage and divorce has been analyzed in a number of papers since Landes (1978). The framework developed in section 2 can be employed to review and evaluate the ideas in this literature as well as issues not previously addressed. To do so, it is useful to categorize the types of legal rules (and changes therein) into three categories: changes in the size of divorce settlements, the expanding scope of marital property, and fault vs. no-fault.

3.1   Changes in the Size of Divorce Settlements

The earliest examination of the consequence of legal change for marriage and divorce was found in the analysis of the function and consequence of alimony in Landes (1978). Her model, in the literal sense, addressed the incentives of one spouse ('the wife') to invest implicitly in the other's ('the husband's') labor-market human capital. Greater investment arose from more complete specialization by the 'wife' to household production and less allocation of time to labor-market production by her. Landes compared the extent of household-based specialization by the wife under alternative legal regimes: (1) no post-divorce compensation (to her) associated with the value of her husband's labor-market earnings vs. (2) the level of post-divorce compensation ('alimony') that induces cooperation between husband and wife to maximize their combined income (accounting for the possibility of divorce). Formally, Landes demonstrates that allowing the wife to claim on her investments in her husband's labor-market capital elicits a welfare-improving expansion in her willingness to make such investments.

The Landes result can be embedded within the more general and broader model sketched in this chapter. Specifically, providing/increasing alimony can be construed as an increase in the fraction $1 - a$ (of divorce output D) that the legal system obligates H (who gains from divorce) to pay W (who loses from divorce). In the polar case where H and W can readily transact, altering the value of $1 - a$ is irrelevant to any marital outcome, since H and W could write enforceable contracts that internalize any externalities. This can be seen directly by appreciating that with no obstacles to bargaining or contracting, H and W would maximize their joint income, as given by:

$$I_T = I_H + I_W$$
$$= [bmM + \pi(a - b)mM + \pi a\Phi + \pi\Phi_H + h(1 - m)M + M_{HS}]$$
$$+ [(1 - b)mM + \pi(b - a)mM + \pi(1 - a)\Phi + \pi\Phi_W + (1 - h)(1 - m)M + M_{WS}]$$
$$= M + M_{HS} + M_{WS} + \pi(\Phi + \Phi_H + \Phi_W) \tag{11.12}$$

Examination of this expression reveals that $1 - a$ simply operates as a transfer, and thus drops out of the simplified expression for I_T. This 'Coase Theorem' result can also be observed in comparing H's gains to divorce with W's gains to marriage:

$$\Delta D_H = D_H - M_H$$
$$= (a - b)mM + a\Phi + \Phi_H > 0 \tag{11.8}$$

and

$$\Delta M_W = M_W - D_W$$
$$= (a - b)mM - (1 - a)\Phi - \Phi_W > 0 \tag{11.9}$$

Clearly, increasing $1 - a$, and thereby decreasing a, leads to offsetting reductions in both ΔD_H and ΔM_W. Reducing H's gain to divorce by the same amount that W's gain to marriage is decreased leaves the surplus to divorce (marriage) unaltered.

If obstacles to bargaining exist, however, then H and W will not allocate time in order to maximize joint income, but will instead choose time allocations that serve private goals, such as the Nash best-response allocations. As derived in section 2, the conditions under which each person individually maximizes are:

$$[(1 - \pi)bm + \pi am + h(1 - m)]\frac{\partial M}{\partial t_{HM}} = \frac{\partial M_{HS}}{\partial t_{HM}}, \tag{11.14}$$

and

$$[(1 - \pi)(1 - b)m + \pi(1 - a)m + (1 - h)(1 - m)]\frac{\partial M}{\partial t_{WM}} = \frac{\partial M_{WS}}{\partial t_{WM}}. \tag{11.15}$$

Equation (11.15), the first-order condition for W, illustrates Landes's central point: more generous alimony, i.e., larger $1 - a$ (or smaller a), increases the expected private marginal benefit to W of investing in M, as $[\pi(b - a)m]\partial M/\partial t_{WM}$ is enlarged. This serves to increase W's private marginal benefit, increasing her effort towards the quantity that satisfies the social optimality condition:

$$\frac{\partial M}{\partial t_{WM}} = \frac{\partial M_{WS}}{\partial t_{WM}} \tag{11.13B}$$

It is within the context of this sort of model that Landes generates the policy implication that increasing the size of alimony is welfare-improving, as greater effort by W increases M and thereby H's share of M, ceteris paribus. However, in treating H's labor-market capital as a univariate function of W's effort, Landes's model omits an important reality: that H's effort also influences the size of H's labor-market capital. In the context of the model in this chapter, this means that, as assumed in equation (11.1):

$$M = M(t_{HM}, t_{WM})$$ (11.1)

In other words, when $1 - a$ increases, not only W's incentives, but also those of H, are affected. Equation (11.14) illustrates this effect on H; because $[\pi(a - b)m]\partial M/\partial t_{HM}$ falls when a falls, H's expected private marginal benefit of expending effort in producing M falls. This reduces M, and pushes H's effort farther below the socially optimal level, at which:

$$\frac{\partial M}{\partial t_{HM}} = \frac{\partial M_{HS}}{\partial t_{HM}}$$ (11.13A)

This implies that a policy to expand the generosity of alimony or other forms of divorce settlement does not unambiguously increase marital output and thereby reduce dead-weight loss; the effect on M depends on the relative magnitudes of the opposing effects on W (to increase M) and H (to decrease M).

3.2   Expanding Scope of Marital Property

Beyond the question of how the gains to divorce, and hence marital property, are divided is the issue of defining which gains are marital property, and hence divisible. Considerable attention has been devoted, in both scholarly and practical contexts, to the implication of a more expansive definition of marital property. Analyses have investigated particular forms of marital property, such as advanced degrees and professional licenses (Borenstein and Courant, 1989; Polsby and Zelder, 1993), pensions, and other topics.

Whether an advanced degree or professional license constitutes marital property is an issue still being evaluated by the legal system. There have been steps in the direction of regarding degrees/licenses as marital property, with courts in some states ruling in this manner. The leading case in this line is *O'Brien v. O'Brien* (1985), a New York divorce case in which the divorced wife argued that she had invested in her physician husband's medical training during the marriage. The court decided in the wife's favor, holding that the husband's medical license was marital property and therefore subject to equitable division under which the wife would receive a portion (40 percent, in this case) of the present value of the medical license. Analysis of this holding, by Borenstein and Courant (1989) and Polsby and Zelder (1993), has provided an economic efficiency justification for it (or a variation on it), which can be outlined in the context of the model presented in this chapter.

Within the model, developed in section 2, the parameter m captures the breadth of marital property as construed by the legal system. In choosing how much effort to devote to producing M, the spouses H and W each consider that the proportion m, which is chosen by the legal system, determines the fraction of M that is 'marital' in a legal sense. Hence, common-law or statutory expansion in the range of property, such as advanced degrees, that are considered 'marital' property entails an increase in m. The comparative-static implications of increasing m can then be assessed formally.

As in the analysis of changes in a in the previous subsection, changes in the law are only relevant, in an efficiency sense, when obstacles to bargaining exist. Without obstacles, H and W can just contract around whatever m is chosen by the legal system. In the presence of such obstacles, however, H and W each maximize own utility, and thus do not completely internalize external costs and benefit to one another. Changes in m are therefore pertinent for both H and W; the specific implications can be discerned by examining the private-optimum first-order conditions for H and W:

$$[(1 - \pi)bm + \pi am + h(1 - m)]\frac{\partial M}{\partial t_{HM}} = \frac{\partial M_{HS}}{\partial t_{HM}}, \quad (11.14)$$

and

$$[(1 - \pi)(1 - b)m + \pi(1 - a)m + (1 - h)(1 - m)]\frac{\partial M}{\partial t_{WM}} = \frac{\partial M_{WS}}{\partial t_{WM}}. \quad (11.15)$$

For analytical purposes, these can be rewritten as:

$$[bm + \pi(a - b)m + h(1 - m)]\frac{\partial M}{\partial t_{HM}} = \frac{\partial M_{HS}}{\partial t_{HM}}, \quad (11.14')$$

and

$$[(1 - b)m + \pi(b - a)m + (1 - h)(1 - m)]\frac{\partial M}{\partial t_{WM}} = \frac{\partial M_{WS}}{\partial t_{WM}}. \quad (11.15')$$

Consider first equation (11.14′), the first-order condition for H's privately optimal choice of t_{HM}. An increase in m affects each of the three components of H's private marginal benefit of t_{HM}. The first term, $bm(\partial M)/(\partial t_{HM})$, increases in m, reflecting the fact that larger m increases the reward to H, on the margin, from increasing his time devoted to the production of marital property mM (in which he shares at the rate b whether married or divorced). The direction in which the second term, $[\pi(a - b)m]\partial M/\partial t_{HM}$, changes as m increases depends on whether $a > b$ or $a < b$. Intuitively, this means that increased m benefits H in the event of divorce if $a > b$, and harms H if $a < b$. Finally, the third term, $[h(1 - m)]\partial M/\partial t_{HM}$, decreases in m, conveying the fact that with higher m, less of H's investment in M is regarded as separate property, of which he receives the share h. Moreover, it is plausible that this third-term effect is larger than the second-term effect, even if the latter is positive. Specifically, imagine that $h > a$: a large share of their joint investment in separate property goes to H (e.g., H's human capital). Consequently, it must be the case that $h > \pi(a - b)$, even if $a > b$. Hence, the net effect of an increase in m on the second and third terms combined is negative; in the event of divorce, higher m means that H receives a smaller share of M. Because the effect of increased m on the first term is positive, the net effect of increased m on H's private marginal benefit of t_{HM} is ambiguous, and, as h is larger, increasing m is more likely to *reduce* H's effort in the production of M.

An analogous result can be obtained for W based upon (11.15′). When the definition of marital property is expanded, each of the three components of W's private marginal benefit of t_{WM} is affected. The first term, $[(1 - b)m]\partial M/\partial t_{HM}$, increases in m, reflecting the fact that larger m increases the reward to W, on the margin, from increasing her time devoted to the production of marital property mM (in which she shares at the rate $1 - b$ whether married or divorced). The direction in which the second term, $[\pi(b - a)m]\partial M/\partial t_{HM}$, changes as m increases depends on whether $a > b$ or $a < b$.

Intuitively, this means that increased m benefits W in the event of divorce if $a < b$, and harms W if $a > b$. Finally, the third term, $[(1 - h)(1 - m)]\partial M/\partial t_{HM}$, decreases in m, conveying the fact that with higher m, less of W's investment in M is regarded as separate property, of which she receives the share $1 - h$. Moreover, it is plausible that this third-term effect is smaller than the second-term effect, even if the latter is positive. Imagining, again, that $h > a$ gives the implication that $1 - h < 1 - a$, making it more likely that $1 - h < \pi(b - a)$, especially as h approaches 1 (i.e., H receives most of the income from their joint investment in separate property). Hence, the net effect on the second and third terms of an increase in m is more likely to be positive if $a < b$. Because the effect of increased m on the first term is positive, the net effect of increased m on W's private marginal benefit of t_{WM} is ambiguous, and, as h is larger, increasing m is more likely to *increase* W's effort in the production of M.

3.3   The Switch to No-fault Divorce

Another area of legal change in which economic analysis of marital property has been significant is the evaluation of the grounds for divorce. Economists' scrutiny of this issue has primarily concerned the transition from fault to no-fault that occurred in the US and elsewhere from the 1970s onward. In this analysis, marital property has played an important role, both in conceptual and formal senses. Developments along both of these lines can be considered in light of the model described in section 2.

Conceptually, the nature of marital property, in the context of no-fault, matters for the analysis of spousal bargaining. In the simplest analysis in which transacting occurs with little impediment, the switch from fault to no-fault would have no impact on divorce rates or other aspects of marriage. This 'Coase Theorem' result was first illustrated by Landes (1978), and can be briefly reviewed here as a benchmark for additional analyses. To see this, recall the expressions describing the circumstances in which H gains from divorce and W gains from continued marriage:

$$\Delta D_H = D_H - M_H$$
$$= (a - b)mM + a\Phi + \Phi_H > 0 \qquad (11.8)$$

and

$$\Delta M_W = M_W - D_W$$
$$= (a - b)mM - (1 - a)\Phi - \Phi_W > 0 \qquad (11.9)$$

When bargaining is essentially unimpeded, the occurrence of divorce is invariant to the governing legal regime: fault, or no-fault, where fault essentially requires W's mutual consent, and no-fault can be obtained by H without W's consent. Instead, the outcome (divorce, or continued marriage) depends solely on the comparison of H's gain to divorce (ΔD_H) and W's gain to marriage (ΔM_W). Specifically, when $\Delta D_H > \Delta M_W$, divorce occurs under either fault or no-fault. Under fault, H can compensate W via the divorce settlement, leaving both better off, while under no-fault, W is unable to compensate H (by renegotiating the marriage contract) because her gains to marriage are too small (smaller than his loss from continued marriage, i.e., forgone gains from divorce). Conversely, when $\Delta D_H < \Delta M_W$, marriage continues under either fault or no-fault. Under fault, H does not have enough surplus to compensate W for forgoing her gain to marriage, while under no-fault, W possesses enough surplus to improve H's share of marital output enough to induce him to prefer continued marriage.

It is well understood that this Coasean invariance result breaks down if there are obstacles to bargaining, such as prohibitive transactions costs or market failures in bargaining (see Zelder (1998a) for a thorough discussion of the Coase Theorem in general, and Zelder (2002) for a review of the bargaining literature pertaining to marriage and divorce). Of particular relevance to the discussion of marital property contained in this chapter are two strands of prior literature. One concerns the way in which gains to marriage (practical if not per se legal marital property) are received. The other concerns the manner in which family law influences investment in legally-defined marital property.

Consider first the issue of the practical form of marital property. One interesting and important aspect of this involves the form in which gains to marriage are received. In particular, consumption within marriage can, by definition, be either private to H, private to W, or public (collective) to both H and W. In fact, it is realistic to think that public goods – children, sex, conversation, love – are a prominent feature of marriage. Incorporating this aspect into the analysis of marriage and divorce, and the impact of legal change, is therefore potentially crucial.

To do this, define marital property mM as consisting of the proportion γ public goods and the proportion $1 - \gamma$ private goods. Hence, the expressions for income within marriage for H and W can be rewritten as:

$$M_H = \gamma mM' + b(1 - \gamma)mM' + M_{HS} + h(1 - m)M' \qquad (11.4A')$$

$$M_W = \gamma mM' + (1 - b)(1 - \gamma)mM' + M_{WS} + (1 - h)(1 - m)M' \quad (11.4B')$$

H and W jointly consume $\gamma mM'$ while married to each other, leaving marital private goods $(1 - \gamma)mM'$ to be divided between them at the rates b and $1 - b$, respectively. For the purposes of this analysis, assume that the portion γ of mM' only functions as a public good within marriage, but not within divorce.[10] As a result, the gain to marriage for W can be rewritten as:

$$\Delta M_W = M_W - D_W$$
$$= [\gamma mM' + (1 - b)(1 - \gamma)mM' + M_{WS} + (1 - h)(1 - m)M']$$
$$- [(1 - a)(mM' + \Phi) + M_{WS} + (1 - h)(1 - m)M' + \Phi_W]$$
$$= (a - b + b\gamma)mM' - (1 - a)\Phi - \Phi_W > 0 \qquad (11.9')$$

Of this, $b\gamma mM'$ constitutes W's public-good gains to marriage.

Given this, consider the effect on spousal bargaining. Because some of W's gains to marriage are public, they are consequently non-transferable to H within marriage. This conclusion derives from the reality that W cannot induce H to change his behavior (i.e., regarding whether or not to divorce) using public goods, since the $b\gamma mM'$ she might wish to transfer is already, by nature, consumed by H (who already gets $\gamma m M'$ within marriage). As a result, some of W's gains to marriage are unusable in bargaining. This has implications for the equilibrium divorce rate under fault and no-fault divorce.

Specifically, consider the case in which $\Delta M_W > \Delta D_H$. Under fault divorce, H must compensate W, by means of a more generous divorce settlement, to induce her to consent to divorce. But when $\Delta M_W > \Delta D_H$, his gains from divorce are inadequate to induce her consent, and marriage continues. Under no-fault, however, a different equilibrium is possible (Zelder, 1993). Suppose that W's public-good gains to marriage, $b\gamma m M'$, are a relatively large fraction of her total gains to marriage. Then, it is possible that:

$$\Delta M_W = (a - b + b\gamma)mM' - (1 - a)\Phi - \Phi_W > \Delta D_H$$

$$= (a - b + b\gamma)mM' + a\Phi + \Phi_H$$

$$> \Delta M_{WPr} = \alpha[(1 - b)(1 - \gamma)mM' + M_{WS} + (1 - h)(1 - m)M'], \quad (11.16)$$

where ΔM_{WPr} constitutes the maximum transfer W is willing to make to remain married (such that she remains better off within marriage). Specifically, α is the fraction of her total *private-good* marital income that she can give up while still remaining better off within marriage.[11] If (11.16) holds, then despite W having greater gains to marriage than H has gains to divorce, she is unable to induce him to stay married, under no-fault, if:

$$\Delta D_H = (a - b + b\gamma)mM' + a\Phi + \Phi_H > \Delta M_{WPr} = (a - b)mM' - (1 - a)\Phi - \Phi_W$$

Because $\Delta M_W > \Delta D_H$, however, divorces that occur under the condition outlined in (11.16) are Kaldor-Hicks inefficient: H gains less from divorce than W loses. Thus, in looking at marital property in a functional (although not legal) sense, as it is composed of a larger component of public goods, it becomes more likely that additional divorces, which would not occur under fault, will occur, and the divorce rate will exceed the social optimum (Zelder, 1993).

Other analyses of the consequences of the legal transition to no-fault focus instead on the impact of no-fault on property rights within divorce and the implications for the division of marital output. In this context, the shift to no-fault (and other legal changes) can be viewed as altering the divorce threat point (i.e., the reservation level of consumption/utility within divorce). The direction in which the threat point moves is a subject of some discussion in the literature.

The underlying assumption in some of these analyses is that the switch to no-fault made divorce (or the possibility thereof) more prevalent. This assumption is the subject of much empirical analysis concerning the impact of no-fault on the divorce rate; a comprehensive review of much of this literature (Zelder, 1998b) concludes that the strongest evidence favors the hypothesis that no-fault did indeed increase the divorce rate.[12] In any case, portions of the following discussion will rely upon this assumption; if the assumption is unreasonable, then those specific conclusions must be modified.

One approach views more prevalent divorce under no-fault as serving to weaken the divorce threat point of the person who would be harmed by divorce (assumed to be W in this analysis), in that exit is more credible (Dee, 2003; Stevenson, 2007). Another approach depicts no-fault divorce as exposing divorced individuals to greater financial hardship than did fault divorce (Brinig and Crafton, 1994). The idea here is that the removal of fault grounds often coincided, historically, with reduction in alimony, thus reducing the reservation utility of those who had previously received alimony, predominantly women.[13] Whichever direction the threat point moves, there is corresponding movement in the distribution of utility within marriage. To see how this works, reconsider utility within marriage for both *H* and *W*:

$$M_H = bmM + M_{HS} + h(1 - m)M \qquad (11.4A)$$

$$M_W = (1 - b)mM + M_{WS} + (1 - h)(1 - m)M \qquad (11.4B)$$

Given this setup, regard *W* as the one at risk of divorce (consistent with the earlier assumption that she gains from continued marriage). A change in *W*'s divorce threat point, due to a shift to no-fault, can then be inferred to induce a change in *b*, the share of marital output *mM* consumed by *H*. Hence, if no-fault improves *W*'s divorce threat point, this will decrease *b*, the share received within marriage by *H*, thereby increasing $1 - b$, the share received by *W*. Conversely, if no-fault weakens *W*'s bargaining position, *b* will increase and $1 - b$ will decrease.

Empirically, *b* can be represented by spousal consumption as well as the incidence of domestic violence (Brinig and Crafton, 1994; Dee, 2003). As Dee (2003) points out, domestic violence can be viewed as serving both 'instrumental' and 'expressive' functions, the former inducing behavioral modification by victims, and the latter generating nonmonetary benefits for abusers. Under either interpretation, therefore, domestic violence serves to increase abuser utility while decreasing victim utility within an ongoing relationship. Hence, the switch to no-fault, by altering divorce reservation utility, has the potential to alter consumption, in the broadest sense, within marriage. Brinig and Crafton (1994) hypothesized that no-fault reforms would be meaningful in this context when their unilateral consent divorce *grounds* were coupled with the removal of marital fault as a determinant of the size of divorce *settlements* (what we can refer to as 'full no-fault' states). Specifically, disconnecting the magnitude of the settlement payment from spousal behavior was predicted by Bring and Crafton to increase the incidence of behavior previously regarded as marital fault. The particular measure of marital 'opportunism' investigated by Brinig and Crafton was spousal abuse, as represented by the rate of calls to domestic violence crisis centers. They analyzed cross-sectional data for 1987, predicting variation in crisis-center call rates, by state, as a function of whether the state had adopted 'full no-fault', either prior to 1975 or between 1975 and 1987 (as well as covariates for per capita income, urbanization, violent crime rates, religious affiliation, and political affiliation). They estimated that crisis-center calls occurred at a higher rate in states which had adopted 'full no-fault' prior to 1975, as compared with non-adopting states, while later-adopting states (between 1975 and 1987) displayed no difference in crisis-center calls. Their interpretation is that early adoption of 'full no-fault', by reducing the threat point for women, therefore reduced the share they receive of marital income $(1 - b)$, as reflected by the greater rate of domestic violence to which they were exposed.

This analysis of no-fault and domestic violence is refined and expanded upon by Dee (2003). He recognizes that a critical limitation of the Brinig–Crafton estimates is their failure to account for state-specific heterogeneity. Specifically, Dee correctly argues that Brinig and Crafton cannot identify no-fault 'effects' on domestic violence because of the possibility that states adopting no-fault during his sample period, 1968–1978, differ unobservably from states that did not (and that early and late adopters might differ unobservably as well). Hence, he includes state fixed effects in his regressions. Dee also controls for a set of observables (police per capita, unemployment rate, per capita income) similar to those of Brinig and Crafton, as well as covariates (presence of death penalty, rate of 'stranger' (unrelated individual) homicides) directly relevant to the two outcomes he endeavors to explain: number of wives murdered by husbands, number of husbands murdered by wives. By using an outcome measure that directly reflects the cost of domestic violence, he also enables his estimates to address more directly the impact of divorce law on this phenomenon (as opposed to a more remote measure such as crisis-center calls). As well, Dee distinguishes male-against-female and female-against-male murders, permitting the detection of gender-specific effects. Finally, Dee also uses count-data regression methods (Poisson, negative binomial) to generate more reliable inferences from his murder-count data.

After including state fixed effects (and using negative binomial regression to ensure that his standard errors are not understated), Dee estimates that no-fault had no impact on the murder of wives by husbands, but that it did increase the rate at which husbands were murdered by wives. He also usefully tests whether access to no-fault had differential effects on divorce threat points depending on the underlying marital property regime: community property, equitable distribution, and common law.[14] He finds that a switch to no-fault still had no impact on homicides *against* wives, regardless of marital property regime, while the murder of husbands by wives was more common after the switch to no-fault but only in equitable distribution and common law states. Dee interprets these two regimes, equitable distribution and common law, as less financially favorable to wives. Thus, in Dee's interpretation, by lowering wives' divorce threat points, no-fault (within these less financially generous regimes) exposed women to greater risk of non-lethal domestic violence from their husbands, making women more likely to resort to lethal self-defense.

In addition to examining the evidence regarding the shifts in marital consumption shares b and $1 - b$, it is also worth considering the predicted impact of the changes in these shares (and in the corresponding divorce threat-point shares a and $1 - a$) on the efficiency of spousal time allocation. Consider first the wife W's Nash first-order condition:

$$[(1 - \pi)(1 - b)m + \pi(1 - a)m + (1 - h)(1 - m)]\frac{\partial M}{\partial t_{WM}} = \frac{\partial M_{WS}}{\partial t_{WM}}. \quad (11.15)$$

As above, the shift to no-fault can be viewed as a reduction in the wife's share of the divorce settlement, $1 - b$, and an increase in the husband's share, b. A reduction in $1 - b$ associated with a shift to no-fault along with a less generous financial settlement, would, by itself, reduce the first component of W's marginal benefit of investing in the production of marital output M, namely, $[(1 - \pi)(1 - b)m]\partial M/\partial t_{WM}$, reducing time devoted by W to the production of M, while increasing her time devoted to producing separate property. This effect would be further reinforced to the extent that reduced $1 - b$ lowers $1 - a$, W's share of marital output within marriage, due to her weakened bargaining position. Thus, given these considerations, Gray (1998) and others have investigated whether the shift to no-fault has led women to reallocate time away from household production. Specifically, they have considered the impact on the allocation of time to the labor market, the typical other use of time in such models. Analytically, predictions about the impact on labor-market time are identical to predictions regarding the impact on separate-property-production time in the model analyzed here. Hence, these labor-supply analyses predicted that no-fault would disproportionately increase female labor supply in those states with less favorable property-division regimes, namely equitable-distribution and common-law states.

Gray, in fact, finds differing effects of no-fault on female labor supply, depending on whether the property division regime was equitable, common-law, or community property. Specifically, in analysis of both CPS and PSID data, he detects that no-fault neither increased nor decreased female labor force participation (or hours) in equitable distribution states, while no-fault decreased female labor supply in common-law states, and increased female labor supply in community property states. He interprets this as consistent with differing changes in women's bargaining power within marriage. Hence, because increased risk of divorce under no-fault lessened women's bargaining power in common-law states, they were less able to bargain for (preferred) time allocated to the labor market, leading to reductions in such time. Conversely, because increased risk of divorce under no-fault enhanced women's bargaining power in community-property states, they were better able to bargain for (preferred) time allocated to the labor market, leading to increases in such time. Stevenson (2007), by contrast, attempts to replicate Gray's result for 'newly-weds' (less than two years of marriage) in Census data, and finds that female labor supply is greater under no-fault, regardless of the prevailing property-division regime. She interprets this and a similar result for having children (reduced likelihood under no-fault, regardless of property-division regime) as indicating diminished value for marriage-specific invest-ments (and increased value for marriage-general investments) under no-fault.

4. CONCLUSION

Economists have been writing about family law for the past 30 years, enabling real progress to be made in understanding the treatment and function of marital property. Hence, real insights have been generated pertaining to the impact of divorce settlements on behavior within marriage, the efficient treatment of newer marital property forms such as advanced degrees, and the unexpected consequences for marital transacting of the switch to no-fault. However, much remains unsettled. Included in this list are: how to provide efficient compensation for investments in marital property, and resolving conflicting results regarding the impact of no-fault divorce and how these results differ depending on the property regime and functional sorts of property held within mar-riages. Thus, it is quite likely that economics will continue to lend considerable insight to the analysis of marital property for years to come.

NOTES

1. Goods inputs are omitted from the production function M(•) for purposes of simplification, although their inclusion would not materially alter the analysis later in the chapter.

2. As is standard, the marginal products of t_{HM} and t_{WM} are both assumed to be positive but diminishing.
3. As for the production of M, the marginal products of t_{HS} and t_{WS} are both assumed to be positive but diminishing.
4. While these shares b and $1 - b$ are treated as exogenously determined, it is understood that they arise endogenously as the result of bargaining between H and W. The endogeneity of b will be addressed later in the chapter.
5. The shares h and $1 - h$ are also treated as exogenous, although they are undoubtedly endogenous to the bargaining process, for the purposes of simplifying the analysis.
6. 'Income' and 'consumption' are used interchangeably throughout to refer to the quantity of marital output allocated to each spouse.
7. The original expression for this aspect of her gain is written as: $[(1 - b) - (1 - a)]mM$, where $1 - b$ and $1 - a$ are her shares of mM within marriage and divorce, respectively. This simplifies to $(a - b)mM$.
8. See Zelder (1998a) for a comprehensive discussion of the circumstances in which bargaining is not successful.
9. For tractability, a and h are treated as exogenous.
10. This assumption can be justified in several ways: coresidence of H and W is necessary for joint consumption, or public goods are marriage-specific and their value therefore dissolves upon divorce.
11. As Zelder (1993) points out, ΔM_{WPr} exceeds W's private-good gain to marriage, in that W is willing to give up *more* than her total private-good gain to marriage due to the fact that she is unable to transfer any of the *public*-good gain to marriage.
12. Much of the more recent literature curiously ignores a substantial number of earlier papers that are reviewed in Zelder (1998b).
13. As with the impact of no-fault on the divorce rate, the financial impact of no-fault is also an empirical question.
14. Community property regimes treat much of marital property as being held jointly by husband and wife, and thus subject to distribution, and equitable distribution similarly allows judges to distribute property in an equitable fashion regardless of its original owner, while common law regimes regard property as owned by the title-holder, disproportionately husbands in Dee's data.

REFERENCES

Borenstein, Severin and Paul Courant. (1989). 'How to Carve a Medical Degree: Human Capital Assets in Divorce Settlements'. *American Economic Review*, 79, 992–1009.
Brinig, Margaret F. and Steven M. Crafton. (1994). 'Marriage and Opportunism'. *Journal of Legal Studies*, 23, 869–894.
Dee, Thomas S. (2003). 'Until Death Do You Part: The Effects of Unilateral Divorce on Spousal Homicides'. *Economic Inquiry*, 41, 163–182.
Gray, Jeffrey S. (1998). 'Divorce-Law Changes, Household Bargaining, and Married Women's Labor Supply'. *American Economic Review*, 88, 628–642.
Landes, Elisabeth M. (1978). 'Economics of Alimony'. *Journal of Legal Studies*, 7, 35–63.
Polsby, Daniel D. and Martin Zelder. (1993). 'Risk-Adjusted Valuation of Professional Degrees in Divorce', *Journal of Legal Studies*, 23, 273–285.
Stevenson, Betsey. (2007). 'The Impact of Divorce Laws on Marriage-Specific Capital'. *Journal of Labor Economics*, 25, 75–94.
Zelder, Martin. (1993). 'Inefficient Dissolutions as a Consequence of Public Goods: The Case of No-Fault Divorce', *Journal of Legal Studies*, 22, 503–520.
Zelder, Martin. (1998a). 'The Cost of Accosting Coase: A Reconciliatory Survey of Proofs and Disproofs of the Coase Theorem', in Steven G. Medema (ed.) *Coasean Economics: Law and Economics and the New Institutional Economics*, Kluwer Academic Publishers, pp. 65–94.
Zelder, Martin. (1998b). 'Did No-Fault Divorce Law Increase the Divorce Rate? A Critical Review of the Evidence'. Unpublished manuscript.
Zelder, Martin. (2002). 'For Better or For Worse? Is Bargaining in Marriage and Divorce Efficient?', in Antony Dnes and Robert Rowthorn (eds) *The Law and Economics of Marriage and Divorce*, Cambridge University Press, pp. 157–170.

12 Property titling and conveyancing
Benito Arruñada*

I. ENFORCEMENT BENEFITS VS. 'CONSENT' COSTS

Rights to land and many other assets can be enforced as property rights, *iura in rem*, claimable against the asset itself and therefore valid against all persons, *erga omnes*.[1] These property rights are said to 'run with the land,' meaning that they survive unaltered through all kinds of transactions and transformations dealing with other rights on the same parcel of land or on a neighboring parcel. For example, the mortgagee keeps the same claim on the land even after the mortgagor sells it. Property rights oblige all people: the new owner who has purchased the land is obliged to respect both the mortgage and, in particular, the right to foreclose in case the guaranteed debt is not paid. Enforcement of a property right is independent of who holds other rights on the same asset. Alternatively, rights on assets can be contract rights, enforceable against a specific person, *inter partes*. To clarify the difference between property and contract rights, consider what happens in the case of a lease of land, this being a right that in many jurisdictions may be structured as either a contractual or a property right. Assume that the land is sold during the life of the lease. If the lease is a contract right, the lessee loses the right of occupation, and gains instead a contract right against the lessor. However, if the lease is a property right, the lessee keeps the right of occupation. It is then the land purchaser who may have a contract right against the seller, if the sale was made free of leases. The buyer is subrogated into the seller's position. There is no change to the lease, which has run with the land from the seller to the buyer, surviving intact after the sale.

When the law enforces a right as a right *in rem*, consent of the right holder is required for the right to be affected, that is, damaged, in any way. This requirement of consent – either real or constructive – provides precious enforcement benefits for rights on durable and immovable assets. On the other hand, the enforcement of contract rights depends on the availability, resources and legal status of persons, who are mobile and may become unavailable or judgment proof when obliged to pay. For durable assets, a property right is therefore much more valuable than a contract right having the same content – that is, when the only difference between them is that the latter lacks *in rem* enforceability.

These enforcement benefits come at a cost, however. When multiple rights exist on an asset, transactions do not convey property rights with the promised *in rem* extent until all affected right holders have consented. In other words, to produce perfect property – that is, *in rem* – rights, some kind of explicit or implicit contracting has to take place between the transactors and each of the affected right holders in order for the latter to give their consent. Many institutions in the field of property law are designed to make these 'contracts' with affected right holders possible. Consent can be given explicitly, by private agreement, declaring to a register or in court proceedings, as well as implicitly, by the simple passing of time. Consent can also be produced at the moment the relevant transaction takes place. Consequently, the rights resulting from the transaction will be free of uncertainty as to whom the true legal right holder is and as to their precise nature. Alternatively, consent can be postponed, and the relevant transaction then produces rights which are burdened with the survival of any property rights whose right holders have not yet consented.

In any case, without the consent of affected right holders, transactions produce a mix of property and contract rights: property – *in rem* – effects to the extent compatible with the surviving property rights held by others, and contract rights for the difference. The proportion of property and contract rights in the mix varies with the kind of conflicting right. In the extreme case of a fraudulent conveyance, the grantee gets only a contract right against the grantor, who is not the true legal owner. More generally, any intended property right is in fact partially contractual if an affected right holder keeps a contradictory or concurrent right against it.

Property rights thus face a tradeoff with positive and negative effects. On the one hand, they facilitate specialization by ensuring enforcement, given that right holders' consent is required to affect them. However, for the same reason, their survival after conveyance of the asset or any other transformation of rights requires costly institutions and resources in order to organize the process of searching, bargaining and contracting for consent. In particular, the possibility of hidden property rights increases the information asymmetry between the conveying parties: the seller knows better than the acquirer about hidden property rights. More generally, the need of knowing which conflicting property rights exist, finding out who their right holders are, bargaining with such right holders to obtain their consent and contracting or somehow formalizing an agreement with them, all increase the costs of transforming and conveying rights. This may in turn hamper investment, trade and specialization.[2]

II. TITLING SYSTEMS

A. Privacy of Rights as a Benchmark

Under the Roman Law tradition of private conveyance that was dominant in Europe until the 19th century, private contracts on land had *in rem* effects on third parties even if they were kept secret. In cases of conflict, courts 'established title' (that is, they allocated property and contract rights) on the basis of evidence on possession and past transactions, whether or not these transactions had remained hidden. This potential enforcement of adverse hidden rights made full consent impossible to reach *ex ante*, hindering trade and specialization. All transactions in land then gave rise, totally or partially, to contract rights and the enforcement advantage of property rights remained unfulfilled, especially with respect to abstract rights, such as mortgages.

Whatever the palliatives being applied (mainly, reliance on possession and the chain of title deeds), the costs of contracting property rights under a regime of pure privacy are such that modern systems of property law have abandoned privacy. At a minimum, the law requires the publicity of contracts as a prerequisite for them to attain *in rem* effects – i.e. to convey property rights and not mere contract rights. If they keep their rights private, right holders lose or risk losing *in rem* effects. Private contracts may create obligations among the parties but do not bind third parties – all other right holders and, especially, potential future buyers and lenders. Publicity therefore facilitates the search for which property rights are alive, making it possible to reach consent *ex ante*, purging titles, and reducing information asymmetries between the parties.

B. Recording of Deeds

Legal systems vary substantially, however, with respect to how and when any contradiction with other property rights must be purged by obtaining the consent of the holders of these affected rights. The two paradigms are recorders of deeds and registers of rights.

Recorders of deeds are still used in most of the US, France and some other countries, many of which have a French legal background. They enroll and keep private transaction documents ('title deeds') and thus provide evidence on property claims. This evidence is used by the courts to allocate property rights *ex post* – after litigation. In practice, the system is effective if courts apply a non-standard priority rule and, when deciding on a conflict with third parties, they determine the priority of claims from the date of recording in the public office and not from the date of the deed. This priority rule effectively motivates parties to record from fear of losing title through, for example, a wrongful second 'double sale' to an innocent acquirer. If such a second sale were recorded first, it would gain priority over the first one.[3] Consequently, all relevant evidence on property rights is publicly available by inspecting both the public records and the land itself.[4] From the point of view of third parties, the record, in principle, is complete. Some other claims may not be recorded and may well be binding for the parties conveying them, but these hidden claims have no effect on third parties (more precisely, on bona fide acquirers for value).

This inclusiveness of the record makes it possible to produce information on the quality of title ('title reports') by having different experts examine all relevant deeds, which are only those that have been recorded.[5] These experts form an industry which, despite adopting different forms in each country (mainly, that of notaries public in countries such as France, and abstractors, attorneys, title insurance agents and title insurance underwriters in the US[6]), performs similar functions in all of them as it (1) reduces information asymmetry between the parties, (2) reallocates risk from the acquirer to the expert, and (3) makes it possible to clean title clouds by obtaining the consent of the affected third parties. If these clouds are not removed, the grantee will not transact or will insist on modifying the transaction, reducing the price or including additional warranties, in compensation for the survival of property rights that are contradictory to those that were contracted.

Despite private incentives to purge rights *ex ante*, the public record *may*, however, contain evidence on potentially contradictory rights. The recording office is obliged by law to accept all deeds respecting certain formal requirements (mainly, the date of the contract and the names of the parties), whatever their legality and their collision with preexisting property rights. It will therefore contain potentially three kinds of deed: (1) those resulting from transactions made without previous examination; (2) those granted after an examination but without having all defects removed; and (3) those that define purged and non-contradictory property rights. Experts examining the title of a parcel do not know *a priori* which of these kinds of deed are recorded concerning it. For each transaction, they will therefore examine all relevant deeds dealing with that parcel in the past.

C.   Registration of Rights

Registers of rights such as those in Australia, Germany, England or Spain go one step further: instead of merely providing information on claims, they define the rights. They thus require a previous, complete purge of property claims. As in deed recording, private contracts gain priority when they are first lodged to the register. They are then subject, however, to substantive review by the registrar, in order to detect any potential conflict which might damage other property rights. Rights are registered (antedating the effects of registration to the filing date[7]) only when the registrar determines that they do not affect any other property right, or the holders of affected rights have consented. Otherwise, registration is denied and the parties have to restructure their contract or obtain the relevant consents. Information on the register is simplified in parallel with the purge of rights. Rights defined in each new contract are registered together with all surviving rights on the same parcel of land. Extinguished rights are removed or deleted, however, which makes access to the register very simple. Effective identification of each parcel of land is necessary for the system to work, as is the use of a tract index to locate all rights in each parcel.

Given that any contradictions are purged *ex ante*, the register is able to provide 'conclusive,' 'indefeasible' title, meaning that a good faith third party for value acquires a property right if the purchase is based on the information provided by the register. If the seller's right is later shown to be defective, the buyer keeps the property right and the original owner gets contract rights against the seller and the register. The property right is allocated in these exceptional cases to the acquirer, but this happens only when there has been a failure in the register.[8] No contradiction should appear in most cases, however, so property enforcement is based on right-holders' consent. Registration thus interferes with private property much less than is often claimed, as its intervention focuses on the timing and the completeness of the private purging of rights. Registration is regulated by registrars or judges but ultimate decisions are made by right holders by giving consent. Privacy and recording allow parties more discretion on the timing and heavier reliance on privately produced information. Rights therefore seem to be more the product of private decisions, but this perception is deceptive because even recorded rights retain a higher contractual content, given the survival of conflicting claims *in rem*. Additional public intervention by the court is required to transform them into property rights at an *in rem* level equivalent to that provided by registration. Furthermore, this additional judgment is also subject to the possibility of allocation failure.

III.   THE ROLE OF CONVEYANCING SERVICES IN EACH TITLING SYSTEM

All three public titling systems share functional similarities: all three are based on enforcing individual consent as a requirement. As a consequence, contracting proceeds in two steps: first, parties agree to the transaction; second, they gather the consent of affected right holders. By making this gathering of consent more or less difficult, the three titling systems induce different demands for private 'conveyancing services', these being understood as services provided by notaries, lawyers or other professionals that support contracting between the parties.[9]

A. Conveyancing under Privacy

Under privacy, property rights would eventually be enforced *in rem* even if the transaction remained hidden. By themselves, private contracts could not damage third parties: the baseline principle *nemo dat quod non habet* (no one can deliver what one does not have) fully applies. For instance, if B_2 is purchasing land from O, B_2 should be worried that O might have previously sold the land to B_1 or mortgaged the same land to L. However, B_1 is fully protected because, assuming neither of the two buyers took possession, the courts will establish title according to the date of the contract and give the land to B_1, with B_2 having only a contractual claim on O. Buyer B_1 should be worried, however, about the possibility that O and B_2 may fraudulently antedate their contract.

This system maximizes the complexity of conveyancing services. It first generates demand for lawyers to design and evaluate title guarantees offered by sellers and third parties which, even if they do not protect buyers *in rem*, at least provide some protection *in personam*. Second, reducing transaction costs when rights are embodied in titles also requires protecting the titles against fraud.[10] From early times, legal systems required the presence of witnesses, surely the simplest solution, often qualified in terms of number, age, expertise and authority. In addition, titles are protected by requiring that specialists (lawyers or notaries) are involved in producing them. A common solution making fraud difficult is for grantees and mortgagees to demand delivery of the full chain of titles from grantors and mortgagors, so that the risk of previous competing transactions is reduced and later transactions would require faking a full chain of titles. In a sense, the chain of titles is used as a private record but without any guarantee that it is exhaustive.

The role of conveyancers is greatest under this privacy system, because they act as both producers and depositories of the main body of evidence used to establish title. In this context, reducing competition between professionals may serve two purposes.

First, sharing information on their contracts among conveyancers will substantially save on the costs of structuring new deals and make them more secure. This process could be observed recently in Andorra, a small country between France and Spain, which still applies a relatively pure system of Roman Law, including privacy for real estate transactions. The few Andorran notaries started to share information on mortgages after a new regulation was enacted in 1998.[11]

Second, reducing competition will lessen the incentives of conveyancers to cheat each other, and may provide some support for the protection of third parties against fraud. The system hinges, however, on conveyancers dating deeds faithfully. For instance, notaries chronologically enter all documents into the notary's protocol, which provides an additional safeguard on the dating of documents. But the system may be prone to fraud as can be seen in some Latin American countries where, given the sorry state of their land registers, judges tend to refer to the date of deeds, falling back *de facto* into a privacy system and thus increasing the motivation to fraudulently antedate deed notarization, apparently a common occurrence (Arruñada, in press).

B. Conveyancing under Recording

Under recording, private contracts and other documents are filed in a public office that only sets the filing date and reviews the formalities required to index it. The need to safeguard the contract is limited compared to privacy because recording avoids a typical fraud under privacy – antedating a sale or a mortgage. The role of conveyancers as depositories of documents also becomes less relevant and tends to disappear. Something similar happens to the demand for writing sophisticated title guarantees, to the extent that the filing system makes them superfluous.

Conversely, recording does not avoid the risk of a double sale or mortgage. In the previous example, the recording office will not object to recording the second sale by O to B_2, even if the first sale to B_1 is already on record. Nor will it object to recording a sale to B_2 free of charges even if a mortgage of the land to L has previously been recorded. Buyers will therefore be aware that the apparent owner might have sold or mortgaged beforehand, and this deed might have been recorded and gained priority.

Furthermore, finding the relevant information in the public record is not easy, because it contains a mix of relevant and irrelevant deeds resulting from all the previous transactions, and the deeds are often indexed on a personal basis, using name or grantor–grantee indexes. To avoid nasty surprises and receive a report on the quality of title, parties will retain some sort of title agent to search the record fully and detect any previous sales or other title cloud. Consequently, the role of these title agents in searching and reporting on the quality of title remains important, creating a substantial demand for conveyancers.

However, the better the organization of the recording office, the less important the function of title agents. Two innovations with respect to pure recording as described above are crucial: monitoring by the recording office that the grantor figures on record as right holder of the right being conveyed and use of a tract index, both of which have been applied, for example, in France since 1955 *(règle de l'effet relatif* and *fichier immobilier)* but not in most of the US.[12] First, the quality of the recorded information improves substantially when the recording office requires that only those already recorded as right holders can be grantors in a new transaction, thus eliminating the risk of double sales. Similarly, a well-functioning recording office will require the lender's consent before canceling a mortgage. Second, the use of tract indexes, instead of relying on personal indexes of grantors and grantees, is essential for avoiding filing errors. When the records are poorly organized (as in many US counties), it seems natural to develop private 'title plants,' that is, well-organized replicas of the public records. The investment required to build such plants will move the comparative advantage from individual title agents to the operators of the plants, who then play the leading role in the whole process

C.   Conveyancing under Registration

Under registration, the register not only establishes the date but also performs a substantive review of the transaction, impeding any potential collision with property rights held by third parties. This drastically diminishes the demand for high-value services in the preparation of the private contract. There is no role for title guarantees, and the register itself performs the title search and produces a title certificate.

Moreover, under registration, an innocent purchaser who relied on the register keeps the land to the detriment of the original owner. This switch in the adjudication rule drastically changes the incentives of lawyers and notaries. They are no longer indirectly motivated by the interest of their clients to identify and avoid potential title defects, as they were under privacy and recording. Rather, they become the advocates of the parties to the register, which is now the only instance protecting the interest of third parties, whose property rights would turn into contract rights in case of registration error. In other words, given that under registration courts adjudicate conflicting rights to innocent acquirers, parties tend to encourage conveyancers and title examiners to disguise the facts before the register instead of preventing such title conflicts, a change that further reduces the former gatekeeping function of these professionals.

Understandably, the demand for conveyancers to authenticate contracts also diminishes, for several reasons. First, registers are well placed to authenticate documents by themselves. In contrast to mere recording offices, registers perform a highly technical task when testing the legality of private contracts. The knowledge and safeguards necessary to perform such a task can easily be applied to a relatively less technical task such as authentication. This is shown empirically by the existence and effectiveness of registers of rights in Scandinavian countries, which require neither notarized deeds nor intervention by lawyers but simply rely on witnesses. Second, banks are now the real experts at identifying individuals, and this also diminishes the role of lawyers and notaries in contracts to which banks are parties. Third, the development of digital authentication (often called electronic *notarization*) allows parties to disintermediate the notary and dispense with witnesses for authenticating purposes. This may even be more effective than traditional methods, now that urban lawyers and notaries do not personally know most of the parties, as they did in the past, and have to rely on indirect proof such as ID cards. Finally, such lack of personal knowledge also destroys professionals' ability to evaluate the parties' mental capacity.

Nor is it necessary for lawyers to be involved in the start-up stages of a registration system. Given that start-up costs are high, if a reliable supply of party-independent (and, therefore, monopolistic) conveyancing services is available, a way of saving on start-up costs could be to make use of conveyancers to purge titles and improve the quality of deeds.[13] However, provisional registration of possessory rights provides an alternative, cheaper and probably more effective solution. Furthermore, reliance on conveyancers for the start-up stage poses the risk that this mandatory intervention may extend beyond their useful life, as a functional, steady-state register clears titles on registered land effectively and at low cost without such intervention.

This shrinking of conveyancing under registration helps to explain why conveyancers tend to oppose registration. Indeed, conveyancers have often managed to impede the development of registers, monopolizing entry into existing registers or debasing their legal effects – for instance, by reinforcing the effects of possession or title deeds against those of the register.[14] Partly as a consequence of this, many real systems are hybrids in transition. In particular, registration systems are often plagued by the presence of 'overriding interests': rights which are enforced *in rem* despite not being registered (for instance, due taxes and possessory rights) or rights filed in separate administrative registers (as typically happens with municipalities' zoning and preemption rights). This implies that in many countries the role of conveyancers is also a hybrid one, with them playing a greater role with respect to unregistered rights. For example, French notaries play a preventive role, similar to that of US title insurers with respect to the preemption rights held by tenants and municipalities (Willman and Pillebout, 2002), but very different with respect to ownership rights, because the French recording office checks that the grantor's title is on record, in application of the *règle de l'effet relatif.*

D.   How to Regulate Conveyancing

The private and social value of legal assistance in conveyancing services has therefore been declining. Regulation should be adapted accordingly, as both the information asymmetry and externality rationales for restrictive regulation hold less and less water over time, as a consequence of market and institutional changes. Moreover, regulation should be consistent with the reduced functions required of professionals. In particular, restrictive professional licensing is less justified to the extent that comparative advantage in the provision of externalities lies now in public registers and that of overcoming information asymmetries lies with large private firms. Regulation should also be consistent in preserving or, where needed, enhancing the effectiveness of public registers.

For standard transactions, the horizon of regulation is a sort of industrialized production of property rights with low costs and no defects. This Toyota-like manufacturing of property rights requires only a few changes in countries with properly-functioning registers: simplifying overriding interests, standardizing forms and allowing digital access to the registry. In this way, standard rights in real estate would end up being contracted as commodities, ideally in a way resembling financial derivatives, with much lower transaction costs than today.

The role of law professionals in formalizing these standard transactions would be understandably small. Recent reforms and tendencies are moving in this direction, focusing the use of lawyers only on those transactions for which they are really needed. In most of the US, lawyers do not intervene in residential transactions and mortgages. In most cases, title companies, through lay employees, search the title, prepare the documents and close the transaction (Palomar, 1999). These tasks have been performed in England by licensed conveyancers since 1986. The fact that the US uses recording of deeds and England registration of rights shows that these changes are viable under both systems of public titling.

Liberalization does not therefore entail that lawyers and notaries quit providing conveyancing services, but does require them to focus their services on tailoring high-value transactions. They will also be needed for exceptional cases of lower value, but in these they will intervene within an organized hierarchy that filters cases, matching their complexity with the human capital of the professionals handling them. Liberalization also encourages all sorts of providers to offer additional services, including a fuller guarantee – e.g. strict liability and no-fault errors and omissions insurance (Arruñada, 2002) – and the gathering of additional information (for instance, on the physical quality of residential real estate and zoning restrictions, which is now underprovided in many countries). Trends in countries that have been pioneers in liberalization also indicate that there will also be a good deal of vertical integration, with competition amongst organizations that combine different mixes of legal, insurance, financial, distribution and mediation services in order to both reduce conflicts of interest and provide more valuable service to end users.

IV.   EMPIRICAL ARGUMENTS FOR A COMPARATIVE ANALYSIS

The analysis in the previous two sections reached two conclusions. First, public titling is needed to overcome the difficulties of privacy in modern economies. Second, the demand for regulated private conveyancing services decreases with the development of public titling. The present section analyzes the remaining question: the choice between the two public titling systems – recording and registration. It first clarifies two of the main theoretical arguments in the old controversy about these systems – the superiority of recording with respect to costs and its inferiority with respect to effectiveness,[15] identifying which factors can substantially modify these theoretical comparative advantages in practice. After this analysis of the supply of titling services, attention switches to demand for them, exploring how different owners and economies demand titling of different quality, and how this may affect the social choice of titling system. Lastly, a tentative quantitative comparison is made of the performance of both titling systems.

A.   The Dubious Cost Advantage of Recording

Recording of deeds may enjoy an advantage over registration of rights in terms of lower costs, even when adding the additional cost of services needed for examining and assuring title quality, which are provided by lawyers, title agents, title insurers, notaries and the like.[16] This advantage would stem from incentives in both the demand and the supply sides of the industry: under recording, title examination and purging are voluntary, and most supporting services are provided on the basis of private enterprise. However, registration requires *ex ante* purging organized by a public authority.

A main benefit of having an optional purge is that any defects not worth purging can be insured on a casualty basis either by the parties themselves or by a third party insurer. Under registration, the requirement to remove these minor defects may cause holdouts with substantial bargaining costs.[17] These occurrences are probably less frequent with a stricter *numerus clausus*, but this may in turn be costly in terms of flexibility and specialization.[18] Recording is also thought to enjoy the advantage of private incentives in the supply of title assurance and insurance services.[19] Under recording, titles are examined and consents are gathered by business firms or professionals paid with a residual profit. Assuming competition, costs will tend to be minimized, including rapid innovation and adaptation to changes in technology and demand.

These cost advantages may be illusory, however, given the actual incentives of both users and suppliers. Voluntary title assurance may incur costs similar to if not higher than those of public registration because of duplicated efforts and lost economies of scope. Private organization of support services also suffers, as many of such services are natural monopolies and are heavily regulated. We will see below some empirical data which is consistent with these doubts, as established registration systems are not only more effective but also less costly than recording systems in European countries.

Recording suffers a substantial degree of duplication even when a mature title assurance sector develops. First, title plants have to file information on all transactions and relevant facts, not only on the rights being transacted or examined. Consequently, there is less advantage in being able to choose between *ex ante* or *ex post* purging. Second, title plants only serve companies' internal administrative functions, as they have no legal effect. This means that the whole chain of title is examined for each transaction. (Marketable title statutes limiting the time required for title searches reduce this cost but may also threaten the security of property rights.) Third, a double duplication of costs takes place in the US system. Private title plants duplicate the information of the public registers. In addition, different title plants hold duplicate information, given that in many areas there is more than one title plant. Some duplication can be avoided with better-organized recording offices – mainly, by using a tract index. General automation may also facilitate gathering information from public records and reduce the extent and cost of archive duplication in the near future. It is, however, unlikely to avoid the need for filtering this information or to reduce duplication in repeated examination of old titles.

Potential economies of scope in information production and purging of rights and of register information are also hard to reach under recording. Information on the quality of titles is under-utilized and has to be produced repeatedly. This is also due to the voluntary nature of purging, as in some cases title defects are not removed after being identified by the title report. Furthermore, even when defects are removed, the information on the public records is not simplified accordingly. The public record accumulates information on all kinds of rights, defective and clean, dead and alive.[20] This mix of rights increases the cost of future title searches. Potential savings will be incomplete and will depend on hiring the same expert. Private title plants can simplify their information, but they still face similar problems.[21]

Lastly, with respect to suppliers' incentives, the two main title assurance industries developed under recording of deeds have been heavily regulated. Both in France and the US they have administered pricing, entry barriers and comprehensive rules on products and processes, partly as an end result of incidents of fraud and bankruptcy.[22] In particular, as title plants enjoy decreasing unit costs,[23] suppliers are good candidates for becoming natural monopolies. Understandably, their behavior has been repeatedly scrutinized and sanctioned by competition authorities.[24]

Moreover, registers of rights are not always slow and ineffective bureaucracies. Countries with registration of rights display a variety of incentive structures and results in terms of, at least apparent, productivity. Some of the most appalling results were produced by registers with standard fixed-salary bureaucracies (Cook County, Puerto Rico, England before 1990). More professional, judicial-style bureaucracies, as in Germany or Scandinavia, seem to produce different outcomes, however, especially when each registrar is compensated with the profits of his or her office.[25] A corporate version of this Ancient Regime predecessor of private franchise management has also been used to set up registration in some developing countries.[26] This possibility shows that the conversion of private title plants into registers of rights, once defended by Janczyk (1977: 226–27) is not as strange as it might appear.

B.   The Risk of Ineffectual Registration

It is also often believed that registration is more costly but provides more security for property rights, for several reasons. Mainly, registration makes it possible to fully protect good faith acquirers. In principle, the protection granted by recording is intrinsically inferior in that it is largely contractual in nature so does not take advantage of all the enforcement benefits of property rights. Moreover, as argued above, the protection given to registered right holders by a surviving registration system cannot be detrimental to current right holders. As pointed out by Baird and Jackson, '[i]n a world where information is not perfect, we can protect a later owner's interest fully, or we can protect the earlier owner's interest fully. But we cannot do both' (1984: 300). The assertion is accurate but the assumption is crucial: registration is designed to produce perfect information and thus protect both the earlier and the later owners.[27] If it fails to protect owners on a significant number of occasions its chances of survival are very limited.[28] Finally, a registration system that clearly defines property rights may be useful even without proper third-party enforcement, if such clear definition enhances an owner's loss aversion and 'endowment effect,' and this deters seizures. In other words, with badly defined property rights, several parties have endowment effects on the same asset, motivating them to apply force to secure the asset (Mullainathan, 2005).

However, effectiveness is not guaranteed when creating a new register. It is even at risk in functioning registers, because of several systematic but not universal inadequacies. Established registers mainly fail to fulfill the promises of registration by being slow and incomplete. Oddly, they also fail by being too effective.

Slowness means that a long time is needed to get registration. Meanwhile, private deeds are given priority conditional to final registration so that, during the 'registration gap,' the register functions as a record of deeds.[29] The registers of Cook County, England and Puerto Rico saw chronic episodes of registration delay, which resulted in very different outcomes – closure, successful reform, and title insurance and reform, respectively. The lesson is that registration can only function properly with sound incentives. Governments are not always prepared to provide or keep them, however.

Incompleteness of registration is driven by both legal and judicial decisions which lead to enforcement as property – *in rem* – rights of interests which are not registered.[30] This causes some difficulty for those 'overriding interests' which are easily observable (such as possessory rights), but poses a more serious problem for abstract overriding interests (such as tacit liens produced by operation of the law, held by employees and governments, for instance). Any proposed solution to the problem comes up against not only legislative barriers but also conveyancers' and judicial opposition. Conveyancers often seek to protect their market: the weaker the effects of registration, the greater the demand for private title assurance services. Registration of rights also constrains the monopoly of the courts in deciding cases. If registration decisions are conclusive, courts cannot allocate property rights but only contract rights, and this may limit their freedom to decide on the basis of fairness.[31] It is understandable that courts tend to defend their monopoly when the registers are not part of the court system, which is a common occurrence because malfunctioning of the courts is a main motivation for creating a land register. Even when registers do not err often, judges are only too keen to deny the conclusiveness of registration, thus debasing the system. These problems have been suffered by many registers, not only in the US. This is perhaps why one of the most complete registers, the German *Grundbuch*, has traditionally been under the responsibility of judges.[32]

Finally, governments find it useful to use effective registers as gatekeepers for all kinds of public obligations.[33] This has always been done by explicitly defining a certain obligation as a property burden. Land taxation is an old example for privacy, recording and registration.[34] Public use regulation is a more recent case. It is tempting for governments to require even minor obligations to be fulfilled before a right can be registered, implicitly granting them *in rem* protection.[35] Taken to extremes, this may lead users to avoid the register. Furthermore, when the obligations are generally perceived as inefficient, there will be a temptation to dilute enforcement instead of changing the law.

C.   The Need for Adaptation

The social choice of titling system should also be influenced by the actual demand for title quality. In particular, demand for titling services may vary substantially across countries due to differences in the distribution of land value. Essentially, property titling can be seen as a procedure for defining a set of property rights with a certain degree of precision. The pioneering argument drawn up by Demsetz (1967) is applicable here. It states that economic agents demand greater precision in the definition of rights for the most valuable goods or, in dynamic terms, as goods increase in value.

This argument has been developed in the field of titling by Arruñada and Garoupa (2005). In our model, the value of property rights depends on the probability that claimants with better legal rights may appear. The three legal systems we consider – privacy, and the two public systems of recording of deeds and registers of rights – are assumed, following widespread experts' judgment, to increasingly reduce this probability but involve proportionately higher costs.

In our model, once a public titling system is in place, land owners choose to rely on public titling or to keep their rights private. Consequently, the optimum titling system depends on the costs and value of the different systems and on how the value of land is distributed throughout the economy. In particular, social choice of titling system is given by the net balance of several effects: recording causes under-assurance of higher value land, while registration causes crowding out and over-assurance of lower value land. The net balance of these effects and, therefore, the optimal title system are determined by the relative cost effectiveness and pricing of titling (including private 'title assurance services'). Recording triggers under-assurance of land which is recorded under recording but, given its greater value, would be efficiently registered. Conversely, crowding out happens under registration because its higher price leads owners to keep private some lower-value land which otherwise would have been recorded. Similarly, some mid-value land that would have been recorded under recording is registered under registration, causing over-assurance.

The net balance of such effects and, therefore, the optimum system are determined by the distribution of firms and the effectiveness and relative costs of the different systems, including those of the private assurance services that may act as complements or substitutes of the public titling system. Optimal policy decisions will, therefore, require substantial adaptation to local circumstances.

D.   A Quantitative Comparison

Arruñada and Garoupa (2005) conclude that the efficient choice of titling system is an empirical issue that cannot be solved on purely theoretical grounds.[36] Studies such as those carried out by the European Mortgage Federation (EMF) put together the type of data suitable for clarifying these matters empirically.[37] At the price of a small sample

Table 12.1   *Performance indicators of eight developed titling systems (simple averages for two samples of EU countries with different titling systems)*

	Recording of deeds[1][a]	Registration of rights[2][a]	Ratio[1]/[2]
A. Performance indicators of titling systems:			
Mortgage adjusted price [b, c]	1.04%	0.93%	111.56%
Operating cost of mortgage provision for lenders, as a % of outstanding lending [c]	0.59%	0.39%	150.64%
Mortgage registration time, in days [d]	37.19	13.40	277.50%
Mortgage repossession time, in months [e]	37.03	9.25	400.36%
B. Performance indicators of judicial systems. Judicial enforcement of a contractual dispute related to a sale of goods:[f]			
Number of procedures	32.50	32.25	97.74%
Days from when the plaintiff files the lawsuit until actual payment	658.00	423.25	155.46%
Cost, in % of claim	21.48	19.58	109.71%

Notes: [a] Classification of titling systems and from UN-ECE (2000). Registration countries are Denmark, Germany, Spain and the UK; while recording countries are France, Italy, Portugal and The Netherlands.
[b] Adjusted mortgage prices are based on a composite of prices for all lenders and are adjusted for differences in product mix, interest rate risk, credit risk and prepayment risk, so that they represent a comparable price to the borrower. [c] Data for 2003 from Low, Sebag-Montefiore and Dübel (2003: 34). [d] Data for 2006 from EMF (2007, p. 11). [e] Data for 2006 from EMF (2007: 174–91). [f] Data for 2007 from the *Doing Business 2009* survey (World Bank, 2008). Averages drawn up by the author.

size, this data offers two main advantages over alternative studies. First, it measures not only the costs – mainly, time and fees – of titling but also titling benefits, as it estimates two indicators of legal certainty: mortgage repossession time after default and lenders' operating costs. Second, it considers all standard procedures instead of only those which are formally compulsory. For instance, it computes the cost of retaining professional conveyancers when most transactors do retain them, even if they are not obliged to do so and could prepare the contracts by themselves.[38] The latter is also a feature of the data developed by the University of Bremen's Centre of European Law and Politics for the European Commission (ZERP, 2007). It will be used here to compare costs because it surveys a much larger sample of countries.

According to this data, summarized in the attached tables, European registration systems are not only more effective but also less costly than recording systems.

First, as expected, registers of rights exhibit far superior performance as regards the value and quality of registration services. This can be seen in the indicators presented in the first panel of Table 12.1. Faster and safer registration and repossession are main drivers behind lower prices for mortgages, adjusted for differences in product mix, interest rate risk, credit risk and prepayment risk, so that they represent a comparable price to the borrower; and lower operating costs for mortgage lenders, measured as a percentage of outstanding lending.[39] The fact that mortgage repossession is faster in countries with registers of rights is fully consistent with the theory, as they are expected to provide better information on current valid rights and their priority. They therefore facilitate calculation of what is owed, establish priority amongst the various mortgages in a reliable way, and avoid litigation over the ownership and capacity of the contracting parties, drastically reducing the number of legal defenses that can be used by the mortgagor after default.

Of course, these observations are open to alternative interpretations. On the one hand, part of the observed differences could be attributed to variables that have been omitted in the analysis, mainly differential court performance. In fact, data in panel *B* comparing average judicial performance in both samples of countries lends some credit to this explanation. Nevertheless, the differences in judicial performance seem too small to account for the whole difference in repossession time. It is therefore likely that registration improves the mortgage repossession process by providing it with better inputs. On the other hand, the choice between recording and registration could be endogenous, having been influenced by the overall efficiency of the legal system, so that countries with less efficient legal systems should *optimally* rely on recording rather than registration. European history provides a natural experiment that could refute this argument. The French region of Alsace-Moselle has a land registration system (*Livre foncier*) because it was part of the German empire between 1870 and 1918.[40] The system has two key features of registration: it is run by judges who examine the legality of each transaction and the registered rights are presumed valid. Interestingly, French authors consider it safer for users (Piedelièvre, 2000: 20) and advantageous (Simler and Delebecque, 2000: 622).

Second, registers of rights also lead to much lower legal transaction costs than recording of deeds. As shown in panel *A* of Table 12.2, the typical home sale with a mortgage loan for 70% of the home value is 86.47% costlier in countries with recording of deeds. Only a small part of this difference could be attributable to lower average home values in countries with recording, as shown in panel *B*, which compares across countries the transaction costs of buying homes of three different values. For other analyses, results are likely to differ more, however, given that most countries set *ad valorem* price schedules, many of which imply cross-subsidies among transactions of different value.

Comparing costs for the average home transaction is a way of summarizing the information and focusing on the transactions which are most relevant in each country. An alternative solution is to measure the transactions costs of the same transaction in all countries (let us say, a €100,000 home) and then dividing such costs by some measure of each country's *per capita* income (as done, e.g., in the 'Registering Property' index of *Doing Business* (World Bank, 2003–2009)). Such an exercise is performed in panel *C*, expressing costs in purchasing power standard units of GDP per capita. Results are also very similar to those in panels *A* and *B*, because countries and average transactions in the sample are relatively similar. However, if we were comparing countries at widely different levels of economic development, this third method could produce unrepresentative results, because the transaction taken as reference may be of little relevance for both the more developed and the less developed countries, a problem compounded when purchasing power differences are neglected.

Table 12.2 Transaction legal costs (simple averages for samples of 20 EU countries with different titling systems)

	Recording of deeds[1][a]	Registration of rights[2][a]	Ratio[1]/[2]
A. For the average home in each country, as a percentage of home value:			
Solicitors' or notary fees [b]	1.48%	0.69%	214.72%
Property and mortgage registration [c]	0.30%	0.26%	112.67%
Total legal costs	1.78%	0.95%	186.47%
Average home value (€)	150,737	164,724	91.51%
B. For homes of different representative values, as a percentage of home value:			
For a €100,000 home:			
Solicitors' or notary fees [b]	1.74%	0.94%	185.50%
Property and mortgage registration [c]	0.32%	0.31%	103.79%
Total legal costs	2.07%	1.25%	165.23%
For a €250,000 home:			
Solicitors' or notary fees [b]	1.19%	0.51%	234.43%
Property and mortgage registration [c]	0.26%	0.24%	109.71%
Total legal costs	1.45%	0.75%	194.33%
For a €500,000 home:			
Solicitors' or notary fees [b]	0.93%	0.35%	268.72%
Property and mortgage registration [c]	0.24%	0.21%	111.41%
Total legal costs	1.17%	0.56%	208.65%
C. For a €100,000 home, measured in terms of the GDP per capita of each country in purchasing power standards (EU-27=100): [d]			
Solicitors' or notary fees [b]	1,914.30	958.05	199.81%
Property and mortgage registration [c]	340.31	266.78	127.57%
Total legal costs	2,254.61	1,224.83	184.08%

Notes: Data for 2007 from ZERP (2007). [a] Classification of titling systems from UN-ECE (2000). Registration countries are Austria, The Czech Republic, Denmark, England, Finland, Germany, Ireland, Poland, Scotland, Slovakia, Slovenia, Spain and Sweden; while recording countries are Belgium, France, Greece, Hungary, Italy, Portugal and The Netherlands. [b] Solicitors' or notary fees, as well as legal fees charged by real estate agents in Denmark and Sweden. [c] The transaction includes a mortgage loan for 70% of the value. Denmark's data were corrected to exclude transaction taxes. Averages drawn up by the author. [d] Data for 2007. Source of GDP data: Eurostat.

As expected, the difference in total legal transaction costs is caused by substantially lower conveyancing costs in registration, which are reduced by about half. This result is consistent with the substitution argument between conveyancing and public titling. Results also show lower registration costs for registers of rights but differences here are much less significant.

These comparisons of performances and costs are provided here mainly to show which variables we need to measure in order to examine these institutions empirically.

However, even if these results seem relevant, it would be premature to interpret them as causal effects, given the small samples involved. In addition, all countries in these samples are relatively developed, and the relative performance of titling systems could be different in less developed countries. For instance, they may find it harder to avoid a regression of registers of rights to de facto recorders of deeds.

NOTES

*   E-mail: benito.arrunada@upf.edu. I thank Kenneth Ayotte, Manuel Bagüés, Henry E. Smith and Giorgio Zanarone for very helpful comments. Usual disclaimers apply. This work received support from the European Commission through the Integrated Project CIT3-513420 and the Spanish Ministry of Science and Innovation, through grant ECO2008-01116.

1.   The analysis in sections I and II draws on the material presented in Arruñada (2003).

2.   The tradeoff is between the strength of one's rights and their transferability at low cost. The tradeoff is more or less explicit in, among many others, Baird and Jackson (1984), Epstein (1987), Levmore (1987) and Rose (1988), as well as in more recent works which have mostly focused on the role of the *numerus clausus* of property rights, such as Heller (1999), Merrill and Smith (2000), and Hansmann and Kraakman (2002). A version of the tradeoff is also present in the classic work by Calabresi and Melamed (1972). Our analysis, however, focuses on a three-party sequence of two transactions instead of a taking affecting two parties. Moreover, Calabresi and Melamed's property rule is weaker, referring only to the ability to force a would-be taker to bargain for a consensual transfer, and thus arguably has little to do with a right *in rem*.

3.   In most jurisdictions, this priority-of-recording rule applies only to innocent or good faith acquirers, and judges infer that such good faith is lacking when the acquirer knew (had 'notice') of the previous transactions. See, for instance, Merrill and Smith (2007: 919–23) for the four different systems being applied in different parts of the US.

4.   In most jurisdictions, it is necessary to inspect the land to find out about physical possession. On the role played by possession in the transfer of property rights in different kinds of assets, see Baird and Jackson (1984).

5.   Statutory law usually limits the time required for title searches, making it unnecessary to examine the whole chain of titles. For example, 30 states in the US have marketable title acts setting periods of between 30 and 75 years (Boackle, 1997).

6.   Arruñada (2002) compares the role of title insurance under recording and registration.

7.   A register of rights can thus be seen as a double register: it is both a temporary record of deeds (the 'presentment' book that dates titles) and a definitive register of rights.

8.   Because registration failure reduces enforcement of pre-existing rights, there must necessarily be few of such failures. Otherwise, registration would not survive, due to the pressure and desertion of owners.

9.   Section III is largely based on Arruñada (2007b). In addition to analyzing how changes in titling institutions affect the demand for conveyancing, the article analyzes parallel changes in the markets, such as the emergence of large and reputable parties, the tendency to use standardized transactions, and the appearance of electronic notarization.

10.   The pervasiveness of compulsory proof and the ingenuity applied to developing it attest to the importance of restraining fraudulent conveyance. For historical references, see Arruñada (2003: 407).

11.   Section 12 of the Andorran 1996 Notary Act *(Llei del notariat 28-11-1996*, BOPA, 27 December 1996) and Temporary Rule 2 of the Andorran 1998 Notary Regulation *(Reglament general del notariat 20-2-1998,* BOPA, 25 February 1998).

12.   See, for instance, Piedelièvre (2000: mainly 12–13 and 50–55) and Simler and Delebecque (2000: 659–62 and 670–74), about the situation in France, and Dukeminier and Krier (1998: 653–57) about the US.

13.   As claimed by solicitors in the transition between titling systems in Ontario, Canada, where the conversion of deed recording (there called 'Registry' system) into a register of rights ('Land Titles') is claimed to have been made possible by the cumulative work of lawyers in examining and purging titles (Troister and Waters, 1996).

14.   For example, it has been argued that one of the reasons why Torrens registration failed in the US was the opposition of lawyers, abstracters and title insurers (for example, Bostick, 1987: 64, n. 23, citing Quintin Johnstone; Dukeminier and Krier, 1998: 721). Similarly, English solicitors stopped registration in the 19th century (Anderson, 1992) and finally delayed its expansion for a century by requiring county votes (Bostick, 1987: 59, n. 7). Notaries' resistance to change has often also been linked to their monopoly. See,

for example, the cases of France in Suleiman (1987: 92–106), Belgium in Raucent (1998: 129) and Spain in Arruñada (2001).

15. See, for instance, the opinions along these lines of Cribbet (1975: 318), Janczyk (1977), Baird and Jackson (1984: 305) and Bostick (1987). Other authors, considering the US experience with Torrens registration, conclude that registration is costlier and less effective (Shick and Plotkin, 1978). The issues have been controversial almost everywhere. See on this, for Australia, Whalan (1982: 3–12); England, Anderson (1992); France, Picod (1999: 535); Spain, Oliver (1892); and, for the US controversy of the 1930s, Powell (1938) and McDougal and Brabner-Smith (1939).

16. Both registration and recording can be complemented with different degrees of casualty-based title insurance. This complementarity is being shown by the introduction of title insurance in jurisdictions with registration, analyzed in Arruñada (2002).

17. This can be seen as an example of the 'anticommons' problem analyzed by Heller (1998), Heller and Eisenberg (1998) and Buchanan and Yoon (2000).

18. On the *numerus clausus*, see Heller (1999), who points out the role it plays in solving the so-called 'anti-commons' problems; Merrill and Smith (2000), who argue that it serves to reduce the information costs in transfers of property; and Hansmann and Kraakman (2002), who emphasize the verifiability costs faced by acquirers.

19. As Dukeminier and Krier assert, 'title registration puts title assurance in the hands of the government whereas the recording system puts title assurance in private hands using the public records' (1998: 721). This might allow recording to produce better information on title quality, supposedly overcoming its information difficulties, as 'the private company with a profit motive will do a better job of identifying flaws up front as compared to the government' (Miceli and Sirmans, 1995: 86).

20. This perverse effect may be reduced if the legal system or the interest in inducing demand drives notaries or lawyers to purge all titles before recording the deeds. (See n. 13 above for an example in which lawyers claimed to have performed this role.) Observe, however, that the recording system then loses the previously mentioned advantage of 'insuring over' instead of curing minor title clouds.

21. Relying on their own old title reports is risky because the law may have changed since the previous examination (Johnson, 1966: 401). In fact, even if a new insurer is retained in a later transaction, it will frequently examine the full chain of title again. These problems are shown by the diversity of practices and proposals regarding reliance on prior examinations (McCormack, 1992: 126) and reissue discounts (Boackle, 1997).

22. See ZERP (2007), for European notaries, Suleiman (1987) for French notaries; and Lipshutz (1994), Nyce and Boyer (1998), Burke (2000, chapters 14 and 15) and Palomar (2000, chapters 15 and 18) for US title insurance.

23. The costs of building and maintaining title plants are fixed (Lipshutz, 1994: 28) and account for up to half the total costs of title insurance companies (Plotkin, cited by Villani and Simonson, 1982: 274, n. 6).

24. See FDC (1999) for references to two acquisitions which led to consolidation of title plants in several markets. Divestures were required by antitrust authorities later.

25. In this case, a government department manages the relation with a professional network of civil servants. The department regulates entry, processes and prices. Each civil servant then manages an office, recruiting its employees, who are not civil servants and may also be paid with a share of the residual. (A similar hybrid organization was analyzed in Arruñada [1996]). This old arrangement is similar to the one being applied in modern public services reforms. These, however, often have grander plans but weaker incentives, as shown by the paradigmatic 'internal market' and 'fund-holding' doctors introduced by the 1989 reform of the British NHS.

26. A move in this direction was the transformation in 1990 of the English Land Register into a semi-privatized executive agency, with huge productivity improvements (Sparkes, 1999: 18). A similar transformation took place in The Netherlands in 1994 (Jong, 1998).

27. Referring to recording but in a similar vein, Epstein (1987: 18) asserts, '[t]he basic system of recordation is best understood as an *institutional* response to the structural weaknesses in *any* common-law resolution of the ostensible ownership problem. Common-law solutions attempt to reduce the total loss by assigning it to one party or another. Institutional responses seek to eliminate the loss by a more comprehensive system of social control' (Epstein, 1987: 18, emphases in the original).

28. Some formal models differ from this when assuming that recording (plus title insurance) and registration are on an equal footing with the incidence of claims – that is, the same level of surviving defects. For example, Miceli and Sirmans (1995), Miceli, Sirmans and Turnbull (1998), and Miceli, Sirmans and Turnbull (2000). In contrast, Miceli, Sirmans and Kieyah (2001), and Arruñada and Garoupa (2005) assume unequal incidence.

29. The registration of 'caveats,' giving notice of uncertain outstanding interests, has a similar effect (McCormack, 1992: 91), but only on those titles affected.

30. Rose summarizes this tendency graphically when she points out the repeated failed attempts at clarifying

property law: 'legislatures pass new versions of crystalline record systems – only to be overruled later, when courts once again reinstate mud in a different form' (1988: 580). For history and references, see mainly 585–90.

31. As analyzed by Rose (1988, especially at 584–85 and 597–601).
32. Something similar can be said about the land court of Massachusetts that is responsible for administering its Torrens register: 'Unlike other jurisdictions, the Massachusetts courts have not carved out any additional exceptions to the legal conclusiveness of the certificate of title' (Shick and Plotkin, 1978: 106). Furthermore, the register is relatively complete with, for instance, mandatory registration of boundaries (at 118).
33. See Kraakman (1986) for a theory of legal gatekeeping.
34. Policy reformers in the 18th and 19th centuries were conscious of this issue: their original decisions to place the registers within the realm of the Ministry of Finance (France) or the Ministry of Justice (Germany, Spain) were related to their primary goals of making them an instrument for tax collection and private contracting, respectively.
35. Making information on registers freely available to the public imposes an additional cost on owners, by reducing their privacy and increasing the risk of fraud. It may therefore have a similar detrimental effect for registration, aggravated by the power of new technologies to bring together data from many sources. This effect could be reduced by limiting access to the register to those so authorized by owners and those with a legitimate interest. However, the public files were wholly open to the public in 28 of the 42 jurisdictions surveyed by the UN-ECE (2000).
36. A substantial body of empirical literature has examined the effects of land titling on many social and economic variables, such as employment, credit, investment, violence, market beliefs and even health. See, amongst others, Besley (1995), Alston *et al.* (1996, 1999), Lanjouw and Levy (2002), Field (2004, 2005, 2007), Galiani and Schargrodsky (2004, 2010) and Di Tella, Galiani and Schargrodsky (2007). A recurring problem in most of this literature is the potential influence that hidden causal variables may have on both the titling decision and its supposed consequences. Most of these titling efforts have applied some form of registration, which helps explain why there is little evidence on the differential effects of recording and registration.
37. Mainly EMF (2007), and Low, Sebag-Montefiore and Dübel (2003).
38. They therefore overcome two of the main criticisms raised in Arruñada (2007a) against alternative measures such as the World Bank's Doing Business indicators. In addition, Doing Business data does not distinguish the type of title system in place in each country, which drastically limits its usefulness. E.g., Amin and Haidar (2008) find that, according to the Doing Business data, registering property in civil law countries costs 22% more. However, they forget that Doing Business computes notary costs but not the lawyer and conveyancing costs typically but not mandatorily incurred in common law countries. The error term in their regression is therefore correlated with their main explanatory variable. Moreover, they implicitly assume that the value provided by titling systems is the same in all countries without considering even the most basic difference – that between recording and registration. (As shown by Arruñada [2003: 416–20], the common versus civil law divide is not correlated with any particular titling system.) Lastly, their measure of total cost includes transaction taxes. Countries with high taxes on land transactions often have lower taxes on land tenure, and this difference should be considered separately when comparing legal systems.
39. See Low, Sebag-Montefiore and Dübel (2003: 43–44).
40. See, e.g., Piedelièvre (2000: 17) and Simler and Delebecque (2000: 620–22).

REFERENCES

Alston, Lee J., Gary D. Libecap and Bernardo Mueller. 1999. *Titles, Conflict and Land Use: The Development of Property Rights and Land Reform on the Brazilian Frontier*. Ann Arbor, MI: University of Michigan Press.
Alston, Lee J., Gary D. Libecap and Robert Schneider. 1996. 'The Determinants and Impact of Property Rights: Land Title on the Brazilian Frontier', 12 *Journal of Law, Economics and Organization*, 25–61.
Amin, Mohammad and Jamal Ibrahim Haidar. 2008. 'The Cost of Registering Property: Does Legal Origin Matter?', The World Bank, October 20 (http://ssrn.com/abstract=1287217, visited 22 November, 2008).
Anderson, J. Stuart. 1992. *Lawyers and the Making of English Land Law, 1832–1940*. Oxford: Clarendon Press.
Arruñada, Benito. 1996. 'The Economics of Notaries', 3 *European Journal of Law and Economics*, 5–37.
Arruñada, Benito. 2001. 'Pasado, presente y futuro del notariado', 2 *Folio Real: Revista Peruana de Derecho Registral y Notarial*, 135–53.
Arruñada, Benito. 2002. 'A Transaction-Cost View of Title Insurance and its Role in Different Legal Systems', 27 *The Geneva Papers of Risk and Insurance*, 582–601.

Arruñada, Benito. 2003. 'Property Enforcement as Organized Consent', 19 *Journal of Law, Economics, and Organization*, 401–44.

Arruñada, Benito. 2007a. 'Pitfalls to Avoid when Measuring the Institutional Environment: Is "Doing Business" Damaging Business?', 35 *Journal of Comparative Economics*, 729–47.

Arruñada, Benito. 2007b. 'Market and Institutional Determinants in the Regulation of Conveyancers', 23 *European Journal of Law and Economics*, 93–116.

Arruñada, Benito. In press. *Business formalization: Costs versus institutional efficiency (Formalización de empresas: Costes frente a eficiencia institucional)*, Cizur Menor: Thomson.

Arruñada, Benito and Nuno Garoupa. 2005. 'The Choice of Titling System in Land', 48 *Journal of Law and Economics*, 709–727.

Baird, Douglas G. and Thomas H. Jackson. 1984. 'Information, Uncertainty, and the Transfer of Property', 13 *Journal of Legal Studies*, 299–320.

Besley, Timothy. 1995. 'Property Rights and Investment Incentives: Theory and Evidence from Ghana', 103 *Journal of Political Economy*, 903–37.

Boackle, Kenneth F. 1997. *Real Estate Closing Deskbook: A Lawyer's Reference Guide & State-By-State Summary*. Chicago, IL: General Practice, Solo and Small Firm Section, American Bar Association.

Bostick, C. Dent. 1987. 'Land Title Registration: An English Solution to an American Problem', 63 *Indiana Law Journal*, 55–111.

Buchanan, James M. and Yong J. Yoon. 2000. 'Symmetric Tragedies: Commons and Anticommons', 43 *Journal of Law and Economics*, 1–13.

Burke, D. Barlow. 2000. *Law of Title Insurance*, 3rd edn (1st edn, 1986). New York: Aspen Law and Business.

Calabresi, Guido, and A. Douglas Melamed. 1972. 'Property Rules, Liability Rules, and Inalienability: One View of the Cathedral', 85 *Harvard Law Review*, 1089–128.

Cribbet, John E. 1975. *Principles of the Law of Property*. 2nd edn. Mineola, NY: The Foundation Press.

Demsetz, Harold. 1967. 'Toward a Theory of Property Rights', 57 *American Economic Review*, 347–59.

Di Tella, Rafael, Sebastián Galiani, and Ernesto Schargrodsky. 2007. 'The Formation of Beliefs: Evidence from the Allocation of Land Titles to Squatters', 122 *Quarterly Journal of Economics*, 209–41.

Dukeminier, Jesse and James E. Krier. 1998. *Property*, 4th edn. New York: Aspen Law and Business.

EMF, European Mortgage Federation. 2007. *Study on the Efficiency of the Mortgage Collateral in the European Union*, Brussels: EMF.

Epstein, Richard A. 1987. 'Inducement of Breach of Contract as a Problem of Ostensible Ownership', 16 *Journal of Legal Studies*, 1–41.

FDC, Federal Trade Commission. 1999. *Annual Report to Congress. Fiscal Year 1998*. Washington, DC: Department of Justice Antitrust Division.

Field, Erica. 2004. 'Property Rights, Community Public Goods and Household Time Allocation in Urban Squatter Communities', 45 *William and Mary Law Review*, 837–87.

Field, Erica. 2005. 'Property Rights and Investment in Urban Slums', 3 *Journal of the European Economic Association Papers and Proceedings*, 279–90.

Field, Erica. 2007. 'Entitled to Work: Urban Property Rights and Labor Supply in Peru', 122 *Quarterly Journal of Economics*, 1561–602.

Galiani, Sebastián and Ernesto Schargrodsky. 2004. 'The Health Effects of Land Titling', 2 *Economics and Human Biology*, 353–72.

Galiani, Sebastián and Ernesto Schargrodsky. 2010. 'Property Rights for the Poor: Effects of Land Titling', 94 *Journal of Public Economics*, 700–729, doi: 10.1016/j.jpubeco.2010.06.002.

Hansmann, Henry and Reinier Kraakman. 2002. 'Property, Contract, and Verification: The *Numerus Clausus* Problem and the Divisibility of Rights', 31 *Journal of Legal Studies*, S373–S420.

Heller, Michael A. 1998. 'The Tragedy of the Anticommons: Property in the Transition from Marx to Markets', 111 *Harvard Law Review*, 621–88.

Heller, Michael A. 1999. 'The Boundaries of Private Property', 108 *Yale Law Journal*, 1163–223.

Heller, Michael A. and Rebecca S. Eisenberg. 1998. 'Can Patents Deter Innovation? The Anticommons in Biomedical Research', 280 *Science*, 698–701.

Janczyk, Joseph T. 1977. 'An Economic Analysis of the Land Systems for Transferring Real Property', 6 *Journal of Legal Studies*, 213–33.

Johnson, Harry M. 1966. 'The Nature of Title Insurance', 33 *Journal of Risk and Insurance*, 393–410.

Jong, Jitske de. 1998. 'Access to Geo-information in the Netherlands: A Policy Review', in J. Zevenbergen, *Free Accessibility of Geo-Information in the Netherlands, the United States and the European Community*. Delft: Delft University Press.

Kraakman, Reinier H. 1986. 'Gatekeepers: The Anatomy of a Third-Party Enforcement Strategy', 2 *Journal of Law, Economics and Organization*, 53–105.

Lanjouw, Jean, and Philip Levy. 2002. 'Untitled: A Study of Formal and Informal Property Rights in Urban Ecuador', 112 *Economic Journal*, 986–1019.

Levmore, Saul. 1987. 'Variety and Uniformity in the Treatment of the Good-Faith Purchaser', 16 *Journal of Legal Studies*, 43–65.

Lipshutz, Nelson R. 1994. *The Regulatory Economics of Title Insurance*. Westport, CT: Praeger.

Low, Simon, Matthew Sebag-Montefiore and Achim Dübel. 2003. *Study on the Financial Integration of European Mortgage Markets*. Brussels: European Mortgage Federation and Mercer Oliver Wyman.

McCormack, John L. 1992. 'Torrens and Recording: Land Title Assurance in the Computer Age', 18 *William Mitchell Law Review*, 61–129.

McDougal, Myres S. and John W. Brabner-Smith. 1939. 'Land Title Transfer: A Regression', 48 *Yale Law Journal*, 1125–51.

Merrill, Thomas W. and Henry E. Smith. 2000. 'Optimal Standardization in the Law of Property: The *Numerus Clausus* Principle', 110 *Yale Law Journal*, 1–70.

Merrill, Thomas W. and Henry E. Smith. 2007. *Property: Principles and Policies*, New York: Foundation Press.

Miceli, Thomas J. and C.F. Sirmans. 1995. 'The Economics of Land Transfer and Title Insurance', 10 *Journal of Real Estate Finance and Economics*, 81–88.

Miceli, Thomas J., C.F. Sirmans and Joseph Kieyah. 2001. 'The Demand for Land Title Registration: Theory with Evidence from Kenya', 3 *American Law and Economics Review*, 275–87.

Miceli, Thomas J., C.F. Sirmans and Geoffrey K. Turnbull. 1998. 'Title Assurance and Incentives for Efficient Land Use', 6 *European Journal of Law Economics*, 305–23.

Miceli, Thomas J., C.F. Sirmans and Geoffrey K. Turnbull. 2000. 'The Dynamic Effects of Land Title Systems', 47 *Journal of Urban Economics*, 370–89.

Mullainathan, Sendhil. 2005. 'Development Economics through the Lens of Psychology', in F. Bourguignon and B. Pleskovic (eds), *Proceedings of the Annual Bank Conference on Development Economics: Lessons of Experience*. Washington and New York: The World Bank and Oxford University Press, 45–70.

Nyce, Charles and M. Martin Boyer. 1998. 'An Analysis of the Title Insurance Industry', 17 *Journal of Insurance Regulation*, 213–56.

Oliver y Esteller, Bienvenido. 1892. *Derecho inmobiliario español: Exposición fundamental y sistemática de la Ley Hipotecaria*, vol. 1. Madrid: Sucesores de Rivadeneyra.

Palomar, Joyce D. 1999. 'The War Between Attorneys and Lay Conveyancers – Empirical Evidence Says "Cease Fire!"', 31 *Connecticut Law Review*, 423–546.

Palomar, Joyce D. 2000. *Title Insurance Law*. St. Paul, MN: West. (1st edn, 1994. Last revised: July 6, 2000).

Picod, Yves. 1999. *Sûretés: Publicité foncière*, 7th edn, in H. Mazeaud, L. Mazeaud, J. Mazeaud and F. Chabas (eds), Leçons de Droit Civil, tome 3, vol. 1. Paris: Montchrestien.

Piedelièvre, Stéphane. 2000. *Real Property Publicity (La publicité foncière)*. Paris: Librairie Général de Droit et Jurisprudence.

Powell, Richard R.B. 1938. *Registration of the Title to Land in the State of New York*. Rochester, NY: Lawyers Co-Operative Publishing Company.

Raucent, Léon. 1998. *Fonction et statuts des notaires*, 10th edn. Louvain: Académia-Bruylant.

Rose, Carol M. 1988. 'Crystals and Mud in Property Law', 40 *Stanford Law Review*, 577–610.

Shick, Blair C. and Irving H. Plotkin. 1978. *Torrens in the United States: A Legal and Economic Analysis of American Land Registration Systems*. Lexington, CT: Heath.

Simler, Philippe, and Philippe Delebecque. 2000. *Private Law: Securities, Real Property Publicity (Droit Civil: Les sûretés, la publicité foncière)*, 3rd edn. Paris: Dalloz.

Sparkes, Peter. 1999. *A New Land Law*. Oxford and Portland: Hart Publishing.

Suleiman, Ezra N. 1987. *Private Power and Centralization in France: The Notaries and the State*. Princeton, NJ: Princeton University Press.

Troister, Sidney H. and Kathleen A. Waters. 1996. 'Real Estate Conveyancing in Ontario: A Nineties Perspective', *mimeo*. Toronto: Lawyers' Professional Indemnity Company.

UN-ECE (United Nations Economic Commission for Europe). 2000. *Study on Key Aspects of Land Registration and Cadastral Legislation*. London: Her Majesty Land Register.

Villani, Kevin and John Simonson. 1982. 'Real Estate Settlement Pricing: A Theoretical Framework', 10 *American Real Estate and Urban Economics Association Journal*, 249–75.

Whalan, Douglas J. 1982. *The Torrens System in Australia*. Sidney: Law Book Company.

Willman, Raymond, and Jean-François Pillebout. 2002. *Buying or Selling a Home: The Notary's Mission*, 3rd edn. Paris: Mémos de Conseils par des Notaires.

World Bank. 2003–2009. *Doing Business*. Washington, DC: World Bank.

ZERP. 2007. *Conveyancing Services Market (Study COMP/2006/D3/003, Final Report)*. Brussels: Centre of European Law and Politics, University of Bremen (ZERP).

13 Land demarcation systems
*Gary D. Libecap and Dean Lueck**

I. INTRODUCTION

Land demarcation systems are ancient human artifacts and are fundamental to property law, use, and markets. In this chapter we develop an economic framework for examining systems of land demarcation and examine the economic history of demarcation in the United States and elsewhere. Land demarcation is one of the earliest actions of organized human groups. Territories to hunting and gathering sites have been marked and defended among the most primitive peoples (Bailey 1992). The earliest agricultural societies defined rights to plots of land for farming (Ellickson 1993). In modern societies rights are designated for residential and commercial use in dense urban areas, for farmland in highly mechanized large-scale fields, for landscapes allocated primarily as wildlife refuges or wilderness parks, and for such related resources as minerals and water. Yet, despite the somewhat obvious point that a system of demarcating rights to land will be important in determining its utilization and value, the literatures in economics and in law have not addressed these issues in any depth.

In this chapter we examine the economic structure and function of land demarcation systems. We direct attention to the two systems that have dominated land demarcation: metes and bounds (MB) and the rectangular system (RS). Under MB land claimants define property boundaries in order to capture valuable land and to minimize the individual costs of definition and enforcement. Individual surveys do not occur before settlement, and they are not governed by a standardized method of measurement or parcel shape. Property is demarcated by local, natural features of the land (trees, streams, rocks) and relatively permanent human structures (walls, bridges, monuments). Moreover, properties can be comprised of multiple small parcels, leaving unclaimed tracts as open gaps. Further, where incongruent individual plots collide, there also can be gaps of unclaimed land that remain essentially open-access. As these lands ultimately become valued they are inevitably subject to competing and wasteful claims by the adjacent parties.

By contrast under RS, demarcation of individual plots is governed by a common system of plot shapes, sizes, and boundary descriptions. Further, properties are not fractured, but cover all land claimed within a single parcel. As we argue in this chapter, the rectangular survey tends to lower the costs of land development and exchange through its measurement, enforcement, and incentive effects as compared to using metes and bounds to demarcate land ownership boundaries. The latter are necessarily vague and imprecise ('four paces from the most northerly rock pile . . .'), temporary (trees disappear, stream beds change, so that boundary markers had to be periodically investigated to insure that they were still visible), idiosyncratic (different terms used locally), and for all of these reasons, subject to dispute and conflict. The idiosyncratic nature of measurement limits the size of the land market because remote purchasers have little knowledge of local land features and have to rely on localized interpretation of their meaning for property boundaries. Infrastructure development, such as for roads, may be more costly because of the inexact nature and multitude of land boundaries that must be crossed, raising coordination costs.

A centralized rectangular system defines land ownership in a manner that reduces the costs of measurement, enforcement, and exchange. By bearing upfront costs of systematic survey prior to occupancy the marginal costs of demarcating and establishing boundaries are lower compared to metes and bounds. Individual plots are aligned north–south, boundaries are clear, precise, and uniformly positioned, and the system of description is uniform across the region covered.

While the demarcation of land is fundamental to a system of property law it is largely unexplored by property law scholars and instead simply, or implicitly, taken for granted. Indeed Dukeminier and Krier (2002: 675–679) do not mention the distinction between the two systems but only describe the rectangular system. Merrill and Smith (2007) and Thompson and Goldstein (2006) similarly describe the rectangular system. Neither of the comprehensive treatises on law and economics by Posner (2002) and Shavell (2007) mentions land demarcation.[1]

This chapter begins with a survey of land demarcation systems used around the world, with a focus on the US, including rectangular and metes and bounds systems, but also other less common practices. In section III we outline an economic framework for analyzing the demarcation of land generally as well as under both metes and bounds and the rectangular systems. In Section IV we explore some empirical implications of our model in metes and bounds, in the US rectangular system, and in rectangular systems in urban areas and foreign countries. The chapter concludes with a discussion of the findings, implications for property law, and areas for further study.

II.   A BRIEF SURVEY OF LAND DEMARCATION SYSTEMS

Throughout the world and through history, land demarcation has been dominated by indiscriminate or unsystematic systems such as metes and bounds (Brown 1995; Estopinal 1998; Gates 1968; Linklater 2002; Marschner 1960; McEntyre 1978; Price 1995; Thrower 1966).[2] While these systems vary and tend to be highly local in details, they share a method of defining land boundaries in terms of natural features of the land and even some human structures. The dominance of metes and bounds systems indicate that there are substantive costs of establishing organized rectangular systems. Metes and bounds systems are effective and likely efficient when land is not traded regularly in land markets involving buyers remote from the site, and where agriculture is small-scale, not requiring larger, well-defined fields for cultivation or for pasture for livestock. Metes and bounds allows individuals to mold their land holdings around local contours to lower measurement and bounding costs of individual plots and to include only the best land in areas where land is heterogeneous in quality.

In cases where land and agricultural commodity market are more developed, however, metes and bounds is less satisfactory, as we discuss in more detail below. As described by Barzel (1982), markets require standardized measurement of items traded so that sellers and buyers know what is being exchanged and can agree to a market-clearing price. The greater the precision and transparency of measurement, the lower the transaction costs of exchange and the greater reach of markets. Measurement, however, is costly, and hence the accuracy of property rights definition and bounding depends in part on the value of the asset to be traded (Demsetz 1967). Higher valued assets merit more investment in measurement and demarcation to protect them from other claimants and to promote market trading by generating information about the asset. Market transactions, in turn, raise asset values by facilitating its reallocation to those who value it more highly than current owners.

For these reasons, metes and bounds limits market trades because outsiders have little knowledge of local conditions and topography to determine the exact location and nature of parcels to be traded. Moreover irregularly-shaped, scattered small plots may limit cultivation and pasturing practices that allow for economies of scale and use of mechanized capital equipment, as well as raise overall fencing and bounding costs relative to more consolidated, regularly-shaped parcels.

Although MB has dominated in history, people have occasionally used more systematic demarcation methods. [3] These have tended to be rectangular, much like the modern US system, and can be found in many parts of the world. In the ancient world the most famous of these was the Roman system known as centuriation. This system was established in the Second Century BC and used a square unit called the *centuria quadrata* with a side of 710 meters (Bradford 1957; Dilke 1971). This had a hundred square *heredia* or 132 acres which was allotted to a *curia* or 100 families (Johnson 1976). At the center of the centuria an axis intersected at a right angle making four quarters. Unlike the US practice, however, centurialism was not designed for continuous stretches, but rather was reinitiated at each new cross-point and thus varied somewhat with natural land features. In addition centuria were not always aligned on a north-south axis but rather were aligned for topographical reasons (e.g., water drainage). Today, traces of centuriation (in the form of rectangular plots and field) have been found in northern Italy, Braga in Portugal, Chester in England, Tarragona and Merida in Spain, Cologne and Trier in Germany, and Carthage in Tunisia (Stanislawski 1946). Other RS were present in ancient India and the Indus Valley.

Based on the theoretical framework and cases discussed in this chapter, we are able to draw some conclusions about when a rectangular system will be chosen over the more common metes and bounds system. First, RS is more likely when some party or organization is in a position to capture the overall gains of the 'grid', such as a government or urban/rural land developer. Second, RS is more likely when the land has high potential market value under the grid, such as urban/suburban properties. Third, RS is more likely when the upfront costs of the RS are relatively low. This situation can occur when the land is relatively flat; when the land is not already demarcated as MB;[4] when the land is occupied and demarcated as MB, but current occupants have no political standing (e.g., after an invasion and capture); or when infrastructure such as roads have not been established. Figure 13.1 shows an early example of rectangular property demarcation under Roman law. Table 13.1 summarizes features of the major historical and contemporary rectangular systems.

Note: Latitude and Longitude: 36°N 10°E.

Source: Google Earth.

Figure 13.1   Roman rectangular demarcation in present-day Carthage, Tunisia

A.   Land Demarcation in the United States

As indicated in Figure 13.2, the United States uses both metes and bounds and rectangular systems. Metes and bounds generally is dominant in the original 13 states as well as Hawaii, Kentucky, Maine, Tennessee, Vermont, and West Virginia. Further, metes and bounds were used where Spanish and Mexican land grants were prevalent in parts of Texas, New Mexico, Arizona, and California. The rest of the US, as well as parts of Canada, Australia, New Zealand, and South Africa, is covered by RS (Powell 1970; Williams 1974).

Metes and bounds
The use of metes and bounds was brought to North America from practices in Europe (Price 1995: 11). Land availability was the most important lure in the decision to migrate and immigrants needed a familiar means of marking their land claims in the new land: '[i]mmigrant colonists gazing at a wilderness envisioned its taming and imagined new markets bounding the edges of their own fields and meadows. The men who could measure the metes and bounds of those fields held the key to transforming a worthless, uncultivated territory into individual farms' (quoted in Kain and Baigent 1992: 265). The idiosyncratic and localized nature of MB demarcation is illustrated in the following quote:

Table 13.1   Rectangular demarcation systems around the world

Location (authority)	Date	Parcel Shape	Dimensions	Alignment
Greece	479 BC–c.146 BC	Rectangle	Not uniform	Unknown
Ancient Rome	170 BC–Fall of the Roman Empire c. 500 AD	Square	0.44 miles x 0.44 miles	North–South
Ancient India	Inconclusively placed at several centuries before Christ	Rectangle	0.72–0.87 miles x 0.94–1.09 miles	North–South
Indus Valley Civilization	3300–1700 BC	Squares and rectangles	–	North–South
Netherlands	11th century	Square	Not uniform	Not uniform
Mexico	1523-1656	Rectangle	Central square: 0.113 miles x 0.075 miles	–
Long lot farms in Quebec	1620	Elongated rectangles	1 mile x 0.1 miles	Aligned according to rivers
New England colonies	17th century	Square	6 mile x 6 mile townships	
Philadelphia	1681	Rectangle	0.123 miles x 0.075 miles for a city block	Boundaries on north and south sides for area fronting the Delaware River
USA (federal government)	1785	Square	1 mile x 1 mile section	North–South
Canada	1871	Square	1 mile x 1 mile	North–South
Australia	1821 New South Wales	Square	Not uniform	

Sources: Barnes (1935); Bradford (1957); Dilke (1971, 1985); Dutt (1925); Jeans (1966); Johnson (1976); Kain and Baigent (1992); Marshall (1931); Nelson (1963); Stanislawski (1946); and Wainright (1956).

Beginning at a white oak in the fork of four mile run called the long branch & running No 88° Wt three hundred thirty eight poles to the Line of Capt. Pearson, then with the line of Person No 34° Et One hundred Eighty-eight poles to a Gum on the So Wt side of the run corner to persons red oak & chestnut land, then down the run & binding therewith So 54° Et Two hundred & ninety poles to the beginning, Containing One hundred Sixty six Acres, [Stetson (1935: 90)]

As described above, MB systems were characterized as 'unsystematic' or 'indiscriminant' because the land was not surveyed prior to occupation and because the surveys were not governed by a standardized method of measurement or shape. Metes and bounds was especially common in frontier regions of the southeastern US where land quality varied, where native opposition to settlement was more muted than in the North,

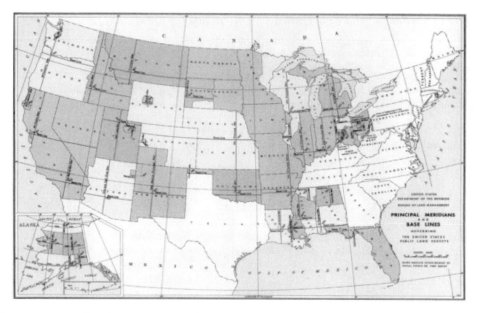

Source: Bureau of Land Management website: www.nationalatlas.gov/articles/boundaries/a_plss.html.

Figure 13.2   Land demarcation systems in the US and the location of principal meridians and baselines under the rectangular survey

allowing for sporadic, dispersed holdings, and where the climate accommodated small-scale, subsistence agricultural production in the interior. Indeed, the two major land demarcation systems in the British North American colonies were the New England system with townships as discussed below and the Virginia system of metes and bounds. Both initially used the same survey technologies (Gunter's chain) and defined holdings in acres (Kain and Baigent 1992: 268).

Figure 13.3 shows Gunter's chain which was developed in 17th century England, and was an indispensable tool for all surveyors in the colonial US because it provided for the standardized measurement land for survey (Linklater 2002: 5). One chain equaled four rods (16 ½ feet, 22 yards, 66 feet or 1/80th of a mile). Each chain equals 100 links with each link 7.92 inches and 1 square link is 1/100,000 of an acre.[5] As settlement increased over time and as land values rose, there was a need to update survey instructions and practices, leading to the publication of numerous surveying textbooks in the mid 18th century, such as John Carter's *Young Surveyor's Instructor: or, An Introduction to the Art of Surveying* and Robert Gibson's *Treatise of Practical Surveying* (Kain and Baigent 1992: 268).

In the southern colonies, most land was distributed to individual settlers via head-rights, whereby individuals could receive warrants for 500 or more acres of land. Under MB, migrants could move inland; pick and chose their parcels; and stake their claims individually, with little coordination with their neighbors. Once the periphery of their land holdings was marked on trees and rocks, claimants would file their warrants and land claims at local government land offices and have the boundaries surveyed. Once

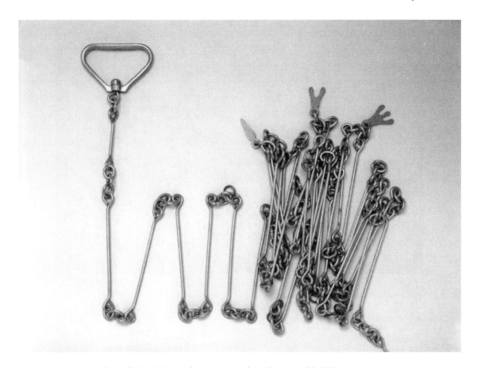

Source: www.tngenweb.org/tnland/terms.htm, accessed on January 29, 2010.

Figure 13.3   Edmund Gunter's chain

surveyed, title could be granted (Linklater 2002: 37; Kain and Baigent 1992: 273). Figure 13.4 shows the pattern of land parcels that developed in Virginia where metes and bounds were used.

Other systematic land demarcation systems
On very productive alluvial land along rivers, where land values were high, particularly in Virginia, Louisiana, Texas, and along the Ohio River long lots were used rather than metes and bounds. Long lots involved more systematically surveying plots of land with axes perpendicular to the river. Long lots were long rectangles of generally definite shapes and boundaries. They facilitated river access for transport and cultivation of the land, and reduced the potential for disputes. Long lot practices were recognized in both Spanish and French land grants (Kain and Baigent 1992: 279). Figure 13.5 shows a map of long lot demarcation in southern Louisiana where the French long lot system was established.

More systematic demarcations of property boundaries also were found in parts of the northern colonies. In the New England colonies of Massachusetts Bay, Rhode Island, coastal New Hampshire and Maine, as well as the Connecticut Valley, the frontier was more constrained by hostile natives, climate and topography than in the South. Accordingly, coastal and valley land values were somewhat higher and the need for coordinated settlement greater. We address these issues in more detail below.

Under the New England system, townships, generally of 6 square miles, were granted

Note: Latitude and Longitude: 36°N 76°W.

Source: Google Earth.

Figure 13.4   Land parcels under metes and bounds in Walters, Virginia

Note: Latitude and Longitude: 31°N 92°W.

Source: Kain and Baigent (1992: 280) and Google Earth.

Figure 13.5   Long Lot Demarcation in Cheneyville, Louisiana

to groups of settlers for occupancy after survey. The internal parcels were not always uniform in shape or size, but were less irregular than found under the Virginia system (Kain and Baigent 1992: 285–6; Price 1995: 27–85). They encouraged denser development and followed the English open-field village model (Price 1995: 32, 44–7, 54, 58). Outside of these settled towns, however, lands in New England were demarcated under metes and bounds (Price 1995: 82).

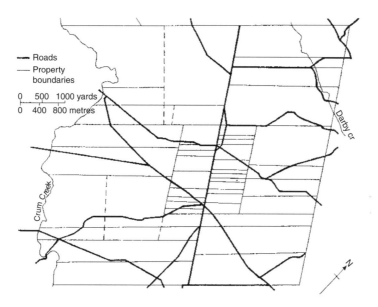

Source: Kain and Baigent (1992: 286) and Google Earth.

Figure 13.6   Demarcation under the William Penn Land Grant

Somewhat similar practices were followed in eastern Pennsylvania by William Penn: 'We do settle in the way of Township or Villages each of which contains 5,000 acres, in square and at least Ten Families . . .' (Kain and Baigent 1992: 287; Price 1995: 259–61). Although metes and bounds were common in New York state, in northwestern New York, rectangular systems were also used by land developers. These developers purchased large tracts of land from the Iroquois, and also secured other large military tracts, and then, divided these large properties into townships and surveyed them before sale. For example, in subdivisions, such as Cooper's tract, a rectangular grid was used dividing the land into 100 square lots of up to 600 acres each and then marketed to settlers (Price 1995: 232–6). In Ohio, the Ohio Company of Associates secured 1,000,000 acres of land divided into townships 6 miles square from the federal government in 1787 and followed the same procedures as the government in surveying and selling the property as a grid (Linklater 2002: 81). Figure 13.6 shows land demarcation in eastern Pennsylvania in the late 17th century. While the borders are linear they are not aligned north–south, nor are the parcels the same size and shape.

A.   The rectangular survey in the United States

The geographical extent of metes and bounds in the United States was halted by the enactment of the Land Ordinance of 1785. The 1785 law required that the federal public domain be surveyed prior to settlement and that it follow a rectangular system. Land sales were the primary source of revenue for the federal government, and the government bore the upfront costs of survey prior to allocation in order to provide for a uniform grid of property boundaries that were standard regardless of location and terrain.

Note: Latitude and Longitude: 47°N 104°W.

Source: Google Earth.

Figure 13.7   Land demarcation in the US under the federal land survey in Belfield, North Dakota

The rectangular survey, as the RS was called in the US, west and north of the Ohio River and west of the Mississippi north of Texas as indicated in Figure 13.2. This rectangular survey system uses a surveyed grid of meridians, baselines, townships and ranges to describe land (Brown 1995; Dukeminier and Krier 2002; Ellickson 1993; Estopinal 1998; Hubbard 2009; Pattison 1957b; Thrower 1966; White 1983).[6] Figure 13.7 illustrates the regularity provided by this RS.

The survey began with the establishment of an Initial Point with a definite latitude and longitude. Next, a Principal Meridian (a true north–south line) and a Baseline (an east–west line perpendicular to the meridian) were run through the Initial Point. On each side of the Principal Meridian, land was divided into square (6 miles by 6 miles) units called townships. A tier of townships running north and south was called a 'range.' Each township was divided into 36 sections; each section was one mile square and contained 640 acres and 160 square rods. These sections were numbered 1 to 36 beginning in the northeast corner of the township and ending in the southeast corner.

Each section can be subdivided into halves and quarters (or aliquot parts). Each quarter section of 160 acres was identified by a compass direction (NE, SE, SW, NW). Each township is identified by its relation to the Principal Meridian and Baseline. For example, the seventh township north of the baseline, third west of the Principal Meridian would be T7N, R3W, 6th Principal Meridian. There are 37 sets of Principal Meridians/Baselines – 34 in the continental United States and 3 in Alaska. Figure 13.2 shows the

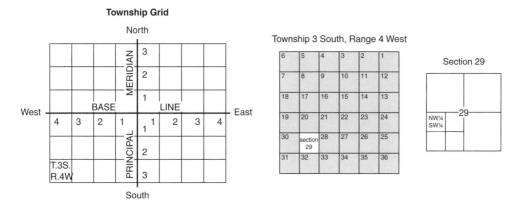

Source: Merrill and Smith (2007).

Figure 13.8   *Details of US rectangular demarcation system*

Principal Meridians and Baselines for the lower 48 states. Figure 13.8 shows the details of the rectangular system.

In the fall of 1785, the survey for this system began in Ohio on the border with Pennsylvania at what is now called the *Point of Beginning* (Linklater 2002: 71). The first townships to be surveyed are known as the 'Seven Ranges' (a north–south tier of townships) in eastern Ohio. Ohio was surveyed in several major subdivisions, each with its own range and base descriptions. Figure 13.9 shows the initial federal survey at the *Point of Beginning*.

The early surveying, particularly in Ohio, was performed with more speed than care, with the result that many of the oldest townships and sections vary considerably from their specified shape (square) and area (640 acres). Proceeding westward, accuracy became more of a consideration than rapid sale, and the system was simplified by establishing one major north–south line (principal meridian) and one east–west (base) line that control descriptions for an entire state. County lines frequently follow the survey, explaining why there are many rectangular counties in the western two-thirds of the nation (Stein 2008). There are no federal meridians or baselines in Texas because there were no federal lands in Texas. Instead, Texas has its own system of land demarcation that is similar to, but not part of, the US rectangular system.[7]

Under the federal rectangular survey, the land was surveyed before any settlement, by first marking out corners at the interval of every mile along the boundaries of the townships usually with monuments or notches on trees to establish the grid (Pattison 1957a: 159, 164). Initially, all surveys were to be done by surveyors hired by the Geographer of the United States (White 1983: 14).

Rectangular systems in Canada and Australia
In the modern era several other countries have also adopted rectangular systems, primarily countries once part of the British Empire where immigration took place to secure land and where land markets developed as an essential part of the new economy.[8] As early as 1783 there was some rectangular demarcation in Canada. 6x6

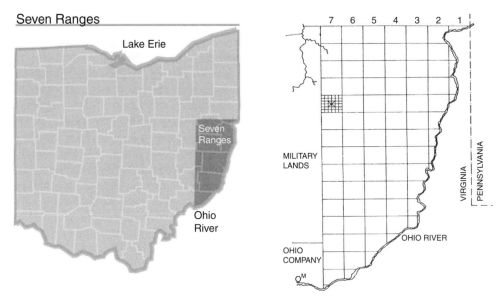

Sources: Morris (1994); and www.ohiohistorycentral.org/image.php?img=634 (accessed on October 17, 2008).

Figure 13.9   Map of Ohio showing the Seven Ranges and the Point of Beginning

mile townships were laid out in Ontario (Kain and Baigent 1992: 298). The township was the settlement unit adopted for the area along the upper St. Lawrence River. After 1784, the township dimensions were increased to 9x12 square miles. Unlike in the US the Canadian surveys experimented with different dimensions and internal subdivisions until the 1860s.

In 1869 the system of land survey mandated 9-mile square townships and 600 acre sections in ranges running east and west of the Winnipeg Meridian. In 1871 the Dominion Land Survey was established and the dimensions were reset at 6x6 mile townships to conform to the US on the southern border with the state of Minnesota and the Dakota Territory (Kain and Baigent 1992: 303). Canada was competing with the US for settlers to the prairies and likely sought to have similar demarcation practices.

The Dominion Survery began on July 10, 1871 and divided the land into one square mile sections.[9] As in the US system, there were Meridians running north–south and Base Lines running east–west. The only difference was that the section numbering system started with Section 1 in the southeast corner of the township rather than the northeast corner as shown in Figure 13.10.

In Australia a rectangular system was established in the state of New South Wales (Kain and Baigent 1992) in 1821. At that time Governor Brisbane set out to survey land following the American system identically with 6x6 mile townships. Later, however, Governor Darling came from London with a new set of instructions. These townships were abandoned and there were introduced 40 mile-square counties, 10 mile-square hundreds and 25 square-mile parishes to facilitate the creation of contiguous and close settlements (Kain and Baigent 1992: 309). These competing policies did not use a common

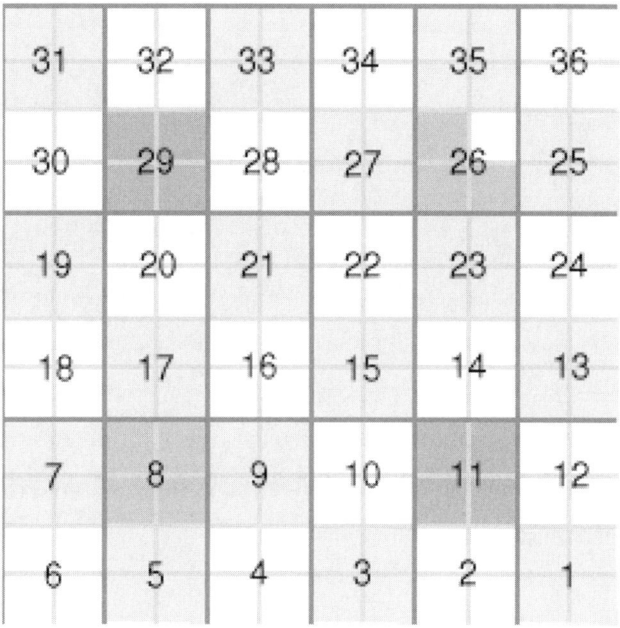

31	32	33	34	35	36
30	29	28	27	26	25
19	20	21	22	23	24
18	17	16	15	14	13
7	8	9	10	11	12
6	5	4	3	2	1

Source: http://en.wikipedia.org/wiki/Dominion_Land_Survey.

Figure 13.10   *Section numbering system according to the Canadian Dominion Land Survey*

baseline and meridian to reference the coordinates, and hence what became of it was a series of regional grids with confounding alignments as seen in Figure 13.11.

Urban land demarcation patterns
In western North America where the rectangular demarcation has been established on a continental scale there are many cities, such as Chicago, San Francisco, Phoenix, Denver, and Calgary, with grid systems. These were all settled to be commercial centers and land markets were active. There are, in addition, examples of rectangular demarcation in cities surrounded by metes and bounds demarcation. These include New York City, Barcelona, Philadelphia, Brasila, and elsewhere.[10] Such urban rectangular systems have been established by local governments and by private developers, typically with the intention to increase commercial activity.

Philadelphia.   In 1682 William Penn, who held the royal charter to Pennsylvania, drew up a plan for the new settlement of Philadelphia, which was to be the market center of the new colony. He instructed three commissioners to lay out a city 2 miles long and 1 mile wide stretching across a peninsula between the Delaware and Schuylkill Rivers. There were to be two main cross streets, each 100 feet wide, 8 east–west streets and 20 north–south minor streets that were each to be 50 feet wide. The main central square was 10 acres and 4 minor squares were 8 acres each (Morris 1994: 339). Figure 13.12 shows the layout of his plan.

Note: Latitude and Longitude: 32°S 147°E.

Source: Google Earth.

Figure 13.11   Rectangular demarcation in New South Wales, Australia

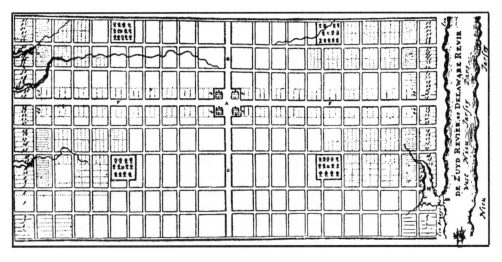

Source: Morris (1994).

Figure 13.12   William Penn's plan for Philadelphia

New York City.   Unlike Philadelphia, New York started without a plan and was settled under metes and bounds for roughly 150 years. By the late 18th century the city was spreading northward in a tangle of independently laid-out grids by developers who were converting meadows and marshland into urban real estate (Morris 1994; and Kostof

Note: Latitude and Longitude: 40°N 73°W.

Source: Google Earth.

Figure 13.13 *Rectangular demarcation in Lower Manhattan, New York City*

1991: 343). In 1807 the city was authorized by New York state to appoint commissioners to plan the undeveloped parts of Manhattan Island, north of Washington Square. The Commissioners' plan of 1811 imposed a uniform grid on the rest of Manhattan. Twelve 100-foot-wide north–south avenues and 155 east–west streets 60 feet wide were established between the Hudson and East Rivers. Figure 13.13 shows a satellite picture of the grid in Lower Manhattan today.

Barcelona.   The city of Barcelona in northeastern Spain developed over time in a seemingly haphazard manner typical of cities governed by metes and bounds demarcation (Kostof 1991: 152). In 1860 a government surveyor Ildefonso Cerda y Suner was given government authority to demolish old and obsolete fortifications of the city and create a general plan for future commercial growth. Ildefonso Cerda began to spread a grid across 10 square miles of flat land. According to his plan, streets were to have an equal width of 66 feet each and square blocks would have cut-off corners to match this width. Figure 13.14 shows Cerda's plan and a satellite picture of modern Barcelona. The plan depicts the irregular pattern of the medieval city core (dark area at the lower left) as being sliced by the grid of boulevards.

Chandigarh, India.   India is a country dominated by metes and bounds demarcation, and its cities are notoriously confusing and congested. Chandigarh, the capital city of the northern state of Punjab, however, is unique within this larger system (Kostof 1991).[11] In 1951, shortly after Indian independence from Great Britain, the government assigned French architect Le Corbusier to design the city. Le Corbusier created a well-ordered matrix that comprised a regular grid of fast traffic roads that defined a neighborhood unit or 'sector'. The sectors measured 0.5 miles by 0.75 miles on a NW–SE alignment. Each block was bisected by one major market street, forming a linear shopping system.

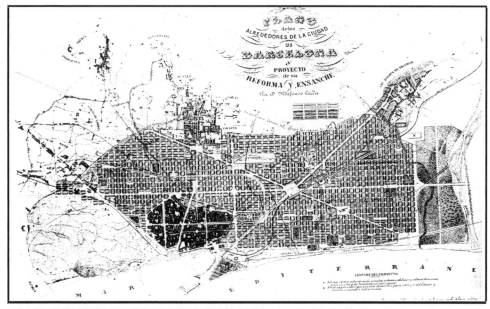

Note: * Latitude and Longitude: 41°N 2°E.

Source: Kostof (1991); and Google Earth.

Figure 13.14   Cerda's plan for Barcelona, Spain and satellite picture of the city*

The civic center was at the intersection of the two major axes just like a forum in a Roman grid system.

The governmental complex was designed on a module of rectangles measuring 800 meters by 400 meters. The residential pattern was characterized by a loose grid pattern of primary roads that defined super-blocks. There were also provisions made for green belts, sites for schools and sports facilities. Figure 13.15 shows the plan and a modern satellite photograph.

III.   AN ECONOMIC FRAMEWORK FOR UNDERSTANDING LAND DEMARCATION

In this section we develop an economic framework for understanding the functions and impacts of land demarcation systems. We focus on rectangular and metes and bounds systems but also consider land demarcation as an economic choice more generally. We begin by considering how a decentralized system of land claiming would generate patterns of land holdings that would be unsystematic and depend on natural topography and the characteristics of the claimant population. We then consider the potential gains from a centralized and coordinated land demarcation system that governs a large region. In this analysis we focus on the particular features of the American rectangular system.

A.   Land Demarcation in a Decentralized System

Consider a large tract of land available to a large group of potential claimants, where the external boundary is enforced collectively or otherwise, so that only internal and shared borders are considered by individual decision makers. Within the external borders, there is no coordination or contracting among claimants.[12] In the simple case where all claimants have the same productivity and the same enforcement costs, the problem for each party might be to simply minimize the border demarcation and enforcement costs, constrained by the productivity of the land. Alternatively the question is what shape generates the largest area (and thus the lower enforcement costs per area) for a given perimeter – this is the ancient and famous *isoperimetric problem*.[13]

The answer to the isoperimetric problem is that a circle will maximize the area for a given perimeter, providing the lowest perimeter-to-area ratio. If enforcement costs depend on the perimeter or the perimeter relative to area we should see circular plots. Figure 13.16 shows such a pattern of land ownership for a 5 mile by 5 mile tract of land. Consider a circular plot with a 4 mile perimeter. The area will be $4 / \pi = 1.27$ square miles. A square parcel with a 4 mile perimeter will have an area of just 1 square mile. Figure 13.16 also shows the same 5 mile by 5 mile landscape with hexagons and triangles.

However, the enforcement cost function is likely to be more complex than simply minimizing the perimeter for a given area. Further, as Figure 13.16 shows circular plots leave large areas of unclaimed land. In fact the unclaimed corners in the circular pattern amount to about 22 percent of the total tract.[14] These unclaimed open access areas would not only dissipate rents derived from the land but might create locales where intruders can threaten the border of the circular plot thus adding to the costs of demarcation and enforcement. They may also lead to disputes if the land later became valuable or if the circular claims overlapped rather than were perfectly adjacent as in Figure 13.16.

Given these problems with a circular landscape, we narrow the set of plausible equilibrium parcel shapes to regular polygons. Regular polygons maximize the area enclosed by a given perimeter (Dunham 1994) and have the potential to eliminate open access

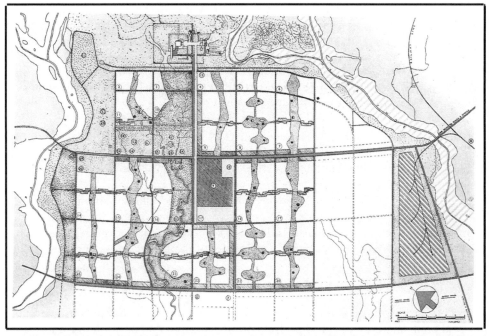

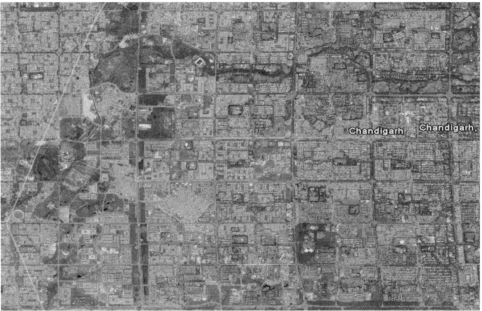

Note: Latitude and Longitude: 30°N 76°E.

Source: Kostof (1991); and Google Earth.

Figure 13.15   Chandigarh, India: Le Corbusier's plan for and current satellite view

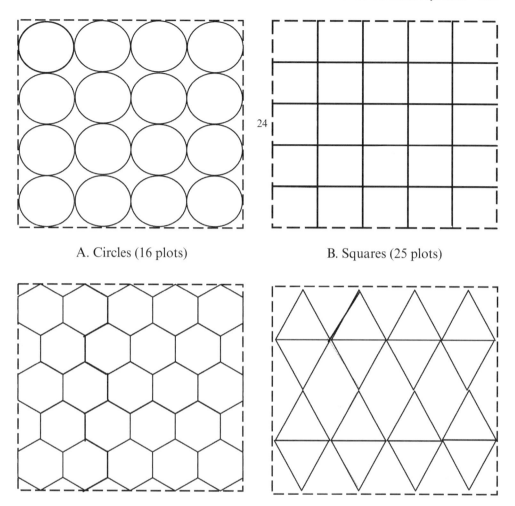

A. Circles (16 plots)   B. Squares (25 plots)

Source: Authors' calculations; also in Libecap and Lueck (2009).

Figure 13.16   Possible parcel configurations

waste between parcels within a given tract. In fact, there are only three regular polygons – triangles, squares, and hexagons – that will allow patterns, with a common vertex, that have no interstices (space) between the parcels.

The choice among triangles, squares, and hexagons can be examined by further analysis of enforcement costs and the economic value of alternative shapes. The perimeter to area ratio (*p*/*a*) generates the following ranking from lowest to highest: hexagons, squares, triangles. The number of shared borders may affect enforcement costs. Another factor is that survey and fencing costs should be lower with fewer angles and longer straight boundary stretches. This clearly favors squares over triangles and hexagons. In addition square parcels are likely to have more efficient shapes for productive uses such as agricultural fields and urban buildings compared to triangles and hexagons.

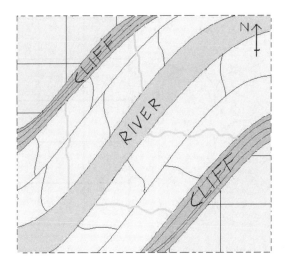

Figure 13.17   Decentralized claiming in non-planar topography

This discussion implies that with homogeneous (flat) land and homogeneous parties (in both productivity and enforcement ability) a decentralized metes and bounds system will yield a land ownership pattern of identical square parcels. Under these conditions a decentralized MB system could lead to individual square plots like a RS system.

Adding heterogeneous terrain and heterogeneous claimants (either in land use value or in costs of demarcation and enforcement) could yield a pattern of land ownership that would appear almost random to an aerial observer. If demarcation and enforcement costs depend on terrain (because of surveying or fencing or road building costs), we would expect borders to roughly follow the topography. To take an extreme example, suppose a deep canyon cut through a fertile plateau. The cost (and benefits) of demarcating and enforcing a border across the canyon may be so excessive that the canyon edge becomes the optimal boundary. Figure 13.17 shows such a case where rugged topography makes linear boundaries too costly so that boundaries are square only on the flat plateau but are irregular in the canyon itself. The canyon itself might remain as unclaimed open access land. Thus we also expect that with heterogeneous land and parties (in both productivity and enforcement ability) a decentralized metes and bounds system will yield a land ownership pattern of parcels whose borders mimic the topography and vary in size with no particular alignment.

We thus expect a pattern of parcel sizes and shapes that depends on the character of the land (topography, vegetation, soil) and of the potential claimants (farming productivity, violence and monitoring productivity, and so on). Adding land heterogeneity (river, broken terrain) leads to non-linear claims as well as unclaimed areas – the so-called 'gaps and gores' described by many historians of MB land systems. This illustrates a tradeoff between the two systems. With RS plots of land are created as squares, irrespective of the quality and features of the land. With MB, however, plots are separated into attractive and unattractive plots. RS then avoids the problem of later conflict over these areas,

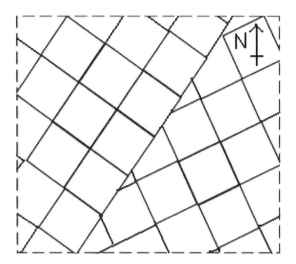

Source: Authors' creation.

Figure 13.18   Colliding rectangular demarcation systems with decentralized alignment

while RS requires that even currently unvalued areas be claimed and enforced within a larger plot. We examine these implications in Section IV below.

B.   Coordination and Collective Action in a Land Demarcation System

The previous analysis shows how land rights would be privately demarcated in an indiscriminate system with individual claiming and enforcement. It is apparent, however, that there are potential gains from a centralized system. First, there can be enforcement cost savings from coordinating on common borders. Second, and more generally, a common system provides information about the location of individual parcels and is thus a public good and will have greater net value if spread over a larger region. Third, coordination results in similarly aligned properties and avoids the gaps of unclaimed land that arise when unsynchronized demarcation systems collide.

Consider adjacent areas settled under metes and bounds. Even with homogeneous terrain (flat, uniform) and homogeneous claimants, there is no reason to expect these patterns of squares to be aligned in the same direction as nearby claims without some sort of convention or other coordinating device. Without such coordination, individual rectangular claims or clusters of claims could collide with other such claims at odd angles, thus creating a series of slivered triangular parcels which are expected to be less valuable. A north–south or other uniform alignment then requires either a social convention or centralized direction.

Figure 13.18 shows a case in which two sections of homogeneous flat land with square plots might have different alignments. Gaps between these claims and overlapping claims might also result from imprecision in location recording and no communication or coordination among the parties. Finally, a coordinated survey of heterogeneous land prior to allocation fixes individual land claim borders and avoids the incentives of claimants to initially 'float' boundaries to cover the most productive land. Such opportunistic border adjustments could result in long-term border and ownership disputes among adjacent properties.

C.   Land Demarcation in a Rectangular System

Many possible centralized land demarcation systems can be imagined and some historical rectangular systems were noted above. The American RS is a particular type of centralized land demarcation system. Land claims under MB required individual surveys without the aggregate coordination benefits described above. Nevertheless, there were likely substantial upfront costs of providing coordinated surveys through designing the details (size of squares), implementing the survey (determining initial points and conducting the surveys), and controlling access until the survey was completed. Generally, because of these costs, only agents who expected to internalize gains of an RS would adopt such a system. Their returns would accrue through the revenues of land sales to claimants who did not have to bear individual survey costs and who benefitted from the other advantages of the rectangular survey. This implies that large land holders, such as sovereign government, rural land and suburban developers or other organizations where entry could be controlled, would adopt a rectangular survey.

The effects of the American rectangular survey have been discussed by historians and geographers but there is no literature on how the rectangular survey might affect incentives and thus affect such outcomes as land value, boundary disputes, land transactions, and land-based public infrastructure. The rectangular system creates linear and geographic-based borders that are fixed and thus impervious to changes in the land and verifiable using standard surveying techniques. This is a distinct difference compared to the impermanent and locally described borders in metes and bounds.

The rectangular system creates a public good information structure that expands the market (Linklater 2002). Expanding the market and lowering transaction costs should make it cheaper for land parcels to be reorganized as market conditions change. This should be observed as a greater number of transactions such as mortgages and conveyances per unit of land. This should also increase the value of land on a per unit basis and should also lead to more uniformity in the size and shape of parcels in a region. For example, in a competitive market with access to a common technology, farms within homogeneous regions should be roughly the same size and shape. This discussion implies that there will be certeris paribus: 1) more land transactions under the rectangular survey than under metes and bounds; 2) less variance in the size and shape of parcels under RS than MB; and 3) higher (per acre) land values under the rectangular survey than under metes and bounds.

The clarity and linearity of the rectangular system are also expected to have an impact on public infrastructure such as roads and other systems that require long right-of-way stretches. Identification of property lines is likely to be cheaper and contiguous linear borders should lower the cost of assembling such rights of way even if eminent domain is required. This implies that there will be more roads per unit of land under the rectangular system than under metes and bounds. Because surveys are standardized and aligned under the RS, there are no unclaimed gaps or gores in property claims. RS also brings coordinated survey and fixed boundaries. These factors imply there will be fewer legal disputes (and litigation) over boundaries and titles under the rectangular survey than under metes and bounds. These implications are tested in Libecap and Lueck (2009), and generally there is strong empirical support for the hypotheses.

Modern Geographic Information Systems (GIS) could potentially allow for the more precise positioning and demarcation of land thus reducing some of the costs of metes and bounds. But, as we discuss below, the coordinating function of a large scale rectangular survey remains an important advantage in avoiding conflicting or overlapping boundaries, in providing usable and recognizable parcel shapes and sizes, in reducing the amount of initially unclaimed gaps of land unmarked and costly to place into production, and in providing a clear set of addresses for all parcels, regardless of location and terrain.

To this point we have stressed the benefits of the rectangular system over metes and bounds but we have ignored the costs of establishing such a centralized and systematic regime. In cases of rugged or extreme terrain forcing a square grid on the landscape can lead to extremely costly surveys, fence lines, and roads. Under a metes and bounds system property boundaries would tend to avoid such extreme topography thus reducing such costs. Indeed in some of the most remote and rugged parts of the western United States the most obvious components of the rectangular survey simply disappear from the landscape.

For example, in rugged terrain in the US, even using the RS, roads do not follow section lines but rather natural contours, and in some cases only simple fences mark the property boundaries. Fields, too, often lose their rectangular shape in rugged terrain. In addition, where the land use requires relatively large parcels (forests, national parks) the rectangular survey system might lead to overinvestment in land demarcation. Note that the borders of such US National Parks as the Grand Canyon, Mount Rainier, and Yellowstone have linear borders even in some of the most rugged terrain. Yellowstone and Mount Rainier are virtually squares, while others comprise combinations of linear and geographic borders. Figure 13.19 shows Zion National Park which is extremely rugged terrain (in southwest Utah), yet its border is almost completely comprised of linear segments.

IV. ECONOMIC IMPLICATIONS AND ECONOMIC HISTORY

The framework we developed above generates a wide range of implications for both the choice of land demarcation systems and the effects of those systems. In this section we examine some of the economic history of land demarcation systems in light of these implications. We divide this analysis into four sections. First, we examine land demarcation under metes and bounds. Second, we examine the determinants of the adoption of rectangular demarcation in the United States and some of the effects of this system. Third, we examine rectangular demarcation systems in urban areas and in areas outside the United States. Fourth, we examine the rather unique system of circular land demarcation in Cuba that illuminates many issues discussed above.

While we use a variety of data sources in this section a significant portion of our findings are from south central Ohio, where the Virginia Military District, a region of 4.2 million acres and 22 counties totally or partially within it, was governed by metes and

Sources: www.utah.com/maps/zion/index.htm.

Figure 13.19   Border of Zion Canyon National Park, Utah

bounds, while the federal rectangular survey governed the remaining 22 million acres and 66 counties in the state.[15] These two land systems have been adjacent for roughly two centuries and, hence, provide a natural experiment for examining the comparative effects of the two methods of land demarcation.

A.   Demarcation under Metes and Bounds

Under metes and bounds demarcation individuals choose and shape parcels more or less unconstrained by explicit links to other existing or potential landowners. A number of choices can be examined including the size and shape of the parcels, the alignment of the parcels, and the disputes over borders. All of these are examined below and compared ultimately with these choices under rectangular demarcation.

Size and shape of parcels

In Section III we hypothesized that with homogeneous (flat) land and homogeneous parties (in both productivity and enforcement ability) a decentralized metes and bounds system will yield a land ownership pattern of identical square parcels. Conversely, we hypothesized that with heterogeneous land and parties a decentralized metes and

A   Parcel boundaries in flat topography (Highland and Clermont countries)

B   Parcel boundaries in rugged topography (Pike County)

Source: Libecap and Lueck (2009).

Figure 13.20   Topographic and demarcation correlation under metes and bounds

bounds system will yield a land ownership pattern of parcels whose borders mimic the topography and vary in size with no particular alignment.

We can examine these implications through visual inspection of topography and parcel size and shape within the central Virginia Military District of Ohio where metes and bounds was used to demarcate property. Figure 13.20, Panel A shows a section of flat land in Highland and Clermont counties. It is clear that the parcels are rectangular and even square as predicted. In the Virginia Military District there were large sections of land that had been assembled by speculators who purchased warrants from veterans. The pattern shows evidence of organized grid-like surveying of small blocks of land, where groups of tracts are aligned in the same directions, but not typically north–south as in the rectangular system.[16] In the case where different grids abut one another, the results are triangular parcels, some of which were unclaimed originally.

Panel B shows a similarly sized area in Pike County (eastern Virginia Military District) where the terrain is more rugged Here the parcels tend to have much more variation in parcel shape, with the boundaries often following natural land features such as rivers and valleys. Additionally, there is greater variation in parcel size, with many very small parcels and a few extremely large parcels. There is no evidence of coordinated parcel boundary alignment as seen in Panel A.

A   Virginia Military District   B   Crowell

Note: Latitude and Longitude: 33°N 99°W.

Source: Libecap and Lueck (2009); and Google Earth.

*Figure 13.21   Colliding Tracts of Rectangular Parcels in the Virginia Military District
(Highland and Clermont counties) and Crowell, Texas*

Alignment of parcels
As the analysis above shows, when the land is flat we expect and find that parcels under
metes and bounds tend to be rectangles and even squares. But, as we argued in Section
III, without a central coordinating system it is likely that sets of square parcels will not
be aligned because their original alignment will be focused on nearby settlements or
transportation routes. Thus we expect to find collisions between chunks of squares and
the attendant slivers of triangular parcels that result. Figure 13.21 (Panel A) again shows
this in the Virginia Military District in Clermont and Highland counties, where these
patterns of colliding grids are evident. A similar outcome is seen in Texas (Figure 13.21
Panel B) where there were several distinct rectangular systems.

Boundary conflicts under metes and bounds
In his examination of Ohio lands, William Peters (1930: 26, 30, 135) concluded that
there was more litigation due to overlapping entries, uncertainty of location, unreliable
local property markers, and confusion of ownership in the 19th century in the Virginia
Military District under metes and bounds than in the rest of Ohio combined. Seeing
confusion over land boundaries in Kentucky and Tennessee, Stephen Austin had Texas
adopt rectangular grid surveys where possible and thereby avoided the litigation associated with metes and bounds in other southern states. As noted by Linklater (2002:
241): 'The advantages inherent in the square-based federal land survey gave the state's
economy a vigor its neighbours lacked.'

   The same flexibility that allowed for open entry in land claiming also encouraged
boundary disputes and fraud. As Linklater (2002: 165) described: 'A metes and bounds
survey did not just produce shapes that only the best surveyors could measure, it
created a maze of bureaucratic form-filling that invited fraud and wholesale corruption.'
Competing claimants burned blazed trees that marked parcel boundaries or moved monuments so that claims often exceeded the amounts stipulated in their warrants and no

longer fitted the property description filed at the land office. The irregular shapes of land holdings made it difficult to clearly define boundaries and properties often overlapped. In eastern Georgia, where the maximum land grant was 1,000 acres, more than 100 individuals put in multiple headright claims for in total more than 100,000 acres. Georgia's area in 1796 covered 8,717,960 acres, but, as Kain and Baigent (1992: 275) report, land claims within the state exceeded 29,000,000 acres, more than three times the total land area within the state's borders.

Under metes and bounds settlers had incentives to leave boundaries vague and flexible for at least two reasons. One was that in a wilderness it was costly to locate precise boundaries during the initial land claim, and hence difficult for the surveyor who followed to find those boundary markers. Second and more important, given the lack of information about the location of the most desirable lands at the time of the initial land entry, claimants did not want to be bound to absolute markers. Rather, they wanted the original boundaries left sufficiently indistinct so that they could be moved during the survey to encompass more valuable areas that had been missed. Indeed, a major reason for fragmenting holdings under MB was to secure only the best lands. These practices made boundaries much more costly to survey and mark.

Metes and bounds also encouraged property conflict because irregularities in one property's boundaries affected the perimeters of all neighboring properties. Lacking an overall framework for positioning and demarcating property boundaries under metes and mounds, each successive land claim typically was designated or 'chained' with respect to existing adjoining property descriptions, their surveys, and monuments. Consider, for example, a parcel description from one Ohio case: '[s]urveyed for Thomas Perkins, assignee 1,866 2/3 acres of land, on a military warrant, No 3,442, and part of 3,530, on the waters of Three Mile and Eagle creek, beginning at two lynns, a sugar tree and white oak, southwest corner of Humphrey Brooks' survey, 1,690; thence south 30 degrees west 227 poles to a white walnut, hackberry and buckeye, southwest corner of Benjamin Beasley's survey' (*Nash v. Atherton* (10 Ohio 163, 165 (1840))). Whenever the adjacent property corners could not be verified; when that property's survey was found to be faulty (covering too much land or land that did not fit the property description at the land office); or if the surveys overlapped, then the boundaries and titles for all of the affected, chained properties could be clouded and potentially be declared invalid by the courts because they did not conform to one another or legal descriptions.[17]

Land values in the southern frontier typically were lower than in the North, as discussed below. This situation encouraged careless survey: '[w]hen land was thought of as limitless, there was little incentive to accuracy' (Kain and Baigent 1992: 271). For these reasons, metes and bound areas, especially in the US Southeast – interior Virginia, Tennessee, Kentucky, Alabama, Mississippi, and Georgia – were characterized by land conflicts: '[i]n effect the metes and bounds system was skewed in favour of those with deep enough pockets to hire lawyers and land jobbers, and to keep sweet an army of state officials' (Linklater 2002: 166). These overlapping and confused boundaries also encouraged title disputes (Kain and Baigent 1992: 274–75).

Complexity of the metes and bounds system
Another cost of the metes and bounds system is that it is a very local system using local language and local surveys as reference points. This has two costs. First, descriptions are

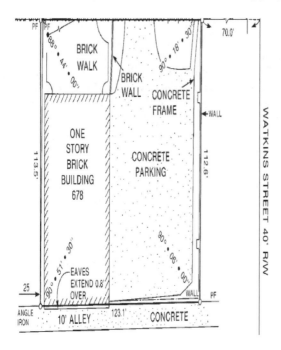

'Beginning at an iron pin found on the south side of 10th Street 70 feet west of the center line of Watkins Street as measured along the south side of 10th street; thence south and forming an interior angle of 90°18'30" from 10 Street 112.6 feet to a 3 inch steel fence post on the north side of an alley; thence, west along the north side of said alley and forming an interior angle of 90°06' from the preceding call 123.1 feet to a 3 inch steel fence post; thence north and forming an interior angle of 90°51'30" from the preceding call 113.5 feet to a 3 inch steel fence post on the south side of 10th Street; thence east along the south side of 10t Street and forming an interior angle of 88°44' from the preceding call 125 feet to the point of beginning.'

Source: Hinkel (2003).

Figure 13.22   Plot description under metes and bounds, Fulton County, Georgia

simply complicated and thus costly to use and convey. Second, it is difficult for someone outside the local market to understand the nature of the property and thus to interact in the market. Local systems like metes are bounds act as barriers to entry into the land market.

As noted earlier, new technology, such as Geographic Information Systems (GIS), may mitigate some of the costs associated with metes and bounds. With GIS, individual property boundaries, demarcated by local terrain and geographic characteristics, can be determined more precisely without knowledge of narrow idiosyncratic factors. Even with this technology, the absence of a centralizing coordinating mechanism provided by the rectangular survey remains. Under metes and bounds overlapping or colliding boundaries are still possible; complex property descriptions persist; oddly shaped parcels remain; and the opportunistic bounding of the best lands leaves gaps of less desirable lands unmarked and difficult to place into effective production.

To illustrate the cumbersome nature of property description and definition under metes and bounds consider the description of a square plot of land. In the rectangular system a square plot would simply be noted, for example, as Section 12, in a certain township related to a particular principal meridian. As described above this is typically a one line address. Under metes and bounds even a simple square parcel cannot be described simply. Figure 13.22 illustrates this complexity of property demarcation under metes and bounds measurement with a lot description – of a nearly square parcel no less – in Fulton County, Georgia.[18]

B.   Demarcation under the US Rectangular System

The history of the adoption and use of rectangular demarcation in the United States allows us to examine many of the implications of our economic framework. In particular we examine the forces that led to the adoption of the rectangular system and its effects on land markets, land use and land disputes.

Adoption of the American rectangular system

We argue that the RS provides a public good in terms of systematic location of properties, coordinated survey, and reduced title conflict. We also note that there are considerable initial costs associated with employing an initial rectangular survey prior to entry. These arguments suggest that the RS would be used only when these benefits could be internalized to offset the costs of systematic survey. Governments, large land grantees or land speculators who planned to subsequently subdivide and sell, as well as suburban real estate developers, are examples of cases where the RS would be used. These owners would capture the resulting higher land values.

The discussion of the history of the Federal Land Law of 1785 and the motivating incentive to raise revenue through the use of systematic demarcation outlined in Section III is consistent with this implication. Moreover, the use of centralized land demarcation in New England townships, the William Penn land grant in Pennsylvania, and for land company holdings in colonial New York likely reflects the ability of the parties to capture the benefits of coordinated land demarcation and settlement. Finally, these benefits are also reflected in the adoption of grids in commercial urban subdivisions, where the value of land was relatively high compared to political urban settings where other demarcation practices were used.

Between 1781 and 1802, the Federal Government acquired 267,730,560 acres of land in cessions from the states. Ultimately, with the Louisiana Purchase, annexation of Texas, acquisition of Oregon and Mexican lands, the public domain included 1,309,591,680 acres, a huge estate (Hibbard 1965: 31). Lacking other sources of revenue in the late 18th and early 19th centuries the Federal Government sought a land demarcation system that would maximize land value, while encouraging orderly, dense settlement.

The Virginia metes and bounds and the New England township system were the dominant and available competing models. Southern representatives to the Continental Congress generally supported metes and bound demarcation, but key southerners including Jefferson, Washington, and William Grayson,[19] along with northern representatives, supported the New England plan. In debating the legislation, Thomas Jefferson and others in the Continental Congress pushed for the establishment of the rectangular survey because they were frustrated with the metes and bounds system and expected a positive impact on land values that would raise federal revenues from land sales.[20] Jefferson was head of a committee of the Continental Congress organized to choose the best way to survey and sell land.

The pervasive Virginia method allowed claimants to choose their property, survey by metes and bounds, and then purchase it. This was ruled out by the committee, which instead called for survey before occupation with properties to be marked in squares, aligned with each other, 'so that no land would be left vacant,' to prevent overlapping claims, and to simplify registering deeds.[21] Under this approach the US could sell land to raise money and would have the system 'decimalized.'[22] Squares also reduced survey costs because only two sides of each township and smaller parcel had to be surveyed.[23]

Alexander Hamilton stressed the importance of land sales for the US Treasury and supported Jefferson: '[t]he public lands should continue to be surveyed and laid out as a grid before they were sold.' The importance of revenue in the selection of the RS is indicated in the *Letters of the Members of the Continental Congress*. For example, Arthur Lee wrote to Joseph Reed on April 5, 1784: 'General Clarke, Wolcot, Green, Butler, and Mr. Higgenson are appointed to negotiate a treaty and purchase from the Indians their claims, which will secure the settlements in that Country, and enable us to satisfy the demands of the Army, and sink the public debt by the sale of the Lands. A consummation devoutly to be wished' (Burnett 1934: 485). Additionally, the New Hampshire Delegates wrote May 5, 1784: 'We flatter ourselves these Lands will prove a considerable resource for sinking the national debt, and, if rightly conducted, liten the burthens of our fellow-citizens on account of Taxes as well as give relief to the creditors of the United States.' (Burnett, 1934: 513).

Demarcation prior to settlement was also seen as a means of generating information about the value of federal lands before sale: '[i]t was pointed out that congressional surveys would disclose a great deal of valuable information concerning the western lands.'[24] Jefferson's committee also argued that survey before sale was necessary to prevent overlapping claims and to simplify registring and deeds. A rectangular system would prevent gaps and gores, making the buyer take the good land with the bad. Every man's land was to share a boundary with his neighbor's. The existence and costs of thousands of boundary disputes in the courts made the proposed rectangular system and prior survey sound attractive, even to the Southern delegates (White 1983: 9). For all of these reasons, Jefferson's recommendation became incorporated in the Land Ordinance of May 20, 1785 for disposing lands in the western territory.[25]

The gains from coordination

The coordinating influence of the federal land survey is dramatically different from what was found under metes and bounds. Instead of irregular, localized plots defined by topography and natural monuments, each property under the RS was anchored by the federal survey to a location within a specific section, township and range, such as a 80-acre tract in '. . . the west half of section 13, T[ownship] 3, R[ange] 4, east of M.D' or a 40-acre tract at 'R[ange] 4, T[ownship] 3, S[ection] 13, p. N. . .' (*Treon's Lessee v. Emerick* 6 O 391, 392) or '¼ South-West, ¼ Section North–West, Section 8 Township 22 North, Range 4 West, Fifth Principal Meridian' (Linklater 2002: 181).

Because MB demarcation defines property borders relative to neighboring properties, it is common for boundary disputes to arise and have effects even on non-adjacent properties. This cannot happen under RS because demarcation does not rely on the demarcation of other properties. Instead, the RS provided a uniform structure that coordinated the location of all parcel boundaries with respect to township and range lines that were tied to latitude and longitude coordinates. Accordingly, a property could be located precisely without resort to the knowledge of local, idiosyncratic land characteristics, trees, rocks, and other monuments. Further, all lands within the specified parcel were included, regardless of quality. It was not possible to gerrymander the claim under the rectangular system could be done under metes and bounds. As a result there were fewer gaps of unclaimed, open terrain as were common in metes and bounds. All of this likely reduced individual survey costs under the rectangular system; made boundaries and titles more definite than under metes and bounds; and removed sources of boundary and title disputes.[26]

The advantages of the RS grid were demonstrated as early as 1788 when the first patent to Ohio lands was issued at the New York City land office to John Martin who paid $640 for a square mile section: Lot 20 Township 7, Range 4. It was in the frontier but 'once it had been surveyed and entered on the grid, it could be picked out from every other square mile of territory, and be bought from an office three hundred miles away on the coast' (Linklater 2002: 84). This simple statement illustrates how the RS creates information that greatly expands and simplifies the market for land.

In 1787, the Northwest Land Ordinance was passed reaffirming the use of the RS called for in 1785. The rectangular survey provided for a systematic, simple, uniform method of allocating land on the frontier in a manner that could generate income for the government and at the same time meet the demand for land coming from immigrants to North America. New base lines and meridians were selected as settlement moved west.[27] These new points of origin became important starting points for surveying in new territories as the country grew and new areas were settled. The first Principal Meridian was a mile from the Ohio–Indiana border and the second Principal Meridian was placed in southern Indiana (Linklater 2002: 176–7), and they moved across the continent as indicated in Figure 13.1.

Linklater (2002: 181) describes the benefit of this regular survey system: '[t]he beauty of the land survey as refined by Jared Mansfield was that it made buying simple, whether by squatter, settler or speculator. The system gave every parcel of virgin ground a unique identity, beginning with the township. Within the township, the thirty-six sections were numbered in an idiosyncratic fashion established by the 1796 Act, beginning with section 1 in the north-east corner, and continuing first westward then eastward, back and forth. . .'.

C.   Land Markets

Because of historical accident, there is a portion of central Ohio in which the RS and MB regimes are adjacent. In short, the state of Virginia was granted ownership of 4 million acres of Ohio as compensation for its Revolutionary War veterans and settled this land using MB. This area was named the Virginia Military District (VMD). Simultaneously, the RS was implemented in the rest of the state and in the countries surrounding the VMD.[28]

Libecap and Lueck (2009) study this natural experiment in land demarcation and examine the effects of MB and RS on land disputes, values and markets, using a wide range of data from the area surrounding the Virginia Military District.

Property disputes

As Libecap and Lueck (2009) find, the Ohio courts repeatedly noted the difficulty of titles in the Virginia Military District. A typical comment was found in an 1840 property dispute from Brown County in *Nash v. Atherton* (10 O 163, 167): 'This case involves principles which are important, and upon its correct decision must depend in some measure the security of titles within the Virginia military district, which at the best, have been heretofore considered as somewhat precarious, and have been, and still continue to be, subject to much litigation.'[29]

Indistinct property boundaries resulted in competing land claims. To designate property for titling under metes and bounds and to inform subsequent locators so that they could make their own claims with respect to the property's boundaries, Ohio law required that borders be defined clearly with corner monuments, which could be natural or artificial; the direction or courses be described precisely; and the distances involved measured accurately. Unfortunately few properties met these requirements and many titles were voided. But when one property's boundaries and title were questioned, all adjacent boundaries and titles were clouded because original land entries were made with respect to one another.

Mistakes by one surveyor or opportunism by a claimant either by over claiming beyond the amount of land authorized in the land warrant or by subsequently floating boundaries to include the best lands had a contagious effect on nearby parcels when the original property was challenged in court. Because of these linkages, the court called for definite boundaries, rejecting the common practice of adding an adjustment factor to each survey line: '[w]here a chain of entries of land in the Virginia military district are made dependent upon each other, each calling for a line of a specified distance and the next commencing at the termination of that distance, the actual location of each must be ascertained by measuring the number of poles called for in the entry. An extension of these distances is not allowable upon an alleged custom of extending at a distance of five percent.'[30]

Market transactions, land values, and infrastructure investment

Libecap and Lueck (2009) use Ohio county data from 1860 of the number of mortgages and conveyances as measures of land market activity and find that controlling for population, number of farms, farm acreage, land value, and land topography, there were significantly more mortgages per acre, land conveyances, land conveyances per acre, and per capita in RS counties relative to MB counties. When the dependent variables are evaluated at their means, counties within the RS system had 50 percent more conveyances compared to adjacent MB counties.

Using data from the 1850 and 1860 agricultural and population census manuscripts for matched parcels taken from C.E. Sherman's (1925) map of original Ohio parcels, Libecap and Lueck estimate average land value per acre by townships, controlling for a variety of natural and demographic factors, they find that the pre-acre property values were substantially higher under the RS system relative to those under MB.[31] Contributing to these surprisingly large effects of land demarcation is the finding that there were fewer roads and railroads, all else equal, in the MB regions, relative to RS areas.

Earlier, scholars of land demarcation have noted this possibility. In his detailed study of the RS and MB in parts of four counties in northwestern Ohio in 1955 Thrower (1966: 86, 88–97, 123) stated that: 'perhaps the most obvious difference between the systematic and the unsystematic surveys is the nature of the road network developed under these contrasting types of land subdivision' with greater road density in the RS areas.

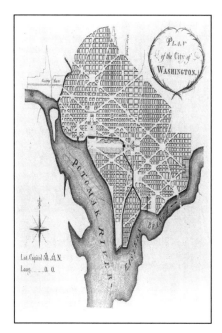

Source: Morris (1994).

Figure 13.23 Land demarcation in Washington, DC and New York City

D. Demarcation in Urban Areas

Throughout human history most cities have developed piecemeal under metes and bounds or similar indiscriminate land demarcation systems. As noted above, however, there are notable cases in which rectangular systems were adopted by cities operating within a larger metes and bounds system. The impacts of these systems on economic growth and urban land markets are hard to assess, but in this section we briefly summarize both the choice to adopt rectangular systems and the effects of these systems. We start by examining two relatively modern national capitals – Brasilia and Washington, DC. Next we examine some major cities where rectangular systems were chosen.

National capitals

Washington, DC. President George Washington was authorized by the Residence Act of 1790 to select a 10 mile square site for the US capital on the Potomac River and appoint a committee of three surveyors to set up the city by the year 1800 (Morris 1994: 351). Washington, DC was designed to be a political, rather than commercial, center and had its major streets laid out as spokes radiating from circles (Morris 1994: 351). The distinct differences between DC and NYC are shown in Figure 13.23 that shows the initial plat map for Washington, DC as well as Manhattan as of 1802.[32]

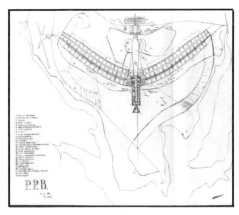

Source: www.infobrasilia.com.br/pilot_plan.htm and www.aboutbrasilia.com/facts/history.html.

Figure 13.24   Brasilia – Costa's cross design and satellite picture

Brasilia.   Ever since the 18th century the Portuguese King, the Brazilian Emperors and the Brazilian Presidents of the Republic were interested in moving the capital to an interior area, thereby minimizing exposure to maritime raids.[33] In 1823, J.B. de Andrade e Silva, a leader in Brazilian Independence, proposed this move and suggested the name of Brasília. An area of 14,400 square kilometers was reserved for the capital, and over 100 years later, in 1956–1957 a public contest was announced accepting designs for the new capital that would be remote from the commercial centers of Rio de Janeiro and Sao Paulo. Lúcio Costa won the competition with his innovative design known as the *Plano Piloto* (Pilot Plan). The plan resulted in a rather unusual grid as seen in Figure 13.24. Costa designed a portion of Brasilia in 1957 on the basis of a cross, with two axes crossing at right-angles. He adapted this cross to the local topography of the city. One of the axes was curved in such a way as to fit into an equilateral triangle that would limit the urbanized area.[34] The emphasis of the plan was on design befitting a capital and not to promote land market transactions.

Cities with rectangular systems

There are no systematic studies available to definitively answer how much economic activity was stimulated by the adoption of rectangular systems in places like Barcelona, New York and Philadelphia, but there is some historical evidence to suggest it was important for commercial development. For New York City, the grid appears to have facilitated its expansion as the country's major commercial center with active land markets. The process of filling empty spaces in the grid continued over time and reached 42nd Street by 1850, and the entire island of Manhattan was covered by 1890.[35]

E.   The Cuban Circular System

Earlier we argued that circles were unlikely to be used because of the high cost of bounding, division, wasted space, and overlapping claims. The Cuban experience seems to

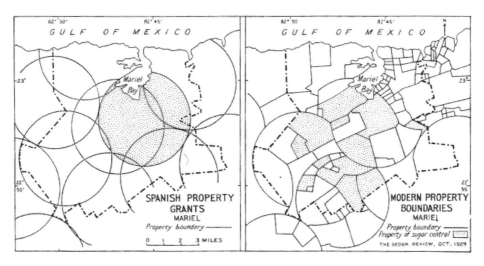

Source: Platt (1929).

Figure 13.25 Circular royal grants and subsequent subdivision of plots

support these notions. During the 16th century, land grants were made by the King of Spain for stock-raising in circular corrals (Platt 1929: 604). These were 1 league (3.45 miles) in radius from a given center, thus having an area of 37 square miles. Land was cheap and there were few settlers. The initial selection of a center was important and boundaries were not as areas distant from ranch centers were not valuable, and thus not likely to be contested or requiring active enforcement.

As the population grew, however, boundaries became more important and reassembling the lands into sugar plantations became desirable. The circular grants were difficult to survey, resulting in legal battles over title. Sugar cultivation could occur on smaller plots, but the division of circles was costly, contributing to uneconomically small residual plots and waste as indicated in Figure 13.25.

IV. SUMMARY AND CONCLUSION

The demarcation of land is an ancient human practice likely beginning with large-scale fluid hunting territories established by hunter-gather groups. This chapter has examined the economic structure of land demarcation systems. We focused on two major practices, metes and bounds and rectangular systems primarily as they have been used in the US. We explain the nature of metes and bounds and the rectangular systems in the US and the legislative history and motivation for its adoption of RS in the Land Law of 1785. We also explain how RS has been adopted in parts of Canada and Australia and cities in other parts of the world.

Given this background, we explored the causes and consequences of these two dominant systems. We postulated that a decentralized system of land claiming would generate patterns of land holdings that would be uncoordinated and depend on natural topography and the characteristics of the claimant population. We then showed how a centralized, rectangular system are expected to generate different ownership patterns and incentives for land use, land markets, investment, and border disputes. We discussed some empirical findings from a comparative analysis of MB and RS in Ohio, other parts of the US, Canada, and Australia, as well as urban areas in a variety of locations. We find that RS is adopted when land values are potentially high and those values can be captured by a land developer (private or government). We also find evidence that RS increases land values by promoting land markets, reducing land boundary disputes, and stimulating investment in infrastructure. For these reasons, more attention should be placed on these fundamental institutions and their roles in influencing property rights to land and the transactions costs of exchange.

It is difficult to separate the shape and the standard location (i.e., system) effects of a rectangular system. Yet, we find even under metes and bounds squares predominate in areas that are flat, but there is no overall coordinating mechanism, so that where tracts of parcels collide there will be oddly formed shaped parcels. This effect is avoided in a large rectangular system where parcels do not collide nor overlap and where squares are generally imposed regardless of topography. Accordingly, uniform productive shapes and standard, identifiable locations are the benefits of a rectangular system as a *coordinating* institution. For these reasons we believe that a centralized land demarcation system is a fundamentally important and overlooked institutional innovation for promoting production and markets for land.

NOTES

*   Libecap@bren.ucsb.edu and lueck@email.arizona.edu. Research support was provided by National Science Foundation through grants SES-0518572 and 0817249. Support was also provided by the Cardon Endowment for Agricultural and Resource Economics at the University of Arizona. We also thank Adrian Lopes, Trevor O'Grady, and Andrew Knauer for valuable research assistance.

1. There is, however, a practical literature in real estate law that is well aware of the difference in land demarcation systems. See, for example, Eldridge, *Evidence and Procedures for Boundary Location* (1962).
2. The term 'metes and bounds' is primarily an English term though we use it to describe a decentralized, topography-based demarcation system. Geographers, such as Thrower (1966) use the term 'indiscriminant' survey.
3. It is possible that a centralized land demarcation system could use nonlinear boundaries but we are unaware of any such system. The 19th century soldier and explorer John Wesley Powell (1878), however, proposed a land demarcation system based on river drainages. He also, however, called for large, rectangular homesteads in the semi-arid West that were larger than those designed for the eastern US.
4. In that case, resurvey and RS marking may pose uncertain redistribution and hence be resisted by current occupants;
5. The history of the development of the chain is detailed in Linklater (2002).
6. It is now called the Public Land Survey System or PLSS; see www.nationalatlas.gov/plssm.html.
7. Below we discuss the rather unique case of Texas.
8. Libecap, Lucek and O'Grady (2010) examine the factors leading to the adoption of the rectangular survey in parts of the British Empire.
9. http://en.wikipedia.org/wiki/Dominion_Land_Survey.
10. Note some other cities with substantial grids.
11. See also http://whc.unesco.org/en/tentativelists/5082/.
12. For more detailed development, see Libecap and Lueck (2009).
13. See Dunham (1994) for history and analysis and http://en.wikipedia.org/wiki/Isoperimetry for an overview of the problem.

14. In fact, it is possible to pack circular plots together by having each parcel touch six others in what is called 'hexagonal packing'.
15. Libecap and Lueck (2009) give a detailed discussion and analysis of the Virginia Military District.
16. Libecap and Lueck (2009) find further statistical support for this correlation between topography and parcel size and shape.
17. Libecap and Lueck (2009) examine land disputes under RS and MB in Ohio more systematically and find more boundary and title conflicts under MB.
18. This is taken from Hinkel (2003: 88). This parcel is not perfectly square but the closest we were able to discover.
19. Grayson was a delegate from Virginia and member of the committee to draft a land ordinance.
20. Ford (1910: 55); Treat (1910: 16); Pattison (1957a: 87), Webster (1791: 493–95); White (1983: 9).
21. Linklater (2002: 68–70); White (1983: 9).
22. Linklater (2002: 68–70).
23. Burnett (1934: 563).
24. Taylor (1922: 12).
25. Linklater (2002: 116, 117), Gates (1968: 59–67), Treat (1910: 24).
26. If a parcel did not become private property it remained owned by the Federal government. In many cases, such unclaimed or unsold land became part of the national parks or national forests.
27. Indeed, forces such as mineral discoveries and white–Indian relations dramatically influenced the pattern of settlement and the demand for land.
28. Libecap and Lueck (2009) discuss this history in detail.
29. See also Porter v Robb, 7 Ohio (Pt. 1) 206, 210–211 (1835): 'To relieve would shake more than half the titles between the Scioto and Little Miami rivers. . ..;' and Lessee of Cadwallader Wallace v Richard Seymour and H. Rennick, 7 Ohio 156, 158 (1836): '. . .a variety of questions are presented of more than ordinary difficulty, in consequence of the nature of the titles in the Virginia military district. . .'.
30. Andrew Huston v Duncan McArthur, 7 Ohio (Pt. 2) 54, 55 (1835).
31. Libecap, Lopes and Lueck (2009) find even larger positive effects from RS in a study of 19th century agriculture in California.
32. www.library.cornell.edu/Reps/DOCS/nyc1811plan.jpg http://en.wikipedia.org/wiki/Image:L%27Enfant_plan.jpg.
33. See www.infobrasilia.com.br/pilot_plan.htm and http://www.aboutbrasilia.com/facts/history.html accessed on October, 13, 2008.
34. Super-blocks were assigned numbers and residential buildings were given letters and apartments with numbers. Therefore a typical address would read for instance: N-S3-L, apt. 201.
35. See Atack and Margo (1996) for discussion of the development of NYC land markets.

BIBLIOGRAPHY

Atack, Jeremy and Robert A. Margo. 1996. 'Location, Location, Location! The Market for Vacant Urban Land: New York 1835–1900', *National Bureau of Economic Research, Working Paper* No. H0091.

Bailey, Martin. 1992. 'The Approximate Optimality of Aboriginal Property Rights', *Journal of Law and Economics*, 35, 183–198.

Barnes, Carlton P. 1935. 'Economies of the Long Lot Farm', *Geographical Review* 25, 298–301.

Barzel, Yoram. 1982. 'Measurement Cost and the Organization of Markets', *Journal of Law and Economics*, 25, 27–48.

Bradford, J. 1957. *Ancient Landscapes*. London.

Brown, Curtis M. 1995. *Boundary Control and Legal Principles*, 4th edn.

Brown, C.M. and W.H. Eldridge. 1962. *Evidence and Procedures for Boundary Location*, New York: John Wiley and Sons.

Burnett, Edmund C. (ed.). 1934. *Letters of the Members of the Continental Congress*, Vol. 7. Washington, DC: Carnegie Institution of Washington.

Demsetz, Harold. 1967. 'Towards a Theory of Property Rights', *American Economic Review*, 57, 347–59.

Dilke, Oswald A.W. 1971. *The Roman Land Surveyors: An Introduction to the Agrimensores*. Newton Abbot.

Dilke, Oswald A.W. 1985. *Greek and Roman Maps*. Cornell University Press.

Dukeminier, Jesse and James E. Krier. 2002. *Property*, 5th edn. New York: Aspen Law & Business.

Dunham, William. 1994. *The Mathematical Universe: An Alphabetic Journey through the Great Proofs, Problems and Personalities*. New York: John Wiley & Sons.

Dutt, B.B. 1925. *Town Planning in Ancient India*. Calcutta.

Ellickson, Robert C. 1993. 'Property in Land', *Yale Law Journal*, 102, 1315–1400.
Estopinal, Stephen V. 1998. *A Guide to Understanding Land Surveys*. 2nd edn. New York: John Wiley & Sons.
Ford, Amelia Clewley. 1910. *Colonial Precedents of Our National Land System As It Existed in 1800*, Bulletin of the University of Wisconsin No 352, Madison, WI, 321–477.
Gates, Paul W. 1968. *History of Public Land Law*. Washington, DC: Public Land Law Review Commission.
Hibbard, B.H. 1965. *A History of the Public Land Policies*. Madison, WI: The University of Wisconsin Press.
Hinkel, D.F. 2003. *Essentials of Practical Real Estate Law*. 3rd edn. New York: Delmar Cengage Learning.
Hubbard, Bill Jr. 2009. *American Boundaries: The Nation, The States and the Rectangular Survey*. Chicago, IL: University of Chicago Press.
Jeans, Dennis N. 1996. 'The Breakdown of Australia's First Rectangular Grid Survey', *Australian Geographical Studies*, 4, 119–28.
Johnson, Frank M. 1924. *The Rectangular System of Surveying*. Washington, DC: Department of the Interior, GLO.
Johnson, Hildegard B. 1957. 'Rational & Ecological Aspects of the Quarter Section', *Geographical Review*, July.
Johnson, Hildegard Binder. 1975. 'The US Land Survey as a Principle of Order', in Ralph E. Ehrenberg, ed. *Pattern and Process: Research in Historical Geography*. Washington, DC: Howard University Press.
Johnson, Hildegard Binder. 1976. *Order Upon the Land: The US Rectangular Survey and the Upper Mississippi Country*. London: Oxford University Press.
Kain, Roger J.P. and Elizabeth Baigent. 1992. *The Cadastral Map in the Service of the State: A History of Property Mapping*. Chicago, IL: The University of Chicago Press.
Kostof, S. 1991. *The City Shaped: Urban Patterns and Meanings Through History*. London: Thames & Hudson.
Libecap, Gary D. and Dean Lueck. 2009. 'The Demarcation of Land and the Role of Coordinating Institutions', NBER working paper no. 14962, May.
Libecap, Gary D., Adrian Lopes and Dean Lueck. 2009. 'Land Demarcation and Agriculture in 19th century California', working paper, University of California – Santa Barbara.
Libecap, Gary D., Dean Lueck and Trevor O'Grady (2010), 'Large Scale Institutional Changes: Land Demarcation within the British Empire', *Journal of Law and Economics*, forthcoming.
Linklater, Andro. 2002. *Measuring America*. London: Harper Collins.
Longley, P.A., M.F. Goodchild, D.J. Maguire and D.W. Rhind. 2005. *Geographic Information Systems and Science*. London: John Wiley and Sons.
McEntyre, John G. 1978. *Land Survey Systems*. New York: Wiley and Sons.
Marschner, Francis Joseph. 1960. 'Boundaries and Records in the Territory of Early Settlement from Canada to Florida', Agricultural Research Service USDA.
Marshall, Sir John H. 1931. *Mohenjo-Daro and the Indus Civilization*, Vol. 1. London: Arthur Probsthian.
Merrill, T.W. and Henry E. Smith. 2007. *Property: Principles and Policies*. New York: Foundation Press, Thomson/West.
Morris, A.E.J. 1994. *History of Urban Form: Before the Industrial Revolutions*. 3rd edn. Harlow: Pearson Education Limited.
Nelson, H.J. 1963. 'Townscapes of Mexico: An Example of the Regional Variation of Townscapes' *Economic Geography*, 39 (1), 74–83.
Pattison, William D. 1957a. 'Beginnings of the American Rectangular Land Survey System, 1784–1800', Ph.D. thesis, University of Chicago (Department of Geography), December.
Pattison, William D. 1957b. 'The Original Plan for an American Rectangular Land Survey, Surveying and Mapping', 21: 339–345.
Paullin, Charles O. 1932. *Atlas of the Historical Geography of the United States*. John K. Wright, ed. Washington, DC: Carnegie Institute of Washington and the American geographical society of New York.
Peters, William E. 1930. *Ohio Lands and their History*. 3rd edn. Athens, Oh: Lawhead Press.
Platt, R.S. 1929. 'Geography of a Sugar District: Mariel, Cuba', *Geographical Review*, 19 (4), 603–612.
Posner, Richard A. 2002. *Economic Analysis of the Law*. 6th edn. Boston, MA: Little, Brown.
Powell, J.M. 1970. *The Public Lands of Australia*. Oxford University Press.
Powell, John Wesley. 1878. 'Report on the Lands of the Arid Region of the United States with a More Detailed Account of the Land of Utah'. 45th Cong., 2nd Session, H. Doc. 73. Washington, DC: Government Printing Office.
Price, Edward T. 1995. *Dividing the Land: Early American Beginnings of Our Private Poperty Mosaic*. Chicago, IL: University of Chicago Press.
Shavell, Steven. 2007. *Foundations of Economic Analysis of Law*. Cambridge, MA: Harvard University Press.
Stanislawski, D. 1946. 'The Origin and Spread of the Grid-Pattern Town', *Geographical Review*, 36.
Stein, Mark C. 2008. *How the States Got Their Shapes*. Washington, DC: Smithsonian Press.
Stetson, C.W. 1935. *Four Mile Run Land Grants*. Washington, DC: Mimeoform Press.

Taylor, H.C. 1922. *Educational Significance of the Early Federal Land Ordinances*. New York: Teachers College, Columbia University, reprinted, Ayer Publishing, 1978.

Thompson, Barton H., Jr. and Paul Goldstein. 2006. *Property Law: Ownership, Use, and Conservation* New York: West.

Thrower, Norman W. 1966. *Original Survey and Land Subdivision*. Monograph Series of the American Association of Geographers. Chicago, IL: Rand McNally and Company.

Treat, Payson J. 1910. *The National Land System, 1785–1820*. New York: E.B. Treat, reprinted in 1967 and 2003.

Wainwright, Nicholas B. 1956. 'The Pennsylvania Magazine of History and Biography', 80, 164–226.

Webster, Pelatiah. 1791. *Political Essays on the Nature and Operation of Money, Public Finances, and Other Subjects: Published During the American War, and Continued Up to the Present Year, 1791*. Philadelphia, PA: Joseph Crukshank. *Early American Imprints*. 11 July 2008, http://docs.newsbank.com.proxy.library.ucsb.edu:2048/openurl?ctx_ver=z39.88-2004&rft_id=info:sid/iw.newsbank.com:EVANL.

White, C.A. 1983. *A History of the Rectangular Survey System*. Washington, DC: US Dept. of the Interior, Bureau of Land Management.

Williams, M. 1974. *The Making of the South Australian landscape: A Study in the Historical Geography of Australia*. London and New York: Academic Press.

14 Servitudes
Carol M. Rose

In popular democracies, any legal doctrine with the name 'servitude' has a strike against it. According to the law of servitudes, generally speaking, one property is subordinate to another for some specified set of purposes, presumably in a kind of 'service' to the other. As if these intimations of hierararchy were not enough, in the United States, the servitudes that most readily come to mind for most people are racially restrictive covenants, now unenforceable for decades but still remembered as a part of a race-ridden history. Servitudes raise misgivings for another reason as well: their reputation for head-breaking and deal-breaking complexity.

In spite of these caveats, servitudes are tremendously useful. They lie at the heart of sophisticated modern land developments as varied as shopping malls, common interest residential developments, and environmentally oriented land conservation arrangements. They now appear to be poised for an alternative life in intellectual property, where various devices have now come to the fore to enable promises to 'run' with software or information.[1]

None of these developments, of course, could have occurred without a considerable number of alterations in traditional servitude law, or without the development of a supporting legal institutional infrastructure. Perhaps the most dramatic signal of these changes is the arrival in 2000 of the American Law Institute's new 'Restatement' of servitude law, in which this non-radical assemblage of notable lawyers and academics endorsed a dramatic simplification and paring-back of the bristling complications of traditional servitude law.[2]

These developments raise interesting issues about the general evolution of property rights. A recurring story in property theory is that, roughly speaking, property rights evolve to meet changing needs for resource management. This narrative is implicit in John Locke's *Second Treatise of Government*, and explicit in Blackstone's *Commentaries*; it has been spelled out even more explicitly in the work of the modern economist Harold Demsetz as well as other modern economists.[3] The changes in servitude law would appear to confirm this evolutionary thesis.

Nevertheless, this happy sequence is not quite the whole story. In servitude law, the most visible evolutionary pattern begins with a great array of complex formal categories and then moves away from formalism toward seemingly simpler and more flexible guideposts. Simplification has made servitude law an increasingly pliable tool, stimulating new kinds of projects and servitude uses. Yet these new projects and uses have generated their own issues, once again re-complicating servitude law. Moreover, re-complications occur in predictable ways: they recreate, in different language, the reasoning behind the old and seemingly obfuscatory categories of traditional servitude law.

The plan of this chapter is to outline the ways in which certain kinds of concerns initially produced complex formal rules in traditional servitudes, as well as the ways in which newer property institutions – particularly record systems and expanded equity jurisprudence – made it possible to simplify the older rules. The chapter will then turn to three areas in which streamlined servitude doctrines assisted in great expansions of servitude use during the twentieth and now twenty-first centuries: racial residential restrictions, common interest communities, and conservation servitudes. In all these areas, however, newly-expanded servitude uses triggered a resurgence of traditional concerns, albeit in new guises. Along the way of describing these events, this chapter will take several excursions into areas in which servitudes cross-hatch with more general controversies in property law and theory, particularly issues about the role of information in property institutions, the transactions costs generated by the proliferation of property interests, and issues of flexibility and governance.

I. SERVITUDES AND THE WORRIES ABOUT THEM

Imagine a homeowner, Anne, who needs the neighbors' help if she is to make some desirable improvements to her property. First, her house is on a bit of a rise, and her driveway is very steep. She would like to re-route the driveway to a flatter spot, but she needs the consent of her neighbor Bart, because the new driveway would cut across a now-unused corner of his lot. Second, she wants to secure a view from her front window down across the valley, but here too she needs Bart's help, specifically some reassurance that he will either not plant trees or not let them grow so high as to impede her view. Finally, in a considerably bolder move, she wants all the neighbors on the block to agree to some aesthetic principles about housing decor, and to contribute funds to a neighborhood improvement association to which they will all belong.

Anne may get Bart and the other neighbors to agree, but that will not do her much good unless the agreements last beyond the ownership of the particular persons involved. Consider her wish for an unimpeded view: if Bart agrees but then sells to Charles, Charles might plant trees – or threaten to do so unless Anne pays a price reflecting her valuation on the view rather than his own disvalue in going tree-less. Without assurance about the future, Anne, fearing exactly this result, may never strike the deal with Bart and may forgo the window that would have delivered such a beautiful view. By the same token, Anne will want the *benefit* of her deal with Bart to outlast her own ownership of her house, so that if and when she sells her house, her purchaser Ned will also enjoy (and pay more for) the easement and the other amenities that Anne has negotiated.

Servitudes are the legal instruments that deal with Anne's desiderata. The central feature of servitudes is that *they enable current interest-holders to make commitments about their properties that will also bind and benefit future owners*. This central feature of servitude law – that servitudes 'run' to successive interest-holders in the property – is the source of both its advantages and its complications.

The greatest overall advantage of servitudes is that they give stability to property arrangements over both time and space. The time element is obvious – Anne can rely on Bart's successors to keep the trees in trim. This longterm control is of course most valuable with goods that have long duration, notably land, which is one reason why chattels are not often loaded with servitudes.[4] The space element time allows owners to have rights that control certain aspects of other people's property. Like landlord–tenant law – another example of temporally and spatially divided interests in property – servitudes permit owners to tailor the intensity of their control over land, and to layer their varying interests out beyond their own boundaries.

One way to envision the benefits of servitudes is to consider them in the light of what Robert Ellickson designated (with tongue in cheek) his 'highly sophisticated' division of land uses into events with small, medium, and large effects.[5] Individual owners need not worry much about 'small' events on the neighbor's property (e.g. planting a flower).[6] Where servitudes have a good deal of bite is with respect to medium events (e.g. covenants against loud music or garish nonconforming architecture). Servitudes are not normally very helpful for controlling large events (e.g. contributions to greenhouse gases), although even here covenants can have some effect, as in in restricting land uses to carbon-sequestering forestry uses. As we shall see, however, the extension of servitudes to large areas and events brings some additional problems.

Another way to envision the advantages of servitudes is to compare them to the most obvious alternative: in order to control the unwanted activities of neighbors, one might avoid having neighbors altogether. To secure her view, Anne might buy the whole swath of land that includes Bart's house. But large lot ownership means that one is stuck with a large parcel that one might not want to use intensely for one's self. The temptation would be to subdivide or rent out a portion with conditions (no loud parties, only trimmed trees). But how are these conditions to be imposed on the tenants, particularly if the tenants assign the lease to someone else? Once again, the answer is servitudes. Indeed, covenants running with the land began in England in the landlord–tenant context.

Given all these benefits of servitudes, it seems at first blush rather odd that they have generated so much hostility from so many quarters. Some nineteenth century judges sharply criticized them for stirring confusion about and tying up real estate,[7] and modern courts, even when upholding servitudes, routinely caution that the law disfavors any such constraints on free alienability.[8] Meanwhile, journalists and commentators treat the modern permutations of servitudes – especially those in gated communities – with barely disguised disapproval.[9]

Clearly servitudes raise issues aside from their usefulness to landowners. One way to get a sense of those issues is to observe the ways that earlier courts constrained efforts to create and enforce servitudes 'running with the land.'

II.   TRADITIONAL CONCERNS, TRADITIONAL FORMALITIES

A conventional law-and-economics approach would predict that the chief constraints on servitudes would address the usual sources of market failures – transactions costs and externalities. Servitude law did indeed confront those problems, but it divided the terrain in a somewhat different way. Some transaction costs derive from information issues, matters that were especially prominent in the doctrines that constrain servitudes. A second source of transaction costs revolves around what I will call 'renegotiability' – that is, protecting the capacity to renegotiate these instruments from a potentially disparate and fragmented set of interest-holders. Third party effects or externalities were generally a somewhat muted concern in traditional servitude law, but they could be swept in under a third set of constraining doctrines, those that effectively imposed a kind of cost/benefit or 'value' test on these instruments.

Taken as a whole, the legal concerns over servitudes fall into these three basic but often overlapping categories: information, renegotiability, and value.[10] Of these three, traditional servitude law paid most attention to the first, information, or, as it was often called, notice, with the other concerns playing a somewhat secondary role. In more modern law, information problems have been much relieved by the availability of recording, but in part as a result, renegotiability and value have loomed larger.

A. The Information or Notice Concern

Let us return to Anne and her neighbor Bart, and let us suppose that she has secured all the agreements that she sought. Traditional servitude law would have designated her interests in several distinct categories. First, her driveway across Bart's place would have been classed as an 'easement.' Second, Bart's agreement not to plant trees or to let any already-planted trees grow too high is more ambiguous: it could have been classed as a 'negative easement,' or it could have been classed as a 'covenant running with the land,' or, if enforced in a court of equity, as an 'equitable servitude.' Her last desideratum, a neighborhood agreement involving duties and dues, would almost certainly have been classed as a covenant or equitable servitude, but it would have been an especially problematic one.

This difference in nomenclature reveals a pattern in which the courts imposed increasingly intrusive limits on servitudes when moving from the driveway through the trees to the neighborhood organization. This basic pattern can be stated in the following general rule: *legal hedges arose in proportion to information dissipation.*

1. Information and easements – 'in gross' vs 'appurtenant'
The simplest case is the driveway, traditionally designated as an easement (or even a 'positive easement'). Anne's use of Bart's land here is information-rich and, correspondingly, it had few legal hedges. Bart can see it, and so can any potential purchaser of Bart's property. There are only two parties involved, and the easement runs across one parcel to an adjacent one, so that each owner knows where to find the other if either one (or a successor in interest) wishes to negotiate a release from or modification of the easement.

But suppose Anne buys an easement that is unattached to any property of hers; suppose, for example, she owns no property near a beach, and she purchases a right-of-way across Bart's waterfront property in order to get beach access. In this case, information has been lost about *who* owns the easement rights. Unlike Anne's driveway, this right-of-way does not lead to other property that Anne owns. If Bart or a successor changes his mind, it will be harder to find Anne to bargain for a release. It would be even harder if Anne could sell her easement to someone else, say Ned. How does anyone know anything about this this free-floating Ned?

The unattached easement is an example of information-dissipation, and the response of the common law judges was, first, to give this kind of easement a distinctive name, and, second, to add a limitation. They called it an 'easement in gross' to distinguish it from the adjacent 'easement appurtenant'; the chief consequence was that transfer of the easement in gross would destroy it. Bart presumably could remember who Anne was, and he could also tell his buyer, Charles, but he could not be expected to keep track if she alienated the right-of-way to someone else.

Modern law and economic scholarship might find judicial intervention in such cases unnecessary, since presumably Anne and Bart themselves would take into account the information problems that their future purchasers would encounter. Here as in other instances in servitude law that we shall see shortly,[11] however, the courts may not have entirely trusted the parties' ability to discount for clogs on alienability over the very long life that land would enjoy.

Nevertheless, courts did find ways to back away from the quite draconian rule against transfer of easements in gross. In keeping with the information dissipation model, courts modified the rule where the beneficiary was more likely to be observed. For example, if Ned bought Anne's easement in gross for business purposes, he would be likely to install features (like a ticket booth) that would make Ned identifiable. A good land record system can eliminate the who-owns-it problem altogether, and in the United States, where recording is routine, the rule against transfer of easements in gross is for all practical purposes a non-entity.[12]

The details of this highly technical sideshow would scarcely be worth mentioning if they did not convey a larger lesson: that information dissipation brings increased judicial supervision over servitudes, and conversely, that greater access to information reduces supervision.

2.   Easements vs. covenants and the 'horizontal privity' puzzle

A further area where information sensitivity appeared in traditional servitude law was the distinction between easements and covenants. Backtracking for a moment, the information dissipation in 'easements in gross' concerns the *identity* of the interest-holder, that non-landowning Anne (or Ned) who has the right to cross over Bart's property to get to the beach. A different kind of information loss, however, can occur about the *content* of the interest, and it is that information loss that drives the easement/covenant distinction.

Consider Anne's second desideratum: she wants a view over Bart's property, which entails an arrangement whereby Bart cannot maintain tall trees on his lot. The arrangement might even include some obligation on Bart's part, like clipping the trees back periodically. In a sense, the rights that Anne wants look like a classic easement: that is, she has the right to use the property of another, here for a view. But this use is information-impoverished, by comparison to Anne's using a driveway across Bart's lot. If Bart sells to Charles, Charles will be able to see Anne's driveway, but what notice does Charles have that Anne is entitled to *look* across his lot? Even worse, what notice does Charles have that he, Charles, is expected to clip the shrubs? The fact that the shrubs are clipped right now gives very little notice of any requirement that they *must* be clipped.

Taking Anne and Bart so far (and leaving out her ambitious plan for a neighborhood improvement association), we could then characterize their interests in the following way:

#1   Anne has the right to do X on Bart's land.
#2   Anne has the right to have Bart *not* do Y on Bart's land.
#3   Anne has the right to have Bart do Z on Bart's land.

In negotiations between themselves, Anne and Bart can make whatever contract arrangements of this sort they want, but the servitude issue is whether Bart's agreed-upon obligation will bind Charles and Charles' successors, the persons who agree to nothing but merely buy land once belonging to Bart. Here information to Charles (and his successors) becomes critical: only Interest #1 (i.e., the driveway) is likely to give clear signals of its content to Charles *et al.* Interests #2 (no tall trees) and #3 (trim the trees) are considerably more ambiguous from the physical nature of the property, and as we shall see shortly, #3 has other objections as well.

Neither American nor English courts would have treated an obligation to trim the trees – i.e. Interest #3 – as a mere easement. This obligation would be classed as a covenant, although some courts would not allow it run to Charles at all, refusing to enforce 'positive' covenants that required some kind of act or performance.[13] The English courts also treated the negative obligation #2 as a covenant. Why a covenant? Because in order to 'run with the land,' a covenant had to jump through more hoops than was the case for easements, and those hoops tended to demand more information.

One of the most important hoops acquired the unlovely name 'horizontal privity'; it required that the parties to the original agreement be in some kind of special relationship. In England, only landlords and tenants were considered to be in the appropriate relationship of horizontal privity; in the United States, courts expanded the relationship to include buyers and sellers.

The driving idea behind horizontal privity was to give information to later purchasers about the content of their covenant obligations. If covenants were initially hit upon by landlord and tenant, or by seller and buyer, the covenant upon which they agreed would be very likely to appear in some major document of transfer (a lease or a deed). The later purchaser or tenant would presumably ask to see these documents, and he would thus be notified of the covenant obligations they contained.[14]

One practical consequence of the horizontal privity requirement, however, was that agreements simply between neighbors would not pass the test, since no major documents of transfer memorialized them. American courts, with recording as a back-up information system, soon found ways to relax this rule in equity jurisprudence, as we will see in the unfortunate case of racially restrictive covenants. In practice, however, the horizontal privity rule is one reason, although certainly not the only one, that many neighborhood restrictions begin with a developer, who can incorporate the entire array of restrictions into the original deeds.[15] Another major reason, of course, is transactions costs: it is difficult for larger numbers of neighbors to come to agreement after the fact – the more complex the development, the less amenable to post-hoc agreement.[16]

With respect to the content of rights and obligations running with the land, then, what now seem formalistic anachronisms are instructive in showing the relevance of information. Particularly in England, where recording was not generally used, it was important that information-poor obligations be characterized as covenants, because one of the major features of the covenant designation was to push such claims into a more information-rich structure.

B.   The Renegotiability Concern

Information dissipation was clearly one of the chief concerns that drove traditional servitude law toward information-producing constraints. But a concern that the parties be able to modify or escape servitude obligations was another important consideration. The

easement-in-gross rule was itself was not only about information but also about renegotiability; if Bart could not find Anne or her successor, he might never be able to alter
or buy out her right to cross his property. Similarly, the easement/covenant distinction
had a renegotiability component; covenants generally can sweep in many more interest
holders than easements, and can include many more types of arrangements. Those features made covenants more supple but also available to larger and more heterogenous
groups than easements, and hence covenants raised special concerns for negotiation.

As with information, a general rule can be stated for renegotiability concerns in traditional servitude law: *legal hedges increased in proportion to potential renegotiability
breakdowns.*

As if horizontal privity were not grim enough as a requirement for covenants to run,
traditional covenants would not run with the land unless they satisfied another kind of
privity, commonly dubbed 'vertical.' In fact, vertical privity has little to do with enhancing information, the main thrust of so-called horizontal privity. Instead, vertical privity
is aimed at reining in the number and types of potential claimants with an interest in the
property of others, thus reducing transactions costs for change.

Unlike horizontal privity, which relates to the two property holders who originally
agree on a covenant, vertical privity governs the relationship between the original interest holders and their successors in interest – in the examples above, the relationship of
Anne to purchaser Ned, or of Bart to purchaser Charles. According to the vertical privity
doctrine, only a successor in interest who has some kind of interest in a predecessor's
land (like Ned, who purchased from Anne) could assert rights under a servitude. An even
more stringent requirement applied on the burdened side: Charles could not be bound
to fill obligations running with Bart's land unless Charles held exactly the same kind of
interest as Bart.

The result and probable motivation for this rule on the benefitted side was that it cut
back the numbers and types of interest-holders who could assert a claim to covenant
rights, concentrating enforcement rights in the hands of the persons most likely to value
them. Suppose, for example, that Anne and Bart and the neighbors are bound by a covenant to keep the house colors pastel. If Bart decides that he wants to paint the house
scarlet instead, he will have to negotiate a release with all those owners. But the vertical
privity rule, in a crude way, makes sure that he does not have to negotiate with others –
for example, the pedestrians and the local architectural society, who in a certain way also
'benefit' from his covenant obligation.

The concern for renegotiability links servitude law to a much-discussed issue in
modern property scholarship: the worry that excessive fragmentation of interests will
quash value-enhancing transactions and leave property unusable – a concern that has
now acquired the name of the 'anticommons.'[17] In an 'anticommons' scenario, an asset
is subject to so many and such diverse interests that the interest-holders cannot negotiate
their way to unified control of the asset. The anticommons standoff is especially problematic where a property would have higher value in some *new* use, since the fragmentation of interests impedes what would otherwise be a normal transition from less to more
valuable uses. The vertical privity requirement is one minor gesture through which traditional servitude law responded to the anticommons issue and the threat of an ensuing
transaction-cost-induced obsolescence.

A more direct and significant response to renegotiability problems – and the attendant threat of obsolescence – came from the treatment of covenants in courts of equity.[18] These courts developed a special kind of sunset rule for obsolescent covenants, in a doctrinal development known as 'changed circumstances.' Under this doctrine, if a covenant can be shown to have no further value for its purported beneficiaries, the courts can dispense with it. It is worth noting once again that the changed circumstance doctrine applies only to covenants and not to easements, for the very good reason that easements generally are one-on-one affairs. While easement renegotiations may give rise to bargaining breakdowns,[19] they are much less vulnerable to fragmentation than are covenants.

Despite the availability of 'changed circumstance' as an antifragmentation or renegotiability device, however, courts generally have applied the doctrine very sparingly, suggesting that they have been uneasy about assessing the value of landed interests in such way as to override objecting claimants.[20] Modern scholarship might suggest that liability rules could loosen this reluctance – i.e., permitting change if the party seeking change were willing to pay damages. Indeed, a provocative article by Ian Ayres and Eric Talley argued that liability rules even in small number contexts can eliminate strategic bargaining and force the two sides to reveal their true valuations.[21] Others have countered, however, that in the absence of serious transactions costs, liability rules undermine the stability of property rights, along with the investment incentives that security enhances.[22] Traditional courts were reluctant to allow a forced buyout even where transactions costs appeared high.[23] But if modern courts come to accept liability rules more freely, this attitude could change.[24]

C. The Value Concern – Chiefly of 'Touch and Concern'

In the case of the complicated covenants – as opposed to the generally less problematic easements – traditional doctrine revealed another concern: that servitudes be able to pass a very rough equivalent of a net value or cost-benefit test. Here too, the traditional doctrines addressed more than one concern at a time. The doctrine of changed circumstance, for example, is one that straddles questions of renegotiability and value. For all their reluctance in granting claims of changed circumstance, the courts, in admitting the doctrine at all, accepted the task of deciding whether a covenant has continuing value to the parties – a kind of Kaldor-Hicks assignment of the entitlement to the highest value user where transactions are impeded.

'Changed circumstance' is a doctrine that has survived the modern Restatement's radical surgery of servitude law, but another traditional value doctrine did not. That is the requirement that covenants 'touch and concern' land – a doctrine that may lose influence as the Restatement takes hold in the courts, but that is still useful as a chief example of the value concerns of traditional servitude law.

Unlike easements, covenants might potentially include anything that might be done on a property – no dancing, residency limited to Methodists, a jig must be done every Monday at 8 p.m. on the patio.[25] Parties can satisfy any of these special tastes by contract, but the touch and concern (T&C) doctrine constrained some of these purported covenants from running to subsequent interest-holders. The doctrine, however, was and still is a rather loose one. A literalistic view requires that the covenant relate to some physical use of land. But this is a highly restrictive interpretation, eliminating such useful obligations as dues to the property owners' association.

Modern law and economics scholarship is helpful in demonstrating a more generous and realistic understanding of the basic idea behind T&C, namely, permitting promises that enhance the joint value of two or more properties, while excluding promises that do not. One might ask how an owner might use the land if the two (or more) properties were in single ownership. The restriction passes the T&C test if the property burdened with a restriction (e.g., no scarlet paint) loses less than the benefitted property or properties gain (neighborhood color coordination). If a cognizable segment of the market conceivably consists of paint-color-conservative neighbors, the covenant passes the test.

A closely related way to understand the T&C requirement is to consider it in the light of a series of contracts: would two or more landowners be likely to cut a deal for the restriction in question?[26] If the restriction burdens one but benefits the other even more, the answer is likely to be yes, they would so agree, since the benefitted party could offer a suitable side payment to the burdened party; and with that answer, one can say that the original covenantors' deal did indeed touch and concern the respective properties, and that it binds subsequent owners as well, without the need for renegotiation. With these more generous interpretations of T&C, it is easy to see that promises to pay money are likely to have substantial value to common interest communities – otherwise all the lawn-mowing and re-roofing would have to be performed personally.[27] On the other hand, Bart's promise to pay for Anne's vacation in Hawaii has little relationship to the joint value of their properties – no T&C.

A deeper question about T&C, however, is why covenant law should be concerned about assessing value in covenants at all, particularly from the ex ante perspective taken by T&C. As with the potential information difficulties in so-called easements in gross,[28] a law and economics perspective might raise the question why the courts would not simply leave the issue to the parties themselves, who should discount any costs and benefits into their own calculations, and who should be left to enjoy (or suffer from) their own choices.

Richard Epstein argued this position very forcefully some years ago.[29] To be sure, a value or cost/benefit calculation operates as a surrogate for normal market transactions under conditions of market failure, including the informational problems that are so important in servitude law. Yet even if one treats information gaps as a market failure justifying intervention, nevertheless, as Epstein argued, the recording system should make the older information-forcing doctrines unnecessary, and T&C unnecessary too as a backstop for those doctrines.

The virtual evaporation of information concerns suggests that the role of T&C in American law may have lain elsewhere. Renegotiability concerns are a prominent candidate, since negotiation difficulties may hinder the movement of resources from lower-value to higher-value uses. As James Krier argued several decades ago, courts can use T&C to screen for value-enhancing servitudes, allowing them to continue without the need for onerous renegotiations with every transfer, while dropping generally unwanted servitudes whose enforcement would only provide a temptation to rent-seeking.[30] Things change over time, and as Uriel Reichman observed somewhat later, idiosyncratic requirements are likely to become obsolescent relatively rapidly.[31] Indeed, looked at ex post, as in the changed circumstance doctrine, the persistence of an obsolescent covenant signals that there has in fact been some obstacle to negotiation. Moreover, a doctrine like T&C, by confining servitudes to land-related parcels, also acted as an aid to renegotiability; like the vertical privity rule, it reduced the numbers of persons whose consent would be needed to alter a given servitude. In all those ways, a value doctrine like T&C moved in where renegotiability might have been an issue, notably in the large-number covenants as opposed to the small-number easements.

Having said all this, a more hardcore economic approach might apply the Epsteinian objection to renegotiation problems as well – that is, the possibility of future negotiation breakdown should be understood by the initial parties to a servitude transaction, and those parties should discount potential problems into the prices that they pay and receive for servitude rights. In the case of an exceedingly durable resource like land, however, it may be that the courts implicitly distrusted the discounting ability of present parties. Certainly their frequent remarks about servitudes' tendency to clog real estate suggest that view. Perhaps the courts saw themselves as longer-term stewards of a public weal that would continue after the contemporary parties' present-value considerations had reached a vanishing point. In that light, renegotiability limitations merged with a third standard concern in the economics of property, namely externality – here the external effects of servitudes on longterm potential future owners.[32]

Indeed, the traditional value doctrines – T&C and changed circumstance – to some degree did patrol for third party effects, but overt consideration of externalities was not a major feature of traditional servitude law. For example – a point we shall revisit with conservation servitudes – obsolete servitudes may adversely affect non-party neighbors; but the traditional doctrine of changed circumstance took neighborhood effects into account in only the most limited of ways, focusing instead on the continuing value of the servitudes to the parties themselves and not to third party owners.[33]

One place where third party effects did appear more openly was in some courts' reluctance to enforce covenants not to compete. The doctrinal rubric was T&C, but the courts' statements clearly showed an unwillingness to enforce an agreement that seemingly smacked of monopoly, with its attendant effect on consumers.[34] In subsequent decades, some antitrust scholarship, especially about retail sales price maintenance and territorial sale agreements, argued that these kinds of constraints may carry social benefits after all, since they can reduce free riding in advertising and service.[35] Perhaps not surprisingly, more recent servitude cases have relaxed the early rejection of covenants not to compete.[36] But the earlier decisions illustrate that courts thought that they needed to police servitudes at least minimally for these potential negative externalities.

One aspect of value still remains as something of a mystery, however: that is the rejection of covenants that bound parties to positive obligations, like clipping the hedges or, for that matter, paying money. These were covenants of which the purchasers were on notice, and which did not necessarily present either negotiation difficulties or apparent third party effects. Yet at least some courts rejected them.[37] Why not enforce them? The rationale may escape the usual law and economics rationales of information costs, transactions costs and externalities, which do indeed explain much of early servitude law. The closest analogy was the courts' antipathy to involuntary servitude, even if agreed upon by contract by sophisticated players like opera singers.[38] As we shall see, there is more than a trace of this attitude in more recent legal developments in common interest communities, where residents who should have known of their obligations still complain bitterly about them – and sometimes get the sympathetic attention of others.

D.   A Reprise of the Traditions from the Perspective of Modern Scholarship: the Numerus Clausus, Information, and the Courts of Equity

Traditional legal institutions permitted parties to create servitudes that would bind future owners, and to that extent they recognized the great usefulness of these devices. The overwhelming concern of the older servitude jurisprudence, however, was information: would purchasers and potential purchasers be on notice of these obligations? Most of the legal hedges around servitudes included at least some element of notice; even in the United States, where recording was routine in most states, courts borrowed the English information-forcing doctrines.

Since information was the dominating concern of the earlier servitude law, this body of law most directly engages modern property scholarship on information. In this area, the most influential work of the last several years has been by Thomas Merrill and Henry Smith, most notably their article on 'optimal standardization,' as embodied in the civil law doctrine of the Numerus Clausus or 'closed number.'[39] The Numerus Clausus is the idea that property instruments must be kept to a relatively limited number of standardized forms. Otherwise, to put it succinctly, potential purchasers have to look out for too many things. If parties A and B can make idiosyncratic arrangements that bind future users of their land, they increase the search costs for C, who now has to look out for 'fancy' arrangements as well as normal ones. Increased search costs in turn impede smooth market transfers, so that A and B's 'fancies' have external costs to others in the market. According to Merrill and Smith, the Numerus Clausus is thus a way to arrive at optimal standardization, allowing some flexibility but reducing information costs in the real estate market generally. In the case of servitudes, Numerus Clausus considerations are reflected in the way that different types of servitudes acquired their own categorical names, and that they had to meet differing requirements that also had categorical names of their own. Moreover, as we have seen, those requirements did respond to the density of information of any given servitude type.

Other authors, however, have argued that methods and institutions other than standard forms are perfectly capable of conveying information.[40] For land transfers, recording and registration systems are the most important of these institutions; with recordation, buyers and sellers can meaningfully allocate between themselves the responsibility for finding title information, either through warranty deeds (seller responsible) or quitclaim deeds (buyer responsible).

What, then, is the continuing role of the Numerus Clausus? Traditional servitude law suggests that the relationship between these information institutions is not entirely straightforward. Thus while U.S. law relaxed some of the British constraints on servitudes, distinctions reminiscent of Numerus Clausus thinking persisted in U.S. servitude law, some to this day, in spite of the American states' widespread use of recording.

One straw in the wind about this puzzling lag comes from civil law, the home of the Numerus Clausus. Civil law countries not only use the Numerus Clausus as an information system, but they also use registration systems. The latter are far more rigorous and reliable than recording systems in conveying title information, virtually guaranteeing the state of the title from the face of the registry.[41] Why use standard forms when the registration system itself is so complete?

The civil law example suggests that standardization and record systems may not be alternative information sources, but rather supplementary ones. The Numerus Clausus polices the civil law registration system ex ante, disallowing 'fancies' from registration and thus preventing the threat of information overload on the registration system itself.[42] The American recording system, on the other hand, makes few demands on the instruments recorded; like the joke about the elderly German Chancellor Hindenburg, on whose desk you supposedly could not leave your lunch without his signing it, the recording office will accept just about any document. Insofar as a Numerus Clausus appears in American law, it polices the recording system ex post (for salience) rather than ex ante (for recordability); it lets all kinds of documents in, but indicates that one need pay attention only to certain kinds of recorded interests.[43]

The Numerus Clausus and standardization more generally hint at another aspect of traditional servitude law, one involving the role of the courts. When courts apply standardized categories, they are most likely to take an ex ante posture, even if they do so artificially, asking whether some claimed interest met the formal requirements from the outset. The strictest and most formalistic of requirements of servitude law (the two privities, easements in gross) came from at-law jurisprudence, where decisions are made by juries. These facts in turn suggest that in the Anglo-American context Numerus Clausus-like features are at least in part an artifact of civil procedure, and particularly of the jury trial.

In instructing a jury, a court is apt to take a formalistic approach, giving the jury a laundry list of ex ante requirements to check off, rather than allowing these lay persons to make a holistic decision; such a decision might be too easily affected by unprofessional emotion and confusion. At equity, on the other hand, decisions are made by the judge alone, who is supposedly learned in the law and who is unswayed by advocates' obfuscations and appeals to emotion. The judge acting in equity can make a reasoned decision on matters ex post, asking directly, for example, whether the relevant parties did in fact have notice of their obligations, instead of reaching the notice question indirectly, through a formalistic, gatekeeping check-off list.

In the United States, unlike in England, the recording system allowed even at-law jurisprudence to relax at least one of the formalities of servitude law: U.S. courts allowed horizontal privity to include not only landlords and tenants but also sellers and buyers, since all could record their interests. This relaxation greatly extended the use of servitudes in new residential developments. But perhaps equally important, the recording system permitted U.S. courts to take equity's relaxed approach to information in a much larger array of cases, because through recording the parties could or did have information about the state of obligations that ran with title. As we shall see, this larger set of cases included some of the most unattractive of all servitudes, namely a widely-used type of racially restrictive covenant.

As was noted above, it has been something of a puzzle why courts in the United States retained some of the British formal categories at all, given the wide use of recording. One possible answer is that there was little pressure to change because the U.S. courts in fact ceased to deploy those formalities in any significant manner. Instead, as we shall see in the next section, U.S. courts used equity jurisprudence and the recording system to dispense with the formal requirements – perhaps reducing any major effort to change the doctrines.

III. PUSHING THE ENVELOPE: NEW USES OF SERVITUDES, OLD AND NEW WORRIES ABOUT THEM

As we have seen, several concerns drove traditional servitude law toward complexity – most notably to assure information, especially to potentially burdened parties, but also to some degree to reduce renegotiation costs, and to assure that at the end of the day servitude obligations resulted in net positive values, taking into account primarily the parties involved but sometimes also third parties. The doctrines that spoke to those concerns were sometimes incomplete and often redundant. But by addressing the problem areas of information, renegotiability and value, traditional doctrines in fact enabled servitudes to expand, meeting the needs of property owners under conditions where their own interests became more complex and layered.

Moreover, when alternative institutions – especially recording systems and equity jurisprudence – addressed these same concerns, traditional servitude doctrine could relax and simplify. But the same growing institutional capacity that made doctrinal streamlining possible has had another consequence as well: people started to deploy servitudes' purposes far beyond their earlier uses.

The next sections will explore three areas in which servitudes expanded quite dramatically during the twentieth century, and in two of the three cases continue to do so in the twenty-first. All of these expansions depended on modifications of older servitude law, but they all also raised considerable uneasiness, both for the traditional reasons and for some new twists on those reasons. The first case is the nasty but thankfully fairly short-lived history of racially restrictive covenants, which more or less began and ended in the first half of the twentieth century. The second case is the emergence of large private communities, generally a development after the Second World War. The third and most recent case is the growth of conservation easements for environmental and historic preservation purposes. As with traditional servitude law, these more recent extensions give ample opportunity to pause to consider the perspectives of modern property scholarship on this dynamic area of the law.

A.   The Short Unhappy Life of Enforceable Racially Restrictive Covenants

Racially restrictive covenants on residential property began to emerge in noticeable numbers in the United States just after the turn of the twentieth century, largely in urban areas. Their advent coincided with the so-called City Beautiful movement, a mix of efforts to clean up cities and make them both functional and attractive. Many early twentieth-century urban and suburban residential developers thought that racial restrictions were a part of that mix, and in older deeds one finds racial restrictions listed matter-of-factly alongside restrictions on such matters as setback, design, or uses.[44]

The chief function of racial covenants was to keep African Americans (and to a lesser extent Asians) out of white neighborhoods. They shared the stage for a time with racial zoning, but in 1917 the United States Supreme Court ruled that racial zoning was unconstitutional, because it was too great a governmental intrusion on private property.[45] Thereafter, racially restrictive covenants – as ostensibly private arrangements – seemed to be the only safe legal alternative to assure neighborhood segregation. As a consequence, racial covenants picked up considerably in the 1920s, fueled then and later by the avid support of real estate professionals.

In the 1920s as well, a new form of racial covenant began to emerge, especially in older, built-out cities that were often the destination of newly-urbanizing minority migrants. This new form of covenant was the neighborhood agreement, created not by a developer at the time of platting new homes, but rather by enterprising residents in existing neighborhoods. It was not always easy to get other neighbors to join, however. Historian Wendy Plotkin's groundbreaking research on racial covenants in Chicago points out that these arrangements often suffered from a first-mover problem: no one wanted to sign first, taking the risk of getting stuck with an unsaleable property if others did not join in as the neighborhood 'turned.'[46]

According to Plotkin, the most successful neighborhood covenant drives were organized by what would now be called 'norm entrepreneurs,' including the University of Chicago on the city's south side.[47] Real estate professionals also assisted, taking the view that racial covenants enhanced neighborhood stability and enhanced property values for their customers. The National Association of Real Estate Boards devised a model neighborhood racial covenant, and it incorporated racial steering into its realtors' code of ethics.[48] In the 1930s, another major player emerged: the new Federal Housing Administration, which included racially restrictive covenants as one of the desiderata for underwriting home loans.[49]

None of the resident-driven neighborhood racial covenants might have taken hold, however, if the courts had not been willing to overlook a legal problem that distinguished them from the developer-created covenants. Even though neighbor covenants were recorded, they lacked horizontal privity, the requirement that the originators be in a special relationship that would force the covenant information into a major real estate transfer document, like a deed or a lease. In the absence of this formal criterion, the creators of neighborhood racial covenants tried to gussy them up with much formal language of 'whereas' and 'hereto' and 'in consideration of the premises.' [50]

While courts occasionally noted the irregular origins of these neighborhood covenants, they accepted them nonetheless, ironically enough, on the basis of equity jurisprudence.[51] So long as a complaining party requested an injunction (an equitable remedy) to enforce the racial covenant, the courts asked only about notice to the purchaser of the covenanted property – and since the recording system normally gave record notice, albeit of a then-unconventional document, the racial covenant was enforceable. The courts' willingness to grant equitable remedies for these neighbor-created racial restrictions illustrates a point made earlier: formal servitude requirements may have lingered so long in U.S. law because they could be evaded so easily as to lose practical importance.[52] As a legal matter, the courts in equity recognized that the recording system had effectively solved the information issue that horizontal privity had attempted to address. But unfortunately, neighborhood racial covenants were an early beneficiary.

In solving the information problem, recording and equity jurisprudence made servitudes easier to use. Easy use, however, generated two other problems, one chiefly about renegotiability and the other and more important one about value. To begin with renegotiability: relaxation of the servitude rules meant that racial covenants now became widely available to older urban neighborhoods, which were often those most directly in the path of minority expansion, and whose residents were undoubtedly the most panicky.[53]

But once the covenants were in place, white owners could eventually find themselves with houses that no other white purchasers would buy, and that the owners were legally barred from selling to minority purchasers. In a number of neighborhoods, racial covenants appear to have fallen apart by lack of enforcement, a kind of tacit consent by the fleeing white owners. In others, some white owners struggled to extricate themselves from the covenants while their neighbors insisted on enforcement.[54] Defecting owners sought a familiar judicial solution: they argued that 'changed circumstances' should make the covenants unenforceable.[55]

As usual, these cases raised an underlying issue of continuing value to the parties ostensibly benefitting from the racial servitudes. But a more important value problem also emerged, if only very faintly – that is, value, or rather disvalue, to non-parties. This other kind of value issue emerged at least in part as a result of the very relaxation of formalities that propelled the expanded use of racial covenants. As one judge noted in the mid-1940s, the horizontal privity rule had limited covenants to whatever land a developer included in his plan. But neighborhood covenants had no such limits, and they could potentially spread across great swaths of urban geography.[56]

Size, however, carries third-party implications that smaller sets of restrictions do not: very widespread covenants threaten seriously to limit the options of excluded groups. In an era of expanding African American urbanization, racial covenants became a source of acute resentment and a target of civil rights activism, particularly as African-American veterans returned from service in the Second World War. A few judges started to listen, arguing that third party effects should be considered in enforcement cases.[57]

As if to put an exclamation point on the issue of size, Levittown, an immense new postwar housing development on Long Island, included racially restrictive covenants in its first sales in late 1947.[58] These developer-created covenants had no horizontal privity problems. But as the neighborhood agreements had done previously, Levittown extended racial covenants over a very large area, and strongly hinted that much more was to come: Levitt's eyepopping new development was a portent of the mass-produced subdivisions that were soon to surround cities all over the United States. Less than a year after the first Levittown house went on sale, the United States Supreme Court had decided, in *Shelley v. Kraemer* (1948), that judicial enforcement of privately-created racially restrictive covenants was not simply private but instead counted as state action, in violation of the Constitutional prohibition on racial discrimination by governmental bodies.[59]

Much ink has been spilled over the constitutional basis of *Shelley*, particularly its interpretation of what counts as 'state action.' But from a property perspective, the case showed the re-emergence of third-party effects in servitude jurisprudence, somewhat akin to older courts' refusal to enforce covenants not to compete. In the case of racial covenants, the sheer scale of servitude coverage may well have played a role in bringing third-party effects to the fore, not only in tightening minority housing but also in handing a ready-made issue to the United States' adversaries in an emerging Cold War. The large scale of racial covenants, in turn, had rested in part on the judicial willingness to relax the rules on their behalf.

As befits an issue with such tremendous moral, political and historical overtones in American law, modern law and economics scholarship gives rise to further reflections on racially restrictive covenants. Just as modern antitrust scholars have questioned the old constraints on covenants not to compete, other scholars have reconsidered racial restrictions in the light of public choice and game theory, opening up some issues that await further exploration.

First, legal scholar David Bernstein and economist William Fischel, in arguing that racial zoning would have been much more damaging than racial covenants, implicitly question whether racial covenants really did have substantial third party effects. Under racial servitudes, unlike racial zoning, the enforcement costs of neighborhood segregation could not be externalized onto the public at large. The neighbors had to do their own enforcing, the two scholars argue, and in many cases they did not bother.[60] Meanwhile, it might be added, there were arbitrage agents on the other side, who made money by 'blockbusting' servitude-laden white neighborhoods. In the light of these pressures, there is some question how much difference racial covenants really made to minority housing opportunities, despite the outcry about them prior to *Shelley*.

A second set of issues derive from game theory as well as norm theory, and they raise the question whether racial covenants made any difference to *segregation* (as opposed to simply the quantity of minority housing). Housing segregation certainly did not halt when racial servitudes became unenforceable. In one explanation, Thomas Schelling's influential thought experiment of some years ago illustrated that a quite modest taste for discrimination can result in a highly segregated residential pattern.[61] If that is the case, then legal enforcement of racial servitudes may well have been peripheral to neighborhood segregation all along.

Similarly, Richard Brooks has pointed out that racial covenants continued to be incorporated into deeds for some time after *Shelley* made them unenforceable, suggesting that servitudes drew their efficacy from their ability to signal neighbor preferences, rather than from their hardball litigation potential. His position implies that segregation depended more on social norms than on the availability of legal enforcement.[62] Along the same lines, Lior Strahilevitz has argued that persons intent on segregation can find other signaling devices, thus making explicit racial servitudes less important.[63] He focuses on the prevalence of non-golf-playing residents in golf-course-centered planned communities, and he argues that a golf course may function as a signal that a particular community is likely to have few minority members.

All these new scholarly perspectives suggest that, as with the older courts' adverse reaction to covenants not to compete, the external third party effects of racial servitudes might have been exaggerated with respect to housing, although not with respect to profound dignitary harms. This is obviously a controversial position. But however the future debates evolve on that question, it is clear that since *Shelley*, the courts' attitude to third party effects has changed. As servitudes have spread out into new uses, for better or for worse, the relatively limited issues of 'touch-and-concern' and 'changed circumstance' have morphed into much more expansive doctrines like 'reasonableness' and 'public policy.'

B. Common Interest Communities, or, Don't even Think about Leaving your Trash Cans in front of the Garage

Over the last decade, a substantial percentage of the new housing built in the United States has been structured in common interest communities (CICs), a type of development whose popularity, it appears, can only be curbed by more general slumps in real estate.[64] The legal foundation of each CIC is a recorded 'declaration' – a more or less elaborate set of servitudes that forms the legal basis for the ongoing rights and obligations of the property owners.

In some ways the CIC declaration is quite typical of servitudes more generally: the declaration allows each property owner to control her own individual residence most intensely, but she has a layered set of more specific interests in the properties of her neighbors and of the community as a whole, and in turn, they have layered interests in her property. What is different about the CIC servitudes is, first, their allocation of self-government to the property owners, and, second, the potential size and complexity of the communities so governed. While CICs vary greatly in size, the larger ones may include thousands of individual units, along with common areas like lawns, clubhouses and swimming pools. All aspects of the properties may be subject to a great array of rules about physical configurations (e.g. size of structure, material color, vegetation), and even the behavior of the residents (e.g. where to park, when not to play musical instruments).

Arrangements with this level of complexity require management, and in order for any kind of CIC to develop, servitudes too had to evolve, particularly to overcome the negotiation impasses that would be encountered if every decision required unanimity. One might regard the evolution of CIC servitudes as a more benign version of the evolution of racial covenants: it is a story of growing confidence in property institutions – notably recording and equity jurisprudence – followed by relaxation of the formal constraints on servitudes, then followed by vastly expanded use of these servitudes, and finally followed by new forms of constraints that to some degree mimic the old ones. There are differences in these stories, however. Public intervention into racially restrictive covenants involved only a single and highly freighted issue. Common interest communities take many more shapes and present a considerably more diverse array of controls on land uses and property owners, and not surprisingly, as we shall see, there is much more debate about the appropriateness of public intervention into their workings.

Having said that, however, CICs are widely disliked both in popular and academic literature, in spite of, or perhaps because of, the popularity they enjoy with home purchasers. A number of academics argue that, like the widespread racial covenants of an earlier day, the now-proliferating CICs are so prevalent as to inflict harm on the larger public, though usually for different reasons. One frequent argument is that CICs and especially large gated communities remove resources and empathy from the larger community. The insiders, it is said, refuse to take their share of problem land uses and public services; meanwhile they assess themselves for nice playgrounds while they refuse to vote for bond issues for city parks.[65]

This position about external harm has had an echo in some cases about CICs. One legacy of *Shelley v. Kraemer* is that some courts have been willing to impose loosely-defined constraints of 'public policy' on CICs,[66] particularly nullifying CIC efforts to exclude various kinds of social service group homes.[67] As with *Shelley*, the intuition appears to be that if an institution becomes really large or widespread, it has public policy implications, if only by limiting opportunities for those on the outside. This view, however, is sharply opposed by libertarian thinkers, who argue that CICs are no different from any other kind of property with respect to external effects, and that free market transactions are preferable to public intervention for avoiding externalities.[68] In any event, CICs come in great varieties, and because they can serve such varied interests they arguably expand choices rather than contracting them.

Even richer developments in servitude law, however, have not revolved around CICs' external effects, but rather around their internal organization, and especially the critically important emergence of governance mechanisms to overcome negotiation problems. If there is a single case that can be said to have made common interest communities legally plausible, it is *Neponsit Property Owners' Association v. Emigrant Industrial Savings Bank* (1938).[69] *Neponsit* was a private beach community near New York City; its developer organized it in such a way as to require each homeowner to pay dues, initially to the developer but later to a Property Owners' Association. This now entirely recognizable arrangement was duly recorded and annotated in all the owners' deeds, but it was still problematic under traditional servitude law. The reasons were, first, because the promise to pay money did not 'touch and concern' land; and, second, because the Property Owners' Association itself owned no land and thus under the 'vertical privity' constraint could not claim the benefit of a servitude.

The development documents, however, structured unpaid dues not as a personal debt but rather as a lien against the property – that is to say, an equitable remedy. Consequently, when the Bank acquired the property and refused to pay unpaid dues, the New York Court of Appeals could reconsider the formalities of the common law in the more direct fashion of equity jurisprudence. It disposed of the 'touch and concern' problem by reasoning that dues payment was a value-enhancing assurance that the streets and beach would be maintained. And it disposed of the vertical privity issue by noting that the Property Owners' Association actually represented the homeowners – close enough to ownership to claim the right to benefit from the Bank's servitude obligations.[70]

With the *Neponsit* case, CICs were ready for prime time, at least legally, although in fact prime time did not arrive until the 1970s, when Florida and California real estate developers began to make extensive use of these new residential arrangements.[71] Since that time, CICs have expanded dramatically, including everything from urban apartments to horse- or golf-centered single-family developments, enormous gated communities supposedly full of right-wing Republicans and small co-housing communities supposedly full of left-wing Democrats. But legally, the *Neponsit* case was an important element in making all these possible. After *Neponsit*, developers could create residential communities that entailed regular assessments and homeowner associations for management, thus greatly enhancing the CICs' ability to handle ongoing maintenance, common expenses, and any other common concerns.[72] In a dramatic departure from the renegotiability problems of earlier servitudes, CICs could now operate on the basis of representation and something less than unanimity in decisionmaking, effectively becoming private governments: as Richard Epstein has described them, the original covenants – recorded, of course – act as a kind of constitution, the rules and rule changes act as legislation, and the dues serve as taxes.[73]

CICs thus illustrate another case where relaxation of the servitude rules opened the door to a whole new type of real estate structure. But these new organizational structures have created tensions of their own, and some are very familiar from earlier servitude law – particularly concerns about value. One much reported complaint is that boards are simply too intrusive, although it seems likely that certain highly publicized instances

– e.g., about pets, flags, and kissing your boyfriend in your car – overstate this issue.[74] Nevertheless, legal scholar Paula Franzese argues in effect that CICs' proliferation of rules and regulations exceeds what one might call 'optimal regimentation,' and that CICs would be more peaceable and better-managed with fewer rules and more room for the development of community norms.[75]

These complaints require some explanation, since one might have expected developers to supply a variety of CIC governance arrangements to match varying tastes for controls. One explanation is that developers may stick with a limited number of tried-and-true rule structures out of caution about old judicial doctrines, regulatory demands, and perhaps especially the insistence of financial institutions on standardized CIC organizational components.[76] But if that is so, then this standardization, like a new iteration of the Numerus Clausus, might reduce variety but also economize on information costs – and it should mean that purchasers ought to know what they are getting into in CICs.

Do purchasers know what they are getting into? In the late 1980s, a very high percentage of CIC purchasers appeared to have had only a dim understanding of covenants and POA governance,[77] perhaps suggesting that at least as of that time standard forms that were familiar to judges, public officials and financial officers were not so well known to consumers. Generally, however, the courts are not very sympathetic to residents' complaints about POA activities, taking the position that purchasers either knew or should have known about the servitudes and POA arrangements, and they signed on anyway.[78]

There are indeed exceptions to this position, and they suggest some patterns familiar from more traditional covenant law. For one thing, the courts give considerable latitude to servitude obligations that are information-rich, while riding herd on those that are information-poor. CIC servitudes bind property owners to follow not only the 'constitutional' servitudes of the recorded declaration, but also POAs' 'legislative' bylaw changes and rule interpretations. Information about the original servitudes is relatively thick, but information about ongoing governance – rule changes and POA interpretations – is necessarily much thinner; the latter cannot be perused ex ante, and thus they put the property owner at a greater potential risk. Whether or not purchasers should know more than they do about basic governance patterns, it may overtax human foresight to anticipate the changes in circumstance that occasion changes in CIC rules – whether these circumstances be the increasing burden of obsolescent older rules,[79] or simply changes in the overall wishes of the community.

Notice that with respect to ongoing governance, CICs differ both from landlord–tenant relations and from public governments. A landlord is constrained by market demand for his own property, and he is unlikely to adopt rules that tenants find unpalatable or unreasonable. A public government passes regulations that affect other people's property, but it has to follow constitutional provisions that prevent it from, say, stopping religious expression or confiscating residents' property. But in a POA, a majority group might well be willing to interfere with the interests of a minority, without either the landlord's economic constraints or the municipality's constitutional ones.[80] An early case from Florida gave an example; in what was obviously a heated internal battle, the condominium association held a referendum and thereafter banned the use of liquor in the clubhouse, apparently much to the dismay of the clubhouse drinkers.[81] Under such circumstances, modern courts have in effect replayed the concerns of the traditional ones, especially the concern for information. The name of the review has changed to 'reasonableness,' but on the whole, the underlying inquiry is whether, given the basic character of the CIC, a resident could have expected rule changes of this sort.[82]

As with traditional T&C review, then, reasonableness review of CICs generally has a link to information issues, but also to value issues. What purchasers knew or could have expected provides the frame for judicial policing of CIC activities. As to value, these decisions generally stress fairness rather than a direct cost/benefit calculation, but cost/benefit re-emerges when one considers CICs taken as a collectivity. The availability of external post-hoc readjustments may make CICs more palatable to a larger market; potential purchasers are less likely to be frightened away from this form of residential arrangement, knowing that if push comes to shove a court can intervene to correct association overreaching.

Perhaps most controversial is the claim that CICs, like the racial restrictions at issue in *Shelley v. Kraemer*, are now such a dominant form of new housing that they actually limit free choice – and hence, for the sake of the residents themselves, CICs require external supervision based on values of the larger community. Some state legislatures and the U.S. Congress appear to echo this underlying idea, insofar as they have limited CIC restrictions on displays of flags and signs, and, in the case of California, CIC restrictions on pets.[83] The flag laws might be read as a response to something exceptional, a kind of legislative 'changed circumstance' doctrine in the wake of 9/11. But some legal commentators take a more broad-brush approach, arguing that CICs are comparable to public governments, and that as such they should be subject to constitutional restraints, particularly on issues of speech and assembly.[84] Legal scholar Gregory Alexander has called for wide-ranging judicial intervention into CIC governance on the related but somewhat unusual ground that it is needed for the preservation of republican governance within the community itself.[85]

Not surprisingly, other scholars hotly contest the idea that CICs' internal governance requires supervision based on external values, particularly those scholars who have more confidence in the market's ability to supply various types of CICs and in consumers' ability to understand and choose the type they want. From a law-and-economics standpoint, perhaps the most interesting defense is that certain structural features make CICs self-correcting with respect to the risk of arbitrary behavior. Some arguments along these lines are the following: developers have an ex ante incentive to structure the appropriate mixes of security and flexibility;[86] the much-decried homogeneity of CICs itself tends to reduce internal conflict;[87] the difficulty of exit, like bilateral monopoly, forces participants into tit-for-tat cooperative solutions;[88] and finally, as a matter of comparative institutional competence, courts are not obviously better than the residents at finding appropriate solutions in most instances,[89] and overmuch judicialization could even undermine CICs' ability to make the dynamic changes that reduce conflicts over the long run.[90]

At bottom, these controversies reflect an ongoing debate about whether *value* should be an independent basis for intervention into the operation of servitudes. The CIC form ratified by *Neponsit* would appear to solve both the information and renegotiability problems so typical of servitudes. But if the CIC declaration informs residents what to expect, and if POA governance overcomes transactions costs and holdouts, what need is there to intervene on the basis of some external weighing of costs and benefits? Here again, the persistence of the value issue suggests the pattern in which elegant legal modifications invite new extensions of covenants, and new extensions then re-raise the older concerns. *Neponsit*, while a large planned community in its day, was a much simpler and smaller community than the modern CICs like Columbia, Maryland or Sun City, Arizona.[91] The sheer size, complexity and pervasiveness of modern CICs invites a value based or cost/benefit critique, both with respect to externalities and with respect to internal operations. While some of these critiques may be overblown, the growth and development of modern CICs suggests that servitude uses can evolve and expand in such a way that they constantly re-invigorate questions into their value, both to the participants over time and to outsiders.

C.   Conservation Servitudes and the Shadow of the Future

Conservation servitudes, like CIC declarations, are a product of the post WWII era, and they may have their roots in the same frenetic real estate development that marked those years. As new housing developments marched out into the suburbs, historic properties were left behind to decay – and to be removed, in part by private enterpreneurs (who were encouraged by favorable tax treatment of demolitions), and in part by governmentally-sponsored roadbuilding and urban renewal projects. The same real estate development frenzy appeared to be eating up once-rural fields and forests and replacing them with tract homes. Those interested in conservation of historic structures and wildlands were a large and diffuse group, and this pattern meant that conservation had at least some public-good characteristics.[92] But certain dramatic events particularly focused public attention, among others the demolition of the iconic Penn Station in New York in 1964, and of course Earth Day in 1970.

Governments began their own conservation programs as early as the nineteenth century parks, later adding historic preservation ordinances and environmental planning and conservation measures. But insofar as these measures affected private property, governmental bodies have had to be sensitive to takings claims from aggrieved landowners. One potential solution arrived in the 1970s: this was to bifurcate land ownership from development rights, and to offer landowners a form of compensation in the form of transferable development rights or, as they came to be known, TDRs. Under a TDR program, an owner who was prohibited from building on a historic site or natural area instead got the right to exceed the normal density limits elsewhere, or even to transfer his development rights to someone else.[93] There was something of a 'funny money' aspect to TDRs, since their value depended on the density limits themselves, but they introduced a separation between land ownership and development rights that was then picked up in conservation servitidudes.

The conservation servitude, like the TDR, is a legal device for separating land ownership from development rights. One who buys a conservation servitude leaves the land ownership with the original owner, who then may sell the underlying land to another – but without the development rights. These devices have become an extraordinarily successful way to pump private money into conservation, and their size and numbers have grown dramatically in the last few years.[94] They are favorably cited by free market environmentalists, who believe that private investment and voluntary agreements will do more to preserve environmental goods than government ever can.[95] But they have also been favored by governments, notably through tax code provisions that treat the dedication of a perpetual conservation easement as a charitable donation.[96] Thus a ranch owner unhappy about seeing the old family spread turn into ranchettes can work with a conservation group or governmental agency to donate a conservation easement, and then take the tax deduction or the payment, knowing that the land can stay in ranching uses forever, or at least as close to forever as anything can be in property law.[97] Developers too find conservation servitudes a useful way to finance amenity values, although conservation easements for golf courses, for example, have raised some red flags.[98] But, as legal scholar Barton Thompson argues, all these motivations suggest that conservation servitudes mix public goods characteristics with private ones[99] – and, as we shall see, that fact raises uneasiness about them from quite different directions.

Needless to say, a recording or registration system is critical to negative servitudes of this kind. From the physical character of a property alone it would be well-nigh impossible to discern a servitude requiring that an old structure *not* be altered or a natural area *not* be developed.[100] But quite aside from recording, conservation easements could not exist without relaxations of several of the formal requirements of earlier servitude law. Taken together, the single most important feature of these relaxations is that the conservation easement can be enforced even though there is no benefitted land.[101]

Why does this matter? There are three main reasons: first, the linkage of a servitude to benefitted land conveys information about the character of the servitude obligations. Second, this linkage also reveals the identity of claimants and reduces their numbers, thus preserving renegotiability. And third, the presence of some benefitted land is a benchmark that the servitude has continuing value. Traditional requirements (especially easement in gross rules, along with touch and concern) supported those considerations, and while the modern conservation easement has been liberated from the old rules, it has not been liberated altogether from the concerns that underlay them – information, renegotiability, and value.

Recording should be sufficient to give everyone sufficient information about the content of servitude rights and obligations, as well as the identity of the interest-holders. But renegotiability is another matter: if no benefitted land is required, people from anywhere in the world may contribute to a conservation easement in, say, an Amazon-region forest, and they then may claim enforcement rights against alterations. Modern conservation servitude legislation does attempt to deal with this potentially extreme fragmentation of interests: it limits ownership of conservation easements to governmental bodies and charitable conservation organizations.[102] These limitations sharply reduce the numbers and kinds of rights-holders in conservation servitudes and, like the old vertical privity rules, they mean that enforcement rights will generally be centralized in the kinds of organization that one would normally expect to hold them and to protect them over time.

But what about value? What is to assure the original value of a conservation easement, and, perhaps more important, what is to assure that it does not outlive its value, inflicting costs not only on the parties directly involved but also on third parties? Views on this issue diverge dramatically, with some arguing that conservation servitudes are too rigid and too likely to cause problems of obsolescence, and others arguing that these servitudes are too loose and too easily abandoned prematurely. In the sharpest attack to date on conservation servitudes, Julia Mahoney takes the too-rigid position; she argues that environmental conditions change over time, as do tastes and knowledge about them, making it especially likely that conservation servitudes will one day outlive their useful-ness – precisely because they are supposed to be 'permanent.'[103] She argues further that obsolete conservation servitudes could create substantial externalities for future genera-tions, damaging third parties who would have benefitted from alternative uses of these restricted properties (e.g., for housing), but who have no leverage to shake these restric-tions loose from their outmoded aims.[104]

A central though unstated element in Mahoney's obsolescence argument, however, is that, in effect, the chief measure to solve the renegotiability problem – limiting owner-ship to governmental bodies and conservation groups – has backfired, creating another kind of renegotiability problem that makes these servitudes difficult to modify and hence susceptible to inescapable losses of value. The nub of the argument is that governments and nonprofit organizations are not good long-term decision-makers about property. The reasons are that these bodies spend other people's money, respond overmuch to feckless environmentalist constituencies, and pay insufficient attention to the costs that future third parties will have to bear if a low-value conservation area blocks newer uses or higher-value development.[105]

Other commentators point out, however, that existing servitude law has answers to the obsolescence issue, including that old standby, the doctrine of changed circum-stances, not to speak of the newer rubric of 'public policy.'[106] But more importantly, the counterargument is that if public and nonprofit groups have weaknesses as owners, those weaknesses cut in the opposite direction, permitting conservation servitudes to be neglected, altered or abandoned too freely rather than too parsimoniously, all on behalf of development interests.[107] Aside from these familiar public choice points, another reason might be drawn from traditional servitude law: if there is no benefitted land, there is also no benefitted landowner who might sharpen the resistance to management lapses and alterations of obligations.

These issues have given rise to a variety of proposals for supervising and safeguard-ing the operation and especially the potential termination of conservation servitudes. Among others, these proposals have focused on third party interventions in the form of certification boards, public input, and judicial weighing of costs and benefits, *inter alia*; perhaps most interesting for law-and-economics scholars is the re-emergence of pro-posed liability rules in the form of eminent domain for extinguishment.[108]

In the larger view, critiques of conservation servitudes from all sides suggest that these devices are still in quest of an appropriately-developed property infrastructure. Among other things, some substitute needs to be found for 'benefitted land,' in order to assure that these servitudes are valuable in the first place (particularly to the public that is subsi-dizing them), that they can be protected over time when they continue to be valuable, and that they can be let go when they become outmoded. In this sense of an underdeveloped property infrastructure, conservation easements give a preview of what may be the next frontier in servitude law – that is, servitudes in software and electronically-distributed content that is dedicated to the public but with certain supposedly perpetual limitations. These new servitudes are, if anything, even more deracinated from 'benefitted property' than are conservation servitudes, which normally have some local connections,[109] and they too are showing growing pains that resemble the newer land-based servitudes for conservation purposes. And, as Molly Van Houweling argues, they too are unlikely to shake off the concerns of traditional servitude law.[110]

CONCLUSION

In many ways, the modern history of servitudes is a vindication of the familiar and optimistic evolutionary story about property rights – that they evolve to meet new resource management needs. Nevertheless, this history also teaches that through all the innovations, the concerns remain the same, notably about information, renegotiability, and value. Perhaps even more interesting, the evolution in servitude law suggests a kind of self-replicating pattern, in which a streamlined answer to one kind of problem – say, information – allows developers and others to push the envelope with new uses of servitudes, and then those uses in turn generate issues with respect to some other problem areas like renegotiability or value. Recording and equity jurisprudence solved the information problem for racially restrictive covenants, but racial covenants ran in a direction that raised very serious value concerns. The *Neponsit* case and homeowners' associations cut through the renegotiability issue for CICs, but CICs themselves raised other questions as to their value both to insiders and outsiders. Conservation servitudes have provided a way for private parties to invest in valuable environmental resources, but they too raise new issues of renegotiability and ultimately value over time.

Information and renegotiability concerns are elements of the more general topic of transactions costs, and as such these issues in servitude law clearly engage economic issues that affect all of property law. Indeed, it is significant that two of the most influential scholarly pieces on the economics of property law in the last decade deal, respectively, with information on the one hand and fragmentation/renegotiability on the other.[111]

Concerns about *value* have a somewhat more mixed pedigree. In part, as we have seen, older servitude doctrines about value simply served as a backstop to assure information and renegotiability. Moreover, insofar as doctrines of value reflect external effects on third parties, the value question is also familiar to economic reasoning. But at the same time, value *to the participants* runs through servitude law as a recognizably separate consideration, generally as a kind of residual cussedness about subjecting any person to certain kinds of obligations simply because he or she bought a particular piece of property. This is an oldfashioned view reminiscent of early servititude law, but one hears a noticeable echo in the positive response that CIC residents receive when they complain about no-flag rules and pet restrictions, even though it is certainly arguable that they should have known about the rules and governance procedures when they bought.

An even more potent factor that sets off issues of value, however, is once again the phenomenon of pushing the envelope, and with it the perception that some set of servitudes has expanded so mightily as to affect third parties' and even the participants' own choice set. No one would know or care much about CICs or conservation easements if they had remained idiosyncratic and sparse. No one might even have cared much about racially restrictive covenants if they had remained no more than mean-spirited demands of odd-ball owners. In each of the cases discussed in this chapter, however, a streamlined set of servitude doctrines helped these devices to expand to proportions that made them threatening to outsiders or dictatorial to participants, eliciting judicial and political responses even where economists might think the reaction overstated.

Servitudes on the whole are property arrangements that serve a free market economy; they allow individuals to slice and dice their interests over time and space, within the boundaries of constraining rules that cut information costs and prevent servitudes from becoming non-negotiable and hence frozen in place. The additional constraint of value is looser and potentially more intrusive, and hence unattractive to free marketeers. But modern servitudes have expanded so as to touch the lives of many different persons, over long time periods. Under those enlarged circumstances, the value constraint is a reminder that a property regime is 'in rem,' affecting not only the immediate owners but also the world around them – and the rest of the world may have something to say about their costs and benefits.

NOTES

1. Molly Shaffer Van Houweling, The New Servitudes, 96 Geo. L. J. 885 (2008).
2. Restatement (Third) of Property: Servitudes (2000) (hereinafter Restatement).
3. For a description and critique of this evolutionary story, see Carol M. Rose, Property as Storytelling: Perspectives from Game Theory, Narrative Theory, Feminist Theory, in Carol M. Rose, Property and Persuasion: Essays on the History, Theory, and Rhetoric of Ownership 25 (1994).
4. Carol M. Rose, What Property Can Do for Government (and Vice Versa), in The Fundamental Interrelations Between Government and Property 209, 213–14 (1999) (noting special connection of servitudes and records with land); cf. Henry Hansmann and Reinier Kraakman, Property, Contract, and Verification: The Numerus Clausus Problem and the Divisibility of Rights, 31 J. Legal Stud. 373, 407–408 (2002) (attributing relative dearth of chattel servitudes to lesser need for coordination of uses).
5. Robert C. Ellickson, Property in Land, 102 Yale L. J. 1315, 1325 (1993).
6. Common interest community rules, however, do suggest that neighbors can be quite concerned about quite minor details of the property uses of others. See Part II. B., infra.
7. Keppell v. Bailey, 39 Eng. Rep. 1042, 1049 (Ch. 1834) (famous case expressing disfavor to servitudes as tying up land); cf. Tulk v. Moxhay, 41 Eng. Rep. 1143 (1848) (famous case giving favorable treatment to servitude of which buyer was on notice).
8. See, e.g. Dawes v. Johnson, 856 N.E.2d 769, 772 (Ind. App. 2006); cf. Restatement at sec 3.1 (presumption in favor of servitudes).
9. See, e.g., Evan McKenzie, Privatopia: Homeowner Associations and the Rise of Residential Private Government 25–26, 186–87 (1994); Timothy Egan, The Serene Fortress: A Special Report; Many Seek Security in Private Communities, N.Y. Times, Sept. 3, 1995, at 1, 1, col. 2.
10. Molly van Houweling, supra note 1, identifies roughly the same set of concerns in a very helpful typology of the constraining features on servitudes. Her typology differs slightly from that presented here, but the basic approach is very similar.
11. See sec. II.C. infra.
12. The identification problem can continue, however, if an easement in gross is acquired outside the recording system, notably by prescription; here the identity of the prescriptive owner might be obvious because of the requirements of prescription itself, but not the identity of a *purchaser* of a prescriptive easement. Cf. Miller v. Lutheran Conference & Camp Association, 200 A. 646 (Pa. 1938) (permitting transfer of easement in gross that was acquired by prescription).
13. See, e.g. Miller v. Clary, 103 N.E. 1114 (N.Y. 1913) (refusing to enforce covenant that required maintainance of mill shaft and delivery of power, citing English authority although also some contrary cases).
14. It is telling that horizontal privity was only required where the issue was whether the subsequent owner was *burdened* by covenant obligations, and not whether for the *benefit* of a covenant ran to a subsequent purchaser. A moment's reflection reveals the information-related reason: those who buy the benefitted property are much more likely to be informed by the seller, who has an interest in informing prospective buyers about arrangements that benefit the property.
15. For an especially interesting example, see Charles M. Haar and Lance Liebman, Property and Law 770–784 (1st edn 1977) (reproducing documents through which the firm that developed Columbia, Maryland, established the complex servitudes in that community by incorporating them into a nominal conveyance of the entire property to a particular individual for $5.00).
16. By comparison to ordinary servitudes, some states allow Business Improvement Districts, which permit sub-municipal urban districts to organize ex post to collect fees for highly local services; but these depend on special legislation that permits them to organize through petitions and local governmental approval rather than unanimous agreement of the participants. Robert Ellickson has proposed similar

organization of block-level neighborhood residential associations; see Robert C. Ellickson, New Institutions for Old Neighborhoods, 48 Duke L. J. 75 (1998).

17. The major article on this issue is Michael Heller, The Tragedy of the Anticommons: Property in Transition from Marx to Markets, 111 Harv. L. Rev. 621 (1998) [hereinafter, Heller, Anticommons].

18. All kinds of servitudes are subject to other traditional equitable rules like laches, estoppel and prescription, which basically cut off stale claims ex post, by barring the reassertion of formal rights that have been violated for long periods or with some kind of implicit consent.

19. See, e.g., Brown v. Voss, 715 P.2d 514 (Wash. 1986); see also Robert Cooter, The Cost of Coase, 11 J. Legal Stud. 1 (1982) (discussing strategic bargaining and other transaction issues in bilateral monopolies).

20. See, e.g., Western Lands v. Truskolaski, 495 P.2d 624 (Nev. 1972); Hrisomalos v. Smith, 600 N.E. 2d 1363 (Ind. App. 1992).

21. Ian Ayres and Eric Talley, Solomonic Bargaining: Dividing a Legal Entitlement to Facilitate Coasian Trades, 104 Yale L. J. 1027 (1995).

22. See, e.g., Thomas Merrill and Henry E. Smith, What Happened to Property in Law and Economics, 111 Yale L. J. 357, 379–83 (2001); Carol M. Rose, The Shadow of the Cathedral, 106 Yale L. J. 2175, 2182–89 (1997); Louis Kaplow and Steven Shavell, Property Rules versus Liability Rules: An Economic Analysis, 109 Harv. L. Rev. 713, 767–68 (1996); see also Henry E. Smith, Property and Property Rules, 79 N.Y.U. L. Rev. 1719, 1781, 1797–98 (2004) (analyzing information advantages of property rules over liability rules).

23. See, e.g., Evangelical Lutheran Church of the Ascension of Snyder v. Sahlem 172 N.E. 455 (N.Y. 1930) (offer of compensation for holdout ruled insufficient to void covenant right).

24. See, e.g., Warsaw v. Chicago Metallic Ceilings, Inc, 676 P.2d 584 (Cal.1984); Blakeley v. Gorin, 313 N.E.2d 903 (Mass. 1974).

25. Property scholar Laura Underkuffler unearthed a sale transaction that hinged on inclusion of a covenant to prohibit any use of the property 'for any purpose contradicting the teachings or doctrines' of a particular church. Email to Property Professors' Listserve, July 30, 2008.

26. James E. Krier, Book Review (reviewing Richard A. Posner, Economic Analysis of Law), 122 U.Pa. L. Rev. 1664, 1678–81 (1974).

27. The leading case on this point is Neponsit Property Owners Ass'n v. Emigrant Industrial Savings Bank, 15 N.E.2d 793 (N.Y. 1938), to be discussed below.

28. See sec. II.A.1, supra.

29. Richard A. Epstein, Notice and Freedom of Contract in the Law of Servitudes, 55 So. Cal. L. Rev. 1353 (1982).

30. Krier, supra note 26, at 1678–81. Cf. E.G. Jeffrey Toward an Economic Understanding of Touch and Concern, 1988 Duke L. J. 925, 935–39 (arguing that T&C allows courts to allocate benefits and burdens efficiently as between original contractors and successors; necessitated by high bargaining costs of correcting errors).

31. See Uriel Reichman, Toward a Unified Concept of Servitudes, 55 S. Cal. L. Rev. 1177, 1232–33 (1982) (arguing that the T&C requirement was a brake on obsolescence, since idiosyncratic promises are likely to go out of date rapidly). Another traditional ex ante constraint on obsolescence was the Rule Against Perpetuities (RAP), which is very complex in application but generally limits any owner's ability to control future uses to a period in which his or her grandchildren can reach maturity. Servitudes are not now considered subject to the RAP, but early twentieth-century developers were evidently not certain of this, and some attempted to structure servitudes in such a way as to escape or conform to the RAP. See Carol M. Rose, Shelley v. Kraemer, in Property Stories 169, 179–80 (2004). Still another brake on obsolescence was the English confinement of covenants to leases, which meant that servitudes expired with the lease. However, this rule can be avoided with a long-term lease.

32. For the general issue of servitudes and future externalities, see Van Houweling, supra note 1, at 900–901.

33. See Rombauer v. Compton Heights Christian Church, 40 S.W.2d 545 (Mo. 1931) (giving lesser weight to changes outside the covenanted area, over which the beneficiaries had no control).

34. Norcross v. James, 2 N.E. 946, 949 (Mass. 1885) (Holmes opin.).

35. Lester Telser, Why Should Manufacturers Want Fair Trade? 3 J. Law & Econ. 67 (1960); see also Leegin Creative Leather Products v. PSKS, [551 U.S. 877], 127 S.Ct. 2705 (2007) (overturning rule that resale price maintenance is a per se antitrust violation, noting controversy among economists about anticompetitive or procompetitive effects).

36. Whitinsville Plaza, Inc., v. Kotseas 390 N.E. 243 (Mass. 1979) (partially overturning Norcross doctrine after extensive review of newer developments and critiques). See also Restatement (Third), sec. 3.6 (invalidating servitudes that impose 'unreasonable' restraints on trade or commerce).

37. See, e.g., Miller v. Clary, 103 N.E. 1114 (N.Y. 1914); Guaranty Trust Co. of New York v. Queens County Ry. Co, 170 N.E. 887, 892 (N.Y. 1930).

38. See Lea S. VanderVelde, The Gendered Origins of the Lumley Doctrine: Binding Men's Consciences and Women's Fidelity, 101 Yale L. J. 775 (1992) (describing free labor ideology of later nineteenth century, partial retreat in cases beginning with opera singers); see also Reichman, supra note 31, at 1233 (describing T&C in part as bulwark against 'feudal serfdom'). The easiest doctrinal explanation is that this aspect of T&C extends the contract doctrine against assignment of personal service contracts, but that doctrine raises similar issues.

39. Thomas W. Merrill and Henry E. Smith, Optimal Standardization in the Law of Property: The Numerus Clausus Principle, 110 Yale L. J. 1 (2000) [hereinafter Merrill and Smith, Optimal Standardization].

40. See, e.g., Hansmann and Kraakman, supra note 4, at 384–85, 390, 393 (citing possession, labeling, and registry as noice-giving devices); Glen O. Robinson, Personal Property Servitudes, 71 U.Chi. L. Rev. 1449, 1486–87 (2004) (citing mandatory seller disclosure, physical characteristics).

41. Benito Arruñada, The Choice of Titling System in Land, 48 J. L. & Econ. 709–11 (2005).

42. See C. Dent Bostwick, Land Title Registration: An English Solution to an American Problem, 63 Ind. L. J. 55, 61 (1988) (arguing that an ideal title registration system must sharply curtail the numbers and types of interests); cf. Michael Heller, The Boundaries of Private Property, 108 Yale L. J. 1163, 1176–78 (1999) (discussing the Numerus Clausus as an anti-fragmentation device).

43. Cf. Benito Arruñada, Property Enforcement as Organized Consent, 19 J. L. Econ. & Org. 401, 416–17 (arguing that the Numerus Clausus is larger in recording than in registration systems).

44. See, e.g., Parmalee v. Morris, 188 N.W. 330 (1922) (reciting deed's racial restrictions along with requirement of minimum setback and prohibition of use as liquor store); Porter v. Barrett, 206 N.W. 532 (1925) (racial restriction listed along with prohibition on use for slaughterhouse, liquor business or 'any other thing obnoxious to a good residential neighborhood').

45. Buchanan v. Warley, 245 U.S. 60 (1917).

46. Wendy Plotkin, Deeds of Mistrust: Race, Housing and Restrictive Covenants in Chicago, 1900–1950, at 71–75 (Doctoral dissertation, Univ. of Ill. Chicago, 1999) . To avoid the first mover issue, many neighborhood covenants were conditioned on the signatures of a certain percentage of the property owners. This could create problems for later enforcement, especially when minority purchasers and civil rights groups challenged signatures. See, e.g., Stone v. Jones, 152 P.2d 19 (Cal. App. 1944) (challenge to signatures on neighborhood covenant).

47. Plotkin, supra note 46, at 117.

48. Ibid., at 45–48, 66.

49. FHA Underwriting Manual sec. 980(3)(g) (1938).

50. See, e.g., Mays v. Burgess, 147 F.2d 869 (1945) (quoting 1925 neighborhood covenant in District of Columbia).

51. See, e.g., Wayt v. Patee, 269 P. 660, 662 (Cal. 1928).

52. While equitable remedies are supposed to be reserved for extraordinary circumstances where money damages do not suffice, equity decisions are very common in real estate law, given the standard doctrine that all real estate is unique and hence damages are not calculable.

53. See Pickel v. McCawley, 44 S.W. 2d 857 (Mo. 1931) (giving an interesting description of the organizing efforts following minority expansion, including the use of forms from the St. Louis Real Estate Exchange).

54. See, e.g., Russell v. Wallace, 30 F.2d 981 (D.C. Cir. 1929).

55. See, e.g., Pickel (changed circumstance argument succeeded); Hundley v. Gorewitz 132 F2d 23 (D.C. Cir. 1942) (same); Letteau v. Ellis, 10 P.2d 496 (Cal. App. 1932) (same); cf. Stone v. Jones, 152 P.2d 119 (Cal. App. 1944) (argument failed); Koehler v. Rowland, 205 S.W. 217 (Mo. 1918) (same).

56. Mays v. Burgess, 147 F.2d 869, 873, 876-77 (D.C. Cir. 1945) (Edgerton, diss.) (noting the lack of horizontal privity and stating that neighbor-created covenants, unlike covenants created 'by deed', could have the result that 'unlimited quantities of land may rapidly be subjected to the restraint.'

57. Id.; Fairchild v. Raines, 151 P.2d 260, 267–68 (Cal. 1944) (Traynor, conc.).

58. Barbara M. Kelly: Expanding the American Dream: Building and Rebuilding Levittown 30–33, 60 (1993).

59. Shelley v. Kraemer, 334 U.S. 1 (1948).

60. David E. Bernstein, Philip Sober Controlling Philip Drunk: Buchanan v. Warley in Historical Perspective, 51 Vand. L. Rev. 797, 865–66 (1998); William A. Fischel, Why Judicial Reversal of Apartheid Made a Difference, 51 Vand. L. Rev. 975, 978 (1998).

61. Thomas C. Schelling, Sorting and Mixing: Race and Sex, in Micromotives and Macrobehavior 135 (1978).

62. Richard Brooks, Covenants and Conventions (forthcoming).

63. Lior Jacob Strahilevitz, Exclusionary Amenities in Residential Communities, 92 Va. L. Rev. 437 (2006).

64. According to the Community Associations Institute, in 2008 there were 300,800 association-governed communities with over 24 million housing units and 59.5 million residents. The 1970 figures were,

respectively, 10,000, 701,000, and 2.1 million. CAI Industry Data, National Statistics, available at www. caionline.org/info/research/Pages/default.aspx.

65. See, e.g., McKenzie, supra note 9, at 180–92; Egan, supra note 9, citing, among others, Harvard law professor Gerald Frug; Sheryll D. Cashin, Privatized Communities and the 'Secession of the Successful': Democracy and Fairness Beyond the Gate, 28 Fordham Urb. L. J. 1675 (2001); David J. Kennedy, Note, Residential Communities as State Actors: Regulating the Impact of Gated Communities on Nonmembers, 105 Yale L. J. 761, 763 (1995).

66. See, e.g., Hrisomalos v. Smith, 600 N.E. 2d 1363, 1366 (Ind. App. 1992) (stating that 'public policy' requires the voiding of obsolete servitudes); Restatement (Third), at sec. 3.1.

67. A leading case is Crane Neck Ass'n v. New York City/Long Island Co. SVCS Group, 460 N.E.2d 1336 (N.Y. 1984).

68. See Richard A. Epstein, Covenants and Constitutions, 73 Corn. L.Rev. 906, 916–26 (1988).

69. Neponsit Property Owners' Ass'n v. Emigrant Industrial Sav. Bank, 15 N.E. 2d 793 (N.Y. 1938).

70. For a more detailed description of the case, see Stewart E. Sterk, Neponsit Property Owners' Association v. Emigrant Industrial Savings Bank, in Property Stories 301 (2004).

71. Id., at 321–22; see also Evan McKenzie, supra note 9, 10–12 (thumbnail sketch of CIC growth); Wayne C. Hyatt, Common Interest Communities: Evolution and Reinvention, 31 John Marshall L. Rev. 303, 319–23 (1998) (same, particularly legal evolution).

72. Henry Hansmann has argued that multiple-unit structures are a kind of natural monarchy, most efficiently managed by a landlord, and thus many CICs would appear to be driven by the tax advantages of homeownership. H. Hansmann, Condominium and Cooperative Housing: Transactional Efficiency, Tax Subsidies, and Tenure Choice 20 J. Legal Stud. 25 (1991). This may be less applicable to a community like Neponsit, as well as many more modern developments, in which the individual units are single family houses.

73. Epstein, supra note 68, at 910, 923.

74. James L. Winokur, The Mixed Blessings of Promissory Servitudes: Toward Optimizing Economic Utility, Individual Liberty, and Personal Identity 1989 Wis. L. Rev. 1, 62–65 (noting wide disaffection among CIC residents with governance, citing surveys and litigation); but see Foundation for Community Association Research, What Americans Say About Their Community Associations, available at www. cairf.org/research/survey.pdf (reporting on 2005–2007 survey data reporting wide satisfaction, unwillingness to have greater supervision by public bodies). See also Kevin Johnson, Feuds Take Homeowner Groups to Legal Limits, L.A. Times, Sept. 18, 1994, at 1 (describing, *inter alia*, complaints about POA restrictions on overweight pets, bamboo balcony shades, kissing one's boyfriend in the car); Pamela Dittmer McKuen, Wave of Patriotism Relaxes Rules About Flying the Flag, Chicago Trib. Oct. 19, 2000, at 24.

75. Paula A. Franzese, Building Community in Common Interest Communities: The Promise of the Restatement (Third) of Servitudes, 38 Real Prop. Prob. & Tr. J. 17 (2003).

76. Winokur, supra note 74, at 59; Hyatt, supra note 71, at 323, 334, 359, 361–64; see also Mark Fenster, Community by Covenant, Process and Design: Co-Housing and the Contemporary Common Interest Community, 15 J. Land Use & Envtl. L. 3, 21, 26–27, 46 (1999) (noting financing problems of co-housing, an unfamiliar community form, leading founders to organize as condominiums).

77. Winokur, supra note 74, at 59, note 246 (citing 1987 Denver area survey that as many as 85% of CIC purchasers were unaware of servitudes and homeowner associations).

78. David C. Drewes, Note: Putting the 'Community' Back in Common Interest Communities: A Proposal for Participation-Enhancing Judicial Review, 101 Colum. L. Rev. 314, 326–27 (2001) (asserting that the 'consent paradigm' has generally won out in the courts, although the author disagrees).

79. See, e.g., Gerald Korngold, Resolving the Intergenerational Conflicts of Real Property Law: Preserving Free Markets and Personal Autonomy for Future Generations, 56 Am. U. L. Rev. 1525, 1572–73 (2007) (noting that some early CIC covenants required fixed dues that were insufficient for later maintenance costs).

80. See also Herbert Hovenkamp, Bargaining in Coasian Markets: Servitudes and Alternative Land Use Controls, 27 J. Corp. L. 519, 529–33 (2002) (describing instances in which the underlying covenants could be changed by vote and raising the issue of cycling among decisions).

81. Hidden Harbor Estates v. Norman, 309 So.2d 180 (Ct.App. Fla. 1975). The very high referendum vote suggests a heated controversy, though the complainants lost the case.

82. Hyatt, supra note 71, at 355 ('The appropriate standard is one that fairly responds to owner expectations and to association purposes'); Stewart E. Sterk, Minority Protection in Residential Private Governments, 77 B.U. L. Rev. 273, 329, 333–37 (1997) (noting that courts readily enforce many CIC association decisions, but not those violating specific owner expectations). See also Nahrstedt v. Lakeside Village Condominium Ass'n, 878 P.2d 1275 (Cal. 1994) (applying a greater presumption of reasonableness to covenants in original declaration than to later rules, in spite of statutory language subjecting all

rules and rule changes to general 'reasonableness' standard); cf. Villa de las Palmas Homeowners' Ass'n v. Terifaj, 90 P.3d 1223 (Cal. 2004) (reading statute to apply same standard of 'reasonableness' review to subsequent amendments as to measures in the declaration).

83. For the laws limiting U.S. and state flag prohibitions, see, e.g. N.C. Genl. Stat. secs. 47C-3-121, sec. 47F-3-121 (2007); Freedom to Display the American Flag Act of 2005, P.L. 109-243, 120 Stat. 572 (HR 42); for California's law limiting pet restrictions, West's Ann. Cal. Civ. Code sec. 1360.5 (providing that CICs may not prohibit owners from keeping at least one pet).

84. See, e.g., Lisa J. Chadderdon, No Political Speech Allowed: Common Interest Developments, Homeowners Associations, and Restrictions on Free Speech, 21 J. Land Use & Envtl L. 233 (2006) (arguing that CICs' actions can be classed as 'state action').

85. Gregory S. Alexander, Dilemmas of Group Autonomy: Residential Associations and Community, 75 Corn. L. Rev. 1, 7, 55–56 (1989).

86. Epstein, supra note 68, at 921–22.

87. Clayton Gillette, Courts, Covenants, and Communities, 61 U.Chi. L. Rev. 1375, 1412–13 (1994) (arguing that CICs' tendency toward homogeneity reduces likelihood of conflict).

88. Id, at 1416–17; see also Hanoch Dagan and Michael A. Heller, The Liberal Commons, 110 Yale L. J. 549 (2001) (describing role of several features, including exit constraints, in enhancing cooperation and protecting residents in common property regimes).

89. See, e.g., Glen O. Robinson, Explaining Contingent Rights: The Puzzle of 'Obsolete' Covenants, 91 Colum. L. Rev. 546, 576–79 (expressing skepticism whether intervention is preferable to market) (1991).

90. Gillette, supra note 87, at 1420–25; see also Sterk, supra note 82, at 336–340 (arguing that CICs avoid extremes and generally do not require intervention).

91. Neponsit initially had 1,600 residential lots; see Sterk, supra note 70, at 302; it is currently described as comprising a community 4 blocks wide and less than 1/10 square mile; see www.neponsit.org/ (last visited Sep. 18, 2008). Columbia, Md., began with 14,000 acres that were divided into nine 'villages' and a city center, with a current population of just under 100,000 people. See the Columbia websites, www. columbia-md.com/columbiaindex.html and www.columbia-md.com/columbiahistory.html (last visited Sept. 18, 2008); Sun City, Arizona, is a retirement CIC of approximately 40,000 persons; see www.sun-cityaz.org/index.htm (last visited Sept. 18, 2008).

92. See Barton H. Thompson, Conservation Easements: Toward a Greater Private Role, 21Va. Envtl. L. J. 245, 251–53 (2002) (describing public good argument but noting considerable private interest in conservation).

93. An early and much-cited scholarly discussion was John J. Costonis, The Chicago Plan: Incentive Zoning and the Preservation of Urban Landmarks, 85 Harv. L. Rev. 574 (1972); probably the most cited case involving TDRs is Penn Central Transportation Corp. v. City of New York, 438 U.S. 104 (1978).

94. See Gerald Korngold, Solving the Contentious Issues of Conservation Easements: Promoting Flexibility for the Future and Engaging the Public Land Use Process, 2007 Utah L. Rev. 1039, 1046–48 (documenting spectacular growth of conservation servitudes in last decade); Barton H. Thompson, Jr., The Trouble With Time: Influencing the Conservation Choices of Future Generations, 44 Nat. Res. J. 601, 604 (2004) (same). Acreage covered by conservation servitudes has grown from 2.5 million acres in 2000 to 6.2 million in 2005, not counting the Nature Conservancy holdings of 2.7 million in 2005, for a total area four times the size of Yellowstone National Park; this also does not include servitude acreage held by local, state and federal governments. See Nancy A. McLaughlin, Condemning Conservation Easements: Protecting the Public Interest and Investment in Conservation, 41 U.C. Davis L. Rev. 1897, 1903, note 13 (2008).

95. See, e.g., Linda Platts, Greener Pastures, PERC Reports, September 2003, at 15, available at www.perc. org/pdf/sept03.pdf.

96. I.R.C. , sec. 170 (h); Susan French, Perpetual Trusts, Conservation Servitudes, and the Problem of the Future, 27 Cardozo L. Rev. 2523, 2525 (2006).

97. Conservation servitudes have also become important in alleviating tensions over owner responsibilities under the Endangered Species Act; see Felicity Barringer, Aware of Political Ecosystem, Property Rights Advocate Embraces Conservation Plan, N.Y. Times, Dec. 27, 2005, at A16.

98. Jonathan Weber, A Class War Runs Through It, N.Y. Times, Sept. 6, 2005, at A27.

99. Thompson, supra note 92, at 252–58.

100. Information poverty has been a notorious problem for maintaining property in wilderness condition, since the usual ways to signal claims to land involve altering it from a natural state – cutting the trees, plowing the prairies grasses, building a house. See, e.g., Carol M. Rose, From H2O to CO2: Lessons of Water Rights for Carbon Trading, 50 Ariz. L. Rev. 91, 100–102 (2008) (noting that property rights established through physical alteration are contrary to passive uses); John G. Sprankling, An Environmental Critique of Adverse Possession, 79 Cornell L. Rev. 816, 856–57 (1994) (noting anti-environmental character of prescriptive claims).

101. Unif. Conservation Easement Act, sec. 4; Federico Cheever, Public Good and Private Magic in the Law of Land Trusts and Conservation Easements: A Happy Present and a Troubled Future, 73 Denv. U. L. Rev. 1077, 1083–85 (1996).

102. Unif. Conservation Easement Act, sec. 1(2).

103. Julia D. Mahoney, Perpetual Restrictions on Land and the Problem of the Future, 88 Va. L. Rev. 573 (2002). An earlier though less hostile critique of perpetual conservation servitudes was Gerald Korngold, Privately Held Conservation Servitudes: A Policy Analysis in the Context of In Gross Real Covenants and Easements, 63 Tex. L. Rev. 433 (1984).

104. Mahoney, supra note 103, at 586.

105. Id., at 773–76. Gerald Korngold takes a similar position about private nonprofit groups, but not about governmental owners; see Korngold, supra note 103, at 490–92 (arguing in favor of limiting conservation servitude ownership to public bodies on ground that they will be more accountable than private owners); Korngold, supra note 94, at 1065 (arguing that voters control public owners but not private ones and nonprofits).

106. Thompson, supra note 94, at 609–11 (citing Uniform Conservation Easement Act, sec. 2); Korngold, supra note 103, at 493; see also Hrisomalos v. Smith, 600 N.E. 2d 1363, 1366 (Ind. App. 1992) (stating that 'public policy' requires the voiding of obsolete servitudes).

107. Cheever, supra note 101, at 1093–1100 (giving a variety of real and hypothetical lenient extinguishments, arguing that development interests can overwhelm servitudes holders); see also Jeff Holz, Land Trust Chief Charged with Marijuana Possession, N.Y. Times, Oct. 8, 2006, at 5.

108. For a recounting of these and other proposals, see Korngold, supra note 94, at 1066–1084; see also, e.g., French, supra note 96, at 2535 (proposing public intervention in termination process); Nancy A. McLaughlin, Rethinking the Perpetual Nature of Conservation Servitudes, 29 Harv. Envtl. L. Rev. 421 (2005) (proposing application of cy pres doctrine from trust law); McLaughlin, supra note 94 (proposing eminent domain with just compensation for extinguishment).

109. See Federico Cheever, Confronting Our Shared Legacy of Incongruous Land Ownership: Notes for a Research Agenda, 83 U. Denv. L. Rev. 1039, 1048–52 (2006) (citing 'local-ness' of many conservation servitudes as safeguard against errors and obsolescence).

110. Van Houweling, supra note 1.

111. Merrill and Smith, Optimal Standardization, supra note 39; Heller, supra note 17.

15 The economics of nuisance law
*Keith N. Hylton**

I. INTRODUCTION

Nuisance law has been described as an impenetrable jungle.[1] Judging by the dearth of efforts to codify it in the form of blackletter rules, this appears to have been an opinion shared by most legal scholars.[2] The lack of clearly stated rules has probably delayed attempts to use economics to explain nuisance doctrine.

In spite of this, some efforts have been made to provide an economic theory of nuisance law. Most of those efforts, stemming from Coase,[3] have relied on the theory of transaction costs to explain the functional distinction between nuisance and trespass law.[4] But the core of nuisance doctrine involves balancing tests and limitations on scope that are not easily understood on the basis of transaction cost theory. This chapter aims to explain the core doctrines of nuisance law. Instead of transaction cost analysis, I will rely on an approach that I will refer to as the externality model.

In contrast to the traditional legal commentary, I find nuisance law a coherent body of rules that serves an explainable function. Nuisance law optimally regulates activity levels. Nuisance law induces actors to choose socially optimal activity levels by imposing liability when externalized costs are far in excess of externalized benefits or far in excess of background external costs. Proximate cause doctrine plays an important role, in this analysis, in generating optimal activity levels.

II. ECONOMICS OF NUISANCES

The literature on the economics of nuisance law can be divided into two branches. One is the *transaction cost framework*, which began with Coase's discussion of nuisance in his famous article on transaction costs and resource allocation.[5] The transaction cost approach emphasizes the functional differences between nuisance and trespass law, and provides a positive theory of the boundary between nuisance and trespass.[6] It has also been applied to explain the law on priority ('coming to the nuisance').[7]

The other branch of work on the economics of nuisance law can be labeled the *externality model*, which focuses on the regulatory function of nuisance law.[8] The externality approach offers a sparse model of the function of nuisance liability, and a positive theory of the core doctrines of nuisance. The core doctrines examined under the externality model are those of intent, reasonableness, and proximate cause.

While the transaction cost model explains why nuisance law may be socially preferable to trespass law under certain conditions, the externality model attempts to explain the specific features of nuisance law. Alternatively, one could say that the transaction cost model addresses the boundary of nuisance law; explaining matters such as the choice between trespass and nuisance, the exclusion of liability for aesthetic disturbances, and rules on priority. The externality model addresses the law's function within the boundary.

Because I will examine the core nuisance rules here, I will focus on the externality model. The transaction cost models will be discussed as comparison points and largely in the margins. The distinction between activity and care levels is the starting point for the externality model.

A. Activity Levels, Care Levels, and Externalities

The law and economics literature distinguishes care and activity levels.[9] The care level refers to the level of instantaneous precaution that an actor takes when engaged in some activity. For example, an actor can take more care while in the activity of driving by moderating his speed or looking more frequently to both sides of the road. The activity level refers to the actor's decision with respect to the frequency or location of his activity. If, for example, the activity of concern is driving, it can be reduced by driving less frequently.

The invasions associated with nuisance law can be viewed as external costs associated with activity level choices. Consider, for example, a manufacturer who dumps toxic chemicals into the water as a byproduct of its manufacturing activity. Suppose the manufacturer is taking the level of care required by negligence law (reasonable care), and, in spite of this, the manufacturing process leads to some level of discharge of toxic chemicals. In this case, the environmental harm is a negative externality associated with the manufacturer's activity level choice.

Whether we are considering the activity of driving a car or that of manufacturing, the model examined here is of activities that impose external costs on society even when they are carried out with reasonable care. The question I consider is how the law can regulate activity levels in a way that leads to socially optimal decisions. I will argue that nuisance law appears to accomplish this goal.

I assume in the model below that there are two liability rules that can be applied to actors, strict liability and negligence.[10] Under either rule, actors are assumed to take reasonable care.

B. The Economics of Activity Level Choices

For any activity, the actor engaged in it will set his privately optimal level at the point which maximizes his utility from that activity. That means the actor will consider the benefits he derives from the activity as well as the costs, and choose a level at which the excess of private benefits over private costs is at its maximum. If $b(y)$ represents the private benefit enjoyed by the actor at activity level y, and $c(y)$ represents the private cost, the actor will increase his activity level until

$$b'(y) = c'(y),$$ (15.1)

where $b'(y)$ represents the marginal private benefit (MPB) to the actor and $c'(y)$ represents the marginal private cost (MPC). The actor's privately optimal activity level choice is given by the intersection of MPB and MPC in Figure 15.1 (point A).[11]

There are negative externalities (or external costs) associated with many activities.

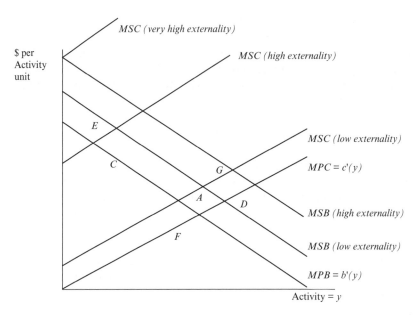

Source: Keith N. Hylton, *Duty in Tort Law: An Economic Approach*, 75 Fordham L. Rev. 1501, 1506 (2006).

Figure 15.1   Levels of externalization of costs and benefits

Suppose the activity is driving. With each mile driven, the actor imposes some risk of harm from an accident or from pollution on the public in general. Or, if the activity is manufacturing, with each widget produced, a manufacturer who discharges chemicals in the water imposes clean-up costs on others. The marginal social cost of the actor's activity is simply the sum of the marginal private cost and the marginal external cost imposed on society. Thus if $v(y)$ represents the external cost of the activity, the marginal social cost (MSC) is $c'(y) + v'(y)$.

1.   Cost and benefit externalization: single activity model

There may be benefits to society generated by the actor's activity. For example, the provision of water to a building, even when carried out with great care, puts the tenant's property at risk of damage from escaping water, but also benefits society by enhancing sanitation.[12] Similarly, providing internet service to a home puts the resident's computer at risk through the transmission of computer viruses, but also enhances the spread of information across society.[13] And consider driving again. If the number of drivers increases from one to two, both drivers will have the added safety that if anything goes wrong on the road (e.g., a car falls into a pothole), they will find someone who can help them or call for help.

The marginal social benefit is the sum of the marginal private benefit and the marginal external benefit of an additional unit of activity. Thus, if $z(y)$ represents the external benefit, the marginal social benefit (MSB) is $b'(y) + z'(y)$.

The final step of this economic analysis of activity level choices is to consider the differences between private and social incentives. Social welfare is optimized when

$$b'(y) + z'(y) = c'(y) + v'(y). \tag{15.2}$$

The level of activity that satisfies the social optimality condition may differ from the privately optimal level. The socially and privately optimal activity levels will be the same if the cost and benefit externalities are equal; that is, $v'(y) = z'(y)$. If the external cost exceeds the external benefit at all activity levels, $v'(y) > z'(y)$, then the privately optimal activity choice will exceed the socially optimal level; and the converse holds as well.[14]

Figure 15.1 can be used to elaborate. Consider the case of low and roughly equivalent externalities on both the cost and benefit sides, as shown by *MSC (low externality)* and *MSB (low externality)*. The socially optimal level of activity, which equates the marginal social benefit and the marginal social cost, is found at the point *B* in Figure 15.1. The socially optimal level of activity (*B*) is roughly the same as the privately optimal level of activity (*A*). The reason is that the modest positive and negative externalities cancel each other out.

Consider the case of high externality on the cost side and low externality on the benefit side, as shown by the intersection of the *MSC (high externality)* and *MSB (low externality)*, or point *C* in Figure 15.1. Now there is a wide divergence between the privately optimal level of activity (*A*) and the socially optimal level of activity (*C*). In this case it appears desirable for the government to intervene to reduce the level of activity. Indeed, in the case of very high externality on the cost side (*MSC (very high externality)*) it may be desirable to shut down the activity completely.

Finally, consider the case of low externality on the cost side and high externality on the benefit side, as shown at point *D* in Figure 15.1. The privately optimal level of activity (*A*) is substantially below the socially optimal level (*D*). The law should intervene to increase the level of activity.

2. Cross externalization of costs and benefits: dual activity model

In many settings, actors cross-externalize benefits and risk. For example, on the roads, drivers impose accident risks on each other even when driving with reasonable care. In addition, drivers may externalize benefits. The presence of other drivers may reduce some risks to certain drivers – e.g., the risk of being stranded by the side of the road may be lower if other drivers are present. The same may be true in a more general sense of neighboring activities. The noise from one factory may at times disturb the work of a neighboring business. But the factory's presence may draw suppliers, employees, and customers to the area, to the benefit of other local businesses.[15] Agglomeration externalities may make particular locations ideal for certain industries, even in the presence of substantial external costs.[16]

Consider two actors S and T. In the case of risk externalization, the activity total cost function for their activities can be represented as

$$c(y_S) + c(y_T) + V(y_S, y_T) \tag{15.3}$$

where $V(y_S, y_T)$ represents the total externalized social cost of both of their activities.

For example, $V(y_S, y_T)$ might represent the costs imposed on society by a cloud of pollution that results directly from the activities of S and T. Alternatively, $V(y_S, y_T)$ could represent the costs to society from specific and independent invasions from S to T and vice versa. For example, S may emit noise that disturbs T, and T may emit a cloud of black smoke over S's property.

The total social cost of activity can be broken down as follows:

$$c(y_S) + c(y_T) + v_S(y_S, y_T) + v_T(y_S, y_T) \qquad (15.4)$$

where $v_S(y_S, y_T)$ represents the portion of the total externality cost borne by S and $v_T(y_S, y_T)$ represents the total of the externality cost borne by T. Return to the example of pollution. The breakdown in (15.4) assumes that the total cost of pollution is borne by S and T alone, so the total cost can be decomposed into the portions borne by both. The pollution example is complicated because it may be difficult to disentangle the specific contributions of S and T to the general harm. The alternative example of independent cross-externalization (e.g., S emits noise, T emits smoke) is simpler, because the specific contributions are easily identified and separated.

To simplify the discussion, assume we are dealing with a case of independent cross-externalization – i.e., S emits noise that disturbs T, and T emits smoke that disturbs S. In this case, the total social cost of the activity can be represented as

$$c(y_S) + c(y_T) + v_{TS}(y_S, y_T) + v_{ST}(y_S, y_T) \qquad (15.5)$$

where v_{ST} represents the cost (or risk) externalized from S to T as a function of both activity levels and v_{TS} represents the cost externalized from T to S. Assuming, for simplicity, that no benefits are externalized, the privately optimal activity level for S will be determined by the condition

$$b'(y_S) = c'(y_S) + \frac{\partial v_{TS}}{\partial y_S}, \qquad (15.6)$$

and a similar result holds for actor T. It should be clear that both actors will constrain their activity levels more than in the single activity case considered above, because they will take into account the risks they personally incur when increasing activity. If the benefit and cost functions are the same for both actors, and $\partial v_{TS}/\partial y_S = \partial v_{ST}/\partial y_T$, they will choose the same activity levels.

In the absence of externalized benefits, the privately optimal activity levels will be greater than the socially optimal levels. This is easy to see because the socially optimal activity level will be determined by:

$$b'(y_S) = c'(y_S) + \frac{\partial v_{TS}}{\partial y_S} + \frac{\partial v_{ST}}{\partial y_S}. \qquad (15.7)$$

As long as the cost externalized by S to T is responsive to changes in S's activity level, S will choose an activity level that is too high from society's perspective.

If benefits are externalized, then it is no longer clear that the privately optimal activity levels are socially excessive. Whether the privately optimal activity levels coincide with the socially optimal levels depends on the relationship between externalized benefits and externalized costs. In the case of externalized benefits, the privately optimal activity level will be determined by the condition

$$b'(y_S) + \frac{\partial z_{TS}}{\partial y_S} = c'(y_S) + \frac{\partial v_{TS}}{\partial y_S}, \qquad (15.8)$$

where z_{TS} represents the benefit externalized from T to S (assuming an independent cross-externalization setting). The socially optimal level of activity is determined by the condition

$$b'(y_S) + \frac{\partial z_{TS}}{\partial y_S} + \frac{\partial z_{ST}}{\partial y_S} = c'(y_S) + \frac{\partial v_{TS}}{\partial y_S} + \frac{\partial v_{ST}}{\partial y_S}. \qquad (15.9)$$

It should be clear that the level of activity that satisfies the private optimality condition may differ from the level that satisfies the social optimality condition.

C. Law

Since the actors are assumed to be taking reasonable care, the negligence rule cannot influence their activity level choices. The negligence rule holds the actor liable only when he fails to take reasonable care. Since the actors are assumed to have taken reasonable care, the negligence rule will not lead to any findings of liability.[17]

Strict liability has the property that it imposes liability on actors even when they have taken reasonable care. The legal system can influence activity levels through imposing strict liability. In this part, I will examine the conditions under which strict liability leads to optimal activity levels.

1. Single activity case

Consider the case in which externality is high on the cost side and low on the benefit side. The socially optimal scale in this case is point C in Figure 15.1. In the absence of strict liability, the privately optimal scale is point A. Imposing strict liability on the actor is probably desirable in this case. When strict liability is imposed on the actor, his marginal private cost schedule becomes equivalent to the marginal social cost schedule. In the case of high externality on the cost side coupled with low externality on the benefit side, the actor's privately optimal activity level under strict liability will be point E. It is not the socially optimal level, which is at point C, but it is close. Social welfare will most likely be improved by using liability to lead the actor to choose level E rather than the socially excessive level A. I will argue below that proximate cause doctrine serves to adjust the activity level to the socially optimal point.

Now consider the case in which externality is low both on the cost and on the benefit sides. The socially optimal scale of activity is associated with point B. The privately optimal level of activity is associated with point A. These are the same activity levels. If strict liability is imposed on the actor, it will reduce his activity level below the socially optimal scale, and therefore reduce social welfare.[18] Strict liability will lead him to choose the scale F, which is below the socially optimal scale.

It follows from the foregoing that *strict liability* is *desirable in the single activity case only when the external costs of the activity substantially exceed the external benefits associated with the activity*. In this case imposing strict liability reduces activity levels to a point that is closer to the socially optimal scale than would be observed under the negligence rule. When the external benefits are roughly equal to or greater than the social costs associated with the activity, strict liability is not socially desirable.

2.   Dual activity case

To simplify, assume there are no external benefits. When negligence is the legal rule that applies, the privately optimal level of activity in the cross-externalization model is given by condition (15.6).

When strict liability is the legal rule, the privately optimal level of activity will depend on the type of strict liability rule adopted. Suppose the law adopts a rule of symmetric strict liability, which holds both S and T strictly liable for harms. Under the symmetric strict liability rule, the privately optimal activity level for actor S is determined by:

$$b'(y_S) = c'(y_S) + \frac{\partial v_{ST}}{\partial y_S}. \tag{15.10}$$

Note, comparing (15.6) and (15.10), that strict liability and negligence lead to the same activity levels if

$$\frac{\partial v_{ST}}{\partial y_S} = \frac{\partial v_{TS}}{\partial y_S}. \tag{15.11}$$

In other words, as long as the harm externalized by S to T is the same as the harm externalized by T to S, strict liability and negligence result in the same privately optimal activity levels. When the actors cross-externalize reciprocal harms, strict liability and negligence result in the same activity levels.

This generates the following *Reciprocal Harm Theorem: when the costs externalized by two actors to each other are reciprocal, strict liability is not socially preferable to negligence.*[19] The reason is that under strict liability, you will pay for harms to others, while under negligence (again, everyone is complying with the negligence standard in this model) you will pay for only the harms you suffer. Since those harms are the same, activity levels will not differ under the two regimes.

Given the condition governing socially optimal activity in (15.7), it should be clear that neither (symmetric) strict liability nor negligence will lead to socially optimal care. Still, if $\partial v_{TS}/\partial y_S$ is substantially less than $\partial v_{ST}/\partial y_S$, then it follows that strict liability will generate an activity level for S that is closer to the socially optimal level than will the negligence rule. This suggests that if S externalizes much more cost to T than T externalizes to S, strict liability will be socially preferable to negligence.

Now consider asymmetric strict liability. Suppose S is subject to strict liability and T is subject to the negligence rule. Under asymmetric strict liability, the following conditions govern the activity levels chosen by S and T.

$$b'(y_S) = c'(y_S) + \frac{\partial v_{TS}}{\partial y_S} + \frac{\partial v_{ST}}{\partial y_S}$$

$$b'(y_T) = c'(y_T) \tag{15.12}$$

These conditions imply that S will exercise the socially optimal level of activity, because he will pay for the harms he externalizes to T and he will also have to pay for the harms externalized by T. T will not exercise the socially optimal level of activity. If, however, S's external costs are substantial and T's are trivial, this is a better solution than the one provided by the negligence rule.

III. THEORY OF NUISANCE LAW

I have presented an economic analysis of activity level choices and considered its implications for law. In this part I examine the law to see if it conforms to the predictions of the model.

Some parts of the doctrine are easily interpreted in light of similar tort rules. Consider the legal definition of a nuisance: an intentional, nontrespassory and unreasonable invasion into the quiet use and enjoyment of property. Intentional, in nuisance law, has always had a meaning similar to its meaning in the context of trespass law: it is enough if the defendant was aware of the nuisance, and the plaintiff is not required to prove that the defendant aimed to harm him. The term nontrespassory has always had the effect of distinguishing between invasions that interfere with exclusive possession of property or a portion of it (e.g., an invading boulder) and invasions that merely make it less desirable to remain in possession of property (e.g., smoke). I will go beyond these comparisons with trespass doctrine to examine how this chapter's model justifies the definition and doctrines of nuisance.

A. Nontrespassory Invasions

The definition of a nuisance as a nontrespassory invasion distinguishes nuisances from trespasses and also from consensual transactions. If the interference is the result of the consent of the victim, then it is not properly characterized as an invasion.

The invasiveness requirement is implicated by the externality model. If the interference is consensual, in the sense that the affected party is fully aware of the nature of the interference and still contracts with the offending actor, then there is no need for the law to intervene to control the activity level of the offending actor. The activity level will be regulated to the optimal level by the market. Thus, if a person contracts with another to install a noisy furnace, and he is fully aware of the noise that will be emitted by the furnace when he enters the contract, he has no basis to bring a nuisance claim against the furnace supplier for the noise interference.

This argument can be put in terms of the single-activity model. Suppose buyers are contracting with a seller whose product generates a negative externality – for example, the seller markets widgets that explode, but no one knows about the risk. Assume there is no positive externality associated with the product. Obviously, the buyers were not aware of the negative externality – otherwise it would not be an externality. The market equilibrium would occur at the output scale where the marginal private benefit of consumption equaled the marginal private cost of supply: $b'(y) = c'(y)$. But this would result in socially excessive consumption, because the socially optimal output scale occurs where $b'(y) = c'(y) + v'(y)$. If the buyers are aware of the negative feature of the product, then the effective market demand schedule would be $b'(y) - v'(y)$. The market equilibrium would occur where $b'(y) - v'(y) = c'(y)$, which is socially optimal.[20]

B.   Intentional Invasions

The externality model provides a theory of intent in nuisance law. The purpose of strict liability is to regulate activity levels. In order to carry out this function, liability must be applied to actors that have sufficient information to have their activity level choices influenced by liability. For example, an actor that decides to locate a smoke-belching factory next to a residential area must be aware of the invasions caused by the smoke from his factory if strict liability is going to have any impact on his initial location decision.[21] In the cross-externalization model examined earlier, strict liability led to optimal incentives on the part of the nuisance generator because the marginal cost of his activity became $c'(y_S) + \partial v_{TS}/\partial y_S + \partial v_{ST}/\partial y_S$. But if the nuisance generator does not have enough information to be aware of his imposition on others ($\partial v_{ST}/\partial y_S$), the threat of strict liability cannot regulate his activity level choices.

Suppose, for example, the nuisance generator's activity causes toxic chemicals to leach into the soil and contaminate a tributary to the groundwater supply used by the victim. If the nuisance generator is unaware that chemicals are leaching into the soil, or (more likely) of the existence of the tributary, then the intentionality requirement would not be satisfied.[22]

It follows that intention in nuisance law, at its core, does not mean intending to harm the victim, or intending to interfere with the victim's use of his property. It is sufficient that the actor has enough information to either be aware of or to easily foresee the harmful impact of his activity on others.

C.   Unreasonable Invasions

Perhaps the most important term in the definition of nuisance is unreasonable. The theory of this chapter suggests a clear interpretation for the reasonableness test of nuisance law. The model presented in the previous part suggests that an unreasonable invasion is one that is associated with an activity for which: (a) the external costs substantially exceed the external benefits, or (b) the external costs thrown off by the defendant's activity are not reciprocal to the external costs thrown off by other local activities.[23] These two conditions describe the settings in which the law should intervene to reduce an actor's activity level. Provided that the intentionality and nontrespassory descriptions apply to a particular invasion, the law should impose strict liability when the external costs exceed external benefits or are non-reciprocal.

Nuisance doctrine is closely related to the law and theory of strict liability articulated in *Rylands v. Fletcher*.[24] The *Rylands* court described several nuisance cases as falling within the rationale of its decision. This is useful because the law on *Rylands*-based strict liability has been set out with much greater clarity than nuisance law.

Using the theory of *Rylands* as the closest doctrinal source for nuisance law, we can set out the following test for a nuisance:

(a)   existence of a high degree of interference with the quiet use and enjoyment of land of others;
(b)   inability to eliminate the interference by the exercise of reasonable care;
(c)   extent to which the activity is not a matter of common usage;

(d)   inappropriateness of the activity to the place where it is carried on; and
(e)   extent to which its value to the community is outweighed by its obnoxious attributes.

I will refer to this below as the nuisance test. These factors are based on the Second Restatement's articulation of the *Rylands* doctrine in the form of a set of rules, in Section 520. The foregoing five-factor test is an attempt to examine whether the external costs thrown off by a nuisance substantially exceed external benefits, or are reciprocated by background external costs of other activities.[25]

The first two factors of this test require that the interference be substantial even when the actor is taking reasonable care. As in the case of abnormally dangerous activities, the first two factors should be treated as minimal requirements for nuisance liability. If, in other words, the interference would be trivial if the actor took reasonable care, then the interference should not be considered a nuisance, and there is no need to examine the remaining factors of the test.[26]

The remaining three components present the core of the reasonableness test in nuisance law. The third factor, common usage, helps identify activities for which the risks are reciprocal to those of other common activities. If an activity is one of common usage, then actors engaged in the activity will impose reciprocal risks on each other, and there is no basis for adopting strict liability over negligence.[27]

The fourth factor, inappropriateness, is both another way of determining whether the activity imposes a reciprocated risk and a way of assessing whether the risks are balanced off by the external benefits. Since the fourth factor focuses on the location, it should be treated as a type of assumption of risk test. An activity would be considered appropriate or reasonable for its location if its costs are typical of other activities in the locale, or if its externalized benefits would make it reasonable for someone in the area to tolerate the costs (because the externalized benefits exceed the externalized costs).

The last factor asks the court to directly compare the benefits externalized by the activity and the costs externalized. When the benefits are substantial, the last factor suggests that the court should be reluctant to impose liability on a nuisance theory. Consider, for example, the noise generated by a fire station. Suppose it is a particularly busy fire station. The noise generated by fire trucks constantly moving in and out of the station with their alarms running could be deemed to substantially interfere with the quiet use and enjoyment of land by neighbors. However, the neighbors also benefit by being located close to the fire station. Since those benefits are substantial and widely dispersed, the neighbors should not be allowed to impose strict liability on a nuisance theory against the fire station. There is no economic basis for using liability as an incentive to force the fire station to cut back on its activity or to reconsider its location decision.[28]

In *Baines v. Baker*,[29] the defendants proposed to erect a hospital for treating smallpox patients in Coldbath Fields, London. The plaintiff, an owner of rental property in the area, sued to enjoin the building as a nuisance. The court refused to enjoin on the ground that the plaintiff's property-value losses due to fears, even though rational, were not recoverable through a nuisance action; and that the public benefits of the hospital would justify the external costs.

The most famous nuisance case involving the balancing of external costs and benefits is *Pennsylvania Coal Co. v. Sanderson*.[30] The defendants operated a coal mine, and in the process of operation brought up underground water. The water brought up by the mining operation flowed into and polluted a surface stream that was used three miles away by the plaintiff as a source of water for the home. The court described the case as pitting the interests of the leading industry of the state against riparian property owners. It also characterized the case as a purely private nuisance, not affecting general access to usable water, because the community had 'abundant pure water from other sources.'[31] The court held that the plaintiff's activity had to yield because of the importance of the defendant's activity to the local economy.[32]

The externality balancing test implies a movement toward expanding strict liability as an economy becomes wealthier. For a subsistence level economy, the introduction of industry should have enormous beneficial externalities. But as the wealth and industry expand, the positive externalities of industrial expansion probably diminish.[33] And wealthier consumers will attach a greater valuation to recreational and aesthetic interests.

D. Scope of Liability: Proximate Cause, Extra-Sensitive Plaintiffs, and Coming to the Nuisance

Under the proximate cause rule courts have limited the scope of nuisance liability to injuries that are connected in a predictable way to the externalized risk. Injuries that are not predictably related to the externalized risk are not within the scope of strict nuisance liability. The externality model suggests a reason for this: to focus liability on the cost-externalizing features of the defendant's activity rather than the activity per se. Suppose the victim drives his car into the defendant's malarial pond. To permit a strict liability action would fail to tax the defendant's activity for the specific risk creation – i.e., the risk of malaria – that nuisance law aims to discourage.

A clearer justification for the proximate cause rule in nuisance law can be based on the model of the previous section. Return to the single-activity model and let the externalized risk component, $v(y)$, be separated into two subcomponents,

$$v(y) = v_1(y) + v_2(y),$$
(15.13)

where $v_1(y)$ is the normal risk externalized by activities of the defendant's type and $v_2(y)$ is the extraordinary risk that makes the defendant's activity a nuisance. For example, in the case of a malarial pond, $v_1(y)$ is the risk externalized by any water storage, and $v_2(y)$ is the malaria risk. The proximate cause rule excludes liability for the normal risk component. If, as nuisance law implicitly assumes, normal risks are balanced off by (normal) positive externalities, then excluding liability for normal risk leads to optimal activity levels.

To see this, note that the social optimum would require the level of care to be set so that $b'(y) + z'(y) = c'(y) + v_1'(y) + v_2'(y)$. If most normal negative externalities (background risks) are cancelled out by normal positive externalities, $z'(y) = v_1'(y)$. Thus, the social optimum is achieved where $b'(y) = c'(y) + v_2'(y)$. The proximate cause rule leads to the social optimum in activity by excluding the normal risk component, $v_1(y)$, as a source of liability. In terms of Figure 15.1, suppose $v_1'(y)$ represents the 'low externality' cost increment (*MSC (low externality)*), and suppose $v_2'(y)$ represents the 'high externality' cost increment (*MSC (high externality)*). If normal positive externalities are present (i.e., *MSB (low externality)* measures the marginal social benefit of the activity), the socially optimal activity level is that associated with point *C*. However, strict liability applied without any offset based on the proximate cause rule would lead the actor to choose the activity level associated with point E. Applying the proximate cause rule of nuisance law, which limits application of strict liability to those injuries attributable to the extraordinary risk, leads the actor to choose the socially optimal activity level (point C). The extra-sensitive plaintiff problem is closely related to the proximate cause issue. Nuisance law does not provide for compensation to the extra-sensitive plaintiff, such as one who complains of illnesses caused by such ordinary activity as the ringing of church bells.[34] The justification for this settled piece of the law is best understood in terms of the theory offered here. A nuisance exists when the externalized costs associated with an activity are substantially in excess of externalized benefits, or the externalized costs are not reciprocated by the external costs of other background activities. The comparison of externalized costs and benefits is made with respect to statistical averages, not to any particular plaintiff. If, on the basis of statistical averages, the externalized costs associated with an activity are not substantially greater than the externalized benefits (or background external costs), then the activity is not a nuisance, under this framework, even though an individual within the community might suffer an injury from it.

In terms of the model, the extra-sensitive plaintiff rule, as well as other rules, can be understood by introducing random components to the external cost. In the single-activity model, let

$$v(y) = v_1(y) + e_1(y) + v_2(y) + e_2(y) \tag{15.14}$$

where the error terms represent random shocks that might alter the externality level in specific instances beyond the average level. The law, however, has to be determined by and for average cases. Thus, the optimal activity condition is $b'(y) + z'(y) = c'(y) + v_1'(y) + v_2'(y)$, and since on average $z'(y) = v_1'(y)$, the optimal activity condition simplifies to $b'(y) = c'(y) + v_2'(y)$.

This analysis implies that if the average risk associated with the activity is only the background level $v_1(y)$, the activity is not a nuisance even if the associated random shock component ($e_1(y)$) is substantial in a specific instance. The activity of ringing church bells emits a normal background risk. In a specific instance, it may lead to an unusual harm, such as causing a church neighbor to suffer a rare neurosis. The harm observed in that specific instance does not alter the finding that the activity itself does not constitute a nuisance.

In the same sense $v_2(y)$ can be taken to represent the expected risk associated with the extraordinary externalization component. Because social optimality requires $b'(y) = c'(y) + v_2'(y)$, strict liability is imposed for this component of the external cost. The error term e_2 can be taken to represent remote risks. For example, suppose the actor emits an unusual amount of black smoke, sufficient to create a public nuisance for passersby on the roads. Suppose the smoke does not interfere with a passerby, but the passerby stops to look at the smoke. After the passerby returns to the road he gets into an accident. The smoke emission would be a 'but-for cause' of the accident, but it would be considered a remote injury in relation to the extraordinary externalization component. By excluding liability for remotely related injuries, nuisance law maintains incentives for socially optimal activity levels.

A better sense of the motivation for the proximate cause test in the case in which the specific extraordinary risk has been realized can be suggested by writing the risk decomposition as

$$v(y) = v_1(y) + v_2(y)(1 + v_{1|2}(y) + \ldots + v_{N|2}(y)) \tag{15.15}$$

where each component $v_{1|2}(y)$ through $v_{N|2}(y)$ represents a conditional risk based on the realization of the extraordinary risk $v_2(y)$. When the extraordinary risk is realized – e.g., a continuing release of black smoke or loud noise – many other events may change as a result, generating injuries. Those other events can be viewed as conditional risks; again, consider the example of the passerby who delays his travel as he looks at the black smoke and then gets hit by a bolt of lightning two minutes later. The release of the extraordinary risk reshuffles the deck, in a sense, and changes the path of later events. But if the nuisance generator is held liable because the release of the extraordinary risk has 'reshuffled the deck', then he will be potentially liable for an infinite number of injuries. If courts held defendants liable for the conditional risks, the liability would be virtually limitless. The proximate cause test reduces the risk of limitless liability and generally avoids excessive liability.

E.   Coming to the Nuisance

Sometimes defendants argue that plaintiffs should not be able to recover because they 'came to the nuisance'. The coming to the nuisance defense is valid in some cases, but not in all. The theory of this chapter provides a justification for the ambiguous treatment of the coming-to-the-nuisance defense.

Since the goal of nuisance liability is to optimally regulate activity levels, a victim's decision to come to the nuisance is certainly a relevant piece of information. The victim's decision to move is no different from the case of the buyer who contracts with a seller to purchase some item with a latent and dangerous defect. If the buyers are aware of the negative feature of the product, then the effective market demand schedule would be described by $b'(y) - v'(y)$. The market equilibrium would occur where $b'(y) - v'(y) = c'(y)$, which is socially optimal. Thus, if a smoke-belching factory sits alone in an area, and the victim moves next door to it, there would be no reason to view the factory's activity as socially excessive. In this case, the coming-to-the-nuisance defense applies.

There are two reasons that the coming-to-the-nuisance defense might not be desirable in this model. First, the victim may not have been aware of the offender's activity when purchasing his property. In *Ensign v. Walls*,[35] the defendant maintained a dog-breeding business in a residential area of Detroit. The invasions (odors, noise, occasional escapes, filth) caused by the defendant's activity may not have been obvious to prospective residents; most probably they became aware of the nuisance after moving in. Using the single-activity model for the purposes of analogy, in this sort of case the market equilibrium would occur where $b'(y) = c'(y)$ (because the invasive feature of the defendant's activity was not apparent to the new resident), while the social optimum would occur where $b'(y) - v'(y) = c'(y)$.

The second reason the coming-to-the-nuisance defense may not be desirable is that the market for real property can be distinguished from most other markets for goods or services. Suppose the community consists of one smoke-belching factory and 99 residents. It is clear in this case that the reciprocal harm condition would not be satisfied ($\partial v_{TS}/\partial y_S \neq \partial v_{ST}/\partial y_S$); the background risks externalized by the residents would be trivial in comparison to the cost externalized by the factory. If the coming-to-the-nuisance defense were allowed, there would be no mechanism to control the activity level of the factory. The factory could double its level of activity without meeting any liability. This is distinguishable from the ordinary market setting in which the market transaction involves a fixed level of risk (e.g., a widget that explodes with probability .01), and in which the turnover of buyers continually constrains the consumption of risky products.[36]

As a general matter, strict nuisance liability hinges on a comparison of externalized costs to externalized benefits or to reciprocal background risks. The historical pattern should not be controlling.

The justifications for the law on priority offered within this model do not diminish the more traditional transaction-cost-based understanding. A rule favoring priority would encourage socially wasteful races and expropriation.[37] My argument suggests that one can account for the law on priority without resorting to the transaction cost theory.

F. Shut Downs

Notice that in Figure 15.1 if external costs are very high and external benefits are non-existent, the optimal scale of the offending activity is zero. Another way of expressing the same point is in terms of total benefit and total costs. A shut down of activity should occur when $b(y) + z(y) < c(y) + v(y)$; or equivalently when $b(y) - c(y) < v(y) - z(y)$. In other words, a shut down should occur when the net external cost exceeds the joint surplus from the activity.[38]

The theoretical recommendation that a cost-benefit test should apply to the issuance of injunctions is consistent with nuisance law. In *Boomer v. Atlantic Cement Co.*,[39] the New York court reversed a preexisting state doctrine that favored the granting of injunctions for any substantial unreasonable invasions. The court held that in the presence of a great disparity between the economic value of the nuisance generator's activity and the harm imposed on the victims, courts should issue damage awards rather than injunctions. The reason underlying the decision was consistent with long-standing principles of equity, which most courts follow on the matter of injunctions. Under those principles, an injunction would be appropriate only when the benefits of an injunction appeared to be greater than the costs.

If damages payments accurately reflected all of the losses suffered by victims, there would never be a need to issue an injunction. Every case involving extremely high external costs would be shut down, in effect, by damages awards.[40] Given this, why are injunctions are ever issued?

The economic case for injunctions is that damages awards do not compensate for all of the losses suffered by victims of nuisances. The more specific reasons differ in the private and public nuisance settings. In the private nuisance setting, a sufficiently offensive invasion will impose large subjective losses on victims. For example, suppose the offending activity sends so much black smoke over the plaintiff's property that it is impossible to live on the property. Then the defendant has effectively seized the property of the plaintiff. A damages award in this case would compensate the plaintiff for the market value of the property, but not for the subjective loss from expropriation. The injunction is preferable because it forces offending activities to either pay for the full losses (objective and subjective) or shut down. In the public nuisance setting, the damages awards will also fail to compensate plaintiffs for all of their losses. The rule governing damages does not provide compensation for ordinary inconveniences. However, even if victims could be compensated for ordinary inconveniences, most would not sue because the cost of suit would be too high relative to the likely damages awards. Given this, the injunction is socially preferable.

The injunctions can be viewed in both cases as minimizing error costs. Damages awards could in theory lead to optimal shut down decisions, but the types of error built into the strict liability system are obvious. Subjective losses are not compensated in the private nuisance cases and the standard inconveniences are not compensated through public nuisance lawsuits. Because of these gaps, nuisances that should be shut down may easily escape that outcome in a system in which courts applied only liability rules to nuisance activities.

VI.   REMAINING NOTES ON THE TRANSACTION COST MODEL AND BOUNDARY ISSUES

A complete economic model of nuisance law would consist of the transaction cost model and the externality model, with the transaction cost model used to explain the boundaries of nuisance law and the externality model used to explain its regulatory function. The foregoing analysis deemphasizes the boundary question that has been the focus of transaction cost analysis. The strategic decision to deemphasize the boundary question does not at all imply that it, and the transaction cost model, are in any sense less important.

I have already noted some of the boundary questions examined under the transaction cost model; specifically the choice between trespass and nuisance, and the rule on priority. The transaction cost model appears to be superior to the externality model as a theory of the boundary between nuisance and trespass law. However, both the transaction cost and externality models provide justifications for the law's treatment of priority.

One other boundary question, unexamined so far, is the exclusion of protection under nuisance law for aesthetic interests, such as the right to sunlight or to a view of the mountains.[41] The exclusion of aesthetic interests appears to be better explained by the transaction cost model than by the externality model. It is obviously an externality, in the technical sense, when a landowner erects a fence that blocks the sunlight to another adjacent landowner. There is no reason suggested by the externality model for not treating the harm to the adjacent landowner as potentially a nuisance.

Under the transaction cost model, there is a clearer economic case for excluding liability for aesthetic harms (such as blocked sunlight). If aesthetic interests were protected by nuisance law, there would immediately be questions of information and proof. If one adjacent landowner can sue the owner of a hotel for blocking sunlight, why not allow other adjacent landowners? The transaction costs of resolving these disputes in the bargaining process would be enormous. On the other hand, if the law refuses to protect aesthetic interests, then the transaction costs of resolving disputes would be much more manageable.

VII. CONCLUSION

Nuisance doctrine is complicated and covers a wide array of cases, but at its core it is simple and straightforward. The long-standing complaints about its incoherence are invalid. The law generates optimal activity levels by imposing strict liability when externalized risks are far in excess of externalized benefits or far in excess of background risks. Existing nuisance doctrine is consistent with this theory.

NOTES

*   knhylton@bu.edu. I prepared this chapter for the Research Handbook on the Economics of Property Law edited by Kenneth Ayotte and Henry Smith, and it has benefited from their suggestions. Haoqing Zhang provided research assistance. I take responsibility for errors and omissions.
1.   WILLIAM L. PROSSER, HANDBOOK OF THE LAW OF TORTS 571 (1971).
2.   One effort to 'codify' nuisance doctrine is Section 826 of the Second Restatement of Torts, which says: 'An intentional invasion of another's interest in the use and enjoyment of land is unreasonable if: (a) the gravity of the harm outweighs the utility of the actor's conduct, or (b) the harm caused by the conduct is serious and the financial burden of compensating for this and similar harm to others would not make the continuation of the conduct not feasible.' Restatement (Second) of Torts: Unreasonableness of Intentional Invasion § 826 (1977). This effort is of questionable value because it refers to the actor's conduct rather than his activity. The reference to conduct could easily lead readers to believe that Section 826 is equivalent to the balancing test observed in negligence law – i.e., the Hand Formula. Moreover, Section 826 implies that strict liability should be applied to any activity that has a nontrivial interference with the plaintiff's use and enjoyment of property. The difficult question in nuisance law is determining how to balance externalized risks and externalized benefits.
3.   The economic theory of nuisance doctrine can be traced to its brief treatment by Coase. Ronald H. Coase, *The Problem of Social Cost*, 3 J. L. & ECON. 1 (1960).
4.   The first detailed examination of the economics of nuisance law is that of Merrill, see Thomas W. Merrill, *Trespass, Nuisance, and the Costs of Determining. Property Rights*, 14 J. LEG. STUD. 13 (1985). Building on Coase, Merrill provides a transaction-cost theory of nuisance law. The transaction-cost analysis is also rooted at least in part in the property-versus-liability rule analysis of Calabresi and Melamed, see Guido Calabresi & A. Douglas Melamed, *Property Rules, Liability Rules, and Inalienability: One View of the Cathedral*, 85 HARV L. REV 1089 (1972). More recently, the transaction-cost theory has been extended by Henry E. Smith, see Henry E. Smith, *Exclusion and Property Rules in the Law of Nuisance*, 90 VA. L. REV. 965 (2004). The transaction-cost approach is essential for understanding the reasons trespass law cannot serve as a functional substitute to nuisance law. However, the doctrines of nuisance law reflect considerations that go beyond the transaction-cost theory.
5.   Coase, supra note 3.
6.   Merrill, supra note 4; Smith, supra note 4.
7.   Donald A. Wittman, *First Come, First Served: An Economic Analysis of 'Coming to the Nuisance'*, 9 J. LEG. STUD. 557 (1980); Christopher M. Snyder and Rohan Pitchford, *Coming to the Nuisance: An Economic Analysis from an Incomplete Contracts Perspective*, 19 J. LAW, ECON. & ORG. 491 (2003).
8.   Keith N. Hylton, *A Missing Markets Theory of Tort Law*, 90 NW. U. L. REV. 977 (1996); Hylton, *A Positive Theory of Strict Liability*, 4 REV. LAW & ECON. 153 (2008). Many of the arguments in this article are drawn from Keith N. Hylton, *The Economics of Public Nuisance and the New Enforcement Actions*; 18 Supreme Court Economic Review 43 (2010). The notion that liability rules can be used to control externalities has been well understood for a long time in the law and economics literature, see, e.g., A. Mitchell Polinsky, *Controlling Externalities and Protecting Entitlements: Property Right, Liability Rule, and Tax-Subsidy Approaches*, 8 J. LEG. STUD. 1 (1979). The externality (or missing markets) model uses this basic insight to understand the specific nuisance law rules.
9.   See Steven Shavell, *Strict Liability Versus Negligence*, 9 J. LEG. STUD. 1 (1980).
10. The model in this chapter builds on a simpler model developed in Hylton, *Positive Theory*, supra note 8. By distinguishing incentives under strict liability and under negligence, the model is sufficiently general to be applied to trespass law. However, I will focus on nuisance law. This focus can be justified by the assumption that the invasions (externalities) examined here are of the type generally falling under nuisance doctrine – such as smoke, noise, odors, etc.

11. Figure 15.1 assumes that marginal benefits diminish as the actor increases his activity level, which implies that the marginal private benefit schedule can be represented by a downward sloping line. Marginal private benefits decline because the actor gains less in utility from an additional unit of the activity as his activity level expands. The marginal private cost schedule is assumed to increase as the actor increases his level of activity (see *MPC* in Figure 15.1).

12. See Rickards v. Lothian [1913] A.C. 263.

13. See Keith N. Hylton, *Property Rules, Liability Rules, and Immunity: An Application to Cyberspace*, 87 B.U. L. Rev. 1 (2007).

14. All externalities are real or technological externalities in this analysis. Moreover, I assume that all externalities are relevant in the sense of Buchanan and Stubblebine, see James M. Buchanan and William C. Stubblebine, *Externality*, 29 Economica 371–84 (1962).

15. Paul Krugman, *Increasing Returns and Economic Geography*, 99 J. Pol. Econ. 483 (1991).

16. These aspects of the economics of cities have been recognized in the nuisance case law, see Gilbert v. Showerman, 23 Mich. 448 (1871).

17. This assumes courts operate without error and that litigation is not costly. If courts make mistakes and litigation is costly, compliance with the negligence standard does not reduce liability costs to zero. On litigation costs and judicial error, see Keith N. Hylton, *Costly Litigation and Legal Error under Negligence*, 6 J. Law, Econ. & Org. 433 (1990).

18. One could say that the externality is irrelevant, in the sense of Buchanan and Stubblebine, supra note 10, because the net marginal effect on the third party is zero (note that the marginal negative externality is just balanced off by the marginal positive externality). Alternatively, one could view this analysis as an exercise in 'second best theory'. Intervention to correct a market failure is sometimes ill-advised under second-best theory because the negative externality created by an actor may be offset by a positive externality (perhaps on another market). On the theory of second best, see Richard G. Lipsey and Kelvin Lancaster, *The General Theory of Second Best*, 24 Rev. Econ. Stud. 11 (1956).

19. On the 'reciprocal harm' proposition, see Hylton, *Missing Markets*, supra note 8; Hylton, *Positive Theory*, 2008; supra note 8.

20. Invasiveness, viewed from an economic perspective, means that the negative externality was not the result of a consensual, fully informed transaction. Otherwise, the market would generate optimal consumption (activity) levels. It should be clear that there is no bright line economic definition of the invasiveness concept.

21. It is quite likely that strict liability will have ex post effects on an actor's scale or location decision. After moving to a location, the burden of strict liability probably would induce a nuisance generator to scale back its activity and perhaps to move it to another location, even if the generator was not aware of the costs imposed on victims. However, strict liability cannot affect ex ante incentives if the generator is unaware of the costs externalized to victims.

22. There is an underlying question of what it means to be 'unaware' of the harm imposed on the victim. To some extent, this is a problem running through all of intentional torts. At some point, awareness of danger reaches the level where an actor's conduct has to be described as intentional. The courts have never attempted to set out probability thresholds that would determine an awareness of harm that would require the label intentional. For an early and rather complete examination of intent and probability in the law, see Oliver Wendell Holmes, Jr., The Common Law 52–59 (1881).

23. Many of the activities subjected to strict liability can be viewed as aggregations of risk rather than as different in kind from ordinary risks. For example, the risk created by storing explosives is simply an aggregation of the risk anyone creates by storing something that can explode. The unusual risk creation that justifies strict liability can therefore be viewed as an aggregation or consolidation of risks which are ordinarily confronted in a dispersed and uncorrelated form.

24. L.R. 3 H.L. 330 (1868). The *Rylands* case treats ultrahazardous and nuisance cases as all part of the same general doctrine. On the connection between *Rylands* and nuisance doctrine, see also Hylton, *Positive Theory of Strict Liability*, supra note 8.

25. The Second Restatement has another provision, Section 826, that sets out a test specifically for nuisance law (discussed supra, note 2). However, Section 826 fails to appropriately distinguish nuisance and negligence doctrine, and to give a proper sense of the balancing test implicit in nuisance doctrine. In contrast, Section 520 of Restatement (Second) provides a fairly accurate description of the *Rylands* common law, which is equivalent at its core to the nuisance common law.

26. Judge Posner's decision in Indiana Harbor Belt R.R. v. American Cyanamid Co., 916 F.2d 1174 (7th Cir. 1990), an ultrahazardous activity strict liability case, is consistent with this proposition.

27. One strand of the property-rights (or trespass law) perspective (discussed supra, note 4) has suggested that the reciprocal harms concept can be understood as a softening of property rights in settings in which transaction costs could justify it. See Richard Epstein, *Nuisance Law: Corrective Justice and Its Utilitarian Constraints*, 8 J. Legal. Stud. 49 (1979). The corrective justice theory is quite different from the economic

model examined here. Corrective justice theories sometimes reach conclusions that are consistent with economic models, as in this case, but they tend to be based on a style of argument that eschews formal analysis. Moreover, within an economic framework, one of the important questions examined in any attempt to provide a positive theory of the law is whether the legal rule at issue is likely to lead to a socially optimal equilibrium. That question is unaddressed in the corrective justice context.

28. See Malhame v. Borough of Demarest, 162 N.J. 248, 392 A. 2d 652 (Law Div. 1978).
29. (1752) Ambler 158; for a summary, see Nathaniel Cleveland Moak & John Thomas Cook, Reports of Cases Decided by English Courts: with Notes and References (1884), at 368–69, text available online at: http://books.google.com/books?id=i3UyAAAAIAAJ.
30. 113 Pa. 126; 6 Atl. 453 (1886). For an insightful discussion of *Sanderson*, see Todd J. Zywicki, *A Unanimity-Reinforcing Model of Efficiency in the Common Law: An Institutional Comparison of Common Law and Legislative Solutions to the Large-Number Externality Problems*, 46 Case W. Res. L. Rev. 961, 1017–20 (1996).
31. Id., at 459.
32. Id.
33. In particular, the positive externalities created by the enhancement of market infrastructure and other social benefits from industrialization diminish. However, even in a wealthy industrialized economy, there may be commercial activities that throw off external benefits. For example, information technology, by enhancing the dissemination of information through society, carries significant positive externalities.
34. Rogers v. Elliott, 15 N.E. 768 (Mass. 1888).
35. 34 N.W.2d 549 (Mich. 1948).
36. The key problem is the ability of the factory to increase the invasion without facing any additional cost. In the case of the widget seller, the risk of explosion is fixed with every widget. Moreover, if the widget seller causes the risk of explosion to increase, that will affect the widget market – assuming buyers know the risk. The market constrains the widget seller, to some extent, from increasing the risk. In the nuisance context, suppose a new resident purchases property knowing the risk of an invasion, so the cost of the invasion is capitalized into the property price. But for any given expectation of risk, the nuisance-generating factory can always make it worse later. If the nuisance-generator could assert priority as a defense, the cost of making it worse for residents would be zero on the margin.
37. Wittman, supra note 7; Snyder and Pitchford, supra note 7; Epstein, supra note 27; Smith, supra note 4.
38. The shut down point is reached where the net social benefit from the activity is obviously negative. Although Calabresi and Melamed did not examine nuisance doctrine, the general notion that injunctions could be appropriately applied to activities for which the social costs clearly outweighed the social gains was explored, largely in the margins, of their famous article on property rules, see Calabresi and Melamed, supra note 4. For a more extensive model, see Keith N. Hylton, *Property Rules and Liability Rules, Once Again*, 2 Rev. Law & Economics 137 (2006). This is also consistent with Cooter's prices and sanctions model, see Robert D. Cooter, *Prices and Sanctions*, 84 Colum. L. Rev. 1523 (1984).
39. 26 N.Y.2d 219, 257 N.E. 2d 871, 309 N.Y.S.2d 312 (1970).
40. See, e.g., A. Mitchell Polinsky, *Resolving Nuisance Disputes: The Simple Economics of Injunctive and Damage Remedies*, 32 Stan, L. Rev. 1075 (1980).
41. See, e.g., Fountainebleau Hotel Corp. v. Forty-Five Twenty-Five, Inc., 114 So. 2d 357 (Fla. App. 1959).

16 Acquiring land through eminent domain: justifications, limitations, and alternatives
*Daniel B. Kelly**

I. INTRODUCTION

The government often seeks to acquire land, either for itself (for roads, schools and other public projects) or on behalf of private parties (such as real-estate developers and corporations) whose private projects may entail certain public benefits. Typically, the government can acquire such land in one of two ways: (i) it can purchase the land through consensual transactions; or (ii) it can take the land using eminent domain. Consensual transactions require the government to buy parcels from existing landowners at bargained-for prices that are mutually acceptable. Eminent domain allows a government (the 'condemnor') to condemn land, even if one or more of the existing owners is unwilling to sell, in exchange for providing owners (the 'condemnees') with just compensation based on the 'fair market value' of their property. This chapter explores the justifications for, limitations of and alternatives to the government's use of eminent domain.

The primary functional justifications for eminent domain involve bargaining problems, including the holdout problem, the bilateral monopoly problem and other transaction costs, as well as the existence of externalities. The holdout problem is particularly noteworthy, and this chapter analyzes three types of holdouts, depending on whether the failure in bargaining is the result of strategic behavior among owners, the presence of a large number of owners or a single owner who is unwilling to sell because of a highly idiosyncratic valuation (see infra Part II).

Although eminent domain solves any potential bargaining problems by transferring land directly from existing owners to the government, eminent domain has limitations as well. The primary limitations are the difficulty of valuing parcels, the potential for secondary rent seeking and the existence of administrative costs. Valuing parcels is especially problematic because, in the absence of perfect information, the government may underestimate the valuations of existing owners or overestimate the valuations of future owners. In either case, eminent domain may increase the likelihood of an undesirable transfer, i.e., a transfer in which the existing owners value the land more than the future owners, even if public officials are acting to maximize social welfare rather than advance their own, or other private, interests (see infra Part III).

Because of these limitations, scholars have proposed various alternatives for acquiring land, three of which I discuss below: (i) secret purchases; (ii) land assembly districts; and (iii) auction mechanisms. Comparing eminent domain with each of these alternatives is necessary to determine whether, or under what circumstances, it is desirable for the government to invoke eminent domain, a determination that ultimately depends on a number of important, yet relatively unexplored, empirical questions (see infra Part IV).

The final section provides a summary of the main conclusions (see infra Part V).

II.   JUSTIFICATIONS FOR EMINENT DOMAIN

The eminent domain power, the government's power to take private property for 'public use', is said to derive from the government's authority as sovereign. Grotius (1625) first used the Latin phrase *dominium eminens* (literally, supreme lordship) to emphasize that 'the property of subjects is under the eminent domain of the state' so that the state may use, alienate, or destroy such property 'not only in the case of extreme necessity . . . but for ends of public utility.' In the United States, eminent domain is considered 'an inherent attribute of sovereignty, recognized by all fifty States and the federal government' (Dana and Merrill 2002: 3). The U.S. Supreme Court has emphasized that the federal government's power to 'appropriate lands or other property within the States for its own uses' is 'inseparable from sovereignty, unless denied to it by its fundamental law.'[1]

Although the original justification for eminent domain is relatively clear as an historical matter, it is worthwhile to inquire what purpose eminent domain serves today.[2] If the government wishes to acquire property, it usually can do so, like other buyers, by attempting to purchase the property through consensual transactions. The primary advantage of these consensual transactions is that, presumably, any transfer that does occur makes both buyer and seller better off, while any transfer that does not occur would not have been socially desirable.[3] Indeed, because of eminent domain's administrative costs (see infra Part III.C), public officials often prefer to purchase, rather than condemn, property, assuming they can bargain successfully with existing owners.[4] Of course, the difficulty with relying solely on consensual transactions is that, if the government cannot in fact bargain successfully with existing owners (i.e., if there are impediments to consensual exchange), the highest-value user may not obtain the property.

Therefore, the primary functional justifications for eminent domain involve three types of bargaining problems. First, if the government is seeking to assemble multiple parcels of land, the government might be unable to purchase the parcels if existing owners have an incentive to hold out for a higher price. I discuss three variations of this 'holdout problem' in Part II.A. Second, if the government is seeking to purchase a particular parcel, the government may have difficulty acquiring the parcel because this type of situation, involving a single buyer and a single seller, creates a bilateral monopoly. I discuss this 'bilateral monopoly problem' in Part II.B. Third, even if neither the holdout problem nor the bilateral monopoly problem is a concern, the government might be unable to purchase one or more parcels if the cost of bargaining with the existing owner(s) is prohibitive. I discuss this problem involving other transaction costs in Part II.C. Finally, some courts have relied on the existence of positive externalities to justify eminent domain. I discuss this problem involving externalities in Part II.D.

A.   The Holdout Problem

One of the major plausible justifications for allowing the government to invoke eminent domain for its own projects or for private projects that may have public benefits is the holdout problem. The holdout problem can arise in several different circumstances. Specifically, the holdout problem can arise if existing owners realize the government is attempting to purchase several contiguous parcels because owners might demand a higher price than they otherwise would and thus act as *strategic owners*; the holdout problem also can arise, even if existing owners are not acting strategically, if the government's information is imperfect and the government needs to buy parcels from *a large number of owners*; and the holdout problem can arise, even if existing owners are not acting strategically and even if the number of existing owners is not large, if one or more of the owners are unwilling to sell at any price or are otherwise *idiosyncratic owners*.

1. Strategic owners

Imagine the government is attempting to build an interstate highway or railroad from New York to San Francisco. In the absence of eminent domain, the government would have to purchase contiguous parcels of land along the entire route. Conceivably, if the government is willing to offer the owner of each parcel a price that is above the owner's valuation, many existing owners would sell their land to the government.

However, because the government must acquire each parcel, certain strategic owners may attempt to obtain an inflated price by holding out. These owners realize their parcels are each necessary to effectuate the entire project. Any existing owner is thus in the position of a monopolist with whom the government must negotiate. Certain owners might therefore refuse to sell at a given price even though, in the absence of the assembly, they would have sold at this price because the government's offer exceeds their actual valuation. This type of strategic behavior could prevent the transaction and, therefore, the entire project from occurring. Recognizing that owners may hold out, the government might decide to forego this type of project altogether.

Similarly, if General Motors (GM) is attempting to assemble a contiguous parcel of land for a new automobile factory in Detroit, GM might have difficulty acquiring the land through a series of consensual purchases. Once again, the reason for the assembler's difficulty is that existing owners, realizing GM cannot build the factory without acquiring each of their parcels, might hold out and attempt to extract a higher payment. Thus, in the absence of eminent domain, the government or a private party like GM might confront strategic sellers who hold out in situations requiring the assembly of multiple contiguous parcels.[5]

According to the conventional justification, governments, as well as private parties like GM, need the power of eminent domain to overcome this threat that strategic owners may hold out. Courts have long recognized that one justification for eminent domain is the holdout problem. For example, in 1926, the New Jersey Supreme Court pointed out that 'the power of eminent domain is absolutely necessary' because, '[i]f this were not the law, then a single individual could hold up a state project.'[6] Contemporary courts, including the U.S. Supreme Court, also have identified the holdout problem as a major justification for the government's use of eminent domain.[7]

2. A large number of owners

The holdout problem is also possible even if existing owners are not acting strategically. Specifically, if the government is attempting to acquire land from a large number of owners and the valuations of these owners are heterogeneous, certain owners may refuse to sell if the government has imperfect information about their valuations. With imperfect information, the government's optimal offer may not be the highest possible price that would guarantee that all existing owners would agree to sell. Although a very high offer might ensure that the government could acquire each parcel, the government would be overcompensating any owner whose valuation was below the highest owner's valuation. Because of this trade-off between the likelihood of acquiring all parcels and the possibility that the government is unwilling or unable to overpay for some of the parcels, the government's offer might be lower than the highest offer it would have made if it knew each owner's valuation. If the government's offer is lower than the highest valuation, this lower offer might result in one or more existing owners refusing to sell.

For example, suppose ten owners each value their property at \$55,000 for a total of \$550,000. The government values the parcel, as assembled, at \$850,000. Under these circumstances, assembling the parcels would create a surplus of \$300,000. Here, the government might offer to purchase each parcel for \$60,000, or \$600,000 overall. The owners would sell their land because the offer, \$60,000, is greater than each of their valuations, \$55,000. Thus, the assembly would occur, the socially desirable outcome.

By contrast, suppose that these ten owners value their parcels at \$550,000, but that their valuations vary from \$10,000 (for Owner 1), \$20,000 (for Owner 2) and so on up through \$100,000 (for Owner 10). Again, the government values the land, as assembled, at \$850,000, so the assembly would create a surplus of \$300,000. However, if the government's information is imperfect (i.e., if the government does not know the owners' valuations and is required to make a single offer to each owner without varying the price), the highest price the government would be willing to offer is \$85,000 (i.e., \$850,000/10). Although Owners 1–8 might accept this offer, Owner 9, who values her parcel at \$90,000, and Owner 10, who values her parcel at \$100,000, would reject the offer because \$85,000 is less than \$90,000 and \$100,000. Thus, the government would be unable to assemble the land, even though the assembly is socially desirable.

The type of holdout that arises because of a large number of owners does not occur if valuations are homogenous. With homogeneity, increasing the number of owners does not increase the likelihood that the government's offer will be too low for certain owners. The government's offer is the same for each owner, and, assuming the government's offer is above the owners' valuation, each owner will accept. This type of holdout also does not arise if the government's offer is based on perfect information. With perfect information, increasing the number of owners does not increase the likelihood that the government's offer will be too low for certain owners. The government offers each owner the optimal amount (i.e., just enough to convince to owner to sell but no more), even though that amount varies from one owner to the next.

Shavell (2010) develops a formal model of this type of holdout, which he describes as an 'honest holdout.' He posits that, if the government needs *all* owners in a particular area to sell, the 'necessity of such unanimity in owners' decisions to sell constitutes an acute disadvantage of the policy of purchase when the number of owners grows large, for in that context the likelihood that some owner will reject any given government price offer becomes high.' He also distinguishes strategic holdouts, which arise because owners may delay and negotiate for a high price to extract a portion of the assembly's surplus, from honest holdouts, which arise as a result of the unwillingness of owners to sell for less than their true valuations. Shavell concludes that, because honest holdouts are possible whenever owners' valuations are heterogeneous and the government's information is imperfect, 'the policy of eminent domain tends to be appealing in the model when the number of owners is large, whereas the policy of purchase tends to be better when the number of owners is low.'

3. Idiosyncratic owners

A final variation of the holdout problem is possible if an owner is unwilling to sell at any price or is willing to sell only at an elevated price because of a highly idiosyncratic valuation. For the government to purchase property from an owner, there must be a mutually agreeable price. However, existing owners may derive substantial utility from their property or little utility from the government's offer. Under these circumstances, it is possible, as Shavell (2004: 125) points out, that 'no mutually agreeable price may exist' for a number of reasons: 'a person might hold a sentimental attachment to his land, have sufficient wealth to meet his needs, and be unwilling to sell the land for any price that the state is willing to offer.'

For example, in *Kelo v. City of New London*, one of the plaintiffs who refused to sell, Wilhelmina Dery, was born in her house in 1918 and lived there her entire life, including for over 60 years with her husband, Charles, another plaintiff in the case.[8] Presumably, the Derys were not holding out strategically; instead, they probably attached a great deal of sentimental value to their land. Indeed, the Derys may have preferred to remain in their home during their final years, rather than relocate, irrespective of the City's offer. Alternatively, suppose that Donald Trump owns a parcel of land in Las Vegas. Unlike the Derys, Trump has no special attachment to his land, but the amount of money the city is offering to buy Trump's property may have only a nominal effect on Trump's utility. For both the Derys and Trump, the utility from money, no matter how much paid, might be less than the utility from their property.

This variation of the holdout problem is distinct from the problem of strategic holdouts and the problem of honest holdouts. Strategic holdouts may refuse to sell if they recognize that their parcel is necessary for an assembly, even though, in the absence of the assembly, they would have sold. By contrast, idiosyncratic owners may refuse to sell, irrespective of whether the government is attempting to purchase one parcel or assemble multiple parcels, because no mutually agreeable price exists. Honest holdouts may refuse to sell if the government's offer is too low as a result of a large number of heterogeneous owners and imperfect information. By contrast, idiosyncratic owners may refuse to sell, even if there are not a large number of owners and even if the government has perfect information about the owners' valuations.

Whether the possibility of a highly idiosyncratic owner provides an adequate justification for eminent domain is somewhat controversial. On one hand, proponents of using eminent domain to condemn an idiosyncratic owner can plausibly argue that a single owner, with an unusually high utility from property or low utility from money, should not be able to prevent a project that would otherwise be in the public interest. On the other hand, opponents of using eminent domain to condemn such an owner might plausibly claim either that the existing owner's unwillingness to sell should be taken as *prima facie* evidence that the owner values the parcel more than the government or that there is no practicable way of drawing a line between condemning an idiosyncratic owner with an unusually high valuation and condemning an owner whose valuation, like the valuations of many other owners, exceeds the fair market value of the land.

B. The Bilateral Monopoly Problem

The holdout problem usually arises in situations involving the assembly of multiple parcels (or, as just noted, in situations involving an owner with a highly idiosyncratic valuation). By contrast, the bilateral monopoly problem provides a possible justification for eminent domain in situations involving a single buyer and a single seller. A single buyer and single seller may not be able to reach a mutually agreeable price, even though one exists, because neither the buyer nor the seller has any alternative party with whom to bargain. The result is excessive haggling over the surplus, and this haggling may entail transaction costs that are high and, in some instances, prohibitive if they exceed the gains-from-trade.[9]

For example, suppose that a California resident purchases a beach house that borders the ocean (on the west), steep cliffs (to the east), a neighbor (to the south) and a road (to the north). Through no fault of the landowner, the road north of the home is destroyed as the result of a storm surge. If the only alternative for accessing a local road requires the owner to cut through the neighbor's backyard, the landowner and neighbor are in a bilateral monopoly. As Sterk (1987: 57–58) explains: 'A landowner who wishes access to a lake or road may find that only one neighbor can provide him with access, or that only that neighbor can do so at reasonable cost. The neighbor, on the other hand, may find that the only prospective purchaser of an access right is the landowner without access from his own lot.' The result is a bilateral monopoly problem, a problem that not only occurs in situations involving landlocked parcels but also, as Merrill and Smith (2007: 39) point out, is 'extremely prevalent in property law.'

In these bilateral monopoly situations, courts may allow a private party, or the government, to force a transfer from an existing owner. For example, Kelly (2009b) notes that, 'when an individual owns a landlocked parcel, courts will sometimes grant an easement by necessity' because of the 'potential bilateral monopoly problem that might exist between the landlocked owner and her neighbor.' The U.S. Supreme Court has recognized that such an easement by necessity is functionally equivalent to a type of '"private" eminent domain.'[10] The bilateral monopoly problem is also a justification for the government's use of eminent domain. The government has invoked eminent domain in a number of circumstances involving this problem including landlocked property, unique property and the expansion of existing facilities.[11]

C.   Other Transaction Costs

Even if neither the holdout problem nor the bilateral monopoly problem is a concern, acquiring property through consensual transactions may prevent certain socially desirable transfers from occurring if transaction costs are significant. Specifically, if the costs of purchasing property from one or more existing owners exceed the benefits of the assembly, a consensual transfer will not occur even though such a transfer would be desirable.

For example, suppose an existing owner values her land at $150,000, and the government values the parcel at $155,000. If there are no transaction costs (and assuming that the bilateral monopoly problem does not exist), then the government can purchase the property from the existing owner at a price between $150,000 and $155,000. By contrast, if the transaction costs are $3,000 for the existing owner and $3,000 for the government, then the transfer will not occur even though the government is the higher-value user. Here, the total transaction costs, $6,000 (i.e., $3,000 + $3,000), are greater than the assembly surplus, $5,000 (i.e., $155,000 - $150,000). Thus, a transfer will not occur even though, in the absence of transaction costs, such a transfer is desirable.

The possibility that transaction costs may be significant, despite the fact that neither the holdout nor bilateral monopoly problem is a concern, suggests another justification for eminent domain. Namely, eminent domain allows the government to acquire land, either for its own projects or on behalf of private parties, in situations in which the costs of bargaining with existing owners exceed the benefits of the transaction.[12]

D. Externalities

In addition to the justifications for eminent domain based on bargaining problems, some courts have asserted that the government's use of eminent domain on behalf of private parties is necessary because of external effects or 'externalities' that affect the surrounding community. This section investigates under what circumstances the existence of positive externalities may justify using eminent domain to promote economic development.

The justification for using eminent domain in situations involving externalities is based on the possibility that a private developer may not be able to internalize certain benefits of the assembly that accrue to the community. Suppose five owners value their parcels at $1 million or $5 million overall. In addition, suppose the assembly entails a positive externality such that the social benefit of the project is $6 million but the developer can only internalize a private benefit of $4 million. In this situation, the private benefit would not be large enough to induce the developer to purchase the property because the benefit to the developer ($4 million) is less than the value to the existing owners ($5 million), even though the assembly is socially desirable because the social benefit ($6 million) exceeds the value to existing owners ($5 million).

Of course, even if a significant positive externality exists, eminent domain may be unnecessary. Specifically, if the private value of assembly is greater than the value to existing owners, a party already will have a sufficient incentive to assemble the land. Likewise, if the social value of the assembly is less than the value to existing owners, the transfer is undesirable because, even with the external benefits, the social value of the project is too low. The only situation in which eminent domain may be necessary is if an assembly is desirable from a social perspective but the private incentive to assemble is insufficient, i.e., if the social value of the assembly is greater than the value to existing owners but the value to existing owners is greater than the private value to the assembler.

Moreover, even if the externality is determinative, whether this externality justifies using eminent domain is a difficult determination. The determination depends in part on whether the government is able to provide an incentive to assemble through other means. In the case of public projects involving externalities, eminent domain is probably unnecessary (assuming other bargaining problems do not exist) because the government can take into account all benefits, not just its own benefits, in deciding how much to offer. In the case of private projects involving externalities, eminent domain may be necessary if the government is unable to subsidize the assembly. It may be feasible for the government to subsidize private parties whose projects entail positive externalities, but it is also possible that such a subsidy would exacerbate the holdout problems discussed above (see Part II.A). Thus, although positive externalities do not appear to provide an independent justification for eminent domain, they may bolster the justification based on bargaining problems.[13]

III.   LIMITATIONS OF EMINENT DOMAIN

As discussed above (see supra Part II), the justifications for eminent domain are that it may be necessary to overcome various bargaining problems, including the holdout problem, bilateral monopoly problem and other transaction costs, and to enable certain projects involving externalities. Yet eminent domain also has limitations. First, deciding whether or not to invoke eminent domain requires the government to value parcels accurately, but valuation difficulties can arise, creating a risk of undesirable transfers and increasing the costs of property assessments. I discuss these valuation problems in Part III.A. Second, the use of eminent domain on behalf of private parties may entail secondary rent seeking as private parties attempt to convince the government to condemn property on their behalf, especially if a taking involves concentrated benefits and diffuse costs. I discuss the possibility of secondary rent seeking in Part III.B. Third, eminent domain also involves various administrative costs, which I discuss in Part III.C.

A.   Valuation Difficulties

1.   The risk of undesirable transfers

In distinguishing between two modes of protecting entitlements, property rules and liability rules, Calabresi and Melamed (1972: 1107–08) cite eminent domain as an example of how a liability rule might allow parties to avoid the holdout problem even if bargaining costs are high: '[i]f society can remove from the market the valuation of each tract of land, decide the value collectively, and impose it, then the holdout problem is gone.' But Calabresi and Melamed are quick to acknowledge that 'the problems with liability rules are equally real.' They point out that a landowner 'may be sentimentally attached to his land' and, consequently, 'eminent domain may grossly undervalue what [the landowner] would actually sell for, even if it sought to give him his true valuation of his tract.' Because of the difficulty of determining the landowner's actual valuation, 'eminent domain simply gives him what the land is worth "objectively," in the full knowledge that this may result in over or under compensation.'

The U.S. Supreme Court has recognized as well that there is no effective mechanism for determining how much existing owners value their property. The actual value of an owner's property, the subjective value an owner attaches to the land, includes the consumer surplus the owner enjoys from the land (not just the purchase price). This actual value includes sentimental attachments (such as the value of continuing to reside where memories abound) as well as idiosyncratic attachments (such as personalized adjustments the owner has made to the property that are not valued by the market generally). But this true value is difficult to quantify. Moreover, self-valuations are generally impracticable because, in response to the government's offer to purchase or a just compensation determination, existing owners have an incentive to inflate their valuations.[14]

As a result, in calculating just compensation, courts ignore the owner's true value and instead rely on 'fair market value' as an objective measure of damages.[15] The government calculates fair market value by estimating the price at which a marginal buyer and marginal seller would have agreed in a hypothetical market. However, this objectively determined value neither calculates nor compensates a taking's full costs. As Krier and Schwab (1995: 457) point out: 'Quite obviously, objective damages can understate the truth of the matter; they neglect [a party's] consumer surplus or sentimental value, and hence they can promote error in a very systematic fashion.'[16]

Just as the courts in calculating just compensation do not have perfect information regarding owners' valuations, the government in deciding whether to invoke eminent domain does not have perfect information regarding owners' valuations as well. Because the government's information is imperfect, the use of eminent domain creates the risk of socially undesirable transfers.[17]

First, eminent domain may cause a socially undesirable transfer if the government *underestimates* the existing owners' valuations. The government may not take into account an owner's true value in deciding whether to invoke eminent domain, either because the government anticipates that courts will systematically underestimate the owners' valuations or because the government itself may have the same difficulty as the courts in calculating the owners' valuations.[18]

For example, suppose the value of several parcels of land is $5 million to the existing owners and $4.5 million to an assembler. In this case, the use of eminent domain to transfer the property from the existing owners to the assembler would be socially undesirable because the existing owners' valuation ($5 million) is greater than the assembler's valuation ($4.5 million). The government, however, may mistakenly estimate that the value of the land to the existing owners is $4 million (perhaps because $4 million is the 'fair market value' of the property according to an appraiser's valuation). If so, the government might invoke eminent domain to transfer the property because the government calculates that the value to the assembler ($4.5 million) exceeds the compensation owed to the existing owners ($4 million), even though such a transfer is socially undesirable.

Second, eminent domain may cause a socially undesirable transfer if the government *overestimates* a project's expected benefits. The government may overestimate benefits because it may not have perfect information regarding the valuations of future owners. Such determinations are often speculative and difficult to predict. Real estate developers, corporations and other private parties also may have an incentive to exaggerate the expected benefits of their projects to convince the government to invoke eminent domain on their behalf. And these private parties may do so in situations in which they would not have exaggerated the benefits were they attempting to buy the property themselves.

For example, suppose the value of several parcels of land to the existing owners is $5 million and the government knows this valuation. If a private developer values the land at $4.5 million, the assembly would be socially undesirable. However, if the government believes, based on its own estimation or as a consequence of the developer's assertions, that the developer actually values the land at $5.5 million, the government might mistakenly invoke eminent domain on the developer's behalf.

Thus, one limitation of eminent domain is that, if the government underestimates existing owners' valuations or overestimates a future owner's valuation, the government may invoke eminent domain even though the assembly is socially undesirable.[19] In these situations, an undesirable transfer may occur even if public officials are genuinely acting on behalf of the public interest. Of course, the motivations of public officials may not always be so benevolent. Officials who have the authority to condemn may decide to invoke the power of eminent domain, if it is in their own personal interest or the interest of other private parties, regardless of whether or not the condemnation is socially desirable.[20]

2. Assessment costs

As noted above (see Part III.A.1), the conventional wisdom is that if transaction costs are high liability-rule protection is superior to property-rule protection. Liability rules allow for the possibility that an entitlement might be transferred to the highest-valued user even if the original assignment of the entitlement was erroneous and even if transaction costs are high. Accordingly, because the assembly of multiple parcels might entail high transaction costs as a result of the holdout problem, eminent domain might be necessary to ensure a socially desirable assembly. Likewise, because a situation involving a single buyer and single seller might entail high transaction costs as the result of the bilateral monopoly problem, eminent domain might be necessary to ensure a socially desirable transfer. However, Polinsky (1980) challenges this conventional wisdom and concludes that, if courts have imperfect information, liability rules are not necessarily superior.

Krier and Schwab (1995: 453–55) expand on Polinsky's criticism of liability rules like eminent domain. They assert that, '[j]ust as obstacles to bargaining (transaction costs) might impede efficient exchanges by the parties in property rule cases, so problems in obtaining and processing information (assessment costs) might impede efficient damage calculations by the judge in liability rule cases.' Krier and Schwab conclude that 'when (a) assessment costs promote inaccurate damage awards by the judge, and (b) bargaining between the parties is at the same time impeded by transaction costs, there is no *a priori* basis for favoring liability rules over property rules. If (a) and (b) are the real-world conditions – and we think they regularly are – then the conventional preference for liability rules makes no sense.'

Merrill and Smith (2007: 61) also point out that the argument for the superiority of liability-rule regimes, like the use of eminent domain to acquire property, 'assumes that the process of assessing damages is not fraught with the same problems that would be encountered in trying to negotiate the buyout of an entitlement.' They conclude that: 'Damages must be calculated by the court, and if they vary from person to person or are difficult to measure, the assessment process may also encounter analogous difficulties that render the apparent advantage of liability rules illusory.'

One might add that, even if it is feasible for an appraiser to calculate 'fair market value' or for the court to calculate 'just compensation' accurately, the costs of making an accurate determination may be relatively high. Indeed, it is likely that the accuracy of an appraisal is directly correlated with the amount of time and money expended on the appraisal (presumably with a diminishing marginal return for each additional hour or dollar that is spent). Thus, a low-cost appraisal is more likely to result in an inaccurate assessment (or an assessment in which the probability of underestimation or overestimation is relatively high), and a high-cost appraisal is more likely to result in an accurate assessment (or an assessment in which the probability of underestimation or overestimation is relatively low). If the costs of making an accurate assessment are relatively high, these assessment costs constitute a significant limitation on using eminent domain, just as high bargaining costs constitute a significant justification for invoking eminent domain. The problem is complicated further, as Krier and Schwab (1995: 459–60) suggest, because, at least in certain situations, 'the very circumstances that make for high or low transaction costs also make for high or low assessment costs.'

B. Secondary Rent Seeking

1. Lobbying for and against condemnation

Merrill (1986a: 85–86) points out that the use of eminent domain creates a surplus whenever the value of the parcels as assembled is greater than the value of the parcels prior to the assembly. Because the just compensation determination is based on the 'fair market value' of the land in its highest pre-condemnation use, the condemnor effectively receives 100% of this surplus.[21] As a result, the possibility of utilizing eminent domain may produce a type of 'secondary rent seeking' because, as Merrill points out, 'competing interest groups [may] attempt to acquire or defeat a legislative grant of the power of eminent domain.' Indeed, under certain circumstances, 'the expenditures undertaken to obtain or defeat a grant of eminent domain could completely offset the expected surplus that would be generated by the use of eminent domain.'

For example, suppose that a city with a relatively high unemployment rate is hoping to convince a major biotechnology or pharmaceutical firm to relocate its corporate headquarters and manufacturing facility to the city. City officials are considering the possibility of invoking eminent domain to assemble several parcels of land for the site. The value of the parcels as assembled is $15 million, the existing owners' true valuation is $14 million and the fair market value of the parcels to the existing owners is $13 million. Thus, the actual surplus of using eminent domain to assemble the land is $1 million (i.e., $15 million − $14 million), although, assuming that a firm is eventually willing to purchase the property from the city at its fair market value, the surplus to the firm would be $2 million.

Under these circumstances, two types of secondary rent seeking may occur. First, realizing there is a potential surplus of $2 million, various firms might lobby the condemnor and engage in other measures to acquire a legislative grant of eminent domain. Suppose three firms each spend $300,000 or $900,000 overall in attempting to convince the city to invoke eminent domain on their behalf. Second, realizing that just compensation based on fair market value ($13 million) is lower than their true valuation ($14 million), the existing owners might lobby, litigate and engage in other defensive measures to oppose the condemnor and defeat a legislative grant of eminent domain. Suppose the existing owners spend $200,000 attempting to convince the city not to invoke eminent domain. Under these circumstances, the costs of secondary rent seeking, $1.1 million ($900,000 + $200,000), outweigh the assembly surplus, $1 million, so the city's decision to use eminent domain on behalf of the firm creates a net social loss.[22]

As this numerical example illustrates, rent seeking may be problematic even if the potential private beneficiary is required to pay the 'fair market value' of the property. But Merrill (1986a: 88 n. 91), as well as Alexander (2005), notes that a condemnation followed by retransfer is 'especially likely to engender rent seeking if . . . the price charged by the government on retransfer is less than the compensation awarded under the opportunity cost formula.' In fact, many private parties that benefit from the government's use of eminent domain are not required to reimburse the government for the costs of the condemnation. For example, in *Poletown Neighborhood Council v. City of Detroit*,[23] Detroit transferred the land to General Motors for $8 million, even though the estimated cost of the project to the public was $200 million.[24] Likewise, in the numerical example above, suppose that the city paid the existing owners $13 million in just compensation but that the city subsequently transferred the land to the firm for $1 million. At this price, the surplus to the firm is $14 million (not just $1 million, as before), so competing firms will have an incentive to expend even more resources attempting to convince the government to invoke eminent domain on their behalf.

Because they may be able to capture a significant surplus, developers, corporations and other private parties have a powerful incentive to use various means, including intensive lobbying, political contributions, expensive lawyers, threats to relocate and bribery, to obtain the takings power for their own projects. And these private parties often will have an incentive to capture the eminent domain process for their own advantage, even though they may not have sought or acquired the same land if they had been required to pay the property's actual value through consensual purchases with existing owners or even the property's 'fair market value' in a direct transfer from the government.[25]

2.   Concentrated benefits, diffuse costs

Consider a taking primarily for a private benefit. For example, a real-estate developer may want to assemble land for a new condominium development. If the government decides to invoke eminent domain, the single beneficiary of the taking, the developer, is able to obtain a relatively concentrated benefit. By contrast, consider a taking primarily for the public benefit. For example, a local government may want to assemble land for a new elementary school. If the government decides to invoke eminent domain, the multiple beneficiaries of the taking, the future students and their parents, each obtain only a small portion of the benefit because the benefit is relatively dispersed among many individuals. These two scenarios suggest that private parties that directly benefit from the government's use of eminent domain may have a greater incentive than members of the general public to subvert the takings power for their own advantage.

Moreover, while a private party can use inordinate influence to obtain a concentrated benefit, the costs of the taking will be relatively dispersed among existing owners and taxpayers. Although existing owners might appear to have a relatively concentrated interest in opposing the taking of their land, several factors may undercut their incentive to oppose the government's use of eminent domain. Many owners may sell under the threat of condemnation because, as Cohen (2006: 557) points out, 'property owners frequently lack the resources, political clout, or sophistication to contest an attempt to take their property by eminent domain.' An assembly project that involves multiple condemnations also creates coordination difficulties because existing owners will have an incentive to free ride off their neighbors' efforts to oppose the taking. In addition, while condemnees usually do not receive full compensation, even partial compensation decreases the incentive for individual owners to oppose a taking.[26] Similarly, because the costs of just compensation are widely dispersed among all taxpayers, individual taxpayers usually have neither the relevant information nor a sufficient incentive to oppose particular condemnations, even if they believed that a taking was socially undesirable.

C.   Administrative Costs

Merrill (1986a: 77) also points out that eminent domain entails various administrative costs. He asserts that, like the transaction costs associated with market exchange, these administrative costs are 'another important factor' in determining the circumstances in which eminent domain is appropriate. Consequently, it is necessary to analyze the administrative costs of eminent domain as well as the transaction costs of market exchange.

Eminent domain entails administrative costs at various stages of the condemnation process. These stages include authorizing the use of eminent domain, invoking and exercising eminent domain in a manner consistent with procedural due process, appraising the property that is subject to condemnation in order to determine its fair market value and litigating claims about the legality of the condemnation or the adequacy of the compensation. Merrill (1986a) succinctly describes this process and the administrative costs associated with each step:

> First, and most important, legislatures must authorize the exercise of eminent domain. It is thus necessary to persuade a legislature to grant the power of eminent domain, or, if a general grant of the power already exists, to persuade officials to exercise it. Second, the due process clauses of the fifth and fourteenth amendments, as well as local statutes and rules, impose various procedural requirements upon the exercise of eminent domain. At a minimum, these include drafting and filing a formal judicial complaint and service of process on the owner. Third, nearly all jurisdictions require at least one professional appraisal of the condemned property, something generally not done (or not done as formally) in a private sale. Finally, both court-made and statutory law guarantee a person whose property is subject to condemnation some sort of hearing on the condemnation's legality and the amount of compensation due. Of course, the parties to condemnation proceedings, like the parties to most civil litigation, typically settle before a trial. But the possibility of trial clearly increases the expected administrative costs of condemnation.

The appraisal costs described in the third step are one aspect of the assessment costs that, as discussed above (see Part III.A.2), are necessary for the government to incur in attempting to value parcels accurately. These costs, as well as the other administrative costs that Merrill describes, are additional costs that, like the transaction costs of bargaining, should be taken into account in comparing eminent domain with any of the alternative mechanisms for assembling land.[27]

IV.   ALTERNATIVES TO EMINENT DOMAIN

As discussed above, eminent domain has a number of justifications based on its effectiveness in overcoming bargaining problems (see Part II), but it also has limitations, including the difficulty of valuing parcels accurately, the possibility of secondary rent seeking and the existence of administrative costs (see Part III). However, an adequate investigation of eminent domain requires not only examining the justifications and limitations of eminent domain but also considering how eminent domain compares with alternative mechanisms for acquiring land, both for public projects and for private projects that may entail public benefits. Below, I explore three alternatives: (i) secret purchases (Part IV.A); (ii) land assembly districts (Part IV.B); and (iii) auction mechanisms (Part IV.C). The analysis highlights several theoretical considerations and suggests the need for future empirical work on both eminent domain and its alternatives.

A. Secret Purchases

Several scholars, including Munch (1976), Posner (1977), Merrill (1986a) and Cohen (1991), have noted that developers and other private parties sometimes rely on buying agents to assemble land. Kelly (2006) investigates this strategy for acquiring land through the use of secret purchases. He concludes that secret purchases may be superior to eminent domain (at least in situations in which such purchases are feasible). Moreover, the general ability of private parties, but not the government, to utilize buying agents may provide a justification for distinguishing between the use of eminent domain for government projects and the use of eminent domain on behalf of private parties.

Secret purchases are relatively effective at assembling land because they allow a buyer to purchase property without revealing the identity of the assembler or the nature of the assembly. Under this strategy, a buyer is able to purchase land through third-party agents, so existing owners do not realize that their land is being purchased for a larger assembly. The existing owners do not, therefore, have an incentive to inflate their asking prices and hold out strategically. These owners will sell if the assembler's offer price exceeds their actual valuation. In this way, acquiring land through secret purchases circumvents the problem of strategic holdouts.

At the same time, secret purchases also eliminate the risk of an erroneous transfer, one of the primary disadvantages of eminent domain. As discussed above, although the government can invoke eminent domain to overcome bargaining problems (see Part II.A-C), eminent domain may force a socially undesirable transfer if the government underestimates existing owners' valuations or overestimates a future owner's valuation (see supra Part III.A.1). By contrast, because an existing owner will sell her property to a buying agent only if the agent's offer exceeds the owner's valuation, buying agents take into account an owner's actual valuation. Buying agents also eliminate any incentive for assemblers to exaggerate their expected benefits from a project; an assembler will purchase a property only if the assembler's valuation truly exceeds the owners' valuations.

Private parties have utilized the strategy based on secret purchases in a number of situations. Harvard University used buying agents to expand its campus by purchasing fourteen parcels of land in Allston, a section of Boston, Massachusetts, for $88 million. Disney used buying agents to avoid the holdout problem and assemble thousands of acres in Orlando, Florida for Walt Disney World. And several courts have begun to note that the use of buying agents is a common practice among developers for assembling land for shopping centers and other urban projects.[28]

Importantly, unlike private parties, the government normally cannot rely on buying agents to acquire property for its own projects. Although private parties usually can choose not to disclose the nature of their projects, most government projects are subject to democratic deliberation and public scrutiny and thus known in advance.[29] Moreover, even if the government were able to maintain the secrecy of a project, the need to buy off potential holdouts raises a significant danger of corruption between public officials and existing owners, as Merrill (1986a: 82) points out.[30] Consequently, whereas private parties may not need the government's use of eminent domain to overcome strategic holdouts, the government typically does need the power of eminent domain for its own projects.[31]

Of course, even for private parties, relying on secret purchases to acquire land entails certain costs.[32] Hiring buying agents and monitoring their performance increases the costs of real estate transactions.[33] There is also some risk, especially for assemblies in densely populated areas, for situations in which an assembler must acquire land quickly or for circumstances in which zoning or other regulatory approvals are required, that existing owners will detect the presence of buying agents.[34] The strategy based on secret purchases also implicitly assumes that the valuation of a seller does not vary based on the identity of the buyer.[35]

In addition, secret purchases are effective primarily in enabling an assembler to overcome the problem of strategic owners. It is less clear whether secret purchases are useful in overcoming holdout problems involving a large number of owners (unless the assembler can make multiple offers) or idiosyncratic owners (unless an owner is idiosyncratic only with respect to a particular buyer). Secret purchases also may not be effective in mitigating the bilateral monopoly problem if the parties believe they are still in a situation involving a single buyer and single seller. And because of the additional costs of hiring and monitoring buying agents, secret purchases may increase the number of transfers that do not occur simply because of other transaction costs.

Finally, whether secret purchases are an effective alternative to eminent domain for assembling land for projects with externalities is also ambiguous. Although the government may subsidize any project, including the assembly of land through secret purchases, an ex ante subsidy may not be feasible while maintaining the anonymity of buying agents. Such a subsidy may be possible ex post, i.e., after the assembly. For example, the government may provide such a subsidy if it is concerned about the reputational effects of not providing the subsidy. Alternatively, the government may decide to subsidize the private party's intended development of the land (e.g., the construction of a factory), which may entail external benefits, rather than the land assembly, which by itself is unlikely to involve any external benefits. If so, the government might provide a subsidy after the party assembles the land but before the party initiates the development.[36]

B.   Land Assembly Districts

Heller and Hills (2008) propose a novel property rights arrangement, a Land Assembly District ('LAD'), that they believe is superior to eminent domain. A LAD is a district of property owners that has 'the power, by a majority vote, to approve or disapprove the sale of the[ir] neighborhood to a developer or municipality seeking to consolidate the land into a single parcel.' Voting rights within the LAD are allocated in proportion to each owner's share of the land within the district. With majority approval, the assembler obtains title to the entire district, and owners receive their proportional percentage of the bargained-for sale price. Without majority approval, owners retain their property, and neither the assembler nor the LAD is permitted to use eminent domain.

Heller and Hills claim LADs are advantageous because they: (i) overcome the holdout problem; (ii) reduce the risk of an undesirable transfer; and (iii) allow owners to share in the assembly surplus. First, by requiring existing owners to make a collective decision (viz., to assemble or not to assemble), LADs overcome the problem of obtaining unanimous consent from existing owners. Second, if the LAD assembler does not offer a satisfactory price, existing owners have a veto over whether or not to proceed with the assembly. Third, LADs allow owners to bargain for a share of the assembly surplus and thus have the ability to diffuse any potential opposition among existing owners.

However, one significant problem with LADs is that the assembler is only concerned with the median owner's valuation. If there is heterogeneity among the owners' valuations, the median valuation can be either above or below the average valuation. If the median is below the mean, there is a risk of *overassembly*: the assembler can offer the median and obtain all the land, even though the offer is less than the total value of the parcels to the owners. If the median is above the mean, there is a risk of *underassembly*: the assembler must offer at least the median to obtain all the land, but this offer is greater than the total value of the parcels to the owners. Thus, because of heterogeneity, majority voting may cause LADs to approve socially undesirable assemblies or disapprove socially desirable ones.

Consider an example. Five homeowners each own a parcel in the same neighborhood. (For simplicity, I assume each parcel is the same size, that all valuations are observable and that there are no external effects.) Although each parcel has a fair market value of $100,000, the owners value their properties differently. Owner 1 values her parcel at $110,000; Owners 2 and 3 value their parcels at $120,000; and Owners 4 and 5 value their parcels at $175,000. A developer values the parcels, as assembled, at $650,000. Overall, because the existing owners value their properties at $700,000 ($110,000 + $120,000 + $120,000 + $175,000 + $175,000) and the developer values the properties at $650,000, an assembly would be socially undesirable, and the optimal result is for the assembly not to occur.

Allowing the government to use eminent domain on behalf of the developer leads to this optimal result. A beneficent government, observing these valuations, would exercise eminent domain if and only if the developer valued the land more than the existing owners. Here, because the developer values the land at $650,000 and the existing owners value the land at $700,000, the government would not invoke eminent domain.

Yet, using a LAD, the developer could make an offer slightly above the median owner's valuation, say $125,000 per parcel. The developer is willing to make this offer because her valuation, $650,000, is higher than $625,000 (i.e., $125,000 x 5), the sale price if the LAD approved the assembly. Although Owners 4 and 5 would reject the offer because $125,000 is less than $175,000, Owners 1, 2 and 3 would accept the offer because $125,000 is greater than their existing valuations. Consequently, the assembly would occur because three of the five existing owners, a majority, have approved the sale, even though the assembly is socially undesirable.

Now suppose that Owner 3, the median voter, values her parcel at $170,000 (instead of $120,000). Thus, the existing owners value their properties at $750,000 ($110,000 + $120,000 + $170,000 + $175,000 + $175,000). Here, an assembly would be socially desirable if the developer values the land at more than $750,000 and socially undesirable if the developer values the land at less than $750,000. Suppose the developer values the land at $840,000, so that the optimal outcome is for the assembly to occur.

Here, allowing the government to use eminent domain on behalf of the developer again leads to the optimal result. The government would invoke eminent domain and assemble the property because the developer's valuation, $840,000, is higher than the existing owners' valuation, $750,000.

By contrast, using a LAD, a developer would need to make an offer slightly above the median owner's valuation, say $175,000 per parcel, for a price of $875,000 (i.e., $175,000 x 5). If a developer made an offer of $825,000 (or $165,000 per parcel), a majority of the owners (Owners 3, 4 and 5) would vote against the assembly even though the offer, $825,000, is greater than the owners' valuation, $750,000. In fact, because of heterogeneity, any developer who valued the property at more than $750,00 but less than $850,000 could not assemble the land using a LAD even though such an assembly would be desirable. Thus, heterogeneity means LADs may not only approve certain assemblies that are socially undesirable but also disapprove certain assemblies that are socially desirable.

Like eminent domain, LADs also entail certain administrative costs. As Heller and Hills (2008: 1489–90) point out, creating a LAD requires, among other things, 'defining LAD boundaries, establishing a LAD Board, and selecting governing directors.' Moreover, '[t]o educate the neighbors about the potential benefits and costs of a LAD, the government would hold a series of hearings in which the private land assembler could make the case for land assembly to the neighbors.' Thus, one of the primary benefits of LADs, community participation and the ability of owners to decide for themselves whether or not to accept an assembler's offer, also entails certain costs.[37]

To be sure, using eminent domain has costs as well (see supra Part III). Whether LADs are superior to eminent domain thus depends on whether, empirically, the costs of heterogeneity and the administrative costs of LADs are less than the valuation problems, secondary rent seeking and administrative costs of eminent domain. This determination requires knowing, for both LADs and eminent domain, the value lost because of socially undesirable assemblies that do occur and socially desirable transfers that do not occur. But there is no reason to assume *a priori* that LADs are necessarily superior to eminent domain for circumventing strategic owners and assembling land.

Although the determination of whether LADs or eminent domain is superior for circumventing strategic owners is ambiguous, any comparative advantage that LADs may have appears to diminish as the number of owners increases. As discussed above (see Part II.A.2), if the government's information is imperfect, holdouts are possible if owners' valuations are heterogeneous. However, by relying on majority voting, LADs are especially susceptible to the problems of overassembly and underassembly under conditions of heterogeneity.

In addition, according to Heller and Hills (2008: 1492–93), LADs apply only in situations involving fragmented property, not unique property. Thus, LADs are not necessarily effective in overcoming the bargaining problems that may occur with regard to unique parcels or other situations in which a bilateral monopoly problem might arise. To a certain extent, LADS may exacerbate the bilateral monopoly problem. Because LADs require the assembler and a group of existing owners to negotiate over a project's assembly value, these negotiations may create a bilateral monopoly problem, even in situations that did not originally involve a single buyer and a single seller.

On the other hand, like eminent domain, LADs would prevent the holdout problem caused by highly idiosyncratic owners, unless these idiosyncratic owners constitute a majority of existing owners. Moreover, the government presumably could provide a subsidy to LADs for projects involving positive externalities (although Heller and Hills suggest that eminent domain, rather than LADs, is appropriate for situations involving negative externalities).

C.   Auction Mechanisms

Recently, several commentators have suggested various types of auction mechanisms for overcoming the holdout problem and assembling land. Typically, the objective of these mechanisms is to induce existing owners to reveal their true valuations and thereby facilitate socially desirable assemblies.

For example, building off Heller and Hills (2008), as well as Lehavi and Licht (2007), Shapiro and Pincus (2008) and (2009) propose an 'SP' auction mechanism. The SP assembly mechanism involves a single auction of all relevant properties taken as a whole, with each property owner within a delineated zone being required to nominate the minimum price required for his or her own property. According to Shapiro and Pincus (2009), the SP auction induces every potentially displaced owner to 'state their preferred value for the auction reserve as equal to their own reservation price for their own property, divided by their share of the auction proceeds.' The auction also entails a secret reserve, such that 'the aggregated property will sell only if the winning bid is at least sufficient to pay the reservation prices that the owners will place on their individual properties.'

Compared with eminent domain, the SP auction has a major advantage and a major disadvantage. On the upside, the SP auction provides a test to determine whether the government's use of eminent domain actually 'generates more benefits than costs, including local externalities.' On the downside, as Shapiro and Pincus admit, the SP mechanism 'may sometimes reject what would have been an efficient change in land use.' Thus, although an SP auction might prevent the problem of overassembly, there is still some risk of underassembly.

Likewise, Kelly (2009a) notes that, because of the problems with majority voting if preferences are heterogeneous, economists have proposed the use of 'pivot mechanisms' in a variety of circumstances for solving collective action problems like the holdout problem. A pivot mechanism, essentially a Vickrey-Clarke Groves (or 'VCG') auction, is a sealed-bid auction that assigns an entitlement in a socially optimal manner by charging each bidder for the harm that he or she imposes on other bidders.[38] Kominers and Weyl (2009) develop a formal model to explore several auction possibilities for solving the holdout problem. Ultimately, they advocate a VCG auction, supplemented by a Pigouvian tax refund to balance the budget and deter collusion. Other scholars, including Yengin (2008) and Plassmann and Tideman (2007), also have investigated the possibility of using pivot mechanisms to assemble land.

The various auction mechanisms currently being explored in working papers, including Shapiro and Pincus (2009), Kominers and Weyl (2009), Yengin (2008) and Plassmann and Tideman (2007), are promising steps toward innovative solutions to the bargaining problems that eminent domain is able to overcome only imperfectly because of valuation difficulties, secondary rent seeking and administrative costs. However, unlike the strategy based on secret purchases, these auction mechanisms, as well as land assembly districts, have yet to be implemented in any real-world settings involving the acquisition of land. It is thus premature to assess the efficacy of such auctions, not only because the theoretical frameworks are still being developed but also because it is difficult to evaluate the actual effects of any auction prior to its implementation.

For example, one question that often arises, especially with regard to relatively sophisticated auction mechanisms, is whether the relevant parties (here, the local governments and private developers that may be interested in acquiring land as well as the existing owners that will be required to bid in such auctions) are able to participate effectively, notwithstanding the complexity of the underlying mechanism.[39] In addition, there is a nontrivial danger that reliance on an auction could induce additional rent seeking, unless the auction mechanism is established exogenously and is not subject to revision or manipulation.[40]

* * *

Overall, a meaningful comparison between eminent domain and any of these alternatives, secret purchases, land assembly districts or auction mechanisms, will require a significant amount of empirical analysis to address a number of important, yet relatively unexplored, issues. These issues include, among other things, the extent of the holdout problem, the magnitude of transaction costs and administrative costs and the risk of facilitating socially undesirable transfers or impeding socially desirable transfers. With a few exceptions, there has been very little empirical investigation of eminent domain itself,[41] let alone the use of secret purchases or proposals such as land assembly districts and auctions, a fact several commentators have noted.[42] Ultimately, such empirical work is critical for determining the circumstances in which it is optimal for the government to acquire land using eminent domain.

V.   CONCLUSION

Whether the government should acquire land using eminent domain, either for its own projects or on behalf of private parties whose projects may entail certain public benefits, depends on a number of theoretical and empirical considerations.

There are several possible justifications for the government's use of eminent domain. The primary justification is the holdout problem. In situations involving the assembly of multiple parcels of land, certain strategic owners may hold out and prevent an assembly even though these owners would have sold in the absence of the assembly. If owners are not strategic, the holdout problem still may occur if there are a large number of owners, the owners' valuations are heterogeneous and the government's information is imperfect. Under these circumstances, certain owners will refuse to sell if the government's offer is lower than their valuation (at least if the government is unable or unwilling to discriminate between high- and low-value owners through multiple offers). A final situation in which the holdout problem may occur is if one or more of the existing owners is a highly idiosyncratic owner and no mutually agreeable price exists because the owner derives either a high utility from property or a low utility from money.

Although the holdout problem is the primary justification for eminent domain, there are other bargaining problems that may justify the use of eminent domain as well. In situations involving a single buyer and single seller, eminent domain may be necessary to overcome the risk of excessive haggling, haggling that ultimately may dissipate the entire surplus as the result of this bilateral monopoly problem. The existence of transaction costs, which may arise even in the absence of the holdout problem or bilateral monopoly problem, also might impede an otherwise socially desirable transfer. In addition, although positive externalities are sometimes cited as a justification for eminent domain, such externalities may exacerbate the bargaining problems discussed above but probably do not provide an independent justification for eminent domain. Typically, the government can take into account external benefits in deciding whether to invoke eminent domain for its own projects or directly subsidize projects that entail external benefits in deciding whether to invoke eminent domain for private parties.

However, using eminent domain to acquire land has certain limitations. First, because the government's information is imperfect, the government may confront several difficulties in estimating the value of land. The government may underestimate the valuations of existing owners or overestimate the valuations of future owners. As a result, eminent domain creates a risk that the government may force a socially undesirable transfer, a risk that is only exacerbated if public officials are acting to advance their own, or other private, interests, rather than the public interest. Moreover, in attempting to determine these valuations, the government must incur certain assessment costs, the costs of obtaining and processing information about owners' valuations, and these costs, like transaction costs, should be taken into account. Second, the use of eminent domain may result in secondary rent seeking. Many parties will have an interest in seeking to persuade or dissuade the government from invoking eminent domain, especially if the benefits of a taking are concentrated in a relatively small number of private parties and the costs of a taking are diffused among a relatively large number of landowners or taxpayers. The costs of such rent seeking might exceed any surplus created by the transfer. Third, just as purchasing land through consensual exchange involves certain transaction costs, taking land through eminent domain entails certain administrative costs, and these costs also should be taken into account.

Of course, determining the circumstances in which eminent domain may be necessary requires not only an examination of its justifications and limitations but also a comparison of eminent domain with potential alternatives. The three alternatives explored above are the use of secret purchases, land assembly districts and auction mechanisms. These alternatives appear to be superior to eminent domain under certain conditions but inferior or ambiguous in other circumstances.

The strategy based on secret purchases, which utilizes buying agents to hide the identity of the assembler as well as the nature of the assembly, is relatively effective in overcoming the problem of strategic holdouts. This strategy also eliminates the risk of socially undesirable transfers. By preventing existing owners from acting opportunistically and by requiring potential assemblers to purchase parcels from existing owners, the strategy based on secret purchases ensures that the assembler actually values the land more than the existing owners. The fact that the government is usually unable to purchase land through buying agents, while private parties are able to rely on such agents, suggests a reason for generally limiting eminent domain to government projects. However, the strategy based on secret purchases will not necessarily be able to overcome holdouts who are unwilling to sell at any price, the bilateral monopoly problem, or the existence of other transaction costs (which may be higher because of the need to hire buying agents). Whether secret purchases are capable of assembling land for a project that entails an externality depends on whether a party already has a sufficient incentive to assemble the land, or, if it does not, whether the government is capable of subsidizing the activity without disrupting bargaining.

Land assembly districts or 'LADs', a property rights arrangement that requires existing owners to decide whether or not to sell their neighborhood to an assembler through majority voting, are also superior to eminent domain in certain respects. By mandating a collective decision by the existing owners, LADs overcome the holdout problem, and, by giving existing owners a veto over whether or not to proceed with the assembly, LADs may prevent certain undesirable transfers that eminent domain enables. However, if there is heterogeneity among the owners' valuations, LADs may result in either over-assembly or underassembly. With majority voting, the assembler is only concerned with the median owner's valuation, but, if the median diverges from the mean, LADs may approve socially undesirable transfers or disapprove socially desirable ones. LADs may be problematic as well in those assemblies involving a large number of owners if heterogeneity exists. And, because LADs require the assembler to negotiate over a project's assembly value with a group of existing owners, LADs may increase the number of situations in which there is a bilateral monopoly problem.

Utilizing auction mechanisms, mechanisms in which existing owners and interested assemblers bid to determine whether or not a transfer should occur, is another alternative that scholars have proposed for solving the holdout problem. The format of auction mechanisms varies, from reliance on a traditional auction with a secret reserve to implementation of a pivot mechanism (or VCG auction) that charges each bidder for the harm that he or she imposes on other bidders. Like LADS, these auction mechanisms have not yet been implemented, so it is somewhat premature to evaluate their effectiveness as an alternative to eminent domain. However, even assuming that these auction mechanisms will induce owners to reveal their true valuations, implementation of such mechanisms raises several issues including whether the mechanisms are too complex for participants to understand and whether the mechanisms might induce rent seeking.

Ultimately, determining whether, and under what circumstances, it is necessary for the government to invoke eminent domain is a complicated issue. It requires consideration of the theoretical justifications for, limitations of and alternatives to eminent domain. But it also requires investigation into the effects of using eminent domain as well as potential alternatives, an investigation that is just beginning.

NOTES

*   daniel.kelly@nd.edu. I gratefully acknowledge the permission of the *Cornell Law Review* and *Harvard Law Review* for allowing me to incorporate excerpts from two earlier articles, Kelly (2006) and Kelly (2009a), at various points in this chapter.

1.   *Kohl v. United States*, 91 U.S. 367, 371–72 (1875). The Public Use (or 'Takings') Clause of the Fifth Amendment – 'nor shall private property be taken for public use, without just compensation' – restricts the federal government's use of the eminent domain, although it does not authorize the power of eminent domain itself. *See* Dana and Merrill (2002: 1) ('Takings Clause directly constrains the federal government.') The U.S. Supreme Court has interpreted the Takings Clause to apply to the states, *see Chicago, Burlington & Quincy R.R. Co. v. City of Chicago*, 166 U.S. 226 (1897), almost all of which also have similar provisions in their state constitutions.

2.   For seminal contributions to the literature on eminent domain and takings, *see* Merrill (1986a); Epstein (1985); Munch (1976); Berger (1974); Calabresi and Melamed (1972); Sax (1971); and Michelman (1967). For recent summaries of the economically-orientated literature, *see* Miceli and Segerson (2007a) and Miceli and Segerson (2000). For background on the constitutional history of property rights and the

public use requirement, *see generally* Ely (2007); Merrill and Smith (2007: 1220–1374); Dana and Merrill (2002); Treanor (1995); and Ackerman (1977).

3. Obviously, this presumption is somewhat of an oversimplification as there are a number of factors – the initial distribution of entitlements, the endowment effect, the divergence between willingness and ability to pay, disparities in bargaining power and asymmetric information, just to name a few – that may affect whether a transfer occurs, irrespective of whether the transfer is desirable from a social perspective. On the distinction between socially desirable and socially undesirable transfers, *see* infra note 17.

4. *Compare* Kaplow and Shavell (1996: 757 n.143) (noting that 'most property the government acquires is purchased, rather than forcibly taken' and citing 'defense procurement and an endless variety of routine purchases, as well as many acquisitions of land' as examples).

5. For additional examples of holdouts, *see, for example*, Alpern and Durst (1997) and Alpern and Durst (1984). For further analysis of the holdout problem, *see* Miceli and Segerson (2007a) (modeling holdout problem in a bargaining framework, in which a developer seeks to purchase several parcels of land, and showing that holdouts are a significant cost in the absence of eminent domain); Menezes and Pitchford (2004) (modeling land assembly problem and concluding that strategic delay among sellers is source for the inefficient allocation of land); Strange (1995) (solving for perfect Bayesian equilibria of land assembly game and concluding that holdout problem exists and that likelihood of assembly decreases as number of landowners increases); Cohen (1991) (discussing theoretical problem of holdouts and distinguishing holdouts from free riders); Eckart (1985) (exploring model of land assembly problem in which existing owners can collude with each other or act independently).

6. *Everett W. Cox Co. v. State Highway Comm'n*, 133 A. 419, 513 (N.J. 1926); *see also Varner v. Martin*, 21 W.Va. 534, 556–57 (1883) ('One man by his obstinacy or excessive avarice might readily prevent the building of a railroad. For in many instances it would be physically impossible to run around or avoid passing through his farm, and but for the power of condemning his land he could prevent the public from having the use of a railroad, which might be almost indispensable to the progress and development of the country.').

7. *See Kelo v. City of New London*, 545 U.S. 469, 489 n. 24 (2005) (noting debate about whether eminent domain is necessary 'to overcome holdout problems and assemble lands for genuinely profitable projects'); *Diginet, Inc. v. City of Chicago*, 958 F.2d 1388, 1400 (7th Cir. 1992) (Posner, J.) (pointing out that 'hold-up potential is the principal argument for investing right of way companies with the power of eminent domain'); *Cottonwood Christian Ctr. v. Cypress Redevelopment Agency*, 218 F. Supp. 2d 1203, 1231 (C.D. Cal. 2002) ('Eminent domain can even be an effective tool against free-riders who hold-out for exorbitant prices when private developers are attempting to assemble parcels for public places such as an arena or sports stadium.').

8. *See Kelo*, 545 U.S. at 475; *id.* at 494 (O'Connor, J., dissenting).

9. In discussing the bilateral monopoly problem, Merrill and Smith (2007: 40) explain that, in a bilateral monopoly situation, 'each of the parties has nowhere else to turn in order to engage in an equivalent transaction. Thus, if parties disagree about the price or terms for an exchange of resources, prolonged haggling can result. Perhaps one or both parties, perceiving that the other party has no good options, will bargain strategically to try to get an especially favorable deal.'

10. *See Leo Sheep Co. v. United States*, 440 U.S. 668, 679–80 & nn.14–17 (1979); *compare* Berger (1978: 225) (examining judicial opinions and concluding that 'the major categories of nongovernmental takings (for example, cases involving landlocked owners, public utilities, mill acts, irrigation, and drainage problems, and slum clearance) all involve some element of condemnee monopoly').

11. *See* Merrill (1986a: 97–102) (surveying number of cases in which the government invokes eminent domain in these situations); *see also* Wilk (2004) (updating Merrill's survey).

12. Similarly, Michael Heller has pointed out that it is sometimes difficult to assemble land and other property interests if property has become excessively fragmented. *See generally* Heller (2008) and Heller (1998). Heller suggests that this problem, the 'tragedy of the anticommons,' can arise in situations in which the costs of negotiating with each owner are prohibitive as well as situations in which existing owners are holding out strategically. *See* Heller (1998: 640) (pointing out that 'the market route to bundling rights might fail altogether if the transaction costs of bundling exceed the gains from conversion, or if owners engage in strategic behavior such as holding out for the conversion premium').

13. Some courts also have asserted that the government can use eminent domain to eliminate 'blight' because of negative externalities. Here, the concern is the external costs that other members of the community might bear as a result of an existing owner's detrimental use of land but that the existing owner does not have an incentive to take into account. As Fennell (2004: 984–85) points out: 'The case for clearing blighted land is essentially a nuisance-control rationale that hinges on the negative externalities generated by the land in its present condition.' For example, abandoned buildings or substandard housing conditions may cause external effects on neighbors by increasing criminal activity or deterring potential buyers. However, there is a considerable debate over whether eminent domain is necessary to address such

negative externalities, a question that is ultimately beyond the scope of this chapter. For further analysis of eminent domain and urban blight, *see, for example*, Lefcoe (2008); Eagle (2007); Gordon (2004); Pritchett (2003); and O'Flaherty (1994). The seminal U.S. Supreme Court case involving condemnations based on blight is *Berman v. Parker*, 348 U.S. 26 (1954).

14. On the possibility of using self-valuation mechanisms, *see, for example*, Plassmann and Tideman (2007) and Levmore (1982).

15. For a sampling of the vast literature on just compensation and the conditions in which it is desirable for the government to pay compensation, a question this chapter addresses only tangentially, see Miceli (2008); Bell and Parchomovsky (2007); Wyman (2007); Serkin (2005); Shavell (2004: 127–34); Krier and Serkin (2004); Calandrillo (2003); Nosal (2001); Heller and Krier (1999); Hermalin (1995); Farber (1992a); Farber (1992b); Burrows (1991); Fischel and Shapiro (1988); Kaplow (1986); Durham (1985); Blume and Rubinfeld (1984); Blume, Rubinfeld, and Shapiro (1984); Quinn and Trebilcock (1982); and Knetsch and Borcherding (1979).

16. In calculating fair market value, courts also do not consider the 'demoralization costs' that condemnees may experience from certain uncompensated losses. *See* Michelman (1967: 1215–16).

17. A *socially desirable transfer* is a transfer in which property moves from A to B and B values the property more than A. For example, if a buyer's offer price (say, $100,000) is higher than a seller's asking price (say, $90,000), at any price between the offer and asking price (that is, $90,000 ≤ P ≤ $100,000), a trade would be mutually beneficial for both parties. By contrast, a *socially undesirable transfer* is a transfer in which property moves from A to B but A values the property more than B. For example, if a buyer's offer price (say, $90,000) is lower than a seller's asking price (say, $100,000), the government's use of eminent domain to transfer the property would be undesirable because $90,000 is less than $100,000.

18. Garnett (2006: 104) argues that the problem of undercompensation may not be as severe as scholars have assumed: 'Takers operate under incentives that may minimize the risk of undercompensation: They need to avoid holdouts and the political fallout from negative publicity. They are legally obligated to bargain with property owners and are penalized financially if these negotiations fail. And they almost always are legally required to provide substantial relocation assistance to displaced owners.'

19. A socially undesirable transfer is possible even if the government does not invoke eminent domain if existing owners are bargaining with the government or a private party in the shadow of eminent domain. *See* Miceli and Segerson (2007a) (modeling holdout problem and showing that, if a developer has the power to invoke eminent domain, all existing owners will bargain but that these owners may negotiate prices below their true value, which may result in excessive transfers to the developer).

20. For public choice perspectives on the circumstances in which the government may choose to invoke the takings power for reasons other than the public interest, *see* Fischel (2004); Shavell (2004: 129–30); Garnett (2003: 51–61); Dana and Merrill (2002: 46–52); Nosal (2001); Levinson (2000: 375–77); Kochan (1998); Levmore (1991); and Fischel and Shapiro (1989).

21. *See United States v. Miller*, 317 U.S. 369 (1943).

22. For analysis of this type of rent dissipation, *see* Barzel (1997: 30–32); Mueller (1989: 232); and Anderson and Hill (1983: 441, 447). Because of this concern about secondary rent seeking, Epstein (1985: 161–81) proposed that eminent domain should be limited to those situations involving the procurement or creation of public goods, a controversial proposal that provoked a number of responses. *See, e.g.*, Symposium (1986); Paul (1986); and Merrill (1986b).

23. 304 N.W.2d 455 (Mich. 1981).

24. *See* Somin (2004: 1016–19). For other examples, *see* Kelly (2006: 37–38).

25. Another concern with the possibility of private parties acquiring land at little or no cost from the government is that, if circumstances change, these parties may have a greater incentive to 'back out' of projects, even if the projects entail public benefits, than if they had purchased the property themselves. *See* Kelly (2006: 38–39 & n.192).

26. *See* Shavell (2004: 130) (pointing out that, 'if compensation is paid for takings, then victims of takings will have less reason to resist them, so that a problem of excessive takings could arise *because* of the practice of paying compensation').

27. In order to pay just compensation, the government must raise funds through taxation, which, as Shavell (2004: 125–26) points out, entails administrative costs and distorts private behavior. However, the government would also be required to raise these funds to purchase land, so the implicit costs of raising funds through taxation do not appear to favor either consensual purchases or eminent domain.

28. *See, e.g.*, *Kelo*, 545 U.S. at 489 n. 24; *Westgate Vill. Shopping Ctr. v. Lion Dry Goods Co.*, No. 93-3760, 1994 WL 108959, at *7 (6th Cir. Mar. 30, 1994); *County of Wayne v. Hathcock*, 684 N.W. 2d 765, 783–84 (Mich. 2004); *see also* Brief for John Norquist, President, Congress for New Urbanism as *Amicus Curiae* Supporting Petitioners, at 5–6, *Kelo v. City of New London*, 545 U.S. 469 (2005) (No. 04-108) (describing assemblies in Las Vegas, Providence, and West Palm Beach). In addition, the government traditionally has invoked eminent domain for private parties in situations involving the instrumentalities of commerce

(e.g., railroads, canals, and private highways) or utilities (e.g., telephone lines, oil pipes, and electric wires). But these exceptions, which involve long, thin, continuous pieces of land, further illustrate the relevance of buying agents in determining when eminent domain is appropriate; buying agents are ineffective in precisely those circumstances in which there is widespread agreement that using eminent domain on behalf of private parties is justified. *See* Kelly (2006: 59–61); *see also* Epstein (2003: 324) ('The basic insight is that the takings power works best to weave the threads of infrastructure – highways, railroads, telephone easements, rivers, and the like – and not for squarish plots of land used for other purposes.').

29. *See* Shavell (2004: 125 n. 23) ('[G]overnment is often unable to keep its plans quiet (indeed, the plans may have come about through a public decisionmaking process), and if so, the secret purchase option is not feasible.'); Fischel (2004: 950) ('Unlike private developers of such activities, who can use straw-buyers and other subterfuges, community planning must take place in the open, and holdouts will be far more problematic.'); Merrill (1986: 82) ('[A]lthough buying agents, option agreements, and straw transactions may work well for private developers, it is unclear whether government can use these devices effectively.').

30. Fischel (1995: 69–70) describes how Los Angeles was severely criticized for acquiring Owens Valley water rights privately and covertly and bypassing eminent domain: 'The bypass allowed the city to escape public scrutiny of its plans. Because of the public's anxiety about secrecy, modern governments almost always have to operate in the open, and the holdout problem surely remains.'

31. For a suggestion that this distinction should have been relevant to the Court's analysis in *Kelo*, see Posner (2005: 96) (citing discussion paper later published as Kelly (2006)). For a contrary view, arguing that 'private takings' also should be permitted because eminent domain is just as necessary to circumvent strategic owners in private transactions as it is for government acquisitions, *see* Bell (2009).

32. For objections to the strategy based on secret purchases, *see* Seidenfeld (2008: 317–321); Dana (2007: 137–140); and Mihaly (2007: 27).

33. *See* Heller and Hills (2008: 1473) (asserting that, '[e]ven where developers successfully assemble land by using dummy corporations and shill buyers, the transaction costs of the assembly are so high that only a small fraction of the most valuable projects go forward').

34. *See* Bell (2009: 567) (noting public nature of zoning proceedings). But compare Hellman (1974), *reprinted in* Ellickson and Been (2005), for an interesting account of how buying agents were used to assemble an entire block in New York City.

35. *Compare* Restatement (Third) of Agency § 6.11 & cmt. d (2006).

36. It is worth noting that, in addition to secret purchases, private parties may rely on other methods of acquiring land. For a brief discussion of one such method, precommitment strategies, *see* Somin (2007) (pointing out that 'precommitment may be a more difficult strategy [than secret purchases] to implement effectively because it requires that the buyer predetermine a set price for each lot to be purchased in advance of beginning the assembly process [and thus] increases the likelihood of making a mistake' and noting that, unlike the use of secret purchases, there do not appear to be 'real-world examples of successful use of this strategy for major development projects').

37. *See also* Lehavi and Licht (2007: 1728 n.110) (noting 'the transaction and coordination costs of setting up and operating a multitude of LADs').

38. For a particularly clear introduction to VCG auctions, *see* Kreps (1990).

39. *Compare* Bajari, McMillan, and Tadelis (2009: 375) (conducting empirical analysis of private sector building contracts to compare auctions and negotiation and concluding that 'some of our stylized facts, particularly the positive correlation between auctions and measures of complexity, challenge the conventional view about the widespread benefits of auctions').

40. For evidence that rent seeking may be a problem in the context of spectrum auctions, *see, for example,* Rose (2007) and Wilkie (2007: iv) (arguing that 'both economic theory and marketplace evidence hold that spectrum auctions are not always a cure since the very processes of designing and conducting auctions at the FCC are prone to anti-competitive rent-seeking behavior by entrenched market actors').

41. *See, e.g.,* Chang (2010) (regression analyzing compensation in eminent domain settlements in New York City, 1990–2002); Turnbull and Salvino (2009) (regression analyzing correlation between using eminent domain for private development and government size); Morriss (2009) (regression analyzing state responses to U.S. Supreme Court's decision in *Kelo*); Merrill (1986a) (survey cataloguing 'all indexed federal and state appellate opinions since 1954 involving a contested public use issue'); Munch (1976) (regression comparing just compensation paid and fair market value in 798 condemnation cases in Chicago from 1962 to 1970); and Burger and Rohan (1967) (study comparing settled compensation with appraisers' assessments for 1,221 settlements in Nassau County, New York between 1960 and 1964). In addition, in the thirty-three years following Munch (1976), there were only four empirical studies examining just compensation, according to Chang (2010) (citing Kades (2008); Garnett (2006); Clauretie, Kuhn, and Schwer (2004); and Guidry and Do (1998)). *See also* Aycock and Black (2008).

42. *See, e.g.,* Pritchett (2006: 908) ('little empirical data on the extent to which eminent domain is used, the impact that condemnation has on individuals and communities, or the outcomes resulting from

government seizure of property'); Claeys (2006: 876) ('very few empirical studies about how eminent domain works in practice').

REFERENCES

Ackerman, Bruce A. 1977. PRIVATE PROPERTY AND THE CONSTITUTION. Yale University Press.
Alexander, Gregory S. 2005. *Eminent Domain and Secondary Rent-Seeking*, 1 NYU J. L. & LIBERTY 958.
Alpern, Andrew and Seymour Durst. 1984. HOLDOUTS! McGraw-Hill.
Alpern, Andrew and Seymour Durst. 1997. NEW YORK'S ARCHITECTURAL HOLDOUTS. Dover Publications.
Anderson, Terry L. and Peter J. Hill. 1983. *Privatizing the Commons: An Improvement?* 50 S. ECON. J. 438.
Aycock, S. Alan and Roy Black. 2008. *Special Master Bias in Eminent Domain Cases*, 33 REAL ESTATE ISSUES 53.
Bajari, Patrick, Robert McMillan and Steven Tadelis. 2009. *Auctions versus Negotiations in Procurement: An Empirical Analysis*, 25 J.L. ECON. & ORG. 372.
Barzel, Yoram. 1997. ECONOMIC ANALYSIS OF PROPERTY RIGHTS. 2d edn. Cambridge University Press.
Bell, Abraham. 2009. *Private Takings*, 76 U. CHI. L. REV. 517.
Bell, Abraham and Gideon Parchomovsky. 2007. *Taking Compensation Private*, 59 STAN. L. REV. 871.
Berger, Lawrence. 1974. *A Policy Analysis of the Taking Problem*, 49 N.Y.U. L. REV. 165.
Berger, Lawrence. 1978. *The Public Use Requirement in Eminent Domain*, 57 OR. L. REV. 203.
Blume, Lawrence and Daniel L. Rubinfeld. 1984. *Compensation for Takings: An Economic Analysis*, 72 CAL. L. REV. 569.
Blume, Lawrence, Daniel L. Rubinfeld and Perry Shapiro. 1984. *The Taking of Land: When Should Compensation Be Paid?*, 99 Q. J. ECON. 71.
Burger, Curtis J. and Patrick J. Rohan. 1967. *The Nassau County Study: An Empirical Look Into the Practices of Condemnation*, 67 COLUM. L. REV. 430.
Burrows, Paul. 1991. *Compensation for Compulsory Acquisition*, 67 LAND ECON. 49.
Calabresi, Guido and A. Douglas Melamed. 1972. *Property Rules, Liability Rules, and Inalienability: One View of the Cathedral*, 85 HARV. L. REV. 1089.
Calandrillo, Steve P. 2003. *Eminent Domain Economics: Should 'Just Compensation' Be Abolished, and Would 'Takings Insurance' Work Instead?*, 64 OHIO ST. L.J. 451.
Chang, Yun-chien. 2010. *An Empirical Study of Compensation Paid in Eminent Domain Settlements: New York City 1990–2002*, 39 J. LEG. STUD. 201.
Claeys, Eric R. 2006. *That '70s Show: Eminent Domain Reform and the Administrative Law Revolution*, 46 SANTA CLARA L. REV. 867.
Clauretie, Terrence M., William Kuhn and R. Keith Schwer. 2004. *Residential Properties Taken Under Eminent Domain: Do Government Appraisers Track Market Values?*, 26 J. REAL ESTATE RESEARCH 317.
Cohen, Charles E. 2006. *Eminent Domain After Kelo v. City of New London: An Argument for Banning Economic Development Takings*, 29 HARV. J.L. & PUB. POL'Y 491.
Cohen, Lloyd R. 1991. *Holdouts and Free Riders*, 20 J. LEG. STUD. 351.
Dana, David A. 2007. *Reframing Eminent Domain: Unsupported Advocacy, Ambiguous Economics, and the Case for a New Public Use Test*, 32 VT. L. REV. 129.
Dana, David A. and Thomas W. Merrill. 2002. PROPERTY: TAKINGS. Foundation Press.
Durham, James Geoffrey. 1985. *Efficient Just Compensation as a Limit on Eminent Domain*, 69 MINN. L. REV. 1277.
Eagle, Steven J. 2007. *Does Blight Really Justify Condemnation?* 39 URB. LAW. 833.
Eckart, Wolfgang. 1985. *On the Land Assembly Problem*, 18 J. OF URB. ECON. 364.
Ellickson, Robert C. and Vicki L. Been. 2005. LAND USE CONTROLS. 3rd edn. Aspen Publishers.
Ely, James W., Jr. 2007. THE GUARDIAN OF EVERY OTHER RIGHT: A CONSTITUTIONAL HISTORY OF PROPERTY RIGHTS. 3rd edn. Oxford University Press.
Epstein, Richard A. 1985. TAKINGS: PRIVATE PROPERTY AND THE POWER OF EMINENT DOMAIN. Harvard University Press.
Epstein, Richard A. 2003. *In and Out of Public Solution: The Hidden Perils of Forced and Unforced Property Transfer*, in PROPERTY RIGHTS: COOPERATION, CONFLICT, AND LAW. Terry L. Anderson and Fred S. McChesney, eds. Princeton University Press.
Farber, Daniel A. 1992a. *Economic Analysis and Just Compensation*, 12 INT'L REV. L. ECON. 125.
Farber, Daniel A. 1992b. *Public Choice and Just Compensation*, 9 CONST. COMMENT. 279.
Fennell, Lee Anne. 2004. *Taking Eminent Domain Apart*, MICH. ST. L. REV. 957.
Fischel, William A. 1995. REGULATORY TAKINGS: LAW, ECONOMICS, AND POLITICS. Harvard University Press.

Fischel, William A. 2004. *The Political Economy of Public Use in* Poletown*: How Federal Grants Encourage Excessive Use of Eminent Domain*, MICH. ST. L. REV. 929.

Fischel, William A. and Perry Shapiro. 1988. *Takings, Insurance, and Michelman: Comments on Economic Interpretations of 'Just Compensation' Law*, 17 J. LEGAL STUD. 269.

Fischel, William and Perry Shapiro. 1989. *A Constitutional Choice Model of Compensation for Takings*, 9 INT'L REV. L. ECON. 115.

Garnett, Nicole Stelle. 2003. *The Public-Use Question as a Takings Problem*, 71 GEO. WASH L. REV. 936.

Garnett, Nicole Stelle. 2006. *The Neglected Political Economy of Eminent Domain*, 105 MICH. L. REV. 101.

Gordon, Colin. 2004. *Blighting the Way: Urban Renewal, Economic Development, and the Elusive Definition of Blight*, 31 FORDHAM URB. L.J. 305.

Grotius, Hugo. 1625. DE JURE BELLI AC PACIS. Translated by Francis Kelsey. Bobbs-Merrill, 1925.

Guidry, Krisandra and A. Quang Do, 1998, *Eminent Domain and Just Compensation for Single-Family Homes*, 66 APPRAISAL J. 231.

Heller, Michael A. 1998. *The Tragedy of the Anticommons: Property in the Transition from Marx to Markets*, 111 HARV. L. REV. 621.

Heller, Michael A. 2008. THE GRIDLOCK ECONOMY: HOW TOO MUCH OWNERSHIP WRECKS MARKETS, STOPS INNOVATION, AND COSTS LIVES. Basic Books.

Heller, Michael A. and Rick Hills. 2008. *Land Assembly Districts*, 121 HARV. L. REV. 1465.

Heller, Michael A. and James E. Krier. 1999. *Deterrence and Distribution in the Law of Takings*, 112 HARV. L. REV. 997.

Hellman, Peter. 1974. *How They Assembled the Most Expensive Block in New York's History*, N.Y. MAG. (Feb. 25).

Hermalin, Benjamin E. 1995. *An Economic Analysis of Takings*, 11 J. L. ECON & ORG. 64.

Kades, Eric A. 2008. 'A Positive Theory of Eminent Domain' (3rd Annual Conference on Empirical Leg. Studies Papers), *available at* http://ssrn.com/abstract=1086789.

Kaplow, Louis. 1986. *An Economic Analysis of Legal Transitions*, 99 HARV. L. REV. 509.

Kaplow, Louis and Steven M. Shavell. 1996. *Property Rules versus Liability Rules: An Economic Analysis*, 109 HARV. L. REV. 713.

Kelly, Daniel B. 2006. *The 'Public Use' Requirement in Eminent Domain Law: A Rationale Based on Secret Purchases and Private Influence*, 92 CORNELL L. REV. 1.

Kelly, Daniel B. 2009a. *The Limitations of Majoritarian Land Assembly*, 122 HARV. L. REV. F. 7, *available at* www.harvardlawreview.org/media/pdf/kelly.pdf.

Kelly, Daniel B. 2009b. *Pretextual Takings: Private Developers, Local Governments, and Impermissible Favoritism*, 17 SUP. CT. ECON. REV. 173.

Knetsch, Jack L. and Thomas E. Borcherding. 1979. *Expropriation of Private Property and the Basis for Compensation*, 29 U. TORONTO L.J. 237.

Kochan, Donald J. 1998. *'Public Use' and the Independent Judiciary: Condemnation in an Interest-Group Perspective*, 3 TEX. REV. L. & POL. 49.

Kominers, Scott Duke and E. Glen Weyl. 2009. 'Solving the Holdout Problem' (Working Paper, on file with the author).

Kreps, David M. 1990. A COURSE IN MICROECONOMIC THEORY. Princeton University Press.

Krier, James E. and Stewart J. Schwab. 1995. *Property Rules and Liability Rules: The Cathedral in Another Light*, 70 N.Y.U. L. REV. 440.

Krier, James E. and Christopher Serkin. 2004. *Public Ruses*, 2004 MICH. ST. L. REV. 859.

Lefcoe, George. 2008. *Redevelopment Takings After* Kelo*: What's Blight Got To Do With It?*, 17 S. CAL. REV. L. & SOC. JUST. 803.

Lehavi, Amnon and Amir N. Licht. 2007. *Eminent Domain, Inc.*, 107 COLUM. L. REV. 1704.

Levinson, Daryl J. 2000. *Making Government Pay: Markets, Politics, and the Allocation of Constitutional Costs*, 67 U. CHI. L. REV. 345.

Levmore, Saul. 1982. *Self-Assessed Valuation Systems for Tort and Other Law*, 68 VA. L. REV. 771.

Levmore, Saul. 1991. *Takings, Torts, and Special Interests*, 77 VA. L. REV. 1333.

Menezes, Flavio, and Rohan Pitchford. 2004. *The Land Assembly Problem Revisited*, 34 REGIONAL SCIENCE AND URBAN ECON. 155.

Merrill, Thomas W. 1986a. *The Economics of Public Use*, 72 CORNELL L. REV. 61.

Merrill, Thomas W. 1986b. Book Review, *Rent Seeking and the Compensation Principle*, 80 NW. U. L. REV. 1561.

Merrill, Thomas W. and Henry E. Smith. 2007. PROPERTY: PRINCIPLES AND POLICIES. Foundation Press.

Miceli, Thomas J. 2008. *Public Goods, Taxes, and Takings*, 28 INT'L REV. L. & ECON. 287.

Miceli, Thomas J. and Kathleen Segerson. 2000. *Takings, in* ENCYCLOPEDIA OF LAW AND ECONOMICS. Boudewijn Bouckaert and Gerrit De Geest, eds. Edward Elgar.

Miceli, Thomas J. and Kathleen Segerson. 2007a. *The Economics of Eminent Domain: Private Property, Public*

Use, and Just Compensation, in FOUNDATIONS AND TRENDS IN MICROECONOMICS. W. Kip Viscusi, ed. Now Publishers.

Miceli, Thomas J. and Kathleen Segerson. 2007b. *A Bargaining Model of Holdouts and Takings*, 9 AM. L. & ECON. REV. 160.

Michelman, Frank I. 1967. *Property, Utility, and Fairness: Comments on the Ethical Foundations of 'Just Compensation' Law*, 80 HARV. L. REV. 1165.

Mihaly, Marc B. 2007. *Living in the Past: The* Kelo *Court and Public-Private Economic Redevelopment*, 34 ECOLOGY L.Q. 1.

Morriss, Andrew P. 2009. *Symbol or Substance? An Empirical Assessment of States Responses to* Kelo, 17 SUP. CT. ECON. REV. 237.

Mueller, Dennis C. 1989. PUBLIC CHOICE II. Cambridge University Press.

Munch, Patricia. 1976. *An Economic Analysis of Eminent Domain*, 84 J. POL. ECON. 473.

Nosal, Ed. 2001. *The Taking of Land: Market Value Compensation Should be Paid*, 82 J. OF PUB. ECON. 431.

O'Flaherty, Brendan. 1994. *Land Assembly and Urban Renewal*, 24 REGIONAL SCIENCE & URBAN ECON. 287.

Paul, Ellen Frankel. 1986. Book Review, *Moral Constraints and Eminent Domain: A Review Essay of Richard Epstein's Takings: Private Property and the Power of Eminent Domain*, 55 GEO. WASH. L. REV. 152.

Plassmann, Florenz and T. Nicolaus Tideman. 2007. 'Efficient Urban Renewal Without Takings: Two Solutions to the Land Assembly Problem' (version of March 12), *available at* http://ideas.repec.org/p/vpi/wpaper/e07-8.html.

Polinsky, A. Mitchell. 1980. *Resolving Nuisance Disputes: The Simple Economics of Injunctive and Damage Remedies*, 32 STAN. L. REV. 1075.

Posner, Richard A. 1977. ECONOMIC ANALYSIS OF LAW. 2nd edn. Aspen Publishers.

Posner, Richard A. 2005. *Foreword: A Political Court*, 119 HARV. L. REV. 31.

Pritchett, Wendell E. 2003. *The 'Public Menace' of Blight: Urban Renewal and the Private Uses of Eminent Domain*, 21 YALE L. & POL'Y REV. 1.

Pritchett, Wendell E. 2006. *Beyond* Kelo: *Thinking About Urban Development in the 21st Century*, 22 GA. ST. U. L. REV. 895.

Quinn, John, and Michael J. Trebilcock. 1982. *Compensation, Transition Costs, and Regulatory Change*, 32 U. OF TORONTO L.J. 117.

Rose, Gregory. 2007. *Spectrum Auction Breakdown: How Incumbents Manipulate FCC Auction Rules to Block Broadband Competition* (June), *available at* www.newamerica.net/files/WorkingPaper18_FCCAuctionRules_Rose_FINAL.pdf.

Sax, Joseph L. 1971. *Takings, Private Property, and Public Rights*, 81 YALE L.J. 149.

Seidenfeld, Mark B. 2008. *In Search of Robin Hood: Suggested Legislative Responses to* Kelo, 23 J. LAND USE & ENVTL. L. 305.

Serkin, Christopher. 2005. *The Meaning of Value: Assessing Just Compensation for Regulatory Takings*, 99 NW. U. L. REV. 677.

Shapiro, Perry and Jonathan Pincus. 2008. 'The L2H2 Action: Efficiency and Equity in the Assemblage of Land for Public Use', (Working Paper), *available at* http://www.economics.adelaide.edu.au/research/papers/doc/wp2008-06.pdf.

Shapiro, Perry and Jonathan Pincus. 2009. 'Name Your Price: Efficiency and Equity in the Use of Eminent Domain with Local Externalities', (Working Paper, on file with the author, version of June 25).

Shavell, Steven. 2004. FOUNDATIONS OF ECONOMIC ANALYSIS OF LAW. Harvard University Press.

Shavell, Steven. 2010. *Eminent Domain versus Government Purchase of Land Given Imperfect Information About Owners' Valuations*, 53 J. L. & ECON. 1.

Somin, Ilya. 2004. *Overcoming* Poletown: County of Wayne v. Hathcock*, Economic Development Takings, and the Future of Public Use*, MICH. ST. L. REV. 1005.

Somin, Ilya. 2007. *Controlling the Grasping Hand: Economic Development Takings After* Kelo, 15 SUP. CT. ECON. REV. 183.

Sterk, Stewart E. 1987. *Neighbors in American Land Law*, 87 COLUM. L. REV. 72.

Strange, William C. 1995. *Information, Holdouts, and Land Assembly*, 38 J. URB. ECON. 317.

Symposium. 1986. on Richard Epstein's *Takings: Private Property and the Power of Eminent Domain*, 41 U. MIAMI L. REV. 21.

Treanor, William Michael. 1995. *The Original Understanding of the Takings Clause and the Political Process*, 95 COLUM. L. REV. 782.

Turnbull, Geoffrey K. and Robert F Salvino. 2009. *Do Broader Eminent Domain Powers Increase Government Size?*, 5 REV. OF LAW & ECON. 785, *available at* www.bepress.com/cgi/viewcontent.cgi?article=1395&context=rle.

Wilk, Corey J. 2004. *The Struggle Over The Public Use Clause: Survey of Holdings and Trends, 1986–2003*, 39 REAL PROP. PROB. & TR. J. 251.

Wilkie, Simon. 2007. *Spectrum Auctions are not a Panacea: Theory and Evidence of Anti-Competitive and*

Rent-Seeking Behavior in FCC Rulemakings and Auction Design (March), *available at* www.m2znetworks. com/xres/uploads/documents/Wilkie%202%20Auctions%20No%20Panacea%20Wilkie.pdf.

Wyman, Katrina Miriam. 2007. *The Measure of Just Compensation*, 41 U.C. Davis L. Rev. 239.

Yengin, Duygu. 2008. 'The Super-Fair Groves Mechanisms and Fair Compensation in Government Requisitions and Condemnations' (Working Paper), *available at* www.adelaide.edu.au/directory/duygu. yengin?dsn=directory.file;field=data;id=6233;m=view.

17 The rest of Michelman 1967

William A. Fischel*

Frank Michelman's 1967 article, 'Property, Utility, and Fairness: Comments on the Ethical Foundations of "Just Compensation" Law,' is the most influential article on the takings issue and one of the most-cited articles in law. This review is a description of the structure of his article and its major points. My purpose in publishing this is derived from my observation that Michelman's article is usually presented to students of takings law by way of excerpts. The parts excerpted are almost always the utilitarian and Rawlsian criteria for deciding when to compensate disappointed claimants and when to leave their losses where they lie. Although these are important parts (and will be discussed below), the structure of Michelman's whole article reflects an approach to takings that strongly qualifies his famous criteria. This chapter reflects my opinions, not those of Michelman. The present chapter is intended primarily to induce students of regulatory takings to look at the rest of Michelman's enduringly famous article. For that reason, it is brief, and I omit most citations that are found in his article.[1] Parenthetical page numbers refer to those in 80 *Harvard Law Review*.

Michelman starts *Part I* with a philosophical conundrum. How can scholars reconcile philosopher Leonard Hobhouse's rigid insistence that society should not sacrifice the well-being of a single person for the benefit of many with the 'worldly wise' view of Oliver Wendell Holmes, Jr., that government should not sacrifice the citizen 'more than it can help' (p. 1166)? Michelman goes on to indicate a line he will *not* pursue, which I would call 'connect the dots' legal scholarship, which involves reviewing opinions, particularly those of the Supreme Court, and seeing if one can make a rule that fits the decisions (p. 1171). He motivates this with a review of the 'jarring' decisions that are inconsistent with one another (p. 1170). His prime examples are the coal-mine case, Pennsylvania Coal v. Mahon, 260 U.S. 393 (1922), in which compensation to the coal company for eliminating its right to mine without regard to damaging structures on the surface was held to be warranted, and the brickyard case, Hadacheck v. Los Angeles, 239 U.S. 394 (1915), in which compensation for closing a pre-existing brickyard was not required (p. 1170). Michelman is unsatisfied with the present state of takings law and wants to advance a better way: 'I hope to show that the test of fairness. . .is not a truism; that departures from it in practice are common and can often be identified with confidence. . .' (p. 1172).

The next stage of the article – the beginning of the analytical part – is a discussion of 'The Purposes of Collective Action' (p. 1172). It is telling to me that Michelman does not start with the principles of property. The takings problem arises from actions by the government. In starting here, it is as if he wants to convince readers that the government is up to something good now and then. (For a contrary view, affirming the centrality of the common law of property and evincing a profound skepticism of government intentions, see Epstein (1985).) Michelman gets right into the Kaldor/Hicks criterion so familiar to economists. The criterion holds simply that if the dollar value of the benefits of a public action exceeds its costs, the action should be regarded as economically efficient (p. 1174). A revised zoning ordinance, for example, meets this if the gains to homeowners, as manifested by higher property values, from its additional protections exceed the costs – forgone profits – by would-be developers.

Michelman then asks, why, if the proposed project adds to the value of property within its jurisdiction, does the government not simply obtain the consent of the property owners who suffer losses (p. 1174)? I would take this to mean Pareto superiority, which holds that a change is desirable if someone is better off – as is usually implied by consent – and no one else is worse off. One of Michelman's answers is that Pareto superiority is too hard to arrange, and society would forgo all of the benefits of collective action if we rigidly adhered to it. He points particularly to the excess transaction costs of compensating everyone involved, citing (p. 1176) Coase (1960) and Calabresi (1965). I would note that Kaldor (1939) and Hicks (1939) came up with their now-famous criterion for the same reason – the transaction costs of compensating all the losers would have forestalled the adoption of nineteenth-century Britain's most illustrious liberal cause, the abolition of the protectionist Corn Laws.

There is some discussion of the problem of public goods and free riders (p. 1175), but the question of how governments make decisions, which occupies the field of public economics, is not central to Michelman's analysis. Nor is there any sustained discussion of the meaning of 'public use' for which property is taken, which has exercised the takings issue so much since Kelo v. City of New London, 545 U.S. 469 (2005). Michelman proceeds in almost every instance with the presumption that the government's proposed taking is valid and that the main question of interest is when to supply the remedy of 'just compensation.'

Michelman makes a brief detour into the log-rolling theory that compensation is implicitly provided because *on average* losses will be offset by gains over time (p. 1177). (This has been explored by Farber 1992.) He does not go down that route, even while admitting its attractions, because, as James Madison warned in the Federalist Papers and civil rights issues of the time demonstrated, there is good reason to be skeptical of the proposition that things just average out for everyone in the long run (p. 1178). Lack of compensation is also problematical because legislators have a problem calculating social efficiency without actually having to pay.

The ideal tests of social efficiency are unanimity or, if there are dissenters, compensation for those who do not consent (p. 1180). On this point, Michelman criticizes the view that government should not compensate because it will be too costly to the government: 'What society cannot, indeed, afford is to impoverish itself' (p. 1181). He goes on, however, to justify coercive redistribution of wealth, but only if it 'has a general and apparent "equalizing" tendency. . . .' (p. 1182). The possibility that an 'equalizing tendency' might be carried so far as to cause society to 'impoverish itself' is not explored, nor is the notion that taxation might also be seen as a taking of property. In this regard, Michelman's analysis follows conventional legal principles, which keep taxes and redistribution analytically separate from property issues.

Leaving general principles, Michelman devotes *Part II* (p. 1183) to his famous critique of the common rules of takings decision, and he finds them all wanting. Michelman derides the distinction between taking by physical invasion and taking by regulation as 'wordplay' and 'form-over-substance' (pp. 1185–86). He notes specifically that the distinction could allow for the substitution of regulation for taking in the case of scenic easements (1186). That is, instead of purchasing the land or an easement to keep it from being developed, the government burdens the landowner with a regulation that prevents development. He also points out that the distinction may result in overcompensation by some formulas, since often the physical invasion is trivial or even beneficial, as in taking the edges of parcels for a public sidewalk (p. 1185).

Diminution of value, derived from *Pennsylvania Coal*, is suspect because the baseline from which compensation should be calculated is not clear (p. 1191). Should it be the use that existed previously; the use that maximizes sale value, regardless of its effect on neighbors; or the use consistent with neighboring uses? The diminution-of-value standard is also complicated by the divisibility of property interests (p. 1193), which could allow owners to carve out a stick from an otherwise profitable bundle that has been 'taken' by the regulation.

The balancing test asks whether there is enough public gain to justify the private loss. This merely restates the Kaldor/Hicks criterion without resolving the compensation question (p. 1196). Another test, the harm-benefit rule, holds that government actions that extract benefits from the private sector should be compensated, but actions that prevent nuisances or other 'harms' should not. The distinction is criticized on the basis of Michelman's sympathy for the brickmaker in *Hadacheck* (who was made to shut his works down without compensation): '. . . there is no basis for a general rule dispensing with compensation in respect of all regulations apparently of the 'nuisance-prevention' type. . . .' (p. 1197). Miller v. Schoene, 276 U.S. 272 (1928) which upheld the destruction of cedars in order to save apple trees (discussed below), is also invoked to show that cause of nuisance not so clear (p. 1198).

Having shown that the usual tests do not make much sense – though he does concede the intuitive appeal of several of them – Michelman turns in *Part III* to theories of property (p. 1202). (Recall he has already discussed theories of government.) The search is for a theory in which both compensation and noncompensation make sense. That is, it is easy to build a theory of property in which you always compensate (e.g., the usual reading of Blackstone) or never compensate (e.g., Marx). Michelman's idea of property in this context hinges on 'some degree of permanence of distribution' (p. 1203).

The first theories he examines are 'desert' and 'personality' (p. 1203). Personality theory regards property as an extension of one's self. Artistic creations, for example, are said not to be mere fungible commodities, and no amount of compensation would seem to offset deliberate injuries to property owners under these theories. John Locke's labor theory is an ancient example of a 'desert' theory: Mixing one's labor with something creates an entitlement to keep it. This class of theories share a common disregard for the social consequences of property ownership. Michelman concludes that the 'absolutist implication' of such theories makes them unhelpful as the basis for a theory of compensation (p. 1204).

The second property theory Michelman considers is 'social functionary' (p. 1206), which holds that production would be impossible (or too costly) without property. Property in this view is defined largely by what it accomplishes as an ingredient of production. But this theory does not preclude some rather arbitrary redistributions (p. 1207). All sorts of demoralizing losses might not be compensable if the social value of the regulation exceeded the loss of incentive effects of noncompensation. This is not quite the same as the Kaldor/Hicks criterion (where benefits just have to exceed costs), because a social functionary approach would insist on considering more than just the dollar costs of resources taken; the adverse incentive effects would have to be calculated as well. The difference between social functionary theory and the next theory to be considered, utilitarianism, seems to be that individuals do not count by themselves, but only for their value as agents of social production. That there might be a special, additional loss from failure to compensate – 'demoralization costs' under the utilitarian rubric next considered – is not counted under social functionary theory.

The theory that comes closest to dealing in a balanced way with compensation issues is utilitarianism, as developed by Jeremy Bentham (p. 1208). Michelman takes Bentham as providing 'the germ of a theoretically satisfying approach to the compensation questions' (p. 1211). The realization that stability of expectation is *useful* is what condemns unprincipled transfers (p. 1211). It is not that property is absolutely necessary for production that makes security important, but that security itself is a good thing. This distinguishes utilitarianism from social functionary theories. The latter would jettison property (and compensation) if doing so aided production, while utilitarianism would hesitate before doing so because the (*ex ante*) feeling of insecurity would still remain.

The loss of well-being of an individual who thinks of himself or herself as being treated arbitrarily counts for something in utilitarianism, but not necessarily in social functionary theory. This is implicit in Bentham's theory of property as 'a basis of expectations' (p. 1212). Property is not itself an expectation, for some expectations may be unreasonable or unwarranted. The existence of property is instead the institutionalization of feelings of security. Undermining such a basis is itself a bad thing because of the anxieties it creates in individuals.

Part IV (p. 1214) presents the famous tests for compensation that are so often reprinted in property texts. Their separation from the previous parts of Michelman's article in casebooks probably explains why they are so poorly understood. The reader who has not had to wrestle with the theories of the state, the paradoxes of existing compensation tests, and competing theories of property is usually puzzled by the utilitarian criteria that form the first test of compensation, which is based on Bentham's utilitarian theory.

The test is simple. Assume a project is efficient in that it meets the KaldorHicks criterion that total social benefit (B) exceeds the opportunity costs (C) of the resources involved. That is, we initially assume that the government is up to something with positive net social benefit, $B > C$. Whether compensation should be made depends on comparing demoralization costs, D, with settlement costs, S. Demoralization costs are all the bad (for a utilitarian) things that happen when compensation is not made. They include two elements: the disutility (measurable in dollars) of those not compensated (and that of their sympathizers), plus the lost value of future production caused by their acting on this new knowledge. (I would note that a social functionary theory would count only the latter loss – forgone future production – in deciding whether to compensate.) Given that utilitarianism emphasizes the sense of security that property provides, one might call demoralization costs 'insecurity costs'.

Settlement costs arise when society *does* decide to make compensation. These are the transaction costs of identifying losers, winnowing out false claimants, negotiating, having a trial (if that's the method), and raising taxes (with their associated deadweight losses) to pay for the project or foregoing some other public project. Once these two costs (demoralization and settlement) are ascertained, the utilitarian rule is to pay if D > S, but not if S > D. It's simple economics: choose to endure the lower costs.

In teaching these concepts for many years, I have found that even economics students are easily confused about the settlement costs of taxes. It is not the amount of taxation that is the settlement cost. If compensation is perfect – if it pays for all costs – and thus eliminates all demoralization cost, the taxes (or other public revenue) raised are simply a transfer whose value is equal to the term C in the B ≥ C efficiency criterion. The settlement cost elements of taxation comprise the additional administrative costs of raising new tax revenue and the deadweight loss of tax avoidance from higher taxes (or from forgoing other public projects). This is not an easy number to calculate, but just using taxes themselves is both economically wrong (because deadweight loss may be greater or less than tax collections) and inconsistent with Michelman's categories.

What is seemingly noneconomic about Michelman's utilitarian criteria is the element of disappointment and insecurity in demoralization costs. Economists overlook this element because it is so hard to measure: Individual demoralization is 'private information' that can easily be overstated. Economists are much more comfortable with the lost future production element of demoralization cost, but that then puts economists into the social functionary category. Many economists may be comfortable with that, but they should not be. Modern demand theory uses utilitarianism to a larger extent than we like to admit. If it was only the loss of measurable future production that counted in demoralization, we could indeed fall into the habit that Hobhouse proscribed, that of sacrificing individuals for the benefit of the larger number or at least, in Holmes's formulation, sacrificing them more than can be helped.

Michelman in an important note (p. 1215, n. 100) says that *courts* do not necessarily have to make calculation about settlement and demoralization costs. Indeed, doing so could greatly raise settlement costs. What Michelman suggests is that courts carve out some core areas that the political process is apt not to balance. (How the politics works is discussed later and hardly ever adverted to in the legal literature.)

Michelman realizes that demoralization costs are tricky, so he goes on to describe them in more detail. 'Deliberate' social actions from 'majoritarian exploitation' are most serious (p. 1216). The 'only one possible way' to justify the special majoritarian anxiety is that it is 'purposive,' as opposed to random (p. 1217). Insurance can handle the random hazards. Here again is a reason for reading the previous sections of Michelman's article. Economists are apt to treat all losses as insurable (most notably Blume and Rubinfeld 1984), but the utilitarian's concern about security of possession makes losses deliberately caused by the majority seem especially bad (Fischel and Shapiro 1988). Michelman in fact adverts to Calabresi's (1965) analysis of risk in an earlier footnote (p. 1169, n. 5):

> There is, however, an important difference, warranting separate treatment, between compensating for individualized losses which are the foreseeable results of deliberate collective choices, and compensating for losses which are, from society's collective vantage point, pure accidents. The former practices, but not the latter, may imply a distinctive policy of forestalling exploitation, or the suggestion thereof, by the many of the selected or identified few. It could be said to be a subsidiary purpose of this article to clarify and elaborate upon this distinction.

The famous list (more nuanced than a list, of course) of contributors to demoralization costs starts on p. 1217. Demoralization costs are larger (even if unintentional) if:

(1)   Settlement costs are low. This seems to mix the other side of the compensation ledger (settlement costs themselves), but not really. When it would have been easy to compensate losers but society decides not to, it is obvious that the victim sustains a disproportionate loss, and general feelings of insecurity are heightened.

(2)   It appears doubtful that B > C, so that the government action looks more like unprincipled redistribution than one done for the public weal. This implies that efficiency itself is partly a balm for demoralization.

(3)   The individual burden is especially large, not of the type that are typically scattered around.

(4)   The burden is not offset by some reciprocity of advantage, such as the gain a homeowner gets from a zoning law that forces both her and her neighbor to forego certain types of use. This actually amounts to the possibility that compensation has been paid in the form of the benefits of the regulation itself, though one cannot just wave one's hands about the benefits of a civilized society or the whole basis for compensation is undermined.

(5)   Most interesting to me, demoralization costs are larger if the victim lacks influence in the political process to have extracted some concessions 'in kind' that might not be noticeable from the particular action in question (p. 1218).

To put the abstract criteria in a more concrete perspective, consider a famous but puzzling takings case whose background and denouement I have researched (Fischel 2007; I had earlier and less completely discussed this in Fischel 1995). The case is Miller v. Schoene, 276 U.S. 272 (1928), which Michelman calls 'celebrated' (p. 1198). In 1914, the Virginia legislature passed a law that required the cutting down of red cedar trees whose proximity to apple trees resulted in a damaging fungus or 'rust' that harmed the apple crop but did no harm to the cedar trees. The botanical peculiarity of the fungus was that its life cycle required a back-and-forth trip between the apples and the cedars. If the two species were not within a mile or two of one another, the rust was not produced at all. Despite the ambiguity of which species was the victim of the other, the Virginia and U.S. Supreme Courts upheld the measure, for which no compensation to the owners of the cedars was constitutionally required.

I found that the law as originally written *did* offer compensation for the supposedly small set of cedar owners whose trees had economic value as windbreaks or ornamental hedges. Most other cedars were volunteers that sprung up in fence rows and untended farm fields and had little value to their owners. I found, however, that offers of compensation to a few induced many more cedar owners to demand compensation, and this threatened the financial viability of the rust control program. In response, the apple growers persuaded the courts to eliminate compensation, though the orchardists continued to pay for disruptions to cedar owners' farming operations caused by the teams of cedar cutters. Cedar owners acceded to this, I argue, because they recognized the high value of apples as compared to cedars and that the apple industry was important for the local economy.

In terms of Michelman's utilitarian criteria, the original law (calling for compensation but requiring cutting) can be thought of as regarding settlement costs to be lower than demoralization costs. Demoralization costs were not especially high because it was clear to almost everyone that benefits exceeded costs; the widespread distribution of usually-low-value cedars mitigated feelings of being singled out; there was a general reciprocity of advantage in that the apple industry was widely accepted as the basis for local (Shenandoah Valley) agricultural prosperity (even complaining cedar owners conceded this); and cedar owners, though unorganized (there were no cedar plantations), enjoyed political representation in the legislature that passed the laws. (My most dumbfounding discovery was that the plaintiff in the case, Dr. Casper Otto Miller, had served in the legislature and voted for the cedar-cutting law.)

Despite the modest demoralization costs, proponents of the law – mainly the apple orchard owners, who were well organized – understood that owners of ornamental cedars should be compensated for their cutting. The orchardists thought that this would involve only modest settlement costs, and they were actually willing to tax themselves (and not Virginians as a whole) to pay for compensation when damages were warranted. Thus, apple orchard owners originally conformed to the utilitarian prescription that held that compensation was warranted when $D > S$, assuming, as was clearly true in this instance, that $B > C$. But the orchard owners found after a few years' experience that settlement costs were spiraling out of control. Owners of cedars that contributed almost no value to their property were demanding compensation for their cutting. Apple-orchard taxes were rising so much that enduring cedar rust was seeming preferable to cutting cedars.

In this chastened and alarmed mood, the orchardists attempted to limit the compensation from their open-ended law against a determined and deep-pocketed plaintiff, Daniel Kelleher, in Kelleher v. Schoene, 14 F.2d 341 (1926). Kelleher almost certainly financed Dr. Miller's litigation, and Miller's was the case that reached the U.S. Supreme Court. Both the Virginia and U.S. Supreme Courts brushed off the plain language of compensation in the 1914 Act and held that compensation was not required under any circumstance. Despite this victory, apple orchardists continued to pay for the cutting themselves and also a limited set of consequential damage (disruption of farming from cutting cedars) until advances in fungicide technology after World War II made cedar cutting unnecessary.

Leaving the utilitarian concern, Michelman takes up his equally famous (though not mutually exclusive) Rawlsian criteria (p. 1218). This is remarkable in part because Rawls was not yet famous as a social philosopher for his *Theory of Justice* (1971). Michelman got an early read on Rawls from philosophy journals of the type law professors seldom read. His motive for invoking Rawls was apparently unease with utilitarianism, a doctrine that modern philosophers were increasingly inclined to criticize (p. 1219).

Under Rawlsian thinking, the question of compensation is removed far from the historically determined roots of property law and its utilitarian concern for security. The issue of compensation (among many other social practices) is to be viewed as part of the creation of a social contract in a hypothetical 'convention of the circumspect' (p. 1220). The convention meets behind a veil of ignorance about who owns what. Behind this veil, members of the polity have to make rules for when the veil is lifted. Knowing that they may be on the bottom of the wealth distribution, they become, it is assumed, highly equalitarian. They regard each other as equals behind the veil and agree to continue such equality once it is lifted. This is the 'equal liberty' principle. However, such equality could be unproductive, so they agree to adopt only those measures that make the least-advantaged person better off. Inequality in social arrangements is acceptable, but only if its effect is to make poorest better off. This is what Rawls later called the 'maximin' principle.

Because Rawls's theory was later embraced as a defense of the modern welfare state, it is an odd theory to invoke in defense of property. It must be understood, however, that under its conditions, the 'lifting of the veil' assumes that a satisfactory distribution of wealth has been agreed upon (p. 1221). Hence deviations from it for the common good should not alter the distribution. When collective improvements require the sacrifice of someone's wellbeing, the equal liberty principle requires full compensation, since lack of compensation would leave some people unequally benefited by the measure. However, Rawls's second principle – the maximin – allows for the possibility that those left uncompensated might themselves realize, at some remove, that they would be better off if sometimes the government did not have to pay compensation. The conditions under which this is acceptable are that the disappointed claimant ought to be able to have seen that, in the long run, she would be worse off if the rule were always to compensate (p. 1221).

This leads to Michelman's famous triple-negative rule: '[a] decision not to compensate is not unfair as long as the disappointed claimant ought to be able to appreciate how such decisions might fit into a consistent practice which holds forth a lesser long-run risk to people like him than would any consistent practice which is naturally suggested by the opposite decision' (p. 1223). How he ought to appreciate it is essentially to invoke the aforementioned utilitarian criteria, which is to minimize the sum of demoralization and settlement costs, subject to the condition that an action's net benefits are deemed to be greater than either cost.

This rather round-about convergence of Benthamite utilitarianism and Rawlsian contractarianism is not perfect. Michelman points to two situations in which they might give different results. In one, government might be able to deceive other people about an individual loss and thus not spread demoralization costs, which would then warrant less compensation on the everyday utilitarian calculus (pp. 1223–24). Michelman points out that this is an unlikely condition in an open society. The other divergence arises if those not compensated are stubborn about not seeing their long run advantage, as they should have in the Rawlsian convention of the circumspect. Because utilitarians supposedly take people as they are, not as philosophers would like to see them in a thought experiment, the utilitarian approach is actually more likely to offer compensation than the supposedly more equalitarian Rawlsian principle (p. 1224).

Part V (p. 1224) revisits the judicial rules (e.g., physical invasion, diminution of value) in light of the 'parallel' utilitarian and fairness criteria (p. 1226). The traditional judicial rules do not look so absurd in this context, though all of them are only partial clues to how to settle the takings issue. Physical invasion adverts to the disproportionate burden of demoralization costs and the settlement cost of line-drawing (p. 1227). But Michelman still has little to say in favor of it as an exclusive criterion, and it cannot by itself meet the fairness test (p. 1229).

Diminution of value is defended gingerly as a way of identifying the 'crystallized' or 'investment backed' expectations that seem more important than potential gains and losses (p. 1233). Michelman is clearly uneasy with this, even though he uses it to justify the process of grandfathering nonconforming uses in zoning. Here is another point at which the fame of Michelman's article is misunderstood. Several commentators and Supreme Court opinions (e.g., Penn Central v. New York, 438 U. S. 104, 128) cite without qualification 'investment-backed expectations' as a principle that Michelman supports and apply it to a regulation that does not seem to meet his criteria.

The rule about balancing social gain against private loss (that is, the Kaldor/Hick test) is seen as an imperfect effort to identify situations in which the gain is so especially large that the individual's demoralization costs might be reduced, but Michelman still finds little aid in this rule (p. 1235). Harm and benefit is rehabilitated as establishing a potentially efficient benchmark from which to judge compensation. Activities judged 'harmful' are akin to being 'theft-like' and hence require no compensation (p. 1236). But Michelman does not move to the economists' notion of least-cost avoider, which endorses the harm-benefit distinction (Ellickson 1977). Instead, Michelman deprecates the harm-benefit rule by criticizing the *Hadacheck* decision, in which the neighborhood 'harm' of brickmaking was reason not to pay for shutting down the brickyard. The notion that Hadacheck should have anticipated that his formerly isolated factory would be surrounded by residential uses is met with quiet exasperation: 'But he is, after all, a brickmaker' (p. 1243).

In my opinion Mr. Hadacheck's willingness to go to jail (the writ was habeas corpus, not certiorari) rather than comply with the shut-down rule should not obscure the general virtues of the harm-benefit rule as one that the convention of the circumspect (as well as everyday utilitarians) might easily choose. And Hadacheck's famous civil disobedience may have been the reason that the nascent law of zoning was soon altered to allow pre-existing nonconforming uses to persist (Weiss 1987: 87). One might say that the display of demoralization by Hadacheck was sufficient to subsequently change zoning practice.[2]

The most neglected section of Michelman's article is *Part VI*: 'Institutional Arrangements for Securing Just Compensation' (p. 1245). Michelman first points out that the fairness problem would not arise if public decisions were decided on by unanimity. The biggest fairness problem arises when there are 'stable factions able to engage in a more or less systematic ganging-up – a malfunction most difficult to prevent under simple majority voting' (pp. 1245–46). This hazard would most often arise in local government (Ellickson 1977), but Michelman never invokes the local/state/national distinction or distinctions as to types of politics beyond the majoritarian model. Courts of law have shown no interest in the distinction, either (Rose 2007). Although Michelman starts with takings as a problem of fair politics, variations in the nature of political processes are not explored further.

Michelman frames the problem as choosing between a 'fairness machine' (fair politics) and a 'fairness discipline' (judicial review). His general argument is that legislatures have to shoulder more responsibility for imposing a fairness discipline on themselves. This is because of the complexity of the issues involved, which makes it difficult for judges to decide what is fair, and because reliance on the judges makes the legislators ethically lazy: They may think that if it's about fairness, it's for the judges to decide (p. 1251).

Michelman briefly invokes another law and economics device: Try to resolve a case as if there were a fairness machine operating (p. 1248). (This would be similar to deciding the optimal amount of nuisance if emitter and victim were the same or were on property owned by a single party.) But judges have a difficult time making subjective judgments like that because the idea behind judging is the supposedly objective, impersonal application of external criteria (p. 1249). This accounts for the formal rules (e.g., physical invasion) that are so unsatisfying. Michelman then goes on to suggest that judges at least try for a decision rule that goes part of the way, and it sounds remarkably like the decision patterns adopted in U.S. Supreme Court cases: 'compensation is due only when there has been either (a) a physical occupation or (b) a nearly total destruction of some previously crystallized value which did not originate under clearly speculative or hazardous conditions' (p. 1250). Michelman thinks this was already in force. 'But it rather clearly leads to denial of compensation in cases where fairness requires otherwise' (p. 1251).

Michelman nonetheless thinks that political authorities can and should take up fairness more than they have. He points out that they already do so to some extent, offering compensation in private bills that are not constitutionally called for (p. 1252). (I would add that it was the Virginia legislators, not the courts, who called for compensation in the cedar-apple controversy in *Miller v. Schoene*.) He goes on to point out that legislatures can cobble together compensation schemes that would be beyond the ability of courts, and that these schemes may reduce both demoralization and settlement costs (p. 1254). He points to urban renewal relocation costs as an example of this need, and he indicates that some such costs are compensated. His example of administrators overlooking the demoralization costs to tenants (not owners) of running a highway through a block of modest dwellings (p. 1257) has also been addressed, with predictable economic results: The higher cost of building highways indeed discouraged their construction (Cordes and Weisbrod 1979).

CONCLUSION

This chapter has been brief so as to help readers see the larger structure of Michelman's 1967 classic and to encourage them to read the original article. The continuing relevance of the article is due to its comprehensive, scholarly view of the just compensation question. However, Michelman's hope that 'the test of fairness' could serve as 'a guide to public policy' (p. 1172) seems largely unfulfilled. Passage of the Environmental Protection Act of 1970 and related state and local expansions of the scope of property regulation raised the stakes for takings claims. Claims of the past (those Michelman considered) had largely been localized and episodic. After 1970 they were nationalized and pervasive. 'Just compensation' now appeared as a cudgel to beat back the government, a possibility that delighted libertarians and alarmed environmentalists. Presented with cases that had stakes that were large and whose remedies were difficult to cabin, courts have largely fallen back to formulaic rules such as physical invasion and elimination of all economic use, as in Lucas v. South Carolina Coastal Council, 505 U.S. 1003 (1992). A process that balances the interests of private owners and the public at large, which is at the heart of Michelman's endeavor, seems beyond the capacity of most judicial and legislative bodies. That such balancing remedies are still appealing to scholars is one reason for the durability of Michelman's 1967 article.

NOTES

*   bill.fischel@dartmouth.edu.
1.   Scholarly commentary on Michelman is vast. My own views are in Fischel (1995, chap. 4) and Fischel (1988), as well as in two articles with Perry Shapiro (Fischel and Shapiro 1988; 1989). Michelman was awarded the inaugural Brigham-Kanner Property Rights Prize by the William and Mary Law School in 2004. Commentary on his work on that occasion by distinguished scholars is contained in 15 WILLIAM AND

MARY BILL OF RIGHTS JOURNAL 369 (2006–2007). A small sample of works that critically build on his work (aside from those mentioned in the text below) includes Ackerman (1977), Miceli and Segerson (1996), Ghosh (1997), Dagan (1999), Eagle (2000), Bell and Parchamovsky (2001), and Serkin (2006).
2.   For an excellent history of the context and influence of Hadacheck on the development of zoning, see Kolnick (2008).

REFERENCES

Ackerman, Bruce A. 1977. Private Property and the Constitution. New Haven: Yale University Press.
Bell, Abraham and Gideon Parchomovsky. 2001. Givings, 111 Yale Law Journal 547.
Blume, Lawrence E. and Daniel L. Rubinfeld. 1984. Compensation for Takings, 72 California Law Review 569.
Calabresi, Guido. 1965. The Decision for Accidents: An Approach to Nonfault Allocation of Costs, 78 Harvard Law Review 713.
Coase, Ronald H. 1960. The Problem of Social Cost, 3 Journal of Law and Economics 1.
Cordes, Joseph J. and Burton A. Weisbrod. 1979. Government Behavior in Response to Compensation Requirements, 11 Journal of Public Economics 47.
Dagan, Hanoch. 1999. Takings and Distributive Justice, 85 Virginia Law Review 741.
Eagle, Steven J. 2000. The Rise and Rise of 'Investment-Backed Expectations', 32 Urban Lawyer 438.
Ellickson, Robert C. 1977. Suburban Growth Controls: An Economic and Legal Analysis, 86 Yale Law Journal 385.
Epstein, Richard A. 1985. Takings: Private Property and the Power of Eminent Domain. Cambridge: Harvard University Press.
Farber, Daniel A. 1992. Public Choice and Just Compensation, 9 Constitutional Commentary 279.
Fischel, William A. 1988. Introduction: Utilitarian Balancing and Formalism in Takings, 88 Columbia Law Review 1581.
Fischel, William A. 1995. Regulatory Takings. Cambridge: Harvard University Press.
Fischel, William A. 2007. The Law and Economics of Cedar-Apple Rust: State Action and Just Compensation in *Miller v. Schoene*, 3 Review of Law and Economics 133.
Fischel, William A. and Perry Shapiro. 1988. Takings, Insurance, and Michelman: Comments on Economic Interpretations of 'Just Compensation' Law. 17 Journal of Legal Studies 269.
Fischel, William A. and Perry Shapiro. 1989. A Constitutional Choice Model of Compensation for Takings, 9 International Review of Law and Economics 115.
Ghosh, Shubha. 1997. Takings, the Exit Option and Just Compensation. 17 International Review of Law and Economics 157.
Hicks, John R. 1939. The Foundations of Welfare Economics. 49 Economic Journal 696.
Kaldor, Nicholas. 1939. Welfare Propositions of Economics and Interpersonal Comparisons of Utility, 49 Economic Journal 549.
Kolnick, Kathy A. 2008. Order Before Zoning: Lane Use Regulation in Los Angeles, 1880–1915. PhD Dissertation, University of Southern California (Planning).
Miceli, Thomas J. and Kathleen Segerson. 1996. Compensation for regulatory takings: an economic analysis with applications. Greenwich, CT: JAI Press.
Michelman, Frank I. 1967. Property, Utility, and Fairness: Comments on the Ethical Foundations of 'Just Compensation' Law, 80 Harvard Law Review 1165.
Rawls, John. 1971. A Theory of Justice. Cambridge: Harvard University Press.
Rose, Carol M. 2007. What Federalism Tells Us About Takings Jurisprudence, 54 UCLA Law Review 1681.
Serkin, Christopher. 2006. Big Differences for Small Governments: Local Governments and the Takings Clause, 82 N.Y.U. Law Review 1624.
Weiss, Marc A. 1987. The Rise of the Community Builders. New York: Columbia University Press.

Index